AF179860

GLOBAL PRICE FIXING

STUDIES IN INDUSTRIAL ORGANIZATION
Volume 24

Series Editors:
H.W. de Jong, *University of Amsterdam, Amsterdam, The Netherlands*
W.G. Shepherd, *University of Massachusetts, Amherst, U.S.A.*

Advisory Board:
W.Adams, *Michigan State University, East Lansing, (Mich.), U.S.A.*
R.E. Caves, *Harvard Univetrsity, Cambridge, (Mass.), U.S.A.*
K.D. George, *University College of Swansea, Singleton Park, U.K.*
E. Heusz, *Friedrich Alexander University, Erlangen-Nürnberg, Germany*
A.P. Jacquemin, *University of Louvain, Louvain, Belgium* and
Commission of the European Communities, Brussels, Belgium
E. Kantzenbach, *University of Hamburg, Hamburg, Germany*
H.W. Lambers, *Erasmus University, Rotterdam, The Netherlands*
R. Prodi, *University of Bologna, Bologna, Italy* and
Instituto per la Ricostruzione Industriale, Bologna, Italy
F.M. Scherer, *Harvard University, Cambridge, (Mass.), U.S.A.*

GLOBAL PRICE FIXING

Our Customers are the Enemy

John M. Connor

Professor, Purdue University, Indiana, USA

Kluwer Academic Publishers

Boston/Dordrecht/London

Distributors for North, Central and South America:
Kluwer Academic Publishers
101 Philip Drive
Assinippi Park
Norwell, Massachusetts 02061 USA
Telephone (781) 871-6600
Fax (781) 681-9045
E-Mail <kluwer@wkap.com>

Distributors for all other countries:
Kluwer Academic Publishers Group
Distribution Centre
Post Office Box 322
3300 AH Dordrecht, THE NETHERLANDS
Telephone 31 78 6392 392
Fax 31 78 6392 254
E-Mail <services@wkap.nl>

Electronic Services <http://www.wkap.nl>

Library of Congress Cataloging-in-Publication Data
Connor, John M.
Global price fixing: our customers are the enemy / John M. Connor
p.cm--(Studies in industrial organization; v.24)

ISBN-13: 978-1-4613-7982-9 e-ISBN-13: 978-1-4613-0293-3
DOI: 10.1007/978-1-4613-0293-3

1. Price fixing--Case studies. 2. Cartels--Case studies. I. Title. II. Series.

HF5417.C58 2001
338.5'23--dc21 2001034435

Copyright © 2001 by Kluwer Academic Publishers.

Softcover reprint of the harcover 1st edition 2001

All rights reserved. No part of this publication may be reproduced, stored in a retrieval system or transmitted in any form or by any means, mechanical, photo-copying, recording, or otherwise, without the prior written permission of the publisher, Kluwer Academic Publishers, 101 Philip Drive, Assinippi Park, Norwell, Massachusetts 02061

Printed on acid-free paper.

DEDICATION

For Willard F. Mueller,
mentor, friend, and inspiration.

TABLE OF CONTENTS

PREFACE

Some books get written, others write themselves. This book is the latter type.

I have devoted myself to studying the economic organization of industries related to food and agriculture for almost twenty-five years. It has been my good fortune to work at places that tolerated my gadfly approach to research. So long as I produced a few publications each year and wooed a few graduate students to share those interests, I was free to pursue an array of topics: why firms diversify, the competitive role of advertising, strategies for selling in overseas markets, measuring market power, and many others. Although firmly anchored in the eclectic analytical framework of industrial economics and focused on the food system, I traversed a wide field at will.

Some years ago, I had pretty much convinced myself that naked price fixing was not a high priority for scholarship in these industries. True, collusion was rife in a few food industries, such as bid-rigging among suppliers of fluid milk to school districts in isolated rural districts. Ripping off milk money from school children is reprehensible enough, but the size of the economic losses from localized price fixing paled besides other sources of imperfect competition. Moreover, there were no great policy debates about the wisdom of enforcing the price-fixing prohibitions in the Nation's antitrust laws. The more exciting areas of research for the field were the panoply of behaviors placed under the rubric of "non-cooperative" or tacit collusion. These were more subtle forms of conduct that were the subjects of research on the frontier of the discipline's expanding frontier of knowledge, and they were more policy-relevant.

The policy debates by competition-law experts on both sides of the Atlantic Ocean concentrated on the standards for merger enforcement, practices that might bolster the vertical transmission of market power, the competitive consequences of brand loyalty on conditions of entry, or the rationality of price discrimination. No, I had decided, naked horizontal price fixing was largely a thing of the past, well under control by the century-old Sherman Act.

My attitude on the importance of cartels in the food and agriculture system did a *volte-face* in 1995 and 1996. Like hundreds of thousands of other readers of the *Wall Street Journal*, I read with increasing fascination the legal travails of what was one of the nation's most admired agribusiness firms, the Archer Daniels Midland Company. When ADM and two other makers of lysine proposed settling with lysine buyers, the amount they offered seemed to me woefully inadequate, so I wrote a letter to a *Journal* writer expressing that opinion. That letter was never published, but by happenstance it became the instrument of my personal involvement in the ADM saga. Beginning with the federal class-action antitrust case in lysine, I have served as an expert in several cases that alleged global price fixing by manufacturers of food and feed ingredients. These cases gave me access to internal company documents that economists rarely see. While most of the documents exchanged during the pre-trial discovery stage are confidential and protected by court seals, analysis of such data helps inform the judgement of a writer who must make his case from public documents. Footnotes in the chapters that follow will disclose my roles as consultant to various parties in the legal actions described. The references list most of the opinions I wrote for clients.

The longer I followed the news on the exposure and prosecution of these global cartels, the more convinced I became of their historical importance. Unlike the historical instances of localized price fixing in the U.S. food industries with which I was familiar, these cartels were different. They were huge, complex, geographically extensive, culturally pluralistic, illustrative of a major technological shift, and resulting in new forms of social sanctions by antitrust enforcers. Perhaps equally important, the vast publicity generated by government indictments and civil litigation provided a paper trail about price fixing that was unsurpassed in the history of trusts, monopoly, and cartels. What might have been viewed as simply another sordid example of corporate crime and personal venality began to evolve in quite another direction. As my notes, clippings and e-files on the new cartels began to mount, I became consumed with the necessity of telling their stories, first in a series of talks at professional conferences, later in refereed journal articles, and now in this full-blown monograph.

Immersion in these cases gave me a valuable cross-cartel perspective. There were a large number of similarities to the schemes, though the differences were also instructive. I decided to limit the scope of this book primarily to three of the largest and precedent-setting global cartels: lysine, citric acid, and vitamins. These were the best documented cartels in the public records, and indeed as a group very likely the best documented price-fixing cases ever from the economic perspective. They were also cases in which I had deep personal involvement. The economic details that have emerged into the public record permit a degree of precision of measurement of the cartels' sizes and impacts that is unequaled. At this writing, new global cartels continue to be investigated, prosecuted, and litigated. Most of the biggest ones involve food or feed ingredients. Others may well have gone undetected.

Professional economists may find my writing style somewhat unconventional. The chapters that follow display much of the cool, rational, and dispassionate style that is the preferred hallmark of a modern social science. Yet, interwoven with more orthodox legal-economic discourse are narratives of the events surrounding the formation, operation, and legal prosecutions of these global cartels. I have also been so bold as to focus on a few of the major defendants. Narrative is rarely employed in scientific writing in the social sciences. My purposes are to make the material more accessible to lay audiences, to relieve tedium that can come from bloodless economic writing, and to add to the readers' understanding of personal motives and corporate strategies. After all, in essence, economics is the study of individual decision making about material matters. In my view, narrative can add a richness of psychological detail that lends credibility and explanatory power to putatively rational decision making.

Despite my inclination to include information on corporate and personal histories, legal principles and procedures, and sociopolitical environments, this book is fundamentally a study in economic history. The stories told here are meant to illustrate the explanatory power of economic models of real world phenomena. While economic abstractions and jargon are kept to a minimum, there are some. Most of the economic theories and empirical studies relevant to cartels are relegated to the second chapter. The three long central chapters illustrate the economic dimensions of the cartels with graphs and simple tables. The more detailed statistics are relegated to technical appendices. The latter chapters focus mainly on the legal battles and their consequences.

I hope that the episodes narrated in this book will strike the readers as more than a historical footnote. It is intended to be more than a voyeuristic examination of criminal behavior, profit-seeking gone awry, and the tragic destruction of managerial careers and corporate reputations. It will become, I hope, a permanent reminder of the constant vigilance that must be exercised by a modern nation's legal system to restrain and correct the behaviors of companies that wield power in their markets.

West Lafayette, Indiana
December 2000

ACKNOWLEDGEMENTS

Many of my students and colleagues helped me write this book by tolerating my role as raconteur about these global cartels with at least feigned interest. Indeed, the first time that I put some thoughts on global cartels to paper was in a Departmental Seminar at Purdue University in March 1997. The enthusiasm of that audience helped persuade me that there was a need for this book.

I especially wish to thank a wide circle of professional friends for reading and commenting on early drafts of various chapters of this book or the academic articles incorporated in them. This circle includes: Kenneth Adams, Jay Akridge, Harry Ayers, Michael Boehlje, Donald M. Brown, Peter Carstensen, Ronald Cotterill, James DeCoursey, Nicolas de Roos, Robert M. Durante, Catherine Durham, James Eales, Paul Farris, Luke Froeb, Jeffrey Hyde, James B. Lieber, James MacDonald, William Masters, Francis Moro, Adair Morse, Willard F. Mueller, Brian Posewitz, Lee Schrader, William G. Shepherd, C. Robert Taylor, Gregory Werden, Ed Whitelaw, Thomas Wilson, Karl Zimmer, and several anonymous reviewers of academic journals. Also due for thanks are the many fine economists who helped me sharpen my analyses on the existence and size of the cartel injuries through an adverserial relationship. The latter group includes Lawrence J. White, Frederick Warren-Boulton, Charles Chicchetti, Kenneth Elzinga, Fred S. McChesney, and Jeffrey A. Dubin.

Several members of my Department's staff contributed to the preparation of this book's manuscript. Carrie Hancock is the skillful desktop publisher of this book. Debby Weber, Matt Mooney, Brenda Pearl, Anastasia Macaya, Megan Wilson, and Carol Wood also assisted with preparation of the manuscript.

Finally, I would like to express my appreciations to the School of Agriculture of Purdue University for its material support during 1997-2000.

Chapter 1

INTRODUCTION

For a while it was the best of times, and then it was the worst of times.

This book tells the story of how a modest number of highly placed managers in prominent multinational companies built and ran three global cartels, a way of doing business that had rarely been seen for half a century. For periods ranging from three to 11 years, these food-and-feed ingredient enterprises enjoyed profits that were near the maximum that market conditions could generate. Although highly lucrative for the participants in these cartels, the tragic reality was that financial fortunes were created for the few at the expense of the many. The cartels' effectiveness rested on the exploitation of their customers and their customers' customers who traded in markets that were twisted out of their natural shapes. Although these clandestine conspiracies operated with impunity for several years, through a combination of serendipity and routine police work the cartels were discovered, investigated, and their members convicted. All the corporate participants and nearly all of the individual ringleaders were punished by several of the world's antitrust agencies at levels that set historical precedents for severity. In the aftermath of prosecutorial victories lay shattered corporate reputations, broken careers, and a glimmer of hope that the next generation leaders might learn from the mistakes of the past.

PURPOSE AND SCOPE

The goal of this book is to describe and analyze the origins, operation, and impacts of global cartels in the markets for lysine, citric acid, and vitamins. These products are organic chemicals purchased in bulk by tens of thousands of food and animal-feed manufactures. They are essential and unique ingredients in thousands of food, feed, and medicinal products purchased by nearly all the world's population. In each case, the products originate in industries that are dominated by a very small number of multinational producers. In most cases the dominant suppliers employ advanced biotechnologies to make these chemical intermediates. Whether complex biotechnologies or sophisticated chemical synthesis, the production processes somewhat insulate the established manufactures from new competition because of patents or technological secrecy. In other words, the lysine, citric acid, and vitamins industries are classic oligopolies protected by substantial barriers to entry that are eminently positioned to exploit their customers by exercising market power.

Market power can be wielded in ways both legal and illegal. This book will document that the leading suppliers in the lysine, citric acid, and vitamins chose the path of illegality. In each case, top executives of the major producers formed conspiracies in 1990-1992 that aimed at raising prices and restrained industry output. There is some evidence that the formations of the three cartels were linked, with the financial success of the first cartel inspiring the establishment of several others within a year or two. The conspiracies were effective in raising market prices for periods ranging from three to eleven years. In each case, the participants of these cartels were prosecuted by the U.S. Department of Justice (DOJ) during 1996-2000, hounded in the courts by thousands of aggrieved customers, and forced to disgorge much if not all of their monopoly profits. The antitrust prosecutions in the United States rippled throughout the world's major industrial countries. In legal actions still unfolding in Canada, Mexico, Europe, Asia, and Latin America, local antitrust agencies are duplicating the well-publicized prosecutorial victories of the DOJ's Antitrust Division. In many cases, non-U.S. antitrust officials have discovered the inadequacy of their laws, procedures, or sanctions to cope with huge global dimensions presented by these cartels' operations. In several jurisdictions, including the United States, reforms are underway that will grant government prosecutors new investigative tools and enhanced powers to punish price-fixing behavior.

The unavoidable stars of this book's morality tale are the giant U.S. agribusiness company Archer Daniels Midland Co. (ADM) and several of the firm's top executives. Until its illegal activities became known to the public, ADM was routinely described as one of the most admired corporations in America and an exemplar of the country's prowess in global agribusiness. ADM's fortunes were uniformly credited to its long-serving chairman, Dwayne Orville Andreas. A diminutive titan of industry, Andreas had shaped his company into his own image: well-informed, flexible, bold, risk-taking, ruthless, and above all *connected*. Much of ADM's financial success was ascribed to Dwayne Andreas' dense network of ties to farm organizations, news media, foreign leaders, and the corridors of power in Washington, DC. As a result of his efforts, ADM had over the years become perhaps the federal government's most coddled corporation.

In the early 1990s, both Dwayne Andreas and ADM's president were in their 70s. Power was devolving toward Dwayne Andreas' anointed successor, his son Michael Andreas, ADM's Vice Chairman and sole Executive Vice President. The younger Andreas was his father's devoted disciple. It was he who hatched the plans to create global cartels in citric acid and lysine, two product lines recently acquired by ADM. Michael Andreas assigned the details of his plans to two of ADM's division presidents, Terrance Wilson and Mark Whitacre, the first an impeccably loyal lieutenant, the second a brilliantly devious plotter.

This book gives ADM and its leading managers an especially intense scrutiny because they were the single leaders in two of the best-documented global cartels of the 20th century. While there are more than 20 companies deserving of having their roles as cartel participants fully explained, more is known about ADM's pivotal scheming than any of the others. Partly this is because ADM is the only publicly traded U.S. corporation among the co-conspirators; the others are privately owned, subsidiaries of foreign corporations, or headquartered in Europe or Asia where stockholder reports are not so detailed. However, the main reason so much can be learned about ADM's otherwise clandestine activities is that ADM's officers were prosecuted in a federal court in Chicago.[1] They alone resisted bargaining for terms with DOJ prosecutors prior to trial, and as a result generated the most complete public record of any of the cartels' misdeeds. As one legal scholar put it:

> "The bizarre, tabloid like tale of . . . Mark Whitacre . . . and the morality play that was subsequently presented in a Chicago courtroom will alter forever the antitrust enforcement landscape" (Klawiter 1998: 203).

ADM pleaded guilty to criminal price-fixing charges in late 1996, and it was testimony of one of the company's own officers that may have been the most decisive in the jury's decision to find Andreas, Wilson, and Whitacre guilty. In April 2000, a three judge appeals panel confirmed their guilt and effectively increased their sentences. Like divine thunder from on high, the appeals court decision was unrestrained in condemning the company and its three convicted officers:

> "For many years, Archer Daniels Midland Co.'s philosophy of customer relations could be summed up by a quote from former ADM President James Randall: 'Our competitors are our friends. Our customers are the enemy.' This motto animated the company's business dealings and ultimately led to blatant violations of U.S. antitrust law, a guilty plea and a staggering criminal fine against the company . . . The facts involved in this case reflect an inexplicable lack of business ethics and an atmosphere of general lawlessness that infected the very heart of one of America's leading corporate citizens. Top executives at ADM and its Asian co-conspirators throughout the early 1990s spied on each other, fabricated aliases and front organizations to hide their activities, hired prostitutes to gather information from

> competitors, lied, cheated, embezzled, extorted and obstructed justice" (Kanne *et al.* 2000:1-2).

IMPORTANCE OF THE CASES

Economists have long lamented the paucity of information on price-fixing conspiracies in general and global conspiracies in particular. One would like to have information on the size of the markets affected and of the economic injuries caused by cartel's operations. To gauge the size of the injuries to buyers, the price effects are critical. However, in general, most criminal antitrust cases require no testimony on economic effects, most civil cases never make it to trial, and the forensic economic analyses prepared for such cases are kept sealed by court orders. "Comprehensive studies of the effects of cartels upon prices are not available" (Edwards 1976:12). A more recent survey by Dick (1998) cites relatively few empirical studies of the price effects of cartels, and all of them are domestic conspiracies. This book is able to present fairly precise estimates of the effects of global cartels on prices, production, and profits.

Besides the quantitative analysis of the economic impact of cartels, this study is important for several other reasons. First, although the focus is on three specific cartels, they are illustrative of more than a dozen other international cartel cases already prosecuted and a score more still being investigated. Lysine, citric acid, and vitamins are part of a worldwide epidemic of global price fixing not seen since the 1940s. Second, the cases examined herein demonstrate an important shift in antitrust enforcement policy in the United States and elsewhere toward greater attention on global cartels. Third, the size of the industries involved in cartelization and the severity of the injuries caused has reached unprecedented levels. Fourth, the prosecution of these global cartels involved new methods of investigation, novel types of sanctions, and fresh legal issues. Fifth, these cases illuminate with great clarity the motives for global cartel formation and the methods of cartel operation. Finally, the increased attention to anticartel enforcement has met with continued broad-based political support.

A Renaissance in Global Enforcement

Antitrust was not an issue in the 1992 U.S. presidential election campaign, yet President Clinton made appointments in the Justice Department that ensured a more assertive posture in antitrust enforcement than was seen in the 1980s (Balto 1999).[2] Late in the Clinton administration in particular it became apparent that the DOJ was unafraid to launch dozens of high-profile cases in the price fixing, merger, and monopoly areas. However, commentators of all stripes have noted that attention to global cartels was a hallmark of the late Clinton administration.[3] In an article highlighting seven major antitrust achievements in the late 1990s, David Balto states: "In its greatest single antitrust achievement, the Clinton administration has dramatically refocused criminal enforcement . . . to international cartels" (*ibid.* p. 25). Writing just a few months after the ADM convictions at the Chicago trial, a leading antitrust scholar predicted that:

> "The most significant and enduring antitrust enforcement initiative of this era will be the aggressive criminal enforcement of international cartels by the antitrust division" (Klawiter 1998:201).

Among the factors driving this change in policy emphasis, argued Klawiter, were success in prosecutions, improved procedures for gathering evidence outside the United States, and greater international cooperation among antitrust agencies. Journalists tended to mention a confluence of personal and political factors to explain the Antitrust Division's "renewed vigor" in prosecuting global cartels:

> "The aggressive posture has been driven by a mix of political opportunism, frustration with past missteps, attractive inducements to whistle-blowers, and other factors" (*Los Angeles Times* May 22,1999:A1).

Among the other factors mentioned were the DOJ's defeat in the *Industrial Diamonds* case in 1994, bipartisan support for antitrust in the U.S. Congress, and the recognized phenomenon that presidential administrations display less caution about offending business constituencies when re-election is not a concern.

These comments by outside observers were echoed by speeches given by Antitrust Division officials. As early as 1995, the Division head stated that: "The Antitrust Division is . . . substantially expanding investigations and cases with significant international aspects" (Bingaman 1995). The annual reports of the Division and subsequent speeches by its top officials confirm that a substantial real location of resources tools place toward global price-fixing matters in 1994 and 1995 (Spratling 1999). In a speech given before competition-law officials from around the world gathered to consider anticartel enforcement, Assistant Attorney General for Antitrust Joel Klein noted that from 1950 to 1995

> ". . . our international cartel cases became few and far between . . . simply because we didn't have any evidence that international

> cartels continued to be a problem. That has all changed" (Klein 1999:3).

The mere fact that officials from 30 antitrust agencies had assembled at such a conference ". . . reflects the dawn of a new era in antitrust enforcement against international cartels" (*ibid.*). The private antitrust bar began to echo the sentiments of DOJ lawyers in the late 1990s. Adler and Laing (1997) called the ADM/lysine case part of an "explosion" of international price-fixing.

A symbol of the sea change in enforcement priorities is the fact that the DOJ's Antitrust Division did not bother to distinguish purely domestic matters from international ones until 1998. Since then, armed with a precise if rather broad definition of "international", the Division has noted the remarkable globalization of its activities on several occasions. A striking statistic concerns the proportion of corporate or individual defendants that were indicated for criminal price-fixing violations by the DOJ. Prior to 1995, less than 1 percent were foreign-based corporations or foreign residents, but in 1998-1999 the proportion had risen to a startling 50 percent of such indictments (figure 1.1).

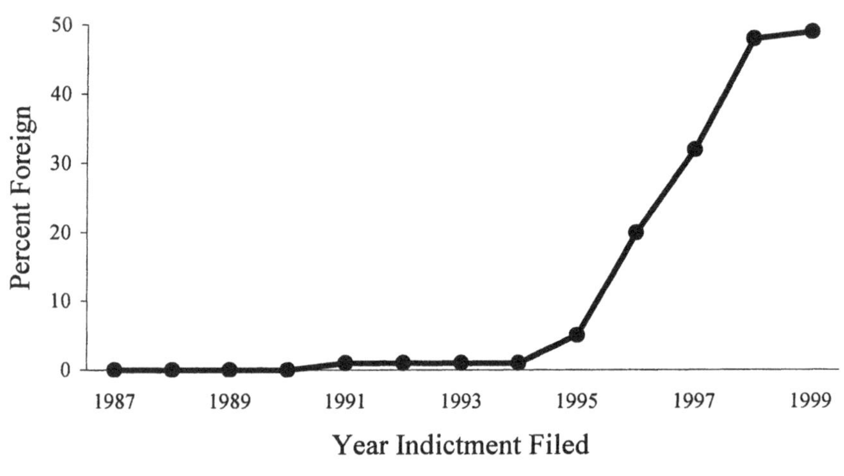

Figure 1.1. Proportion of Corporate Defendants in U.S. Criminal Cartel Cases that were Foreign, 1987-1999.

Source: ICPAC (2000).

Another quantitative indicator is the fines secured by the DOJ for price-fixing violations, virtually all as a result of corporate guilty pleas. Prior to 1994, the largest such fine was $2,000,000. Since 1994, record fines have been obtained in nearly every year (figure 1.2). In 1994 and 1995, the record price-fixing fines grew out of purely *domestic* cartels, but all the subsequent record fines were from members of *global* cartels. Joel Klein, chief of the Antitrust Division at the time, said that the $900-million-plus in fines in fiscal year 1999 is more than the entire history of U.S. antitrust enforcement (Klein 1999). Moreover, from 1996 to 1999, fully 76 percent of all the $10-million-plus corporate fines were imposed on non-U.S. corporations (*ibid.*). Individual convictions show a similar pattern. In the vitamin cartel cases alone, the DOJ was able to secure 24 criminal convictions by the end of the year 2000.

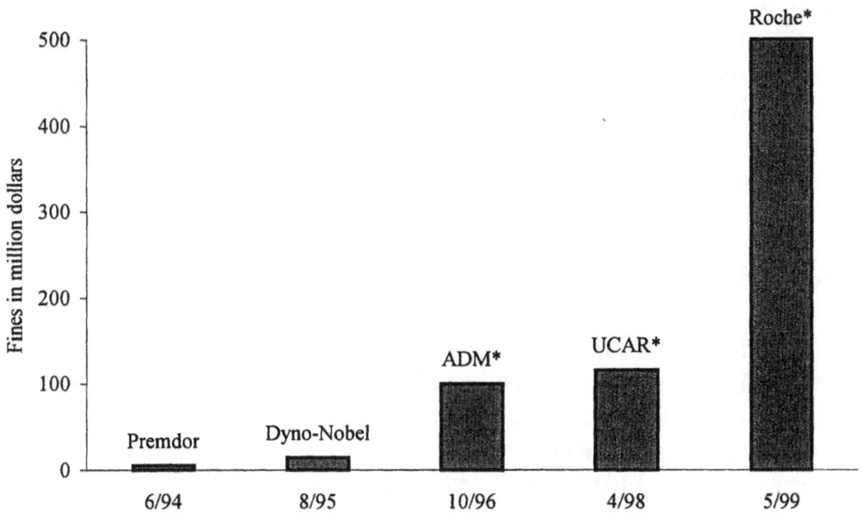

Figure 1.2. Record Criminal Antitrust Fines for Corporations, 1994-1999.

Sources: Bell and Laskin, Connor (2000).
* = Members of global cartel

The DOJ is not alone in targeting foreign firms for price fixing. Canada's Competition Bureau and the European Commission's DG-IV have likewise investigated and fined predominantly firms not headquartered in their respective jurisdictions. In 1999, the United Kingdom's Restrictive Practices Court imposed sanctions on members of an international cartel for the first time in its history; the two firms were members of the lysine cartel. A 1999 survey of legal experts in antitrust law found clear evidence that competition-law prosecutors from around the world were "imbued with anticartel fever" (*Business Crimes Law Report* January 2000). Mario Monte, the EU's competition law commissioner, made fervent speeches about the necessity of tough anticartel enforcement. He called global cartels "cancers on the open market economy" (*The Guardian* September

19, 2000). Besides evidence from Canada and the EU, the experts noted that in 1999 Germany's Federal Cartel office had imposed its largest cartel fine ever. Even the somewhat cautious Japan Fair Trade Commission had fined at least two non-Japanese companies in 1998-1999. However, on balance, the JFTC was notable for its back of activity in the area of global price fixing, even though Japanese firms were involved in several cartels.

Indictments and prosecutions of global cartels are likely to continue at a rapid pace during the first decade of the new millennium. In 1999, the Antitrust Division had more than 35 grand juries in session investigating possible criminal antitrust violations (Klein 1999). Nearly all of them were probing alleged international cartel activity. Government investigations outside the United States typically trail U.S. actions by a year or two. The biggest issue of international antitrust enforcement in the 1960s – the extraterritorial reach of U.S. law – has faded to unimportance. Extraterritorial prosecutions are now practically a customary rule of international law.

Affected Sales and Injuries Are Huge

"Affected Sales" is the term used to describe the total turnover in a market during a price-fixing conspiracy.[4] A characteristic of the three food-and-feed ingredient cartels examined below is that their products comprise a small share of the total ingredients purchased and mixed into the final product. The cost of lysine or vitamins added to hog feeds is tiny compared to the cost of the rough grains used in the finished feed, and the cost of citric acid is negligible in a food product like yogurt. Nevertheless, the huge size of the world's food manufacturing industries guarantees that even minor ingredients can be substantial industries in their own rights.

In a speech given just before the big vitamin cartels cases were announced, DOJ official Gary Spratling (1999) stated that global cartels prosecuted since October 1996 had affected U.S. markets with $10 billion in sales. By the end of 1999, total U.S. affected sales would be $17 billion.

Global sales of lysine during the 1992-1995 conspiracy period amounted to about $1.8 billion. Citric acid sales were about twice as high per year, and the cartel persisted for almost four years; affected global sales were roughly $4 billion. Affected sales in the bulk vitamins industries are more difficult to calculate because the conspiracies covered at least ten vitamin markets, and they varied from four to eleven years in duration. The DOJ's press release suggested that U.S. affected sales were $5.5 billion, but private plaintiffs counsel estimated sales at $8.4 billion using a somewhat broader product mix. In all three global cartels, purchases of cartelized products in the United States represented 25 to 35 percent of global purchases. Thus, affected global sales of vitamins and vitamin products were in the $20 to $30 billion range.

The three cartels that are the focus of this book account for a fairly large share of all the global cartels charged and prosecuted in the United States. The affected U.S. sales of all global cartels indicted over the four years beginning in October 1996 amounted to about $16 billion. Lysine, citric acid, and vitamins had U.S. affected sales of about $10 billion, or 63 percent of the total.

A major objective of the present work is to provide accurate estimate of the economic costs imposed on market participants by global cartels. As explained in chapter 2, the most widely accepted measure of price fixing harm is the *overcharge* to customers of a cartel during the period when prices were elevated above their non-conspiracy levels. The customer overcharge is a conservative measure of economic injury because it does not count the efficiency losses caused by the distorted prices.[5] In the United States, the 1992-1995 lysine overcharges amounted to $80 million, or 17 percent of affected market sales (see Chapter 9). The citric acid cartel overcharged U.S. customers between $116 and $309 million, or 14 to 21 percent of sales (Chapter 6). However, the largest of the global cartels were those manufacturing bulk vitamin products (Chapter 12). Estimates of the overcharges to U.S. buyers vary from $1.1 billion on sales of $5.5 billion (a 20% rate) to $3.0 billion on $8.4 billion in sales (36%).[6] Taken altogether the vitamins cartels were probably the most destructive global conspiracies of all time, with world wide customers overcharged by $4 to $9 billion.[7]

New Antitrust Enforcement Tools

The 1990s saw a number of significant improvements in law enforcement methods first applied in the global cartel cases that are the focus of this book. Innovations were seen during the investigation, negotiation, litigation, and sentencing phases of prosecution. Of course, luck played a role in the eventual prosecutorial victories, but the new methods and stiffer sanctions appear to have raised the effectiveness of government antitrust enforcement. In addition, changes in federal and state class-action procedures and larger settlements for opt-out firms have increased private damage penalties in the United States. Finally, anticartel practices of several overseas competition law agencies have become clarified, and a movement toward greater use of civil suits is also evident. The upshot of all these changes is a significant increase in the potential liability facing participants in global cartels. Consequently, there is some expectation that the elevated enforcement competencies of the 1990s will instill greater deterrence for global price fixing in the 2000s.

Among the major improvements in global price-fixing investigation procedures is the introduction of automatic amnesty for the first corporate whistle-blower. Under certain publicized conditions, the first company to come forward with reliable information about a conspiracy in restraint of trade is guaranteed full forgiveness of government fines. Later arrivals to cooperation with prosecutor are promised partial reduction in their sentences under federal guidelines that came into widespread use in the early 1990s. Countries other than the United States are beginning to institute similar plans. By the late 1990s, the U.S. DOJ was getting almost two tips per month from companies seeking amnesty. Another innovative program that stimulates cooperation from individual cartel participants who may be facing felony convictions stems from a memorandum of understanding between the DOJ and the Immigration and Naturalization Service. This agreement allows the DOJ to offer a foreign resident guaranteed future movement across U.S. borders, even if the individual is subsequently convicted for a felony and serves prison time.

Both these incentives for corporate or personal cooperation with investigators have helped to solve the historically knotty problem of collecting overseas evidence in international cases. Another innovation that ameliorates this problem is the burgeoning and multiple forms of cooperation between the world's antitrust agencies. Scores of agreements of several kinds now permit simultaneous raids by multiple national antitrust agencies, the sharing of investigative evidence, and easier transnational access to potential witnesses or targets of an investigation. A widening zone of countries with extradition treaties for criminal price fixers is making it harder for cartel participants to escape the consequences of their conspiracies.

In the United States especially, but abroad as well, the FBI and its sister agencies have begun to use the full panoply of its intimidating arsenal: large-scale "raids" on offices and homes, telephone taps, body wires, and offers of amnesty for informers. The lysine case clearly demonstrated the importance of one more investigative technique that had never been used prior to 1993 for price-fixing allegations. With the cooperation of Mexican authorities, the FBI was able to record the first of several non-U.S. conspiracy meetings through a tape recorder operated by a cooperating witness. Similar cooperation was afforded for the FBI in Japan. Even more crucial to the lysine prosecution was the FBI's use of videotapes for several meetings that occurred in the United States. In a jury system operating in the television age, nothing is more persuasive than capturing the words, facial expressions, and body language of conspirators in action for replay on a monitor in court.

While the business community may abhor the following institutional innovation, the appearance in the United States of what are tentatively called "social reform" law firms has in all likelihood made life more difficult for cartel participants. These firms bring class-action suits in a broad array of perceived injustices that are not being addressed by the congress or regulatory agencies. The actions are made possible by subsidizing high-risk cases from the retained legal fees of more conventional class-action suits. A change in federal court rules in 1996 allowed law firms to represent a class whose members fit a group of potentially injured persons. The rule change has increased the incentives to file civil antitrust cases quickly even though the odds are against winning.[8]

In this connection, it is worth mentioning that civil price-fixing cases brought by the U.S. Federal Trade Commission have suddenly grown a new set of teeth. On the basis of 1999-2000 federal court decisions in *U.S. vs. Mylan Laboratories*, the FTC is now empowered to seek disgorgement of illicit profit (essentially single damages) from participants in price fixing schemes; previously the FTC was confined to seeking only injunctive relief. [9] Although the FTC does not have access to some of the investigative powers of the DOJ and cannot seek double damages or criminal penalties, its enhanced fine-making powers have almost doubled the anticartel resources of the federal government.

New Insights into Cartel Operations

The outbreak of global cartelization after nearly fifty years of dormancy may be compared to biological contagion. Price fixing behavior on a global scale had erupted in the decades just before World War I and again just prior to World War II. U.S. prosecutions in the late 1940s (and in one famous case in 1960) helped douse the fires of conspiracy for two decades or more, but in the remarkably short period of 1989-1991 several new cartels sprung into action. The conspiracies also resemble contagion in the sense that within some firms with multiple lines of business, once one product line was proving the profitability of price fixing, it infected another line of business. There is evidence that a conspiracy in the global market for vitamins that began in 1990 spread within and across multinational companies to citric aid in 1991 and lysine in 1992. Although the years 1989-1991 includes a worldwide recession, a more common characteristic that weakened a company's resistance to price fixing seems to have been a booming drop in profit after a high plateau of profitability.

The lysine, citric acid, vitamins, and other global cartels that were discovered and prosecuted after 1995 share several features (Spratling 1999, Griffin 2000, and following chapters). These cartels were formed and operated by the company's top executives who typically had decades of seniority. Initially, only two or three officers were involved in the planning and execution of the conspiracies, but eventually each company would contribute at least ten men to a cartel's maintenance.[10] The conspirators "without exemption" were ". . . fully aware that they [were] violating the law in the United States and elsewhere." (Spratling 1999:9) and showed in their conversations ". . . contempt and utter disregard . . . for antitrust enforcement" (Griffin 2000:5) and for their customer-victims. Even seasoned antitrust lawyers were shocked by the crudeness of the lysine conspirator's conversation: "People literally could not believe how direct and brazen it all was" (*USA Today* July 10, 2000). Yet, the conspirators had a special fear of what they perceived to be tougher U.S. antitrust enforcement. "Defendants in several recent cases have revealed that the cartels changed their practices and began avoiding contracts in the United States at all costs . . ." (Spratling 1999:10). Cartels frequently utilized industry trade associations as covers for their illegal meetings, prepared false agendas and false minutes, and took many other steps to hide their conspiracies.

Although assisted by electronic methods of communications, nearly all the cartels required quarterly face-to-face meetings to revise their agreements and check on progress toward their goals. In nearly all cases, list prices (target prices, floor prices, or ranges) were set with great precision, and transaction prices inevitably responded within days or weeks. While strictly speaking unnecessary, ". . . most cartels recognize that price-fixing schemes are more effective if the cartel also allocates sales volume among the firms" (Spratling 1999:11). With volume agreements in place, price wars and other self-destructive disciplinary tactics were generally avoided. Cheating was also discouraged by internal compensation plans, division of pooled profits, audits by third parties, or simple bullying by dominant members.

Epidemics end when the susceptible hosts disappear or when growing conditions turn unfavorable. Although a few of the corporate members of the global cartels discovered in the late 1990s have left their industries voluntarily, the financial sanctions imposed on them were not high enough to kill them off. The individual conspirators taken out of circulation by prison sentences can hardly dent the supply of potential price fixers. Although only time will tell, it is likely that the severe sentences meted out to both corporate and individual conspirators will dampen the enthusiasm for overt price fixing. The antitrust regulatory atmosphere is clearly more frigid in all the major industrialized countries than was the case in the 1980s. Unfortunately, financial penalties are not enough, as is demonstrated by the fact that there were about a dozen corporate or individual price fixers that became repeat offenders. Corporate antitrust compliance programs have the potential for leveraging the deterrence effect of harsh sentences, yet it appears that these lessons are lost in the space of a decade or two as a new generation of corporate leaders take the helm and institutional memories are lost. What may be needed is something akin to a genetic mutation for many corporations: structural changes in corporate governance that reward ethical behavior.

SOURCES AND METHODS

This book relies on a broad selection of primary and secondary sources of information. Among the primary sources are the transcript of the trial that convicted three lysine cartel conspirators *(U.S. vs. Michael Andreas et al.)*; scores of legal briefs, plea agreements, memoranda, affidavits, and court orders and opinions; copies of original documents submitted as exhibits for trials or obtained under pre-trial discovery processes; speeches and documents released by the DOJ and other antitrust agencies; and corporate web pages and investor reports. Two recent books (Lieber 2000, Eichenwald 2000) shed light on the U.S. investigation and conviction of the lysine and citric acid conspiracies; they quote from direct interviews, audio tapes, video tapes, and FBI interview forms. Among the secondary sources are journalistic articles, law-review articles, pieces from industry trade publications, and editorial opinions. Many of the major sources used are listed in the *References* section at the end of this book, but to avoid unnecessary clutter the majority of the factual sources employed in this book can be found in the chronological appendices of Connor (2000).[11]

This work is fundamentally a historical approach to understanding the interplay among personal motivations, economic forces, and the legal environment. While it is amply illustrated with quantitative information, formal statistical or mathematical analysis is eschewed in the interests of readability. Some of the conclusions reached have been influenced by my role as a forensic economist, but not, I believe, at the expense of rigorous economic reasoning nor in violation of my layman's understanding of legal principles.[12] At times a straightforward narrative of the events surrounding a cartel or legal process was chosen as the most appropriate method of exposition.

ORGANIZATION

The eighteen chapters that follow fall into three groups. Chapters 2 and 3 provide background on the economic theory and legal principals relevant to understanding cartels. Both are fairly elementary treatments of the subjects, so readers with more than a passing knowledge of price analysis and welfare theory can easily skip Chapter 2. Chapter 3 is a broad survey of U.S. and non-U.S. competition law and enforcement procedures. Special attention is paid to anticartel enforcement.

Chapters 4 to 12 comprise the economic core of this book. Three chapters are devoted to each of the three cartels selected for intensive study: citric acid (Chapters 4-6), lysine (Chapters 7-9), and vitamins (Chapters 10-12). In each case, one chapter lays out the demand and supply characteristics of the product market; the second chapter narrates the major events in the life of the cartel; and the third chapter collects what can be learned about the economic impacts of the cartel on prices, profits, trade, and customers.

Four chapters then concentrate on the legal fallout from the exposure of the three cartels. Chapter 13 narrates the U.S. Department of Justice's criminal cases against the international cartels, ending with an assessment of the effectiveness of the prosecutions. Chapter 14 follows similar developments by competition-law units in Canada, the European Union, and elsewhere outside the United States.[13] The 1998-1999 criminal antitrust trial against three senior executives of the Archer Daniels Midland Co. is the subject of Chapter 15.[14] Finally, Chapter 16 covers the civil suits filed against members of the three cartels, most of which were filed by U.S. buyers.

Chapter 17 returns to an economic viewpoint on a few additional selected cartels with features not found in the lysine, citric acid, and vitamin cases. This chapter tries to be forward looking by predicting the prosecution of additional food-and-feed ingredient cartels. Chapter 18 is the final one on legal topics. The point of view is the legal resources that are available to fight or defend cartels, both government and private organizations – the forensic law industry so to speak. The latter parts of Chapter 18 try to assess the adequacy of the laws and enforcement resources available to combat global cartels. The final chapter attempts to identify major themes that appear throughout the book and to provide a summary of the ultimate impact of the global-cartel pandemic of the 1990s.

Chapter 1 Endnotes

[1] The case is uncaptioned as *United States vs. Michael D. Andreas et al.* The trial lasted for more than two months in the summer of 1998, sentencing occurred in July 1999, and the court of appeals rendered its decision in April 2000.

[2] A little known fact is that when Bill Clinton first returned to his native state of Arkansas in the early 1970s, he taught law at the University of Arkansas. His first teaching assignment was a course in antitrust law (Balto 1999).

[3] Non government lists of corporate criminals come to similar conclusions. In its report on the "Top 100 corporate Criminals of the 1990s," *Corporate Crime Reporter* nominated six global price fixers among the top ten.

[4] In principle, sales during intro-conspiracy price wars should not be counted. On the other hand, sales by firms outside a cartel are usually effected as are sales for a while after a cartel is broken up.

[5] The dead-weight static loss is caused by underproduction and is typically five to ten percent of the value of the monopoly overcharge. Some U.S. court circuits accept the dead-weight loss as a compensable harm. In addition, cartels may generate dynamic losses.

[6] It is possible that the *NASDAQ Market-Makers* price-fixing case settled in 1999 had overcharges at the lower end of the vitamin range. A case filed by scores of the largest U.S. retailers against the Visa and MasterCard syndicates in 1997 claims monopolization damages of $8.1 billion (Wilke 1999). When adjusted for inflation, the heavy electrical equipment cases of 1960 affected a greater value of sales but may have had smaller overcharges. These cases were domestic ones.

[7] One of the reasons for the discrepancy is the treatment of the vitamin animal premix market. A few of the conspirators sold both pure bulk vitamins and a value added mixed product. Conspiracies existed in both types of markets.

[8] However another new twist in class actions will have the effect of reducing the size of private settlements. First employed in the vitamin cartel case, the "reverse most-favored-nation clause" dictates that opt-outs settlement rates, if higher, should be applied retroactively to the opt-in class members. Thus the opt-ins free ride on the legal efforts of the opt outs, who usually do negotiate better deals. The effect is to heighten the resistance of defendants to bigger settlements.

[9] The FTC sought $120 million from Mylan Laboratories under a 1975 amendment that was untested in the courts until a July 1999 decision of the U.S. District Court for the District of Columbia. In July 2000, Mylan agreed to pay $100 million to the FTC and 33 U.S. states as well as $8 million in legal costs. (70 percent of the company's fiscal 2000 net revenues).

[10] I use the word "men" intentionally in its strict gender sense. In the more than 200 individuals named so far, none is identifiably female.

[11] This lengthy staff paper is available on a web page sponsored by the American Agricultural Economics Association (http://agecon.lib.umn.edu/index.html) or may be obtained in hard copy by writing to the author at: 1145 Krannert Building, Purdue University, West Lafayette, Indiana 47907-1145. This source cites more than 1000 sources, arranged in several chronologies and indexed.

[12] In the spirit of full disclosure, readers should know that I have served as an expert for U.S. and Canadian plaintiffs in civil antitrust matters that involved the following products: lysine, citric acid, bulk vitamins, methionine, sodium gluconate, and corn sweeteners. I also served as a testifying expert for prosecutors in one criminal case involving an amino acid. Confidential information received in the course of these projects is protected by court orders and by promises to clients. However, some information from publicly available sources taken from reports originally prepared for clients has found its way into this work, and my analyses performed on the basis of confidential data have tempered the conclusions expressed in this book.

[13] The slow pace of the E.U. cartel investigations means that these prosecutions were not all completed as this book was completed.

[14] Interested readers will find far more detailed narration of the Chicago trial in a new book by James Leiber (2000).

Chapter 2

THE ECONOMICS OF PRICE FIXING

This chapter offers a simple nontechnical economic explanation of the causes and effects of price fixing, beginning with a description of how prices are formed in competitive markets and in the presence of a monopoly. These two analytical models of how prices and output evolve in markets are too unrealistic to fit natural markets, yet their contrasting results are useful because they bracket the price/quantity outcomes in real markets. That is, perfect competition and pure monopoly are the extreme points on a continuum of market environments, and the performance of real-world markets tends to be "in between" the two extremes.[1] These "in between" markets are different because they have a small number of sellers or buyers. Small numbers raise the possibility of strategic behavior, of which price fixing is one type. A detailed list of company behaviors that constitute price fixing is provided and discussed. This is followed by an explanation of the five main economic factors that affect the formation and success of cartels. The chapter ends with a brief empirical analysis of the economic harm imposed on market participants by effective cartels and a historical survey of global cartels.

In Chapter 3, the economic theory of cartels is extended to a legal analysis of cartels: the U.S. federal laws on price fixing, selected cases of prosecutions of global cartels, and non-U.S. competition laws that apply to cartels.

BASIC THEORY

Pure Competition and Monopoly

Until the 1930s most students of economics were taught only two diametrically opposed abstract models of how markets worked. The perfectly competitive market model describes a world in which there is a large number of buyers and sellers, all of them well informed about prices and product quality, trading perfectly homogeneous goods according to well established trading rules.[2] Goods are homogeneous when buyers are unwilling to pay more for one seller's product compared to any other's. A key assumption in this model is that if the numbers of buyers or sellers become too few, there is nothing preventing more of them from jumping into the market almost immediately to take advantage of trading profits. Similarly, in the face of negative profits, participants could quickly and costlessly exit the market by selling their assets to large numbers of willing buyers. While this ideally competitive market is a mental construct of economic theorists, some real world markets in agricultural products or stock trading come pretty close to matching its characteristics. Even though few natural markets are perfectly competitive, the model is important because it is a benchmark for comparing the performance of all other markets.

The other model is pure monopoly. In this case, a single firm supplies the entire market for a well-defined product. The monopolist sets the market price on the assumption that entry into its industry is blockaded, perhaps because the firm has unique access to an essential input or production technology or perhaps because it owns patent or trademark that makes its product inimitable. A monopolized good may be homogeneous in the sense that it is simple or comes in only one grade or variety. On the other hand, the many buyers of the monopolist's product perceive that there are no satisfactory substitutes available for purchase; in this sense the monopolist's product is like a unique brand that has no rivals – it is a highly differentiated product. Like the perfectly competitive market, there are few examples of pure monopolies in natural markets, and the few that exist tend to be publicly regulated.

The behavior of sellers in perfectly competitive markets is quite different from that of monopolists, even though both are assumed to be maximizing company profits. Firms in perfectly competitive markets lead pretty dull lives because they are pure price-takers. After checking out the market price, a seller sets the firm's output at the profit-maximizing level, which is the same level at which all other identical firms set their output. Individual firms pay no attention to overall market demand.[3] The seller then purchases an optimal mix of labor, capital, and other inputs from markets that are also perfectly competitive; all sellers choose the same mix of inputs because they all have adopted the same low-cost technology of production. All the sellers earn zero economic profits (which will be a positive rate of return on investment, adjusted for market risk, on the company's financial records). Perfectly competitive firms are unconcerned about creating loyal customers because they can always sell all that they can make at the market price. Neither do they have to worry about the reliability or price of intermediate materials or capital equipment, because these too are perfectly competitive homogeneous product markets.

Behavior by monopolists is quite different, though it too has an air of unreality about it. The monopolist sees the demand for its product as identical with market demand because buyers believe there is no substitute for the monopolist's product. Market supply equates with the output under the control of the monopolist. There is no market price separate from what the monopolist decides to charge; that is, the monopolist is a price-maker not a price-taker. The profit-maximizing price set by a monopolist will depend only on its costs of production and the shape of the market demand curve. The monopoly price will be positively related to the height of production costs and the inelasticity of demand.[4] The most important implication of the monopoly model concerns its effect on market performance. Welfare analysis demonstrates that perfect competition results in the greatest quantity of production at the lowest possible price, which is highly beneficial to consumers (see the Technical Appendix). Monopoly, on the other hand, restricts output to some level below the competitive level, resulting in a loss in consumption and production. This is termed the dead-weight loss. Moreover, the supracompetitive price charged by a monopoly results in the transfer of income from buyers to the owners of the monopoly. While a loss to consumers who still buy at the elevated price, not all of the transfer is a loss to society.[5] A monopolist may set a single price, but the size of the transfer can be increased if the monopolist is able to divide demand into distinct groups that are then charged distinct prices; such price discrimination may be on the basis of size of purchases, buyers' income, or each group's sensitivity to price.

Oligopoly

Firms in perfectly competitive markets have no power over price. Absent government intervention, the possibility of organizing large numbers of sellers into an association that would raise the price for its members' benefits is nearly zero. Perfectly competitive behavior is essentially anonymous. There is no benefit in getting to know competing suppliers because there is no hope of developing a common strategy that would pay. Even if a private trade association could be formed, the free-entry condition would ensure the unprofitability of collective action.

The possibility of group activity aimed at raising profits through purely private actions is much greater in an *oligopoly,* that is, an industry with a few sellers.[6] In essence, when a group of sellers becomes small enough to control a sufficiently large share of sales in the market, the group comes to realize the possibility of collective action that can raise the group's total profits. Similarly, when numbers of sellers are few, they begin to appreciate the fact that their independent decisions over price or output can hurt the profits of their industry rivals. The great early industrial-organization economist Edwin Chamberlin called this "mutual dependence recognized." That is, unlike the atomistically small companies in perfectly competitive markets, oligopolists infer that their business actions (price changes, output adjustments, plant investments, and the like) will affect the profits of their rivals, and vice-versa. Typically, oligopolists form strategic plans that take into account what their industry rivals will do in response to a notable business action. Strategic thinking of this type is folly in a perfectly competitive industry because the actions of one firm can only have an infinitesimally small impact on industry supply or product price. Monopolists, too, can ignore strategic interdependence because there are no rivals of any consequence.[7]

Economists call the formation of market plans that take into account the expected reactions of rivals' *conjectures*. Economic models of strategic behavior of firms fall into two one of two classes, cooperative and noncooperative. *Cooperative* or *overtly collusive* behavior requires a conscious agreement between rivals (established firms already selling into the same market) or between an actual and potential rival. All "conspiracies" in the legal sense are types of strategic behavior that economists class as cooperative. Overtly collusive groups are *cartels* (see box).

Cartel

A cartel is an association of two or more legally independent firms that explicitly agree to coordinate their prices or output for the purpose of increasing their collective profits. The members of a cartel must knowingly and intentionally conspire to raise (lower) the price of the product that they sell (buy) above (below) the price that natural market forces would cause in the absence of the cartel's actions. Affecting price will cause the quantity of product sold in the market to contract, but some cartels reinforce the price distortion by agreements to reduce output, sales, or industry capacity. Cartels can use various subtle techniques to communicate, monitor, and enforce agreements, but those conspiracies that engage in overt agreements about market price and quantity are called "naked" cartels.

The word cartel come into English in the 16th century from the Old Italian word *cartello,* which meant a note or letter of defiance, a preliminary step in the etiquette of dueling. A cartel in this sense is now obsolete. A second meaning of cartel that slipped into the language a little later (and is still in use) is a written agreement between opposing armies for the exchange of prisoners. This meaning was extended by German writers in the 1880s to describe a government coalition that brought together normally antagonistic political parties. Shortly thereafter the word *kartell* was applied to a combination of two or more business rivals for the purpose of regulating prices or output of an industry. The word cartel was first used in English in 1902 in this business sense in three British publications to refer to what were formerly called "producers syndicates" or "trusts' in the sugar and steel industries *(Oxford English Dictionary).*

Noncooperative behavior (also called *tacitly collusive)* involves conjectures that are formed independently by firms. That is, firms develop hypotheses about rivals' strategic behavior without any direct communication with those rivals. Typically, no cooperative conjectures are formed by observing a rival's reactions to historical changes in market conditions or to independent actions of the conjecture-making firm. The classic example of tacit collusion is price followership by firms that take note of public price announcements of leading firms.

PRICE FIXING DEFINED

Price fixing is the quintessential example of cooperative behavior. The aim of oligopolists that enter into an overt agreement on price is to increase the *pool* of profits available to all sellers in an industry. The agreement on price might benefit some sellers outside the collusive group, but to be effective it must raise the pool of profits for those in the club above that amount available prior to the agreement. Once the pool of additional profits is created, the collusive group must assure its members will share the pool as an incentive to join or remain in the group. This type of cooperative behavior is called joint-profit maximization. It is this interest in creating additional joint profits that distinguishes cooperative behavior from non-cooperative behavior. Non-cooperative strategies are pursued with the objective of increasing single-firm profits, possibly at the expense of the profits of the firm's rivals. Some types of price-leadership behavior are non-cooperative oligopolistic conducts. In most price leadership cases, a single firm may be designated as the first mover in announcing price changes. This works as a collusive device because the leader conjectures that it will be followed under certain conditions and because the followers conjecture that a sufficiently large share of leading firms will follow. If such a form of industry behavior evolved through historical repetitions, it is tacit collusion.[8]

Price fixing has long been recognized as a problem in natural markets. Adam Smith, the founder of neoclassical economics, was a keen observer of the business practices of his day. Perhaps referring to behavior he observed in the coffee houses of 16th-century London or Edinburgh, he wrote in his famous 1776 book *The Wealth of Nations* that

> " . . . people of the same trade seldom meet together, even for merriment and diversion, but the conversation ends in a conspiracy against the public, or in some contrivance to raise prices."

This passage neatly describes *horizontal* price fixing, that is, an explicit contrivance among sellers of the same product. It also points to the fact that a conspiracy may involve a wider array of specific agreements besides price fixing *per se.* Indeed, "price fixing" is really just a popular, short, and convenient phrase for the broader class of activities called "restraint of trade," a term that has a complex meaning in economics and the law.

Setting Prices and Conditions of Sales

A more complete list of collusive restraints is shown in Table 2.1. While raising prices (and thereby profits) is the key or ultimate objective, many other actions may be agreed upon to support that objective. There are six categories of trade restraints covered by the general term "price fixing." The first category covers price agreements proper and terms of sale that can directly affect the prices paid by customers. In every case, these decisions by a group of sellers have the effect of reducing the total number of different prices sellers can charge and reducing the discretion of sellers in bargaining over price. By narrowing the array of alternative prices, a cartel reduces the costs of negotiating an initial agreement on prices and the costs of monitoring adherence to an agreement in force.

Most cartels begin by agreeing on list prices, that is, the price quoted to potential buyers in a company's catalog, on its web site, or by fax or telephone by its salespersons. The agreed-upon price tends to be an exact rounded number, such as $1.20 per pound (rather than $1.185 per pound) (Lanzilotti 1996). For ordinary consumers, there is no distinction between list price (also called "posted" or "shelf" prices) and the price at which a transaction will occur. However, for industrial products only the smallest or most anxious buyers will pay the full list price; these are called spot sales. The purchasing managers or agents for major buyers will expect a discount for the large quantities their company expects to purchase, and they may be willing to sign a long term supply contract to enhance their bargaining position. Thus, for large and contract buyers, a list price is simply a guide for the beginning of haggling that is expected to result in significant discounting or rebating after deliveries are made. In some industries, the largest buyers solicit written bids from sellers they believe qualified to serve them. Most price-fixing conspiracies aimed at industrial markets make side agreements on the maximum size or number of discounts to be allowed for each participant.

Table 2.1. Collusive Activities in Restraint of Trade.

Pricing:	• Agreeing on list or transaction prices • Agreeing on delivery charges • Agreeing on discounts, rebates, or premia • Agreeing on bid prices • Agreeing on currency exchange rates • Agreeing on price protection clauses
Shares:	• Setting global sales shares • Setting global quantities per seller • Setting regional or national shares • Allocating specific customers • Allocating winners on bids
Production:	• Agreeing on global output reduction • Agreeing to limits on export destinations • Restricting arbitrage by buyers • Agreeing to restrict production capacities • Refraining from production or sales
Monitoring:	• Sharing frequent, detailed sales information • Agreeing to third-party certification of shares • On-site inspections of facilities or inventory • Meeting-the-competition clauses
Enforcement:	• Dominant firm targets deviants • Periodic compensation mechanism • Marketing agency for pooling sales • Pooling and division of profits • Trigger-price agreements
Cover-up:	• Destroy evidence of travel, meetings, communications, or monitoring • Create or use existing trade association • Use code language or ciphers

In many industrial markets, the conditions of sale are well known, customary, or specified by widely accepted uniform contract provisions. Where this is not the case, conspirators often must negotiate a common set of transactional conditions. These may include payment dates (e.g., due within 30 days of delivery), price protection clauses (limits on purchases made after a price increase is announced but before it is effective), price ratios for different quality grades (if any), and transportation charges. Where quality grades exist, most conspiracies will focus on the purest or most common product form and rely on conventional discounts or premia to be applied to the modal product form. List prices frequently are quoted on the assumption that the seller will provide delivery of a full truckload or rail car within some conventional delivery zone. Smaller loads or more distant deliveries will require price premiums. In some cases customer pick-up discounts will be specified. Unless transportation schedules are set by customary industry practice, cartel members must grapple with creating them; otherwise buyers will be able to use them as bargaining points to obtain discounts that are difficult to detect. Geographic price differences may be quite complex in an extensive market like the United States; collusion will be more difficult if production sites are widely scattered and if imports from multiple plants is significant. Global price fixing is further complicated by the existence of multiple currency regimes whose exchange rates fluctuate. If regional price differences become too pronounced, a price agreement can be undermined by geographic arbitrage by companies outside the cartel. Most of the global cartels covered in this book used the U.S. dollar to shore up regional price uniformity and instituted quarterly price changes.

Fixing Market Shares

The more successful a collusive group is in setting transaction prices at or close to the monopoly level, the greater the incentive for individual members to offer secret discounts to customers. In effect, such cheating on the price agreement will result in an increase in the quantity share of the deviant firm.[9] To counter such tendencies a cartel may assign volume limits or market shares to each cartel member. Negotiating volume or sales shares for its members is not strictly necessary for a cartel, but

> "The members of most cartels recognize that price-fixing schemes are more effective if the cartel also allocates sales volume" (Spratling 1999:11).

One reason that share agreements reinforce cartel cohesion is that quantities can be more easily monitored by the group than the prices of transactions. That is, faithful members of the cartel can use changes in market shares as indicators of cheating more easily than trying to verify allegations of price discounts to particular buyers.

Typically, each member of the agreement is assigned its historical share of whatever market is being cartelized. However, negotiating acceptable shares in a more dynamic setting, particularly where potential members have been gaining shares in the recent past, will be more problematic and may require considerable diplomacy and compromise. The largest members of the cartel may be asked to give up some of their present market share to satisfy newer upstarts. Alternatively, a dominant or low cost member of the cartel may employ threats or coercion against weaker members.

In the case of geographically widespread cartels, the level of calculating the shares must be decided. The simplest agreement is one that encompasses global sales. A global share agreement is also likely to be the easiest to monitor if cartel members share production or sales data frequently. However, in many cartels there is a tendency for members to desire hegemonies in their home markets or others that they have historically dominated. The extreme example of a localized approach to setting shares would be a cartel that assigns specific buyers to specific sellers in the cartel. Although assigning territorial or customer shares is appealing in its simplicity and holds the promise of easy monitoring, there are several disadvantages. It may prove difficult to reach an initial agreement that involves many territories or customers, and once in place customer allocations will increase the number of opportunities for bickering among the conspirators. Perhaps most problematic is the suspicions raised by customers that observe refusals to deal by all but one of the cartel participants, suspicions that could lead to complaints to antitrust authorities.

Limiting Production or Sales

Given the "law of demand" (i.e., prices and quantities demanded are inversely related), raising prices and reducing quantity should be in principle perfect substitute conducts. That is, a cartel would appear to have the option of raising price or contracting output but should not need to do both. In practice, cartels frequently make volume-reduction agreements in order to reinforce previously agreed price increases. Volume restrictions can be global in scope and may involve sales or investment plans. Agreements to avoid plant expansions are particularly appealing ancillary deals because in a growing market the appearance of capacity constraints would in itself raise prices. Moreover, agreements on plant capacities are much easier to monitor than agreements on sales transactions. Failure to expand capacity as quickly as demand insures the cartel of long-term stability because capacity typically takes years to create and full utilization discourages defections from the cartel.

In global cartels, the phenomenon of international trade in the cartelized product may prove vexing. Agreements on export restrictions may have to be reached in order to effectuate regional or territorial share agreements. Even if cartel members are disciplined in their observance in volume agreements, their customers may not be. Wholesalers may engage in geographic arbitrage if regional price differences widen during a conspiracy. Large geographic price differences may especially appear if a cartel engages in geographic price discrimination. The usual answer to such a problem is rather unappealing: cartel sellers must intimidate buyers into observing a no-arbitrage rule.

Monitoring the Agreements

Simple price fixing is readily monitored by individual cartel members because their customers show a willingness to pay more than the pre-conspiracy price. For market-share or volume-reduction agreements, more elaborate information systems may be established by a cartel. One of the most common monitoring systems involves regular reporting of members' sales or production levels to a designated cartel secretary. The secretary in turn totals up the reported sales and prepares "scorecards," running accounts of each participant's market shares or progress toward a volume-reduction goal. Honest reporting that shows movement toward cartel objectives is an indicator of group harmony and discipline.

Misreporting (usually under-reporting) of company sales may spur the cartel to institute a system of third-party verification. International accounting firms are sometimes hired to perform on-site inspections of plant production, sales, and inventory records. The cooperation of an accounting firm is more likely if the client is a trade association.

Enforcement of Agreements

A common feature of cartels is a firm that takes on the role of "the enforcer." Typically a leading or dominant cartel member will threaten adverse actions against potential deviants in the group. The enforcer may poach customers from a potential cheater or organize a broader boycott against the recalcitrant firm possibly supplemented by rumormongering, bribes, or other strong-arm tactics. Sometimes the threat, usually an increase in production so large that it causes a precipitous decline in price, is directed at firms that are reluctant to join the cartel in the first place. Thus, the enforcer must have sufficient excess capacity to make the threat a credible one. The wavering candidates for membership must be convinced that the enforcer both has sufficient excess capacity and is willing to employ it as a competitive weapon. Historically, the formation of cartels is frequently preceded by price wars because these are tangible demonstrations of the power of the enforcer over market price. Once formed, the enforcer may continue to threaten the others in the cartel with price wars, or the cartel may adopt a "trigger mechanism," a side agreement among cartel members to increase output by a specified amount should cheating be detected. However, the price war is a terribly blunt instrument redolent of self-flagellation. The problem with price wars is that it punishes all the members of a cartel, the enforcer included. Moreover, after the deviants surrender the details of the cartel agreement must be renegotiated.

An alternative to a designated enforcer is a mechanism that will redistribute the monopoly profits among cartel members. One such technique is periodic compensation. A disciplined cartel controls supply but has little influence on demand and may be faced with substitute products that have uncontrollable prices. The likelihood of substitution increases as the cartel becomes more successful in raising price. Thus, even a well-intentioned market-share agreement may be difficult to maintain with great precision over time. Some cartel members, despite their best efforts, may overshoot or undershoot their target market shares. This problem can be handled by developing a compensation system whereby cartel members with excess sales transfer product at cost to those who undershot; the recipients then resell at the elevated cartel price, recouping lost profits in the previous period. In effect, cartel members that sell more than their allotted share are penalized, thus providing a deterrence for future violations of the share agreement.

Another mechanism for redistribution of cartel profits requires a high degree of trust among conspirators. It involves the creation of a secret or illegal joint venture. The new subsidiary of the cartel becomes the sole marketing agency for cartel output. In some historical instances the common sales agency actually took title to the product, as would a merchant wholesaler. Quarterly or annually this joint venture would redistribute profits to its "stockholders," the members of the cartel, according to some previously agreed formula. Alternatively, a less formal profit-sharing plan might be developed by a cartel. Periodically, the members will meet and share its internal profit-and-loss statements, calculate the total profits of their profit centers, and apply the formula for redistribution. In the latter case, the level of trust is extraordinary because each of the participants must reveal their costs of production. However, profit pooling is particularly useful for attracting and holding cartel participants with relatively high costs of production.

Covering Up Cartel Activities

Where cartels are legal, no covers need be implemented. Indeed, cartels may prefer to register their contracts with a national administrative body or court system so that legal authorities will help enforce the cartel's agreements. In the United States, Webb-Pomerene export cartels submit reports of their collusive activities annually to the Federal Trade Commission.

However, when a cartel operates without the sanction of law, efforts are made to keep its activities clandestine. Evidence that could help possible future prosecutions is destroyed or kept to an absolute minimum. Face-to-face meetings are still the preferred mode of communication of cartels, because they avoid possible future indictments for mall fraud or wire fraud. If the telephone must be used, code names or ciphers are devised. The major problem with face-to-face meetings, especially for global conspiracies, is that they create a paper trail of travel records. To overcome this problem, cartels often hold meetings concurrent with those of an otherwise legitimate trade association. Commodity trade associations operate for nearly every industry with at least a few hundred million dollars in sales; indeed, the formation of such associations is actively encouraged by the European Commission. In some cases, cartels create sham associations with fake agendas as a cover for illegal price discussions.

CARTEL THEORY

A cartel is organized for the purpose of maximizing the joint profits of its members. If completely effective in meeting this goal, the oligopolists that are parties to the agreement will enjoy collective profits equal to those of a monopoly in the same industry. A cartel may be viewed as a temporary and usually partial merger among rival sellers for the purpose of generating monopoly profits. For various reasons, including the costs of colluding, the inability of a cartel to insure compliance with the agreement, and uncertainty about market conditions, most cartels fall short of generating full monopoly profits.

The first formal theory of cartel behavior is that of George Stigler (1964).[10] According to this model, cartels will be formed if the net present discounted value of the economic expected total profits made during the collusive period exceed profits that would have accrued during the same period in the absence of collusion (Dick 1998). The collusive profits exclude any added costs of monitoring and enforcing the cartel. The but-for profits will be zero if the alternative to collusion is perfect competition, but often the but-for scenario is tacit collusion that would generate positive economic profits. Green and Porter (1984) put Stigler's model in the form of game theory.[11]

The initial formation of a cartel will depend on the predicted collusive profits, predicted costs of managing the cartel, and predicted but-for profits. Because potential cartel participants generally can be expected to ascertain easily their costs of production and distribution, the major items that need to be predicted are the collusive price, the duration of the agreement, the chances of being caught and prosecuted, and the economic costs of the price-fixing penalties.[12] There are likely to be uncertainties and differences of opinion among the potential conspirators on each of these four major factors; the greater the uncertainty and differences, the less likely the cartel will be formed. The expected collusive price may be one of the easier items upon which agreement can be made. An approximate notion of the elasticity of market demand and knowledge about substitutes at anticipated cartel-enhanced price levels will usually suffice. The fact that most cartels are established by sales or marketing managers probably ensures that the conspirators will have the necessary expertise about customer behavior. If the expected cost of discovery and punishment are low enough, then predictions about durability will have little influence on cartel formation because even the short run collusive profits will be positive and high enough to justify launching a cartel. Prior to the mid-1990s, the size of government fines and civil settlements for price fixing *were* small in the major industrialized countries (see Chapter 3 below, Posner 1976). Now corporate price-fixing penalties are much larger, but *personal* penalties are either completely absent (as in the European Union) or treated under the law as civil misdemeanors in all but a few jurisdictions.[13] Finally, the expected costs of collusion are low because the subjective probability of detection is low, as surveys of antitrust lawyers in the United States and Europe verify (Feinberg 1985).[14]

If a cartel agreement is successful in raising market price, individual firms in the cartel can make even more profit by "cheating," that is, selling some of their output at prices below the agreed-upon price. Cartel members incur costs in monitoring the sales activities of co-conspirators. Moreover, one or more of the participants must be prepared to discipline deviants once they are detected. The costs of punishing mavericks may be quite large, especially if a severe price war ensues that drives down profits into negative territory.

Cartels are usually clandestine, and in the absence of third party reporting of market transactions, cheaters may be able to hide their chiseling from their co-conspirators.[15] As a result, cartels will usually attempt to detect cheating indirectly from ambiguous or probabilistic information (Dick 1998). Stigler's model suggests that evidence on cartel cheating can be inferred from the behavior of customers. Evidence of cheating can be inferred from a participant's failure to attract an equal share of first-time buyers, a failure to retain its historical share of loyal customers, and by a decline in the market shares of non-cheaters in the cartel. This last signal would require somewhat reliable and frequent reports of members' market shares and a good notion of total market consumption. No cartel can expect to eliminate all cheating.[16]

The basic task of a cartel is to set a uniform market transaction price. Uncertainty about the costs of monitoring and policing the agreement will often imply that a cartel will start with a price well below the monopoly price. As experience, trust, and discipline grow, the price will ratchet up towards the profit-maximizing monopoly price. Thus, a cartel must regularly meet to reset the price, particularly to take into account shifts in demand or supply conditions. If different grades exist, price discounts and premia must be established and perhaps adjusted over time. The cartel must develop policies that discourage its members from expanding their sales through service differentiation. All these tasks will be made more effective if the cartel can agree to set observable market shares for each participant or divide markets by geography, product form, or class of customer. Meeting-the-competition clauses in sales agreements are a simple method of detecting cheating. All the cartel's customers then have an incentive to expose below-price transactions. Another enforcement mechanism is the trigger-price agreement, in which cartel members agree to expand output by a prescribed amount should the market price fall below some critical level.

CONDITIONS FACILITATING COLLUSION

Economists began analyzing the forces that affect the formation and stability of cartels in the early 20th century. At first modeling this phenomenon was rather intuitive – simply a contrast between the market environments that foster competition with those that are compatible with pure monopoly. In the 1930s, progress in cartel theory was aided by the discovery and development of simple, static oligopoly models. Thinking about cartels was also greatly influenced by legal-economic case studies of the tobacco, steel, aluminum, and other industries with well documented cartel prosecutions. By the late 1950s, industrial organization had taken on a separate identity within economics, with its own specialized textbooks and academic journals. This became known as the structure-conduct-performance (SCP) or "mainstream" school of industrial economies. By the 1960s, the SCP school was heavily involved in statistical studies of markets, including cartelized ones.

The "Chicago School" of industrial economies mounted a number of serious challenges to the orthodoxy of the mainstream in the 1970s. However in the area of cartel analysis, there were few substantive differences between the two schools of thought. The principal difference was the importance of government regulations in supporting cartel behavior. The Chicago School tended to give great weight to regulations as an explanation for the formation and durability of private cartels. While the critical role of governments is clear in cartels like OPEC, mainstream economists tended to dismiss the importance of regulatory bodies in maintaining most cartels organized by corporations.

A greater and more lasting contribution to cartel analysis was the explosion of mathematical models of collusion emanating from the relatively new field of game theory.[17] Game theory is well suited to the study of oligopolistic decision making because of the many analogues between games and oligopolies. Both have a limited number of players, well-defined payoffs (i.e., profits), and strategies for winning. In a market setting, strategies are rules or decision criteria that are limited by the environment (cost and demand conditions) and formed on a basis of conjectures about the anticipated reactions of rivals. Conjectures may be formed *independently* by merely observing rivals actual choices through time as market conditions vary or *cooperatively* by an overt agreement or by signaling intent. Collusion is one cooperative strategy available to those firms in an oligopoly game.

Mathematical game theories vary greatly in the degree of realism embodied in the assumptions (Pearce 1992). Early models assumed that the payoffs were fixed and known with certainty; more recent models allow for variable-sum payoffs in which the total profits can rise or fall as the firms choose alternative strategies. In some, players start out with identical endowments, while in others firms may have access to variable cost configurations. In some models, players choose quantity of production (Cournot) in others price (Bertrand). The earliest games were single-period (comparative-static). Others allow for two stages in which different strategic choices are made, and still others for an infinite sequence of moves and countermoves (so-called supergames). Repeated interaction among firms often leads to outcomes that can be described as cooperative behavior. Cooperation is rewarded by higher profits, but deviation from monopoly output levels is punished by a reversion to non-cooperative levels (often Cournot equilibria) that generate lower profits. More recent models have been able to incorporate environmental uncertainty and learning by the players over time. Repeated games are not necessarily superior to one- or two-stage games; the latter may be better suited to explaining explicit collusion and cartel formation (Nocke 2000).

From formal theorizing and empirical studies of collusive behavior, a number of well accepted facilitating conditions for cartel formation and stability were deduced. Game-theory models tend to result sometimes ambiguous conclusions about the role of market and firm characteristics; put another way, predictions about market equilibria depend crucially upon often small changes in assumptions or parametric values. The rest of this section summarizes the contributions of economic analysis of sellers to collude, with special attention to factors that explain the formation of overt conspiracies.

High Seller Market Concentration

Assuming that there are barriers to entry, the Stigler model and virtually all others predict that the expected market price under collusion will be positively correlated with the degree of seller market concentration. With one or two exceptions this result is a continuous one. That is, there is no threshold level for concentration above which collusion first becomes feasible; also, most models do not require an upper limit on the number of firms to obtain a collusive result. An exceptional model is by Selten (1973).[18] As a rule of thumb, Selten predicts that cartels are unlikely to be formed when there are more than five equal-sized firms (Herfindahl index below 2000). Philips (1995) finds that six is the critical threshold. Dick (1998) asserts that very high levels of concentration are likely to induce tacit rather than overt collusion; moderate to high seller concentration is conducive to cartel formation and persistence.

Empirical studies of discovered and prosecuted U.S. price-fixing conspiracies have confirmed the requirement of small numbers of firms. Fraas and Greer (1977) found that the majority had fewer than eight firms, but there have been successful prosecutions of cartels with up to 30 participants. Cartels with larger numbers of members tended to need formal associations or common sales agencies to pull off their conspiracies. Hay and Kelly found that 80 percent of the cartels in their sample had ten or fewer members.

Low Buyer Concentration

Often overlooked is the structure of the buyers' market. Collusion should be facilitated by an atomistic structure among buyers. The reasoning is straightforward. To achieve the same level of additional sales, a deviant firm will have to make a larger number of price concessions when there are many buyers compared to a more oligopsonistic structure. A large number of price cuts means a greater chance of detection, especially when buyers report their transaction prices to other members of the cartel or to third parties. Furthermore, when there are few buyers paired with few sellers, buyers may be more loyal to their suppliers (Stigler 1964). Stability in buyer identities makes it easier to detect cheating indirectly through changes in market shares.

Buyer concentration is considerably more difficult to measure than seller concentration. Measures of buyer concentration require information on customer lists, and these are typically closely guarded by companies. Perhaps for this reason, little empirical verification can be found among cartel studies that low buyer concentration facilitates cartel behavior.

Homogeneity and Standardization

Product homogeneity is a necessary condition for collusion. By definition, a pure monopolist sells a product that is unique: No other brands exist, and there are no substitutes. Cartels may not require such an extreme form of homogeneity to operate successfully. Certain types of product differentiation will mask price cutting while others will encourage nonprice rivalry. Heterogeneity can originate from several avenues, some of which can be accommodated by a cartel (Scherer and Ross 1990).

First, product differences in tangible or subjective quality can cause heterogeneity. Heterogeneity arising from the first source may be traced to purity, power, durability, or some other gradation in quality that all buyers prefer more of. This type of differentiation (technically vertical differentiation) can be handled by the development of industry grades or product standards. A cartel can accommodate grade-based price differences, though at some additional costs of negotiation and enforcement. The second, subjective type of differentiation arises from a taste for variety among consumers (horizontal differentiation) that can be reinforced through brands and image advertising.[19] This kind of differentiation is most likely to be incompatible with pricing coordination. Carried to its extreme, horizontal differentiation implies that a unique bundle of real or imagined characteristics is sold to each buyer. Custom-made products make for nearly insuperable barriers to price collusion.

A second source of product heterogeneity is spatial differentiation. Customers will often prefer products that originate from certain locations or sellers that are closer to them. When sellers are located in widely separated regions or countries, transportation costs alone will tend to create geographically localized monopolies. While cartels can overcome the effects of spatial heterogeneity, the phenomenon greatly complicates price schemes. As a result, collusion is more common for industries in which production or sales locations are geographically clustered or in which transportation costs are small relative to selling prices.

Third, product designs may change frequently over time. This is true in fashion goods and in industries experiencing rapid technological change. Temporal differentiation frustrates attempts to collude on price because frequent renegotiations of an agreement increase both the costs of operating a cartel and the chances of bickering.

Fourth, heterogeneity among sellers may be due to differences in production processes rather than the products themselves. Or, firms may have asymmetric access to relevant market information such as the total size of the market or the market shares of major rivals. Variations in marginal costs of production across firms will make agreement on an optimal cartel price more difficult (Rothschild 1999). High cost firms will prefer higher prices. While such differences do not make arriving at a consensus impossible, it raises the costs of colluding. In addition to lengthening negotiation time, a profit-pooling arrangement may have to be implemented to attract high-cost participants to the cartel. Alternatively, high-cost participants may have to be granted larger market shares from the cartel than their historical market positions would dictate. If the largest firms have the lowest costs, they may have to intimidate the smaller ones into joining the cartel, which does not bode well for stability of the agreement.

The foregoing discussion suggests that cartels are less likely to be formed during the early years of a new industry than an industry's more mature phase. At an industry's formative stage, there are likely to be several potential production technologies vying for supremacy. Later, the less efficient methods of production will be weeded out leaving a more standardized combination of plant size and input-output relationships across firms. Moreover, when an industry reaches a certain threshold in size, it is more likely to have a trade association or cadre of industry analysts that help spread information around about the industry's best technologies. That is, asymmetry of information will decline. Ample empirical evidence exists showing a relationship between cartel operation and product or technological homogeneity (Dick 1996, Asch and Seneca 1975, Fraas and Greer 1977).

Entry Barriers

High concentration and product homogeneity are usually sufficient conditions for at least some type of collusion in the short run. However, a cartel will not be durable unless entry is slow or difficult.

Many models of collusion assume that entry into the industry is blockaded during the period of analysis (Pearce 1992). Actual entry or the threat of entry will complicate the formation and stability of collusive arrangements. Entry will be slow or forestalled by inaccessibility to low cost production methods by would-be entrants, sunk costs of production (which may be signaled by high fixed costs of production), and customer loyalty (Schmitt and Weder 1998, Scherer and Ross 1990). In addition, the established firms in an industry can pursue strategies that will raise barriers to entry or exit. They may limit prices below the short-run profit-maximizing level or raise rivals' costs (Granitz and Klein 1996). When cartels are successful in raising price, new entry is more likely to be induced but the greater the share of fringe firms, the lower the cartel price will be (Nocke 2000). The ideal mechanism for preventing entry is government sponsorship or regulation of cartels; the power of government can be used to make membership in a cartel compulsory. In the 20th century, cartels were often the favorite tool for governments to "rationalize" industries. Short of sponsorship, government may be induced to use its regulatory powers to slow or prevent entry (Lanzilotti 1996).

Private cartels may have to take steps to slow entry. One method is to reduce the cartel price below the level it considers optimal. The additional stability may generate more profits in the long run than those sacrificed near term by the lower price. Another technique is for the cartel or its leading members develop large excess capacity so as to credibly threaten output increases upon unwelcome entry. Saudi Arabia played this role in the well-known OPEC oil cartel, but in many cartels the designated enforcer may build excess capacity to threaten both would-be deviants and potential entrants. Predatory tactics have been noted in several historical studies of cartels (Scott-Morton 1996, Levenstein 1993).

Growth and Demand

There is a large and somewhat contradictory literature on the role of demand changes in collusive decisions. This literature does not apply so much to seasonality or regular cycles in demand as to unforeseen demand shocks. Unexpected surges in growth are expected to lead to increases in capacity utilization (decreases in excess capacity). The traditional view is that, like monopolists, collusive arrangements would require a "passive sales" rule; that is, rather than adjust price or volume in the face of demand perturbations, collusive firms would want to absorb the changes by building up inventories or increasing orders backlogs (Scherer and Ross 1990). On the other hand, passive sales behavior increases the likelihood that during unanticipated recessions would be tempted to dump excess stocks, thus setting off a price war. When demand is low and excess capacity high, the threat of entry is reduced making the likelihood of cartel formation (and higher prices) higher. Thus, compared to competitive industries, the conventional view is that collusive behavior results in dampened price flexibility and in counter cyclical price change movements (Rotemberg and Saloner 1986, 1989; Schmitt and Weder 1998). Staiger and Wolak (1992) and Goodhue (1998) use somewhat different theoretical approaches to conclude that demand volatility tends to cause more and more severe price wars, but they do not agree with the timing. On the other hand, a model developed by Green and Porter (1984) and generalized by Abreu *et al.* (1986) predicts that cartels would punish deviants with a price war whenever the cartel observes negative demand shocks. That is, cartels would induce procyclical price changes.

The evidence on countercyclical price changes in collusive (or high concentration) industries seems to be supported by some studies (Domowitz *et al.* 1986) as does the tendency for cartels to be formed when demand is low or slowing down (Nocke 2000). The regularity of price wars is not well established empirically, partly because it is difficult to disentangle price wars from mere price reductions (Porter 1985). Moreover, there seems to be an untested presumption in this literature that a tendency toward frequent price wars is to be interpreted as supporting collusive behavior.

Other Factors

Early work is appearing on a host of other possible determinants of collusive behavior. There is a hint in the work of Lambertini (1996) that the shape of the industry demand curve may affect collusion. While most theorists specify linear demand, Lambertini suggests that Cournot behavior is more likely when demand is highly convex, a demand condition associated with differentiated product industries. The attitudes and cultural orientation of cartel managers may affect cartel formation. With long run financial goals uppermost, cost heterogeneity is less likely to inhibit cartels (Scherer and Ross 1990). This hypothesis may explain why cartel formation is more common among firms in Asia, where managers have reputations for focusing on distant profit or market-share goals. Highly localized markets seem more prone to collusion (Dick 1998). This could be a surrogate for high seller concentration, or it may capture a tendency for more uniform business cultures to spawn collusion. If so, both geographic and cultural propinquity will facilitate conspiracies. Even the leadership styles of CEOs are being factored in. Industries that lack innovation may find cartel formation to be more compatible with an autocratic management style (Rotemberg and Saloner 1991).

EFFECTS OF COLLUSION[20]

A successful cartel has the power to move the market price. A sellers' cartel will attempt to raise the price paid by its customers, and a cartel of buyers will aim to lower the price it pays to its suppliers. Figure 2.1 illustrates the first case, market power exercised by sellers. A market consists of two sides, a set of buyers who have different degrees of willingness to pay for a product at different quantities and a set of producers whose technologies of production determines their ability to supply various quantities at different prices. The willingness to buy is summarized in the demand curve shown in Figure 2.1. Demand curves are almost always downward sloping because as the market price falls more customers enter the market and existing customers will be able to afford to buy more. The ability of suppliers to make and sell product is represented by the supply curve which can be either flat or upward sloping. The area on the graph *below* or to the right of the supply curve is an infeasible region because suppliers will not be able to recover their costs.[21] The area *above* and to the right of the demand curve is not a feasible equilibrium zone either. Thus, the point at which the two curves cross represents the maximum quantity (Q_c) that can be sold at price P_t; and at price P_t consumers will purchase all of Q_c placed on the market. The intersection point is the long-run competitive equilibrium point in this market, given the preferences of buyers and the current technology of supply. The price P_t that consumers are willing to pay for quantity Q_c is exactly equal to the full marginal costs of production of supplies M_c.

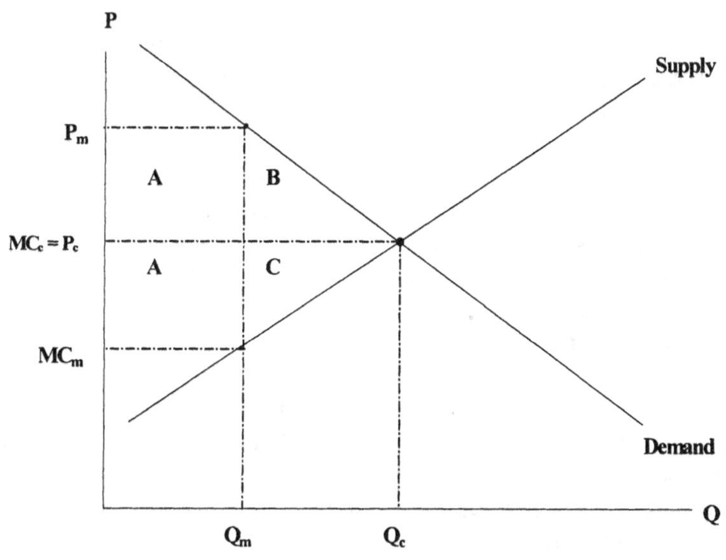

Figure 2.1. Welfare Effects of Collusion.

When a cartel is formed encompassing all suppliers in the industry, it will maximize the profits of all of them by setting the price at P_m, which is what a monopolist would charge in the same market. Given no other changes in this market, when the price jumps from P_o to P_m consumers pull back on their purchases. The maximum quantity that those who remain in the market is willing to buy at price P_m is Q_m. Suppliers have no power to force consumers to buy more than Q_m, so the cartel must reduce its output to Q_m also. This simple one-period model can be made more elaborate by considering changes in inventories and other dynamic features of markets, but it illustrates the main points as it is.

Price fixing has two distinct effects on the market participants. First, there is a change in total market revenues and costs of production. Before the price was increased, consumers bought quantity Q_c at price P_t. Thus, total revenues for producers were P_o*Q_c dollars. When the price rises to P_m, the revenue becomes P_m*Q_m. At the same time, as the quantity of industry output shrinks from Q_c to Q_m, the marginal costs of production falls from MC_c to MC_m. The total costs of producing Q_m is always going to be less than producing Q_c.[22]

The upshot of all these changes is that the aggregate profits of sellers will increase from zero when the price was competitive to the rectangle A when price is P_m. That is, when quantity declines to Q_m, profits will become the difference between total revenues $P_m \cdot Q_m$ and total costs MC_m*Q_m. The profit rate will be $(P_m - MC_m)/P_m$, and this is a direct measure of the degree of market power held by the cartel.[23] In actual market situations, a cartel may fail to attract all the suppliers, may fear impending entry, or may miscalculate. If so, the market price will be somewhat below P_m Similarly, the cartel may incur additional costs in policing its agreement, which would raise its costs above MC_m and cause some reduction in profits. If cartel enforcement costs are to high, it will not be formed. If formed, cartel members must anticipate that its monopoly profits will outweigh the possible costs of discovery and prosecution. No matter what additional costs of colluding might be, the buyers end up paying all of rectangle A as a sort of monopoly tax on their purchases. This *overcharge* is a direct measure of the economic harm done to buyers of a cartelized product. Formally, the overcharge is a transfer of income from buyers to the owner of the supplying companies.[24] Because conspiring is never a free good, the size of the overcharge (the injury) is going to be larger than the amount of monopoly profits generated (the gain). Some economists believe that the additional costs of carrying out a conspiracy and industry lobbying for market power should be counted as a loss for both consumers and producers (a social loss).

The second effect of cartel pricing is entirely a social loss. On figure 2.1 it is represented by the two triangles B and C. The upper triangle is a loss to consumers, and the lower triangle is a loss to producers. These losses are incurred because of the cutback in sales and output from Q_m. For consumers, this loss is a result of their withdrawal from the market due to an unacceptably high price; they are forced to give up consumption of the cartelized product and uses their spendable income on an inferior substitute if any exists. For producers, the contraction in industry output means operating at suboptimal levels or exiting the industry. In either case, some labor and plant resources will lie idle. This monopoly loss is called the *dead-weight loss.* Although not apparent in Figure 2.1, the dead-weight loss is typically many times smaller than the overcharge.

There are relatively few empirical studies of the price and profit effects of cartels. A major early monograph on global cartels was able to find few precise estimates of price increases in cartelized markets (Edwards 1944). A clever study by Bosch and Eckhard (1991) examined the stock market price reactions of listed firms charged with price fixing by U.S. antitrust authorities. They estimated that the 127 firms lost a net present value of $2 billion in profits as a result of these regulatory actions. A similar study of a conspiracy by NASDAQ market makers determined that their bid/offer margins were inflated by 30 percent before their conspiracy was exposed publicly (Christie *et al.* 1994). Stock-price studies are limited by having to make strong assumptions about temporal cost relationships and about the dates of the conspiracy and information shocks to the market. Studies based on product price data have found price elevations due to cartels of from 3 percent (Audretsch 1989) to 23 percent (Froeb *et al.* 1993). In the three global price-fixing cases that are examined most closely in this book, the overcharge rates were estimated to lie in the 15 to 30 percent range (see below). However, there is in theory no strict supper limit to the overcharge rate; in one recent case prosecuted by the Federal Trade Commission, prices on two anti-anxiety drugs were believed to be elevated by 2000 to 3000 percent. There is even less evidence on the long run effects of cartel prosecutions on prices. Sproul (1993) concluded that price-fixing cases did not stimulate lower industry prices. Feinberg (1986) found in a sample of German firms prosecuted for price fixing that while price-cost margins fell, the price effects lasted only for about two years.

CARTEL HISTORIES

Soon after they first appeared in the U.S. economy around the 1870s, popular books were written about the "trusts" that were organized in the sugar, railroad, petroleum, tobacco, and many other industries. Richard Ely's classic book *Monopolies and Trusts* published in 1900 was one of the first serious economic analyses of the phenomenon. "Trusts" was the turn-of-the-century term for large economic combinations, often forged by mergers, for creating and sustaining market power. Today these organizations would be called holding companies, syndicates, pools, joint sales agencies, or simply monopolies.

Around the time of World War II the attention of serious books on economic history turned toward European and especially German cartels.

Indeed, the English word for formal price-fixing coalitions was borrowed from the German word *kartell* with the same meaning. Cartels may be organized to control production, distribution, merchandising, property rights, pricing, or any combination of these business activities. Although the term cartel has many near synonyms, it alone carries the connotation of a combination of normally antagonistic entities whose purpose is the restraint of trade. Syndicates or monopolies are not by themselves illegal, though monopoly behavior usually is.

Among the first historical studies of German cartels were those by Stockder (1924) and Trittelvitz (1939). Modern historians continue to draw lessons from German cartels, many of which began in the 1870s and ended during Word War I (Webb 1997). The German coal and steel cartels have received especially close scrutiny (Weganroth 1964, Peters 1989). Lundqvist (1998) examined the formative period of the Swedish beer cartel in the 1890s. Although it took 15 years of tumultuous negotiations to finally coalesce, the Swedish beer cartel operated quite harmoniously for 50 years (1906-1956), mainly because of the threat of a strong national temperance movement to extinguish the industry. Many U.S. and U.K. cartels also began in the late 19th century. The U.S. bromine cartel operated from 1885 to 1914 (Levenstein 1997). Collusion with the U.S. railroads in the 1870s was an essential ingredient in the predatory tactics that helped establish the Standard Oil monopoly (Granitz and Klein 1996). U.S. railroads began successfully colluding among themselves in the early 1880s (Porter 1983). Even after the U.S. Interstate Commerce Commission was established to regulate railroad transportation rates in 1887 (the very first federal industry regulatory agency), five railroads were able to continue colluding on express passenger trains (Grossman 1996). The U.S. railroad express cartel lasted for an extraordinary 52 years. One reason for the continuing interest in these early cartels is they were entirely legal at the time and there are numerous historical records available. Indeed, most of these cartels received government acquiescence and some got government support.

The most durable private cartel in history was established in 1934 to control the prices of rough gem-quality diamonds. De Beers Consolidated is a South African company that propped up the prices of gem diamonds by controlling the supply of diamonds between the point of mining and the point at which they are cut. In 1934 and other times when demand for diamonds softened because of recessions in the major importing countries, De Beers purchased and held large inventories of rough diamonds. Originally in control of the output of mines only in South Africa, De Beers negotiated often secret supply contracts with governments in the Soviet Union, Zaire, and other parts of tropical Africa. From the 1930s until the mid 1980s, De Beers controlled more than 90 percent of the world's supply of rough gem diamonds. However, as new supplies were discovered in Canada, Australia, and other countries that lay outside De Beers' grasp, its share of global supply slid to 63 percent in 1999 (*Wall Street Journal* July 13, 2000). In 2000, De Beers Centenary AG, the company's Swiss-based operating division, announced that it was abandoning its supply-control activities.[25] The cartel had lasted 66 years.

After 1890, cartels became illegal in the United States and Canada, and federal government victories in the courts against price fixing and monopolies during 1908-1914 led to the disbanding of most U.S. cartels by World War I. However, many private commodity cartels were re-established during the interwar period in Europe. During the 1920s and 1930s several of the formerly "domestic" cartels (some controlled exports) took on an international character. For example, the 1933-1939 international steel export cartel managed production and sales among several of the major continental European steel-producing nations (Barbezat 1993). Stocking and Watkins (1946) wrote about several international cartels that were active in the interwar period. They provided several chapter-length summaries of the magnesium, aluminum, incandescent electric bulb, and several chemical cartels that operated without government intervention. One example was the second dyestuff cartel. The original dyestuffs cartel was a German and Swiss creation that operated internationally in a very aggressive fashion for several decades prior to World War I. In 1927, it was reborn when a French dyes syndicate joined with an already operating German cartel. In 1929, the four Swiss dye manufacturers became members, and in 1931 the UK's Imperial Chemical Industries (ICI) joined. During the 1930s this dyestuffs cartel controlled 60 to 70 percent of world production capacity and well over 80 percent of global exports. Japanese dye manufacturers were not full members of the cartel, but some had brief bilateral agreements with some of the cartel's members. At the time, U.S. dye manufacturers had a tacitly collusive group that affected prices and technology, but they did not join the global cartel.

The high points for publications about cartels were the years following World War II. Several books were written about the role that German cartels and the Japanese *zaibatsu* played in the emergence of totalitarian political structures in the Axis countries in the 1920s and 1930s. (Reimann 1942, Hexner 1946, Martin 1950, Dubois 1952). Several more books on the topic were written by three of the most prominent economists of the fledgling field of industrial organization: Edward Mason (1946), Corwin Edwards (1944, 1967), and George Stocking (Stocking and Watkins 1947, 1948). Edwards and Stocking had direct experience with the German and Japanese cartels as advisors to the Allied occupation authorities just after the war. They were directly responsible for the imposition of U. S. type antitrust laws and the establishment of national agencies to enforce the new laws: the Federal Cartel Office in West Germany and the Japan Fair Trade Commission. The interwar cartels associated with the Axis powers continue to fascinate historians of more recent generations (Levy 1966, Hayes 1987, and Kudo and Hara 1992).

Edwards (1944) provides many examples of interwar collaboration, some of it unwitting, between U.S. and German companies that ultimately aided the Axis war effort. A particularly apt story concerns the interwar relations between Sterling Chemical and Bayer. During World War I, Bayer's assets were seized by the U.S. government's Alien Property Custodian. In 1918, Bayer's seized U.S. assets were sold to Sterling, including the trademark to Bayer's aspirin, on the condition that Sterling would never surrender control of those assets to Bayer. Beginning in 1919, Bayer began a slow but sure bear hug of Sterling. In 1920, Sterling agreed to pay to Bayer 75 percent of its profits on its Latin American sales of Bayer brand products; in 1922, Bayer proposed a secret merger with Sterling, which the latter resisted; in 1923 and 1926 Sterling did sell controlling interests in a U.S. and a U.K. subsidiary to Bayer; throughout the 1920s and 1930s the two companies colluded on tax evasion of exports in the Americas; and in 1934 Sterling and Bayer agreed to boycott U.S. newspapers carrying "anti-German" articles. Edwards relates other instances of cooperation that resulted in militarily valuable technology transfers from U.K to German chemical companies. Similar cooperation occurred between the U.S. and German chemical industries. The formation of international chemical cartels was mainly the result of European mergers in the 1920s. The biggest of them was the I.G. Farben merger in 1925 (Stocking and Watkins 1946). Bayer, BASF, and Hoechst were the lead companies in the merger, but virtually all-German chemical companies were allied with Farben by ownership or through membership in a Farben-led cartel. By 1940 Farben had created 2000 cartels to cover pharmaceuticals, synthetic fibers, and all other chemical lines. Each cartel established joint sales agencies, exclusive supply arrangements, patent pooling, and profit sharing. Farben became an important part of Germany's war effort and profited mightily from it.[26] Farben, ICI, and DuPont created a loose international chemical cartel in the 1930s. Both DuPont and Sterling continued to abide by the terms of their cartel agreements with Farben until the middle of 1941.

The embarrassing role of international cartels in contributing to World War II combined with an active program of prosecutions by the U.S. Department of Justice in the 1940s seems to have caused a hiatus in international cartels for almost 50 years. Very few legal or economic studies were written about post-war international cartels, perhaps because there were so few of consequence. One of the few monographs on the topic was a legal-economic study of a Japanese television conspiracy that resulted in a famous Supreme Court decision (Schwartzman 1993). A cartel of Japanese electronic-products manufacturers was formed in the 1950s under the guidance of Japan's Ministry of International Trade and Industry (MITI). Several U.S.

manufacturers filed suit in 1970 against Matsushita Electric Industrial Co. and six others alleging price fixing and predatory pricing in the U.S. market for televisions. Schwartzman concludes that the television cartel conspired to acquire a large share of the U.S. market by (1) operating a home-market cartel, (2) investing the cartel profits in export-manufacturing capacity, and (3) setting U.S. export prices below long run average total costs for at least four years beginning in 1967. By the mid-1980s the Japanese cartel members had in fact garnered a dominant U.S. market share, but the facts in the case that went to the Supreme Court stopped in 1970. The close 1986 decision in *Matsushita v. Zenith Radio* has been highly controversial because of the theory of predatory pricing employed by the Court's majority (Scherer and Ross 1990: 469-479). The opinion concluded that up until 1970 consumers had benefited greatly from low television prices and that the cartel had not by that time achieved monopoly power in the U.S. market. The majority chose to ignore the cartel's power in its Japanese market, the evidence of strong *geographic* (as opposed to temporal) price discrimination, and any consideration of the injury to Zenith Radio *et al.*

The Electrical Equipment Conspiracy

Although not an international cartel, by far the most publicized price-fixing conspiracy of the post World War II era was in the heavy electrical equipment industry in the 1950s (Herling 1962, Fuller 1962, Sultan 1974, Walton and Cleveland 1964, Scherer and Ross 1990). The products involved were a vast array of components like turbo-generators, transformers, and switchgear that were purchased by electric power utilities through bidding processes. The three largest suppliers were General Electric, Westinghouse Electric, and Allis-Chalmers. These firms and dozens of smaller manufacturers had been involved in agreements to limit competition since the 1880s, though the effectiveness of the schemes had increased after the 1920s when the rate of technological changes had slowed. From 1911 to 1960 General Electric Company was convicted by the DOJ of price fixing 16 times; in addition, it had signed several consent decrees with the FTC. However, in the electrical equipment industry and probably most others as well, Sherman Act violations were viewed as merely naughty behavior (Fuller 1962). These permissive attitudes were reinforced by the mild sanctions imposed for antitrust violations up through 1959. Fines were modest and paid cheerfully by companies as a "minor cost of doing business" (Herling 1962). Corporate antitrust convictions were the equivalent of corporate parking tickets. Moreover, most individuals were not fined and their prison sentences, if any, usually suspended; as misdemeanors, no loss of civil rights occurred. Finally, the DOJ and the courts routinely permitted guilty parties to plea "*nolo contendere*" rather than "guilty," which meant that their pleas had no bearing on follow-up civil damage suits.

Because of the high fixed costs of manufacturing heavy electrical equipment, cyclic overcapacity had long been a feature of the industry. The Korean War had stimulated demand in the early 1950s that led to excess capacity and a fierce price war in 1955 (Walton and Cleveland 1964). Small numbers of sales people began actively colluding on prices and market shares late that year using the annual meeting of the National Electrical Manufacturers Association as a cover. More frequent meetings began in order to coordinate pricing on complex products in 20 lines, with the passive approval of the companies' top managers.[26] In Congressional testimony after the firms were convicted, F.F. Loock, President of the Allen-Bradley Company said:

> "No one attending the [price-fixing meetings] was so stupid that he didn't know the meetings were in violation of the law. But it is the only way a business can be run. It is free enterprise" (Fuller 1962).

The DOJ indictments alleged that the monopoly profits generated by the conspiracy on generators were 40 percent of sales.

In late 1960, five grand juries handed down 160 indictments, covering 45 senior executives and 29 corporations as defendants (many were indicted on multiple counts because 20 products lines were affected). Affected sales were $7 billion for conspiracies that lasted for up to seven years. In current dollars these products had average annual U.S. sales of at least $5 billion, which means that it still has claim to the title of "the greatest price conspiracy of all time" (Herling 1962).[28]

The large number of convictions of high level executives and well known corporations captured the attention of the public in a way never seen before in antitrust cases. Editorials in major newspapers and famous business leaders blasted the scandalous behavior of the defendants. A survey of the nation's newspapers found that 55 percent placed the December 1960 news of the executives' jail sentences on their front pages. Congressional hearings brought further embarrassment to the electrical equipment companies and their former employees. At General Electric Company, the 17 indicted officers all resigned, and the 23 unindicted co-conspirators were demoted. One major effect of the convictions was the DOJ's insistence on the use of simple guilty pleas in this case; today, *nolo contendere* pleas are hardly ever permitted in Sherman Act violations. The more severe penalties and public condemnation of costly illegal activity had a strong impact on altering business attitudes toward price fixing, which is now generally accepted as seriously unethical (Herling 1962).

The direct buyers of heavy electrical equipment, public utilities, were initially reluctant to seek treble damages by filing civil suits (Walton and Cleveland 1964). However, fear of shareholders' suits drove about 1700 of them to initiate actions by early 1962. Among the plaintiffs was the federal government, which for the first time sued under a 1955 law that allowed the U.S. Department of Justice (DOJ) to obtain treble damages for injured federal agencies such as the Tennessee Valley Authority; the government settled with General Electric in 1962 for $7.7 million. Walton and Cleveland (1964) estimate that the federal settlement represented 16 to 20 percent of affected sales. If correct, then the overcharge was $1.1 to $1.4 billion (1962 dollars). The DOJ, then headed by Attorney General Robert Kennedy, got especially good settlement terms. Had all the other plaintiffs settled at the same rate, the 29 guilty manufacturers would have paid an extraordinary $250 to $300 million in penalties (or $1.2 to $1.5 billion in current dollars). Instead, General Electric and its co-conspirators settled the remaining private suits for only about 2.5 percent of sales.[29] Although threatened at one point with a divestiture, General Electric instead signed a consent decree that essentially said "go and sin no more."

General Electric's subsequent behavior throws into doubt the efficacy of consent decrees as devices to prevent recidivism. First in May 1963, General Electric announced a new pricing policy of "book pricing" for turbo generators. Buyers were told that catalog prices would be followed exactly, adjusted by a periodically updated multiplier. Westinghouse and others soon learned how to replicate GE's prices precisely. Until invalidated by yet another DOJ antitrust suit *(U.S. v. General Electric et al.)* decided in 1976, this new form of price leadership was highly effective in raising prices. Lean *et al.* (1985) argue that GE's profits were actually higher with book pricing than the naked cartel of the 1950s. Second, in May 1973, General Electric was found guilty of Sherman Act violations with respect to its pricing of its light bulbs *(New York Times* May 9, 1974 and May 10, 1974). Third, in 1994 General Electric was a defendant in a global price-fixing case called *Industrial Diamonds.* While many observers found the evidence of guilt convincing, the case was dismissed because of the government's inability to access key foreign witnesses and documents.

One of the outcomes of the *Industrial Diamonds* case would have positive benefits for future investigations of global conspiracies. Immediately after its loss, the DOJ negotiated a Memorandum of Understanding with the U.S. Immigration and Naturalization Service (INS) (Klawiter 1998). The memorandum allowed the DOJ to extend the right to cooperating witnesses to travel freely across U.S. borders even if the witness was later convicted of a price-fixing felony. Offering such a concession would later prove to be a powerful incentive for executives with foreign nationalities or foreign residencies to agree to cooperate with DOJ investigators.

Chapter 2 Endnotes

[1] This statement holds constant the technology of the supplying industry (the production function) and the willingness of buyers to pay for the product (the demand function). The equilibrium price of all markets must be equal to or above the competitive level and below the monopoly price.
[2] The classical economists of the nineteenth century implicitly assumed that trading occurred in a double oral auction in which the participants could observe the price of every transaction. In fact, modern economic analysis verifies that auctions of several types do result in clearing prices and quantities exchanged that are quite close to these predicted by the model of pure competition (Marion *et al* 1987, Plott 1989). However, monopoly and oligopoly tend to be associated with other.trading and exchange systems such as private negotiations, posted prices, formula contracting, administered pricing, and various vertical arrangements. A common characteristic in noncompetitive markets is nontransparency of transactions; not all the prices or quantities traded can be observed by market participants.
[3] Nor is there a role for a trade association to stimulate market demand or to create product standards in a perfectly competitive market. However, if government intervenes in the market, such associations may have a lobbying role.
[4] If P is price, MC is the marginal costs of production and distribution, and η is the elasticity of market demand, then the optimal monopoly price is:

$$P_m = \frac{MC}{(1+1/\eta)} \, .$$

Since η is almost always negative, the bigger its absolute value, the bigger is P_m^* holding costs constant. In a perfectly competitive market η is perceived to be negative infinity; thus $P = MC$.
[5] To the extent that the transfer (monopoly profits) is used by the seller to bolster or maintain its monopoly power, this is also a social loss.
[6] The word oligopoly was coined by Sir Thomas Moore, lawyer and saint, in his book *Utopia* published in Latin in 1516 but translated into English a few decades later. The term was revived in one of the first books on the economics of oligopoly, Edwin Chamberlin's *Theory of Monopolistic Competition* (1933). By the 1950s business newspapers in the United States and United Kingdom began to contain articles using the word *(Oxford English Dictionary).*
[7] Monopolists *can* be charged with illegal behavior by taking actions to prevent the entry of future rivals into their market or prevented the growth of tiny rivals. However, monopolization is not a collusive activity because that requires two or more independent entities.
[8] If, however, the leading firms overtly agreed to such a strategy, it could be held illegal.
[9] The ability to detect secret price-cutting is a key feature that explains the effectiveness and longevity of cartels. Stigler (1964) suggested that cartel members could detect cheating by a decline in the proportion of repeat customers, of customers switching from other suppliers, or the proportion of first-time buyers.
[10] Formal models of duopoly or oligopoly date back to Cournot (1838), Bertrand (1883), and Chamberlin (1929), but these presume independent or tacitly collusive behavior.
[11] McCutcheon (1999) has developed a cartel theory based on the interest group theory of government regulation (see also Bork 1978, Posner 1976). Her model depends on the application of quite small penalties to explain why cartels are formed, yet penalties that are large enough to encourage renegotiation of a cartel agreement after a price war. This model would seem to have been made obsolete by the high price-fixing penalties documented in this book.
[12] Costs of production and distribution are usually readily knowable because production will contract to levels observed in the recent past. Management costs of collusion are trivial except

for price wars and personal and corporate legal penalties. Most cartels appear content to use the pre-cartel prices or profit rates as the but-for scenario.

[13] The United States criminalized price-fixing in 1974 and made it a felony in 1994. Canada, Japan, and three European countries have criminal statutes, but these are rarely enforced (see Chapter 3).

[14] Personal communication from Frederick Warren-Boulton (2000).

[15] Indeed, the presence of reliable reporting on transaction prices will generally make illegal conspiracies infeasible. Organized auction markets are unlikely places for collusive price agreements whereas markets that depend on posted prices or bilateral negotiations are fertile grounds for collusion.

[16] Cheating will be tolerated up to the point where the marginal costs of policing the agreement equal the profits gained from preventing cheating.

[17] The field grew out of a seminal book by John von Neumann and Oskar Morgenstern entitled, *Theory of Games and Economic Behavior* (1944). However, analytical difficulties limited progress in the field until the 1970s.

[18] A one-period, homogeneous-product Bertrand oligopoly with identical firms predicts zero profits from collusion with three or more firms (Martin 1993). One-shot models are generally less applicable to the study of cartels.

[19] Sellers can still exercise market power in such situations, but it is unilateral (single-firm) power not multilateral.

[20] This section focuses on the so-called static welfare effects of monopoly pricing. In addition to price increases, cartels will normally cause posted and exchange prices to become less dispersed compared to prices in now conspiracy periods. Price discrimination may become common (and prices more uniform within target segments). Dynamic effects include price variation disjointed from cost variation, reduced capital investment, and a slowdown in innovation (Posner 1976, Lanzilotti 1996, Scherer and Ross 1990).

[21] These are marginal costs of production and distribution including the opportunity cost of capital (i.e., normal profits). In the short run these are roughly equivalent to variable costs; in the long run a producer must cover both variable and fixed costs. We assume long run in this chapter.

[22] The monopoly price is discovered by equating the marginal costs of production (points on the supply curve) with the marginal revenue (not shown, but it passes through the supply curve at the point where $MC_m = Q_m$).

[23] Figure 2.1 implicitly assumes diseconomies of scale in production because unit costs rise as Q rises. With constant costs, the supply curve would be flat, but total costs will still decline. Whether revenues increase depends on the elasticity of demand at Q_c.$(P_m - MC_m)/P_m$ is called the Lerner Index of market power. At the monopoly level of profits, $(P_m - MC_m)/P = HHI/\eta$, where HHI is the Herfindahl Index of concentration and η is the absolute value of the elasticity of market demand.

[24] Note that "supplying companies" includes both cartel members and those non-cartel firms that passively support the cartel by pricing up to P_m. Legally, the cartel is responsible for all the injury caused to the buyers, even non-cartel sales. Free riders gain but are not legally culpable. If some suppliers choose to price competitively, they create no overcharge.

[25] De Beers' inventory had been climbing for some time, reaching about $5 billion in 1999. De Beer's decision was also prompted by the "blood diamonds" controversy, i.e., the use of diamonds to finance interminable civil wars in Angola, Sierra Leone, and other African countries. De Beers now aims to become a marketer of "De Beers" branded diamonds.

[26] Farben's directors began to support the Nazi party financially as early as 1930. Chemical assets in countries conquered by Germany were given to Farben, as was slave labor to run some of its factories. The Farben directors were tried and found guilty of war crimes late in the Nuremberg trials.

[27] The top convicted GE vice president, W.S. Ginn, said at his sentencing hearing that he was ordered to engage in price fixing by the company's top three officers (who were not indicted) and that price fixing was "a way of life" at GE (Fuller 1962). Top officers were "quarantined" from direct involvement. Orders were "vague and elliptical," used code words ("agreeing on arrangements"), and accompanied with winks.

[28] Corrected by the producer price index for industrial equipment.

[29] Each plaintiff had to negotiate a settlement individually with each defendant. Legal costs as well as the reluctance of plaintiffs to sue important suppliers may be the reasons for the low settlement rate. In the 1970's, class actions would simplify prosecutions and strengthen the hands of the plaintiffs.

Chapter 3

ANTICARTEL LAWS AND ENFORCEMENT

MARKET POWER

The principal application of industrial economics to antitrust analysis is to identify exercised market power. In economics and the law, market power is the ability to control exchange prices or to prevent entry by a buyer or seller into a market. The ability to set prices will never be absolute, but a market participant has power over price if it has discretion to influence price over some range. Similarly, a seller need not be able to blockade market entry entirely to have market power – merely the ability to slow down the rate of entry or prevent one new potential seller from entering is enough.

Market power may be *latent* or it may be *exercised.* An example of latent market power is the so-called Good Monopolist, a firm with a monopoly position in a protected market that chooses to set its price at the competitive level knowing that by doing so it is sacrificing potential profits. Latent market power the law deems innocent, but exercised market power is frequently illegal. Exercised market power may derive from the concerted action of buyers or sellers (also called multilateral market power) or from the conduct of a single, typically dominant firm (unilateral market power). Collective action by buyers of sellers that has as its principal aim the increase or maintenance of their market power is called *collusion* in economics and a *conspiracy in restraint of trade* under the competition laws of most modern industrial countries.

Monopoly is the oldest word in the language to describe market power. It came into English through Latin from Greek *(mono* = single plus *polion* = to sell). The first printed reference to monopoly as economic behavior is found in Sir Thomas More's *Utopia* published in 1551:

> "Suffer not these rich men to buy up all, to engross and forestall, and with their monopoly to keep the market alone as please them."

By 1601, treatises and court decisions in English Common Law condemned monopoly behavior as an unlawful business practice that resulted in the enrichment of the monopolist at the expense of the buyer. The legal term often used to described the crime was "engrossing," but "monopoly" too was used to describe price-fixing conspiracies:

> "Setting the price before hand of that which they sell, and that which they buy, and so committing open Monopoly" (J. Wheeler, *Treatise on Commerce,* 1601).

Also during the early 17th century, the term monopoly was used in commentaries to cover exclusive licenses, patents, and unique business charters granted by the crown or Parliament. These, of course, were legal monopolies.

Originally, the word monopoly covered both the case of a single seller and the case of a few sellers, but by the late 19th century the latter situation had come to be called *oligopoly.* Oligopoly is a descriptive term for an industry with a few sellers, but it does not necessarily denote illegal behavior. Other closely related terms are syndicate, trust, or cartel. *Syndicates* are groups of investors created to carry out schemes requiring large amounts of capital. Except in the context of gambling or stock markets, syndicates are not usually illegal conspiracies.[1] The legal concept of *trust* goes back to at least the 15th century as a legal arrangement whereby property is held by a trustee for the benefit of another person. Trusts were often the legal instruments used to hold the combined assets of merged firms and thereby exercise true monopoly power. Thus, by the 1870s "trusts" had taken on a pejorative connotation. In 1890, G.B. Shaw defined trusts as "a combination to destroy competition and to restrain trade." When the Sherman Act was passed in 1890 to control abusive trust behavior, it became popularly known as an "anti-trust" law even though the law applied also to dominant-firm behavior. The word *cartel* was discussed in Chapter 2 above. Although somewhat comparable to a syndicate or trust, it is the most precise term to describe business combinations formed by agreement to regulate production, sales, or prices. Cartels are oligopolies that engage exclusively in multilateral conduct.

Market power is a matter of degree. In economics the most widely accepted measure of the extent of exercised market power is the Lerner Index, also called the price-cost margin. For a given industry, the Lerner index is the difference between the observed market price and marginal costs divided by the market price (in Figure 2.1, $(P_m\text{-}MC)/P_m$). Given the demand and cost conditions in a particular industry, the Lerner index calculates the maximum profit that a monopolist or dominant firm can earn in the industry.[2] In a perfectly competitive industry, the Lerner index will be zero. By inference, the Lerner Index describes the profit rate on sales or the percentage overcharge that can be attained by an effective cartel, whether the cartel controls total supply or simply a dominant share of industry supply.

The time frame is critical in assessing the degree of market power, and it has important implications for antitrust applications. In the short run, some capital costs are *fixed* in that they do not vary with the level of firm or industry output, whereas the remaining portion of total costs are *variable*. Therefore, in the short run fixed costs are irrelevant to maximizing profits, and the appropriate measure of costs in the Lerner Index is *short run marginal costs*. Consequently, the degree of market power in the short run is always greater than or equal to market power in the long run. In the short run, a profit maximizing firm with market power may not be covering its full costs; that is, the firm's economic profits may be negative and it may not be imposing an overcharge on its customers.[3] From the point of view of antitrust analysis, the presence of long run market power is more serious in the sense that it always generates monopoly profits for sellers and always causes injury to buyers. That is, a positive Lerner Index in the long run may be considered evidence of *monopoly power* or, in the phrase used in antitrust case law, "a high degree of market power" (Werden 2000).

U.S. antitrust case law has incorporated the economic definition of market power in decisions of the Supreme Court going back to 1969. Circuit courts of appeal also have adopted the economic concept of market power. However, the term "monopoly power" is the more common term used by the courts. It is "the power to control prices or exclude competition." This formulation may be interpreted as two alternative ways of exercising a high degree of market power: price fixing and raising barriers to entry. Alternatively, the reference to exclusionary conduct may be interpreted as showing concern for durability as an aspect of high degree of market power. In sum, U.S. antitrust decisions seem to equate monopoly power or a high degree of market power with a positive Lerner Index in the long run. High market shares, concentration, and barriers to entry are often cited as practical indicia of monopoly power. The Lerner Index can also be inferred from the own-price elasticity of demand, and increasingly the courts seem to be adopting this approach (Werden 2000).

THE SHERMAN ACT

The Sherman antitrust act was made law in the United States in July 1890 (Hovenkamp 1998). Although it was preceded by similar laws in several states, it would prove to be the world's first effective anticartel statute.[4] The Sherman Act is descended from the English common law that underpins much U.S. law, but its passage was primarily a populist response to abuses by large-scale industrial trusts that first appeared in the 1880s (Sullivan and Fikentscher 1998). The major goal of the Act was to enhance various libertarian economic and political values protected by the U.S. constitution: property, contract, economic opportunity, and political liberty. Simply as law, the Sherman Act may be viewed as federalizing the common law of trade restraints (Hovenkamp 1998). Its emphasis on preserving the competitive process, protecting buyers from exploitive prices, keeping market entry free, and shielding companies from abusive tactics made the Sherman Act a uniquely American invention. In the early 20th century, the goals of antitrust shifted somewhat as the courts interpreted antitrust as a tool for furthering laissez-faire economic policies. Up to the early 1930s, both the presidential administrations and the courts consistently supported anticartel actions. After a brief hiatus in the mid 1930s when antitrust was abandoned, the symbiotic relationship between German cartels and the rise of National Socialism stimulated a renewed animus toward cartels.

The Department of Justice won its first price-fixing case in *U.S. v. Trans-Missouri Freight Assn.* in 1897 (Hovenkamp 1998). One reason for the lag between passage and enforcement was the broad, even vague language of the Act. Congress intended to state general principles of illegal conduct rather than enumerate specific types of conduct. Thus, Section 1 of the Sherman Act rather simply prohibits

> ". . . every contract, combination . . . or conspiracy in restraint of trade or commerce among the several states, or with foreign nations . . ."

In effect, Congress delegated the interpretation of the law to the federal courts.

As is true of any important law, legal battles are fought over nearly every word in the statute. For example, notwithstanding Congress' use of the word "every," the Supreme Court decided as early as 1911 that only *unreasonable* restraints were intended to be prohibited. Some restraints are classified as unreasonable under every circumstance. Conspiracies that involve agreements on common prices, on market shares, on exclusive sales territories, and on boycotts are generally deemed unreasonable. Such cases are decided on a *per se* illegality basis. That is, these behaviors are illegal irrespective of the circumstances or their market impacts. On the other hand, some types of collusive conduct may have pro-competitive effects as well as effects destructive of competition. These cases are decided on a "rule of reason" basis. That is, the courts will entertain economic evidence about the balance between the benefits and the harm caused by the restraint and will examine under which circumstances one effect may dominate the other. In *per se* violations no economic evidence need be presented to the court.

The Sherman Act may be prosecuted by the DOJ as a criminal felony or as a civil matter at the discretion of the courts. Prosecutors will bring forth criminal charges if they judge the price fixing to be a serious violation and if the evidence for prosecution seems strong enough. The burden of proof in a criminal prosecution falls on the government and involves four elements (Bell and Gaskin 1999). First, the prosecutors must demonstrate beyond a reasonable doubt that a conspiracy or *explicit agreement* was entered into by the parties. Normally, one or more of the parties to the agreement must testify that their oral or written communication was in fact a genuine deal or contract. Second, the defendants must have knowingly and *intentionally* entered into the agreement. In the case of a cartel, the intent must be shown to be the goal of increasing prices or profits of the participants. Third, the conduct must fall into the category of unreasonable restraints. Naked cartel behavior always qualifies. Fourth, federal prosecutors must demonstrate that the market spilled across state borders or international borders. Intrastate trade can only be prosecuted under antitrust laws passed in at least 44 of the 50 states.

Although nearly all overt price conspiracies are prosecuted by the Department of Justice as criminal matters, in a small percentage of cases the evidence may not be strong enough to convince a jury "beyond a reasonable doubt." The DOJ then has the option of prosecuting an alleged cartel as a civil matter. In a civil trial only the preponderance of the evidence is required to obtain a conviction. In most price-fixing cases the most difficult element is the question of intent, so in civil proceedings the jury is often presented with circumstantial evidence about the behavior of the firms that may allow it to *infer* that an agreement must have been made. The Federal Trade Commission, the state attorneys general, and parties injured by a cartel also have standing to bring civil suits against alleged cartels. As plaintiffs, they too are required only to show that a conspiracy was more likely to have occurred than not.

Defendants in Sherman Act cases have a number of possible defenses that may let them go free. First, a defendant may present evidence that it withdrew from the conspiracy more than five years before the case was filed. Second, a corporate defendant may attempt to show that the managers who ran the conspiracy did so in direct violation of company policy. Of course, the "rogue managers" are still liable for prosecution. Third, defendants may attempt to prove that the companies involved in the cartel were in fact under common ownership and control. A company cannot conspire with itself, only another independent business can. Fourth, defendants may argue that they have already been prosecuted for the same crime; this is the "double jeopardy" defense. Fifth, defendants may try to establish that they were acting under government authority. Price-fixing agreements may be legal if a municipal, state, or federal regulatory body oversees an industry. Moreover, certain types of organizations are immune from Sherman Act prosecution; most nonprofits are exempt, and since the 1920s farmers' cooperatives and labor unions have been exempt.[5] Sixth, perhaps the most common defense concerns intent. Defendants will frequently argue that their agreements were for some purpose other than raising prices. They might suggest that their meetings were management-training exercises or that they met simply to exchange innocent information. For both prosecutors and defendants, the actual effect on prices is irrelevant to guilt or innocence. Nor can defendants suggest that they were unaware of the law.

The borderline between *per se* violations of the Sherman Act and rule-of-reason violations have shifted somewhat in the last 30 years or so (Gilbert and Williamson 1998). One type of restrictive practice that is no longer considered a *per se* violation is exclusive dealing. Supreme Court reversed itself on the issue in *GTE Sylvania Inc. v. Continental TV, Inc.* (1977). The Court came to the conclusion that exclusive distribution arrangements could provide efficiencies and benefits to consumers. Similarly, some types of vertical price-fixing arrangements have been considered under a rule-of-reason approach. Setting maximum prices to be charged by franchisees is no longer illegal. However, it is nearly impossible to find credible antitrust experts advocating the abandonment of the *per se* rule for horizontal price fixing, even among those writers hostile to antitrust enforcement in general (Bork 1978).[6]

The important distinction between tacit and overt collusion seems to be clearer in economic analysis than it is in the law (Gertner and Rosenfeld 1998). U.S. courts generally use the term price fixing to encompass all forms of cartel behavior and to indicate that it is *per se* illegal. Plaintiffs have an incentive to characterize many forms of collusive behavior as price fixing because then they are relieved of the burden of proving market definition, market power, and market effect – all central elements in a rule-of-reason case. Often the key feature in a case that determines whether the *per se* rule applies is the legal and economic meaning of the "agreement." Naked cartels always meet the test, but not all prosecutions of cartels have evidence of secret meetings with explicit agreements.

A contract between two firms to merge is an explicit agreement that will restrain competition between the two entities, yet mergers are always analyzed under the rule of reason. Moreover, the courts have treated certain types of open joint sales under the rule of reason because they arguably increased output and social welfare (e.g., *Broadcast Music, Inc. v. CBS* 1979). In some cases prosecutors will allege cartel behavior but lack direct evidence of an explicit agreement. In these cases, it will be necessary to present circumstantial evidence about market effects so as to allow the jury to infer that an explicit agreement must have occurred. If this evidence is persuasive, then liability for the price fixing follows the *per se* rule.

Many effective price-raising conducts involve the formation of tacit understandings among rivals. Some types of price leadership require a leading firm to initiate a round of price changes in the industry by an explicit announcement or "signal." The followers need not explicitly express their concurrence with the price change by communicating it to the leader, but they can achieve the same result by announcing a parallel price change to their customers or indirectly to their rivals through trade publications. Such parallel pricing actions have usually been classified as "non-cooperative" behavior in economic models of oligopoly – strategic oligopolistic interdependence that does not constitute overt collusion or conspiracy under the law. Tacit collusive actions usually require a punishment mechanism in order to be effective in raising long run profits. While price wars are the classic form of punishing deviants from a tacitly collusive arrangement, various predatory actions may be targeted against deviants. Strategies covering market segmentation, most-favored-nation contrasts, and early credible price announcements can help discover deviant behavior; these are called facilitating practices. Exchanges of information through trade associations about sales or costs of production can also be facilitating conditions. In general, facilitating devices increase the predictability of future behavior among rivals.

Predatory behavior and facilitating devices may be illegal collusive conduct. Historically parallel behavior, especially in prices, may be used to conclusively infer the existence of an express agreement. In general, absent such an agreement, merely parallel behavior cannot suffice for price-fixing liability. However, evidence of parallelism in behavior can be combined with so-called "plus factors" that may seal the guilt of a group of sellers under the Sherman Act. Among the plus factors are identical bids in sealed-bid auctions, a predictable pattern of winning or losing in auctions, conduct against self interest,[7] exchanges of excessively detailed transaction data, price announcements far in advance of purchase dates, preventing new product introductions, or other evidence of a dramatic change in market performance that could not be due to shifts in demand or supply.

Not all academic writers agree that the *per se* rule of price-fixing prosecution is justified by the savings in judicial resources. Posner (1969) takes the position that there is no substantive difference between cartel behavior and tacit collusion. If so, the logical conclusion is that all price fixing cases should be decided on a rule-of-reason basis with full information presented on market effects (Gertner and Rosenfield 1999). However, so far such opinions remain in the minority. U.S. law on facilitating practices used to further tacit collusion is a bit unsettled. An important case was the issuance of detailed price books by General Electric and Westinghouse during 1963-1974. Combined with a quickly adjusted multiplier and price protection clauses, the two companies perfectly matched their prices on large turbo-generators. In 1977, a consent decree ended the practice (Hay 2000). However, a similar case of advance price signaling by makers of a gasoline additive was overturned on appeal *(Ethyl* 1980). Among the reasons given by the court were that coal signaling practice for the purpose of informing rivals of their pricing intentions and had no efficiency defense, then the practice could be declared a *per se* illegal implicit practice; that is the adoption itself was an *implicit conspiracy*. In the *Airline Tariff Publishing Co.* case (1993), advanced price announcements that involved communications among airlines through their shared reservation system was found to be illegal even though the practice had legitimate business purposes that benefited consumers. The practice was declared illegal because the harm to entry conditions outweighed the benefits of early announcements.

Thus, Hay (2000) argues that an independently adopted industry-wide practice for the purpose of suppressing price or non-price competition may sometimes be declared *per se* violations of the Sherman Act (or Section 5 of the FTC Act). They are probably legal in homogenous-product industries with good price information if (1) the practice does not alter the parallel pricing that would emerge without it anyway or (2) the removal of the practice would not improve market performance. If the practice has no legitimate business purpose, its adoption is probably *per se* illegal. Moreover, even if the practice can be defended as an efficient one, injured parties in a civil case might argue that the harm caused them outweighs any efficiencies.

PROSECUTING PRICE FIXING

Price-fixing allegations may be brought by federal or state antitrust agencies or by private injured parties. The Department of Justice has sole authority under the Sherman Act to bring criminal charges against alleged corporate or individual price-fixers, but civil indictments may be launched by any of the parties just mentioned. The procedures available to the DOJ for prosecuting criminal defendants are quite different from civil cases. The procedures for civil indictments are all fairly similar for plaintiffs, whether government agencies, attorneys general, or private injured parties. However, the Federal Trade Commission is a bit different because the five commissioners make decisions at a level equal to that of a federal district court; moreover, the FTC usually charges price fixers with violations of the Sherman Act and Section 5 of the FTC Act, which prohibits unfair methods of competition. The form and substance of civil antitrust suits pursued in state courts are quite similar to those in federal courts (O'Connor 1996).

Government Suits

Federal antitrust agencies usually open investigations after receiving credible complaints from citizens; less commonly, the agencies' staffs might open an investigation on the basis of press reports. After a preliminary staff analysis that affirms the possibility of a violation and confirms that the market has imperfectly competitive characteristics, a more formal investigation is opened. Determining the feasibility of a market to support price fixing is called screening (Dick 1995).

For a criminal case, when emerging evidence evaluated by DOJ lawyers and economists becomes strong enough, a grand jury will be established with the approval of the Assistant Attorney General for Antitrust (Victor 1998). Most grand juries are set up in major cities where the Division has field offices. Although under the supervision of a judge who ensures that federal rules of procedure are followed, the grand juries are very much tools of a prosecutor. The juries issue subpoenas and hear testimony that is almost always kept secret. Such subpoenas can only be served on persons residing in the United States or to businesses that are registered in U.S. territory. Foreign companies are immune to U.S. subpoenas, unless they have U.S. subsidiaries or agents.

If probable cause is established to the satisfaction of the prosecutors, the jury will vote on whether to indict companies or individuals or to request search warrants from a local magistrate. Warrants will be issued only if a sworn DOJ statement asserts "probable cause" of criminal activity. Requesting search warrants for antitrust matters was rare until the 1990s. Citizens on grand juries can ask questions of those testifying, but their main role is to restrain over-zealous prosecutors. Grand juries usually do not interview the targets of an investigation, but do hear individuals who might provide useful testimony in a trial. The final action of the grand jury, after reviewing testimony and seized documents, is to vote on whether to hand down indictments for specific persons or companies.

Grand juries have no authority to compel appearances from companies or persons resident outside the United States. Therefore, in the case of global cartels, the DOJ may seek the voluntary cooperation of foreign residents or companies. Testimony may be taken in third countries. In potential criminal matters, the DOJ may seek the assistance of foreign ministries of justice under mutual assistance treaties. Joint criminal antitrust investigations can be conducted with a few countries.

Grand juries are used in some state courts, but for the most part civil cases must be filed without sworn testimony of the kind available to grand juries. Most private civil antitrust suits are filed by plaintiffs who are able to convince a law firm to take the case on a contingency basis. After a case is filed in court, evidence is gathered by both sides under a process called "discovery." During discovery, plaintiffs will demand business records or other evidence from defendants relating to a conspiracy. Moreover, defendants or others that may have relevant information are required to be deposed under oath, though most defendants choose to exercise their rights to non-recrimination. If economic or technical evidence is to be presented in court, the written opinions of testifying experts on both sides will be exchanged followed by rebuttals from each; the experts may be deposed as well. In big cases, dozens of experts may be employed to develop briefs and affidavits, but only the testifying experts may be deposed by the opposing sides.

When both sides in a case have had sufficient time to prepare their positions, lawyers from each party will attempt to negotiate a mutually acceptable deal prior to a grand jury vote on indictments or prior to the start of court testimony. A large majority of antitrust cases, both criminal and civil, are settled out of court. A smaller number may even be settled in the midst of formal court hearings, but once guilt has been decreed by judge or jury the only matter subject to negotiation is the severity of the sentence. In criminal cases, prosecutors have a great deal of discretion over which charges to make, the time period of the alleged crime, and how many persons in the conspiracy to charge. The wording of an indictment on a guilty plea agreement can be crucial in determining both the immediate criminal penalties and future civil liability. The plea agreement can include advantageous language on "the scope and duration of the alleged conspiracy" (Victor 1998:501). If a company decides to explore the possibility of cooperating with prosecutors and pleading guilty before trial, prosecutors may agree to grant amnesty to the company or to immunize one or more of the company's employees from indictment. If the company's cooperation comes at an early stage in the multiparty negotiations and the testimony offered is helpful in prosecuting other co-conspirators, a large number of people may be immunized. Lenience less than full immunity may also be negotiated. Prosecutors can also promise to seek reductions in the size of the fine normally required by the U.S. Sentencing Guidelines, subject to court approval. Before concessions are offered, prosecutors need to know in advance how much cooperation they can expect. The degree and type of cooperation is outlined in a proffer letter presented by defense counsel to prosecutors. The last defendants to settle typically have the least useful new information about the conspiracy, so their ability to bargain is much reduced. However, even a latecomer to cooperation may receive significant concessions, even amnesty, for information about price fixing in unrelated markets. Immunity agreements usually contain conditions about the degree of continuing cooperation that permit prosecutors to revoke the immunity of a guilty party that becomes recalcitrant.

The DOJ instituted a formal Leniency Program for corporations in the early 1990s. The program has been successful in attracting a large number of corporate whistle-blowers and resulted in more than 20 price-fixing convictions by the end of the decade. If a corporate conspirator was not the initiator of a cartel, but is the first to offer information about a conspiracy about which the DOJ was unaware, then a full amnesty is automatic (*Legal Times*, May 4, 1998) In some cases, corporate cartel members have been in a "race to be first" to confess (Spratling 2000). However, the DOJ will also reward even the second or third firms that offer to cooperate with significant downward departures from U.S. Sentencing Guidelines levels. The size of the leniency awards will depend on many factors: the quickness of the offer to cooperate with prosecutors, the firm's rank within the cartel, leadership behavior within the cartel, the size of the overcharge, and the degree of involvement by top management. The identity of firms granted full amnesty is kept confidential by the DOJ. Spratling (2000) provides several examples of leniency in fines granted to second or third firms to confess their roles in global cartels. The second firm in a cartel to cooperate may be assessed a fine as much as two-thirds below the fine of the last cartel member to agree to plead guilty.

Prosecutors cannot directly offer relief to defendants from separate civil damage suits by injured buyers. Even those firms that receive amnesty for their cooperation are liable for civil penalties equal to three times the overcharges paid by direct buyers. The guilty pleas or court decisions become *prima facie* (incontestable) evidence of a conspiracy in a civil indictment; moreover, even if an alleged member of a cartel is not indicated or found innocent in a trial, the company can still be made to pay civil damages because in a civil proceeding the standard is the "preponderance of the evidence," not "beyond a reasonable doubt." However, the wording of a company's guilty plea can affect the size of a civil damage award, as can the content of testimony in the rare price-fixing trial. When a criminal investigation is completed, most of the evidence collected that is relevant to assessing a cartel's overcharge is turned over to the plaintiffs during discovery; all the testimony and evidence collected for presentation at trial will become available to the plaintiffs as well. This evidence may bear on the size of the economic injuries. For these reasons, it is usually to the plaintiffs' advantage to delay settling until all criminal matters are completed.

When it becomes known that a grand jury is investigating allegations of criminal price fixing, buyers usually quickly file for civil damages in federal courts where they are located. The lawyers representing buyers will collect information on the industry affected from their clients' public sources, tips from insiders,[8] private investigators, and economists or business consultants. The announcements of criminal indictments or convictions will bring more injured parties forward as plaintiffs because of the publicity itself and because the chances of winning a favorable settlement increase. However, not all civil cases tag along after criminal ones. There are many more private antitrust cases filed in federal courts than there are cases brought by public prosecutors (White 1988). Occasionally, private parties may bring even price-fixing cases that the government has decided not to investigate or litigate because the burden of proof is too onerous.

Since changes in federal rules of procedure in the 1970s, treble-damages suits scattered across several court districts have been consolidated by the courts into "multi-district litigation," more commonly known as class actions. When a panel of judges determines that the alleged violations and defendants are similar enough, the suits filed in multiple U.S. federal court districts are gathered up into one action assigned to one supervising federal judge. The location is often chosen for the convenience of the plaintiffs or defendants but the workload of the court district is also a consideration.

Usually within a year or so of the first filing, the supervising judge will "certify" the federal class, that is, determine that all the plaintiffs have standing to sue for damages from the same set of defendants. Next, the judge chooses one or a very few lead counsel to represent the class; the lead law firm may be proposed by a majority of plaintiffs' counsel or may be appointed by the judge upon application. If a negotiated settlement is proposed prior to a trial (or the conclusion of a trial), the judge holds a "fairness hearing" in which the defendants and class counsel will present arguments and evidence that the settlement amount is "fair and reasonable." This is a fairly elastic standard, particularly if the hearing is scheduled without any prior criminal guilty pleas. Finally, after approval of the settlement, members of the class may agree to take a prorated share of the settlement (net of legal fees and costs), or they may opt to leave the class. The opt-outs usually try to settle later for larger recovery rates, though some may not settle out of court at all. (There once was a feeling among some business people that suing one's suppliers for price-fixing damages was distasteful or ungentlemanly, but such attitudes are becoming rare, partly because shareholders are quick to sue for mismanagement. Privately held firms are more likely to negotiate secret payments or concessions in lieu of formal legal actions). If no settlement can be negotiated, the class action may go to trial and be heard by a jury or, if the defendants prefer, a judge only.

Although the law and rules of legal procedure give government prosecutors great powers, it must not be forgotten that they bear the burden of proof when a case goes to trial. Moreover, the standard of proof – "beyond a reasonable doubt" – is a very high barrier to surmount. The difficulty of prosecuting criminal international conspiracies is even greater because of problems in gathering evidence outside national borders. In the early 1990s the DOJ prosecuted three global cartels: *Plastic Dinnerware*, *Industrial Diamonds*, and *Thermal Fax Paper*. Of the three, the first was a victory for the prosecution, the second an unmitigated loss, and the third a partial loss. The key factor explaining the outcomes was whether the case was settled by means of plea bargain or by trial.

The *Plastic Dinnerware* cases ended in June 1996 with a total of five corporations and nine executives pleading guilty to criminal price fixing. While the fines were not especially large ($40 million), the executives received prison sentences of from four to twenty-one months, the last probably the stiffest ever meted out in a U.S. price-fixing case. The case is also notable for being the first to sentence two Canadian citizens, the first foreigners to be sent to U.S. jails for Sherman Act violations.

The *Industrial Diamonds* case was litigated during November-December 1994 but ended with a dismissal by the presiding judge after the government's case was presented. Analysis by the *New York Times* and *American Lawyer* mention the government's lack of preparation and relatively small team as factors in the government's loss, but the major failure seems to have been the absence of a key witness and documents held by a South African alleged corporate conspirator. As a result, the government was unable to show that prices were exchanged by the two defendants.

In the *Thermal Fax Paper* case, the DOJ alleged that five manufacturers and three wholesalers colluded on prices during 1990-1992. All the meetings were held in Japan but telephone calls were used to complete the agreements within the U.S. market. Five Japanese companies and one Norwegian company pleaded guilty in late 1995 and early 1996, but the largest U.S. supplier, Appleton Papers, Inc. and its vice president, refused to do so. The *Appleton Papers* case was tried before a Wisconsin jury in early 1997. Without tape recordings of the alleged telephone calls, the government was forced to rely on the testimony of one of the convicted Japanese conspirators to make its case. While the prosecution's witness did his best, juries tend to view convicted felons that have received "handsome plea bargains" as no better than "mob enforcers turned stool pigeons" (*American Lawyer April 1997:66*). Performance at trial is a "persistent weakness at the Antitrust Division," with a conviction rate of only about 20 percent *(ibid)*.

U.S. Price-Fixing Fines and Prison Sentences

For 65 years after the Sherman Act first became law, the fines on corporations were modest because the violations were considered misdemeanors. Until amended in 1955, the maximum fine the courts could impose was $5,000 per count (Connor 1997). Creative prosecutors found ways in serious cases to increase the number of counts of violations so as to surpass the $5,000 limit, and additional indictments for mail or wire fraud might be tacked on as well. Yet, the total fines that could be proposed by public prosecutors was typically much smaller than the additional profits earned by the companies from their illegal actions. Prior to 1960, the average corporate fine in federal price-fixing cases was less than $100,000 (Posner 1976). The courts could impose additional penalties in the form of consent decrees that restricted a company's conduct for several years and sometimes required monitoring by federal antitrust agencies. While a violation of these decrees, if detected, could warrant quite serious fines for contempt of court, in general firms regarded the fines and decrees as minor nuisances equivalent to corporate parking tickets (Fuller 1962). Moreover, corporations were frequently allowed to plea *nolo contendere* ("no contest") rather that "guilty." The former plea reduced the company's exposure to civil suits because it was not *prima facie* evidence of a crime having been committed that could be used in follow-up civil proceedings.

Complaints by government prosecutors, members of the antitrust bar, and other antitrust experts got the attention of Congress. The maximum fines for Sherman Act violations were increased in 1955 and 1974. In 1974, the maximum fine for individuals was raised to $100,000 and for corporations or other legal entities to $1 million (Wiley 2001). In 1990, on the centennial of the Act, the maximum corporate criminal fine was raised to $10 million per count (though it is now unlikely that multiple counts will be framed in indictments for single conspiracies). In 1998, the Assistant Attorney General for Antitrust testified before the Senate Judiciary Committee that the size of the economic injuries being caused by cartels in the 1990s required another increase in the statutory maximum (Klein 1998). He proposed that it become $100 million per company.

Two changes in federal sentencing rules have allowed prosecutors to seek corporate fines higher than the statutory limit.[9] First, beginning in 1991 the courts have been obliged to apply the U.S. Sentencing Guidelines to companies that plead guilty or that are convicted by trial. Prosecutors prepare a brief for the court that explains how the guidelines apply to the particulars of the case at hand; at a sentencing hearing after conviction at trial, the defense will submit a brief that will argue for lower culpability. These guidelines require that the government calculate a "base fine" equal to 20 percent of the company's net sales in the cartelized market; if prosecutors have reason to believe that the cartel raised prices by much more than 10 percent due to the conspiracy, it may propose a higher percentage figure. Then the base fine is multiplied by a "culpability score" that rises with the number of aggravating factors (e.g., the company initiated the conspiracy or acted as the cartel's enforcer) and falls with mitigating factors (e.g., it left the conspiracy voluntarily). In many recent cartel cases the culpability multiplier has ranged from about 1.5 to 4.5.[10] That is, the Sentencing Guidelines typically specify fines equal to 30 to 90 percent of affected sales However, prosecutors can and usually do request large downward departures from the fines implied by the Sentencing Guidelines if the company has offered even minimal cooperation with the government's investigation. The discounts granted by the courts are frequently in the 50 to 90 percent range.

Second, and potentially more important, violations of the Sherman Act were declared in 1974 to be *felonies* rather than misdemeanors. A corporation convicted of any federal felony (fraud, tax evasion, price fixing, etc.) is subject to a conceptually simple fine structure: the larger of either twice the harm caused to citizens or twice the illegal gains. In the case of price fixing, twice the harm is double the overcharge, and this is always larger than twice the gain.[11] These felony price-fixing sanctions (18USC §3571(a) and (b)) are usually referred to as the "alternative fine statute." The felony standard for figuring appropriate fines will result in a larger fine than the Sentencing Guidelines whenever the overcharge is greater than about 15 percent of sales and when the corporation's culpability is relatively slight. One disadvantage of the twice-the-harm approach is that in a litigation situation the prosecution would have to present expert economic testimony of the size of the company's overcharge during the sentencing phase, and the defendant would be obligated to rebut the government's estimate. The Sentencing Guidelines require only company sales, about which there is usually little debate.[12]

Because the two approaches will arrive at different proposed fines, which is chosen to justify a fine is an important matter of legal procedure. It is clear that Congress intended to replace the $10 million statutory limit with the Sentencing Guidelines in criminal price-fixing convictions but not civil ones. However, it is not clear when the courts should implement the felony standard instead of the Sentencing Guidelines in criminal cases, except in cases where the overcharge is significantly higher than 10 percent. As a guide for civil plaintiffs, the felony standard is greatly preferred because evidence accepted in sentencing hearings would be presentable in treble-damage suits. From the point of view of deterrence effect, a defensible rule would be to calculate both fines and choose the larger.[13]

The first time that the U.S. government's use of the alternative fine provisions came to the attention of the antitrust bar was in October 1996 when the Archer Daniels Midland Co. agreed to pay a $100-million fine for two price-fixing counts. Corporate defense counsel believe that beginning in 1996 "[t]hat . . . is what the government is going to be pushing in every case" (Victor 1998: 502). In fact, the "two-times rule" has been invoked to impose high fines on corporate price fixers 29 times between October 1996 and September 2000 (*National Law Journal*, September 18, 2000). More than 80 percent of these high fines have been paid by non-U.S. corporations.

Sentences for *individuals* who are convicted for price fixing also fall into three categories. First, the statutory limit for persons is $350,000 and three years' prison time. Prior to 1974, when price fixing was a misdemeanor, the upper limit on prison time was one year, imprisonment was imposed in only eight corporate price-fixing cases, and very few convicted price fixers served more than 30 days. Since 1974, about half of all individuals convicted of criminal price fixing receive prison sentences and the average length had tripled. Second, the Sentencing Guidelines propose that fines ought to be from 1 to 5 percent of affected sales, up to $350,000. Prison time is determined by a long list of specific aggravating and mitigating factors that result in a range of months within which the sentencing judge chooses. Third, fines may also be calculated under the so-called alternative fine provision in force since 1987. In the last case, fines of up to $25 million can be imposed on individuals if the cartel's overcharge is large enough. The alternative fine standard has just begun to be applied to individuals in the late 1990s who make plea agreements, but it has not yet been litigated successfully. Again, there is some ambiguity in the law as to when the alternative fine provisions can or must be used in criminal cases.

Most penalties for price fixers are the result of pre-trial bargaining between prosecutors and defendants. To avoid a protracted trial but also obtain a conviction, prosecutors will offer "downwards departures" from the guidelines to induce defendants' cooperation. Because the U.S. Sentencing Guidelines already take into account corporate leadership, recidivism, and economic impact, the standard for awarding varying "downward departures" below the guidelines range to cartel participants is quite simple: the degree of corporate cooperation in the government's investigation. Since 1978, the DOJ has had a leniency policy that offers automatic full amnesty to companies that are the first to alert the agency about a cartel, so long as the company did not initiate the cartel and no government investigation was in progress (Spratling 1999). A revision of the leniency policy in the early 1990s extended full amnesty to a company that does not quite meet the aforementioned conditions but instead offers evidence of a cartel in another line of business for which there is no DOJ investigation. Besides these unique opportunities for a 100% discount on government fines (civil penalties are not affected), less radical discounts are routinely awarded to any other members of a cartel that agree to plead guilty (Spratling 2000). The first or second companies to offer cooperation in cartel cases have received 60 to 100 percent discounts. The last to agree to plead guilty and cooperate have been rewarded with 20 to 40 percent discounts from the guideline fines. Discounts are justified by the conservation of prosecutorial resources. Without the offer of downward departures in corporate and personal penalties, many more labor-intense courtroom battles would have to be fought by the government.

Besides formal downward departures from the Sentencing Guidelines, which must be approved by a federal judge in an open sentencing hearing, there are other tools available to prosecutors to sweeten the deal for a corporate whistle-blower. One such option concerns the identity of the corporate entity to be named in the plea agreement. Although it is the stated policy of the DOJ to charge both a parent firm and its subsidiary if both engaged in the conspiracy, the DOJ has the flexibility to charge only a subsidiary if it wishes. This option is particularly critical in the case of global cartels because multinational participants often have only minimal assets in the county prosecuting a cartel. Because judges are loath to fine a company in excess of its net assets or ability to pay from revenues, charging a company's small sales office rather than the parent organization can place a very low upper limit on a company's fine. For example, as a reward for its early cooperation, only Sewon America was charged in the lysine prosecution rather than its rich Korean parent company, thus saving the parent millions of dollars in fines. In addition, a company can benefit from the phrasing of its guilty plea agreement, a document that carries the weight of *prima facie* evidence in derivative civil suits. The agreement may use language that defines the cartelized market in a narrow way or minimizes the length of the conspiracy period. In other words, the precise description of the illegal activity can reduce the implied size of the overcharge and, hence, a firm's liability for civil damages.[14] An uncommon concession is for the DOJ to negotiate a favor from another government department for a company willing to plead guilty. An example is failing to disbar a guilty company from signing sales contacts with the federal government. Finally, numerous concessions may be extended to employees of the conspiring companies.

U.S. Prosecution of Global Cartels

The first private international cartels began to operate in the late 19th century, but by 1913 there were more than a hundred.[15] The German dyestuffs cartel was one of the first. Through its leadership in synthetic organic chemistry, the German dyestuffs industry developed an early lead in global production. When manufacturers in France, the United States, and elsewhere tried to imitate the success of the German industry, the German dyestuffs cartel used full-line forcing and predatory pricing tactics to undermine the growth of new entrants. It was these monopolistic tactics that were the main reasons for the seizure and sale of the U.S. chemical assets of Bayer and BASF at the end of World War I.[16]

Perhaps the first lawsuit by the U.S. government against a global cartel was *U.S. v. American Tobacco et al.* that was filed in 1907 and decided by the Supreme Court in 1911 (ICPAC 1999). There were 94 U.S. corporations and individuals and two UK tobacco companies listed as defendants in this massive price-fixing case. One of the indictments brought against the tobacco firms was that they had agreed to a geographic division of world markets for tobacco products. The American Tobacco monopoly was broken up into several entities and all the defendants were enjoined from allocating world geographic markets in the future. For many years after *American Tobacco* there were few international cartel cases launched by U.S. prosecutors (Klein 1999).

In the 1940s, U.S. prosecutors brought a number of cases against international cartels, some of which involved criminal charges. Most of these cases involved allegations of global market-allocation agreements. Estimates made by scholars writing in the late 1940s place the number of documented international cartels operating prior to World War II at around 179 (Edwards 1944). The principal type of company in these cartels was European manufacturers, but at least a few U.S. companies had joined about 60 percent of those cartels. In the 1930s, cartels were believed to control approximately 40 percent of world merchandise trade. These mostly Euro-centric cartels operated quite openly or at least unhindered by concerns of legal prosecution because U.S. antitrust enforcement was more or less suspended during the Great Depression. Among the global cartels indicted for price fixing by the U.S. DOJ were those selling aluminum, dyes, light bulbs, nylon, titanium, tungsten carbide, roller bearings, and precision instruments (ICPAC 1999). Many of these cases involved leading U.S. and European manufacturers engaged in naked price-fixing conspiracies in globally traded products with substantial sales.

Such cases became relatively few for about 40 years after the early 1950s. The U.S. antitrust agencies continued to prosecute price fixing and bid rigging, but nearly all cases were domestic in scope. Even the harshest critics of the U.S. antitrust laws conceded that they had been effective in suppressing cartels:

> "The elimination of the formal [overt] cartel remains the major achievement of American antitrust law" (Posner 1976:39).

Perhaps the only important international price-fixing case during this period is the well-known uranium cartel, prosecuted in 1975 as *In re Westinghouse Electric Corp. Uranium Contracts*. Most of the few remaining international cartel cases focused on more sophisticated collusive mechanisms, such as patent pooling.[17] Caves (1996) attributes the pause in discovered global cartels after the early 1950s to several factors. First was the successful prosecution of many global cartels by U.S. antitrust authorities during the Truman administration. Second, the adoption of antitrust laws in a score of industrialized countries immediately after World War II probably had some deterrence effect on the formation of cartels. Third, the largest U.S. manufacturers shifted their behaviors from cooperative to relatively aggressive behavior in the 1950s. They opportunistically invested in the war-ravaged economies of Europe and Asia and broadened their product lines. U.S. foreign direct investment combined with the rapid recovery of major companies in the industrial sectors of Europe and Japan, caused global concentration to decline in most industries. Finally, the mix of industries shifted away from homogeneous primary materials and intermediate inputs towards those making differentiated consumer or high-tech goods. In general, the gap between collusive and competitive profit levels is lower for differentiated goods than it is for homogeneous goods, so the incentive to form cartels became less as this shift proceeded.

Perhaps Caves' analysis is correct in explaining the relative paucity of global cartels noted between 1955 and 1995. In addition, the 1980s were a period of greatly reduced antitrust enforcement. Partly for ideological reasons, the sizes of the two big federal antitrust agencies were cut substantially (Preston and Connor 1992). The key appointments by the Reagan administration in 1991 (William Baxter in the DOJ and James Miller in the FTC) ushered in a relatively lax period of federal antitrust enforcement. While there was a continuing commitment to prosecution of domestic price fixing, there was little desire by the new leadership to move the agencies in the direction of novel legal territory by prosecuting global price fixing, even if evidence of such conspiracies had been presented. While the reduced resources of the DOJ managed to bring a respectable number of price-fixing cases each year, they were in economic terms little cases.

Price-fixing enforcement patterns shifted markedly during the Reagan-Bush presidencies, which corresponded roughly to the years 1980-1994 in Table 3.1. First, the mix of price fixing cases was altered considerably. Cases against trade associations, which had formerly comprised about a quarter of all price-fixing cases, practically disappeared. Moreover, the proportion of "other" cases, in which the victims were mostly corporate buyers, dropped to less than half of the historical proportion. These types of cases were replaced by allegations of bid-rigging conduct. The bid-rigging cases mostly concerned small companies conspiring against government buyers in small geographic markets. Cement makers and bottlers selling milk to local school boards were typical cases brought during the Reagan-Bush era. While the number of international cartel cases was quite small in the 1960s and 1970s, these types of cases were virtually not on the agenda during 1980-1994. Although only three years of the Clinton administration are shown in table 3.1, a radical shift toward fewer but larger cases is apparent.

Table 3.1. Characteristics of DOJ Price-Fixing Enforcement, 1960-1997.

Characteristic:	1960-1964	1965-1969	1970-1974	1975-1979	1980-1984	1985-1989	1990-1994	1995-1997
1. Number of cases/year:	49	20	27	32	88	55	62	31
Bid-rigging (%)[a]	44	15	24	40	86	75	74	58
Trade & professional orgs. (%)	11	26	29	20	5	0	1	2
Other/ corporate (%)	45	59	47	40	9	25	25	40
2. Geographic extent of market:								
Local or regional (%)	40	48	67	77	94	90	90	67
National (%)	56	49	29	20	5	10	10	20
International (%)	4	2	4	3	1	0	0	13
3. International cases/year:	0.8	0.4	0.8	0.8	0.6	0	0.2	1.0
4. Affected annual sales/ defendant (million 1982 dollars):	1,547[b]	257	716	1,577	211	39	15	101

Source: Gallo *et al.* (2000).

[a] 79% against government units.

[b] Includes the famous electrical equipment conspiracy case.

There was a clear change in antitrust priorities at the federal level in 1993, the first year of the Clinton administration. President Clinton's newly appointed head of the DOJ's Antitrust Division, Anne K. Bingaman, announced the shift in a speech given in October 1993.[18] Bingaman (1993) stated that enforcement of international-cartel prosecutions and greater international antitrust cooperation were necessary because of the increasingly global reach of the U.S. economy. Although unknown to those in the audience, Bingaman was about to follow her words with actions against two big criminal cartel cases that would illustrate the pitfalls and the promise of pursuing global cases. The first case, the prosecution of General Electric Co. and De Beers Consolidated for price fixing in the global market for industrial diamonds, was an unmitigated defeat for the government. The second, the lysine case, would be the first in a string of prosecutorial triumphs for the Department.[19] When Bingaman made her 1993 speech, the Antitrust Division knew that its year-old investigation of the lysine cartel was turning up strong evidence of a vast conspiracy.

The *Industrial Diamonds* case was difficult from the beginning. The government's chief witness was a disaffected former manager from General Electric's plastics division. Although he confirmed the government's allegation of a conspiracy, his testimony did not hold up well during cross-examination. Other GE employees brought to the stand also verified the government's factual assertions, but they would not agree that the purpose of certain meetings was to fix prices. Even more damaging to the prosecution was the fact that three of the four defendants failed to appear at trial and refused to cooperate in pre-trial discovery. One of the missing defendants was a French customer of GE's industrial diamonds department who the government portrayed as the conduit for price exchanges between GE and De Beers.

At the end of five weeks of trial in October-December 1994 during which the government's case was presented, the trial judge dismissed the case. He later wrote that GE's internal memorandums were ambiguous, the chief prosecution witness was not credible, and that there was no evidence that GE's French customer had transmitted de Beer's price agreements to GE. Contributing to the government's defeat was a grave imbalance in legal resources. Prosecutors were outspent, outnumbered, and outlawyered (*American Lawyer* January 1995:57). The DOJ had one experienced trial lawyer, two others with less experience but well versed in the facts of the case, and four junior attorneys. General Electric spent \$20 to \$60 million defending itself with a team of 25 top-flight litigators drawn from three firms.[20] The superior preparation of the legal defense team resulted in its consistently winning objections on evidentiary rules decisions.

The loss of *Industrial Diamonds* was the cause of considerable criticism of the Antitrust Division's thrust towards prosecution of global cartels. Critics charged that big international cases might drain the Division of resources, much as happened in the 1970s when it tackled IBM and AT&T. Getting documents and witnesses located abroad was likely to be a continuing problem, especially for criminal cases. Many members of Congress were skeptical of prosecuting multinational firms in fast-changing, high-tech industries. Critics like William F. Baxter were unsympathetic to pursuing global cartels:

> "[The DOJ] started off with unrealistic ambitions [and a] crusading notion that there's lots and lots of violations . . . The larger companies are well counseled and don't get into the kind of trouble that the Antitrust Division is looking for. So, instead they go after the little companies . . ." (*New York Times* October 22, 1995, §3, p.1).

As prognostication, Baxter's statement is found wanting.

A second important international case was the DOJ's prosecution of a cartel in *Thermal Fax Paper*, a product used in small capacity facsimile machines by households and small businesses. Sales in the United States were about $120 million in 1995 when most of the indictments and guilty pleas were entered in U.S. courts. The global industry was comprised of five dominant manufacturers: Appleton Papers, Inc. of Wisconsin, Elof Hansson AB of Sweden, and three Japanese companies (Mitsubishi Corp., Nippon Paper Industries Co., and New Oji Paper Co.). By April 1996, these five companies and two paper wholesalers had either pleaded guilty or been indicted for criminal price fixing.[21] In addition, six executives of the companies pleaded guilty or were indicted. Two of the companies and most of the individuals resisted pleading guilty because all of the conspiracy meetings were held in Japan in 1990-1992 and because most of the executives resided in Japan. Telephone calls were used to complete the agreements on prices with the U.S.-based paper manufacturers or distributors. The resisting defendants argued that the Sherman Act did not apply to offshore conspiracies, a position rejected by a U.S. court of appeals.

Bingaman and the division persevered throughout 1995 and most of 1996 with scant progress to show for their global-cartel strategy. The October 1996 guilty plea of Archer Daniels Midland Co. for lysine and citric acid price fixing changed all that. On virtually her last day in public office, Anne Bingaman was able to enjoy the fruits of four year's labor and a return to the widespread respect for the antitrust laws that had been the mission of her administration.

Chapters 4 to 12 of this book examine the operations, economic effects, and legal consequences of the lysine, citric acid, and vitamins cartels. As many commentators have noted, the discovery of the lysine cartel in 1992 and its prosecution in 1996 proved to be the "tip of the iceberg." Out of public sight below the waterline, the U.S. DOJ was investigating about 25 more alleged international cartels in a variety of industries. Since 1994, more than 20 global cartels have been revealed to the public, and in most cases the prosecutions and investigations are completed.[22] As in the three cases covered in depth in this book, the U.S. DOJ's lead in prosecuting more global cartels has been followed by private civil suits in North America and by government actions in Canada, Europe, and elsewhere. The aim of the first part of this chapter is to discuss selected global price-fixing cases that illustrate significant additional features of global price fixing arrangements or legal developments. Later sections of the chapter take up some broader questions related to criminal and civil actions directed at global cartels.

Suits By Private Parties

Section 7 of the 1890 Sherman Act permitted private parties to seek the recovery of monetary damages from antitrust violations.[23] Since that time only the U.S. Justice Department has had standing to bring either criminal or civil suits alleging various types of anticompetitive behavior. However, civil suits alleging price fixing may be filed by certain federal agencies (the Federal Trade Commission, for example), direct buyers, or by state attorneys general on behalf of their citizens. The idea of making injured companies or individuals into civil prosecutors was consistent with ancient traditions of English common law that were absorbed into American jurisprudence, yet the United States is one of the few countries in the world in permitting private citizens to prosecute antitrust violators for substantial compensation.[24] Conservative critics of the antitrust laws generally view private enforcement as superior to public enforcement because the former operates by market-like incentives (Posner 1976).

The Sherman Act permits private parties to seek treble damages, which was a feature of the 1623 English Statute of Monopolies (Hovenkamp 1998:654). By specifying that plaintiffs should be awarded settlements equal to *triple* the economic damages inflicted by defendants, Congress intended private parties to inflict punitive sanctions on antitrust violators so as to deter those violators and their potential imitators from repeating their profitable behavior. In addition, the award of treble damages was intended to deny conspirators the fruits of their illegal conduct (the monopoly profits) and to compensate victims for overcharges on their purchases, the costs of investigating possible violations, and legal costs. Because the burden of proof is on the plaintiffs, single damages would in many cases lead to awards that were less than the illegal profits obtained by conspirators.[25] Moreover, given that legal costs are typically 10 to 30 percent of the treble damage awards, plaintiffs would recover much less than their injuries had Congress specified that only single damages could be recovered. The choice of treble damages was somewhat arbitrary, but they are high enough to provide a reasonable incentive for private parties to bring suits that have some deterrence effects. More than treble damages might lead to frivolous suits or the use of antitrust suits to harass rivals (White 2000).

Not all conspiracies in restraint of trade cause compensable harm to buyers or sellers. It is possible for a cartel to be formed with every intention to manipulate a market for the cartel's benefit and yet fail miserably in the enterprise. Ineffectual conspiracies are illegal and are likely to be prosecuted by the government, but they would not invite civil treble-damages suits because no direct harm could be demonstrated. When private plaintiffs believe a price conspiracy was effective, they face three tests.[26] They must prove in court that price fixing *occurred,* using as a standard of proof "reasonable certainty." In addition, plaintiffs must establish that compensable harm was the *direct result* of the conspiracy. The weight of the evidence, must demonstrate that the price effects did not derive from some other market conditions. Finally, plaintiffs must have a reasonable basis on which to base their claims concerning the *size* of the damages, which is where expert economists come into the picture. Therefore, although the standard of proof (the preponderance of the evidence) is lower for civil cases than for criminal cases, the amount of evidence that must be prepared to be presented in court is greater and often more complex. Many civil cases are settled prior to or during actual court proceedings through negotiated settlements.

Estimating Damages

Figure 3.1 illustrates the degree of overlap between economic concepts of injury and the legal treatment of damages in the case of an effective price-fixing conspiracy. There are five potential groups that may be harmed by price-fixing. (Although illustrated by a case of raising the selling price of a finished product, the analysis also applies to cases where cartels collude to reduce the price paid for input).

The first and clearest case of damages occurs in the case of actual *direct purchasers* who pay an inflated price called the overcharge (rectangle A in Figure 3.1). Direct buyers of lysine spend P_mQ_m during the conspiracy, which generates "excess" or "monopoly" profits of $(P_m\text{-MC})Q_m$. Under economic reasoning the entire monopoly profits rectangle A is an income transfer from buyers to the cartel and should be considered damages, but under legal standards only the upper portion of the rectangle $(P_m - P_c)Q_m$ is recoverable as damages. Direct buyers have had standing to recover the overcharge since the first federal case was decided.

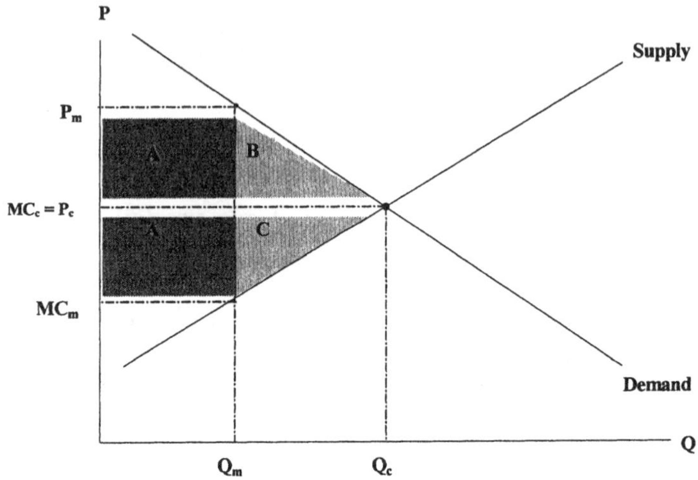

Figure 3.1. Welfare Effects of Collusion.

A portion of the overcharge is passed on to the indirect buyers of products containing the monopolized product Q. For example, hog and poultry farmers who buy prepared animal feeds containing lysine are harmed by a higher price of animal feed. Indeed, if an indirect buyer has a "cost-plus" contract with a feed manufacturer, all of A is passed on to the farmer. With other purchasing methods, rectangle A usually shrinks depending on the location of the *derived* demand and supply curves. In some cases, however, the overcharge on consumers can be larger than the direct overcharge. Under many state antitrust statutes, indirect overcharges are recoverable in state courts, but since the famous *Illinois Brick* decision of the Supreme Court in 1977, no standing is given to indirect buyers in federal courts. Since 1977, bills have been introduced in Congress each year trying to overturn the *Illinois Brick* ruling, but none has yet passed. If federal law did permit indirect-purchaser damages to be awarded, then a good case could be made for awarding only *lost profits* to direct buyers (Hovenkamp 1998:652).

A third group of buyers may be harmed. If a cartel does not enroll all the producers in an industry, it may happen that nonconspirators ("fringe" firms) raise their prices toward the monopoly price P_m (the "umbrella" effect). Direct buyers from noncartel sellers are harmed, while the fringe firms enjoy serendipitous excess profits during the conspiracy period. There is no Supreme Court ruling on standing this case, but while U.S. District Courts are split on the issue, the great majority have allowed standing for this type of injury. Thus, cartel members are liable to pay damages even to direct buyers of output sold by nonparticipating sellers.

A fourth group harmed by price-fixing is those forced to buy inferior substitutes or those who reduce their purchases in response to a higher price. This injury is represented by the consumer portion of the dead weight loss (triangle B in Figure 3.1). Dead weight losses are social losses because both producers and consumers incur harm. Although well accepted as a loss in economic theory, the parties incurring dead weight losses generally have been denied standing. One basis for denial is the legal reasoning that treble damages are meant to deny conspirators the fruits of their illegal conduct, but the dead weight loss is not a gain to conspirators. In addition the courts view these losses as "remote" and identifying which non-buyers are injured, a speculative exercise. Many legal commentators believe actual calculation is problematic, but the formula shown in Figure 3.1 is quite feasible to apply. However, the courts might allow damage claims if parties can show "a regular course of dealing with the conspirators" during non-conspiracy periods. The dead weight loss should be computed when assessing penalties in *public* prosecutions even when they are not permitted in private antitrust suits.

The last injured group is those suppliers of factors of production to the conspirators who lose sales or income due to output contraction. This corresponds to triangle C in Figure 3.1, the supply side of the deadweight loss. The courts do not usually allow standing for such parties, such as workers forced into unemployment, because the injuries are viewed as indirect or remote. A clear exception is that standing is allowed for employees who were fired because they refused to participate in price-fixing arrangements or became whistle blowers.

Estimation of the overcharges to direct buyers is in principal straightforward. P_m, the actual price paid by buyers, and Q_m, the volume sold during the conspiracy can be obtained from the business records of the plaintiffs or more conveniently from the cartel members during pre-trial "discovery." Other information required is P_c, the price that would have governed sales "but for" the illegal conspiracy and the length of the conspiracy period.

Determination of the unobserved "but for" price P_c is often the most contentious area of expert opinion. The correct level of P_c can be calculated in five ways: 1) finding a "yardstick," i.e., a price in a comparable geographic area with no conspiracy; 2) the "before and after" approach (that is, examining price levels immediately before or after the known conspiracy period); 3) predicted prices from theoretical oligopoly models that require information on actual concentration among all sellers (not just the cartel) and elasticity of demand for the cartel's product; 4) economic estimation of demand and supply relationships to obtain the competitive price (a dummy variable can be inserted to model the conspiracy period); and 5) information on cost of production by the conspirators (proprietary information on production capacity, utilization, variable costs, and fixed costs of manufacturing and distribution). In the case of cartels, the defendants are not entitled to presume that they had collective market power prior to their conspiracy. That is, the competitive price is normally the appropriate but-for price (Hovenkamp 1998:660).

In proving the extent of damages incurred by plaintiffs in civil conspiracy cases, the intent of the conspirators must be sharply distinguished from the degree of success in fixing prices. Strictly speaking, even an admission of guilt by the conspirators does not imply that the market's price was affected as intended. For example, conspirators may believe that their initial increase in list prices immediately caused transaction prices to rise, whereas market factors were in fact responsible. Thus, an appropriate damage analysis must be neutral with respect to either allegations or admissions by the defendants. The before-and-after approach is particularly prone to errors of estimation if additional market information is not available to confirm the height of the overcharge and the duration of the conspiracy's effects. Economic theory supports the possibility that the conspirators' prices can be lower than the monopoly price; conspirators may wish to limit entry or conceal their collusive activity. Cheating on cartel agreements may occur. However, in practice, an admission of guilt does lend plaintiffs some strategic advantages in antitrust suits or out-of-court settlement negotiations.

As previously mentioned, the U.S. DOJ may opt to bring a civil suit for price fixing if it determines that the evidence available to prosecutors is unlikely to result in a criminal verdict. The U.S. Federal Trade Commission (FTC) and other federal agencies are empowered only to bring civil cases. The FTC has the authority to order that price fixers disgorge their illegal profits to their customers. The amount is technically not an injury, but in practice is close to single damages. In addition to federal agencies, three other types of plaintiffs may have standing in civil price-fixing suits: direct buyers, indirect buyers, and the states' attorneys general.

Legal Procedures

A relatively new feature of suits by direct purchasers is widespread use of class actions (Calkins 1997).[27] Buyers first file suit in their local U.S. District Courts often without knowing about similar allegations in other court districts. The launching of a class-action suit is chaotic. Tipped off by press reports of a government investigation or simply suspicious behavior by sellers, buyers may approach a lawyer to try to interest the law firm in filing a suit in the court district where the alleged violations took place. Alternatively, price-fixing suits may be instigated by attorneys who learn of grand-jury investigations, possible plea bargains, or impending government indictments. These attorneys then try to identify groups of purchasers who may have been harmed by the conspiracy, alert them about possible settlements the buyers might receive, and sign them up as clients.[28] In either case, as soon as at least one purchaser and one antitrust lawyer judge the suit winnable, a suit is filed alleging price fixing that names the product, defendants and gives other facts about the alleged illegal acts. News of the suit may itself attract more clients as plaintiffs.

The decision to join a suit as a plaintiff may not be an easy one for many companies. Buyers who sue face the disruption of what often times is a comfortable supplier relationship of longstanding. Moreover, because cartels arise in concentrated industries, the number of alternative suppliers is severely limited. Suppliers that have been identified as cartel participants typically are desperate to hold on to their market shares in the tumultuous conditions following disclosure, so they renegotiate better supply conditions with loyal customers. The improved contract terms have the effect of making buyers more reluctant to sue.

For the plaintiffs' law firms themselves, there is often great uncertainty about the odds of winning a settlement and the prospect of negotiations and litigation against typically well financed defense counsel with no compensation for up to five years or more. Nevertheless, as more and more information becomes available about the dimensions of the conspiracy, its time span, and the identities of the conspirators, dozens or scores of law suits may be filed all around the country. As soon as the number of plaintiffs begins to stabilize, their counsel will negotiate a common set of allegations and petition the courts to to consolidate their many cases into one or a few cases.

If the defendants and alleged violations are similar enough, a federal panel consolidates the multi-district suits into one "multi-district litigation" (MDL). The judge assigned the consolidated case holds hearings to certify that the plaintiffs are numerous and have similar complaints. Once the federal class is formed, the judge then chooses a single law firm or co-counsel team to represent the plaintiffs. This process allows many scattered claims to be unified. It enhances efficiency by spreading the more or less fixed costs of litigation over a greater potential settlement amount. If a settlement is offered by defendants, it must be judged fair and reasonable by the court. Individual members of the class may reject the settlement offer and seek a better settlement through a separate action, but if too high a proportion opt out, the settlement may not be approved. The class-action route is particularly important when the buyers are mostly small companies or consumers.[29]

Indirect buyers are those who did not purchase from members of a collusive group yet were injured because a direct buyer passed on all or some of its overcharge when it resold the product (or sold a product containing some of the monopolized goods). If a direct buyer absorbs the entire overcharge, then indirect buyers are unharmed, but most economic models conclude that direct buyers pass on from 50 to 100 percent of their overcharge. Indeed, it is possible that a direct buyer may use the occasion of a cartel-generated price increase to raise its price by a percentage that exceeds the original overcharge percentage (Cotterill *et al. 2000*). Since a 1977

Supreme Court decision uncaptioned as *Illinois Brick*, indirect buyers have had no standing in federal court to sue in price-fixing cases.[30] However, at least 14 states and the District of Columbia do permit indirect-purchaser suits, whether as single or class plaintiffs, and the Supreme Court has decided that the states were within their rights to do so. Indeed, multi-state classes of indirect buyers can be formed. Virtually all of the states have antitrust laws that allow civil antitrust litigation to be decided under principles and procedures that are very similar to federal law.

The final type of plaintiff is the state itself. State governments can of course be parties to suits by virtue of being a direct purchaser from a cartel, but the more interesting case relies on the legal principle of *parens patriae*. Rooted in English constitutional law, this principle allows states to sue in federal court in its sovereign capacity on behalf of its citizens (Calkins 1997). There are *parens* units that predate the formation of the Republic. A couple of high court decisions in the early 1970s threw into doubt the power of states to invoke *parens patriae* to recoup damages from price-fixing conspiracies for their corporate or individual citizens. However, in 1976 Congress enacted Section 4C of the Clayton Act to make such state authority explicit. The clear intent of Congress was to make state attorneys general consumer advocates in the area of antitrust enforcement in recognition of the fact that consumers often have no other recourse to obtain compensation for antitrust injuries. Section 4C empowers state attorneys general to file civil antitrust actions in federal court to seek treble damages for consumers and intermediate buyers that reside in their states. The attorneys general may negotiate or litigate settlements individually or as groups; when litigating as a group, the states essentially form a federal class of plaintiffs.

Enforcement of the U.S. antitrust laws by both the federal and state governments is referred to as "concurrent enforcement". Civil suits for recovery of price-fixing damages to indirect buyers are authorized by the laws of about half of the states. Some recent suits of this kind involved price fixing by manufacturers of fluid milk and infant formulas. However, the largest such action was announced in October 2000, when the attorneys general of 24 states obtained a settlement from the six largest manufacturers of bulk vitamins.[31] In addition, 44 states obtained single damages for their state governments as direct buyers of vitamins. These agreements are subject to the approval of state courts.

The Question of Timing

As mentioned previously, in permitting civil treble-damages suits, Congress envisioned that such suits would follow criminal indictments and convictions obtained by federal antitrust agencies. This is the historical or classic pattern observed in most civil antitrust suits. The great advantage to civil plaintiffs is their ability to enter criminal guilty pleas or verdicts as *prima facie* evidence in civil litigation. However, it may be in the defendants' interests to offer civil settlements after being indicted but before they enter their guilty pleas. Defendants might wish to settle early to avoid bad publicity or to remove an impediment to a planned merger. Defendants may also offer early settlements to private antitrust plaintiffs because to do so would significantly reduce the size of the award compared to what they expect to pay after their pleas are entered. Early settlement offers become beneficial to defendants when during plea bargaining it becomes apparent that the probability of indictment and successful prosecution is quite high. In the months proceeding making their pleas, defendants have a significant information advantage over the plaintiffs who harbor great uncertainty about the size of the expected settlement. Since the new federal sentencing guidelines for criminal antitrust violators began to be implemented in 1995, guilty pleas have been accompanied by information on the defendants' overcharges or the size of the market's sales affected by the cartel. Once this information becomes public, plaintiffs' uncertainty about an appropriate settlement amount is greatly reduced and, consequently, their bargaining position is enhanced. In other words, what might appear to be a generous settlement offer prior to guilty pleas becomes far less tempting after the prosecution lays out its justification for the fines levied in open court.

In recent years, there have been a few cases of civil antitrust suits filed prior to the announcement of indictments and even before word leaked out about the existence of an antitrust investigation.[32] Perhaps the best-known case of this kind is *In re NASDAQ Market Makers Antitrust Litigation* (see box). The NASDAQ case was initially filed in 1994 after an academic study found some statistical irregularities in the differences between the prices at which securities were bought and sold. Defendants were charged with colluding to increase these margins and in 1998 eventually agreed to settle with buyers for more than $1 billion, a record amount for a civil class-action antitrust case. The Department of Justice and the Securities and Exchange Commission opened investigations several months after the case was filed and settled for consent decrees. The DOJ later explained that calculating the overcharges was too complex for it to rationally set fines on the brokerage firms.

Price Fixing Penalties

Chapter 1 recounted how low antitrust fines were prior to 1990 and how these fines have grown in the 1990s in criminal price-fixing cases. Later chapters will demonstrate that civil penalties for price fixing have grown apace. In part, the increased size of criminal and civil penalties reflects the growth in the size of corporations and the markets that they exploited.

The NASDAQ Class Action Antitrust Suit

This enormously complicated suit was unusual for a civil antitrust suit in that it did not follow an investigation or guilty plea prosecuted by federal agencies.

It was initiated by law firms representing more than one million direct purchasers of stocks and bonds sold during the period May 1989 to May 1994. Plaintiffs alleged that so-called market makers on the NASDAQ exchange colluded on the spread between bid and asked prices of 1659 different securities. Eventually 65 law firms represented plaintiffs against 37 securities dealers, including many of Wall Street's best-known houses. The law firms had to finance their investigation for four years before the first defendants began to cave in.

When the class was certified in New York City, four lead co-counsels were appointed. Working like prosecutors everywhere, they offered the weakest firms relatively low settlement amounts. As more of the defendants settled, the cost of settlements per dollar of trading fees rose in each case until the last 30 firms settled *en mass* in late 1998.

The negotiated settlement amount of $1.27 billion was approved by the supervising federal judge on November 9, 1998. Plaintiffs' law firms had requested the judge to approve legal fees at the rate of 17.5 percent of recovery. After noting the extraordinary complexity of the plaintiffs' burden of proof – so difficult that the DOJ found criminal prosecution infeasible – he approved fees and costs of $147 million, which was 14 percent of recovery. This decision marks a return to the traditional method of rewarding plaintiffs' counsel, rather than the "loadstar" method based on actual costs or the sliding scale adopted in the lysine class action.

This was a record settlement that recognized serious and widespread harm. Absent the ability to pool prosecutorial resources, harmed investors might have been without recourse.

In order to deter managers from contemplating the formation of future price-fixing conspiracies, the penalties must rise at least proportionately with the size of the injuries that would be caused. However, there is evidence that the severity of the price-fixing infractions has increased. Not only have most of the cartels prosecuted since 1990 been global in scope (whereas most were national or regional in prior years), but also the percentage overcharges appear to have risen. Combined with the newly assertive stance of the federal antitrust agencies and the expanded opportunities for private suits, fines and settlements have both increased faster than the size of the affected markets.

Private antitrust suits provide complementary deterrence with public prosecutions. Civil class-action suits are a vehicle especially suitable for permitting small buyers – small firms or consumers – to win relief against price-fixing conspirators. The conspirators are mainly large, powerful corporations in highly concentrated industries. Their great wealth and access to legal resources generally brings a David-and-Goliath aspect to antitrust class actions. Yet, there are many legal commentators that have disparaged their use in treble damages cases.

In part, the debate over the desirability of class-action treble-damages suits reflects a wider debate on the social benefits of treble damages themselves. Some believe triple damages to be unnecessarily high to deter (Easterbrook 1986), while others argue that plaintiffs often receive closer to single damages (Lande 1993). If plaintiffs really do get closer to single damages, then civil penalties alone provide virtually no deterrence because only a small portion of all conspiracies are discovered and prosecuted. The best economic study of this issue concluded that only 13 to 17 percent of all illegal U.S. cartels are caught (Bryant and Eckard 1991). If true, then six-times the overcharge is required to deter price fixing. Moreover, buyers who had to exit a market because of cartel-elevated prices are rarely compensated (Page 1996). Another issue that troubles critics of class-action suits is the large size of the legal fees and the incentives they might give for lawyers to file frivolous suits. Calkins (1997:441) suggests that the rise in successful government prosecutions makes the need for supplemental deterrence from civil cases much less justifiable. However, in the three global cartels examined in this book it will be shown that the typical criminal fine imposed in the United States was one-fifth to one-half of the best estimate of actual overcharges, so the need for "supplemental" civil punishment would appear to be still strong. This is particularly true in cases that relied on subtle or innovative methods of price fixing that fall short of the naked cartels documented in this book. Federal class-action suits were filed by direct buyers in each cartel and are fairly well documented. Some of the members of the federal class opted out of the proposed settlements, and many of them settled by means of private negotiation.

The appropriateness of treble damages depends in part on the size of related settlements that are not fully reported. Cartel participants faced many suits outside U.S. courts. Moreover, much less is known about the opt-out U.S. settlements because terms of the settlements typically include non-disclosure clauses. Indirect buyers of these products launched suits in several states and Canadian provinces with varying degrees of success. At least one *parens patriae* action by a large number of state attorneys general was initiated for recovery of indirect damages arising from a global cartel. Finally, related suits for fraud and mismanagement were decided in the lysine case. The global cartels chosen conclusion in this book will allow the full panoply of civil actions to be illustrated.

The role played by economic analysis in antitrust policy-making, public-agency prosecutions, and private litigation has greatly expanded in the last 30 years or so (Einhorn 1993, Coate and Klein 1996). The Bureau of Economics of the FTC employed about 25 economists in the 1960s, but the DOJ's Antitrust Division had far fewer at the time. Now both agencies have hundreds of industrial organization economists on their rosters. These economists have had strong influence on antitrust enforcement since the mid-1970s. "Chicago School" ideas and the "New IO" movement affected the merger, vertical power, and price discrimination areas, but attitudes toward price-fixing did not alter very much if at all (Shepherd 2000). The major change in thinking may have been the issue of whether much observed collusion is achieved tacitly (and therefore putatively legally) (Hay 2000, Gertner and Rosenfield 1998). The great attention focused on merger reviews may have distracted many DOJ economists from giving proper retention to cartel analysis (but see Werden 2000).

A recent book edited by Slottje (1998) has several essays by forensic economists specialized in antitrust legal proceedings. These essays demonstrate the wide array of techniques employed to solve concrete legal questions, the stimulation that law cases provide for new research ideas, and the satisfaction that arises from influencing high-stakes legal battles. Consulting economists have been witnesses in antitrust trials since at least 1920, but increasingly used since the 1960s (Kwoka and White 1994). Many are academics or solo practitioners, but recent decades have seen the rise of economic consulting firms that specialize in regulatory or antitrust matters.

In the prosecution of cartels with sufficient evidence of an explicit agreement, the *per se* rule implies that the role of economic analysis will be limited mainly to rough estimates of the overcharge as a basis for negotiating the fine. If a criminal trial is held, defendants will usually engage economists as advisors to provide arguments as to the ineffectiveness of the cartel. Even though evidence on the issue should be irrelevant, defense counsel will try to sow doubt about price effects in the jury. When only circumstantial evidence of an agreement is available, the testimony of economists may be needed to assist a jury in inferring the existence of an explicit agreement. During the sentencing phase of a criminal trial the size of the monopoly overcharge or dead-weight losses may require economic opinions to guide the presiding judge.

In treble-damages cases, the role of forensic economists is often crucial because the size of injuries is the main issue to be decided or negotiated. The limited sophistication of juries or nonspecialist judges will put a premium on simple analytical approaches and on the persuasive skills of testifying experts. While more advanced theoretical or empirical points will often be presented in expert opinions, these exercises will often serve only to confirm opinions reached by simpler means or to neutralize the weight of the evidence presented by the other side during trials or negotiated settlements.

ANTICARTEL ENFORCEMENT ABROAD

Historical Development

In his magisterial survey of the world's competition laws in the mid-1960s, Edwards (1967) found 24 countries with antitrust laws. Twelve had been adopted prior to World War II, through most of these had fallen into disuse or had been superceded by government policies that actively promoted cartels in the 1930s (Table 3.A.1). Even the United States effectively suspended its antitrust laws during 1933-1937 when depression concerns led to the passage of the National Recovery Act. By in large, prior to 1945 those countries that maintained cartel laws had weak or nonexistent penalties. Often the laws merely permitted investigations or required registration of cartels. Sometimes, as in France, the courts found anticartel laws in conflict with laws that permitted businesses to form industry associations. In other cases, the laws left on the books were simply left unenforced.

Canadian federal competition law dates from 1889. Antitrust allegations are investigated by the Canadian Competition Bureau. Section 45 makes price-fixing conspiracies that "unduly lessen competition" illegal. Although this sounds like a rule-of-reason approach to enforcement, naked cartels are in effect prosecuted by the Ministry of Justice as *per se* offenses. Under Section 47 of Canada's law, covert bid-rigging is a *per se* violation. Finally, there is a special section (46) that empowers the Ministry of Justice to indict cartels that have operated outside of Canadian territory.

Until after World War II Canada and the United States were nearly alone in the world in having a strong commitment to anticartel enforcement. National laws outlawing price fixing were passed in the late 1940s in Japan and Germany as part of the occupation policies of the Allies to prevent the reappearance of concentrated economic and political power in those former Axis countries. Although the Japanese antitrust laws were weakened in the 1950s, those in Germany and the United Kingdom were strengthened in the years just before the Treaty of Rome that created the European Economic Community (EEC) was signed in 1957 (Connor 1997). By the 1960s, the competition laws of the United States and the EEC (now part of the European Union) had become the world's two great legal templates.

In language not unlike that of the Sherman Act, article 85 of the Treaty prohibits agreements and concerted acts in restraint of trade, when that trade is between member countries of the European Union. "Agreements" in

EU parlance are roughly equivalent to overt conspiracies in the U.S. tradition: written or oral agreements or joint announcements about conditions of sales. "Concerted practices" are forms of business cooperation based on mutual understandings or exchanges of information, i.e., tacit agreements (Venit 1996).

All forms of naked cartel behavior are considered serious violations of EU competition law. The European Commission (EC), the executive branch of the EU, has a directorate (the DG-IV) dedicated to competition-law enforcement, and within DG-IV a special anticartel unit was created in the late 1990s. The DG-IV has the power to demand information from potential violators in writing, to conduct on-premise surprise inspections of places of business, to hold hearings on proposed findings, to issue conduct injunctions, to void contracts, and to fine corporate transgressors. Allegations of price fixing are handled by the EC as an administrative proceeding. There is no concept of price fixing as a criminal justice matter under EU competition law. The EC may issue "bloc exemptions" to companies, industries, or trade associations that have inquired about the legality of certain practices; such negative clearances have no parallel in U.S. antitrust enforcement.[33] However, EU law does not permit personal penalties and has no provisions for divestiture of companies. EC remedies may be appealed to the European Court of Justice. As the European Union added more members, national antitrust laws have become *de rigeur* for the new members and those applying for membership.

Like the interstate commerce clause of the U.S. constitution, the EU's competition laws were designed to preserve the smooth functioning of a customs union that is evolving into a single market. However, unlike the competition laws of many other countries, the Sherman Act permits the prosecution of conspiracies in restraint of trade that occur outside U.S. territory so long as those acts affect U.S. trade and commerce. This "extraterritoriality" provision of U.S. antitrust law often remained entirely theoretical because of practical barriers to gathering evidence or serving subpoenas abroad, but in recent years bilateral treaties or protocols have allowed for greater cooperation among the world's many antitrust agencies.

After World War II and up to 1965 a dozen countries adopted new or greatly strengthened antitrust laws (Edwards 1967). Passage was motivated by several factors. The pre-war members of the cartels were politically weak, partly because of abuses revealed by post-war investigations; in some cases cartels were held responsible for inflation, international trade restrictions, or retarded productivity growth; cartels were judged to be incompatible with the dismantling of national planning policies. These national competition laws varied in several respects from those of the United States. Their purpose was to keep prices at "reasonable" levels, protect business from unfair competition, and to maintain economic stability. The U.S. concept of protecting the competitive process for the benefit of consumer welfare is nearly absent in non-U.S. antitrust statutes. Despite the differences in antitrust philosophy, the content of most antitrust laws is quite similar. In about half the cases, price-fixing was strictly prohibited (except for export prices); the remainder prohibited cartels operating “contrary to the public interest”.

Passage of national antitrust laws accelerated in the 1990s because of four factors. First, many countries in the Soviet bloc and Latin America abandoned price controls and centralized economic planning; antitrust laws were viewed as necessary to constrain the market power of privatized firms in concentrated sectors. Second, with the liberalization of international trade and investment rules by many newly industrializing countries, multinational firms began lobbying for a more predictable legal environment for business, including more transparent competition laws. Chile’s highly successful growth strategy was due in part of the clarity of its national antitrust enforcement policies. Third, as many countries turned away from military or dictatorial regimes, antitrust laws were passed as part of the process of democratization, of which the dispersion of economic decision making is seen as one part. South Korea’s Fair Trade Commission is often cited as an example in this regard. The World Bank began making the implementation of effective antitrust enforcement a condition of loans for economic restructuring as early as 1991 in the case of Argentina. Such policies were often welcomed in countries that had relied on heavy investment in state enterprises as a major development strategy, often with disappointing results for employment creation and industrial efficiency.

A fourth reason is the formation of customs unions. When expansions of the EU occurred in the 1990s, the formation of national competition-law agencies with substantive and procedural features compatible with the EU’s became a necessary condition for membership. Poland, Hungary, Turkey, and other prospective EU members have adopted competition laws on the model of the German Federal Cartel Office. In North America, the formation of the North American Free Trade Agreement (NAFTA) area prompted Mexico to pass new competition laws in 1993. The Mexican Federal Competition Commission (COFETEL) had its powers expanded in 1998. Mexican law virtually prohibits price fixing, dividing markets, and bid rigging. COFETEL can and does fine companies for price fixing. Its published findings of violations can be used by private parties as evidence in court to seek compensation for damages.

Anticartel Laws

Cartels have come to be condemned by international bodies (ICPAC 2000). The United Nations’ Commission on Trade and Development (UNCTAD) began holding annual conferences antitrust laws in the mid-1970s. In 1980, UNCTAD issued a set of nonbinding recommendations to its member countries for laws that control restrictive business practices, including clear prohibitions of cartel activities. Prior to 1980, only about five developing countries had instituted competition laws, but during the 1980s UNCTAD was reporting annually on the adoption of about three new national antitrust laws.

Another multilateral agency concerned with cartel policies is the Organization of Economic Co-Operation and Development (OECD). In 1998, its 29 members adopted a set of recommendations on cartel enforcement which ICPAC called "the first consensus statement on an approach to international hard core cartels." The OECD statement defines a hard core cartel as an anticompetitive agreement, concerted practice, or arrangement by competitors to fix prices, rig bids, restrict output, or to divide markets by allocating market shares, customers, suppliers, territories, or lines of business. The OECD recommends the adoption of laws that prohibit cartels and that provide for effective enforcement and sanctions. Moreover, member countries are encouraged to sign mutual assistance agreements between their antitrust agencies and repeal legislation that blocked cooperative enforcement efforts.

Despite the exhortation of UNCTAD and the OECD, anticartel laws and enforcement procedures remain quite variable across the 60 or so jurisdictions that now have such laws. These differences often reflect the general differences in national legal systems. The UNCTAD and OECD recommendations do not have the force of international law; they are more like model laws or workable principles. In general, Canada, Mexico, Germany, and the European Union have the most active programs of anticartel enforcement after the United States. In many other countries in Asia and Latin America (e.g., China, Argentina, and Venezuela) there are laws on the books that are as a practical matter unenforced (Connor 1997). Most other national agencies, including most in Western Europe, fall in between.

Some national antitrust laws specify extensive lists of multilateral conduct that are deemed *per se* illegal, just as price fixing is in the United States, but most national laws follow a rule-of-reason approach even for hard core cartels.[34] The types of sanctions available to the antitrust units or the courts also vary considerably across jurisdictions. Cease-and-desist orders or court injunctions are quite common, and future violations of such orders can bring about very severe additional sanctions.

Government Fine Structures

Monetary fines are frequently imposed on convicted corporate cartel participants, but the limits on such fines or the ways that they are calculated also vary. Anticartel statutes often specify absolute upper limits on the size of corporate fines, such as the $10 million statutory maximum for Sherman Act violations in the United States (Table 3.2). The United States and other jurisdictions have upper limits based on a percentage of "affected sales," that is, sales in the cartelized market during the conspiracy period.[35] Usually the sales concept is geographically or temporally restricted. The percentages mostly fall in the 5 to 20 percent range, but the United States uniquely permits unlimited percentages in the case of felony violations. Typically, national cartel fines are based solely on national sales during the affected period. However, the EU fine structure allows the Competition Directorate to recommend fines up to 10 percent of a violator' s *global* annual sales in all its product lines; U.S. law also permits the use of global sales if a fine based on U.S. sales were to grossly understate the seriousness of the offense. The United States, Canada, and Germany place no limits on the length of the affected period, but other jurisdictions limit the sales from which to calculate the fine to three years or even one year (Table 3.2). Beginning in March 2000, the UK Office of Fair Trade was authorized to assess fines on cartels as high as 30 percent of sales for three years. "The penalties will be on par with those in America" (*Daily Mail* August 12, 1999).

Until 1994 when Sherman Act violations were elevated from the class of misdemeanors to a felony crime, the EU's fine structure was considered to be potentially harsher than that of the United States. However, beginning in 1987, the U.S. Sentencing Guidelines raised the potential liability of corporations to levels comparable to those of the EU or even higher under more extreme circumstances. In January 1998, the Commission of the European Communities issued its first set of sentencing guidelines for antitrust violations. Although similar to the U.S. guidelines in its guiding principles, the EC's criteria are not nearly so detailed.

A comparison is made in Table 3.3 between the two jurisdictions' abilities to levy financial penalties for three global cartel scenarios for a corporate participant that was one of the ringleaders in the cartel. This hypothetical company has annual worldwide sales of $10 billion, but sold only $200 million annually of the product that was the object of price fixing. The company's sales are spread equally across three geographic regions and represent 22 percent of the cartel's sales in the United States, in the European Union, and in the world. That is, the company is simply the average size of the four or five members in the cartel.[36] For simplicity, no discount for cooperation is shown.

In the first scenario (I), the cartel was able to raise global prices by 10 percent for one year (the average overcharge rate envisioned by the U.S. Sentencing Guidelines). In the next two scenarios the overcharge is higher (30 percent), but the duration of the cartel varies from one year (scenario II) to ten years (scenario III). The first column of table 2.3 calculates the harm done to the company's buyers – the overcharge – in the U.S., EU, or global markets. The company's monopoly profits are only slightly lower than the customers' overcharge.

Table 3.2. Price-Fixing Sanctions, Selected Jurisdictions, 2000.

Authority	Maximum Corporate Fines[a]		Maximum Individual		Amnesty Policy
	Fines	Sales Concept	Prison	Fine	
U.S.	$10 million, 20% of sales or twice the loss	Affected U.S., rarely affected world	3 years	$350,000[b]	Yes
Canada	C$10 million	Affected Canadian	5 years	$10,000,000	Yes
European union	10% of sales	Global or EU sales in preceeding year	None	None	Yes
France	5% of sales up to FF10 million	French sales in preceeding year	4 years	FF500,000	No
Germany	Treble the sales gain	Affected German	None	Treble in the gain in sales	No
UK	10% of sales	Affected UK up to 3 years	None	None	Yes
Japan	Criminal: 100 million yen	No guidelines	3 years	5 million yen	No
Japan	Civil: 6% of sales	Affected Japan sales up to 3 years	None	None	No

Sources: ICPAC (2000).

[a] "Loss" is equivalent to the consumer or customer overcharge and perhaps the dead-weight loss. "Gain" is the monopoly profits made from the conspiracy. "Affected" sales are those made in the cartelized market during the entire conspiracy period. Other sales are those made by a company in all lines of business, whether affected or not.

[b] Since 1994, an alternative sentencing provision allows for personal fines of up to $25 million, but fines above $350,000 have not yet been successfully litigated.

Table 3.3. Maximum U.S. and EU Fines for a Company with $200 Million in Affected Sales in a $900-million Global Cartel.

Cartel Scenarios	Economic Harm to Company's Buyers	United States		European Union[a]	
		Sentencing Guidelines	Felony Guidelines	Cartelized Market Sales	Group Sales of $10 Billion
		Million dollars			
I. One year, 10% overcharge					
A. Jurisdiction sales basis[b]	6.7	20-60	13.3	6.7	333
B. Global sales basis[c]	20.0	60-180	40	20.0	1,000
II. One year, 30% overcharge:					
A. Jurisdiction sales basis[b]	20.0	20-60	40	6.7	333
B. Global sales basis[c]	60.0	60-180	120	20.0	1,000
III. Ten years, 30% overcharge:					
A. Jurisdiction sales basis[b]	200.0	200-600	400	6.7	333
B. Global sales basis[c]	600.0	600-1,800	1,200	20.0	1,000

[a] Assumed that the sales of the cartelized product were $66.7 million in the EU out of $200 million in the world.

[b] Assumed that of $900 million in global sales of cartel, $300 million occurred in the U.S. and $300 million in the EU. The company has a 22% share of each geographic market. The USSG multipliers are 1.5 to 4.5, depending on the seriousness of the offense.

[c] Rarely applied by U.S. authorities. More commonly applied (but in a minority of cases) by the European Commission.

By construction, the U.S. Sentencing Guidelines prescribe a fine range that is from one to nine times the company's illegal U.S. profits when only *affected domestic* sales are the basis (scenario A). However, because the guilty company has two-thirds of its sales outside the United States, it is possible that the U.S. fines can be as low as one-third of the company's illicit *global* profits. In those rare instances when the U.S. DOJ decides to request fines on the basis of global sales (scenario B), the maximum fines will always equal or exceed the firm's global monopoly gains. Note that by applying the twice-the-harm rule in felony convictions, the maximum U.S. fine is *lower* than the USSG fine when the cartel's percentage overcharge is low (roughly below 15 percent of sales); the felony standard yields fines *within* the USSG range for moderate to high overcharges; and the felony-based fines are *higher* than the USSG range when the overcharge is quite high (roughly about 50 percent).[37] One notable feature of the felony fine standard is that the resulting fines are more likely to have a deterrence effect (i.e., a punitive component above single damages), especially when the company or the cartel has most of its sales in the United States.

The European Union reserves its highest "basic fines" for naked cartels and certain types of monopoly behavior. Since 1998, this "basic fine" has been specified as 20 million euros or more. This base fine is increased by 50 percent for violations lasting 1-5 years and by 100 percent for duration of 5 years or more. Thus, the minimum base fines for a company determined to have violated the EU's price-fixing laws are 20, 30, or 40 million euros depending on duration of the cartel. The base fine will be further increased if it does not exceed the economic harm caused by the firm's price-fixing activities; that is, if 20 to 40 million euros is less than the overcharge, a fine greater than the overcharge will be assessed so as to have a deterrent effect.[38] The base fine is then further adjusted by a list of aggravating and attenuating factors that are highly reminiscent of the U.S. Sentencing Guidelines except that the EU is less precise about the scores given for varying degrees of culpability. Finally, the EC may recommend fine reductions under its 1996 leniency policy. Cartel leaders can be bestowed 10-50 percent discounts for their cooperation with the EC's investigation; non-leading cooperating defendants will be awarded 75-100 percent reductions if they are the first to cooperate or 50-75 percent if they cooperate at a later stage. Single-product firms usually have less exposure than, as in the example in Table 2.3, a company with many product lines, because by law the EC can impose a fine based on global sales of the parent company's entire organization.

As can be seen in Table 2.3, the maximum fines for a company with identical characteristics are quite similar in the United States (since 1987) and the European Union (since 1998) if the EC chooses to use affected sales for its measuring rod of harm, as it usually does in practice. However, if the EC employs global group sales instead, as EU law permits in theory, then EC fines are potentially far more onerous for short-lived cartels with moderate overcharges than are the U.S. fines. On the other hand, for exceptionally long lasting and harmful cartels (like those in vitamins), the ability of U.S. authorities to impose large fines for exceeds the EC's authority.

European analysts have been critical of the EC's vast discretion in setting fines (Korah 1997). Large discount have been awarded to companies that made low monopoly profits, were first time violators, and cooperated with the EC's investigation. Korah (1997) suggests that there is an unwritten rule that non-EU firms get lower reductions than those headquartered in the EU. Although he rejected a U.S.-style point system as "too transparent" for violators, EC competition Commissioner Karl Van Miert recently reaffirmed the factors be used to determine the discount rates for violators (Alchin 1999). Perhaps most interesting was Van Miert's view that EC fines should be proportionately higher than parallel U.S. fines because Europe has no tradition of individual criminal liability for competition law offenses. This new "U.S. plus" rule was first applied to members of the lysine cartel in May 2000.

Other Price-Fixing Sanctions

The greatest differences in cartel sanctions across countries have to do with the sanctioning of individuals and leniency policies. Like corporations everywhere, individuals guilty of price fixing are typically subject to civil penalties or none at all.[39] Although permitted in Canada, Mexico, and the EU since at least the early 1990s, private damage suits for antitrust violations are uncommon (Venit 1996). The United States, Canada, France, and Japan have criminalized their price-fixing laws, but only the United States regularly prosecutes individuals and seeks prison sentences for the ringleaders of cartel. Canada imposed the first prison sentence for price fixing in 1999. Ireland, Norway, and a few other countries have begun moving in the direction of criminalization. Individual fines are often, capped at modest levels, but Germany allows for treble damages to be assessed on persons. Besides the United States, Canada, the EU, and the UK, have adopted formal corporate leniency policies, though not all have automatic amnesty provisions. As these have been shown to result in significant increases in the discovery of cartels, several other countries are considering their adoption.

Enforcement in Practice

Canada and the EU appear to have the most active anticartel regimes outside the United States. From 1980 to May 2000, the Canadian federal government indicted 75 groups for price-fixing or bid-rigging. (CBC News Release June 16, 2000). Of the 75 cases, 68 percent resulted in convictions, of which 84 percent were negotiated guilty pleas. As in the United States, when defendants went to trial the Crown prevailed in less than one-third of the cases. In the 1990s, the price-fixing cases brought by the Canadian Competition bureau were increasingly international in scope. There were only two global cartel cases prior to 1997, but during 1997-2000, 64 percent were international conspiracies. Antitrust enforcement resources are rather modest in Canada, so about four-fifths of its global cartel convictions have followed U.S. investigations. Canada has had a mutual assistance antitrust agreement with the United States since 1991 and an extradition treaty that applies to criminal antitrust matters.

Since the late 1980s, the European Commission has prosecuted more than 20 price-fixing cartels, though most of them have operated within the EU. Fines have escalated for cartels, reaching about 100 million euros in five cases; the largest single fine imposed was 70 million euros. However, fines have been adjusted downward five times for cartel participants under the EU's 1996 leniency policy. Like the United States, the EU recognizes that it has the power to prosecute offshore conspiracies.

The passage of Japan's Antimonopoly Law in 1947 followed two decades of economic nationalism during which the government actively encouraged and enforced cartel agreements (Schwartzman 1993). A 1932 law made it possible for government ministries to force even unwilling companies to join cartels and prevent capacity expansions that could undermine cartel operations. The 1947 law had weak sanctions and was undermined by the creation of the Ministry of International Trade and Industry (MITI), which was in the 1950s authorized to form cartels in "depressed industries." Japan's Fair Trade Commission (JFTC) had no subpoena powers, could not recommend prison sentences, and could issue only limited cease-and-desist decrees. If companies violated the decrees, the Japanese courts had no contempt powers to sanction them.

In the late 1960s, the JFTC's political position began to improve with the increasing support of academics and consumer organizations. Its actions against the petroleum cartel in the early 1970s were popular and effective. In 1974, the High Court in Tokyo found the cartel guilty of *criminal* price fixing, a first for Japan. In 1977, the Antimonopoly Law was amended, increasing the fines for violations and granting divestiture powers to the JFTC for the first time. However, MITI-sponsored "depression cartels" are still permitted as are legal export cartels. In the early 1970s, 20 export cartels were registered, more than half of them for chemical products.[40]

Although it has a reputation for lackadaisical antitrust enforcement, Japan's Fair Trade Commission (JFTC) has not been inactive in prosecuting cartels. In the ten fiscal years from 1989 to 1998, the JFTC has issued a total of 259 "legal measures." These are administrative actions that include recommendations, cease-and-desist orders, or fines. Of the 259 actions, 73 percent were directed at cartels (ICPAC 2000). Fines, the JFTC's most potent sanction, totaled 47 billion yen (about 250 million yen per cartel or roughly \$2 million).[41] Despite the initiating of regular meetings with U.S. and EU antitrust officials in the 1990s, the JFTC's record on cartel fines shows no upward trend.

Beginning in the mid-1990s, the EC began to discuss the decentralization of competition-law enforcement (Rodger and MacCulloch 1998). One direction involves the transfer of additional enforcement authority from Brussels to the national competition authorities (NCAs) of the member states of the EU. Allowing a national court to handle somewhat localized alleged violations became possible in 1993, so long as the EC declares the case to lack "Community Interest." Devolution of EC antitrust enforcement was prompted mainly by ". . . the lack of resources afforded DG-IV to carry out into tasks" (*ibid.* p.580), but the process has been slow because of the lack of trained professionals in the national agencies. The same motive underlies the complementary use of private suits in the national courts of the EU, a practice encouraged by decisions of the European Court of Justice since at least 1976. Obstacles to this route include the inability of private parties to obtain evidence gathered by the DG-IV (unless published) and disappointingly small damages awards. Although U.S. law has clearly inspired EU antitrust decentralization, adoption of treble damages seems unlikely at this juncture. Like the federal antitrust agencies in the United States, the European competition agency has taken on many additional duties with no expansion in professional staff.

The UK and the Netherlands have responded in the late 1990s with new laws that have strengthened their local competition -law institutions. Progress in using private antitrust suits in national courts has been slower. One problem is that, unlike the United States, information gathered and analyzed by DG-IV officials cannot be shared with private plaintiffs who would like to initiate follow-on actions. Several decisions of the European Court of Justice starting in 1976 have encouraged the use of national courts by private parties, but the few cases brought have resulted in disappointing, weak remedies or penalties. A 1993 EC notice also encouraged private cases where the EC believes there is a lack of "Community interest," a rather vague standard. Many questions relating to standing and sanctions are unresolved. The new UK law (effective March 2000) specifically encourages private antitrust suits, but it appears that indirect buyers will not have standing to sue. Multiple damages seem unlikely to be awarded in any Member State.

INTERNATIONAL COOPERATION

Traditionally, when an antitrust agency needed information located beyond its territory, it could rely on either diplomatic channels or letters from a judge called rogatory requests (ICPAC 2000). National sovereignty made responses to such requests purely voluntary on the basis of comity. Prior to the 1980s, requests for antitrust assistance through these channels were often turned down because of national concerns about foreign interference with national firms, trade secrets, or substantive differences in legal principles. These difficulties were recognized as early as 1930 by the League of Nations (Decugis 1930). In the late 1940s, U.S. prosecution of the rubber, potash, and quinine cartels did not lead to parallel actions by European antitrust agencies in the countries in which the cartels were hatched (Edwards 1967). A 1948 U.S. antitrust suit (*U.S. vs. De Beers Consolidated*) failed mainly because the U.S. locked jurisdiction over cartel participants. However, more recently several DOJ prosecutions of global cartels have involved cooperation with the antitrust agencies of other countries. Moreover, since the early 1980s, DOJ investigations of global price fixing have been relatively unhindered by national blocking statutes abroad that prevented some corporations with headquarters outside the United States from providing documents or depositions even when the firms wished to cooperate. Foreign antitrust units are increasingly imitating the successful investigations or prosecutions initiated by the U.S. DOJ and offering material assistance under various international agreements.

One relatively new development has been the signing of formal bilateral antitrust agreements. The first was signed by the United States and Germany in 1976. By the end of 1999, the United States had six more agreements of this type with Australia (1982), Canada (1984), the EU (1991), and 1999 with Israel, Japan and Brazil. They are not treaties but rather agreements by the Executive Branch of the U.S. government with the ministries of other countries. The purposes of these bilateral agreements include enforcement cooperation, information exchange, regular meetings, technical assistance, and mechanisms for dispute avoidance. Confidential information cannot be shared under these bilateral agreements, so in 1994 Congress passed the International Antitrust Enforcement Assistance Act (IAEAA). The IAEAA permits U.S. antitrust agencies to engage in reciprocal exchange of confidential information with foreign antitrust agencies, except for merger filings. The first IAEAA agreement was signed with Australia in 1999. While exchanges under the IAEAA can occur for either civil or criminal cases, the United States has much more experience with a far larger number of Mutual Legal Assistance Treaties (MLATs). These treaties, which encompass only criminal matters, must be approved by the U.S. Senate. At the end of 1999, the United States had entered into 30 MLATs and another 20 or so were awaiting Senate approval (ICPAC 2000). The Antitrust Division of the DOJ reports many positive experiences in using MLATs, with nearly all such cases involving global price-fixing investigations. Article 15 of the North American Free Trade Agreement requires cooperation and some rudimentary harmonization of antitrust laws among the three signatories. In general, U.S. and foreign antitrust officials favor continuation and deepening of these various bilateral arrangements.

One issue currently facing U.S. antitrust officials is the extent to which the country should cooperate in multi-lateral solutions to antitrust enforcement. The International Trade Organization that was negotiated in 1948 was to have had an important antitrust function, but when the United States Senate declined to ratify the ITO charter, the weaker GATT was established with no antitrust dimensions. Perhaps the first successful international antitrust agency was the 1951 European Coal and Steel Community (ECSC). ECSC rules cover price fixing, mergers, and dominant firm behavior. Although not its principal objective, the ECSC has preserved and increased European competition in the coal and steel markets (Edwards 1967). Indeed, the success of the ECSC was a major stimulus to the formation of the European Economic Community (EEC), to which the ECSC belongs, and the inclusion of competition laws in the 1957 Treaty of Rome.

The General Agreements on Tariffs and Trade (GATT) was recently replaced by the World Trade Organization (WTO). Most of the work of the

WTO's small secretariat has been directed at resolving bilateral trade disputes, but the agency is interested in sponsoring international antitrust rules. While less than half of the WTO's 135 members have antitrust laws, several observers have recommended that the WTO make the development of global antitrust laws a priority. U.S. officials seemed disinclined to cooperate on such a broadening of the WTO's mission. ICPAC (2000) suggested that the WTO needed to expand its expertise in antitrust and then confine itself to government restraints on competition, not private ones, except where private practices may restrain international trade. In late 2000, the U.S. government signaled that it was receptive to the idea of establishing a new international antitrust body unconnected to the WTO. The idea is to have the new agency focus at first on screening of large international mergers, a procedure that would alleviate many companies from the burden of multiple competition-agency filings.

Chapter 3 Endnotes

[1] Syndicate came into English from French in the late 19th century, where it specifically referred to stock-market manipulation. The French term for a collusive group of sellers is *entente,* a term used in diplomacy but not in economics.

[2] It is also the profit-maximizing condition for firms that choose prices in an oligopoly with differentiated brands. In all three cases, the Lerner Index is the inverse of the own-price elasticity of demand facing the firm (market, residual, and brand demand, respectively) (Werden 2000).

[3] Economic profits or rents do not include a normal return to investors or bondholders in the firm, whereas conventional accounting concepts may count these as part of the profits of a firm. In equilibrium, competitive firms earn zero economic profits but may make positive accounting profits.

[4] Several Western and Midwestern states of the United States had antitrust laws in the 1880s, but subnational units had difficulties devising remedies for convicted national firms. France (1790) and Canada (1889) also passed laws against price fixing, but these laws were unenforced for many decades (Connor 1997). See also Table 3.A.1.

[5] In one of the most dubious examples of public policy, Congress exempted soft drink bottles from being sued for creating exclusive supply territories.

[6] McChesney and Shugart (1995) believe that some types of cartels are socially efficient. However, even if the cartels can reduce industry dead-weight losses, these benefits may not outweigh jurists' concerns for conservation of judicial resources or society's concerns for equity or small-business protection. Japan and the EU regularly grant exemptions for cartels in industries with excess capacity.

[7] For example, a buyer of a product might become a net seller on an exchange that sets contract prices. See Mueller and Marion (1999)

[8] Plaintiffs' counsel can obtain information on the testimony of witnesses subpoenaed by grand juries. Both the questions asked by prosecutors and answers given can be revealed by the witnesses themselves. Lawyers may also get hints from federal investigators or prosecutors.

[9] These changes are described in greater detail in Chapter 17 below. Gary Spratling of the DOJ is credited with discovering the applicability of the 1987 and 1990 changes to cartel indictments. The U.S. DOJ has the authority under Section 6 of the Sherman Act to seek forfeiture of property transported in interstate commerce that was owned by the cartel. During 1992-1996, the DOJ exercised this penalty twice, obtaining $28 million in 1992 and $125 million in 1995 (Calkins 1997).

[10] To be more precise, there are two multipliers specified for each level of culpability. The top end of the fine range is double the low end. For prison sentences, the guideline range is narrower.

[11] Some would argue that the injury also includes the dead-weight social loss (Hovenkamp 1998). In any case, profits will be less than the overcharge because collusion is not a free good.

[12] The "affected sales" is normally the company's U.S. sales in the cartelized market during the conspiracy. Lags in price responses could shift the period forward. Moreover, the prosecution has the option of using worldwide sales in specified circumstances.

[13] DOJ economists already perform at least rough overcharge analyses for any price-fixing matter, so such a rule would not unduly burden the agency.

[14] Some cease and desist orders are crafted in ways that resemble house arrest or a suspended prison sentence for an individual. Capital punishment for corporations (i.e., fines that lead to bankruptcy) is pretty much off the table.

[15] One count of the number of global cartels operating just prior to the outbreak of World War I is 112 (Stocking and Watkins 1948). This book does not cover "public" cartels, i.e., those that operate openly with government support or the participation of state-owned corporations.

[16] When the United States declared war on Germany in 1917, the assets of all German companies were sequestered by the U.S. government. Many of these assets were returned in 1919, but the chemical industries were judged to have aided Germany's war effort.
[17] The *Singer* cases (1963) involved a conspiracy to pool patents on sewing machines to eliminate Japanese imports into the U.S. market. The *Canadian Radio Patents* case (1962) was similar. The *Quinine* case (1975) involved an arrangement whereby one European company would bid for U.S. government quinine stocks, but would subsequently share its stock with non bidders (ICPAC 1999).
[18] While Bingaman graciously gave credit to her predecessor, James F. Rill, for initiating some global cartel investigations, there seems to be little evidence that global price fixing was a high priority during 1989-1992. One or two cases were under investigation in 1992.
[19] Joel Klein, head of the Antitrust Division from late 1995, sometimes cites the *Plastic Dinnerware* cartel as an important transitional case. From 1994 to 1996, 14 guilty pleas were obtained (five corporate, nine individual) in this $100-million-per-year industry. It was precedent-setting because of the large fines (more than $40 million) and the prison sentences for two Canadian executives, the first foreigners imprisoned for Sherman Act violations (Klein 1999). However, the cases were only marginally global in scope.
[20] The three firms (Winston & Strawn, Arnold & Porter, and Porter Wright) had more than 1100 lawyers at their disposal, roughly twice the number of the entire Antitrust Division. In addition, GE hired six more top law firms to defend about 40 of its employees. Three or four GE employees called by the prosecution were prevented from testifying.
[21] In four cases, paper wholesalers were charged, three of them subsidiaries of one of the six manufacturers.
[22] ICPAC (2000) listed 19 in Annex 4-A, and DOJ press releases named three more in late 1999 and early 2000. Moreover, as of mid-2000 the DOJ had at least 30 grand juries still active in cases involving allegations of global price fixing.
[23] Now Section 4 of the 1914 Clayton Act. Plaintiffs may also seek court injunctions.
[24] Australia, the U.K., and Canada have recent laws permitting private antitrust suits for single damages. So far, the size of the settlements approved by the courts of countries outside the Unites States has discouraged most private civil suits. Hovenkamp (1998) interprets the Sherman Act provisions that allow buyers to challenge restrictive agreements as a break from common law tradition (p. 51).
[25] Legal practice does not allow defendants to subtract the extra costs associated with operating a cartel from the extra profits made. Nor can the fines and damage awards be counted as costs of doing business for income tax purposes.
[26] There is a fourth test that is usually not an issue. Plaintiffs must show that the last violation occurred no later than four years prior to filing the case.
[27] While not impossible, federal class-action suits were made much easier to file after important amendments to federal court procedures in 1966.
[28] Lawyers specializing in class-action suits used to have relatively low status in the legal akin to that of "ambulance chasers" in the personal-injury field of law. Now they tend to be identified by the more respectable adjective of "entrepreneurial."
[29] The class action *In re Domestic Air Transportation Antitrust Litigation* (N.D. Ga. 1993) had 12.5 million air travelers as plaintiffs. The presiding judge must also be satisfied that plaintiffs' counsel have a feasible plan for contracting all potential award recipients.
[30] Unless the indirect buyer purchased from a direct buyer under a cost-plus contract.
[31] The present author was an advisor to the plaintiffs on the amount of the overcharge incurred by buyers in the United States.
[32] Calkins (1997) cites the *Airlines, NASDAQ,* and *Infant Formula* cases as pertinent examples. Neither DOJ nor *parens patriae* cases were launched. They also required substantial economic analyses that class actions can afford to pay for.
[33] The EC is making increasing use of raids on corporate offices. As many as 20 simultaneous searches have been performed (Venit 1996). However, coercive searches require court orders from the national courts of the Member States of the EU. Moreover, only places of business ay be searched; private homes are off limits.

[34] Sullivan and Fikentscher (1998) assert that in Germany and the EC there is no distinction between antitrust violations such as per se or rule-of-reason. Rather proof allows either the "prohibition" approach or the "abusive conduct" approach; the first requires defendants (e.g., cartel violators) to carry the burden of proof, whereas the second imposes the burden of proof on the plaintiffs.

[35] Besides these shown in Table 3.2, Belgium, Italy, Finland, Sweden, and Spain follow the EU rule of 10 percent of a group's annual sales. Greece allows 15 percent, Austria single overcharges, and Denmark has no upper limit (*Financial Times* August 10, 1999:6)

[36] The resemblance of this company to ADM and of the market to lysine or citric acid is intentional.

[37] The USSG range is sensitive to the culpability score of the company; the range observed in the global cartels examined in this book was about 1.5 to 4.5. The theoretical range is slightly wider.

[38] It is not clear whether the European Commission considers the dead-weight loss part of the consumer harm nor whether the harm to only EU residents is considered.

[39] In lysine, liquid lysine was excluded even though its price was highly correlated with dry lysine. In citric acid, the beginning date of the conspiracy was obfuscated by the DOJ such that the period was foreshortened. In the vitamins case, some cartelized product lines were omitted.

[40] One of the products was glutamate acid, which includes monosodium glutamate (MSG). Both the U.S. and the EU permit export cartels. In the U.S., the Federal Trade Commission registers export cartels on the Webb-Pomerene Act.

[41] Because not all cartels are fined, the average may be higher. Of those cartels fined, the affected Japanese sales amount to between 0.8 and 4.7 trillion yen or up to $40 billion. Criminal sanctions are almost unknown.

Table 3.A.1. The History of Restrictive Business Practices 1790-1965.

Date	Country	Prohibited Conduct	Comments
1790	France	Anticompetitive price fixing	Little enforcement. Overturned in 1926.
1870	Austria	Some cartel provisions. Not enforceable in court	Fell into disuse by 20th century.
1889	Canada	Restrictive cartel practices	
1890	USA	Conspiracies in restraint of trade	Strengthened in 1914, 1936, 1950, 1978, 1990.
1901	Dominican Republic	Certain cartel practices	Rarely enforced.
1906	Australia	Certain monopolistic practices	Fell into disuse. Revived in 1965.
1920s	Norway	Unregistered cartels	Allowed for review of abrasive conduct by a government panel.
1923	Germany	Abusive cartel conduct	Enforcement ceased in 1930s.
1923	Argentina	Abusive conduct of cartels	Little enforcement
1930s	Denmark	Unregistered cartels	Control board to correct abuses.
1930s	Bulgaria	Unregistered cartels	Government could dissolve cartels.
1930s	Yugoslavia	Unregistered cartels	Government could dissolve cartels.
1930s	Romania	Unregistered cartels	Regular government surveillance and review of cartel prices.
1930s	South Africa	Monopolies and restraint of trade	Regular government surveillance and review of cartel prices.
1934	Mexico	Most monopolies and price fixing.	
1936	Portugal	Certain cartel behavior	Never applied
1946	Germany	Conspiracies in restraint of trade	Set up Federal Cartel Office.
1946	Japan	Conspiracies in restraint of trade	Set up Fair Trade Commission.
1946	Sweden	Unregistered restrictive agreements	Authorized investigation.
1946	Argentina	Monopolistic practices, including price fixing	
1948	UK	Set up monopolies Commission	Strengthened 1956, 1964,1965
1949	Denmark	Unapproved price agreements	Commission established. Laws strengthened 1955, 1957, 1963.
1951	Austria	Unregistered cartels	
1953	France	Setting minimum prices	
1953	Ireland	Unfair trading practices	Commission established with enforcement powers.
1953	Japan	Restrictive cartel agreements	Weakened the 1946 law; many exempt industries created 1953-1959.
1953	Norway	Unreasonable prices	Enforced by the King of Norway. Horizontal price fixing declared illegal in 1960.

1955	South Africa	Restrictive agreements contrary to government policy.	
1958	Germany	Broad list of restrictive agreements	Replaced occupation laws.
1958	Netherlands	Unreported cartel agreements	Agreements can be nullified by council.
1958	Finland	Bid rigging	Strengthened in 1964
1958	New Zealand	Unregistered restrictive agreements and unreasonable price effects.	Registration repealed 1961.
1959	Israel	Unregistered restrictive agreements	Set up review board to prohibit certain agreements.
1959	Colombia	Fixing inequitable prices	
1960	Belgium	Abuse of economic power	Authorizes corrective royal orders.
1962	Brazil	Abuse of economic power and attempts to monopolize.	Fines and prohibition orders possible.
1963	Spain	Most restrictive agreements and abuse of dominant position	
1964	Switzerland	Practices that seriously impede competition contrary to the public interest	Courts may annul such practices.
1965	Australia	Collusive bid rigging and unregistered restrictive practices	Can be investigated and terminated.

Source: Edwards (1967).
a) Emphasizes anticartel provisions.

Chapter 4

THE CITRIC ACID INDUSTRY

Citric acid is a product found in thousands of grocery products. This chapter answers the following questions: what is citric acid used for, who makes it, how do they make it, how much is made, and where is it made?

THE PRODUCT

Citric acid is an organic chemical with a unique molecular structure. As an additive in foods like yogurt, sausages, and soft drinks, citric acid is one of several acidulents purchased by food manufacturers. Acidulents serve several useful functions in food formulations: sterilization, bacterial stabilization, flavor fixation, flavor enhancement, and standardization of acid levels. Besides its uses in the food industries, approximately one-third is purchased by detergent manufacturers. Citric acid has been replacing phosphorus in detergents because it does less harm to the ecology of rivers and lakes. Although there are about six other commercially important acidulents, citric acid accounts for more than 80 percent of the value of all acidulents sold in the U.S. market[1] In most food and beverage formulations, citric is the only feasible acid.

TECHNOLOGY AND EARLY DEVELOPMENT

Citric acid may be manufactured in three ways. The oldest method extracts the acid from citrus fruits. In the early 19th century, a cheaper method of making citric acid by chemical synthesis of calcium citrate was put into commercial production in the United Kingdom. However, because the calcium citrate was mainly extracted from Italian lemons, the industry had become an Italian monopoly by the turn of the century.[2] U.S. production by chemical synthesis began around 1880 by the firm Charles Pfizer, Inc., the predecessor of today's Pfizer, Inc.

The dislocation of Italian citric acid production caused by World War I forced prices to very high levels in the early 1920s. The high prices provided an incentive to search for a new method of production that would not require calcium citrate as a feedstock. Chemical experiments in the late 19th century had already shown that traces of citric acid were produced when the *Penicillin* mold was grown in sugar solutions. In 1917, an American chemical scientist published a paper that reported that a different mold, *Aspergillus niger*, produced large amounts of citric acid when it metabolized in a solution of sucrose, salts, and iron. Within six years, this discovery had been put into commercial production by Charles Pfizer, Inc. in its Brooklyn, New York plant. This 1923 manufacturing venture may have been the first commercially successful true biotechnology-based industry. The new technology broke the Italian monopoly on calcium citrate.

Production using the Pfizer fermentation process spread to Europe in the 1930s, starting with a factory in the UK. Fermentation plants using beet sugar molasses were built in Germany, Belgium, and Czechoslovakia. In the post-World War II period, more improvements were made: submerged cultures, higher-yielding yeast strains, and the substitution of glucose for sucrose. Pfizer developed the "shallow pan, deep tank" fermentation process that had become the industry standard by the 1980s.[3] Production of citric acid spread to China in the early 1970s, utilizing sweet potatoes or cassava in small-scale fermentation units.

Citric acid is sold in two product forms and in two quality grades. The two forms are anhydrous and aqueous. The anhydrous (dry) form consists of sodium citrate, potassium citrate, or other salts of citric acid. Citric salts are ideal for most non-food industrial uses such as detergents, where standards of purity are not as high as citric acid to be used in foods or beverages. Most producers of citric acid salts make both quality grades, but until the 1990s, much of the citric acid being exported from China did not meet food-grade standards. Most citric acid shipped internationally is sent in dry form to save on transportation costs, but the majority of citric acid sold for delivery in the U.S. domestic market is shipped in liquid solutions. Aqueous citric acid is usually food grade (highly purified), suitable for processed foods or beverages of many kinds. The liquid form can only be shipped short to moderate distances by tanker truck and requires less labor when handled by food and beverage processors. Although liquid citric acid is the dominant form in U.S. trade, price quotations are usually made on an anhydrous-equivalent basis.

MARKET SIZE AND GROWTH

Market size can be measured at least four ways (see Box). In this section, the focus is on consumption of citric acid and on growth in its demand. The next section discusses industry capacity and supply figures.

Market Size

The total size of a market is indicated by *industry capacity*, *production*, *product demanded* or *consumed*, or *sales*. The first three concepts of size are measured in physical units of weight or volume such as pounds, kilograms, or tons. Sales are the summation of buyer-seller transactions over a period of time, measured in monetary units. Capacity and production are supply-side concepts, whereas consumption views a market from the buyers' perspectives. Sales can be either the total revenues of sellers in a market or the total procurement expenses of buyers.

In manufacturing industries capacity is measured by the maximum or optimal production possible from all plants in a given time period. The most common measure is the annual engineering-design capacity of a plant sometimes called nameplate capacity. This ideal notion of capacity assumes that a plant will operate 24 hours a day for 365 days per year at the maximum levels envisioned by the plant's designers. In practice, plants being operated at full capacity normally require at least 15 to 30 days of down time each year for cleaning or repairs. Thus, maximum feasible production is typically 90 to 95 percent of nameplate capacity. Moreover, the most profitable level of production for a plant (i.e., optimal capacity) is usually somewhat lower than the maximum feasible levels of operation. In most manufacturing industries, during periods of strong demand, plants optimally utilize about 80 to 90 percent of their nameplate capacity.

For a nonstorable commodity, global production will be equal to global consumption. Citric acid, lysine, and vitamins are storable products, so production will exceed consumption only if manufacturers or buyers are building up their inventories. On an annual basis, global production and consumption are likely to be virtually identical. However, regional production and consumption frequently diverge because some regions are net exporters and other regions are net importers.

Global sales are typically the most difficult indicator of market size to measure accurately because of corporate secrecy and multiple national price levels and currencies. In many markets only list prices are public knowledge. List prices rarely equal the transaction prices needed to calculate accurate sales figures. Moreover, sales figures are highly sensitive to the price levels used. Prices may be f.o.b. plant, delivered prices by manufacturers; prices charged by wholesale distributors, or retail prices.

Manufacturers of specialty chemicals like citric acid often have only vague notions about the amount of aggregate production or consumption in their industry. Industry trade magazines faithfully report press releases of plant constructions and expansions, national trade data, or other indicators of industry size, but these publications rarely take the trouble to resolve the often contradictory pieces of information. Proprietary reports by management consultants on an industry's size or growth are sold to a limited number of clients but are sometimes summarized for public consumption. Where they exist, national industry trade associations often collect their members' production figures to arrive at national industry totals. However, these efforts often vary widely in terms of reliability and are of limited use when the industry is global in scope. Moreover, when a national industry consists of only two or three producers, a national trade association is unlikely to be established. In short, manufacturers frequently are in the dark about their national or global market shares, changes in those shares, and rates of growth in consumption or production.

The trade press contains only about a half dozen references to the amounts of citric acid consumed by industrial buyers in the United States and only a couple of estimates of global consumption (Connor 1999). These estimates are not always consistent. For example, in 1993 *Chemical Market Reporter* estimated U.S. consumption at 450 to 500 million pounds, while a Cargill spokesperson said that it was 400 million pounds that year. To derive consistent estimates of demand, the best method seems to be to compile estimates of global and regional capacity, make reasonable estimates of production, and adjust domestic production with international trade data. This approach follows in Tables 4.A.1 and 4.A.2.

Taking 1989 as the base year, U.S. consumption of citric acid was almost 300 million pounds (Figure 4.1). By 1996, U.S. demand reached about 550 million pounds. Thus, demand was growing by about 8 percent per year in the early 1990s. That is about four times faster than the volume growth of the average food ingredient industry and about double the growth rate of the U.S. beverage industries. Presumably, this high rate of growth was being propelled by new uses in food and beverages and by the substitution of citric acid for phosphates by detergent makers[4]

The U.S. market was a large, but declining proportion of global demand for citric acid. U.S. and Canadian consumption of citric acid accounted for about 44 percent of global purchases in 1989 and 31 percent in 1996 (Table 4.A.2). Europe was the second largest market for citric acid, accounting for 47 percent in 1989 and about 33 percent in 1996. Global growth in citric acid demand was about 11 percent per year in the 1990s. Growth of demand was slowest in Europe and in the United States but well above average in Asia and Latin America. Differences in demand growth are largely attributable to differences in consumer demand for beverages. In most of the 1990s, income growth was faster is Asia and Latin America than in the other regions; also, food and beverage demand is more responsive to income changes in low income regions.

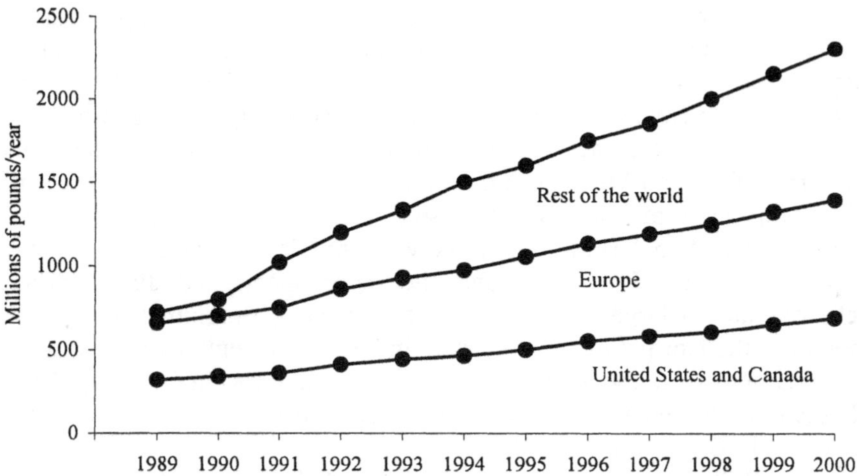

Figure 4.1. Global Consumption of Anhydrous Citric Acid, 1989-2000.

THE STRUCTURE OF PRODUCTION

The North American Market

Until 1989, production of citric acid had been for decades a duopoly in the United States. The oldest American manufacturer, Pfizer, Inc., had long before closed its original Brooklyn plant and replaced it with a medium-size plant in Groton, Connecticut. Pfizer's most modern plant was located in Southport, North Carolina. This plant had a rated citric acid capacity of 80 million pounds per year. Pfizer also operated two small citric acid facilities in Canada and Ireland.

Pfizer's only domestic rival in the North American market was Miles Laboratories, which is headquartered in Elkhart, Indiana and is owned by Germany's Bayer Corporation. In terms of production characteristics, Miles was nearly a twin of Pfizer. Miles too had two U.S. citric acid plants, an older facility in Elkhart that was the same size as Pfizer's Groton plant and a newer facility in Dayton, Ohio that was the same size as Pfizer's North Carolina plant. As far as can be determined, all four U.S. plants were *finishing* facilities only. That is, they purchased their corn sweetener (dextrose) from independent corn refiners and further fermented the feedstock into citric acid. For example, Miles' Dayton, Ohio plant was usually supplied by tanker-car shipments from one of A.E. Staley's corn refining plants in Lafayette, Indiana.

Pfizer's and Miles' U.S. plants gave each of them slightly more than 40 percent of the U.S. supply of citric acid (Table 4.1). "U.S. supply" refers to the theoretical maximum production capacities of the four U.S. plants plus net imports of citric acid. In fact, a small share of U.S. production (about 5 to 10 percent in most years) was exported, to Canada primarily. Taking into account these exports and the fact that U.S. production was less than rated plant capacities, Pfizer and Miles each had U.S. *sales* shares of about 38 percent in 1988, with the remaining quantity sold (23 percent) being supplied by importers. The two largest importers were the large diversified chemical company Hoffmann-La Roche and the more specialized Jungbunzlauer. Roche operated a large citric acid plant in Tienen, Belgium from which it exported to the North American market. In citric acid Junbunglzuer was even larger than Roche; it operated two or three large facilities in Germany, France and Austria. The remaining U.S. imports came from a number of countries, primarily China, Italy, and Israel.

In 1990, two important changes in the U.S. industry took place. The largest U.S. agribusiness firm, Cargill, began production of citric acid from a new plant that it had built at its existing corn wet milling plant at Eddyville, Iowa. Cargill had announced its intention to construct the new finishing facility in November 1987. The highly automated plant required merely 25 to 30 new employees and yet had a rated design capacity of 55 million pounds. What was unusual about Cargill's new plant was the fact that it was physically integrated with Cargill's existing corn wet milling plant. The add-on finishing facility reportedly cost only $40 million to build. When production began in the spring of 1990, the plant added 17 percent to the existing capacity of U.S. production. Cargill's substantial financial resources allowed it to expand its Iowa plant to 80 million pounds in 1991 and to 160 million in 1993.

The second important event in 1990 was ADM's entry into the industry. First signaling its intention to enter with a new plant in early 1990 about the time Cargill's plant was coming on stream, ADM then surprised the industry by announcing in August 1990 that it had agreed to purchase Pfizer's citric acid plants and technology instead of building a new plant. The purchase included Pfizer's Irish and North Carolina plants, with rated capacities of 20 and 100 million pounds. In addition, Pfizer agreed to sell to ADM exclusively up to 40 million pounds of citric acid from its Groton plant for three years.[5] The acquisition of Pfizer's assets was completed in December 1990, thus ending Pfizer's 110-year history of leadership in the U.S. citric acid industry.

ADM's decision to enter citric acid production was almost inevitable once Cargill's move into the industry was known. The history of the two firms is replete with examples of duplication of product lines, though it was more common for Cargill to follow ADM's bold incursions into new fields than the reverse. Both companies had made entry into new biotechnology-based industrial products a high strategic priority beginning in the late 1980s.

This strategic direction was partly a response to the sharp retardation of growth in their sales of high fructose corn syrup around 1986 and partly a response to new low cost starch fermentation techniques for making various organic chemicals traditionally synthesized chemically.

Table 4.1. U.S. Market Shares of Leading Citric acid Suppliers, Selected Years 1988-1998.

Sources of Supply	1988	1991	1995	1998
		Percent		
U.S. Manufacturing Capacity:				
Bayer/Haarmann & Reimer	42	41	28E	0
Pfizer or ADM	42	38	34E	40
Cargill	0	12E	30E	29
Tate & Lyle/A.E. Staley	0	0	0	12
U.S. Imports:[a]				
Hoffmann-La Roche	4	3	2	5
Jungbunzlauer	4	3	3	5
Other importers	6E	3E	3E	10
Subtotal of Top 5 Companies	94	97	97	90
Total Supply[b]	100	100	100	100

Source: Tables 1 and 2 of Connor (1998) and HRA (1992).
E = Estimates by author.
[a] Assumed that Roche accounted for all imports from Belgium and Jungbunzlauer from Germany and Austria where their plants were located. Other imports originated mainly from Italy, Israel, and China.
[b] The total of nameplate finishing capacities of plants located in the United States and U.S. import quantities. A small share of U.S. production was exported to Canada, so the shares shown correspond to U.S. and Canadian shares. Pfizer had a small plant in Canada, not included in the table, that was closed by 1990.

Pfizer's decision to exit the industry it had pioneered in America was doubtless spurred by the appearance of two formidable rivals with reputations for aggressive, growth-oriented tactics. Pfizer may have out-foxed another fox. The profit-and-loss statements of Pfizer's citric acid department may have shown a high rate of return despite its aging plants because prices had been propped up by a cartel in the late 1980's in which Pfizer had participated. Perhaps more important a factor in Pfizer's decision was the fact that ADM and Cargill were the two largest manufacturers of dextrose and other corn sweeteners. Had ADM built a new citric acid plant in 1990, Pfizer would have gone from being one of two manufacturers to one of four U.S. producers, a structure likely to have led to more price competition in citric acid. After entering citric acid manufacturing, Cargill and ADM would have become unwilling suppliers of dextrose to competing citric acid producers, and the number of alternative sources of dextrose was few. Therefore, Pfizer might have been squeezed by higher dextrose prices. Finally, Pfizer was probably aware that backward vertical integration of citric acid manufacturing brought down the cost by several cents per pound.[6] Cargill would become the low cost producer in North America, allowing it to expand its market share at Pfizer's expense.[7] Faced with the likelihood of lower product prices and higher input prices after Cargill's and ADM's entry, Pfizer's decision to withdraw seems eminently sensible in retrospect. ADM's entry left Bayer's U.S. subsidiary, Haarmann & Reimer, alone exposed to this new competitive environment.

In the early 1990s, Cargill's share of the U.S. market grew quickly (Table 4.1). Cargill's new Iowa plant reportedly reached nearly full capacity within a year of its start up, so Cargill expanded its 55-million-pound capacity to 80 million pounds in 1991. Continued success drove Cargill to add more capacity in 1993, bringing the Iowa plant up to 160 million pounds (*Chemical Market Reporter* March 30, 1992). Cargill also began making dry citrates alongside its liquid citric acid. As a result of these investments, Cargill pulled ahead of Bayer/Miles in the U.S. market by 1995. However, ADM had become the largest citric acid manufacturer by expanding its North Carolina plant from 100 million to 180 million pounds in late 1992.[8] A few years later, ADM again expanded its North Carolina plant to 220 million pounds, thus solidifying its dominance in the U.S. market. By 1998, ADM accounted for about 40 percent of U.S. supply, and Cargill was not far behind it (Table 4.1). Bayer had been forced to cede its position as dual leader in 1988 and had shrunk to a dismal 12 percent share of U.S. supply ten years later.

The Global Market

At the end of the 1980s, three of the world's top four manufacturers were European companies. In 1978, Miles Laboratories was acquired by the huge German chemical and pharmaceutical manufacturer, Bayer AG. Bayer later reorganized its U.S. operations by placing the responsibility for marketing citric acid under its fine-chemicals subsidiary Haarmann & Reimer. Although Bayer's headquarters are in Germany, it was in turn owned by a holding company organized under the laws of Switzerland. Similarly, Jungbunzlauer is an Austrian firm with its headquarters in Vienna, but it too was part of a Swiss holding company.[9] Roche is a thoroughly Swiss company headquartered in Basel, Switzerland. Thus, at times it will be convenient to refer to the big three European manufacturers of citric acid as "the Swiss firms." Bayer was the leader in the industry in 1989. In addition to the two plants it acquired in the United States in the late 1970s, Bayer bought a small citric acid plant in Yorkshire, England in August 1990.[10] Bayer dominated citric acid production in Latin America with joint ventures in Mexico, Columbia, and Brazil (*Chemical Week*, August 1990). All told, Bayer controlled some 230 million pounds of citric acid plant capacity in 1989-1990, which was about 25 percent of global capacity at that time (Table 4.2). However, in the mid-1990s Bayer neglected to make many investments to expand its plants, so its share slipped badly.

Table 4.2. Global Capacity Shares of Leading Citric Acid Suppliers, Selected Years 1988-1998.

Sources of Supply	1988	1992	1996	1998
		Percent		
U.S. Manufacturers:	32	30	20	20
Bayer/Miles[a]	16	10	6	0
Pfizer	16	0	0	0
Cargill	0	6	7	7
Archer Daniels Midland	0	10	7	8
Tate & Lyle/A.E. Staley	0	0	0	5
European Manufacturers:	40	38	43	38
Hoffmann-La Roche	9	11	6	6
Jungbunzlauer	15	17	19	17
Biocor	6	4	4	3
Bayer (outside U.S.)[b]	10	9	7	6
Palma Group	0	0	3	3
Asian Manufacturers[c]	22	25	33	39
Total[d]	100	100	100	100

Source: Tables 4.A.1 and 4.A.2.

[a] Bayer reorganized its U.S. operations during this period. Miles continued to manufacture citric acid, but overall marketing responsibility was granted to Bayer's fine-chemicals subsidiary Haarmann & Reimer.

[b] Includes three plants in Latin America and one UK plant sold to Tate & Lyle in 1998.

[c] Mostly Chinese production, but also one Israeli and two Indian plants.

[d] Excludes plants in the former Soviet Union.

By 1993 and for the rest of the 1990s, the leading producer in the world was Jungbunzlauer, with plants in Austria, Germany, and France. In 1991, it began to invest in a series of Asian joint ventures to make citric acid, the first in Sumatra, Indonesia. From one large plant in the early 1990s, the company operated four by 1993. Jungbunzlauer's newest plant in Alsace, France was the vertically integrated type, making both citric acid and its primary feedstock from corn in the same location. Its four production facilities gave Jungbunzlauer about 300 million pounds of capacity in 1993, which was almost one-third of estimated global consumption and about equal to Cargill and ADM's combined capacities. By the late 1990s, Jungbunzlauer's citric acid capacity had reached 500 million pounds.

Europe's third-largest manufacturer of citric acid in the early 1990s was the huge Swiss chemical maker Hoffmann-La Roche (Table 4.2). Roche operated a single large plant in Belgium that in 1990 had a capacity larger than Jungbunzlauer's. However, capacity at Roche's Belgian plant did not expand much in the early 1990s, while Jungbunzlauer was investing heavily in its new plant in Alsace as well as upgrading two older plants in Germany and Austria. As a result, Roche's share of citric acid capacity in Europe fell to about one-third of Jungbunzlauer's by 1996 and was about half of that of Bayer. Thus, while the three Swiss firms each had market shares of 10 to 15 percent in 1989, by 1996 Jungbunzlauer accounted for half of Europe's citric acid capacity and Bayer and Roche only about one-sixth each.[11]

Plants owned by the three Swiss and two smaller Italian firms gave Europe about 40 percent of global production capacity, but Europe consumed less than 30 percent of the world's citric acid. Thus, unlike the North American companies, Europe's producers were quite export-oriented, shipping up to one-third of production to North America and most other parts of the world. Roche and Jungbunzlauer were the two largest exporters to the United States in the late 1980s and early 1990s.

Although ranking third in the size of its citric acid industry, the fastest growth in production and consumption was occurring in Asia, particularly in China. In 1989, Chinese citric acid capacity was about 150 million pounds, or about half as large as U.S. capacity. By 1996, Chinese production capacity had surpassed that of the United States, and by the year 2000 Chinese and European plants are expected to be of equal size (roughly 1 billion pounds each). Production was scattered across scores of small-scale facilities owned by one sort of government entity or another. More than half of China's citric acid output was exported, at prices that were substantially below those in Europe or North America. The low prices reflected both low quality and low production costs.[12] The reason for the suspension is given in Chapter 5 below. With annual growth exceeding 20 percent per year, even in the early 1990s China was seen as a looming threat to existing Western manufacturers, especially European exporters.

MEMBERS OF THE CARTEL

Four companies joined the price-fixing conspiracy that their managers came to call the G-4 or "the club." As will be related in the next chapter, the G-4 was formed one day in March 1991 and fell apart sometime in early 1995.[13] Normally the structure of the market (many sellers, easy entry, or heterogeneous products) or fear of contravening the antitrust laws prevents the formation of a cartel. However, acting in concert, the G-4 was able to perform a feat that most business people can only dream about – moving the global market for its product in a direction that generated profits several times higher than the level in the pre-cartel period. This magical intervention into the normally all-powerful market mechanism by the G-4 was akin to a ship sailing against the wind.

Archer Daniels Midland Co. (ADM) was the G-4's prime mover. The trip made by the company's top two citric acid executives, Wilson and Cox, in January 1991 was the initial contact among the four. Doubtless, ADM's peace offering to the three Swiss firms was well received. Wilson probably explained in subtle ways ADM's corporate philosophy: friendly relations among competitors to achieve the joint exploitation of their customers.

It is useful to digress at this point to provide quick portraits of ADM, Cargill, and the three Swiss companies before moving on to the conspiracy story. These profiles will sketch each of the company's strategies and financial conditions in the early 1990s when the cartel was formed and active. They will focus on organizational or management characteristics that may have made the companies susceptible to opting for conspiracy.

Archer Daniels Midland Co.

ADM is the largest publicly traded agribusiness company in the United States and second largest in the world.[14] Since 1965, when Dwayne O. Andreas was appointed its CEO, ADM had enjoyed a long period of rapid growth, diversification, and profitability. Andreas was a colorful, outspoken agribusiness leader known for his bold strategic moves into new ventures, big international deals, and carefully cultivated political friendships. ADM was Andreas' creature. Its management structure had few layers, investment decisions were quick, and it benefited from numerous government contracts and subsidies (Figure 4.2) Until the lysine price-fixing scandal broke in 1995, ADM was one of the most admired American manufacturers.[15]

In fiscal year 1995, ADM had consolidated net sales of $12.7 billion (ADM).[16] During the decade up to 1995, ADM's net sales increased by 10.1% per year. Although ADM's earnings per dollar of sales were about double those earned by most agribusiness firms, they were quite variable. From fiscal 1986 to fiscal 1990, net earnings rose from $230 million to $484 million (or by 20% per year), but from 1990 to 1994 ADM's net earnings stalled at about $500 million per year. In 1995-1996, the years most affected by price fixing, net annual earnings jumped to $794 million, or 60 percent above the 1990-1994 average

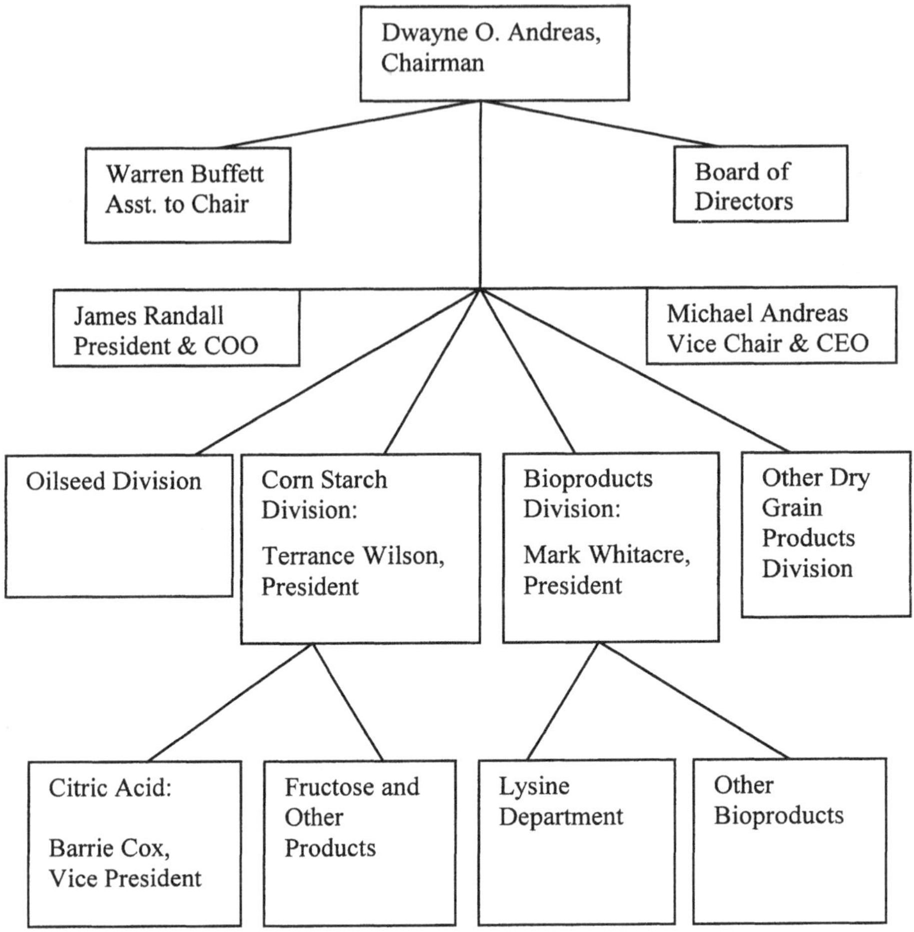

Figure 4.2. ADM's Management Structure, 1991-1995.

Note: May not correspond to the company's formal reporting structure, but reflects the actual decision-making structure of the company

ADM has four major product divisions: oilseed products, corn starch products, bioproducts, and other grains; in 1995 the four divisions contributed about 60, 20, 5, and 15 percent of net sales, respectively. The oilseeds division sells corn, peanut, palm, cottonseed, soybean, canola, and sunflower oils and their byproducts. Specialty products include lecithin, vitamin E, monoglycerides, soy protein concentrate, and soy isolate. The cornstarch division produces corn sweeteners, cornstarch, alcohols, malt, and a host of biotechnology food ingredients (monosodium glutamate, citric acid, ascorbic acid, biotin, lactic acid, sorbitol, and xanthan gum). The amino acids, lysine, methionine, trytophan, and threonine were made by the Bioproducts Division and sold to manufacturers of animal feeds. Within the corn products division, corn sweeteners and ethanol are mature or maturing industries with slow growth and narrowing margins; however, the other bioproducts from corn generate much higher margins and represent ADM's hope for the future. The grains division includes dry milled products such as flours and pastas. Miscellaneous sales consist of aquaculture fish, hydroponic vegetables, grain merchandising, and numerous joint ventures with farmers' cooperatives.

For a company of its size and diversity, ADM is managed by a remarkably small number of managers. Dwayne Andreas and three or four other top managers made all major decisions, largely unfettered by ADM's subservient board of directors. By 1990, Dwayne's son Michael had become the anointed successor to his aging father. Michael had effectively become the company's Chief Executive Officer, while Dwayne concentrated most of his time on broad strategic decisions and external relations. James Randall, an engineer by training, handled ADM's vast physical assets. Until late 1996, the highly paid Board contained a large majority of current and former company officers, relatives of Andreas, long standing close friends of Andreas, or officers of companies that supply goods and services to ADM (agricultural cooperatives or legal services). The company was famously unconcerned about public and investor relations.[17] Strictly speaking, at most two of the Board's 17 members were independent of ADM or Andreas. Members of the press or stock analysts almost never had open contact with ADM officers except rarely with D. Andreas himself. ADM's flexible management style was so admired by multi-billionaire investor Warren Buffett that he sent his son Howard to spend several years as a special assistant to Dwayne Andreas in the early 1990s.

An October 1995 profile of Dwayne Andreas and ADM by the *Wall Street Journal* emphasized the CEO's extraordinary grip on the company. Although he personally owns less than 5% of ADM's stock ". . . Andreas has gained near total control with the help of family members, loyal executives and directors whose combined stakes is nearly 15% . . . He collaborates with his biggest competitors, spends prodigiously to influence the media and public opinion, and spreads large sums among politicians of all stripes." (p.A1). As an example of Andreas' drive to dominate, at an ADM's annual meeting he once cut off a critic's microphone and said "I'm chairman. I'll make the rules as I go along." Such imperious behavior was tolerated because he presided over a period of sterling financial and stock performance for ADM. Unusual among agribusiness companies, ADM has many collaborative arrangements with parties that normally would be considered rivals. Andreas often says, "Keep your friends close and your enemies closer." So, in 1992, ADM built a 3.5-mile pipeline from its Decatur plant to its rival A.E. Staley's plant just before Staley was threatened by a labor strike. ADM owns significant shares in Staley's parent, Tate & Lyle, and has a fructose joint venture with Staley in

Mexico. ADM also has alliances of various kinds with grain cooperatives like Growmark and Goldkist.

Andreas cultivated the image of an international statesman with strong concerns about environmental matters, world hunger, and national food security. His official biography gives him undue credit as one of the major forces behind the U.S. Government's PL 480 Program that ships excess farm commodities to poor countries (Kahn). He is identified as Armand Hammer's successor as the U.S. capitalist with the closest relationship with Kremlin and other Eastern Bloc leaders going back to Joseph Stalin in the 1950s. Andreas built a legendary network of powerful business and government contacts. He was close friends with and contributor to a wide array of farm-state Congressmen and Senators, notably Hubert Humphrey and Robert Dole. He has known personally every U.S. president since Harry Truman.[18] Andreas spends a good deal of his time sponsoring political fund-raising events. ADM has benefited greatly from the U.S. sugar program and from federal ethanol subsidies and usage requirements (Bovard 1995). Lobbying by ADM through its trade associations for these and other government favors is intense and well documented. ADM maintains a palatial suite of rooms in a Washington hotel for the frequent use of Andreas and other officers.

Andreas often appears on *Forbes* magazine's list of the 400 richest people in the United States, and he makes deft use of his wealth. "Andreas, his family, and ADM are by far the largest political contributors in the country" (Hollis). These contributions have resulted in adverse publicity for Andreas at least four times. He wrote a $25,000 check that was given to B.L. Barker, one of the convicted "Watergate Burglars," and a bundle of $100,000 in cash given by Andreas was found in Richard Nixon's White House safe; Andreas avoided testifying about these gifts. Later, Andreas was prosecuted but not convicted for an illegal $100,000 corporate contribution to Hubert Humphrey. In 1993, Andreas and his wife were fined $8,000 by the Federal Election Commission for making excess political contributions.

ADM underwrites the TV broadcasts of the premier political-discussion programs on four television networks: ABC, CBS, NBC, and PBS. During 1994 and January-April 1995, ADM spent at least $16 million supporting the four programs; its support accounts for nearly 27% of the budget of the influential Jim Lehrer News Hour on PBS. ADM owned 10% of the newspaper chain that owns the Chicago Sun-Times. In 1998, ADM created a great deal of discussion among journalists when it hired recently retired ABC anchor David Brinkley to produce "info-mercials" for ADM. ABC eventually decided that it was unseemly to accept these paid commercials which were to have appeared during Mr. Brinkley's former news program. Some commentators have noted little or weak coverage of ADM's legal problems in these ADM financed news media.[19]

There are several ADM management practices that bear the Andreas stamp and that could have made ADM prone to price fixing. ADM made quick and aggressive investment decisions. To enter the citric acid business,

ADM paid top dollar for two aging Pfizer plants primarily to obtain the production technology. In both lysine and citric acid, very large capital expenditures were incurred to expand plants to the largest feasible scales. When production problems occurred with lysine, ADM hired away engineers from their primary competitor, Ajinomoto. Although much of what he says must be treated with skepticism, former ADM vice president Mark Whitacre claims that "stealing technology" was common practice at ADM. Specifically, Whitacre asserted that ADM hired Asian engineers to build and run its Decatur lysine plant and that it stole technology and trade secrets from other companies to begin production of vitamins and medicinal products from corn. Whitacre himself was hired away from the German firm Degussa, the world leader in amino-acid research and production. Ajinomoto sued ADM in late 1996 for patent infringement on production methods for lysine and threonine, and ADM was found guilty in the latter case.

Moreover, Whitacre relates that a culture that fostered or permitted price fixing permeated ADM, at least within the corn-products division. It is clear that Dwayne Andreas has no respect for "free markets," an idea he considers to be a figment of politicians' imaginations (Bovard 1995). That is, Andreas tended to view agricultural markets, both in the U.S. and trade among nations, as political creatures or as the product of personal negotiation between powerful leaders. Markets, he has testified, are essentially creatures of government regulation and power. Whitacre claims that he taped price-fixing discussions within ADM that involved the Chairman (D. Andreas), Vice Chairman (M. Andreas), President (J. Randall), and at least three VPs of operating divisions; he stated that the counsel and assistant counsel of ADM were aware of the activity as well. ADM's participation in three to five cartels tends to support some of Whitacre's charges. Finally, Whitacre asserts that ADM routinely rewarded managers at his level very large bonuses that were paid tax-free into foreign bank accounts by means of phony invoicing schemes. Whitacre himself and three employees he supervised admitted their guilt to such fraud, but how pervasive the practice was in ADM is now much in doubt.

Among people familiar with the agribusiness sector, ADM ". . . long had a reputation for business practices that were close to the edge" (Nicole and Ferguson 1999:50). In 1978, ADM pleaded "no contest" to charges that it had colluded to fix prices on food sold by USDA for international relief programs under Public Law 480. In 1992 and 1994, the company paid $2 million to settle civil antitrust suits alleging that ADM had conspired to fix prices on carbon dioxide, a by-product of its corn fermentation processes. As is typical in such civil settlements, the defendants do not admit their guilt in a formal legal sense. Yet, the impression is conveyed that the defendant judged that there was a good chance that in court the preponderance of the evidence might have turned against them. These early precursors merely hint at the massive price-fixing activities pursued by ADM's top management from 1991 to 1995.

Cargill Corporation

Cargill is the world's largest agribusiness company, but because it is privately owned by a couple hundred members of the founding families, many details of the company's operations, organization, and finances remain hidden from public view. In 1986, Cargill had sales of $32 billion, which were four times the size of ADM's total sales in that year. By 1999, Cargill's total sales were $46 billion, making it the largest privately owned industrial company in the United States. Cargill employs 81,000 people who work at 1000 locations (plants, warehouses, grain elevators, offices, and the like) in 65 countries (Connor 2000: Appendix F).

Until the 1970s, Cargill was, like ADM, narrowly focused on agribusiness products and a few other bulk commodities. The company assembled, transported, stored, sold, and manufactured bulk grains, oilseeds, meats, salt, steel, and other basic commodities. To reduce the cyclic effects of commodity price cycles on its earnings, Cargill began to invest heavily in food processing and branded grocery products in the late 1970s. This diversification program accelerated in the 1980s. By 1993, Cargill's sales of meats and other consumer-ready food products had reached $22 billion, placing it third in the country behind Philip Morris and ConAgra in this segment.

In terms of sales growth, the 1970s were a high point for Cargill. The combination of volume growth, acquisitions, and commodity price inflation raised the company's sales by 1200 percent from 1971 to 1981. Over the longer period 1966 to 1991, Cargill's net worth accumulated at an average annual pace of 16 percent. However, after completing a major purchase in the meatpacking industry in 1987, a five-year period of financial stress plagued Cargill. One major reason was the sharp slowdown in the growth of its corn wet milling business. Following ADM's lead, Cargill had invested heavily in a couple of huge corn refineries that made starch, oil, sweeteners, and other products. Growth of the most profitable product line, high fructose corn syrup (HFCS), hit a wall around 1987 as the opportunities for further substitution for sucrose dried up.

Like ADM, Cargill began to explore opportunities to utilize its large supplies of cheap corn sweeteners to make further-processed, high-value-added agrichemicals by means of advanced fermentation technologies. One of its first biotechnology ventures was citric acid. It was around 1987 that Cargill decided to build finishing capacity to make citric acid from dextrose produced at its newest corn-refining plant in Nebraska. Production of citric acid began in 1991, and after several expansions of capacity in the early 1990s, Cargill became a strong second in the U.S. industry behind arch-rival ADM. Cargill's April 1998 announcement of a new Iowa lysine plant was almost immediately countered by an ADM press release about construction of its *second* lysine facility. A few months later Cargill held a groundbreaking ceremony for its new lysine plant, with a capacity quite a bit bigger than the original announcement. Cargill had formed a partnership with Degussa, the world's leading manufacturer of amino acids, and the company that ADM had prevented from entering the U.S. industry by its preemptive strike in 1989. The Degussa partnership is only one of several that Cargill has formed in order to move decisively into the high-margin bioproducts area. Cargill now makes lactic acid in Nebraska with a Dutch partner and a low-calorie sweetener erythritol with a Japanese partner. These last three bioproducts ventures alone cost Cargill about $200 million. They presage additional large-scale moves into other food and feed ingredients made from corn-fermentation methods.

Bayer AG

Bayer has title to being the world's largest chemical company. In the late 1990s, Bayer's sales were only slightly below those of BASF, but in terms of numbers of employees or profit it was well ahead of BASF. In the late 1980s and early 1990s, it was Hoechst that had the number-one spot, so it is best to think of the big three German chemical firms as jockeying for primacy in the 1990s. All three firms were carved out of the infamous 1925-1947 I.G. Farben chemical monopoly that is best remembered for its collaboration with the Nazi regime and the conviction of its directors for crimes against humanity at the Nuremberg trials (Connor 1999: Appendix F).

Bayer, now headquartered in Leverkusen, Germany, became a leader in the world dyestuffs industry in the late 19th century. Dyes have chemical properties similar to a number of synthetic organic chemicals with pharmaceutical effects. Two important discoveries propelled Bayer to the forefront of the drug industry: aspirin in 1900 and the first sulfa drug in 1908 (sulfa drugs are a class of systemic antibiotics). In 1904, Bayer combined with BASF and some smaller companies to form one of two chemical cartels that monopolized the German chemical industries, then the dominant world supplier of chemicals. In 1925, the two cartels were joined to form the I.G. Farben chemical monopoly, Bayer, BASF, and Hoechst were reborn when I.G. Farben was broken up by the Allied occupation authorities in 1947. Bayer grew rapidly for four decades thereafter.

In 1954, Bayer made its first investment in the United States, a joint venture with Monsanto. During the postwar period the company registered many valuable patents for pesticides, plastics, polyurethane, and pharmaceuticals. By the mid 1970s, Bayer was selling more than 6000 products and generated most of its sales outside Germany. One of its largest foreign investments was the acquisition of Indiana-based Miles Laboratories in 1978. Among Miles' assets were two citric acid plants that gave Bayer half of the U.S. plant capacity for citric acid and about 40 percent of market sales. Testimony at a 1998 antitrust trial reveled that during the 1980s, Miles conspired to fix the U.S. prices of bulk citric acid with the only other U.S. manufacturer, Pfizer Corp. of New York City.[20]

Bayer enjoyed decades of nearly uninterrupted growth until 1987 or 1988, but hit a plateau of financial performance that lasted five or six years. A number of factors were responsible: a lingering recession in Western Europe, political turmoil in Eastern European markets, falling European demand for proprietary drugs, policy restraints on chemical use in the EU, increasing competition from Asian chemical producers, and a failure to contain production costs. From 1988 to 1993, Bayer's sales were stagnant and profits declining. Bayer responded to this crisis by severe cost cutting (including large layoffs of employees in its European plants), an increase in foreign direct investment in fast growing markets, and restructuring of assets. It became the sole producer of citric acid in Latin America, with three or four small plants there, some of them joint ventures. In 1992, Bayer's considerable U.S. assets were grouped under a new U.S. subsidiary named Miles, Inc. with its headquarters in Pittsburgh. One of Miles' subsidiaries was Haarmann & Reimer which marketed citric acid, lactic acid, and other fine chemicals. In 1994, after Bayer's acquisition of Sterling Drug Co. (including the U.S. rights to the Bayer trademark) for $1 billion, its U.S. holding company became Bayer Corporation.

Hoffmann-La Roche AG

Roche Holdings, Ltd., a Swiss holding company, is often better known by the name of its principal operating company, F. Hoffmann-La Roche AG. Headquartered in Basel, Roche has been focused on nutritional and pharmaceutical products from its beginnings in the late 19th century. During the 1920s and 1930s, Roche moved away from its early reliance on medicinal extraction and increasingly applied its extensive R&D resources to chemical synthesis. Among its greatest early successes were the discoveries of synthetic processes for making vitamins C, A, and E. By the early 1970s, Roche controlled 50 to 70 percent of the world market for bulk vitamins. In the 1960s Roche profited greatly by becoming the first to market tranquillizers. However, ten years later the company came under attack by the UK Monopolies Commission for excessive price discrimination when it was discovered that Roche was charging its UK subsidiary fifty times the price of a generic equivalent for its tranquilizer Valium. Compensation was ordered by the Commission for UK buyers. Later, similar actions took place in other European countries. A failure to find profitable replacements for its tranquillizers, the patents on which expired in 1985, placed Roche under some profit pressures in the late 1980s.

In the 1990s, Roche has responded to its reduced prospects for profitability by redirecting its capital investments toward biotechnology ventures. For example, in 1995 Roche paid $5.3 billion to buy the California biotech firm Syntex, now called Roche Bioscience. This acquisition made Roche the world's fourth largest drug company in terms of sales, and first in terms of market capitalization.

In 1997, Roche had global sales of $12.9 billion and employed 51,600 persons. Almost two-thirds of its sales consist of pharmaceuticals, but it was also a world leader in flavors, fragrances, vitamins, carotenoids, and genetic-engineering products. In that year, Roche's net income was an enviable $2.9 billion or 22.8 percent of sales. Its major U.S. subsidiary, Hoffmann-La Roche Inc., had sales of almost $1 billion.

Jungbunzlauer AG

Jungbunzlauer International AG was by far the smallest member of the citric acid conspiracy, but because it was highly specialized in making citric acid, it had one of the highest market shares in the G-4.

This company traces its roots to an alcohol distillery built in Jungbunzlau, Bohemia in 1895. It moved its registered office from Prague to Vienna in 1902. Jungbunzlauer diversified into the production of citric acid in 1962 from its single plant in Pernhofen, Austria, but soon became heavily indebted. A capital infusion from the Swiss holding company, Montana AG, took place in 1967. Controlled by Swiss financier Karl Kahane, this holding company had obtained a majority interest in Jungbunzlauer by the early 1990s. Kahane is now chairman of the company's supervisory board. Sometime around 1994, Jungbunzlauer's headquarters was moved to Basel, Switzerland.

A stock prospectus issued by Jungbunzlauer in 1985 purported to show that the company was fairly profitable, making before-tax profits of 10 percent of sales in the preceding years. However, from 1986 to 1991, Jungbunzlauer's profits and its stock performance were quite unstable. Its five-year moving average of profitability was moving down sharply. Despite its perilous financial condition, Jungbunzlauer made a large investment in a second citric acid plant located in Ladenberg, Germany. That purchase in 1989 made the company the world's third largest manufacturer of citric acid. Moreover, in 1990 Jungbunzlauer began to build a very large citric acid facility on the Rhine River in Alsace, France. This $110 million plant would ferment corn into dextrose or glucose to provide a feedstock for making citric acid and other food ingredients in all three of the company's plants. The company also invested heavily in upgrading and expanding its Austrian and German plants. These projects raised Jungbunzlauer's production capacity to 310 million pounds by 1993, about 20 percent of the world's total, vaulting Jungbunzlauer past Bayer into first place. By 1994, its total capacity reached 460 million pounds, but there were no further increases until the end of the decade (Table 4.A.2).

Jungbunzlauer looks like a small player hell bent on aggressive growth to become one of the biggest in its industries. In its 1991 annual report, the company stated that it had 243 employees generating a mere $96 million in sales. The report boasts that it is Austria's largest producer of ethyl alcohol and that its main products were citric acid, gluconates, and xanthan gum – all made by fermentation. By 1997, Jungbunzlauer reported having 428 employees in its Austrian and German plants with total sales of $300 million. If the French plant was operating as planned, Jungbunzlauer employed about at most 1000 employees in Europe. In October 1998, a trade magazine reported that Jungbunzlauer had initiated a worldwide 10-percent increase in the price of citric acid. Apparently, the company had the industry leadership it craved.

INTERNATIONAL TRADE PATTERNS

International trade provides information that helps in understanding the operation and economic impacts of the global dimensions of the citric acid conspiracy. Citric acid is a storable commodity and in its dry forms (citric salts) sells at a price high enough to justify being shipped internationally. As soon as the price differences between two continents widen to at least five or ten cents per pound, there is sufficient profit incentive for manufacturers or wholesalers to sell abroad, an activity dubbed "geographic arbitrage" by economists.

When a group of sellers tries to form a purely national price-fixing conspiracy, unless trade barriers exist, the sellers are limited in their ability to raise prices because at some level imports will flood the national market. When a cartel is formed that aims at controlling intercontinental prices, it must set those prices at levels that will not permit geographic arbitrageurs to undermine the desired geographic price levels.[21] Because currency exchange rates are uncontrollable and somewhat unpredictable, global price fixing is more complicated than a domestic conspiracy, but if an industry is already globalized, a cartel will have little choice in the matter. Moreover, the daily fluctuations in exchange rates among most major currencies impel would-be price fixers to alter their local prices at frequent intervals. The lysine cartel began by setting target prices only using the U.S. dollar, but with experience eventually set prices in a dozen national currencies. Price quotes were usually kept constant between meetings. As will be seen, the managers of the citric acid and lysine cartels believe that formal quarterly meetings were necessary, supplemented by frequent telephone communication between those meetings.

From 1981 to 1989, the United States imported between 20 million and 65 million pounds of citric acid, with the amount increasing nearly every year (Connor 1998: Figure 2). The imports were responding to relatively high U.S. domestic prices. Most U.S. imports originated in Europe, some coming from Italy, but most from Jungbunzlauer's German plant and Roche's Belgian plant. Most U.S. exports went to Canada and were by comparison quite modest, in the 10 to 20 million pound range. Thus, the U.S. trade balance became increasingly negative from 1981 to 1988.

However, the trade balance made a remarkable turn-around in 1989 and 1990. In response to the impending opening of Cargill's new citric acid plant in Iowa, U.S. prices began to fall in late 1989. List prices had been in the $0.81 to $0.84 per pound range in 1988 and early 1989 (Connor 1998: Appendix Table 1). However, in anticipation of the large additional quantities that Cargill would bring to the market in the spring of 1990, list contract prices suddenly fell to $0.75 per pound in late 1989 and continued to be cut quarterly during 1990. Multiple sources of information indicate that prices of all kinds fell precipitously throughout 1990. Transactions prices for citric acid fell from $0.81 per pound in late 1989 to as low as $0.62 at the end of 1990. Cargill began sales from its new plant in June 1990 and probably cut prices to win over new customers. Moreover, ADM's takeover of Pfizer's plants in late 1990 and its announced intention to expand capacity further depressed U.S. prices. Transaction prices remained low ($0.60 - $0.65 per pound) through June 1991.

As a result of these lower prices, U.S. imports fell by 10 million pounds in 1990 compared with 1989, and exports rose by 25 million pounds. In 1990, U.S. citric acid trade was virtually in balance for the first time in more than a decade. Moreover, exports climbed again in 1991 by nearly 30 million pounds, aided by the expansions of both ADM's and Cargill's plants and prompted by excess production capacity. In 1991, the U.S. experienced its first trade surplus in citric acid for more than a decade.

However, what was good news for the United States' balance of trade must have been viewed with dismay by the Swiss firms. As American exports began to flow to destinations other than Canada, they would have displaced European exports to those countries. Continuing export expansion by Chinese producers merely added to their woes. It is likely that Jungbunzlauer's and Roche's plants in Europe experienced notable declines in capacity utilization, a factor that typically causes production costs to increase. Moreover, these firms probably were being forced to cut prices on the one-fourth to one-third of their production that was historically exported. This was particularly bad news for Jungbunzlauer, which depended on citric acid sales to a greater extent than Roche or Bayer and which was in the midst of a large expansion program. It is also likely that Bayer's Latin American operations were facing a similar squeeze on margins.

Although the newly competitive U.S. industry may have been a temporary phenomenon occasioned by Cargill's large-scale entry, the Swiss firms were very likely in a precarious financial position with respect to their citric acid businesses in the spring of 1991. ADM's peace offering could not have come at a better time. Terrance Wilson's offer of "friendly competition" no doubt fell on receptive ears.

COSTS OF PRODUCTION

Specific information on costs of producing and marketing citric acid by various major sellers is not revealed in the record, but certain inferences can be made from other information. Some idea of costs of production is useful in assessing the strategic behavior of the leading firms and in measuring the economic performance of firms and markets (see Box).

Based upon the trade patterns in the 1980s, it seems quite likely that the costs of producing citric acid in Europe were lower than those in North America. In late 1990 and early 1991, when Cargill's new integrated plant had been up and running for some time, trade patterns reversed in such a way as to suggest that U.S. costs had achieved parity with European costs. However, the low U.S. selling prices may have been a transitory phenomenon, suggesting that U.S. producers may have only been covering their short-run costs at that time. Moreover, one cannot discount the possibility that Cargill might have been willing to sell at a price below long run average total costs in its first year to quickly grab a market share sufficient to achieve the low costs associated with higher levels of plant capacity utilization.

A couple of articles in the trade press provide hints of industry views on production costs (*Chemical Marketing Reporter* June 3, 1991 and July 22, 1991). In late 1990, some buyers were reporting heavily discounted transactions as low as $0.55 per pound, and this price was said to be only slightly above "production costs," which may be taken to be the average total costs of manufacturing alone. When prices were in the $0.60 to $0.65 range, unnamed sources indicated that sales were unprofitable for all U.S. manufacturers, Cargill included. Thus, average total costs may have been as high as $0.70 to $0.75. There were no complaints from sellers about unprofitability when prices were above this range.

Costs of production abroad can provide some information about competitive prices in Europe or America. In December 1998, Mitsubishi Corporation of Japan announced that it would be building a new plant to make citric acid in Thailand. The plant would use inexpensive local supplies of tapioca meal as the principal feedstock for fermentation. What was unusual about this announcement was Mitsubishi's revealing the fact that its marketing plan had calculated that the cost of production, insurance, and freight (the CIF price) of citric acid to Europe or the United States would be $0.58 per pound.[22] Allowing some additional costs for sales brokers and domestic transportation charges suggests an average U.S. delivered price of about $0.65 per pound, well within the range of average total costs from other sources.

One final indicator of costs in the U.S. is what happened to prices after the citric acid cartel ceased operating in early 1995. During 1996 and early 1997, citric acid transactions prices hovered in the narrow range of $0.69 to $0.73 (Connor 1998: Appendix Table 1). On the assumption that this was a relatively competitive period, this price may approximate average total costs. Thus, the indirect and slim evidence available suggests that in the early 1990s average total costs were very likely between $0.65 and $0.75 per pound.[23]

Costs of Production

Economic theory places great weight on costs of production as a determinant of a firm's decision to find its profit-maximizing level of production or for a firm with market power to set its optimal selling price. It is important to distinguish between long-run and short-run costs and between marginal and average costs.

The *short run* is a period of production too short for a new capital investment to make a difference in output. In the context of manufacturing the *long run* is the length of time necessary to plan, design, build, equip and debug a new plant – about two to three years for the citric acid industry. In the short run a company can ignore capital costs when setting prices or output levels (possibly incurring losses in net revenues), but in the long run all costs must be covered.

The economic theory of the firm asserts that firms consider only their marginal costs when optimizing production. However, marginal costs, the incremental costs associated with a one-unit increase in output, are difficult to measure precisely with accounting data. In practical analyses of company or industry performance, accounting data must be utilized. Accounting total costs consist of *variable* costs (costs that change with levels of output) and *fixed* costs. Variable costs include the labor, materials, and energy needed for manufacturing; costs of packaging, delivery, and storage; and selling costs. Fixed costs include such items as capital depreciation, insurance, interest payments on long-term debt, and a reasonable return to the owners of the company's equity. Roughly speaking, in the short run a firm must receive a price sufficient to cover its average variable costs; if the price is too low, it is rational to cease production and sales. In the long run, product price must be at least as high as average total costs.

A very common finding in studies of manufacturing industries is that average variable costs of small plants are higher than medium-size plants. Similarly, new plants operating at low utilization levels have higher costs than plants operating close to optimal levels with experienced personnel. However, the differences in average variable costs of mature medium-size plants and larger plants tend to be negligible. This is an important finding because it implies that over this medium-large size range, long run marginal cost will be equal to average variable costs. Average fixed costs decline continuously as output increases.

SELLING PRACTICES

In the United States most citric acid was sold under annual supply contracts directly by the manufacturers or their agents to the food and detergent manufacturers. The contracts would specify the product form (food grade or industrial grade, liquid or anhydrous), the quantity to be purchased during the upcoming quarter or calendar year, method of delivery, and payment terms. Most large buyers negotiated their contracts in the final quarter of the year. The contract would specify the price to be paid, but sellers had the option of announcing price changes "effective immediately" or at short notice at any time during the life of the contract. However, buyers usually had the option of buying extra product (often one-twelfth of the annual quantity) at the old price at the time an announcement of price increases was made; this is referred to as a "price-protection clause." Price decreases took effect more quickly than increases.

Citric acid manufacturers sent notices to the press and their customers of changes in their "list" price. These were not true list prices, but rather starting points for price negotiations that took place in secret between manufacturers' sales representatives and purchasing managers. The most common list price referred to large lots (full truck loads or tanker-car loads) of anhydrous USP food grade citric acid, delivered to customers near the plant.[24] Standard premiums applied to partial truckloads (four to eight cents per pound) and to deliveries west of Denver (three cents). Once the terms of the contract were set and the types of premiums were known, the only item to be negotiated was the price. The largest and oldest customers often expected discounts in the form of rebates when they signed contracts. Contract customers could request additional quantities during the year, but the price of these supplementary purchases would be renegotiated separately.

In addition to contract sales, manufacturers sold product on a "spot" basis. Spot sales were for immediate delivery and frequently for partial truckloads. Like groceries purchased at a convenience store, such fill-in shopping behavior usually meant paying a premium over contract prices. In early 1990, for example, contract prices were 3 percent lower than list while spot prices were slightly higher than list. In 1995, perhaps a more typical year, contract prices averaged 10 percent below list and spot prices 8 percent below.

There are no organized markets for citric acid with attendant public reporting of transaction prices. Although list prices were faithfully reported by the trade press, fitful articles on transaction prices were normally untrustworthy. Methods of exchange such as those just described for citric acid tilt price information in favor of the few sellers as opposed to the many buyers. The hidden nature of the negotiations makes it difficult for buyers to perform price checks and makes it easy for sellers to bluff about what alternative buyers are paying. Such methods of exchange are highly compatible with and may facilitate price fixing.

Chapter 4 Endnotes

[1] Except for the substitution of citric acid for phosphorus in detergents, the uses of various acidulents appear to be very stable. That is, the demand for acidulents tends to grow and space the demand for the foods and beverages in which they are mixed. The largest use of citric acid is in soft drinks of all kinds. The second largest acidulent, phosphoric acid, is used mainly in cola drinks; the third, lactic acid, mainly in frozen foods; the fourth, malic acid, mainly in candies and tea mixes; and so on (*Chemical Market Reporter*, June 3, 1991).

[2] A profile of the development of the citric acid industry appeared in the British newspaper, *The Independent* on March 9, 1992. This source attributes the discovery of chemical synthesis of citric acid from calcium citrate to John and Edmond Sturge, and dates commercial manufacture in their Selby, Yorkshire plant from 1826. Pfizer's early role is given in *Chemical Market Reporter* July 9, 1990.

[3] A fourth technology that applied yeast fermentation to petroleum-derived n-alkanes was provided to be technologically feasible in the 1960's. In 1975, Miles Laboratories formed a marketing joint venture with Liquichemica Biointensi, which built a plant in Reggio Calabria using this petro-fermentation process (*Chemical Week*, November 12, 1975). The venture was never profitable.

[4] After 1996, volume growth slowed to slightly less than 6 percent per year. The elimination of phosphorus from detergents had been nearly completed by the mid 1990's.

[5] Pfizer announced that in 1989 its sales of citric acid were $180 million, which implies that the North American market was worth $450 to $500 million per year when the transaction price of anhydrous citric acid was $0.80 per pound.

[6] On-site production of liquid dextrose permits pipeline delivery to the citric acid finishing plant. At a typical $0.15 to $0.25 per pound, even rail delivery of dextrose was expensive per dollar of dextrose, especially to Pfizer's two East Coast plants located far from the Corn Belt where most dextrose was made.

[7] Jungbuzlauer in Europe also produced its feedstock at the same location it made citric acid, at least at its newer plants. ADM seems not to make dextrose at its North Carolina plant, but enjoys some economies in supplying its plant with its own dextrose. Bayer's size plants (one in the UK, two in the U.S., and three in Latin America) were not vertically integrated.

[8] Pfizer closed its Groton, Connecticut citric acid plant at the same time.

[9] The full name of the operating company is Jungbunzlauer Spiritus und Chemische Fabrik AG. Around 1994, Jungbunzlauer moved its operational center to Basel. Majority control of Jungbunzlauer is vested in the Swiss holding company Montana AG.

[10] The plant had been owned by Rhône-Poulenc. It had a capacity of 46 million pounds, but in a few years was debottlenecked to 72 million pounds.

[11] Two relatively small Italian plants accounted for the rest of Europe's citric acid production. The older plant located near Pavia was operated by Biacor. This plant was sold by its UK owner in March 1990 and resold in late 1991 to Ferruzzi-Montedison of Milan, now called Erindania Beghin-Say. Italy's second citric acid plant began production in Calitri in early 1993. The two Italian plants had about 130 million pounds of capacity in 1993, much of which was used for export sales.

[12] It appears that the Chinese government provided export subsidies to citric acid exporters at a rate of about 5 to 10 cents per pound until about 1994 when they were suspended.

[13] In November 1992, a fifth firm, Cerestar Bioproducts NV was added to the cartel. Cerestar is a subsidiary of Eridania Beghin-Say, a very large French-Italian agribusiness firm. While Cerestar remained in the cartel (until April 1994), it called itself the G-5.

[14] "Agribusinesses" are companies that primarily trade in or process agricultural commodities, buying from and selling to agricultural producers or other food processors. Unlike most food manufacturers, they do not typically sell finished foods directly to consumers. A fuller profile of ADM and its co-conspirators can be found in Connor (2000: Appendix E).

[15] ADM regularly appeared in the list of the most admired companies prepared annually by *Fortune* magazine. It regularly eked out growth and profit rates far higher than most other agribusiness firms.
[16] However, gross sales, which includes the total sales of merchandised grain and oilseeds, and the sales of unconsolidated joint ventures were approximately $70 billion.
[17] One of Andreas' first acts as CEO was to dissolve ADM's public relations department. Almost unique among publicly owned companies, ADM declined to register quarterly financial results.
[18] Dwayne Andreas was one of the few businessmen to join President Clinton on Air Force One when it flew to the late President Richard Nixon's funeral.
[19] The *Wall Street Journal* published more than 60 articles from 1995 to 1999 that chronicled ADM's or its officers' problems with antitrust investigation or suits. By contrast, Jim Lehrer had one segment devoted to the topic (out of 6,500 segments).
[20] The conspiracy was revealed by an ADM employee in 1996 to the FBI. In 1998, the information was part of the employee's federal court testimony (see Chapter 15). Bayer and Pfizer could not be prosecuted for price-fixing because of the Sherman Act's four-year statute of limitations.
[21] A minor portion of industry output is sold to chemical wholesalers who resell the citric acid to smaller buyers. If geographic differences in prices widen enough, these wholesalers would have an incentive to export some of their stored product.
[22] That is, the cost of production in Thailand would seem to be $0.50 per pound, and might fall as the small plant (15 million pounds per year) is expanded.
[23] This range is also consistent with the Department of Justice's overcharge estimates (Connor 1998: Table 4). The DOJ had access to detailed information on costs of production.
[24] USP is an abbreviation for United States Pharmacopia, one of the standard references for the technical standards required for a food or pharmaceutical product to be sold as suitable for human use.

Table 4.A.1. U.S. Production Capacity and Consumption of Anhydrous Citric Acid, 1989-2000.

Company: Plant	1989	1990	1991	1992	1993	1994	1995	1996	1997	1998	1999	2000
	million pounds per year											
Pfizer/Archer Daniels Midland:[a]	140	140	140	140	200	180	180	180	220[e]	220	220	220
Southport, NC	100	100	100	100	180	180	180	180	220[e]	220	220	220
Groton, CT	40	40	40	40	20	0	0	0	0	0	0	0
Bayer/Haarmann & Reimer:	140	140	150	150	150	150	150	150	150	150	150	150
Dayton, OH	100	100	110	110	110	110	110	110	110	150[c]	150[c]	150[c]
Elkhart, IN	40	40	40	40	40	40	40	40	40	0	0	0
Cargill: Eddyville, IA[b]	0	55	80	80	130	130	160	160	190[e]	190[e]	190[e]	190
U.S. plant capacity	280	335	370	430	480	460	490	490	560	560	560	560
U.S. consumption estimates[d]	300	320	340	390	420	440	475	520	550	570	610	650
U.S. exports	17	21	48	77	50	55	52	68	78	80	67[e]	67[e]
U.S. imports	65	61	50	59	95	109	109	95	119	133	166[e]	180[e]
Implicit U.S. production	252	280	338	408	375	386	418	493	509	517	511	530
Implicit U.S. plants utilization rate (%)	84	84	91	95	78	84	88	95	91	92	91	95

Source: Connor (2000: Appendix B).
[a] ADM acquired Pfizer's North Carolina plant in December 1990, and Pfizer continued to supply additional citric acid from Groton until mid-1993 when the plant was closed. Pfizer had a small plant in Canada in the 1980s.
[b] Cargill made only liquid acid until early 1993 when production of sodium citrate began.
[c] Sold to Tate & Lyle in June 1998 along with a Duluth, MN lactic acid plant and four citric plants outside the U.S. Sales world wide in 1997 were $298 million. Will be operated by A.E. Staley.
[d] Based on occasional trade-press estimates, long-term growth rates of 6% to 8% per year, and some annual variation due to prices.
[e] estimated

Table 4.A.2. Non-U.S. Production and Global Consumption of Anhydrous Citric Acid, 1989-2000.

Company: Plant	1989	1990	1991	1992	1993	1994	1995	1996	1997	1998	1999	2000
						million pounds per year						
Jungbunzlauer (Basel, Switzerland):	132	132	221	243	306	463	463	463	463	463	500[e]	500[e]
Pernhofen, Austria	88	88	155	155	174	220	220	220				
Ladenburg, Germany	44	44	66	88	88	133	133	133				
Marckolsheim, France	0	0	0	0	88	88	88	88				
Sumatra, Indonesia (JV)	0	0	0	0	22	22	22	22				
Bayer (Basel, Switzerland):[a]	90	90	134	134	134	160	160	160	160	160	160	200[e]
Selby, Yorkshire, UK	46	46	46	46	46	72	72	72				
3 Affiliates in Brazil, Mexico, Columbia	44[e]	44[e]	88	88	88	88	88	88				
Hoffmann-La Roche (Switz.): Tienen, Belgium	77[e]	77[e]	154	154	154	154	154	154	154	154	154	154
Biocor: Padova, Italy[b]	53	53	53	53	53	88	88	88	88	88	100[e]	100[e]
Palcitric: Naples, Italy[b]	0	0	0	0	77	77	77	77	77	77	77	77
ADM: Ringskiddy, Ireland[c]	20	20	20	20	20	20	40[e]	40[e]	40[e]	40[e]	40[e]	40[e]
Czech Republic: unknown company	0	0	0	0	66	66	66	66	66	66	66	66
China: many companies[d]	151	186	230	284	351	433	535	661	740	825[e]	920[e]	1,000[e]
Godot Israel: Haifa, Israel	20[e]	20[e]	20[e]	40[e]	40[e]	40[e]	40[e]	40[e]	60[e]	60[e]	60[e]	60[e]
Cargill: India (1994) and Brazil (1999)	0	0	0	0	0	44	44	44	44	88[e]	132[e]	132[e]
A.E. Staley/Bharat Starch: India	22[e]	22[e]	44[e]	44[e]	44[e]	66	66	66	66	110	110	110
Total U.S. capacity	280	335	370	430	480	460	490	490	490	560	560	560
Total non-U.S. capacity[f]	597	630	910	1,015	1,300	1,611	1,800	1,950	2,050	2,200	2,400	2,500
World Capacity, except former USSR	877	965	1,280	1,445	1,780	2,170	2,290	2,440	2,540	2,760	2,960	3,060
U.S. and Canada Consumption	320	340	361	412	443	464	500	550	580	605	650	690
Europe consumption	339[e]	364[e]	390[e]	450	485[e]	510[e]	555[e]	583[e]	610[e]	640[e]	670[e]	700[e]
World consumption[g]	725	800	1,020	1,200	1,330	1,500	1,600	1,750	1,850	2,000	2,150	2,300

Source: Connor (1998).

[e] = Estimate by author

[a] Purchased the UK plant from Rhône-Poulenc in 1990. The three Latin American affiliates of La Roche are in Mexico, Columbia, and Brazil. Their plant capacities were derived from a report on Roche's global capacity of 300 million pounds in 1990.

[b] Palcitric is part of Gruppo Palma of Naples, Italy. Biocor was owned by UK's Sturge Biochemicals until March 1990. In 1991, Biocor was resold to Italy's Ferruzzi-Montedison, now named Eridania.

[c] A fire was reported at this plant in the early 1990s. Excludes Bayer's U.S. plants (see Table 4.A.1).

[d] Annual estimates of capacity are based on constant geometric growth from government capacity figures given for 1987 and 1996. In 1994, China had 103 factories, most of them quite small (74% less than 6.6 mil. lb.), using sweet potato or cassava as the feedstock. Because of low quality, Chinese citric acid sells for 30-40% lower prices than the best quality, but the newest plants are being equipped with modern filtration equipment to improve purity. Some Chinese citric acid is refined and re-exported from Japan.

[f] This line is the total of the non-U.S. plant capacities shown above plus an arbitrary 5% to account for unreported production. Citric acid plants, some quite large, are known to exist in Turkey, India, Indonesia, Korea, Japan, and Latin America. No information is available on the former USSR.

[g] Based on total world capacity with an assumed 75-90% capacity utilization and consistent with reported 3-7 % p.a. volume growth. Excludes former USSR.

Table 4.A.3. U.S. Imports and Exports of Citric Acid and Citric Salts, 1991-1998.

Product[a]	1991	1992	1993	1994	1995	1996	1997	1998	1999[b]
				Million dollars					
Exports (F.O.B. prices):									
Acid	32.7	43.7	27.7	31.1	31.4	38.5	44.3	47.3	40.4
Salts	10.0	17.3	11.6	13.4	11.2	12.5	15.7	13.1	14.8
Totals	42.7	60.9	39.2	44.4	42.6	50.7	60.0	60.4	55.2
Imports (c.i.f. prices):									
Acid	--	--	60.5	67.7	66.2	51.4	58.4	62.3	74.6
Salts	--	--	3.9	3.5	4.1	14.8	15.2	17.2	20.4
Total	--	--	64.4	71.2	70.3	66.2	73.6	79.5	94.9
				Millions of pounds					
Exports:									
Acid	46.8	57.8	35.7	39.6	38.6	54.4	60.1	66.0	53.3
Salts	10.4	18.6	14.1	14.8	12.8	14.0	18.0	14.0	13.4
Imports:									
Acid	50.0	59.0	91.2	106.0	104.7	79.7	96.3	107.6	134.8
Salts	--	--	3.7	3.3	4.1	14.8	22.7	25.6	31.2
				Price(Implicit) in dollars					
Exports:									
Acid	0.68	0.76	0.77	0.78	0.81	0.71	0.73	0.72	0.76
Salts	0.97	0.92	0.82	0.90	0.87	0.89	0.87	0.94	1.10
Imports:									
Acid	--	--	0.66	0.64	0.63	0.64	0.61	0.58	0.55
Salts	--	--	0.72	0.79	0.75	0.69	0.67	0.67	0.65

Source: U.S. Census Bureau, *Stat-USA*, on line service.
-- = Not available
[a]Citric acid is identified under the Harmonized Trade System by number 2918140000. Salts and esters of citric acid (including sodium citrate and potassium citrate) are identified by HTS 2918150000.
[b]Projected from January-April 1999 trade data.

Table 4.A.4. U.S. Citric Acid Imports from Selected Countries, 1988, 1994, 1998.

Country (Company)	1988		1994		1998	
	Quantity	Price	Quantity	Price[a] (Acid)	Quantity	Price[a] (Acid)
	mil lb.	*$/lb.*	*mil lb.*	*$/lb.*	*mil lb.*	*$/lb.*
Canada (Pfizer)	1.3	0.21	0.4	0.64(0.65)	0.3	1.46(1.20)
Mexico (Bayer)	8.9	0.32	2.4	0.72(0.78)	0.0	2.39(--)
UK (Bayer)	2.5	0.31	1.8	0.83(0.54)	0.2	1.68(0.91)
Belgium (Bayer)	41.3	0.29	25.4	0.68(0.68)	12.6	0.67(0.67)
Germany (Jungbunz.)	23.2	0.30	3.0	1.07(0.83)	3.7	0.84(0.63
Austria (Jungbunz.)	20.2	0.30	26.0	0.66(0.67)	32.1	0.59(0.59)
Italy (Ferruzzi)	4.6	0.31	3.0	0.69(0.69)	0.0	-- (--)
Israel (Godot)	19.0	0.35	26.1	0.79(0.78)	37.4	0.64(0.65)
Indonesia	0.0	--	4.9	0.57(0.57)	1.0	0.60(0.60)
China	14.0	0.27	34.8	0.52(0.49)	44.6	0.49(0.49)
Total[b]	139.0	0.30	130.7	0.67(0.59)	133.3	0.60(0.58)

Source: *STAT-USA* online service.
[a] Price of acid and salts (acid only).
[b] Includes countries accounting for less than 1 percent of total imports not shown separately.

Table 4.A.5. U.S. Citric Acid Exports, to Selected Countries, 1990, 1994, 1998.

Country	1990		1994		1998	
	Quantity	Price[a]	Quantity	Price[a]	Quantity	Price[a]
	mil lb.	*$/lb.*	*mil lb.*	*$/lb.*	*mil lb.*	*$/lb.*
Canada	11.0	0.63(0.65)	22.4	0.76(0.79)	39.1	0.71(0.71)
Mexico	3.2	0.69(0.68)	4.9	0.83(0.78)	10.7	0.64(0.63)
Guatamala	0.1	0.19(0.71)	0.0	-- --	1.0	0.65(0.65)
Venezuela	0.0	-- (--)	0.0	-- (0.60)	1.3	0.46(0.46)
Ecuador	0.0	-- (--)	0.1	0.82(0.82)	0.7	0.58(0.59)
Peru	0.0	-- (--)	0.0	-- (1.47)	1.2	0.59(0.60)
Chile	0.0	-- (--)	0.0	-- (--)	0.5	0.62(0.63)
Brazil	0.0	-- (--)	3.6	0.80(0.80)	1.5	0.65(0.65)
Argentina	0.3	-- (0.56)	1.8	-- (0.66)	0.5	(0.60)(0.60)
Germany	0.5	1.10 (--)	0.3	0.88(0.85)	0.8	1.00(0.78)
Netherlands	0.1	-- (2.15)	0.3	1.20(2.44)	0.2	2.52(2.52)
Belgium	0.5	1.92 (--)	2.1	0.95(0.63)	1.1	1.87(0.67)
France	0.7	-- (0.56)	0.2	1.00(2.27)	0.3	1.14(0.96)
Thailand	0.4	0.63(0.62)	2.6	0.81(0.82)	1.2	0.74(0.82)
Singapore	0.0	-- (--)	0.4	0.65(0.86)	0.5	0.67(0.71)
Indonesia	0.2	0.68 (--)	0.7	0.73(0.79)	0.5	0.57(0.75)
Philippines	0.2	0.73 (--)	3.0	0.83(0.83)	0.1	1.32(1.42)
Japan	5.2	0.75(0.70)	5.8	0.75(0.71)	5.4	0.91(0.99)
Australia	1.9	0.57(0.57)	2.4	0.91(0.92)	4.5	0.85(0.89)
New Zealand	1.3	0.56(0.55)	0.7	0.81(0.80)	0.9	0.69(0.65)
Kenya	0.0	-- (--)	0.0	-- (--)	0.5	0.54(0.55)
S. Africa	0.0	-- (--)	0.2	-- (0.45)	0.1	0.85 (--)
Other Africa	2.4	0.78(0.73)	0.01	1.61(1.32)	0.5	-- (0.63)
Total	32.1	0.70(0.65)	54.5	0.81(0.78)	80.0	0.76(0.71)

Source: U.S. Census Bureau (FT 410 and STAT-USA annual data).
-- Insufficient quantity.
[a] Price of acid and salts (price of acid only).

Chapter 5

THE CITRIC ACID CONSPIRACY

INTRODUCTION

In January 1991, Terrance Wilson and Barrie Cox, two top-level officers of the large U.S. agribusiness firm Archer Daniels Midland Company, flew to Europe to meet with representatives of the three largest European manufacturers of citric acid. The two men were unlikely companions. Wilson was a Corporate Vice President and the President of ADM's big corn products division. He had joined ADM decades before, straight from the U.S. Marine Corps, and had worked his way up from near the bottom of the corporate ladder to be only one step removed from the giant company's powerful chairman, Dwayne O. Andreas. Although Wilson lacked a college education, his fierce loyalty to the Chairman and dogged pursuit of ADM's interests had yielded him a position of power and responsibility in ADM unmatched by all but three other officers.

If Wilson by all accounts was untutored, blunt, and profane, British born Barrie Cox was his opposite. Cox was urbane, educated, and knew languages. Unlike Wilson, he had spent nearly his whole career in the citric acid industry, but he had been employed by ADM for only a few weeks. The month before, ADM had acquired Pfizer Company's citric acid business, including two of its three citric acid manufacturing plants. Pfizer had pioneered the manufacturing of citric acid in the United States seventy years earlier. Barrie Cox had worked in marketing citric acid for 21 years in Pfizer's New York headquarters and was among the few of Pfizer's employees selected to keep their jobs and to move to ADM's headquarters in Decatur, Illinois. Among his assets was his personal acquaintance with the managers of the citric acid businesses owned by the leading European chemical manufacturers. In fact, during his late-1999 job interview with Michael Andreas, Cox had been quizzed about the extensiveness of his personal contacts in the European industry. In Cox's first month on the job, his boss Wilson had asked him to set up meetings with the world's three largest citric acid makers: Hoffmann-La Roche; Jungbunzlauer, and Bayer (Tr. 2624).[1]

Wilson and Cox met with the top managers in charge of citric acid at the three companies near their respective headquarters: Andreas Hauri of Hoffmann-La Roche in Basel, Switzerland; Hans Hartmann of Bayer in Hanover, Germany and Rainer Bilchbauer, President of Jungbunzlauer in Vienna, Austria. Years later Cox would describe these January 1991 meetings as simply introductory, get acquainted sessions for Wilson, who was new to the industry. Very likely, Wilson described ADM's intention to modernize and expand Pfizer's biggest plant and to reduce costs by vertically integrating citric acid manufacturing with ADM's production of liquid dextrose, the primary ingredient in the manufacturing process. Wilson also probably attempted to allay any fears the Europeans might have had about ADM's well-earned reputation for hard-ball marketing tactics by saying that ADM should be a "friendly competitor" in the citric acid industry. ADM's policy in the citric acid market would be more like cooperation than confrontation.

Wilson made quick use of his new contacts. Within a month of the European trip, Wilson had arranged a meeting of the four largest makers of citric acid in the world, a group they would jokingly refer to as the G-4 (Tr. 2626).[2] Wilson, Cox and six other top managers of the G-4 met in Basel, Switzerland on March 6, 1991 to discuss a long list of agenda items, among them how to go about raising prices globally. The citric acid cartel was off and running.

TRIGGERING EVENTS

The seminal decision in the history of the citric acid cartel was Cargill's commitment of investment funds for a new high-tech finishing plant in Eddyville, Iowa. What factors prompted that shift in corporate strategy may never be known, but the fact that it was taken in 1987 provides a few clues.

Cargill, like ADM, was a leading manufacturer of sweeteners made from fermentation of corn. Glucose corn syrup and dextrose were mature and slow growing product lines, but high fructose corn syrup (HFCS) was altogether different. HCFS was a miracle of modern science, a cheap process for converting abundant cornstarch into fructose, the sugar found in honey and fruits. Until commercial production of HFCS began in the United States in the late 1960's, fructose that approached and eventually exceeded the sweetness level of sucrose from cane sugar had never been available for purchase by the food processing industries. While its production cost in the 1980's of $0.08 to $0.10 per pound did not make it quite cost competitive with the cheapest imported cane sugar, the prospect of near self-sufficiency in sweeteners prompted Congress to oblige the industry by continuing to keep in place import barriers on foreign sugar.[3] The resulting domestic wholesale price of sugar (about $0.16 per pound in most years of the 1970's and 1980's) guaranteed high profits for HFCS manufacturers. Continued lobbying of Congress ensured periodic renewal of this sweet deal.

From its inception, the HFCS industry enjoyed exceedingly rapid volume growth (20 to 40 percent per year) as the industry converted from sucrose to fructose. The high point in this substitution process was the decision of the major soft drink makers to allow their bottlers to convert from sucrose to HFCS in the mid-1980s. The high growth of HFCS came to a sudden end in 1986 as the last big buyer of sucrose completed its conversion to fructose. ADM, Cargill, and the other five or six producers faced a serious crisis. HFCS would no longer grow any faster than the food processing industries as a whole (only 2 or 3 percent per year) after two decades of heavy growth.

Both ADM and Cargill decided to use their corn refining capacities and expertise to branch out into new sweetener-based, fast growing organic chemicals.[4] Adding fermentors and related equipment to create finishing capacity for new products was less expensive than building stand-alone facilities and yielded production efficiencies as well. Cargill's decision to enter citric acid manufacturing was simply one of the first of a large number of food-and-feed ingredients compatible with its biotechnology thrust. In retrospect, citric acid may have been a fairly obvious first choice among the array of possibilities. Citric acid enjoyed relatively large sales and solid volume growth in the U.S. market of 6 to 10 percent per year. At prices near $0.80 per pound, citric acid sales held out the prospect of a very healthy profit margin, probably between 10 and 25 percent of sales, well above the company's usual returns. It is also likely that Cargill saw the two established U.S. manufacturers, Pfizer and Haarmann & Reimer, as soft targets because their lack of vertical integration imposed higher cost structures. Finally, unlike some of the other possibilities like amino acids or xanthan gum, the technology for producing citric acid from dextrose was more accessible for a newcomer. All in all, citric acid must have looked like a winner to Cargill in 1987.

There is no doubt that Cargill intended to develop a leading position in the citric acid industry. Its Iowa plant when it came on stream in mid-1990 expanded North American production capacity by 17 percent. The new plant took a little more than two years to build. Significant capacity expansions took place at regular intervals: 1991, 1993, and 1995. Cargill's initial U.S. capacity share eventually doubled to 33 percent in 1995, despite parallel expansions at ADM's North Carolina plant. Cargill was proved right in the end about Pfizer and Haarmann & Reimer. Pfizer exited the industry as soon as Cargill entered on the scene. Haarmann & Reimer never made any fresh capacity expansions after 1990, quickly lost its number one position, and was taken out of the industry by its parent seven years later.

In an unusual reversal of their usual roles, ADM in 1990 imitated Cargill's move. ADM announced its intention to enter the citric acid industry three years after Cargill, but took over ownership of Pfizer's plants six months before Cargill began production. How much ADM paid for Pfizer's plants and technology is not known, but the bold decision put ADM well ahead of its long-time principal rival in the contest for production capacity. Due to

Cargill's expansions, ADM's initial 49 percent of U.S. capacity declined to about 37 percent by 1995, but it held on to the number-one position throughout the 1990s by significant plant expansions. ADM's behavior was symptomatic of its oft-stated goal to be at least equal in size to the largest firm in all its industries. Not only did it pull ahead of Cargill in the U.S. but by the mid-1990's ADM was in solid third place globally, behind Jungbunzlauer and Bayer.

Two legal events may have contributed to ADM's decision to initiate the conspiracy in early 1991. Any price fixer must weigh the expected extra profits from creating or joining a cartel against the possible costs of being caught and punished by the antitrust authorities. There is no doubt that the conspiracy netted substantial illicit profits for all the companies involved; how large will be analyzed later. Two legal episodes probably lowered the perception about the chances of being sanctioned.[5] First, after nearly ten years in federal court, the judge dismissed a federal civil prosecution against ADM that alleged ADM had made an anti-competitive acquisition in the HFCS industry. Second, in the early 1990s the Department of Justice was having practical difficulties in prosecuting international cartels. In a case involving Japanese exports of thermal fax paper, the defendants were arguing that offshore price-fixing agreements were beyond the territorial reach of the Sherman Act. In the case of the alleged diamond cartel, the case was dismissed because key documentary evidence and witnesses could not be obtained through normal federal subpoena processes (Daniel *et al.* 1997). Thus, many would-be global price fixers may have got the impression that agreements and meetings conducted offshore were less likely to be sanctioned than domestic conspiracies. The citric acid cartel assiduously avoided meeting on U.S. territory.

MEETING AND METHODS

The opening event in the conspiracy was when Terrance Wilson and Barrie Cox flew to Europe in January 1991 to pay a courtesy call on their big three rivals.[6] To the European managers, ADM's friendly overtures must have seemed like welcome news indeed. Falling U.S. citric acid prices were having negative repercussions on their business worldwide, and the expected future expansions of Cargill and ADM seemed to promise only more grim news. ADM was probably unaware that the companies being contacted had previously colluded with Pfizer in this market and that the breakup of the previous cartel was one reason for falling prices. ADM's hints at its readiness to cooperate would not have gone unnoticed. Wilson also expressed ADM's interest in joining the European Citric Acid Manufacturer's Association (ECAMA), a trade association that was to play a key-facilitating role in the conspiracy. ECAMA's parent organization is the European Chemical Industry Council, an officially recognized unit of the European Commission.

With handshakes all around and business cards exchanged, the two ADM executives returned to Decatur. Unbeknownst to Cox, Wilson afterward quickly contacted the European citric acid managers, informing them of his desire to cooperate in raising citric acid prices. Wilson set up a meeting of all four companies for March 6, 1991 in Basel, Switzerland and instructed Cox to accompany and assist him.[7]

This was the first of many meetings of the G-4 (Table 5.1). There were eight men present at the meeting, two from each company of the G-4.[8] Based on the severity of their sentences, it is clear that the prosecutors of the cartel considered Terrance Wilson and Hans Hartmann of Bayer/H&R to be the group's ringleaders. Hauri of Roche was eventually to take on the role of G-4's executive director. The leading role of Hans Hartmann is not hard to understand. He had been a Bayer employee for almost 40 years and president or executive vice president of Bayer's citric acid business for more than a decade. With his long industry experience, German citizenship, and residence in New Jersey, Hartmann was ideally qualified to act as a liaison between Wilson and the other German-speaking managers. Also, his subsidiary, Haarmann & Reimer, had the most to lose if an effective cartel did not emerge because it was likely the highest-cost producer in the U.S. market.

Table 5.1. Major Meetings of the Citric Acid Cartel, 1991-1995.

Date	Location	Notes
March 6, 1991	Basel, Switzerland	G-4 formed
May 14, 1991	Vienna, Austria (ECAMA)	
November 14, 1991	Brussels, Belgium (ECAMA)	
May 20, 1992	Jerusalem, Israel (ECAMA)	
November 18, 1992	Brussels (ECAMA)	Cerestar joins
June 1, 1993	Kildare Island, Ireland (ECAMA)	
October 27, 1993	Bruges, Belgium (ECAMA)	
May 18, 1994	London, England (ECAMA)	
November 2, 1994	Brussels (ECAMA)	Wilson's last
May, 1995	Brittenau, Switzerland	unplanned meeting

Note: This table lists only the nine meetings that both Terrance Wilson and Barrie Cox of ADM attended and one other. At least eight of these meetings, and possibly all ten, occurred in parallel with official meetings of the European Citric Acid Manufacturers' Association (ECAMA). There were about 25 face-to-face meetings of the whole group and about a dozen bilateral meetings (Tr. 2614-2801).

The agenda for the Basel meeting included several general topics such as the reason for such low prices and the role played by surging Chinese output. The chief representative from Hoffmann-La Roche congratulated ADM on its recent announcement of a U.S. list price increase from $0.65 per pound to $0.68. However, the talk at the Basel meeting soon veered into clearly illegal territory. Violations of the Sherman Act occur if two or more individuals from independent companies knowingly and intentionally attempt to restrain a market's output or prices; it is the agreement to do so that is the crime, not any effects the agreement may have on the market (see Chapter 3). At the Basel meeting, the managers of the four companies agreed to raise their list prices in all regions of the world.[9] They also agreed to allow each company to grant 3 percent price discounts to their five largest customers. A sales quota was established for each member of the cartel for its global sales as well as for three regions (North America, Europe, and the rest of the world). Each company was allocated a 1991 tonnage target based on its 1988-1990 actual sales volume, with an adjustment for anticipated growth. To monitor the volume agreement, each company agreed to submit monthly sale volumes by region to Hauri at Roche's Basel headquarters. Hauri's office would then compile totals and market shares and report the information back to each company. With this information, each cartel member could gauge the adherence of each other member to the allocation agreement. At the end of the year, a buy-back system would be implemented to even out discrepancies between "budgeted" and actual sales. Companies that came in over target would sell citric acid at cost to members that were under target volumes. Finally, they agreed to meet secretly at least twice a year using the official ECAMA meetings as a cover (Table 5.1). In fact, Cox said that the cartel had about 25 formal meetings from 1991 to 1995, plus a dozen or so bilateral meetings. In addition, when things were quiet Cox had at least two telephone calls per week about cartel matters: when there was a lot of activity, calls would occur daily.

The rapidity with which such a complex agreement was hammered out is remarkable. Perhaps a surprising bit of information passed on at the Basel meeting explains why a plan emerged so quickly. Cox learned that his former employer, Pfizer, had been involved in a price-fixing scheme in the 1980's. He was not aware of it at the time and believes that it ended before the ADM takeover in December 1990.[10] The fact that Cox was informed earlier about the price-fixing scheme by the Swiss managers suggests that both Pfizer and the Swiss firms had been co-conspirators. Thus, in a sense, the 1991-1995 citric acid cartel was *re-formed* in 1991 rather than *de novo*.

The official meetings of ECAMA took place at ECAMA's headquarters in Brussels every November and every spring at a different location chosen by one of the member companies. At the open "official" meetings, speeches were made by experts on various subjects, the ECAMA secretary presided and took the minutes and industry data collected by ECAMA were discussed. These open meetings were attended by representatives of manufacturers and buyers alike. In other words, ECAMA had all the trappings of the legitimate trade association that it was.

However, at the parallel "unofficial" conspiracy meetings of the G-4, there were no agendas, no minutes, and no customer representatives present. The manufacturers' representatives at the conspiracy meetings took pains to cover up their activities by destroying any documentary evidence of their conspiracy.[11] These actions reveal that the conspirators knew their "unofficial" meetings were illegal. In fact, Cox testified that Wilson warned him that if the price-fixing were ever discovered, Cox would be "on his own," that is ADM would not pay for Cox's legal expenses should Cox be prosecuted (Tr.2681).[12]

The secret meetings of the G-4 soon became fairly routine events. Full-scale meetings were scheduled on average every eight weeks. A standard format evolved. First, the group would discuss the latest cartel sales reports, which provided information on growth and company market shares. The group then discussed price levels and trends around the world and decided whether to raise prices or keep them firm. Information about competition by companies outside the G-4 was shared. Finally, the group considered "problems effecting the group." This was a euphemism for heated debates about cheating accusations, a psychological phenomenon that afflicts nearly all nonbinding cartel organizations (Scherer and Ross 1990:236-248).[13] Eventually, by late 1994, or early 1995 cheating on their volume agreements became so rampant that the G-4 effectively fell apart. However, for almost four years, the group displayed enough discipline and harmony to have a strong effect on raising prices, the principal aim of the G-4.

CITRIC ACID PRICE MOVEMENTS

U.S. and global prices reached their nadir in the winter of 1990-1991 as Cargill's new plant ramped up its production (Figure 5.1). For three years (1987-1989) U.S. list prices for the most popular form of citric acid had remained unchanged at $0.81 per pound. In anticipation of the vast new supplies from Cargill's plant, by late 1989 buyers began to hold off on their purchases. With their inventories ballooning, the two U.S. manufacturers were forced to cut their list prices four times starting in December 1989 to $0.75. The last list price decrease occurred in July 1990 when Cargill's began sales of citric acid. Cargill announced a list price of $0.63 per pound, a dramatic $0.10 lower than the reigning industry price and 22 percent lower than the price at the end of 1989. Other producers were forced to match Cargill's low-ball price.

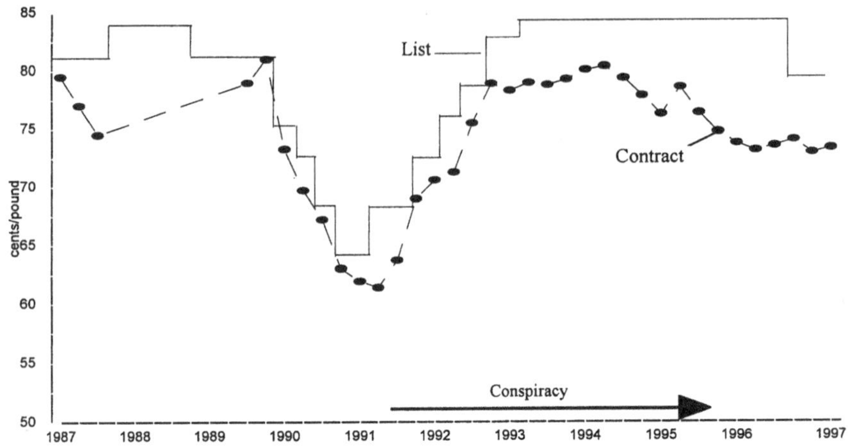

Figure 5.1. List and Contract Prices of Anhydrous Citric Acid, 1987-1997.

Source: Table 3 and Appendix Table 1 of Connor (1998).
Note: List prices are bulk purchase delivered to Midwest points. Contract prices are for bulk orders covering at least 3 months supply needs of the buyers, f.o.b. plant transactions, average for the quarter.

By the end of 1990, Cargill's plant was reportedly producing at close to its optimal level of utilization. In February, Cargill announced a 5-cent list price increase, and its two U.S. rivals (ADM and Haarmann & Reimer) match Cargill's price initiative.[14] Late winter or early spring is a good time to raise prices in any case because demand for citric acid by beverage makers peaks at that time in anticipation of peak summer beverage sales. In August, 1991, Cargill again pushed through a 5-cent price increase, just as annual contract negotiations were about to commence. All the other manufacturers followed Cargill's lead. By this time, the G-4 had begun its price-fixing discussions. As Cargill was not a formal member of the G-4, its leading role in initiating the August price increase is a bit puzzling. Cargill was doing just what the newly formed cartel wished to do, but there is no evidence that Cargill raised its list price by agreements with the G-4 itself.

What is clear is that the cartel took over the responsibility of raising prices after 1991. Beginning in January 1992 and ending in October 1993, Bayer's Haarmann & Riemer subsidiary led four list price increases, each of them for 3 cents. Within a few weeks of Haarmann & Reimer's action, all other major manufacturers matched the increases. For three years, October 1993 to late 1996, the citric acid cartel achieved its central objective: raising and keeping list prices at $0.85 per pound. Because this 35 percent list price increase was followed by a similar increase in transaction prices, profits rose sharply for all producers, whether members of the cartel or not (see Figure 5.1). It is perhaps significant that Haarmann & Reimer was designated to be the firm that initiated the price increases in the U.S. citric acid market. Haarmann & Reimer was doubtless the highest-cost producer in the U.S. industry because it was not vertically integrated into the manufacturing of dextrose and because it ran the smallest, oldest plants. Moreover, of Haarmann & Reimer's citric acid returns were dissipated by noncompetitive, elevated dextrose prices it had to pay to sellers in the alleged corn-sweeteners conspiracy. Cargill was totally vertically integrated from the time it entered production, and ADM achieved the benefits of quasi-integration through optimal scheduling of rail shipments of dextrose.[15] Moreover, both Cargill and ADM had expanded their U.S. plants to a size larger than Haarmann & Reimer's biggest plant by 1993 (Table 4.A.1). Thus, prices that generated merely above average profits for Haarmann & Reimer would generate extraordinarily high profits for ADM and Cargill. Even if there had been no cartel deciding on a collective price level, simply independent price leadership by Haarmann & Reimer would have resulted in the most monopoly-like prices for Cargill and ADM as price followers (Scherer and Ross 1990: 260-261).

In the United States and probably Europe as well, both spot and contract prices fell and rose in sympathy with the list price announcements. Increases in transaction prices took a month or two to take effect after a price list change, partly because of contractual price-protection clauses. From 1987 to the end of 1994, contract prices were from zero to five cents lower than list prices. Cox testified that all the increases in 1992 and 1993 were by agreement of the members of the cartel. The cartel believed that its changes in list prices and effectiveness in restraining the volume sold by the G-4, which controlled 65 to 70 percent of world production, was sufficient to cause transaction prices to rise. However, the cartel might not have been successful if the two largest non-cartel sources of supply – Cargill and Chinese producers – had failed to cooperate.

THE ROLE OF CARGILL

In sworn testimony in federal court, Barrie Cox stated without qualification that neither Cargill nor the numerous Chinese producers were members of the G-4 (Tr. 2674-2676). Hans Hartmann also testified as to Cargill's innocence. While these statements are literally true, the point made about Cargill is at best misleading. Later in the trial, while being cross-examined by Wilson's lawyer, Cox admitted that sometime during 1991-1995 he had "price discussions" with an individual at Cargill (TR.2750). Some of those discussions involved agreeing about the prices Cargill and ADM would bid for certain citric acid accounts.[16] Bid-rigging is, of course, one method of fixing prices.

Almost a year after the Chicago trial, press reports clarified Cargill's role in the citric acid conspiracy (Guebert 1999, *New York Times* June 17, 1999). On October 12, 1996, Barrie Cox was interviewed by the FBI. At the same time, he had been offered immunity from prosecution in return for his complete and truthful cooperation in the FBI's investigation of the citric acid conspiracy. (Perjury during the interview would be grounds for removing Cox's immunity). Cox stated that he had held more than a dozen conversations with William Gruber, his counterpart at Cargill. The conversations dealt with Cargill's plans to raise prices and rig bids to certain customers. Cox said that he agreed to "go along" with Cargill's plan to raise the price of citric acid and restrain ADM's sales volume. Thus, it appears that Cargill and ADM had a bilateral price-fixing agreement separate from the G-4 cartel. Cox informed his boss Wilson about his conversations with Cargill.[17] The three Swiss firms may not have been explicitly informed about the Cox-Gruber conspiracy, though they might easily have inferred it. Cox says that the Swiss firms were aware of his Cargill talks. It is possible that Gruber's actions may not have been known or sanctioned at Cargill.[18]

The import of these facts concerns Cargill's frequent protestations that the company was innocent of price fixing in citric acid and corn sweeteners. In June 1999, Cargill's lawyer denied that the Cox-Gruber conversations ever happened. He also recalled Cox's trial testimony exonerating Cargill:

> "In fact, later in the trial, the government all but held Cargill up as a poster child for good corporate citizenship" (Guebert, 1999).

Indeed, anonymous sources at the Department of Justice confirmed that neither Cargill nor Gruber were targets of investigation in 1999. Nevertheless, Cox's trial testimony was never rebutted in any way by the defendants, even though Cox's testimony was devastating to Terrance Wilson's case (Lieber 2000).

If, as seem likely at this point, the Cox-Gruber conversations were overt price fixing, then Cargill is liable for some of the effects on prices in the U.S. market. Whether top management was aware of Gruber's actions is irrelevant for civil antitrust liability in the United States. Because Cargill was not directly engaged with the G-4, it may not be liable for non-U.S. price effects.[19]

Even if the Cox-Gruber conversations were not illegal, then Cargill was the legal beneficiary of monopoly profits that carry no antitrust liability. Cargill could have made more than $100 million in excess profits during

1992-1995 from its citric acid business. Cargill is entitled to keep these profits even though the G-4 may be required to pay injured parties triple the citric acid overcharges, those resulting from sales by G-4 members as well as nonmembers.[20]

THE CHINA PROBLEM

The citric acid cartel controlled at most two-thirds of the world's supply of citric acid. Even with Cargill's passive acceptance of the cartel's pricing decisions, one set of producers appeared ready to spoil the cartel's effectiveness. Those producers were located in China, and they were intent upon the most rapid expansion of their exports by any means possible, including deep price cuts.

Production of citric acid in China began in the early 1970s. The U.S. trade press began to take notice of Chinese imports in the late 1980s, but China's official news service had begun trumpeting the rapid expansion of its citric acid industry in the early 1980s. By 1988, the Xinhua News Service claimed that citric acid plants in China had 100 million pounds of capacity, or nearly 8 percent of world capacity. Three years later, the Chinese capacity share approached 20 percent. Interest in Chinese joint ventures by Western citric acid manufacturers is noted as early as 1991 and accelerated in the early 1990s. (Foreign investment would also occur in India, Indonesia, and Taiwan in the early 1990s). In 1994, Xinhua reported that actual production in China in 1993 had reached 360 million pounds, but more important for the citric acid cartel was the claim that an astonishing 240 million pounds was exported. If true, these data suggested that in a remarkably short time China had moved into second place behind the United States in terms of national production (third place if one regards the European Union a single market). Most Chinese exports were destined for other Asian countries, but increasingly they were penetrating Europe and North America.

Import data from the United States confirm the looming importance of China as a source of citric acid. In 1991, when citric acid prices were at their lowest level, only 50 million pounds were imported. But when the cartel-induced prices had risen to near $0.80 per pound in 1993, the volume of imports increased by 90 percent. Most of the increase in imports came from Chinese producers. By 1994, one-third of U.S. imports of citric acid originated from China.

Production capacity and exports of citric acid from China was growing at an unsustainable pace. Chinese volume of exports grew by 34 percent per year from 1977 to 1994, though by the early 1990s growth was probably below 20 percent annually. In 1996, national production capacity reached 660 million pounds, which implies that expansion since the late

1980s had reached 15 percent per year. This was double the rate of capacity expansion by members of the G-4.

The impressive growth of China's citric acid industry is part of a larger story of the tremendous industrial growth in China that resulted from a relaxation of centralized planning and socialist economic principles. Production costs are quite low by international standards in most of China's manufacturing industries, and the citric acid industry had three cost advantages worth noting. First, construction costs for new plants in China are significantly lower than plants of comparable size in the West, a feature not lost on the leading European manufacturers when they began forming joint ventures in China in the late 1990s. Second, the starchy raw materials available for fermentation were very low in cost, probably lower than corn in the United States. The major raw material in China was sweet potatoes; some used cassava. Both raw materials are abundant in China. Third, up to at least 1995, China's central government provided export subsidies for many chemical industries, including citric acid. These subsidies may have lowered the price of Chinese citric acid exports by as much as 10 percent.

Chinese citric acid was also cheap because of a reputation for poor quality. The proportion of impurities in much of China's exported citric acid was too high to qualify it for use in foods and beverages, though it may have been acceptable as an ingredient in detergents. Chinese exports to the United States were probably from their best factories that had more advanced filtration equipment, yet trade reports showed the Chinese citric acid sold in the United States at a 5 to 15 percent discount below European imports (Connor 1998: Appendix Table 3). Chinese citric acid plants tended to be tiny by Western standards. In the mid-1990's, 95 percent of its more than 100 plants had capacities of less than 22 million pounds. These smaller plants had to export their citric acid at prices 30 to 40 percent below major Western exporters. Consolidation of production, continuing foreign investment, and upgrading of equipment will in all likelihood raise the quality of Chinese citric acid over time.

The 1992-1994 surge in Chinese exports put the G-4 in a bind. The more successful the cartel became in raising prices, the more Chinese imports flooded into North America and Europe. The cartel's solution to this problem was a masterful political move.

In 1993 and 1994, the United States was embroiled in a dispute with China on the issue of protection of intellectual property rights. The U.S. film, music, and publishing industries were losing millions of dollars of royalties because of widespread and officially tolerated pirating. Press reports told of lobbying of the office of the U.S. Trade Representative by one of the two U.S.-owned manufacturers of citric acid. The lobbying had the desired effect. On February 4, 1995, the U.S. Government announced that it would impose prohibitive 100 percent tariffs on $1.1 billion of goods imported from China in retaliation for Chinese government intransigence. Prominent on the list of imported goods was citric acid. Although last-minute Chinese concessions prevented final imposition of the prohibitive tariffs, the mere threat had the desired effect. In 1995, Chinese exports of citric acid to the United States fell substantially from 1994 levels. Among the Chinese concessions was the removal of the export subsidies that had kept Chinese export prices low. As a result, downward pressure on cartel prices was muted, if not prevented.

The European producers attempted to apply similar pressures on Chinese exporters. Acting as though it was some sort of official government unit, in January 1995 ECAMA officials traveled to China to meet with representatives of China's National Fermentation Association. Their purpose was to warn the citric acid producers to reduce their exports to Europe, otherwise they would initiate an anti-dumping investigation with the European Commission. This threat may have had some credence with the Chinese producers because ECAMA had its secretariat located in Brussels and was affiliated indirectly with the Agriculture Directorate of the European Commission. However, no such investigation was ever publicly announced by the EC.

THE CARTEL IS UNMASKED

On the night of June 27th 1995, approximately 70 FBI agents served subpoenas and exercised search warrants on startled ADM officials, an action popularly known as a "raid."[21] Tiny Decatur, Illinois had never seen anything like it before. The subpoenas were issued by a federal grand jury in Chicago that had been secretly investigating allegations of global price fixing in lysine, citric acid, and corn sweeteners. The FBI interviews initially yielded no useful admissions of illegal activity, but the files at ADM's headquarters contained lots of incriminating evidence of price fixing. FBI raids were repeated at the headquarters of Cargill in Minneapolis, Haarmann & Reimer in New Jersey, and about ten other companies suspected of participating in one of the three alleged cartels.

Knowledge about the citric acid cartel came to the attention of antitrust officials at the U.S. Department of Justice indirectly as a result of its undercover investigation of the lysine cartel (for more details see next chapter). Unbeknownst to Michael Andreas, Terrance Wilson, Barrie Cox, and other top officials at ADM, many of their private business discussions were being recorded on tape recorders provided by the FBI to its "mole." The FBI informant was Mark Whitacre, president of ADM's Biotechnology Division and rising star at ADM. Whitacre had been cooperating since November 1992. In addition to Whitacre's own audio tapes, his information allowed the FBI to set up video cameras in hotels where some of the conspiratorial meetings were held. This videotaped evidence is an historic first in the annals of antitrust investigations.

Whitacre attempted to obtain audio tapes about the citric acid cartel by visiting Barrie Cox's office and trying to engage Cox in discussions that might have revealed inculpatory information about the operations of the G-4. Cox rebuffed Whitacre, much to the latter's disappointment (Tr. 2736-2737). Cox testified that he disliked Whitacre. He considered Whitacre "unnecessarily curious" about ADM's citric acid affairs. Citric acid was one of the few fermentation products that were not part of the Biotechnology Division, so Whitacre had no management responsibility for the product.

The FBI became aware of the citric acid cartel because Wilson repeatedly talked about it when conspiring with ADM's lysine co-conspirators. At several meetings of the lysine cartel, he urged the conspirators to form a trade association for amino-acid manufacturers that would operate just like ECAMA. For example, in June 1992 Wilson explained how the citric acid association used both formal and informal methods for tracking members' sales figures. These figures were used to allocate volume shares among the G-4 participants and confirm adherence to the share agreements. Wilson argued that the share agreements were one way that the cartel instilled cooperation and discipline among its members (Lassar and Griffin: 22-23). At later lysine meetings Wilson touted the advantage of ECAMA in providing a cover for illegal activities. He also urged the lysine producers to choose an accounting firm to independently calculate members' sales volume so as to confirm the accuracy of monthly sales reports, just as ECAMA did.

The day after the June 27th raid, the *Wall Street Journal* and dozens of other major newspapers carried prominently placed articles on the investigation, targeted firms, and alleged illegal price fixing. Formal collusion by the G-4 had stopped about six months earlier. There was an "unplanned" meeting of the G-4 in Switzerland in May 1995 in which the companies tried to put the cartel back on track, but that effort was unsuccessful. The precise causes for the failure to cooperate is not known, but disagreements about volume allocations and cheating on those allocations are good guesses.[22] U.S. contract prices briefly rose to $0.82 in November 1994, but this would prove to be the peak monthly price. Prices slid down after that, then in the first quarter of 1995 rose to about $0.79 per pound, but this could have been helped by the usual seasonal demand spur by the beverage industry. Basically, prices slowly declined each quarter starting in late 1994, reaching $0.70 by early 1997. How long the effects of the cartel's price increases lingered beyond the end of formal collusion is a matter of debate, but the effects seem to have diminished throughout 1995 and vanished by 1996.

Chapter 5 Endnotes

[1] In this book, the transcript of the 1998 trial *U.S. vs. Michael Andreas et al.* is a frequently cited source. The abbreviation "Tr." will be used as a quick reference to this source and its pages. Except for a few major books, and articles, the hundreds of published sources used to write this chapter can be found in Appendix B of Connor (2000).
[2] The moniker G-4 is a conscious imitation of the annual meetings of the heads of the seven largest industrial countries, the G-7. A couple of years later, a fifth company joined the cartel (Cerestar Bioproducts, NV) whereupon the cartel rechristened itself the G-5. The term G-4 will be employed throughout this chapter to describe the citric acid cartel.
[3] The so-called sugar program was originally designed to protect U.S. cane and beet sugar producers from low-cost foreign production. HFCS manufacturers joined forces with the U.S. sugar interests to lobby for trade barriers so as to guarantee high profits at the expense of the U.S. consumers. The program was briefly abandoned in the mid 1970's. Without the help of the HFCS industry, lobbying by sugar-beet and sugar-cane interests might not have been enough to reinstate the program.
[4] A partial list of such products made from corn-sweetener feedstock includes methionine, threonine, tryptophan, sorbitol, lactic acid, gluconates, monosodium gluconates, vitamins (C,E, and biotin), lysine, and citric acid. All of these products were bulk ingredients sold to food or animal-feed manufacturers, ADM and Cargill's tradition consumers.
[5] More accurately, firms must have some subjective perception of the chance of being discovered and sanctioned. What this subjective probability is much debated by economists. Perhaps a consensus figure might oscillate around 10 percent.
[6] Cox later testified that the two met Mr. Hauri of Hoffmann-La Roche, Hans Hartmann, of Bayer's subsidiary Haarmann & Reimer, and Bilchbauer, Lutz, and Kahane of Jungbunzlauer (Tr. 2625).
[7] It is highly unlikely that Wilson did not seek approval from his boss, Michael Andreas, before initiating the conspiracy. At any rate, Andreas was heard on tape discussing the conspiracy at ADM's headquarters. Cox later testified that he was unaware of Pfizer's involvement in fixing critical prices in the late 1980s. Cox may have had little choice, other than resigning. An ADM employee named Wayne Brasser was fired for refusing to cooperate with the scheme.
[8] Besides Wilson and Cox, present were Hartmann and Yamashita from Haarmann & Reimer, Hauri and Marti from Roche, and Bilchbauer and Hummer from Jungbunzlauer. Bilchbauer was president and CEO of Jungbunzlauer; Hartmann was president of H & R; Wilson was president of ADM's corn productions division.
[9] The G-4 had an immediate effect on list prices, but because of the impending start of production by Cargill, U.S. transaction prices did not rise for a few months after the Basel meeting.
[10] The two employees responsible for price-fixing at Pfizer were named Hunter and Moriarty. The conspiracy of the 1980's must have involved Bayer's U.S. subsidiary Miles Laboratories. The European producers were aware of the earlier price-fixing and may well have been active participants. The prior conspiracy cannot be prosecuted because there is a four-year statute of limitations for price-fixing.
[11] Nevertheless, considerable evidence was available to prosecutors after the cartel was exposed. Only three ADM employees were supposed to be informed about the conspiracy (M. Andreas, Wilson, and Cox). Andreas and Wilson never cooperated by giving evidence to prosecutors, but Cox divulged his involvement to an old friend at ADM, VP of Operations Roger Dawson, who also came from Pfizer. Dawson was able to confirm most of Cox's testimony. Documentary evidence survived in the form of travel and expense records of participants at the meetings (travel to non-ECAMA G-4 meetings was damaging), faxes of monthly sales reports, and telephone records. More importantly, tape recordings of Wilson

talking about the citric acid cartel were made at meetings of the lysine cartel. Just after both cartels were exposed, Wilson was taped saying that there was "bad stuff" on those lysine tapes (Tr. 2683-2685).

[12] ADM in fact paid for the legal defense of Andreas and Wilson.

[13] "Nonbinding" means privately enforced by the cartel members themselves. Many cartels are government sponsored and therefore binding.

[14] This was the price increase for which Hauri praised Wilson and Cox when they first met in March 1991. ADM's willingness to follow Cargill's lead in raising prices would be interpreted as a tangible sign of ADM's friendly, cooperative intentions. Cargill's action too must be interpreted as a friendly signal to its rivals in the industry. Cargill was reaching full capacity and thus had if anything lower production costs than in 1990, and in February was a few months early for the seasonal beverage demand increase to be felt on spot purchases.

[15] ADM also operated a new corn wet milling plant in eastern Tennessee that was quite close to its North Carolina citric acid plant. Cargill and ADM were members of the alleged conspiracy to raise prices of corn sweeteners during 1989 to 1995 (see Chapter 13). Thus, from 1991 to 1995 ADM and Cargill may have earned monopoly profits on both citric acid and on sales of its primary input, dextrose.

[16] Why Mark Hulkower, Wilson's lawyer, chose to explore this topic is baffling. Why prosecutor Scott Lassar in his closing argument, ignored the testimony and praised Cargill for its ethical behavior is equally baffling.

[17] He said Wilson showed no surprise at the news, as if Wilson pre-arranged the bilateral deal. The Cargill-initiated price increase must be the August 1991 action. Cox told the FBI that in 1992 or 1993, the G-4 discussed ". . . how to get messages to Cargill, how to control them . . ." Wilson offered to undertake this task.

[18] Michael Andreas was caught on tape saying that Cargill would be unlikely to join "the club" (the G-4) at the beginning, but that it might want to do so later.

[19] It is known that Cargill joined ECAMA at some point during the conspiracy and supplied ECAMA with its monthly sales volumes. It is not clear whether Cargill gave its monthly volume to the G-4 directly. If the ADM-Cargill side deal aided in the propping up prices or allocating volume shares of the G-4 abroad, then Cargill could be sanctioned by the European Commission, Canada, Mexico, and other competition-law agencies.

[20] Compensation for non-member overcharges varies across federal court districts.

[21] Many prosecutors find the term "raid" pejorative because of its connotation of an undisciplined, savage attack. They prefer the blander expression "serving subpoenas and exercising search warrants." The temptation to yield to the concise if colorful term is irresistible.

[22]Jungbunzlauer in particular must have chaffed at the restrictions placed on its sales by the cartel. The company, it will be recalled, had the most ambitious expansion in the G-4 in the early 1990s, and as a result was probably operating at the lowest utilization rate. Moreover, by 1993, its new vertically integrated plant in France was producing low cost feedstock for all of its European plants. Typically, the lowest cost member of a cartel if it has some excess capacity, will have the greatest incentive to cheat or leave a cartel.

Chapter 6

ECONOMIC IMPACTS OF THE CITRIC ACID CARTEL

Market forces facing single producers usually overwhelm any attempts by a firm to deviate from its assigned role in an industry (see Chapter 2 above). With a given plant in place, once a seller in a competitive market observes the market price, it passively sets its output level at the profit-maximizing point. If, as was the case in the global market for citric acid, food-grade product made by alternative sellers was viewed by buyers as perfect substitutes, sellers have few strategic options to try to improve their profitability. Efforts by a firm to distinguish itself on the basis of delivery terms or after-sales service can easily be imitated by rivals. Investing in a lower cost production technology might yield better profits for a few years but carries the danger of operating at inefficiently low levels of utilization or betting on the wrong technology. Price cuts can be quickly matched by other sellers and can lead to a price war that hurts everyone until it is abandoned. Price increases for homogeneous products will lead to an erosion of a firm's market share and a build up in excess capacity that further squeeze margins.

While single-firm actions contrary to market forces are doomed to failure in most commodity markets, joint actions by a group of sellers large enough to dominate supply are another matter. For millennia, sellers have realized that collective action on prices or output levels can raise the profits of all suppliers in a market. The citric acid cartel met these criteria. It chose to raise selling prices simultaneously around the globe. With control of about two-thirds of the world's supply and a system for detecting and compensating for cheating by its members, the cartel clearly was efficacious in raising prices in at least North America and Europe. In this section, the effects of the cartel's collusive behavior on prices, international trade, profits, and consumer welfare in the U.S. market are detailed as precisely as possible.

PRICE EFFECTS

When the G-4 began meeting in 1991, they made agreements to raise their list prices. In some industries, like retail grocery stores, the price listed on the item or shelf is the actual price a buyer will pay at check-out. However, in many other industries, like automobiles, most consumers regard the list price as simply the highest price a seller hopes to get for the product, whereas after searching for alternative offer prices most buyers will purchase an automobile at a negotiated discount. List prices for most industrial commodities like citric acid follow the automobile model of pricing (see "Selling Practices" in Chapter 4 above).[1]

Citric acid prices are hard to find. Chemical-industry magazines occasionally published announcements of list prices of citric acid, particularly when fairly large increases were initiated and when all the major suppliers followed the movement in prices. Somewhat less frequently these magazines would summarize the transaction prices that buyers claimed to be paying (Connor 1998:55).[2] In December 1988, U.S. list prices of the most common type of citric acid were $0.81 per pound (i.e., full truckloads of acid delivered east of the Rockies at a 100% active-content strength). A year later, the list price had dropped to $0.75 per pound and kept falling to the summer and fall quarters of 1990 when it reached a low of $0.63 (see Figure 5.1). Press reports attributed this reduction in list prices by Pfizer and Haarmann & Reimer to the expectation that Cargill's new plant would pour vast quantities of citric acid onto the market. Throughout the latter half of 1990, Cargill fulfilled these expectations. Indeed, Cargill initiated the late 1990 price cuts as a way of quickly attracting new customers. A couple of trade magazine articles asserted that the largest buyers of citric acid were paying 6 to 10 cents per pound less than list price during this period. That is, by late 1990, U.S. manufacturers were selling citric acid to their most favored customers at $0.53 to $0.57 per pound. At those prices even Cargill's efficient operation was probably losing money.

By early 1991 conditions had changed. Pfizer had retreated from the industry, only to be replaced by Cargill's old nemesis, ADM, which was busy learning the new business and upgrading its acquired plant. More importantly, Cargill's plant was approaching its optimal level of utilization, so attracting a lot more market share was no longer such a high priority.[3] Thus, Cargill successfully led a list-price increase in February 1991 and another in August 1991, after which the cartel took over arranging price increases. List prices spiraled upward from February 1991 to October 1993, rising on average every six months by 3 cents per pound. From late 1993 to late 1996, U.S. list prices remained stuck at $0.85 per pound. The cartel was responsible for all the price changes during 1992-1993, and it was responsible for keeping the list price at $0.85 for a couple of years beyond that. Reported transaction prices were not far below list at this time, despite what the trade press called "ample supplies."

Although the citric acid cartel's crime was the agreement to fix *list* prices, the economic injuries caused to buyers must be assessed using *transaction* prices.[4] In a market like citric acid where there is no public price reporting, often only the sellers themselves know what transaction prices really are. Fortunately, a quasi-public source of quarterly average transaction prices was obtained, and there are good reasons to believe that these prices closely track the proprietary price information known to the sellers. U.S.

transaction prices for contract buyers of citric acid are shown in Figure 5.1 (and in more detail in Appendix 1 of Connor (1998) for 1987-1997).

The relationship between (delivered) list prices and (f.o.b.) transaction prices is just what would be expected. Contract prices are equal to or below list prices in every quarter from 1987 to 1997. When list prices fell during November 1989 to July 1990, contract prices fell below list prices within four months, and usually quicker. When list prices climbed from their low in January 1991 to the $0.85 plateau beginning October 1993, contract prices duly responded in the same direction with a short time lag. During the peak period of the cartel's operation in 1994, contract transaction prices hovered just 5 to 7 cents below list, just as had been previously reported by the trade press. The DOJ indictment specifies June 1995 as the end of formal collusion. Although transaction prices slipped slightly in the first quarter of 1995 (to $0.76 or 9 cents below list), they recovered in the second quarter (to $0.79 per pound). However, after June 1995, transaction prices slid slowly downward through 1997 as the power of the cartel faded.

It seems unrebuttable that from some time in 1991 (probably the summer) to at least as late as June 1995, the G-4 had its way with U.S. citric acid prices. Given the large amount of international trade in citric acid, prices in Canada, Mexico, and Western Europe must have responded closely in sympathy with those in the United States. Bayer was the sole manufacturer of citric acid in Latin America, and U.S. exports supplied much of the continent's needs, so it seems highly likely that the cartel was able to effectively raise prices to Latin American buyers as well. The situation in Asian markets is more murky. Here, China was a strong, low cost, and growing source of supply for citric acid, and no Chinese producers were cooperating with the G-4. It is unlikely that buyers in Asia were much affected by the cartel-induced high prices in North America and Europe, save for a few food manufacturers concerned about the levels of impurities found in some citric acid made in Asia.

There is one more price effect that seems to confirm the cartel's grip on market prices during 1991-1995. Recall that there are two kinds of transaction prices, spot and contract. During periods of normal competition, sellers are under pressure to give price concessions to contract buyers because they have time to shop around and because they buy in larger quantities than spot purchasers. That is, competition causes a significant gap between spot and contract prices. In citric acid, this is precisely the case. During every quarter of the pre-conspiracy period in 1990 and early 1991, spot buyers paid 4 percent more than contract buyers (Connor 1998:11). However, as soon as the cartel had begun exercising its collective power, the gap between the two prices practically disappeared. That is, contract buyers stopped getting discounts compared to spot buyers. Cartel discipline was such that searching for a lower price was a fruitless enterprise from late 1991 to early 1995. After the cartel stopped affecting prices, contract prices fell below spot once again.

The G-4 accomplished what it set out to do. Instead of observing a highly dispersed pattern in citric acid prices as one expects in a competitive market, the monopoly power of the cartel raised prices above competitive levels and made price movements over time immune to the forces of demand and supply. List prices were held fixed at $0.85 for an unprecedented 37 months, and contract prices hovered closely below list for much of that time. However, the cartel was successful in tilting the balance of power between buyer and seller. Instead of equally balanced contest of bargaining power over price, buyers were emasculated because the outcome was rigged.[5]

EFFECTS ON PRODUCTION

When a monopolistic group is successful in raising selling prices, most buyers bite their lips and continue buying at the higher prices. Buyers who remain in the market at the elevated price levels simply transfer income they would have earned themselves to the sellers. Most continue to buy because the quantities used of citric acid are relatively fixed. While no published studies of the elasticity of demand can be found, it stands to reason that a price increase for a minor ingredient among many food inputs is likely to continue to be purchased by food processors, particularly as citric acid helps preserve foods. Because demand is highly inelastic, the effects of monopoly pricing on industry efficiency are very small compared to the income-transfer effects (Chapter 2). Analyses of monopoly pricing in the food industries show that effects of power over price are typically at least ten times bigger than the effects on allocative efficiency (Connor *et al.* 1985).

Production was affected by the volume quotas allocated to each member of the G-4. The effective monthly monitoring of sales volumes by Mr. Huari of Hoffmann-La Roche, coupled with annual checking by independent Swiss auditors, left little room for cheating by the conspirators. In May 1991, each member of the G-4 agreed to accept an annual tonnage quota expressed by percentage of global sales volume by the cartel. Bayer/Haarmann & Reimer was awarded the largest share of 34 percent. The other three companies got 27.5 percent (ADM), 24 percent (Jungbunzlauer), and 14.5 percent (Hoffmann-La Roche) of total cartel sales.[6] Actual production by each member adhered very closely to the cartel's planned production (Tr. 2642-2645). Inefficiencies result with fixed quotas of this kind, because lower cost members of the cartel are unable to expand their shares over time at the expense of their less-efficient co-conspirators.

Using percentages of global sales volume as an allocative device was clever from the point of view of preserving cartel harmony. By assigning market shares on a global level, the cartel avoided the discord that would arise from having to negotiate national or regional shares. Any producer is likely to react negatively to an invasion of its traditional home markets by an outsider. Such actions by a fellow member of a cartel would be even more intolerable.

However, the G-4 explicitly avoided assigning such territorial shares. Not only was needless friction avoided, but also the chance of detection by national antitrust authorities was reduced. With exclusive territories, buyers are more likely to complain about refusals to deal by suppliers that had reached their cartel-granted regional limits.

Finally, the pattern of capacity expansions suggests that the cartel's members decided to slow down their rates of investments during 1991-1995.[7] In the U.S. industry, both ADM and Bayer essentially froze in their capacities. (Tables 4.A.1 and 4.A.2). Even Cargill's capacity investments were modest. In Europe, Jungbunzlauer implemented at most one expansion project among its three plants; Bayer may have slightly raised the capacity of one of its six plants; and Hoffmann-La Roche stood pat. To summarize, the four cartel members expanded capacity by about 20 percent from 1993-1997, whereas all other producers of citric acid in the world expanded by 67% (of which Chinese companies grew by 110 percent). As often happens to companies in monopolized industries, they grow fat on profits but lose their dynamism and agility. Moreover, unable to blockade entry, the high cartel-induced prices prompt hungry outsiders to do more than merely nibble from the crumbs that fall from the cartel's table.

EFFECTS ON INTERNATIONAL TRADE

The pattern of trade among nations was notably altered by the cartel's operations. In the United States, just before the cartel was launched the drop in citric acid prices surrounding Cargill's entry in 1990 caused a long-term upward trend in imports to be reversed. At the same time, the vast expansion of capacity created production in excess of domestic needs and prices favorable to a marked jump in exports. However, during the heyday of the cartel, the brief export surplus turned to a huge export deficit for the United States. The deficit was much larger than would have occurred in the absence of the cartel. In addition, there is some evidence that the cartel divided export markets between the European and North American producers and extended their power by price discriminating among destinations for exports. The G-4's attempt to cow Chinese producers into voluntarily reducing exports to the West seems to have had only a temporary impact. The demise of the cartel in early 1995 has led to a restoration of pre-cartel trends in overall imports and exports.

One reason for dwelling on trade patterns is because they are among the few truly transparent pieces of economic activity consistently available before, during, and after the conspiracy. Governments dutifully collect data on traded quantities and values of goods and publish these data even if only one company is responsible for all the imports into or exports out of the country. Sellers in concentrated industries usually follow trade trends carefully to alert them to changes in the locations of production, in pricing policies of rivals, or other strategic indicators of the behavior of rival sellers. U.S. data are particularly detailed: monthly quantities and values are available on the Worldwide Web for both citric acid and citric-salts within three months of actual shipment dates. Up to 80 national destinations are available for citric acid exports. Information on ports of entry and exit for traded goods can provide additional strategic information for geographically dispersed industries.

Imports

Imports of bulk citric chemicals (citric acid, sodium citrate, potassium citrate, and other citric salts) rose throughout the 1980s (Figure 6.1). The two domestic producers continuously lost market share to imports, partly because Pfizer and Bayer's U.S. subsidiary were collusively raising domestic prices during the decade. By 1989, the last year that the U.S. industry was a duopoly, imports accounted for 22 percent of U.S. demand (Table 4.A.1).

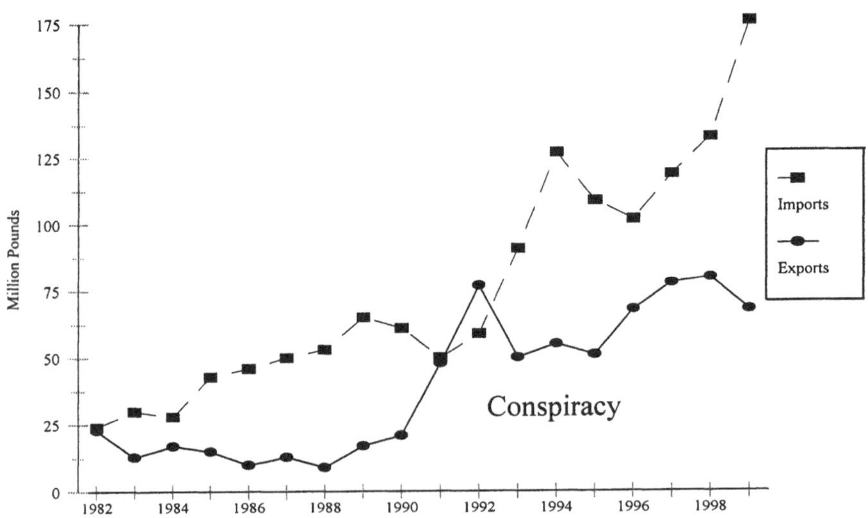

Figure 6.1. U.S. Imports and Exports of Citric Acid and Its Salts, 1982-1999.

In 1988, for example, imports were arriving at U.S. ports from nine major countries (i.e., a country accounting for at least 1 percent of total import volume). Imports were undercutting U.S. producers by selling at $0.30 per pound (Table 4.A.2). However, 90 percent of imported citric acid was imported from five companies with plants located in eight countries. Roche accounted for 36 percent of U.S. imports, four-fifths of that from its big Belgian plant and the rest from Mexico. Jungbunzlauer supplied another 32 percent of the U.S. import volume from its plants in Austria (mostly liquid acid) and Germany (almost all anhydrous salts). The three smaller importers were Godot of Israel (14 percent), the UK firm Sturges (5 percent), and a small plant in Canada owned by Pfizer (1%). The final significant source of citric acid were several small Chinese manufacturers which were able to sell to buyers in the United States at prices 10 percent lower than the other importers. Although supplying only 10 percent of U.S. imports in 1989, China's share had risen throughout the decade, a development that must have been worrisome to the major U.S. and European producers.

The Chinese challenge became a major problem when the cartel successfully raised prices in North America and Europe. Price fixing caused U.S. transactions prices to rise by more than 30 percent from 1991 to 1994 when they reached almost $0.80 per pound. High U.S. prices were a bonanza for exporters to the United States. The volume of Chinese imports exploded, rising by 150 percent from 1988 to 1994 (and by 50% from 1992 to 1994 alone). In 1994, Chinese imports were selling at prices 19 cents lower (28 percent lower) than imports from the cartel. Moreover, with the high prices as an incentive, imports flooded in from Israel, Indonesia, India, and other less developed countries that were able to compete on price even though they lacked the most modern facilities. These imports replaced those by the Swiss cartel members. The share of U.S. imports accounted for by cartel members' plants shrank to less than 45 percent in 1994 from over 70 percent in 1988.

The cartel's solution to the upsurge in Chinese exports to the United States and Europe was quite effective. As recounted earlier in this chapter, one of the cartel's U.S. members lobbied the office of the U.S. Trade Representative, which announced proposed prohibitive tariffs on Chinese imports of citric acid. Last minute concessions by the Chinese government prevented final implementation of this punishment, among which was cancellation of export subsidies for its citric acid makers. The mere threat of tariffs may have been enough because Chinese imports fell substantially from 1994 to 1995. Recall that the cartel also sent a couple of conspirators to the Chinese trade association for citric acid manufacturers threatening an anti-dumping action by the European Union. Voluntary restraints on exports by Chinese manufacturers combined with the end of subsidies might have given the cartel another year or two to prop up prices in their home regions, but the break up of the cartel by May or June of 1995 makes that prediction moot.

By 1998, three years after the cartel ceased to collude formally, imports from Europe had still not recovered to the level of the 1980s. Jungbunzlauer held on about 27 percent of total U.S. imports, but Roche's position had greatly deteriorated (its share was less than one-fourth what it had been in 1988). China and Israel were now supplying over 60 percent of U.S. import volume, and Chinese suppliers still managed to undersell all other importers with prices 22 percent lower.

Exports

The effects of the cartel on U.S. exports of citric acid and salts were even more profound than its impact on imports. The last "normal" year for the U.S. industry seems to be 1990, the first year of operation for Cargill's new plant and the last year before collusion began. The creation overnight of 17 percent more U.S. productive capacity caused prices to decline to the low $0.60 range during most of 1990 and 1991. Otherwise excess capacity was shifted to export sales as foreign demand surged: export volume rose 140 percent one year after and 285 percent two years after the 1990 base year. In 1992, the United States enjoyed its first export surplus in citric acid and salts (Figure 6.1).

However, this renaissance of American international competitiveness was cut short by the G-4's success in raising prices. The high prices in Europe and North America discouraged exports, despite more-than-adequate plant capacities. (Global utilization rates dropped to 69 to 74 percent in 1993-1994 and were probably even lower among the cartel members). U.S. exports during 1992-1995 dropped back to the same quantity as the base year 1990.

As soon as the cartel ceased to operate, U.S. exports once again took off. From the cartel's most disciplined year, 1994, export volume rose by 44 percent in three years, far surpassing even the previous peak in 1992. Thus, through its indisputable impact on U.S. prices, the citric acid conspiracy restrained the volume of exports and artificially stimulated imports. Without the cartel its seems that during the years 1992-1995 the U.S. balance of trade was adversely affected to the tune of about $200 million (Connor 1998:24). This was a significant additional burden on the chronic merchandise trade deficit.

Trade Distortion

Although the cartel's manipulation of prices was probably the main reason for the increase in the overall export gap, there may have been formal and informal restraints on export quantities as well. Formal allocation of exclusive territories to cartel members frequently accompanies price fixing, but there is no hint that this occurred in the G-4's deliberations. Nevertheless, the dictates of cartel harmony may well have encouraged its members to avoid poaching on sales to the home areas of other members, or other regions over which a traditional export hegemony existed.

Looking simply at U.S. exports, there is some support for the idea that U.S. producers forbade exporting to areas historically supplied by Bayer and Jungbunzlauer from their European plant locations. (Bayer's U.S. subsidiary would doubtless be most sensitive to this issue, if not ordered to do so). In 1990, at least 21 percent of the U.S. exported volume of citric acid and its salts was destined to Western Europe. However, during the three high years of the cartel, only 1 percent of U.S. exports ended up in Western Europe; moreover, the small amounts of citric acid that did dribble into Germany, France, and the Netherlands were priced way above the average export price, as though U.S. companies were imposing some kind of private export tariff. As soon as the cartel died, exports to Western Europe resumed forcefully. Export volume during 1996-1998 was *six times* higher than the volume during 1993-1995.

Because of their geographic proximity, Africa and the Middle East (West Asia) are often regarded by European exporters as traditionally hegemonic areas. Even U.S. companies often serve these areas from their European subsidiaries. While the Middle East was too remote to attract significant U.S. exports at any time in the 1990s, African exports fit the pattern of export-forbearance behavior. In 1990, Africa was destination of 7.5 percent of U.S. citric acid exports. During the conspiracy years, they dropped to less than one-tenth of 1 percent of the total exported. Once again, after 1995, African exports bounced back to measurable levels. The regularity and large size of these export cycles offers compelling evidence that ADM and Bayer demonstrated great deference to their European partners, Roche and Jungbunzlauer, by curtailing exports to Europe and Africa. Once the cartel broke up, these became contestable markets for U.S. importers.

On the other hand, U.S. exports to many other more contestable areas show few effects of distortion due to cartel behavior. The share of citric acid being shipped to Canada and Mexico rose throughout the 1990s. Exports to Latin America became more diversified, but the overall share did not change appreciably. U.S. exports to Asia and Oceania rose in relative importance during the early 1990s, but then declined after the cartel's demise. Although Bayer was the dominant producer in Mexico and South America, in this area poaching was permitted or tolerated by the cartel. It is also the case that many Latin American and Asian countries are quite exposed to competition from Chinese producers, so the cartel members may have felt impotent or fatalistic in the face of this strong competitive force. Whatever the explanation, it appears that U.S. manufacturers have been unable to capture even a constant share of the citric acid markets of these two fastest-growing continents.

Geographic Price Discrimination

As a rule, a monopolist can make more money by charging different prices to different customers than by uniform pricing.[8] Whether the cartel took further advantage of its market power by pricing discriminately across export destinations is not clear in the citric acid case.

During the conspiracy years 1992-1995, average annual U.S. export prices were \$0.77, \$0.78, and \$0.81/lb for citric acid. Exports to Canada, which absorbed 39% to 56% of all such exports, were priced at or below the average price (as much as 9% below in 1995), a pattern that continued after the cartel's demise. As these are border prices and the Canadian border was closer to the centroid of U.S. production than the average ocean port, the 2- to 4-cent discount on Canadian export may well be explained by transportation costs. Ignoring very small shipments (less than 10 metric tones per annum), U.S. exports to Western Europe were priced very high by the cartel (and by "nonmember" Cargill), about $1.35/lb or almost double the average price. After the cartel disbanded in 1996-1997, the average price to Western European destinations was much less ($0.86/lb), but still higher than the average global export price of $0.72/lb. Although these averages support the idea of price discrimination between Canada and Western Europe, the practice was not uniform across European destinations. Exports to Mexico, Australia, and New Zealand (all large customers) followed the low-priced Canadian pattern, whereas exports to most Latin American destinations resembled the Western European (very high to slightly high) pattern of prices. What is clear is that the variation in export prices across export destinations was much less after the cartel's break-up than during the conspiracy period. This is not, of course, proof of price discrimination, but it is highly suggestive of geographic third-degree price discrimination, for which market power is a necessary condition.

THE CUSTOMER OVERCHARGE

The principal measure of economic harm caused by an effective price-fixing conspiracy is the consumer (or customer) overcharge.[9] This is a monetary measure of the extra costs incurred by buyers as a direct result of the actions of the conspiratorial group. The overcharge is conceptually identical to the extra profits generated for all sellers in the affected market, save for any extra costs incurred by sellers in operating the cartel. It is doubtful that the managerial costs of operating the cartel amounted to more than a couple of million dollars, so they will be ignored. Note that the overcharge essentially equals the additional profits of *all cooperating suppliers in the market*, not just those that were in the cartel.[10] The size of the overcharge is critical to assessing fines by antitrust officials and to guide private parties in seeking compensation. Defendants in such proceedings may not deduct the costs of operating the cartel nor the costs of legal advice.

In principle, figuring the size of an overcharge is a relatively straightforward arithmetic exercise. However, calculating the size of monopoly overcharges requires accurate information on the volume sold in the relevant market, the length of the conspiracy-effects period, actual selling prices, and the price that would have reigned "but-for" the actions of the conspirators. These data are subject to estimation errors.

The two major sources of data on the size of the U.S. citric (acid and salts) market are not perfectly consistent. The last survey of the U.S.

International Trade Commission on the organic chemical industry reported that total 1994 sales of the three domestic manufacturers were 312.3 million pounds that generated f.o.b. manufacturers' revenues of $251 million (USITC). Net imports of citric products were 54.9 million pounds worth $26.8 million at border prices ($0.651/pound for imports and $0.816/pound for exports). *Delivered* prices for citric products would raise the price of imports in the eastern United States to $0.81/pound; moreover, delivery charges of about 3 cents per pound for average truckload would raise the f.o.b. domestic price from $0.804 to about $0.834 (comfortingly close to the export border price).[11] Thus, the ITC data imply a U.S. buyers' purchase value of $215 million for domestic product (domestic production less export volume) and $89 million for imported material, or $304 million total.

On the other hand, 1994 consumption estimates from seemingly reliable trade sources indicate a much higher 440 million pound level; using delivered prices U.S. buyers paid $350 million for citric acid and its salts (Table 4.A.1). There being no way to reconcile the two sources, we can only present both figures as a range of probable sales.

Overcharge estimates are sensitive to a number of assumptions, most notably the "but-for" price, the market price that would have been observed had there been no cartel. For the seven months prior to the cartel's formation, the contract prices for citric acid ranged from $0.60 to $0.62/pound. Cargill's new plant was already operating nearly at full capacity, so the period January-June 1991 seems like a reasonable one to choose to find a pre-cartel equilibrium price. However, about 18 months after the conspiracy ended, spot transactions prices had drifted only down to $0.67 or $0.68/lb., so the post-cartel period prices suggest that the but-for price could have been as high as $0.68/lb. At $0.68, the overcharges would be a bit over half of the estimates made using $0.60. Under an array of cost assumptions, the citric overcharge estimates vary from $161 to $309 million, or 11% to 21% of purchase value (Table 6.1).

The dates of the conspiracy are also crucial to determining the extent of overcharges imposed on buyers of citric products. In ADM's plea agreement (whose terms were negotiated with the DOJ prior to filing with the Court in October 1996), the period is vaguely identified as commencing "at least as early as January 1993" and ending June 1995 or a minimum of 2.5 years.[12] However, it is now known that collusion by the G-4 began in March 1991, and prices began to respond a few months later. In fact, the DOJ indictments later (1997) filed against ADM's three Swiss co-conspirators, the beginning date for the conspiracy is given to be July 1991. Moreover, it is likely that the price-fixing conspiracy's *effects* on the market lingered well beyond June 1995 even though the conspiracy itself had ended. The longer period July 1991 to December 1995 produces very different estimates, because the quantity purchased rises.

Table 6.1 Estimates of Citric Acid Overcharges in the U.S. Market.

Alternative Conspiracy Periods	"But-For Price" (Competitive Price Assumption)			Implicit Overcharge from DOJ's Criminal Fines[a]
	$0.60	$0.64	$0.68	
			Million Dollars[b]	
Short (1/93-6/95)	205	160	116	180-250
Long (7/91-12/95)	309	233	161	180-250
			Percent of Sales	
Short	24	19	14	17-29
Long	21	16	11	10-17

Source: Author's computations, see text and Table 4.A.2.
[a] Based on fines paid by the most uncooperative cartel members, Hoffmann-La Roche and Jungbunzlauer. The DOJ probably used the short cartel period. (See Chapter 13 for a discussion).
[b] Range is due to uncertainty about the effective cartel period assumed by the DOJ and the existence of discounts on criminal fines awarded to "cooperating" members of the cartel.

The implied overcharge then is from $161 to $309 million. The criminal fines paid by the conspirators provide a cross check on these estimates because the fines are based on overcharge estimates from confidential records. These fines suggest an overcharge well within the other derived estimates.

In sum, the citric acid cartel imposed a monopoly tax on buyers that caused prices to rise from 10 to 25 percent of sales.

CONCLUSIONS

The story of the legal battles that erupted when the citric acid cartel was unmasked is the subject of Chapters 13, 14 and 16. However, the economic side of the story told in this chapter provides a number of important lessons.

First, the citric acid cartel was able to be formed and to operate undetected for three or four years because its members were leading firms in highly concentrated, homogeneous-product oligopolies with substantial entry barriers into the relevant markets. Despite the failure of the citric acid cartel to secure the *direct* participation of the newest U.S. manufacturer, Cargill's indirect or tacit cooperation contributed to the cartel's ability to sustain monopolistic U.S. prices. Overcharges imposed on U.S. buyers of citric acid were at least $116 million but could have reached as high as $309 million. Market structure matters.

Second, the effectiveness of the cartel came about in spite of significant differences in geographic location and business cultures. Bayer's U.S. subsidiary doubtless smoothed such differences when forming the citric acid cartel. Geographic and cultural propinquity may well facilitate joint profit maximization, but it should not be regarded as a necessary condition.

Third in the late 1990s, there were ample signs that the world citric acid industry was becoming less concentrated. While the producers that had been members of the conspiracy continue to announce expansion of capacity in their home markets in North America and Western Europe, the rate of expansion is higher elsewhere. The greatest rates of growth in production of citric acid are now being observed in the larger, newly industrializing countries: Brazil, India, Indonesia, Thailand, and above all China. In a few cases these new plants are being constructed by leading Western firms. Cargill began making citric acid in India in 1994 and in Brazil in 1999; Jungbunzlauer formed an Indonesian joint venture in the early 1990s; Roche started a new plant in China in 1999. However, in the majority of cases the investors are new players. Citric acid plants are beginning production in India (Tate & Lyle), Thailand (Mitsubishi), China (Fuso Chemical), and Saudi Arabia (Bajrai). Most of these latter plants involve local partners. Thus, both the location of production and the ownership of capacity is slowly becoming more dispersed. The formation of naked cartels in the global citric acid industry is becoming correspondingly less likely.

Chapter 6 Endnotes

[1] Technically, supermarket shelf prices are *posted* prices. A posted pricing system guarantees buyers can purchase all the supply available at the listed, nonnegotiable price. In the citric acid market, most sales were by contracts that were *private treaties*. The transaction price was privately negotiated with the list price simply the starting point of the negotiation. Actual prices varied according to the amount purchased and the bargaining abilities of the two parties (Marion *et al.* 1987).

[2] Reports of prices paid by procurement managers must be treated with caution. Knowing that their remarks are likely to be printed, these managers would be tempted to understate their prices out of pride or in order to place pressure on sellers to lower their transaction prices. Alternately, procurement managers, may inflate reported prices if they believe they received an extraordinary discount so as to hide the fact from other buyers who would be tempted to demand such discounts for themselves.

[3] In addition to press reports to this effect, the fact that Cargill increased its plant size by 45 percent in 1991 confirms that it was approaching full utilization in early 1991.

[4] The courtroom testimony by Barrie Cox confirms that the list prices reported by the trade press were also ADM's list prices and that the G-4 was responsible for all but the first two increases (Tr. 2679-2685). Of course, the cartel knew that changes in transaction prices would follow their agreements to fix list prices. The agreements on volume shares and discount policies reinforced the tendency of transaction prices to follow the lead of list prices.

[5] My apologies to modern professional women for apparently sexist terminology. However, I am not aware of a gender neutral term with comparable emotive connotations.

[6] When Ferruzzi (now Eridania) joined the cartel, it was given a 4 percent share and the G-4 members' shares were reduced accordingly.

[7] Allowing for the usual two-year lag between the start of capacity expansion and production, this shows up in annual capacities during 1993-1997.

[8] Profitable third-degree price discrimination requires that demand areas have varying degrees of price elasticity of demand. Moreover, buyers should not be able to resell to each other (geographic arbitrage). Given these two conditions, a cartel will find it more profitable to sell at higher prices in the price-inelastic markets than uniform pricing.

[9] See Chapter 2. The dead weight loss is smaller but also significant. To calculate the dead-weight loss requires information on the over-price elasticity of demand (Peterson and Connor 1997).

[10] Under U.S. antitrust law in most U.S. court districts, guilty conspirators are legally liable for their own ill-gotten gains as well as the monopoly profits of non-conspirators who merely followed the cartel's lead by raising prices independently of any agreement. In the case of the U.S. citric acid market the monopoly profits of Cargill are part of the injury caused to buyers, even if it was not part of the conspiracy. The same applies to the lowest Chinese exporter that in all likelihood was selling citric acid at a price at least 10 cents lower than its cartel rivals.

[11] The actual transaction prices for citric acid were revealed by the four defendants to plaintiffs during the pretrial discovery phase. The transaction prices shown in Figure 1 track the confidential defendants' prices well.

[12] This claim allowed ADM *et al.* to assert that the pre-conspiracy price in December 1992 (hence, arguably the but-for price) was $0.79 per pound. With transaction prices averaging around $0.82 per pound and volume sold out of about 1.3 billion pounds, the ADM overcharge would be only $39 million – which is exactly what ADM offered to pay civil plaintiffs in September 1996! Because civil procedures do not allow plaintiffs access to DOJ files and the plea agreement is considered unimpeachable evidence in a civil trial for damages, the members of the federal class action suit (accounting for two-thirds of purchases) had little choice but to accept the settlement offered by ATM *et al.*

Chapter 7

THE WORLD LYSINE INDUSTRY[1]

The modern lysine industry developed as a result of basic scientific discoveries in biochemistry in the late 1950s. The now dominant method of industrial production of lysine is based on fermentation of liquid sweeteners derived from sugar cane or starches of many kinds. Since being commercially introduced around 1960, manufacturers of mixed animal feeds have grown to view lysine as an essential ingredient. In the last four decades of the 20th century, lysine has grown and developed into a major biochemical product market, attracting more and more biotech companies from Asia, North America, and Europe to the industry. The purpose of this chapter is to sketch the uses, methods of production, market size, and structure of supply of the global lysine market.

THE PRODUCT AND ITS USES

Lysine is an amino acid, an organic chemical essential for the growth of muscle tissue in humans and animals. There are about 20 amino acids manufactured in commercial quantities worldwide. Lysine is one of three amino acids that dominate sales of these types of organic chemicals.[2]

Most animals produce some lysine *in vivo,* but to sustain optimal growth supplies of lysine must be obtained from ingested foods or feeds. Grains and grasses are low in lysine content. Humans and pets usually obtain sufficient amounts of lysine from consuming marine or animal products, but certain vegetables, soybeans in particular, are also good sources of amino acids. During famines when the consumption of seafood, poultry, or meat declines, symptoms of amino-acid deficiency can be observed. However, the principal use of food-grade lysine in high-income countries today is by body-builders aiming to increase muscle mass.

More than 90 percent of the volume of lysine manufactured in the 1990s was purchased by producers of mixed animal feed. Lysine is one of the major ingredients included in the concentrates that are added to rough grains and oilseed meals to make balanced feeds for farm animals.[3] The amino acids in balanced feeds help to stimulate the rate of growth and lean muscle development of poultry, swine, fish, and other monogastric animals.[4] Animal breeders have been developing varieties of swine and poultry that can absorb higher levels of lysine, which allows for shorter growing cycles and brings to market animals with lower fat and higher proportions of muscle tissue. Consumer desires for low-fat meats and farm-raised seafood in high-income countries, coupled with the increased demand for high-protein foods generally in middle-income countries, is ultimately responsible for the rapid growth in demand for lysine and other feed additives.

Feed-grade lysine, the focus of this chapter, is sold in two forms. The original and still dominant product form is a brownish powder sold in bags. For swine, this dry form of lysine is mixed at a rate of about 12 to 24 pounds per short ton of 2000 pounds, so a little bit goes a long way. Dry lysine is storable for at least several months and, because it is so concentrated, is nearly the only type seen in long distance shipments such as international trade. A second type of lysine that was sold in small quantities in the mid 1990s is liquid lysine. This type of lysine was actually an intermediate product of lysine manufacturing that was cheaper to make (on a 100-percent-active basis) because it avoided the extra costs of drying and bagging.[5] However, customers needed special equipment to store and spray the liquid lysine on the animal feed, and the high water content made shipping costs prohibitive for customers more than a couple of hundred miles removed from a lysine factory. Although the liquid form of lysine was growing faster than dry lysine, in 1994 aqueous lysine accounted for less than 2.5 percent of global lysine production volume. The distinction between dry and liquid feed-grade lysine became an issue during the prosecution of the cartel.[6]

Lysine is an organic chemical with a unique molecular structure. Nevertheless, manufactured lysine does have some practically perfect substitutes as additives in animal feeds. Two commonly used high-protein enrichments to feed grains are fish meal and oilseed meals. Both meals are naturally high in lysine. Fish meal is a popular feed additive in Japan and northern Europe. However, because animal and fish products can cause human health problems and indirectly degrade surface water and groundwater supplies, farm producers have been moderating their use of such proteins. In North America soybean cake, a by-product of vegetable-oil processing, is the principal high-protein feed additive. As a general rule, 97 pounds of corn mixed with 3 pounds of manufactured lysine is nutritionally equivalent to 100 pounds of soybean meal as a lysine supplement. So, from the point of view of a swine or poultry producer, if the price of soymeal dips low enough (or if the price of the complementary feed grain rises high enough), the producer will cease buying lysine and switch to soymeal, fishmeal, or another high protein substitute. Thus, grain and oilseed prices at times placed a ceiling on how high lysine prices could go.

TECHNOLOGY OF PRODUCTION

Before 1960, lysine was extracted from vegetable proteins by means of chemical hydrolysis. This process yielded natural lysine that organic chemical companies sold for $3 to $5 per pound. This is still the method employed to make most pharmaceutical-grade lysine, but the selling price makes such lysine too costly to be used by feed manufacturers on a regular basis.

In 1956, a Japanese biochemist (Professor Yoshio Okada of Osaka University) discovered that the metabolic processes of certain strains of bacteria produced an amino acid (glutamic acid). Within a few years, the Japanese food and drug manufacturer Kyowa Hakko was selling commercial quantities of monosodium glutamate (MSG) using this new fermentation process. Kyowa Hakko's technology used sucrose in the form of inexpensive molasses as the feedstock to produce glutamic acid (one of the amino acids) which was then converted into the salt sodium glutamate. By 1958, Kyowa Hakko had developed another commercially viable technology to make lysine from fermentation (Connor 2000:Appendix E).

Working on a parallel scientific track, the larger Japanese food processing company Ajinomoto also exploited the newly discovered fermentation technologies. Ajinomoto had become the world's first manufacturer of MSG soon after the compound was discovered by a scientist at the University of Tokyo in 1908. Between the two world wars, Ajinomoto consolidated its near monopoly on MSG by setting up a vast network of international sales offices. By the late 1950s, Ajinomoto was manufacturing both MSG and pharmaceutical-grade lysine with a process that used dextrose as the feedstock for bacterial fermentation. Because the new technology yielded amino acids at considerably lower costs than the traditional chemical-extraction method, sales of lysine for animal feeds became economical. By 1960, Ajinomoto had begun selling feed-grade lysine in the domestic market. Exports of feed-grade lysine from Japan began before 1970.

Both Kyowa Hakko and Ajinomoto have continued to be leaders in basic and applied research in fermentation processes, genetic engineering, and other biotechnologies that have led to improved methods of manufacturing amino acids, most of which are consumed by the feeds industry. Both companies benefited from substantial research and development (R&D) subsidies for biotech companies organized by Japan's Ministry of International Trade and Industry in the early 1980s. They both own patents on the most efficient microbial strains, and many of the exact details of the lysine production process continue to be protected by company secrecy. For example, the contents of the sweet soup that is fed to the microorganisms may have 20 or more components. Moreover, several of the best genetically modified microbial strains are now zealously protected by patents.

HISTORY OF THE INDUSTRY

Lysine is one of many products of the industry known internationally as the starch industry. Starch is extracted from cereals, tubers, and roots by mechanical, chemical, and biological processes that separate these raw materials' fibers from their proteins (Sansivini and Verzoni 1998). The major types of products of the starch industry included unmodified starches (potato starch, corn starch, tapioca, etc.), sweeteners (fructose, glucose, dextrose, etc.), proteins (corn gluten), vegetable oils, and modified starches. Vitamins and amino acids are the principal examples of modified starches, though they can also be made from other carbohydrates such as sucrose (cane or beet sugar). The world starch industry produced approximately 33 million metric tonnes of starch products in 1992.[7] The manufacturing-level value of global production was roughly $14 billion, of which half originated in the United States.

The largest starchy input was corn (maize), accounting for about 64 percent of the volume of final starch products in 1992. The other major raw materials include sweet potato (13 percent) and cassava or manioc (11 percent) in tropical areas and wheat (6 percent) and potato (6 percent) in temperate zones. The United States is home to almost two-thirds of the world's corn-based starch industry, with most of the rest split between Europe and Asia.

The U.S. starch industry is so highly dependant on maize as its raw material that it is called the corn-wet-milling or corn-refining industry. The U.S. corn-wet-milling industry began as early as the 1840s using chemical separation methods (Connor and Scheik 1997). In addition to corn starch and corn oil, early products included low intensity corn sweeteners. The dollar value of shipments grew by about 7 percent per year in the 19th century, but slowed to 4 to 5 percent from 1900 to 1967 (about 2 to 3 percent in real terms). Around 1967, the industry entered a period of explosive growth that would last almost two decades.

The principal cause of the high growth in corn wet milling from 1968 to about 1986 was the introduction of one new product: high fructose corn syrup (HFCS). The value of shipments of corn sweeteners increased ten-fold from 1967 to 1987 (Connor and Schiek 1997:487), and very little of that growth could be attributed to the industry's traditional sweeteners, dextrose and glucose corn syrup. The volume growth of HFCS was about 10 percent per year, much of it due to substitution of fructose for sucrose, a process that came to a sudden halt about 1986 or 1987.[8] After 1987, volume growth of HFCS slowed to about 3 percent annually. Ironically, the microbial fermentation technology that made the HFCS industry possible was originally licensed from a Japanese Ministry of Agriculture research unit (Mueller *et al.* 1982). This technology was licensed by Clinton Corn Products Company, which was acquired by ADM in the early 1970s. It was ADM's technical experience with the dextrose-fermentation technology used to make HFCS that allowed ADM to consider entering lysine production in the late 1980s.

The Lysine Industry Up to 1990

Ajinomoto and Kyowa Hakko both began manufacturing lysine in Japan around 1960. The first references to the location of their plants in trade magazines is in the 1970s (Connor 1999:8-11). Ajinomoto's plant in Saga Prefecture near the city of Fukuoka used dextrose as its principal intermediate material; Kyowa's plant in Hofu near the western tip of Honshu Island utilized molasses. Increased global demand for lysine soon outstripped the capacity of the two pioneering plants in Japan.

Both companies invested abroad in the decade of the 1970s. First, Ajinomoto established a joint venture in France named Eurolysine in 1974. Ostensibly a 50-50 joint venture between Ajinomoto and Orsan, Eurolysine's plant near Amiens came on stream a few years later.[9] Eurolysine's plant utilized sugar beets as its primary raw material. This plant was expanded at least four times in the 1980s, making it the largest lysine plant in the world from 1980 to 1990. Second, Kyowa Hakko set up a lysine joint venture in Mexico in the late 1970s with Mexican government participation called Fermentaciones Mexicanos (or Fermex). Fermex began production at this Veracruz-area plant on a very small scale in 1980, probably utilizing molasses from the local cane-sugar industry. Two expansions in the 1980s brought the plant up to medium size by 1990.

Thus, until 1980 the world lysine industry was a duopoly consisting of two Japanese firms, each with two plants.[10] Both companies were recognized as leaders in Japan's highly advanced biotechnology industry, indeed both subsequently claimed to have first commercialized the production of lysine via fermentation of sugars. Both were food and beverage manufacturers with sidelines in pharmaceuticals and amino acids. Ajinomoto was larger in terms of sales and employment and was also about twice the size of Kyowa in terms of global lysine market share.

The duopoly became a triopoly in 1980 with the entry of the Miwon Group of South Korea. Miwon was an industrial-financial conglomerate of several operating companies with minority interests in each other but under the ultimate control of one family, the Lims (Connor 2000:Appendix E). These are called *chaebols*. Although Miwon ranks only somewhere between 25th and 30th largest among the country's *chaebols,* the conglomerate was somewhat specialized in consumer processed foods and agri-products processing. Miwon's assets devoted to animal feeds and starch processing operated under the Sewon name. In the late 1970s, Sewon believed itself to be the third largest Asian manufacturer of animal feeds, starch, and related products. The two largest were Japanese firms.

Sewon built a moderate-size lysine plant in Busan, South Korea in the late 1970s which came on stream in early 1980. The type and source of Sewon's technology of production is unknown. It is apparent from its subsequent behavior that Sewon was implementing a marketing strategy fairly common among South Korean manufacturers. Sewon would aim at steadily increasing its global market share by exporting from a single plant in Korea that would be relentlessly expanded through massive borrowing. By 1990, Sewon's plant had been significantly expanded on three occasions to six times its original capacity, and all but a tiny portion of its production would be exported.

The estimated size of lysine plant capacity is shown for the years 1980 to 1990 in Figure 7.1. Size is measured by the announced annual designed finishing capacity for each lysine plant. This so-called nameplate capacity overstates the economically most efficient rate of production by 10 to 20 percent. When a plant first comes on stream in the lysine industry, it typically takes two or three years to reach its optimal level of utilization. However, in the long run a company's share of world capacity closely tracks its share of global production.

In 1980, Ajinomoto's two production units gave it about 60 percent of the global production potential. Large capital expenditures for expansions of its Japanese and French plants as well as new plants in Thailand and the United States, allowed Ajinomoto to hold on to its dominant global position throughout the 1980s. Kyowa built the first plants in North America, beginning with a small plant in Mexico that opened in 1980. Kyowa's U.S. plant was located in Missouri on the Mississippi River, allowing the plant inexpensive access to molasses made in the sugar-cane areas down river. Kyowa's plant, operated by its wholly owned U.S. subsidiary Biokyowa, came on stream in 1984. Ajinomoto's similarly sized plant in Iowa began production two years later; this plant used dextrose piped to it from an adjacent corn refinery operated by Cargill. Ajinomoto's global capacity increased from 44 million pounds in 1980 to 170 million in 1990, yet the other producers were building so quickly that Ajinomoto's share peaked in the late 1980s, slipping to just below 50 percent by 1990 (Figure 7.1). Kyowa Hakko's production capacity rose from about 11 million pounds to more than 90 million during the same period; its share rose from 15 to 27 percent. Finally, Sewon's impressive expansions in South Korea raised its global share from 15 percent in 1980 to 19 percent by 1990.

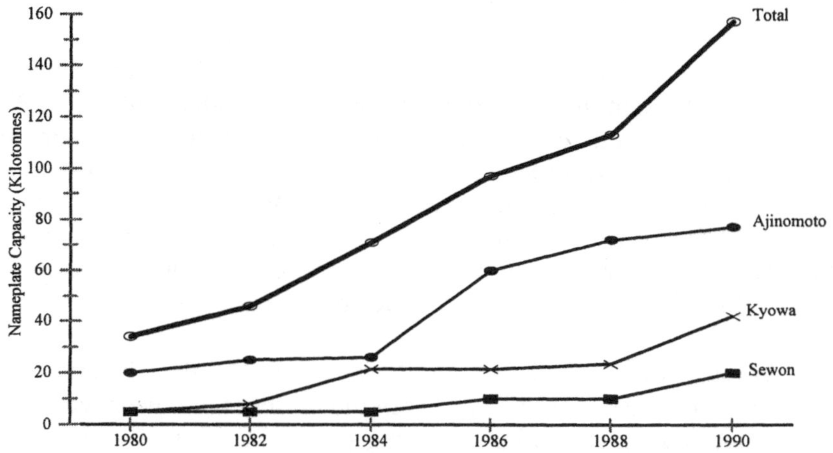

Figure 7.1. The Evolution of Global Lysine Production Capacity, 1980-1990.

Source: Tables 7.A.1 and 7.A.2

Early Price-Fixing Episodes

The 1980s were a heady period for the lysine industry: lysine plant capacities rose on an average annual clip of 16 percent, just about the same pace as demand volume. By anyone's standards, that's a roaring market. With lysine producers scrambling in the 1980s to respond to the strong pressures of robust demand, one might think that market forces would have generated pleasingly high profits.[11] However, it is apparent that sellers believed that they could do better through collective action.

Certainly the structure of the industry favored price fixing in the 1980s. The only three sellers in the world were located fairly close to one another. The small number of plant locations (five plants in four countries in 1980, up to eight plants in 1990) made monitoring of production and exports by each firm feasible. Ajinomoto and Kyowa had very similar business cultures; Miwon Group, like most South Korean conglomerates, demonstrated its abiding respect for Japanese business methods by copying many of them. Lysine is a homogeneous product, an organic chemical with a unique molecular structure and biological function. Until the late 1980s, the threat of entry by new producers seemed unlikely to be realized, partly because of technical barriers reinforced by the Japanese companies' R&D prowess. Antitrust enforcement in Japan is weak, while the newly formed Korean antitrust agency was too new to be effective.

The three Asian manufacturers of lysine participated in at least three price-fixing schemes before 1991. These conspiracies affected the Japanese, European and U.S. markets.[12] The first admitted price-fixing episode began in Europe in 1975 and continued until at least 1992. Eurolysine was established in 1974. While its plant in France did not begin local production until 1977 or 1978, Eurolysine acted as the import and sales agent for Ajinomoto's Japanese-made lysine. In order to set European lysine prices at its desired level, Eurolysine entered into an agreement with Miwon to limit exports to Europe from South Korea. An excerpt from a memorandum of a 1992 meeting summarized a Miwon manager's response to an accusation by Ajinomoto that Miwon had not been "sufficiently loyal:"

> "When your company, Eurolysine, started the lysine production, that is, from 1975 until the present time, we have cooperated by restricting/inhibiting [our exports] to five to ten percent level . . . of the European demand. Such cooperation that has been extended between the two companies for at least 17 years is, I think, a true cooperation." (Tr. 5915-5916).

Although not specifically mentioned, for the European conspiracy to be successful, Kyowa's exports from Japan or Mexico would also have had to be restrained. The companies limited the volume of European imports and local production but did not allocate specific customer accounts among themselves. As one of Eurolysine's CEOs later explained, a refusal to deal is illegal in itself; more importantly, a refusal of all but one supplier to sell will cause buyers to suspect immediately that price fixing is going on and to complain to the antitrust authorities at the European Commission. With its dominant European market share, the practice at Eurolysine in the 1980s was to raise lysine prices as high as the price of substitutes for lysine (soybean meal, fish meal, etc.) would permit.

The second price-fixing conspiracy covered the Japanese market for lysine. One Ajinomoto manager admitted to occasional price fixing when he worked in Tokyo during 1970-1975. Possibly a continuation of the earlier conspiracy, three top managers of Ajinomoto and Kyowa Hakko provided detailed and consistent testimony concerning a more recent period 1986-1990. The conspiracy was preceded by a price war in 1984 that brought Japanese lysine prices down to an historic low of $0.70 per pound (Tr. 4341). However, when Ajinomoto and Kyowa got over their spat in late 1985, they fixed Japanese lysine prices between themselves every month for at least four years (1986-1990). Sewon also joined the conspiracy. The manager of Ajinomoto's Feed Division, which marketed lysine and other feed additives, was at times ordered to engage in the scheme and at times took the initiative himself.[13] This scheme did not involve negotiations over market shares.

Finally, the two Japanese firms admitted to price fixing and to agreeing on territorial market areas in the United States in the late 1980s, a period during which each operated one of the two U.S. lysine plants. Precise dates on the U.S. conspiracy are not given in the transcript record, but the years 1986-1990 seem to be the most likely ones. For a "year or two" Ajinomoto was allocated 55 percent of United States' lysine sales which Kyowa was allocated the remaining 45 percent. In addition, Ajinomoto agreed not to export to Mexico (where Kyowa operated a plant) in return for Kyowa's refraining to export to Thailand (where Ajinomoto had a similar plant). U.S. delivered prices of feed-grade lysine during the conspiracy were above $1.40 per pound, peaking at $3.23 per pound in late 1988.

New Entry

Two large European chemical manufacturers attempted to enter the lysine industry before 1990, but neither was successful. In 1975, chemical-industry magazines carried the announcement that France's largest chemical company, Rhône-Poulenc, was going to build a lysine factory in Lyon, France. Kyowa Hakko was to be a minority partner. This plant was to have begun production with 22 million pounds of capacity in 1978. For reasons that are not clear, this plant was never built. It is likely that Ajinomoto's plans for Eurolysine were well enough advanced that the Rhône-Kyowa joint venture was pre-empted. Lysine would have fitted well with Rhône's extensive portfolio of feed-grade vitamins and agrochemicals, but it has since refrained from making amino acids (Connor 2000:Appendix E).

The second firm to express an interest in manufacturing lysine was the German metals and chemicals company Degussa. Sometime around 1986-1988, Degussa developed a plan to build a lysine plant in the United States.[14] Degussa had significant expertise in manufacturing some other amino acids (it was the world leader in methionine) and had a good R&D base to exploit. Degussa approached ADM to get a bid on a long-term supply contract for dextrose, the intended feedstock for Degussa's new venture. This turned out to be a big mistake for Degussa, because its request simply alerted ADM to an opportunity for itself. ADM decided to take a look at the lysine market itself, liked the high prices and rapid growth it saw, and launched its own feasibility study.[15]

ADM made a firm commitment to enter lysine manufacturing in July 1989. Besides Degussa's expression of interest, ADM had figured out why Japan was importing such large amounts of dextrose. It was the feedstock being purchased by Ajinomoto to make lysine, some of which was then exported from Japan back to the United States (Whitacre 1995). It appeared that selling lysine in the United States was profitable even with considerable long distance freight costs. This fact helped convince ADM's management of a U.S. plant's economic feasibility.

Technical feasibility was another test that had to be satisfied. In April 1988, ADM hired a new research scientist to find an efficient commercial process to make lysine from corn sweeteners.[16] He recommended that ADM purchase the rights to use a patented bacterial strain developed by the Genencor biotechnology division of Eastman Kodak Company. ADM did buy that technology in July 1989, and from August 1989 to November 1990 its R&D laboratory in Clinton, Iowa made lysine on a pilot scale. ADM committed $150 million to build the world's largest lysine manufacturing plant in its home base at Decatur, Illinois. This plant was to become by far the largest in the world with an annual capacity of 250 million pounds, almost three times the size of the largest plant then in existence (Eurolysine's plant in Amiens, France). Contrary to its usual secretiveness, ADM made sure its new bold investment was well publicized, all the better to discourage any would-be interlopers.

In November 1989, ADM hired a brilliant new manager to run its Bioproducts Division. Mark Whitacre was only 30 years old and just a few years beyond finishing his Ph.D. in nutritional biochemistry at Cornell University. His first job after graduating had been briefly with Ralston Purina in St. Louis. Later he worked a few years with Degussa, the very firm that had been blocked from entering the U.S. lysine industry by ADM's quick announcement about its own lysine plant.[17] Over the next four years, Whitacre would hire several of his former colleagues at Degussa to work for him at ADM. Working closely with ADM President James Randall, Whitacre oversaw the construction of the new lysine plant in record time. Previously, smaller lysine facilities had taken ADM's rivals up to four years to complete, but ADM's lysine plant from groundbreaking to production start-up in February 1991 took only 17 months. Randall had a well known tendency to build ADM's plants with copious excess capacity, partly to scare off potential rivals and partly to exploit the lower costs often accompanying large scales of production.

A lot was riding on the success of the lysine venture for ADM because lysine was merely the first of several new products that ADM planned on making with corn fermentation technology. Besides lysine, ADM would soon enter into the production of three more amino acids: methionine, threonine, and tryptophan. By the mid 1990s, ADM was also manufacturing several more organic chemicals based on dextrose: lactic acid, citric acid, bacitracin, sodium gluconate, monosodium glutamate, xanthan gum, and vitamins D, E, and biotin. Lysine was the test case that would determine whether ADM's major new product thrust would be technically feasible and profitable.

Almost simultaneously with ADM, a small lysine plant came into production on the island of Java, Indonesia. The plant was owned by a joint venture formally named Cheil Samsung Astra (CSA). CSA was established in mid-1989 to build a combined MSG and lysine plant. Although the joint venture had the obligatory local ownership of friends of then President Suharto (Astra Group), the great majority of CSA's stock was controlled by Cheil Food and Chemicals Co. of South Korea. Cheil (also called Cheil Jedang) was then part of the huge Samsung Group, South Korea's second largest *chaebol* in the late 1980s. However, Cheil split off to form its own *chaebol* in 1993 (Connor 2000:Appendix E). The MSG/lysine plant was built from money borrowed from Korean and Japanese banks in 1989. Further expansions were financed with a Eurobond placement in 1992. Although Cheil has some expertise in starch and chemical manufacturing, the source of its lysine technology is unknown. Cheil has no known fermentation facilities in South Korea (where Miwon is a monopoly), nor is there evidence that Cheil has strong R&D in the appropriate technical areas.

Cheil would remain the smallest of the five companies, but would relentlessly expand production throughout the 1990s no less than five times. Like its compatriot Sewon, Cheil would aggressively seek increases in its global market share. Unlike Sewon, it had little experience in cooperating with the world's leading producers. In the end Cheil would become a thorn in the side of the cartel.

MARKET SIZE AND GROWTH

The feed-grade lysine industry was fairly new on the world scene in the 1980s. It had formed no producers' association to collect and publish aggregate sales or consumption data. Few governmental organizations published international trade or production data on lysine or even amino acids as a group. Chemical-industry magazines provided only spotty, unattributable, and often inconsistent estimates of national or global market indicators. Lysine manufacturers tended to be secretive in order to protect their technological leads. Thus, when the conspirators first began to meet in 1992, they held many inconsistent notions of the size of the market and, hence, their own market shares. Different beliefs about market size and company shares hindered the formation of the cartel and contributed to distrust among the conspirators until late 1993.

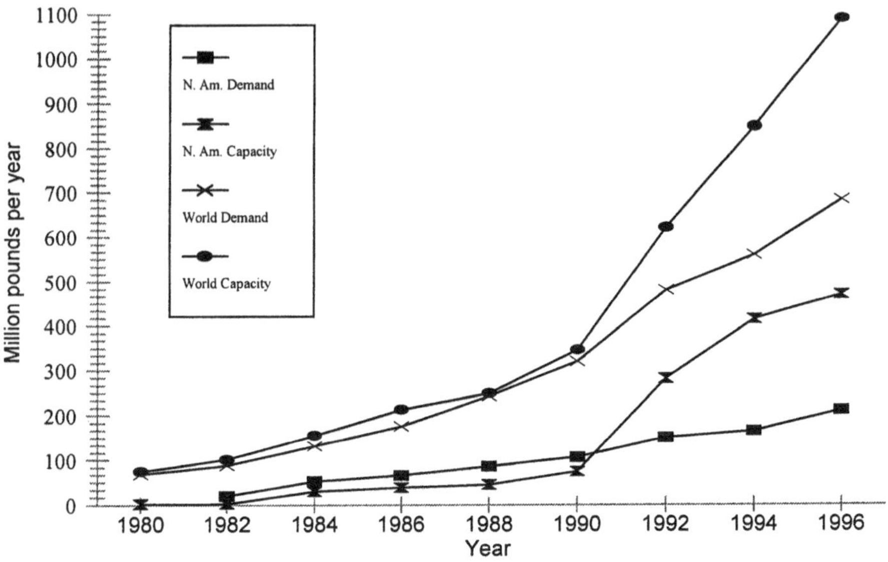

Figure 7.2. Lysine Production Capacity and Consumption, 1980-1996.

Source: Tables 7.A.1 and 7.A.4.

Global demand for lysine in 1980 was just below 70 million pounds (Figure 7.2). During the decade of the 1980s the volume of purchased lysine grew at an annual average of nearly 17 percent, reaching about 320 million pounds by 1990. Growth in demand was mostly smooth from year to year, but in 1993-1994 growth accelerated because of a brief price war in the latter year. Similarly, growth moderated from 1994 to 1996 as higher prices were imposed by the world's three producers in the main consumption areas, Japan, North America, and Europe.

Except for minuscule changes in lysine inventories held by manufacturers and chemical wholesalers, annual global production and global consumption are identical.[18] However, the rated capacity of the world's lysine factories must be several percentage points higher than total production or consumption. The ratio of production volume to rated capacity is termed capacity *utilization.* The utilization rate of the world's lysine plants was close to what is generally considered economically optimal in the food manufacturing industries (i.e., 80 to 90 percent). At times, 1988 for example, it appears that production levels had reached unsustainably high levels of utilization above 95 percent, but then significant plant expansions in South

Korea and North America in 1989 and 1990 relieved these looming capacity constraints.

When lysine buyers knew that major plant expansions would be coming on line, in anticipation of lower selling prices they would often hold off on making purchases for six months or more and consume previously purchased inventories instead. The temporary suspension of purchases typically caused regional prices to drop some 6 to 12 months before new capacity came on stream, only to rise again a year or so later as the new plant capacity became more fully utilized. Sellers with excess capacity exacerbated these cycles by offering low prices temporarily in order to bring their plant utilization levels up to more efficient levels of production. Three of these temporary price breaks can be discerned from reports in the trade press in the decade of the 1980s. First, when Biokyowa's new Missouri plant came on stream in early 1994, U.S. prices declined to a nadir of $0.70 per pound but began to recover by the end of the year. Second, when Ajinomoto's new Iowa plant began production in 1986, U.S. selling prices declined from about $2 per pound down to $0.90; by late 1988 spot lysine prices had jumped to as high as $3.23 per pound and by January 1989 were in the $2.30 to $2.40 range.[19]

North American consumption accounted for as much as 40 percent of global consumption in the early 1980s, but drifted down to about one-third by the end of the decade (Figure 7.2). Western Europe also accounted for about one-third of global sales volume in the mid-to-late 1980s. Both areas contained highly industrialized poultry and pork subsectors, large-scale farm producers who could appreciate the small boosts in productivity that attended the optimization of feed rations, and high income populations with huge appetites for meat in their diets. Demand for lysine was growing by about 10 to 12 percent per year in North America, driven mainly by shifts in consumer preferences for poultry over beef and for lower fat pork products. Similar trends in Japan and Europe were responsible for volume growth averaging 8 to 10 percent per year.[20]

Agricultural producers in both high income regions were early adopters of scientific animal nutrition practices. However, poultry and hog producers in many middle-income countries were just catching on to the benefits of balanced feeds in the 1980s. Moreover, the urban consumers of the many newly industrializing countries of Asia and Latin America were expanding their purchases of meat products far faster than consumers in the industrialized countries. As a result, Asia and Latin America saw demand for lysine grow at far faster rates than Western Europe and North America. In the 1980s, rates of volume growth of lysine in Asia (excluding Japan) and Latin America were in the 12 to 16 percent per year range.

The rate of growth of global demand slowed somewhat in the 1990s. During 1990-1996, it averaged about 13 to 14 percent per year.[21] Although North America and Western Europe had growth slightly below the global rate, the gap between these richer areas and Asia/South America was not as great as formerly. However, the rate of expansion in production capacity far outpaced increases in consumption in the 1990s (Figure 7.2). Consequently, the gap between capacity and production grew in the 1990s. That is, global utilization rates fell to the low 60-percent range during the mid-1990s. With significant excess capacity developing and plants opening in lower cost areas, the two Japanese lysine manufacturers were placed in the painful position of having to close their first manufacturing facilities.[22] These and other changes in the supply side of the lysine market will be explored in the next section.

STRUCTURE OF SUPPLY IN THE 1990s

The years 1989-1991 were a major transition period for the global lysine industry. Throughout the 1980s, production had been dominated by Ajinomoto (50 to 65 percent of global capacity) and the other Japanese pioneer, Kyowa Hakko (20 to 30 percent). The South Korean upstart, Sewon, borrowed mightily to achieve its goal of controlling about 20 percent of world supply, but never quite got there. As recounted above, two new players decided to enter the lysine industry in 1989, and by early 1991 the industry sported five suppliers instead of three. Because ADM's new plant was so huge, it had by far the greatest effect on prices and seller behavior. Little Cheil would not become a nettlesome factor in the industry for a couple of more years.

North America

To recap briefly, there were three lysine plants operating in North America in 1990 (Table 7.A.2). The oldest and smallest plant was operated by Kyowa's joint venture Fermex in Mexico. Four years after Kyowa's production began in Mexico, its U.S. subsidiary Biokyowa had initiated production of lysine in a new Cape Giradeau, Missouri plant. Together with two large plant expansions in Mexico, by 1990 Kyowa Hakko had almost 50-million pounds of lysine production capacity in North America. Kyowa was heavily committed to the North American market, with two of its three plants and more than half of its global capacity located there. The second U.S. lysine plant was built during 1994-1996 by Heartland Lysine, Inc., Ajinomoto's U.S. subsidiary, in Eddyville, Iowa. Twice expanded, by 1990 the Iowa plant had reached a nameplate capacity of 26 million pounds.

Until the Fermex plant started up in 1980, all of North America's needs for feed-grade lysine were supplied by imports from Japan. Total demand in 1980 was only 15 to 20 million pounds, of which 80 to 85 percent was purchased by buyers in the United States. By 1984-1985 when two plants were in operation, imports dropped to 60 to 75 percent of U.S. consumption. Even when all three plants were up and running in the late 1980s, imports continued to account for no less than 40 percent of North American consumption. Most of these imports came from France (Eurolysine) and Japan (Ajinomoto and Kyowa). Only a small amount originated from Sewon's plant in South Korea.

ADM's huge plant in Decatur began selling its production in February 1991. Small at first, the volume sold by ADM rose exponentially to about 4 million pounds per month in the last quarter of 1991 (Connor 2000: Appendix Table A-2). At that rate by year end, ADM's *annual production* had already surpassed Kyowa's total U.S. *capacity* in 1990 and was double Ajinomoto's capacity.

ADM's announced goal of 250 million pounds of capacity was for a while a bit of an exaggeration. The Decatur plant was still having more fermentors installed in 1991 and 1992. It seems from monthly sales volumes, especially during early 1992 and early 1993 when ADM was behaving in an aggressive (indeed punitive) manner, that its plant had at most 130 million pounds capacity through early 1992 and 175 million up to late 1992 (Table 7.A.4).[23] However, by the end of 1993, the Decatur plant had reached its planned capacity of 250 million pounds. ADM's premature announcement was in all likelihood calculated to impress rivals with its ability to increase production quickly for strategic reasons. Up through 1995, ADM's production never reached more than 86 percent utilization of its total capacity and was typically in the 60 to 70 percent range, but after 1995 utilization rates began to rise near their capacity limits. Thus, in 1997 ADM again raised the size of its Decatur plant, this time to 350 million pounds. Moreover, the company built a second lysine plant next to its Cedar Rapids, Iowa corn refinery. This plant opened in 1998 with 100 million pounds of capacity; expansion to 200 million pounds is expected by 2000, giving ADM a total of 550 million pounds of production capacity, which is just about what world capacity was when ADM joined the industry in 1991. Thus, by the end of the 1990s, ADM had reached its overarching corporate goal of becoming equal in size to the number-one producer.

Ajinomoto's and Kyowa's positions slipped badly as a result of ADM's aggressive expansion. Both companies added new capacity at its North American plants. Ajinomoto's plant in Iowa was expanded by 50 percent in 1991, 167 percent in 1993, and another 50 percent in 1996. Despite these heroic investments, Ajinomoto's share of North American lysine capacity fell from 35 percent in 1990 to 14 percent in 1992; it would continue to hover about 20 to 25 percent of the region's capacity through 1998. Kyowa also made substantial investments to expand their plants in Mexico and

Missouri almost every year in the decade. However, Kyowa's share also declined from 65 percent the year before ADM entered to 23 percent two years later. Kyowa was destined to hold onto about 15 to 20 percent of the continent's lysine capacity in the late 1990s.

The Japanese firms' position in the North American market will erode further as a fourth entrant's plant ramps up production in 2000. In early 1999, Cargill and Degussa broke ground on a new lysine plant adjacent to Cargill's newest corn refinery in Blair, Nebraska. The $100-million construction has a planned capacity of 170 million pounds of lysine to be made from liquid dextrose using a Degussa technology. Two less surprising entrants could hardly be imagined: Degussa already operates a small lysine plant in Slovakia, and Cargill tends to imitate ADM's successes in many lines of business. Cargill's expertise in feeds and feed additives should aid the project's ultimate success. Cargill's plant will account for about one-fifth of U.S. capacity in 2000, far behind ADM's 60 percent share.

In the 1990s, most new plant capacity was created by ADM's new Illinois plant and additions made to plants already in operation that were owned by Ajinomoto, Kyowa Hakko, Sewon and Cheil. One minor exception was the purchase by Ajinomoto of a plant that made MSG in Italy. Ajinomoto spent $40 million to buy the 22-million-pound plant and convert it to lysine production. This acquisition gave Eurolysine a total of 125 million pounds of lysine capacity by 1993, which was enough to supply 60 to 70 percent of Western Europe's demand for lysine. In sum, the combination of new plants and plant expansions gave the five members of the lysine cartel control over 97 percent of the world's lysine capacity during the years it operated (Figure 7.3). Except for Cargill's new plant in Nebraska due to come on stream in 2000, there are few instances of new lysine production in the 1990s by companies outside the cartel. The first example of extra-cartel entry occurred in Hungary. A small plant (11 million pounds capacity) began production in 1991 in Kaba, Hungary owned by a joint venture named Agroferm which originally had four partners. The largest owner was a local agricultural processing company HAGE (48 percent); Kyowa Hakko provided technical expertise and about 13 percent of the capital.[24] The plant took four years to build, and by the time it started production local economic conditions were so poor that Agroferm lost money for several years. Sometime in the mid 1990s the Hungarian partners sold a controlling interest to Kyowa which modestly expanded the plant a few times (Table 7.A.5). The Hungarian plant, which exported most of its lysine to Western Europe, never accounted for more than 2 percent of global capacity. A second small lysine venture called Fermas is located in Slovakia. The majority owner is Degussa and the local partner is Biotika. This plant began production of lysine on a very small scale in 1994 (6 million pounds capacity), but it also produces methionine and threonine. Degussa is a leading manufacturer of the latter two amino acids. A third lysine plant began production in Durban, South Africa in 1995. The plant is owned by the AECI Corporation and began with about 25 million pounds of lysine capacity. The plant's technology was licensed from an unnamed European company. There have been no announcements of expansions since 1995, so the financial health of this new venture is somewhat in doubt.

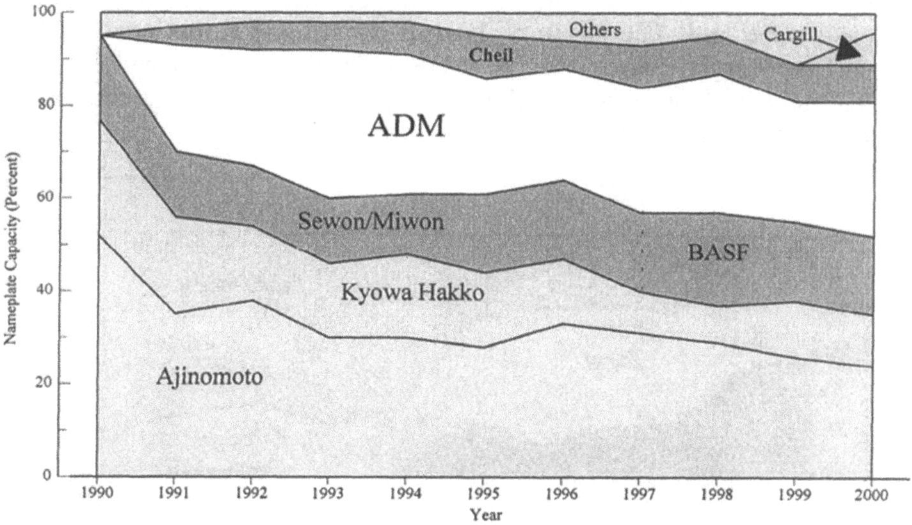

Figure 7.3. Global Capacity Shares of Leading Lysine Producers 1980-2000.

Source: Table 7.A.3

China seems to be the fastest growing spot for new ventures in lysine manufacturing. Ajinomoto established a joint venture in Sichuan Province that began production in 1997 with 34 million pounds capacity. Several smaller joint ventures began producing in China as early as 1993. By 2000, these Chinese operations may have in the aggregate more than 100 million pounds of capacity, or about 13 percent of world capacity.

Thus, the world lysine industry was attracting lots of new capacity in the late 1990s. Most of the new entrants began production after the lysine cartel broke up in 1995, but they would have been a threat to the cartel's continued existence by the end of the 1990s. By the year 2000, capacity created by Cargill, Degussa, AECI, and other companies outside the lysine cartel would reach 15 percent of the global industry (Tables 7.A.4 and 7.A.5). At this level or slightly larger, a cartel of the top five companies would have found it difficult to fix prices at monopoly levels (Scherer and Ross 1990).

Until 1990, the global lysine industry was almost totally owned and controlled by Asian companies.[25] However, the location of production has become more diverse over time (Figure 7.4). In the early 1980s, about two-thirds of lysine capacity was located in Japan and most of the rest in one plant in France. From 1984 to 1990, about half of global capacity was in Asia, of which a small but growing portion was located outside of Japan and Korea; Europe contained 25 to 30 percent; and the Japanese plants in North America about 20 percent. After 1990, the North American (and especially U.S.) share jumped to 40 percent early in the decade and increased to more than 50 percent by the end. The share of Europe, Japan, and Korea continued to shrink. The biggest change was the increase in other Asian locations since 1990; Thailand, Indonesia, and China are the major countries getting more lysine capacity. This trend is expected to continue.

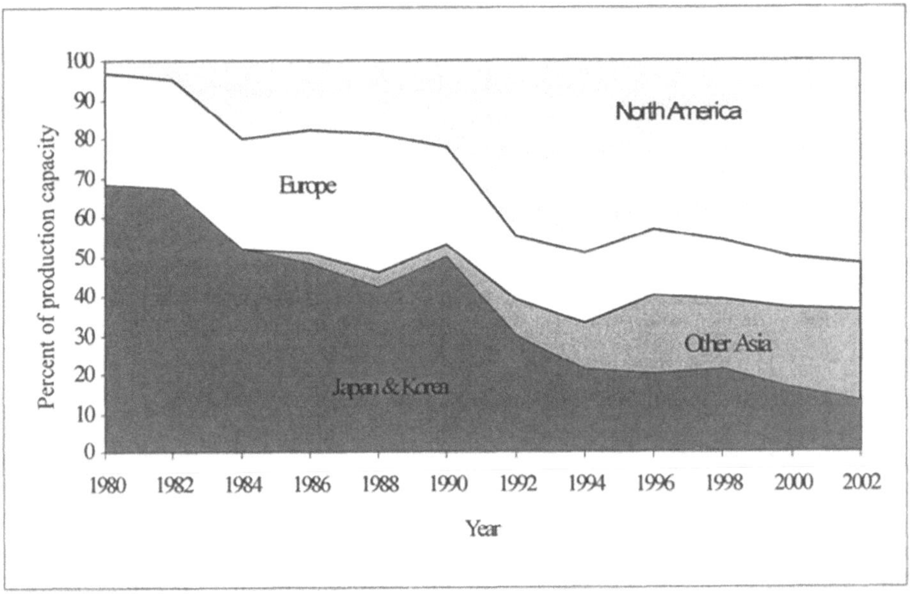

Figure 7.4. Geographic Location of Lysine Production Capacity, 1980-2002.

Source: Tables 7.A.1, 7.A.2, 7.A.4, and 7.A.5.

One indicator of the future global location of a science-based industry like lysine is the location of basic and applied research. Research and development is necessary to overcome technical barriers to building efficient production facilities, continually upgrading those technologies, and providing after-sales technical advice to buyers of biochemicals. While basic scientific knowledge tends to be quite mobile internationally, the applied technologies of production often reside within existing manufacturers or engineering consultants who are tied in to more local networks.

A compilation of scientific publications by food scientists, biochemists, and engineers on the topic of lysine was categorized by the country of residence of the first author (Table 8.A.6 below). These data provide only a rough indicator of national scientific and technical capacities in lysine production techniques because scientists are sometimes restricted by company policy from releasing commercially valuable information prior to the company's applying for a patent. Nevertheless, lysine publications tend to originate from the headquarter's countries of the world's leading lysine manufacturers. Ajinomoto and Kyowa Hakko scientists account for a large share of the Japanese publications on lysine. Scientists working in Germany (where Degussa is headquartered), France (Eurolysine has an R&D laboratory there), and Korea were prominent authors of lysine papers. In the United States, most publications were authored by individuals associated with universities; very few, if any, were ADM employees.[26] During the 1990s, papers by U.S.-based scientists accounted for half of the world total, whereas the Japanese share from one-sixth prior to 1990 to about one-tenth of world output after 1989. The European and Korean shares increased.

MEMBERS OF THE CARTEL

Five companies joined the lysine cartel between 1992 and 1995. ADM, just as it had done in the citric acid conspiracy a year earlier, made the initial overtures in early 1992. Terrance Wilson and Mark Whitacre approached Ajinomoto and Kyowa Hakko in Tokyo in April 1992, ostensibly to form an "amino-acid manufacturers' association." ADM, Ajinomoto, and Kyowa were the first three members of the cartel, which held its first price-fixing meeting in June 1992. ADM requested Ajinomoto and Kyowa to cajole or coerce Sewon and Cheil into joining the cartel. By October 1992, all five companies had met to conspire on lysine prices. What follows are sketches of the five lysine manufacturers that constituted the global lysine cartel.

Archer Daniels Midland Company

ADM has been previously profiled in Chapter 4 above because of its role in the citric acid cartel. That description covered ADM's history, product mix, financial performance, and management style, particularly the dominating role of the Andreas family.

When the news of ADM's involvement in price fixing broke in June 1995 and when numerous legal actions commenced against the company, many candid assessments of ADM's corporate life-style appeared in the business and popular press. This section will assemble the views of this post-cartel literature which has done much to crystalize the public's image of ADM in the late 1990s. These excerpts from longer articles in the press were written after June 1995, at a time when ADM was reeling from allegations and later an admission of guilt of price fixing. In most of them, the journalists were seeking explanations of whether or why the company's unique management style could be responsible for such serious illegal and unethical behavior.

The *Washington Post* characterized ADM as a secretive company best known for ". . . 35 years of unashamed influence-peddling in Washington . . ." Dwayne Andreas was described as ". . . long . . . regarded as the most politically connected agribusinessman in the U.S." (Carlson 1996). ADM had placed a big bet on the success of its Bioproducts Division; its heavy investment was expected to generate as much as 10 percent of ADM's income by 1997 because of its high market shares. ADM is known for ". . . muscling into market position . . ." and for developing "cozy relationships" with rival companies like Tate & Lyle said the article.

The bible of the chemical industry, *Chemical Market Reporter,* normally cautious in criticizing major firms in the industry, echoed these themes. *CMR* noted in 1996 that:

> "Since 1989 . . . Archer Daniels Midland Company has entered over half a dozen . . . biochemical businesses using vertical integration, marketing savvy, deep pockets and . . . aggressive market tactics" (p. 3).

As a result, ADM has "ruffled feathers" and "alienated business rivals." The bioproducts ADM had definitely entered included citric acid, lysine, methionine, tryptophan, sorbitol, lactic acid, vitamin E, monosodium glutamate (MSG), and distilled monoglycerides; "rumored" new products include biotin, vitamin C, sodium gluconate, and xanthan gum.[27]

A front page article in the *Wall Street Journal* drew a sharp portrait of then CEO Dwayne Andreas, who was first appointed a director of ADM in 1965 at the age of 47. Although he personally owned less than 1 percent of ADM's stock in 1995, ". . . Andreas has gained near-total control with the help of family members, loyal executives and directors whose combined stake is nearly 15-percent . . . He collaborates with his biggest competitors, spends prodigiously to influence the media and public opinion, and spreads large sums among politicians of all stripes . . . Over the years, he has moved aggressively to neutralize any obstacles to his dominance . . . [at times employing] rough tactics." All major ADM decisions were made at the top by three or four managers: the Andreases, James Randall, and Terrance Wilson. Meetings were informal and paperwork was kept to a minimum.

ADM's lobbying in Washington is effected primarily through agricultural trade associations, especially the Corn Refiners Association, the Renewable Fuels Association and the National Corn Growers Association (Hollis 1998). ADM is the major beneficiary of the U.S. sugar program and ethanol subsidies. Andreas' political largess is often mentioned as the source of these political favors. Charges of abuse have rarely stuck to Andreas.

The Washington Post printed a similar picture of ADM in 1996, calling the firm insular and rife with cronyism. "[ADM] has been run for 25 years by the iron hand of its chairman, Dwayne O. Andreas, and governed by directors named Archer, Daniels, Andreas and their friends . . . [The ADM board is] handcuffed by company insiders, family members, cronies, and friends of the powerful chairman." More than half of the Board members were 69 or older; at most four of the 17 were independent of ADM or Andreas.

When the ethanol subsidy was unexpectedly renewed for ten years by the Congress in 1997, the political largess by the Andreas family ($4.5 million since 1988) was cited by *Common Cause Magazine* as one of the factors. After continuation of the subsidy was blocked by the Appropriations committees of both houses, the intervention of House Speaker Gingrich and Senate Majority Leader Trent Lott saved the measure at the last minute. Bob Dole, former Majority Leader and Andreas ally, may have been instrumental in lobbying for the subsidy. The ethanol subsidy in its first ten years had cost the U.S. Treasury $7 billion, most of which had been sent to ADM, and had generated few environmental benefits.

It is noteworthy that none of the news analyses suggested that the price fixing was the work of a rogue manager (Mark Whitacre), that the FBI or the Department of Justice was seeking to entrap members of the Andreas family, or that ADM's managers were led astray by foxy Japanese co-conspirators for whom cartels were a way of life – all themes to be sounded by defense counsel in the 1998 criminal trial. While some of the articles are careful to point to ADM's business success, the overall tone is one of wonder or perhaps glee that a master manipulator and his corporate creation had gotten their comeuppance.

Ajinomoto Co., Inc.

Ajinomoto is Japan's largest manufacturer of foods and seasonings (Connor 2000:Appendix E). The fundament of Ajinomoto's fortunes is the flavoring enhancer monosodium glutamate (MSG). The year after it was first isolated by a scientist at the University of Tokyo in 1908, Ajinomoto became the world's first manufacturer of MSG, selling it under the trademark "Aji-No-Moto" ("essence of taste"). The company soon began setting up sales offices in cities all around Asia, and between the world wars extended its sales network to Europe, Latin America, and North America. Ajinomoto's New York sales office was opened in 1917. This office is believed to be the first presence by a Japanese manufacturing company in the United States. Although interrupted by World War II, by the mid-1950s, it had reestablished its international sales network.

MSG was at first extracted chemically from soybean protein, thus explaining Ajinomoto's early move into soybean oil processing. However, the company was quick to capitalize on scientific discoveries in Japan in 1956 that an amino acid (gluconic acid) is a by-product of the metabolism of certain bacteria. Gluconic acid is closely related to the salt sodium glutamate, so within a few years Ajinomoto was manufacturing MSG more cheaply from a proprietary bacterial fermentation process.

Variations on the same process produced several other amino acids, many of them essential for growth and muscle development in humans and animals, such as methionine, tryptophan, and lysine. Optimizing the fermentation process was a difficult technical challenge. The temperature of the nutritive feedstock; the types of sugars, salts, vitamins and other chemicals to add to the mix; and the most productive strains of microbes were the subject of years of research and development. In recent years the microbial strains have been modified by genetic engineering and patented, each an improved strain producing a higher yield of an amino acid for a given amount of sweetener. Despite these long-term technical difficulties, Ajinomoto was manufacturing and selling lysine and other amino acids for the human pharmaceutical market by 1958, and by 1960 the company began selling lysine as an additive for animal feeds. By the 1980s, Japanese biotech companies dominated the world market for the 20 or so amino acids, the majority of them exclusively available from Japanese sources.

In the 1960s, amino acids were still a small side line. Ajinomoto's primary strategic emphasis was the introduction of new highly processed foods and beverages that were in most cases unfamiliar to Japanese consumers. Through numerous joint ventures with U.S. and European food companies, Ajinomoto began to make and sell dried soups, instant coffee, breakfast cereals, and soft drinks. By 1978, Ajinomoto's principal product, seasonings, had shrunk to 22 percent of company sales and processed foods had expanded to 31 percent of sales. However, by the 1980s, the domestic Japanese market for both these product lines had grown quite mature.

To break this constraint on growth, Ajinomoto targeted two areas as top priorities for new investment. First was the establishment of its processed foods lines in foreign markets, especially Asian markets that were fast growing. Second was to branch into pharmaceuticals and other life-sciences-products. Both thrusts would utilize the substantial cash flow from its MSG and domestic food processing lines to finance the R&D and new plant capacities that this new strategic direction would require. In 1987, Ajinomoto created a new life-sciences products division and stepped up its R&D expenditures. By the late 1990s, R&D represented 3.3 percent of sales, a very high level for a food processing company. Its life-sciences division sells amino acids, nucleic acids, enzymes, and medical products for human and animal use.

Ajinomoto's strategic shift seems to have been moderately successful. Sales in fiscal 1998 were $6.4 billion, an increase of 83 percent since 1990 or 8 percent per year (5.7 percent when measured in yen). Employment has reached about 5,100 persons. Operating income in the 1990s has averaged about 6 percent of sales, and before-tax income has generally ranged between 2.4 and 4.6 percent of sales. These profit rates would be considered moderately high for a U.S. food processing company, but low compared to a pharmaceutical company.

Ajinomoto makes lysine in six plants around the world. Its largest plant is located in France (joint venture established in 1974); smaller units operate in Iowa (1982), Thailand (1994), Italy (1993), Brazil (1995), and China (1997). Its oldest plant in Saga, Japan ceased production in 1995.

Kyowa Hakko Kogyu Co., Ltd.

Kyowa Chemical Research Laboratory was established as a joint venture of three Japanese alcohol distillers before World War II. From the beginning Kyowa specialized in fermentation products such as alcohol, acetone, and butane. Following World War II, Kyowa began to make and sell distilled spirits. In 1947, it began manufacturing penicillin (Connor 2000: Appendix E).

In 1949, the company was incorporated under its present name, which means "harmonious fermentation." Shortly thereafter the company gained international recognition for its discovery of the anti-cancer drug mitomycin-C. Like Ajinomoto, Kyowa was quick to take advantage of the 1956 discovery that amino acids were produced from certain microbial fermentations. Within two years, Kyowa was making lysine and MSG commercially from a process that produced glucomic acid from fermentation of molasses, a method that is more cost-effective than traditional methods that extracted amino acids from vegetable proteins. In countries with low cost sugar industries, Kyowa's lysine manufacturing process is as equally cheap as Ajinomoto's dextrose-based process. Since the 1960s, Kyowa has brought to market many new pharmaceutical products and has introduced several improvements in fermentation production processes. In 1983, Kyowa developed one of the first genetically engineered microbes that significantly raised the productivity of fermentation of amino acids. More than 20 percent of its 5,100 employees in the late 1990s were involved in R&D. The company holds more than 1500 patents outside Japan.

Today, Kyowa Hakko is one of the world's leading firms in research in biotechnologies and genetic engineering and in production of amino acids. Besides its major lines of business of pharmaceuticals and agricultural chemicals, Kyowa processes foods and alcoholic beverages. In fiscal 1998, Kyowa Hakko had sales of $3.1 billion and since 1990 sales have grown about 4 percent per year. Pre-tax income in the 1990s ranged from 6.8 to 8.2 percent of sales.

Kyowa operates 8 manufacturing plants in Japan. Its first foreign affiliate was Kyowa Hakko USA, established in 1969 and renamed Biokyowa in 1982. Kyowa also has subsidiaries in the UK (1991), Mexico (1975), Belgium (1976), and Hungary (1987). Kyowa manufactures lysine in three plants that are located in Missouri (construction began in 1982); Orezaba, Mexico (1982); and Kaba, Hungary (1990). Its first lysine plant in Hofu, Japan was retired in 1997, 40 years after it had become the first in the world to employ a fermentation technology to make an amino acid.

Sewon Company

Sewon in the 1980s and 1990s was the second or third largest manufacturer of food and agricultural products in South Korea. (The largest such company, Cheil Food and Chemicals, is profiled below). Until 1994, Sewon was operated as a part of the South Korean conglomerate or *chaebol* Miwon Group. In that year, Miwon's assets were split into two operating companies. The first company, Miwon Co., was given most of the consumer-processed-foods assets of the group. The second, Sewon Co., became an agribusiness-chemicals firm with interests in animal feeds, synthetic resins, lysine, MSG, and other starch products. After 1994, Miwon and Sewon were still loosely tied together in the same *chaebol,* but both were traded separately on the Seoul stock exchange. About 29 percent of Sewon's stock was owned by S.W. Lim in 1997, a son of the Miwon group founder. In November 1997, the *chaebol* changed its name to Daesang Corporation, today one of the 30 largest industrial conglomerates in South Korea as measured by total assets. Miwon and Sewon, after four years apart, were rejoined under Daesang as their holding company.

In 1972, Sewon began making lysine in its plant in Busan, South Korea, but production may have not reached commercially important levels until around 1980. A new and larger plant was built in Kunsan, South Korea in the late 1980s and began production in 1989, and replaced the old plant a year or two later. By the early 1980s, Sewon had become the dominant starch manufacturer in Korea and the third largest in Asia. Sewon spent prodigiously to expand its sole lysine plant, adding to capacity five times between 1990 and 1995. From 1993, Sewon's plant was the second largest in the world, exporting more than 80 percent of its output.

By 1995, Sewon and the conglomerate to which it was affiliated were deeply in debt. Although the company continued to issue rosy pronouncements to the press about its lysine and other starch businesses as late as 1997, it was in dire financial condition. The Miwon Group had large losses in fiscal 1995 and 1996, mainly because of huge debt payments. By mid-1997, Miwon Group could no longer resist the full force of the Asian financial crisis that began in that year and was signaled by huge drops in the value of the Korean won and stock market prices. In late 1997, the Group's debt-to-equity ratio was an astounding 6.5.

In March 1998, the renamed *chaebol* (now Deasang Corp.) appointed a new president from outside of the founding family who took drastic action. Sewon's crown jewel, its lysine business, was sold off to Germany's BASF for $600 million to reduce the group's debt. As of mid-1998, the Daesang group no longer sold lysine, though it did hold on to MSG, aspartame, and some other starch-manufacturing assets.

Cheil Food and Chemicals Co.

Cheil (also called Cheil Jedang) was established as Cheil Sugar in 1953, and it retained its monopoly in sugar refining until the mid 1990s. Cheil was the operating company for the food and agricultural processing businesses of the huge South Korean *chaebol* Samsung until 1993. Samsung began madly diversifying in the mid-1950s and became Korea's largest conglomerate by the mid-1970s, though it dropped to second place behind Hyundai by the late 1990s (Connor 2000: Appendix E).

Throughout the 1980s, Cheil had focused mainly on sugar and other processed foods. By the year 1992, Cheil's sales had reached $1.3 billion, making it the largest Korean food manufacturer. By that time it had already decided to diversify into pharmaceuticals, household chemicals, and fine chemicals. Cheil split off from Samsung in 1993 and embarked on becoming a *chaebol* in its own right. By 1997, Cheil's sales had reached $2.1 billion, having grown by 10 percent per year since 1992. At that time 36 percent of its sales were in sugar, flour, and oils; 31 percent in frozen foods; 17 percent chemicals; and 11 percent animal feeds. Company employment reached a peak of about 2200 in 1996, but the company has since retrenched somewhat. Returns on equity and assets have been low in the 1990s, but Cheil's debts were modest by international standards and very low by a Korean yardstick.

Cheil decided to enter the lysine business around 1988. In 1989, it joined with its parent group Samsung and Indonesia's Astra Group to form PT

Cheil Samsung Astra (CSA). This joint venture borrowed at least $47 million to build a new plant in East Java to manufacture MSG and lysine (22 million pounds of each per year); another $30-million bond issue was successfully floated in 1992 to finance a major expansion. Significant increases in capacity were registered six times between its 1991 start-up year and 1999. Another successful debt placement was reported in early 1999, this one for $83 million. The prospectus issued at the time for the joint venture (slightly renamed as CJ Samsung Indonesia) reports that 1998 sales of MSG and lysine had reached about $155 million and that profits were a striking 17.5 percent of sales. Cheil owns 83 percent of its Indonesian subsidiary, which was prospering in the face of adverse economic conditions in East Asia.

INTERNATIONAL TRADE AND INVESTMENT

Feed-grade lysine was exported from the two pioneering Japanese plants as early as 1970. At that time, the most industrialized poultry and hog operations were located in North America and Western Europe, regions accounting for about two-thirds of potential demand for lysine. While no precise data are available, it is likely that the great majority of Japanese lysine production was being exported to these two regions by the late 1970s. The first foreign direct investment in the industry was Ajinomoto's Eurolysine subsidiary. Its French plant, up and running by 1978, served to supply most of the European market from that time to the present (augmented with by Eurolysine's Bioitalia plant from 1993). Eurolysine also exported to North Africa, the Middle East, and a bit to North America.

Kyowa had announced its intention to build a plant in France in 1975, but gave up when it was pre-empted by Eurolysine. So Kyowa targeted North America instead, first with a Mexican plant opened in 1980 that could have supplied much of North and South America's import needs, then with its Biokyowa plant in Missouri that was opened in 1984. These two plants displaced most of the exports from Japan to the Americans by the latter half of the 1980s. Ajinomoto responded to the impending loss of its North American sales by quickly building a plant in Iowa that was very nearly Biokyowa's twin. It is possible that Kyowa's pique at having been stalemated in North America may have set off the 1984-85 price war. The establishment of four plants in Europe and North America during 1978-1986 caused most exports from Japan to be redirected towards Asia. Sewon's plant in Korea also exported most of its output to Asian markets, partly because of a collusive agreement to restrain its sales to Europe and the United States.

North America imported 100 percent of its lysine needs prior to 1982, but this share declined to 80 percent in 1982, to about 50 percent in 1984-88, and to 40 percent by 1990 (Table 7.A.2). Most of these imports came from

Japan and France at prices of about $1.30 to $1.80 per pound (Connor 1999: Table 4). The United States was a significant exporter of lysine in the 1980s, but nearly all of it was pharmaceutical lysine made by traditional extraction methods in the organic chemicals industry *(ibid.* Table 5). U.S. exports of feed-grade lysine did not begin until 1985, but rose quickly to about 13 million pounds in 1988, which was about one-fourth of U.S. capacity. The majority of U.S. exports of feed-grade lysine in the late 1980s were destined for Canada and Latin America. Trade patterns changed drastically in 1991 when ADM's giant new plant came on stream. However, that story is so bound up with cartel decisions that it is left for the next chapter.

SELLING PRACTICES

Lysine was customarily sold to U.S. feed manufacturers in much the same way as citric acid. Sellers announced a baseline list price for dry lysine based on delivery of full truckloads to specified points in the Midwest near the lysine factories or ports of import. Prices would be higher for deliveries to more distant locations or in partial truckload sizes; discounts were offered if the buyer arranged for transportation. These premiums and discounts were fairly standard across the industry as were payment terms; that is, they were widely viewed as nonnegotiable.

The asking price was usually just the start of price negotiations unless the buyer was seeking immediate delivery. These so-called spot purchases were often concluded at the list price. However, the vast majority of lysine was sold under supply contracts that typically specified an annual quantity that the buyer was obligated to purchase at some predetermined frequency of delivery. Because quality was essentially the same across all sellers, the delivered price was really the only point of the contract negotiations. Usually around the end of the calendar year, buyers or their agents would shop around and haggle sequentially with lysine sales representatives until the buyers felt that they had found the lowest possible price below list. Transaction prices depended on collecting reliable information and the negotiating skills of the parties. Boasting, bluffing, misinformation, nerves, and friendships might sway prices a penny or two in either direction in normal times. The largest and most loyal buyers expected and usually received a conventional 3 percent rebate.

Although the price arrived at was binding for the first delivery, sellers had the option of changing their list or contract prices at any time. Buyers usually were given 30 days' price protection; that is, when list prices increased "effective immediately," contract buyers could buy one-twelfth of their annual contracted volume at the "old price." However, the price on more distant delivery times had to be renegotiated all over again or passively accepted (Tr. 4187).

Most large feed manufacturers dealt directly with the manufacturers' sales representatives. ADM in the mid-1990s maintained three or four sales offices for U.S. transactions, and offices in Miami for Latin American sales, in Singapore for Asian sales, and Germany and the UK for European sales. ADM also sold lysine in some parts of the world through brokers who operated on sales commissions. Merchant wholesalers bought some lysine for resale to smaller customers. Buyers who purchased lysine through wholesalers usually ended up paying several cents above manufacturers' list prices.

The exchange mechanism just described is termed by economists *direct trading,* and the price system is called *private treaty* negotiation. No third parties can observe or record the prices that are used to transfer ownership of the lysine. Specific sales contracts are kept secret between rival buyers and rival sellers, so actual prices paid are subject to misrepresentation and exaggeration. Information about prices is distributed asymmetrically, with the few sellers having the upper hand over buyers that number in the thousands. Such exchange mechanisms are known to foster monopolistic pricing practices (Marion *et al.* 1987:79).

Chapter 7 Endnotes

[1] Most of the facts mentioned in this chapter are from sources cited in Appendix A of a Staff Paper prepared by the author, *Archer Daniels Midland: Price Fixer to the World* (Connor 2000a); its Appendix A is an extensive chronology of events in the lysine industry. An earlier case study of the lysine conspiracy appeared in the academic journal *Review of Agricultural Economics* (Connor 1997); a later study focusing on the lysine overcharge can be found in *The Review of Industrial Organization* (Connor 2000b). The development of the industry and international trade are discussed in another detailed Staff Paper (Connor 1999).

[2] The other two are monosodium glutamate (MSG), a food flavoring, and methionine, another essential amino acid bought mainly by feed manufacturers.

[3] Concentrates consist of vitamins, minerals, salts, trace metals, flavorings, and amino acids tailored to the age, sex, and species of fish or animals being raised. For example, a mature pig of about 100 kg. requires about 0.6 percent lysine in its ration for ideal growth and development, whereas a piglet of 10 to 20 kg. needs feed that is 1.0 to 1.2 percent lysine by weight.

[4] Multi-gastric animals such as cattle have digestive systems that destroy lysine in feed before it can be absorbed. However, lysine makers have recently developed coated pellets that survive and pass through the rumen (the first stomach of ruminants), thus allowing lysine to have a positive nutritional effect.

[5] One experienced Japanese manager testified that only Ajinomoto and ADM sold liquid lysine in 1994 (Tr. 4212-4216). Because of the special holding tanks and spraying equipment required, only 3 or 4 customers were large enough and close enough to the points of manufacture to benefit from lower prices of liquid lysine.

[6] In the Chicago criminal trial (see Chapter 15), defense counsel used the testimony of ADM's comptroller to try to show confusion about the alleged cheating on the cartel's volume agreement by ADM (Tr. 4883-4893). The agreement solely concerned dry lysine.

[7] By convention, the word "tonne" will represent the metric ton of 2205 pounds and "ton" a weight of 2000 pounds.

[8] In 1985 and 1986, the largest buyers of HFCS permitted their bottlers to substitute 100 percent fructose for sugar.

[9] Orsan is short for Les Produits Organiques du Santerre, SA. Orsan was mostly owned by the Lafarge group, a French conglomerate with cement as its primary product. Because Ajinomoto owned a majority share in Orsan, Ajinomoto in effect had a controlling interest in Eurolysine from the beginning.

[10] This statement requires a slight but inconsequential amendment. Press reports mention that Toray Industries, a major manufacturer of synthetic fibers, built a Japanese plant with Kyoto distiller Takara Shozu using Toray's patented lysine technology. This plant was expanded to 18 million pounds in 1982. As late as 1985, Toray was cited as having 10 percent of the global market for lysine, but its sales seem to have been confined to domestic feed manufacturers. No further citations to Toray's lysine business can be found after 1985. It seems quite likely that Toray had withdrawn from lysine production by the early 1990s, if not earlier. Toray was not invited to participate in the lysine cartel when it was formed in 1992.

[11] Lysine was too small a share of total sales to be reported separately in the annual financial reports of the three Asian companies. However, the large investments in new and expanded plants suggest the presence of adequate cash flows from their lysine businesses. Global capacities were quite constrained throughout the 1980s.

[12] These conspiracies were revealed in unrebutted courtroom testimony of two Ajinomoto top managers (Kanji Mimoto, Tr. 908-909, and Hirozaku Ikeda, Tr. 1670-1894), the former CEO of Eurolysine (Alain Crouy, Tr. 2198-2522), and Kyowa Hakko senior manager of Masaru Yamamoto (Tr. 4259-4341). A memorandum written by a Miwon manager (in English) to his

counterpart at Ajinomoto in November 1992 contains explicit reference to 17 years of export restraints by Miwon to Europe (Tr. 5915-5916).

[13] The Ajinomoto division manager from 1985 to his retirement in 1994 was Hirozaku Ikeda. He reported to three bosses during those nine years: Matsumura, Kiosi, Yamamoto, and Kazotoshi Yamada. His superiors were "managing directors," one of six to eight men on the top management committee of Ajinomoto, roughly equivalent to Corporate Vice President in U.S. companies. Ikeda's co-conspirators were Ken Mochi, and Masura Yamamoto at Kyowa and Lee and J.S. Kim at Miwon. Ajinomoto's President Toba was not indicted for the 1992-1995 conspiracy (Tr. 1670-1894). The geographic scope of the cartel of the 1980s is not clear, but most likely affected export prices from Japan and Korea.

[14] Mark Whitacre was a new employee of Degussa in those years. In fact, he was Degussa's chief negotiator with ADM, which proposed a U.S. joint venture in lysine to Degussa in late 1988. Degussa declined the offer.

[15] ADM may have been thinking about lysine as a possible expansion area as early as the early 1980s when one of its scientists performed a literature search on lysine R&D. Notes of a conspiracy meeting in June 1992 made by an Ajinomoto participant quote Wilson saying that Rhône-Poulenc and Degussa were prevented from entering lysine production by ADM's swift announcement of its intention to build huge capacity (Tr. 2333-2348).

[16] Much of this information is drawn from a decision in U.S. Patent Court by Judge Sue Robinson (1998). The scientist was Kenneth Steward. Kodak sold strain number 1051 that yielded 37 grams of lysine per liter of dextrose under laboratory conditions. However, Ajinomoto's patented strains of bacteria yielded up to 41 grams (Robinson 1998:4) in the early 1980s. As dextrose accounted for one-third of ADM's total manufacturing costs (Tr. Ex. 64), Ajinomoto's superior yield translates into about 4 percent cost advantage. Later James Randall of ADM tried to steal Ajinomoto's superior technology.

[17] In fact, in 1988-1989, Whitacre was Degussa's vice president in charge of negotiating a joint venture with ADM. Shortly after, negotiations failed, Whitacre was hired by ADM. In early the 1990s,Whitacre raided Degussa repeatedly for talent for ADM's Bioproducts Division (Eichenwald 2000).

[18] Reliable estimates of global demand were few and rather rough approximations in the 1980s. Capacity figures are more accurate because they are built up from dozens of public references to planned and actual construction projects. In the early 1990s both consumption and capacity data improve in terms of accuracy as members of the lysine cartel of 1992-1995 shared information and arrived at a consensus.

[19] These spot-market price observations were reported in occasional articles in the leading trade magazine, *Chemical Market Reporter*, probably based on interviews of a few buyers. They should be regarded as approximation only. Contract customers generally paid lower prices.

[20] Other areas with relatively modern agricultural sectors would include Australia, New Zealand, and South Africa. The poultry subsectors of many middle income countries in Asia and Latin America had also had modern feeding practices in place.

[21] Growth continued to decelerate in the 1990s; after 1996 demand slowed to about 9 percent per annum.

[22] Although no reference can be found to the event, it is likely that Toray Industries closed its Kyoto plant by the early 1990s. By 1996 or 1998, Japan, the birth place of the global lysine industry, had no feed-grade lysine production left.

[23] This fact is also revealed by discussions among the conspirators in 1992 and 1993, including tours of the plant given to the Asian companies' engineers.

[24] Kyowa was also a minority partner in a small Vietnamese lysine plant (22 million pounds) planned to start up in 1999 or 2000. The other partner is Taiwan's Vedan Enterprises.

[25] The French firm Orsan held minority positions in Eurolysine from 1974 and Heartland Lysine from 1984, but sold out to Ajinomoto in 1994.

[26] ADM has a remarkably small R&D effort for a company its size. ADM's 1998 annual report revealed for the first time its R&D expenditures: $12 to $17 million during fiscal year 1996-1998, a paltry 0.09 to 0.12 percent of sales. Of its six laboratories, only two (Decatur and Clinton, Iowa) deal with starch and bioproducts research. Given what is known about its acquisition of amino acid technology, most of ADM's access to technology came from licensing rights from other companies, hiring experts away from rivals, or from industrial espionage.

[27] Biotin was made for internal use. Sodium gluconate technology was purchased through acquisition of a Finnish company, but was sold only briefly by ADM. Xantham gum for industrial use only was under production in the late 1990s.

Table 7.A.1. World Production Capacity and Consumption of Feed-Grade Lysine, 1980-1990.

Company: Plants Outside North America (Year)	1980	1982	1984	1986	1988	1990
			Thousand metric tonnes/year			
North American capacity[a]	1	2	13.5	17.5	20.5	34
Ajinomoto & Orsan:						
Saga Prefecture, Japan (1960)[b]	10[E]	12[E]	16.0[E]	20.0[E]	20.0[E]	20[E]
Amiens, France (1978-80)	10[E]	13	20.0	30.0	40.0	40[E]
Pathun Thani, Thailand (1986)	0	0	0	3.0	4.5	5[E]
Kyowa Hakko:						
Hofu, Japan (1960)[b]	4	6	8.0	8.0	10.0[E]	20[E]
Sewon (Miwon Group):						
Busan, So. Korea (1980)	5	5	5.0	10.0	10.0	20
World production capacity	34	46	70.5	96.5	113.0	157
World consumption:						
North America	7-10	10-12	24.0[E]	30.0[E]	39.0	43
Rest of the world	21-24	28-30	36.0[E]	50.0[E]	71.0[E]	92
Total world[c]	31	40	60.0[E]	80.0[E]	110.0[E]	135

Sources: Cited in the text.

[E] = Estimated from occasional data points in other years.

[a] From Table 10.2 below.

[b] Dates are the years commercial production began by these pioneer companies, possibly at other production sites.

[c] Assumed smooth growth using published 1982 and 1990 estimates. Total includes one small plant in Kyoto, Japan owned by Toray Industries not shown separately.

Table 7.A.2. North American Production Capacity and Consumption of Feed-Grade Lysine, 1980-1990.

Company: Plant (Year production began)	1980	1982	1984	1986	1988	1989	1990
				Thousand metric tonnes			
Kyowa Hakko/Biokyowa:							
Cape Giradeau, MO (1984)	0	0	7.5	7.5	7.5	7.5	13
Fermentaciones Mexicanas (1980)	1	2	6.0	6.0	6.0[E]	9.0[E]	9[E]
Ajinomoto/Heartland Lysine:							
Eddyville, Iowa (1986)	0	0	0	7.0	7.0[E]	12.0	12
Total plant capacity:							
United States	0	0	7.5	14.5	14.5	19.5	25
Mexico	0	2	6.0	6.0	6.0	9.0	9
North America	0	2	13.5	20.5	20.5	28.5	34
Apparent N. American production[a]	1	2	10.5	17.5	17.5	21.5	30
Estimated consumption:							
United States	6-9	8-11	20[E]	26[E]	33[E]	36	43
Canada	0.5	1[E]	2[E]	2[E]	3[E]	4	4[E]
Mexico	0.5	1[E]	2[E]	2[E]	3[E]	4[E]	4[E]
North America	7-10	10-12	24[E]	30[E]	39	44	51
Net imports[b]	6-9	8-10	18.0[E]	13.5[E]	21.5[E]	22.5[E]	21

Source: Appendix A of Connor (1998) and citations in the text.
[E] = Estimated from assumed trends between more definitive estimates or facts.
[a] Generally 85% of capacity when plants or expansions are mature; closer to 70% of capacity when expansions are new.
[b] The difference between No. American consumption and apparent production, checked for consistency with U.S. trade data (Tables 10.4 and 10.5 below).

Table 7.A.3. Global Capacity Shares of Leading Lysine Manufacturers, 1982-2000.

Company	1982	1984	1986	1988	1990	1992	1994	1996	1998	2000
					Thousand Metric Tonnes					
Ajinomoto & Orsan	25	36	60	72	77	120	113	156	175	190
Kyowa Hakko Kogyo	8	22	22	24	42	52	68	68	62	97
Sewon/Miwon	5	5	10	10	30	40	50	80	135	135
Cheil Sugar Co.	0	0	0	0	0	20	25	30	30	30
Archer Daniels Midland	0	0	0	0	0	80	113	113	205	250
Cargill & Degussa	0	0	0	0	0	0	0	0	0	87
Others	0	0	0	0	0	0	3	36	56	41
Total capacity[a]	46	71	97	113	157	320	375	470	647	830[E]
						Percent				
Ajinomoto	54	50	62	63	52	38	30	33	28	23
Kyowa Hakko	17	31	22	21	25	16	18	14	10	12
Sewon/Miwon	11	7	10	9	18	13	13	17	21	16
Cheil Sugar	0	0	0	0	0	6	7	6	5	4
Archer Daniels Midland	0	0	0	0	0	25	30	24	32	30
Cargill & Degussa	0	0	0	0	0	0	0	0	0	10
Others	0	0	0	0	0	0	1	8	9	5
Total[a]	100	100	100	100	100	100	100	100	100	100

Source: Tables 1, 2, 6 and 7.
[a] Includes a small Japanese plant owned by Toray Industries that is not shown separately. Toray exited the lysine industry after 1986 but before 1995.

Table 7.A.4. North American Production Capacity and Consumption of Feed-Grade Lysine, 1991-2000.

Company: Plants (Year Production Began)	1991	1992	1993	1994	1995	1996	1997	1998	1999	2000
					Thousand metric tonnes/year					
Kyowa Hakko/Biokyowa:										
Cape Giradeau, MO (1984)	13	15	15^E	20^E	20^E	20^E	22	22	28	28
Fermex, Mexico (1980)	15	15	15	15	20	20^E	20^E	22	44	44
Ajinomoto/Heartland:										
Eddyville, IA (1986)	18	20	20	20	40^E	40	60^E	60^E	60^E	60^E
Archer Daniels Midland:										
Decatur, IL (1991)	60	80^E	113	113	113	113	160^E	160	160	160^E
Cedar Rapids, IA (1998)	0	0	0	0	0	0	0	45	45	90^E
Cargill & Degussa:										
Eddyville, IA (2000)	0	0	0	0	0	0	0	0	0	75
Total plant capacity:										
United States	91	155	148	153	173	173	242	289	368	413
Mexico	15	15	15	15	20	20	20	22	44	44
North America	106	130	163	168	193	193	262	311	384	427
Apparent production[a]	65	85	112	124	142	162	176	180	160^E	216^E
Estimated consumption:										
United States	47	48	74	79	83	86	87	100	--	--
Canada[c]	5^E	5	6	7	8	8	9	10	--	--
Mexico	5^E	6^E	6^E	9^E	10^E	10^E	10^E	11	--	--
North America	57	59	86	95	101	104	106	121	128^E	141^E
Net exports, U.S.	5^E	30	34	39	43	59	83^E	68	40^E	--
Net exports, No. America[b]	8^E	26	26	29	41	58	70	59	31^E	75^E

^{E} = Estimated from trends between more definitive statements or published estimates.
Source: Connor (1998a: Appendix A), citations in text, and trial transcript.

[a] In 1991, assumed Kyowa high capacity utilization, ADM low utilization. During 1991-1999, the sum of consumption and net exports. Assumes no change in inventories.

[b] In 1991, a residual. After 1991, accurate U.S. trade data plus estimated Mexican exports less U.S. exports to Canada and Mexico; that is, net NAFTA exports of lysine.

[c] From 1992, equals U.S. exports to Canada, except 1996-1997 when 3,000 tonnes non-U.S. imports assumed.

Table 7.A.5. World Production Capacity and Consumption of Feed-Grade Lysine, 1990-2000.

Company: Plants Outside North America (Year)	1990	1991	1992	1993	1994	1995	1996	1997	1998	1999	2000
	Thousand metric tonnes/year										
North American capacity[a]	34	106	130	163	168	193	193	262	311	384	427
Ajinomoto & Orsan:											
Saga, Japan (ca. 1970)	20[E]	20[E]	20[E]	20[E]	10[E]	10[E]	0	0	0	0	0
Amiens, France (1979)[b]	40[E]	40	40	45[E]	45[E]	50	50	50[E]	60[E]	60[E]	60[E]
Pathun, Thani, Thailand (1986)	5[E]	10[E]	10[E]	10[E]	15[E]	15[E]	15	20[E]	20[E]	20[E]	20[E]
Bottrighe, Italy (1992)[b]	0	0	0	10[E]	15[E]	15[E]	20[E]	20[E]	25[E]	25[E]	25[E]
Sichuan Prov., China (1996)	0	0	0	0	0	0	6	15[E]	15[E]	20[E]	20[E]
Valparaiso, Brazil (1997)	0	0	0	0	0	0	0	15	15	15[E]	20[E]
Kyowa Hakko:											
Hofu, Japan (1977)	20[E]	20[E]	20	20	20	20	0	0	0	0	0
Kaba, Hungary (1991)	0	5	5	8[E]	8[E]	10[E]	10[E]	12	12	15[E]	15[E]
Vietnam (1999)	0	0	0	0	0	0	0	0	0	10[E]	10[E]
Sewon (Miwon Group):											
Busan, So. Korea (1980)	10	0[E]	0	0	0	0	0	0	0	0	0
Kunsan, So. Korea (1989)	20	36	36	50[E]	50	80	80[E]	96	135	135[E]	135[E]
Cheil Sugar Co.:											
Java, Indonesia (1991)	0	9	15[E]	20[E]	20[E]	40[E]	40[E]	50[E]	50[E]	60[E]	60[E]
Degussa/Fermas:											
Slovenska Lupca, Slovakia (1994)	0	0	0	0	3	3	6[E]	6[E]	6[E]	6[E]	12[E]
AECI Chemical:											
Durban, So. Africa (1994)	0	0	0	0	0	11	11	11	11[E]	11[E]	11[E]
Chinese Govt. Companies	0	0	0	0	3	3	19	19	19[E]	25[E]	30[E]
World production capacity	157	254	284	354	365	458	454	580	679	791	848
World Consumption:											
North America[a]	43	57	59	86	95	101	104	106	121[E]	128[E]	141[E]
Rest of the world	102	123	140	150	159	169	206	229	249	277	304
Total world[d]	145	180	199	236	254[c]	270	310[E]	335	370[E]	405[E]	445[E]
Consumption/Capacity Ratio (%)	92	71	70	66	70	60	68	58	54	51	52

Sources: Same as Table 7.A.4.
[a] From Table 7.A.4.
[b] From late 1993, Orsan was no longer a partner in these plants.
[c] The internal business records of ADM estimate world consumption at 245,000 tonnes.
[d] Estimates for the years 1991-1995 are lysine cartel figures taken from trial exhibits. Includes one small plant in Kyoto, Japan owned by Toray Industries that closed some time in the late 1980s or early 1990s. Rest of the world is a residual.

Table 7.A.6. Total U.S. Imports and Exports of Lysine, 1989-1997.

Trade Item[a]	1989	1990	1991	1992	1993	1994	1995	1996	1997[b]
Value:					*Thousand dollars*				
U.S. Imports (c.i.f.)	69966	39394	24811	21408	39564	46218	18272	34830	75269
Food Grade	–	–	–	10890	24100	22173	5792	6113	9381
Feed Grade	–	–	–	10518	15464	24045	12480	28717	65888
U.S. Exports (f.a.s.)	3859	4310	17489	76084	83751	116539	103740	161407	282611
Quantity:					*Metric tonnes*				
U.S. Imports (c.i.f.)	22726	18333	11262	8345	11144	13921	7347	12952	17091
Food Grade	2100[E]	1900[E]	1700[E]	1119	1667	3230	1195	1324	1923
Feed Grade	20626	16433	9562	7226	9477	10691	6152	11628	15168
U.S. exports (f.a.s.)	857	867	6208	37708	43655	51446	49212	71359	104172
Implicit price:					*Dollars per pound*				
U.S. Imports	1.40	2.15	2.20	1.16	1.61	1.51	1.13	1.22	2.00
Food Grade	–	–	–	5.89	5.63	3.11	2.17	2.27	2.06
Feed Grade	–	–	–	0.66	0.74	1.02	0.92	1.12	1.97
U.S. Exports	2.04	2.26	1.27	0.92	0.87	1.03	0.96	1.03	1.23

Source: National Trade Data Bank (CD-Rom).
– = Not available
[E] = Estimated from 1992-1997 food-grade trend.
[a] Feed grade is identified by originating only from Mexico, France, Italy, India, Thailand, Indonesia, Korea, or Japan at prices of less than $4 per pound. The official codes for pharmaceutical or feed grades misclassify some shipments, but these have been corrected.

Chapter 8

THE LYSINE CONSPIRACY

Two top executives of the giant U.S. agribusiness firm Archer Daniels Midland flew from the company's headquarters in Decatur, Illinois to Tokyo, Japan in April 1992. Terrance Wilson, President of the sprawling corn-products division of ADM, disliked long flights because he reacted badly to the effects of jet lag, but he was epitome of the loyal manager and this trip could make tens of millions of dollars for his company if everything went according to plan. Along with Wilson was a brash new ADM vice president, Mark Whitacre, who headed up ADM's new Bioproducts Division. Whitacre was a quickly rising star at ADM. With his Ph.D. in nutritional biochemistry from prestigious Cornell University, he was well equipped to handle the technical side of the high-tech bioproducts business. The product the two men were concerned about was lysine, an essential amino acid that speeds up the formation of lean meat on farm animals. After getting his Ph.D., Whitacre had worked for the German company Degussa that was the world's biggest maker of amino acids, and it was there that Whitacre had discovered he had a flair for salesmanship. It was this rare combination of talents that prompted ADM to depart from company practice and hire him away from Degussa rather than promote from within.

Terry Wilson had come as a young man straight from the U.S. Marine Corps to work for ADM. He loved the company and its charismatic leader, Dwayne O. Andreas, who had several times demonstrated that he personally cared for Wilson and his handicapped son. Wilson applied his tough military ways to his jobs at ADM, so that he rose from near the bottom of the company's organization to very near to its pinnacle in his 25 years with ADM. Although Wilson had never gone to college, he had a thing or two to teach his more polished underling who was twenty years his junior. It was not the sort of thing taught in business schools.

Terry Wilson was going to teach Mark Whitacre how to fix the world price of lysine.

This was a way of doing business that Terry Wilson knew a lot about. Just a year before this trip to Tokyo, Wilson had taken a very similar mission to Europe with his younger colleague Barrie Cox. In a few months under Wilson's tutelage Cox had turned into an accomplished price fixer of citric acid (see Chapter 5). Now was the time to repeat that highly profitable lesson for Whitacre's Biotechnology Division. Like citric acid, lysine was a high-tech product made by fermentation of the corn sweetener dextrose. Like citric acid, ADM had just entered the industry in a big way but wasn't yet the industry's top dog – ADM's ultimate objective in all its lines of business.

Like citric acid, new entry into the industry had precipitated a fierce price war that turned the ink red in all the producer's books.

Now the time was ripe to let ADM's rivals know that it was ready to play ball, to call off their aggressive scramble for market share, and to stanch the outflow of profits precipitated by the bloody yearlong price war. Wilson and Whitacre were on a peace mission to Tokyo to meet their counterparts at Ajinomoto and Kyowa Hakko, the two oldest and still dominant makers of lysine in the world. When the Americans met the Ajinomoto executives for the first time, Wilson made several specific proposals: establishing a lysine trade association, audited sales reports for its members, and a 50 percent increase in price. The sincerity of ADM's offer to cooperate rather than fight would take a while to sink in, but within a few months the managers of all three companies would be toasting their newly formed partnership in crime.

The lysine cartel held its first formal meeting in June 1992. The event that made the conspiracy possible was ADM's decision in 1989 to build the world's biggest lysine plant. Without the demonstrated power of ADM's large production to disrupt the market and to discipline recalcitrant lysine producers, the cartel would never have formed in the first place. ADM used the carrot of profits for all, the stick of its unused capacity, and diplomacy of a high order to get the others to join and cooperate. For the Asian producers a lengthy price war made them pine for the old days when world pricing was simply a sellers' management decision.

THE PRICE WAR OF 1991-1992

ADM's plant in Decatur had a planned capacity three times larger than the biggest then in existence, Eurolysine's French plant. It was so large that the Asian manufacturers doubted that it was technically feasible. To demonstrate its prowess, ADM did the unthinkable in an industry rife with technological secrets: it gave unrestricted plant tours to executives and expert industrial engineers of Ajinomoto, Kyowa, and Sewon. When the Asian lysine makers later met and shared their impressions about the size of the Decatur plant, it is clear that skepticism had shifted to credulity. What they saw was not quite the 250 million pounds of capacity that ADM claimed, but they agreed that at least 130 million pounds of capacity had been installed by early 1992.

What the plant tours had not quite accomplished, the market effects of ADM's entry made crystal clear. As ADM's production ramped up in early 1991, prices plummeted and the sales shares of the three Asian sellers fell dramatically. Indeed, U.S. lysine prices had fallen throughout 1990 in anticipation of ADM's entry. The prospect of lower prices turned out to be a self-fulfilling prophecy. In the three months before ADM's entry, the average U.S. lysine price was $1.32 per pound. Eighteen months later when the price war came to an end, the U.S. transaction price had tumbled to an historic low of $0.68 per pound.[1]

There is little doubt that the vast increases in lysine tonnage from ADM's Decatur plant were the principal reasons for the U.S. price drop. The company sold less than 1 million pounds of lysine in the first quarter of 1991 (Table 8.A.1). By the end of the year, ADM was selling lysine to U.S. customers at an annual rate of 50 million pounds; ADM was by that time supplying 39 percent of U.S. demand, all of it sales taken away from the three Asian manufacturers. ADM's relentless push for market dominance continued through to the summer of 1992, when its U.S. sales reached nearly 80 million pounds on an annual basis, or 71 percent of U.S. consumption. The only way ADM could have zipped from zero to 71 percent of the U.S. market in a year and a half was through large price cuts. Except for a brief period when regular seasonal demand peaked (August-October 1992), prices fell each month from January 1991 to July 1992, a total decline of almost 50 percent. It is obvious that demand for lysine had not weakened during this price war. In fact just the opposite occurred: in response to the low prices, total U.S. consumption of lysine was 11.3 percent higher in 1991 than before the price war in 1990.[2] Thus, the downward movement in lysine prices was nearly entirely explained by ADM's vast supply increase.

By the second quarter of 1992, the Decatur plant was pushing out so much lysine that it exceeded total U.S. market consumption. Anticipating this looming saturation of the domestic market, ADM began exporting just a few months after start up. By the third quarter of 1991, ADM was exporting one-fifth of its tonnage; by the first half of 1992, exports were more than half of the quantity it sold (Table 8.A.1). As will be explored in more detail later, imports of lysine into the United States declined precipitously in 1991 and 1992. Lysine that might have ended up in the United States but for ADM's production was diverted to other world markets. The combined effects of ADM's exports and the diverted U.S. imports caused lysine prices to fall worldwide.

Ajinomoto had begun developing a strategy to cope with ADM's entry as early as April 1990 (Tr. 840). Neither Ajinomoto nor Kyowa had any success in slowing what appeared to them to be ADM's inexorable drive for global dominance. Credible testimony confirms the obvious: all three Asian lysine manufacturers were extremely worried about ADM's huge impact on lysine prices (Tr. 1776-1801). The price impact was worldwide. In France, Eurolysine saw lysine prices plummet 60 percent from 1990 to mid- 1992 (Tr. 2239-42). Internal financial records of Ajinomoto's Heartland Lysine showed that the affiliate lost $1.9 million in fiscal 1992, which its board attributed entirely to ADM's aggressive volume growth (Tr. 2065). Desperate to signal their willingness to cooperate, Ajinomoto and Kyowa attempted to raise prices several times in early 1992 (Tr. 841), but ADM seemed committed to inflicting memorable pain on its rivals. By early 1992, the three Asian manufacturers were holding talks among themselves that led them to seriously consider asking ADM to join them in a more cooperative arrangement (Tr. 1776-1801). With an acceptable offer, the time was ripe for collusion.

ADM shortly thereafter signaled its willingness to engage in softer forms of competition. In April 1992, Mark Whitacre and his boss Terrance Wilson journeyed across the Pacific to meet with top Ajinomoto and Kyowa managers. ADM proposed forming a world lysine association that would meet on a regular basis. The new association would collect and distribute mostly production and market-share information, much like the Corn Refiners Association did for the U.S. corn wet milling products (Tr. 1734-36). Wilson also suggested that, like the European Citric Acid Manufacturers' Association, the new association would provide a convenient cover for illegal price-fixing discussions (Tr. 2186). In a year or two, a lysine association in fact emerged that met quarterly and performed the two functions that Wilson proposed.

Why did ADM initiate these price discussions at this time, and did the discussions cause prices to rise? The answer to the first question revolves around several factors. First, ADM had in early 1992 achieved its strategic goal by accounting for one-third of global sales. Wilson repeatedly assured its Asian rivals that ADM wanted no more than equality with the leading firm (Ajinomoto). Aggressive pricing was no longer necessary to expand its market share beyond this satisfactory level. Second, ADM believed that its rivals were convinced that the Decatur plant could crank up to even more damaging levels of output. Third, unknown to the Asian companies, ADM was having considerable difficulties with low yields due to contamination of its lysine fermentors.[3] Throwing away a bad batch cost ADM millions of dollars each time it happened. Fourth, and perhaps the most pressing reason, ADM had forced prices so low that it was losing money on its lysine operation. Testimony reveals that to overcome initial FBI skepticism about the existence of ADM-related price fixing, Whitacre showed the FBI ADM's financial statements for the lysine department (Tr. 2834-35). Net margins had turned *negative* in the months of July and August 1992 when U.S. lysine prices averaged \$0.66 per pound. Equally interesting is the fact that ADM's lysine profits became positive during September and October 1992 when the price jumped up to \$0.82 and \$0.92, respectively. Whitacre considered this pretty good evidence that the Mexico City Agreement was effective for the cartel. This evidence also supports the notion that ADM's average costs of lysine production were somewhere between \$0.68 and \$0.82 per pound.

MEETINGS AND METHODS

The lysine cartel held ten formal meetings to fix prices. At least three companies were present at these quarterly meetings, and except for Cheil each company sent two or more representatives. (By late 1993, these meetings had become so routine that Terry Wilson also stopped going). In addition, at least 22 other significant face-to-face meetings were held. Eight were bilateral events involving ADM, such as its Decatur plant tours (Connor 2000: Table A4). The remaining 14 meetings were held in Tokyo or Seoul among two or more of the four Asian lysine producers to develop strategies to cope with ADM's proposals on a volume-allocation agreement (Tr. 5018). Finally, there were hundreds of telephone calls made during the conspiracy to coordinate list price changes and to report monthly sales information to the secretary of the lysine association, Kanji Mimoto, head of the feed additives division of Ajinomoto.

The total number of men who attended these various meetings and who were later identified as conspirators in U.S. legal documents was 42.[4] However, this total excludes a unknown number of employees, mostly regional sales managers, who participated in regional price-fixing discussions in Europe, Latin America, and elsewhere later in the conspiracy. At ADM, only ten to 12 men were informed about the lysine conspiracy, of which prosecutors identified three as "cartel managers" or principal co-conspirators. There were six principal conspirators who worked for Ajinomoto or Eurolysine, one for Kyowa, two for Sewon, and one for Cheil. Nearly all of the principal co-conspirators were eventually fined or indicted for their illegal activities.

The Cartel Begins Meeting

In late June 1992, the first of many meetings of what was to become the "lysine association" took place (Connor 2000: Appendix Table A4). In the Nikko Hotel in Mexico City, seven men representing ADM, Ajinomoto, and Kyowa Hakko discussed raising prices and allocating sales shares across several regions of the world. Wilson led the discussion, often repeating ADM's creed:

"The competitor is our friend, and the customer is our enemy."

However, not all competitors were treated as friends. Consistent with its public statements that it was coerced into joining the cartel, federal prosecutors later charged M. Andreas, Wilson and Whitacre with intimidating

Sewon (and possibly Cheil Jedang as well). They threatened to dump huge amounts of lysine onto the market unless Sewon and others joined the cartel and ceded significant market share to ADM.

The lysine conspiracy evolved through two distinct phases: the first from November 1992 to March 1993 and the second from about October 1993 to at least July 1995 (Figure 8.1). During the first phase, the conspirators agreed on prices but were never able to agree on market shares. The conspirators apparently were successful in raising the U.S. price of lysine to $0.98 for three months (November 1992 to March 1993). The agreement broke down in the spring of 1993 when trying to get a consensus on production limits. The second phase was the most harmonious and profitable for the cartel.

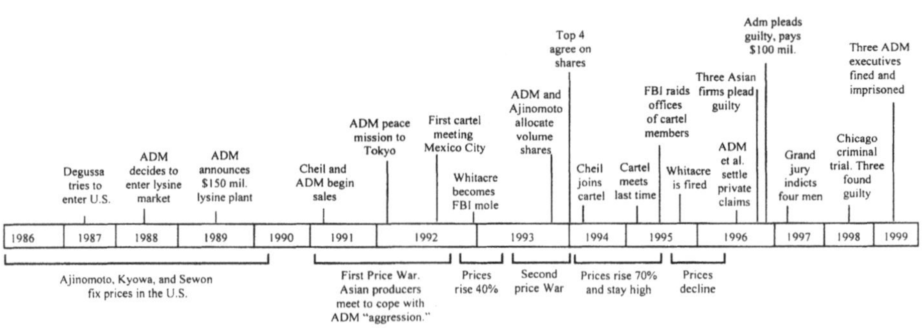

Figure 8.1. Time Line for the Lysine Industry, 1986-1999.

To calm the fears of Ajinomoto in particular, in Mexico City Wilson explained ADM's overall strategic goal in lysine as well as other product markets. As copied into minutes of that meeting circulated to top Ajinomoto managers:

> "ADM's top management has an extremely clear-cut policy on sales share. Their intent is not to insist on having an absolute majority of the sales share, such as 50% or more, but rather to have the same scope of shares as the largest competitor in that industry . . ." (Tr. Ex. 4-T).

Wilson repeated ADM's stance a few months later at the first Paris meeting. As paraphrased in Eurolysine's minutes of that meeting, "ADM considers over 35-40 percent world market share crazy" (Tr. Ex. 34).

The Role of Uncertainty

A cartel resembles a joint venture set up by several partners who independently manufacture a product to be sold through the joint venture. However, unlike a conventional joint venture, the lysine cartel had no corps of middle managers to provide continuity and execute the decisions of top management. In effect, the conspirators were a rotating board of directors that had to implement its own decisions about prices and sales quotas. The absence of a cadre of experienced managers monitoring daily developments in the market meant that the cartel faced somewhat greater uncertainties about market conditions than an on-going company would face. Uncertainty is especially important in cartels because cheating on price or volume agreements is usually profitable for the deviant firm. The existence of cheating can to some extent be detected by unexpected short run price declines or increases in the total quantity sold. Knowing this to be the case, cheaters have an incentive to misrepresent their sales quantities or prices.

The difficulty of ascertaining total production or demand is illustrated by the exchanges of such information at various cartel meetings. Presumably, the major global sellers of lysine were the best informed group on the planet, yet each of them harbored significant misapprehensions about the production levels of other sellers, and, therefore, the global size of the market. These misapprehensions were especially evident prior to and at the beginning of the lysine cartel (Connor 2000: Appendix Table A6). For example, immediately before the cartel was formed, the three largest Asian firms estimated ADM's 1991 production to be only 29 million pounds, which was about 20 percent too low. Two months later, after one collusive meeting, the same group's estimate for ADM in mid-1992 (130 million) was at least 35 percent too low. In 1993, Sewon asserted that Ajinomoto's and Kyowa's production figures were about 10 percent lower than those companies claimed. Similarly, in 1992 and 1993, the two Japanese producers believed that production levels claimed by both Korean upstarts were quite a bit lower than actual production. At the beginning, ADM had greatly underestimated production by its Asian rivals. When ADM first met in Mexico City in June 1992, ADM found that its sales volume figures were far lower than those of the two Japanese firms; it was off by 16 percent for world consumption and 37 percent too low for the Asian region. The conspirators agreed to accept the Japanese numbers.[5]

After pooling their production data in 1993-1995, a consensus on the size of company production and global demand evolved. From mid 1993 to early 1995, disagreement about the size of global demand or company production levels hardly ever erupted. This consensus helped the conspiracy to move forward harmoniously and raise prices to ever higher levels.

Allocating Sales Quotas

Agreeing to raise prices proved to be a much easier decision than agreeing to company-by-company volume quotas. Higher prices lifted everybody's profits, whereas the size of a company's quota was going to determine its share of the pool of monopoly profits generated by the conspiracy. The inability to arrive at an apportionment that did not exceed 100 percent was a major cause of the second price war of early 1993. By June 1993, prices had plunged to an historic low of $0.62, though soon afterwards the usual seasonal forces began to push prices up. The rift was resolved at an October 1993 meeting between ADM and Ajinomoto in Irvine, California. Global sales quotas were adopted by the cartel.

In the end, the great compromise reached by M. Andreas and K. Yamada at the October 1993 Irvine meeting gave ADM substantially less than its goal of one-third the global market. Later, as the dazzling profits from the scheme began to roll in, the rationalization that made this compromise possible was soon forgotten. ADM and Ajinomoto had agreed to share equally almost all the growth in volume of lysine. Mathematically, the two could never quite achieve equality under such a rule, but after many years they would be quite close to parity. According to the follow-up agreement in December 1993 in Tokyo, both Ajinomoto's and ADM's shares were to increase at the expense of the other three companies' shares. It was no time to rock such a profitable boat. In fact, when the time came to apportion expected 1995 global volume among the cartel members, the conspirators' market shares remained exactly the same as their 1994 shares (Tr. Ex. 17-T).

Monitoring the Volume Agreements

Kanji Mimoto of Ajinomoto was assigned the task of preparing monthly "scorecards" for the five members of the cartel as a way of tracking adherence to the volume shares agreed upon. Each month, the five companies telephoned or mailed their lysine volumes of sales to Mimoto, who prepared a running spreadsheet that was handed out and discussed at the quarterly maintenance meetings. Sales volumes were calculated for four regions (North America, Latin America, Europe/Middle East/Africa and Asia/Oceania) and for the world.

A scoresheet covering the calendar year 1994 was submitted as Exhibit 16 by the Government in the Chicago criminal trial. This scoresheet was used to track monthly progress toward the "budgeted" amount of lysine (that is, each company's agreed-upon quota). Because of seasonal demand patterns, most of the companies were below target during the first six months of the year, but this shortfall was made up for in the late summer and early fall when lysine demand surged. By the end of 1994, sales volume reported by the five companies had reached 254,566 metric tonnes, just 1.4% higher than the targeted amount adopted in December 1993. However, the five companies achieved percentage market shares that were remarkably close to the target shares. Sewon was farthest from its allotted share, selling 14.3 percent of the world's lysine instead of 14.7 percent. Had some of the cartel's members been far from their targeted shares, a compensation system had been designed involving intra-cartel sales at the elevated monopoly price by deficit firms (Tr. Ex. 142-T). At its January 1995 meeting in Atlanta, new volume targets were computed based on an assumed 5 percent or 7 percent annual volume growth in lysine.

There were no regional quotas, but because of the locations of their plants, some companies tended to dominate certain regions. In 1994, ADM accounted for 42 percent of U.S. and Canadian lysine sales volume; Ajinomoto and Kyowa each shared about 25 percent of that market. In Latin America, Kyowa controlled nearly half of sales. In Europe, Ajinomoto dominated with 45 percent of sales. The Asian market was more fragmented with Ajinomoto in the lead (34% of sales) followed by Sewon (24 percent), ADM (27 percent), Kyowa (19 percent), and Cheil (11 percent).

The lysine cartel agreed to follow and monitor global quantity shares in late 1993. One reason it took more than a year of negotiations to reach this consensus is that some of the members of the cartel preferred a different method for assigning shares. At an important meeting in Tokyo in May 1993 of the top managers of the three largest Asian producers, the necessity of some sort of volume agreement was accepted, but Ajinomoto and Sewon spoke in favor of exclusive geographic markets as the mechanism (Tr. Ex. 139-T). Sewon proposed that Kyowa be given a monopoly in Japan. Sewon in turn was requested to reduce sales to the U.S. and European markets ". . . upon the principle that a local producer should sell as much as possible in its region" (Tr. Ex. 125-T). The Japanese manufacturers also complained that Sewon had aggressively increased sales in Japan and Mexico, a violation of the principle of home-country hegemony.

There is at first blush an appealing simplicity to assigning exclusive market sales territories to each of the conspirators. Such a system would make monitoring an agreement fairly straightforward, but it raised other contentious issues at the same time. Who would get to sell in the fastest growing markets of Asia and Latin America? No region had supply and demand in balance, so import and export quotas would have had to be devised, a calculus more complicated than that required for a single global quota. Finally, assigning exclusive territories would require four of the companies to refuse to bid for the business in those areas, possibly tipping off antitrust regulators.

The Problem of Geographic Arbitrage

The lysine cartel colluded on list prices for four major world regions. However, the companies expected a degree of downward departure on prices of actual transactions, so long as the discounting was not too severe and did not disrupt progress in achieving the market-share targets. In its December 1993 meeting in Tokyo, the five conspiring companies compared "actual trading price" with the "agreed price" that was to have been charged from November 5, 1993 onward (Tr. Ex. 142-T). Transaction prices were 3 percent below target in the United States and 6 percent below in Europe. Such price differences were partly the result of discounts customarily offered to the largest contracting customers. Also, the larger price gap in Europe might have been due to arbitrage conducted by wholesalers taking advantage of lower North American lysine prices. At their previous meeting in Paris in October 1993, an Ajinomoto memorandum stated that:

> "With the [Deutschmark] strong against the $, presently it is 22% higher than in the U.S. If the difference between Europe and the U.S. becomes bigger, ill-reputed dealers will start working and goods will enter Europe from the U.S. and decrease the price" (Tr. Ex. 10-T).

Finally, in Asia, Latin America, and Oceania, the conspirators believed that December 1993 transactions prices were 10% below the higher target prices set in October. This larger gap could have been the result of somewhat more price cutting by the manufacturers. But at their Tokyo meeting the consensus was that lags in serving export markets were the main reason. "Price increases up to the agreed price can take around 3 months at least (especially, South America and Asia)" (Tr. Ex. 142-T). The three months is reasonable given the normal 30-day price protection in most contracts, coupled with the delays in ocean shipping to the consuming markets with no local lysine production.

Demand Elasticity

In their pricing decisions, members of the lysine cartel were concerned about the elasticity of demand for lysine. They worried at times that total volume demanded might decline rapidly if the cartel raised its price too high in some regional markets (i.e., the elasticity of own-price was less than negative one or "inelastic"). Elsewhere, in more mature markets like Japan, the lysine managers believed that volume was unresponsive to price (i.e., the elasticity was close to zero).

The most extensive discussion of the elasticity of demand (though this particular term was not used) took place at the first Paris meeting in October 1992 (Tr. Ex. 10-T and 128-T). In a discussion of the U.S. market Whitacre opined that: "When the price was increased from $0.95/lb. to $1.05/lb., the demand went down by 10%." This statement means that Whitacre implicitly estimated the demand elasticity to be between -0.95 and -1.05, depending on the price level.

However, Whitacre's estimate was contradicted forcefully by a much more experienced Japanese sales manager. Kanji Mimoto, who had been selling lysine for more than 20 years for Ajinomoto, pointed out that Whitacre had failed to consider the regularly seasonality of demand when making his statement. Mimoto estimated that by increasing the U.S. price from $1.05 to $1.15 per pound, the *annual* impact on U.S. demand (ignoring seasonal factors) would be "less than 8,000-10,000 tonnes." At the then current levels of U.S. annual volume (53 to 59 thousand tonnes), Mimoto's implicit estimate of U.S. demand elasticity was in the range -1.4 to –2.0. The group had the opinion that the demand for lysine was more inelastic for poultry-feed buyers than for swine-feed buyers (the larger of the two groups). This observation led them to consider whether price discrimination between the two types of buyers might be feasible. "What about dual price [customer price differentiation]?," Mimoto asked. In a comment that appears to be out of character, Wilson said he thought it was legally impossible. They also considered, but rejected, a more elaborate system of price discrimination based on customer sizes.

The Shadow Price of Lysine

The conspirators were well aware of the fact that the availability of natural lysine in oilseed meals and fish meal provided a constraint on lysine pricing. Moreover, corn or other rough feed grains needed to be mixed with synthetic lysine when substituted for natural lysine sources. In the United States, soybean meal was by far the dominant source of natural lysine. Thus, soybean meal was a substitute for lysine made by fermentation, but corn was a complement to lysine. If the price of soybean meal fell far enough and the price of corn was high enough, demand for synthetic lysine would disappear unless its price fell below the soybean meal-corn shadow price.

When the ceiling price was well above the market price, the lysine cartel felt comfortable about raising prices. At the 1992 Paris meeting of the five cartel members, there was discussion of soybean meal quality and likely price trends (Tr. Ex. 128-T). "That is, this is a threat to the U.S. price increase . . . However, the corn price went down and the shadow price can be estimated up to U.S. $1.50/lb." In other words, the cartel should not increase its selling price so far that it comes close to $1.50 per pound, especially if soybean prices are likely to decline. The cartel's target price at the time was only $1.05, so the shadow price was really only a distant threat to raising prices.

The conspirators paid close attention to the shadow price "spread," that is, the difference between the shadow price and transactions prices. At a June 1993 meeting in Tokyo, the four Asian producers estimated the spread to be a comfortable $0.90 to $1.00 per pound at a time when the lysine price was very low worldwide (Tr. Ex. 131-T and 132-T). The list price was $0.85 per pound, just about $1.00 below the shadow price (Figure 8.2). Interestingly, these companies used U.S. data on 44%-protein soybean meal to calculate the shadow price, even though fish meal was widely used in Asia as the natural lysine source.

The shadow price continued to receive attention from the conspirators up through 1995 (Tr. Ex. 17-T). In January, the cartel believed that the shadow price spread was somewhat lower, about $0.60 per pound. Even if they were using price data a few months old, the true spread in September or October had been only about $0.40 per pound and was declining rapidly. By January, the ceiling price had fallen slightly below the U.S. transactions price and in January the spread was a negative 15 cents or so. Despite the obviously cooperative mood of the cartel in its January meeting, the transactions price of lysine fell a few cents each month from January to a trough in September 1995. The negative spread during the first five months of 1995 eventually made lysine prices fall, the only period in which the ceiling price forced the market price down during 1991-1995.

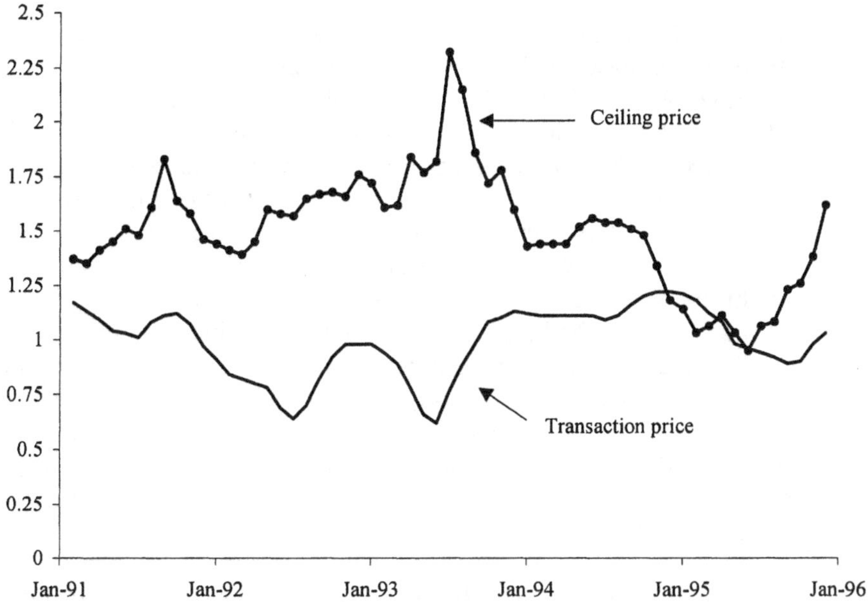

Figure 8.2. Monthly U.S. Transactions and Ceiling Prices of Lysine, 1991-1995.

Sources: Lysine prices supplied by three defendants in a notice to class-action members. Ceiling price based on formula (100 lb. soymeal = 97 lb. corn + 3 lb. lysine) and Illinois cash prices for corn and soybean.

A more technical analysis of the U.S. lysine market by Morse and Hyde (2000) confirms that the shadow price did indeed affect lysine demand. Using the conventional formula based on animal nutrition principles (100 lb. soy meal = 97 lb. corn + 3 lb. lysine) to calculate the shadow price, their model found that variation in the monthly shadow price was positively related to the quantity of lysine sold during 1990-1995. That is, a combination of U.S. soy meal and corn prices behaved as a substitute in the market for lysine. On average, holding the price of lysine itself constant, if the shadow price rose by 10 percent, the quantity of lysine sold would rise 3.5 percent. Thus, the lysine cartel partially adjusted its total sales volume and price in response to movements in the prices of two agricultural products they could not control: soybeans and corn.

Seasonality of Demand

Members of the cartel broadly agreed on the importance of seasonality of demand for lysine. They called it the "winter effect." On-farm use of mixed feeds for swine and poultry operations peaked in the coldest months, January-February in the northern hemisphere.[6] Peak monthly sales for lysine during 1991-1995 was always December (Connor 2000: Table A2). Morse and Hyde (2000) estimated the demand for lysine in the U.S. market during 1990-1995. Taking into account monthly price changes and factors that affect the ultimate demand for meat products, they found that the demand for lysine peaked in the four winter months December through March. This finding would be consistent with the seasonal feed requirements of poultry and hog producers, who would step up the quantities of feed per live animal in the coldest months. U.S. feed manufacturers apparently increase their winter purchases of lysine to prepare mixed feeds for their farm customers and perhaps to build up inventories of prepared feeds or feed concentrates for sales later in the year. The quantity of lysine sold to feed manufacturers in the winters of 1990-1995 was 14 percent above the annual average. For lysine plants serving the U.S. and European markets, seasonal *production* would be elevated in the fall months in order to build inventory for the winter sales peak.

Cartel participants generally believed that the volume of lysine demanded fell 30%, the winter period compared with the peak months (Tr. Ex. 10-T and 128-T). This number seems exaggerated for the U.S. market, and because seasonality is absent in tropical areas, global seasonality ought to be much less pronounced. Also, Southern hemisphere seasonality compensated for some of that in the Northern hemisphere.

Nevertheless, seasonality of sales in the two largest demand regions would normally cause prices to rise in the last quarter of the calendar year. Because prices in 1991-1995 were not those generated by a stable competitive market, it is difficult to estimate the impact of seasonal demand on prices. Given demand elasticities in the -0.9 to -1.6 range, the typical 14 percent increase in the volume of demand from the third to fourth quarters would raise prices by 7 to 16 percent above their summer levels in a completely competitive market.

Seasonality of demand was actually quite useful for the lysine cartel. From the point of view of customer acceptance, the last quarter of the year was an ideal time for the cartel to get its act together. The cartel raised U.S. prices twice by very large amounts. From July to November 1992, transactions prices rose by 53 percent. From June to December 1993, prices rose by 82 percent. Thus, it appears that less than one-third of these price increases can be attributed to seasonal demand factors. On the other hand, the failure of prices to decline in early 1994 must have raised customer suspicions that the market price was not altogether free.

Price Fixing Grew in Complexity

The lysine cartel came to price agreements about 25 times, beginning June 1992 in Mexico City and ending in Hong Kong in April 1995. Prices were set every quarter from the summer of 1992 to the spring of 1995, a total of twelve quarters. However, intra-quarter adjustments were made by telephone and sometimes multiple price increases were specified in one meeting. Towards the end of the cartel's existence, regional sales representatives of the companies began to hold separate meetings on local issues.

The price setting procedures became increasingly elaborate as time went on (Table 8.A.5). At Mexico City, only one price was set for North America and Europe combined, effective about the 1st of October 1992. However, in plans for a December 1992 price increase, the cartel specified three price zones, with the highest price in North America, the lowest in Asia, and Europe in between. These December prices were superceded by an agreement in October 1992 in Paris. At this meeting eight prices were specified, including four in local currencies. From this point on, the European price was set in Deutschmarks at a fairly high level. Latin America was priced separately and four price zones were created for Asia/Oceania. By January 1995, thirteen different regional prices were specified. The CIF prices assigned to various Asian countries give evidence of considerable geographic price discrimination.

Concerns About Entry into the Industry

Members of the lysine cartel were conscious of the possibility of entry by companies outside the cartel. At the three-company meeting in Mexico City in June 1992, Ikeda's notes of the meeting quote Wilson as saying that ADM's rapid and large-scale entry in 1991 prevented two large biotechnology companies from entering the lysine industry (Tr. Ex. 4-7).

> ". . . the fact is [ADM's entry] did stop Rhône-Poulenc and Degussa from entering the lysine business. In particular, Degussa was trying to implement plans to build a 20 thousand ton lysine production plant in North America, but due to the announcement of ADM's plans . . . they abandoned those plans . . . and . . . this had the same effect on Rhône-Poulenc's plans" (Tr. Ex. 4-T).

ADM became aware of Degussa's plan when Degussa requested quotes from ADM for a long-term dextrose supply contract. To cope with the Degussa threat, ADM at first proposed to Degussa that they form a lysine joint venture. When Degussa declined, ADM built its own plant with great haste.

As previously mentioned, both ADM and Cheil began lysine production in February 1991. The first new capacity for lysine production outside the cartel's control was a plant built in Kaba, Hungary in the late 1980s. The plant which began production of lysine in 1991, was owned by a joint venture named Agroferm, which itself had four stockholders, including Kyowa Hakko (13 percent). When the lysine cartel was formed in 1992, Kyowa told its co-conspirators that it had no managerial control of Agroferm. This fact, plus Agroferm's small size (5,000 tonnes) and orientation to the local Hungarian market, convinced the cartel that Agroferm could be ignored as a competitive force in the world lysine market. However, five years later deteriorating economic conditions in Hungary forced Kyowa to become the major investor. Thereafter, Agroferm exported most of its expanded output to Western Europe.

The second actual entry into lysine production by a company outside the cartel occurred in 1994. In 1992, Degussa quietly formed a joint venture named Fermas with a Slovakian company named Biotika. After an investment of 60 million Deutschmarks, the Fermas plant began production of methionine and lysine in 1994. ADM and Sewon knew about Fermas as early as June 1992, but believed that it would have major start-up problems (Tr. Ex. 140-T). Because Fermas' lysine capacity was only 3,000 tonnes and it marketed its lysine in Eastern Europe, the cartel could afford to ignore this small player except as a harbinger of things to come. ADM was aware of conditions in Eastern Europe because it had non-controlling equity investments in a small Ukrainian lysine venture through a partnership with Amylum of France.[7] The size of the Ukrainian plant is not known.

A third example of relatively small-scale entry into lysine occurred in 1995. A plant built by AECI Corporation in Durban, South Africa with about 11,000 tonnes capacity was significant enough for the cartel to take notice. At its January 1995 meeting in Atlanta, the cartel set 1995 global volume quotas for each of its five members, but only after subtracting 3,000 tonnes of sales for the new AECI facility (Tr. Ex. 17-T). The conspirators knew that AECI was beginning production in the second half of 1995 and that the cartel would be able to capture only residual demand once AECI became a source of global supply.

The largest new entry into lysine by non-cartel members was announced after the cartel ceased to operate. In July 1997, Degussa and Cargill made public their plans to build a lysine plant in Blair, Nebraska next to Cargill's newest corn wet milling facility. The joint venture combined Degussa's technical expertise in amino acids with Cargill's efficient dextrose output – a formidable pairing. Although production at this new plant did not begin until late 1999, the scale of the plant (initially 75,000 tonnes) is impressive. Most importantly, it demonstrated that by vertically combining an existing corn wet milling operation with a biotechnology firm can form a source of supply that can easily match ADM for cost efficiency at an investment of $100 million or less.[8] Thus, Tate & Lyle's A.E. Staley subsidiary, CPC International, BASF, and Rhône-Poulenc were but four leading candidates for potential entry in the mid 1990s into lysine. The existence of potential entrants is a competitive factor that limits the exercise of market power, whether by an illegal cartel or a group of firms using tacit methods of cooperation.

The Cartel's Production Capacity

More than 90 percent of new production capacity being created during 1991-1995 were plants controlled by the five cartel members themselves (Figure 8.3). ADM's initial 1991 capacity in Decatur of 60,000 tonnes, was nearly doubled by late 1992 or early 1993 (Connor 1999). Ajinomoto added 22,000 tonnes of capacity to its Iowa plant in 1992 and began another 20,000-tonne expansion in 1994 or 1995. Kyowa's two North American plants had almost 20,000 tonnes of capacity added on during the early 1990s. All in all, North American lysine production capacity rose from 100,000 tonnes in 1991 to 200,000 tonnes by 1995 or 1996.

Capacity rose abroad as well. Ajinomoto added almost 30,000 tonnes of production capacity at its plants in France, Italy, and Thailand. Kyowa added perhaps 10,000 tonnes to its Japanese plant. But the most assertive companies were the two from Korea. Cheil tripled its Indonesian plant's capacity during the conspiracy, adding 20,000 tonnes. Sewon's expansion efforts at its sole plant in South Korea were even greater: 40,000 tonnes of annual capacity were built during the conspiracy.

Members of the cartel were intensely curious about each other's lysine capacities during its formative stage in 1991-1992, but thereafter showed little interest. In June 1992, at the ADM-Ajinomoto-Kyowa meeting in Mexico City, considerable discussion took place about plant and company manufacturing capacities. ADM presented its estimates for each of the 11 lysine plants around the globe (Connor 2000:Appendix Table A5). However, Ajinomoto and Kyowa both claimed capacities that were 50% higher than ADM's estimates (Tr. Ex. 4-T). In that meeting ADM claimed that its Decatur plant had 113,400 tonnes capacity, but just a few days before a Sewon delegation to Decatur had toured the plant and been told that its capacity was 70,000 tonnes (Tr. Ex.140-T). Even a year later despite another plant tour for Ajinomoto officials, the Asian producers thought that the Decatur plant was only capable of 60 to 100,000 tonnes of output (Tr. Ex. 131). It is very likely that ADM's plant did not reach its planned 113,400-tonne capacity until late 1992 or early 1993.

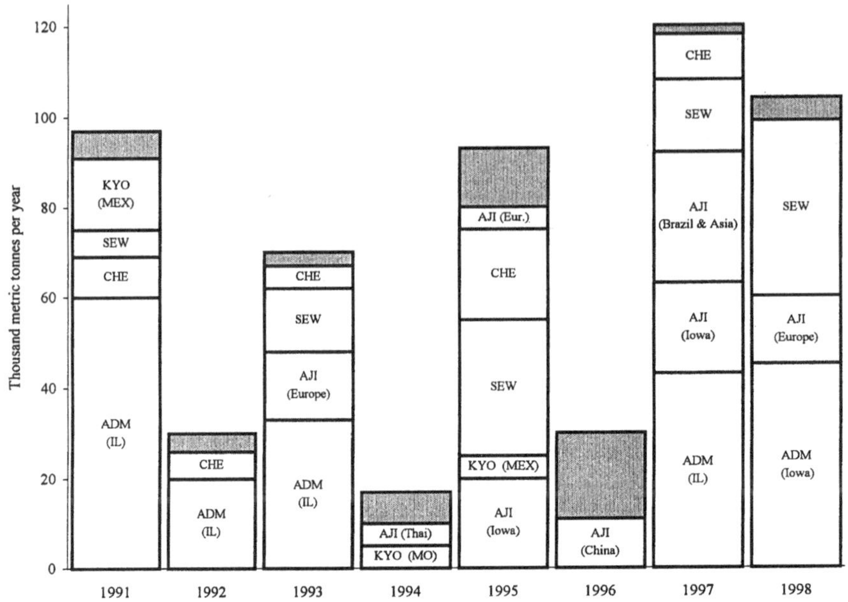

Figure 8.3. Capacity Expansion of Lysine Plants, Completed by Year End 1991-1998.

Source: Connor 1999 (Tables 6 and 7).
Note: Decision to expand or construction normally began about two years prior to completions shown. ADM = Archer Daniels Midland, AJI = Ajinomoto, KYO = Kyowa, SEW = Sewon, CHE = Cheil, and grey = non-cartel. Location follows company name.

In any case, concern about the truthfulness of capacity claims became a moot issue in late 1993 when the cartel came to an agreement on global sales volume quotas for lysine. If the participants adhered to their assigned sales volumes, then the maintenance of excess production capacities or exaggeration about those capacities was of little concern by the group. In fact, in 1992 and subsequent years, global capacity was more than sufficient to satisfy global demand (Connor 2000:Appendix Tables A5 and A6). For example, for December 1992, the best estimate of global capacity is about 300,000 tonnes. This implies that 73 percent to 76 percent of plant capacities were being utilized. In 1994, because of plant expansions begun before the cartel had agreed to volume shares utilization actually dropped to 68 percent.

The rise in excess capacity worldwide may have stemmed from the belief that it would be needed to maintain market share when the cartel broke up.

Costs of Lysine Production

Participants in the cartel were intensely curious about each other's costs of production, but this remained a matter of some uncertainty throughout the conspiracy. Most sellers made statements that exaggerated how low their costs were, but at times some cartel members appeared to be well informed about other seller's costs.[9] Some of the uncertainty stemmed from differential access to the most efficient microbes, but there were also big differences in the types and costs of feedstock (the primary cost of manufacturing) and plant designs (integrated operations probably being more efficient). Another source of confusion, and even intentional obfuscation, concerns which concept of costs was being used. In most cases average total costs (variable and fixed) of manufacturing alone seems to be the most likely concept being articulated, but for short run production decisions, variable costs alone would be the relevant costs to be covered by price. On the other hand, list prices in this industry were quoted as delivered prices for domestic sales (or CIF for export). Thus, in some contexts the appropriate cost concept was average total costs, inclusive of both total manufacturing costs and the (mostly variable) costs of storage, shipping, and selling lysine.

When Sewon officials visited the new Decatur plant in 1992, ADM managers claimed that their costs were only \$0.60 per pound (presumably average total manufacturing costs) (Tr. Ex. 140-T). Whitacre emphasized the huge size of the plant, low corn costs, extensive power co-generation, and cheap dextrose made on the premises as factors contributing to ADM's low costs. Sewon's memorandum of the meeting shows evident concern that their company was at a cost disadvantage because it must export to the U.S. market and is at the mercy of trade barriers. A couple of months later, Sewon lysine manager J.S. Kim reported on an extensive interview of an experienced Japanese lysine expert, one who seems to have been connected with Kyowa. One passage seems to imply that average total costs of exporting lysine from Asia to North American were in the range of \$0.95 to \$1.00 per pound (Tr. Ex. 127-T). This expert takes the reasonable position that Ajinomoto's U.S. operations were disadvantaged by having to purchase liquid dextrose from Cargill at a price about 5 cents per pound more than ADM's own self-supplied dextrose would cost; however, this disadvantage is compensated almost equally by Ajinomoto's superior fermentation yields.[10] In other words, ADM and Ajinomoto's Heartland Lysine had equal costs of manufacturing.

The cost observations were repeated at a meeting in Seoul among the three largest Asian producers in June 1992. Biokyowa and Heartland can at least cover their variable costs at a market price of $0.70 per pound (implying that average total costs would be in the $0.75 to $0.85 range) (Tr. Ex. 125-T). However, if Miwon tries to export to North America when the price is $0.70 per pound, it cannot hope to cover its variable costs because trans-Pacific shipping costs are so large. ADM had a more pessimistic view of Ajinomoto's U.S. costs of production. At a meeting in June 1993, Whitacre opined that Ajinomoto's manufacturing costs were as high as $0.90 per pound (Tr. Ex. 134-T).

Because of exhibits presented at the trial in the case *U.S. vs. M. Andreas et al.,* excellent information on ADM's costs of manufacturing and distribution is in the public domain (Tr. Ex. 60-67). During the year prior to the conspiracy, as output increased from 4 to 10 million pounds per month and as yield failures (contamination episodes) became uncommon, total costs of manufacturing slid systematically from $1.40 to $0.63 per pound. After June 1992, as plant production varied from 10 to 18 million pounds per month, manufacturing costs were predictably close to $0.63 per pound (variable costs of manufacturing alone were positively related to dextrose costs, but averaged $0.53 per pound). During the conspiracy, when one adds worldwide marketing costs, average total costs vary from about $0.73 to $0.78 per pound, but a statistical analysis shows that they did not vary systematically with monthly volume (Figure 8.4). From this information, one can conclude that when output exceeded 10 million pounds per month ADM's average total costs were constant and, therefore, equal to tong-term marginal costs.[11] In a competitive market, price will equal long-run marginal costs plus a reasonable rate of return on investment for the lysine industry (at most 6% of sales seems right).[12]

In sum, the competitive price for the lysine industry, assuming that ADM's were the lowest in the industry, would be expected to have been $0.77 to $0.83 per pound during 1992-1995. Because distribution costs to U.S. customers were lower than the world average, the expected U.S. price would have been a few cents lower.

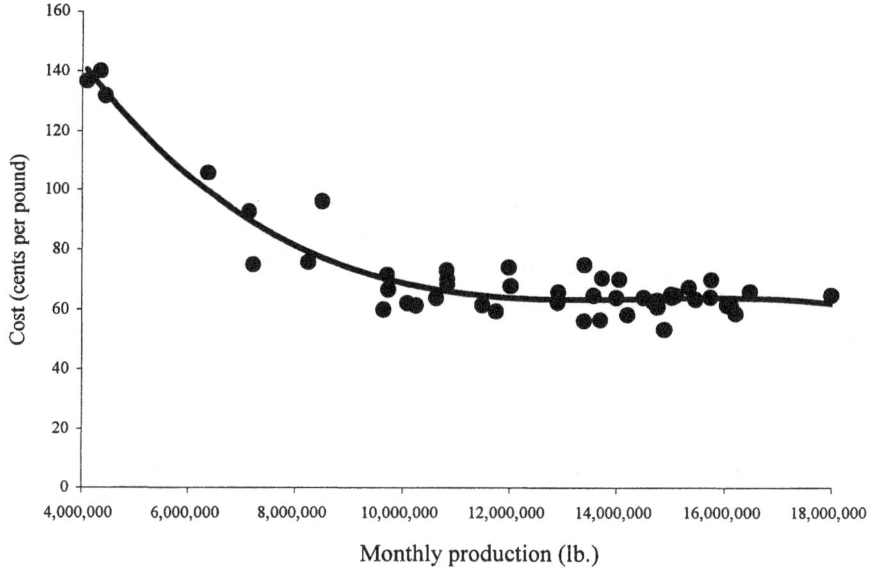

Figure 8.4. ADM's Lysine Manufacturing Costs, 1991-1995.

Capacity Utilization

Capacity and utilization levels of that capacity are key considerations in analyzing competitive conditions in an industry. When all the sellers in a market are operating at maximum feasible capacity, even if an industry is perfectly competitive, short-run prices will rise to level that will cover average total costs (including an opportunity cost of capital) of the highest-cost manufacturer. However, with no capacity constraints, price will gravitate to be equal to the minimum average total cost of the lowest cost producer. Capacity constraints also facilitate non-competitive pricing conduct. In a cartel with capacity constraints the likelihood of cheating on price or on market-share agreements is very low in the short run, and thus, an elaborate system of monitoring prices or sales volume becomes unnecessary. On the other hand, excess capacity (low utilization) helps scare away potential entrants and keep prices high in the long run.

One can compare global sales with rated capacities to develop a utilization figure (cf., Connor 2000: Tables A5 and A6). In 1992, sales volume for lysine was between 210 and 225 thousand tonnes, while capacity was about 300,000 tonnes. Thus, about 70 to 75 percent of global lysine finishing capacity was being utilized. Normally, factories can only run 330 to

350 days per year under ideal conditions; random events would further reduce the maximum sustainable utilization to 85 to 90 percent in a typical year. Thus, in 1992, perhaps 10 to 15 percent of global capacity was truly unutilized. In 1994, the year with the most accurate data, utilization was 69 percent of capacity. In 1995, unutilized capacity seems to have increased a bit more. Thus, the cartel's elevated prices and production constraints brought about increased costs due to excess plant capacities.

At the first Paris meeting, the other lysine producers were told that ADM currently operates at a 60 percent utilization rate in high fructose corn syrup and at 80 to 85 percent in citric acid (Tr. Ex. 34). These figures may be too high if fermentors being used for making related products can be converted quickly and at low cost to manufacture lysine. The trial record contains tantalizing tidbits that suggest that such "swing capacity" existed. In 1992, Ajinomoto bought an existing MSG plant in Italy and was able to convert it quickly to lysine production, but at what cost or rate is not known precisely (Tr. Ex. 127-T). Lysine plants owned by Ajinomoto and Cheil in Asia made both MSG and lysine. Sewon's president is paraphrased at one meeting speculating on reverse conversion of lysine capacity to other high priced biotechnology products (Tr. Ex. 130-T). The fact that ADM was adding the manufacture of other amino acids, food acidulents, and gums suggests that there may be significant economies of scope arising from swing capacity in fermentation products. Therefore, multi-product companies like ADM and Cheil may have had cost advantages over single-product companies like Kyowa and Sewon.

The Lysine Association

From the first contacts made in April 1992 with his Asian rivals, ADM's Terrance Wilson pushed for the formation of a formal lysine association to facilitate the conspiracy. Wilson had in mind two models, the European Citric Acid Manufacturers Association (ECAMA) and the Corn Refiners Association (CRA) in the United States. Both of these organizations held regular meetings to discuss perfectly legal matters of common interest, and both collected members' sales data. ECAMA collected citric acid sales volumes monthly and shared all that information with each of its members, an activity potentially illegal under U.S. antitrust laws (see Chapter 3). The biennial meetings of ECAMA were pretexts for holding secret parallel price-fixing sessions for citric acid.

Wilson met with representatives of the two Japanese lysine manufacturers in April 1992, and they had conveyed the substance of Wilson's proposals to Sewon in Korea soon thereafter (Tr. Ex. 140-T). In June of that year, a high-level delegation from Sewon visited ADM's headquarters and plant in Decatur. At that time, Sewon specifically stated that it was agreeable to the formation of a lysine association. At the Mexico City meeting in June 1992, Wilson again proposed forming an association like ECAMA that would meet at least twice a year and report sales frequently. The sales reports should be independently audited by an international accounting firm, he proposed. All five companies should be members (Tr. Ex. 34).

At the Paris meeting of October 1992, the first at which all five companies sent representatives, Alain Crouy of Eurolysine prepared a fake agenda that included topics such as environmental constraints, animal rights, and "interest of [sic] setting an International Amino Acid Producers Association" (Tr. Ex. 9). In fact, extensive notes taken at the meeting by J.S. Kim of Sewon show the meeting was dominated by price-fixing details and never covered the fake agenda items (Tr. Ex. 128-T). Wilson's opinion was that few people should attend the price-fixing sessions; he also said that ADM would not send representatives to regional meetings of local managers. Regional meetings did occur without ADM's participation. Ajinomoto's Crouy agreed to transmit the substance of such a European meeting on prices by telephone to Whitacre. In June a year later Ajinomoto was still pressing for holding regional price-fixing meetings. Specifically, Ikeda said that J. Ashley, ADM's sales manager for Asia located in Singapore, should be included in local meetings because Mark Whitacre was slow to implement price changes in Asia (Tr. Ex. 131). At that meeting, Kyowa, Miwon, and Ajinomoto favored formation of the association, but Cheil was concerned that ADM would misuse the sales data generated by the association.

It was at the December 1992 meeting that Wilson most fully explained how ADM's arrangements in its citric acid conspiracy could be a useful model for lysine as well. These arrangements included setting market shares and prices in each country or region, elaborate reporting of trade secrets (e.g., prices charged to individual customers in each geographic market), regular audits by professional accountants, and a compensation scheme for members that failed to achieve their targeted sales (Klein 1999).

At the five-company meeting in Vancouver in June 1993, there was also extensive discussion about setting up an association. Except for Cheil, they all agreed that the association would serve at least two useful purposes: collecting information of the size of the lysine market and as a cover-up device (Tr. Ex. 134-T). One proposal would be to create a lysine section within the European Union's International Council for Feed Additives (INCOFA) located in Brussels.

In October 1993, the five members of the cartel had an extensive discussion about the details of the Amino Acid Manufacturers International Association (AAMIA), as their new organization would be called. The key decision was to organize AAMIA as a "working party" affiliated with the European Federation of Feed Additives National Associations (FEFANA).

FEFANA is an organization sponsored by the Agricultural Directorate (DG-VI) of the European Commission in Brussels. The direct members of FEFANA are national organizations of companies in the animal feeds industry, but FEFANA also permits "working parties" of multinational industry groups to join. By October, an AAMIA task force had already met twice and had produced documents that would facilitate recognition as a FEFANA working party in late October. In addition to the five lysine manufacturers, AAMIA would invite six methionine manufacturers to join the group at its first working party meeting in December. (They were Degussa, Nippon Soda, Mitsui, Sumitomo, Novus, and Rhône-Poulenc).

On December 8, 1993 four of the five cartel members met in Tokyo mainly to fix prices (Tr. Ex. 142-T). The four companies agreed to submit an audited report of 1992 sales to the AAMIA by the end of January. Cheil expressed its displeasure by its absence. Apparently, the first formal meeting of AAMIA took place in Tokyo the next day.

The two Korean conspirators, Sewon and Cheil, were the least cooperative with AAMIA in reporting sales volumes to the cartel. Internal memoranda of June and August 1992 meetings with Ajinomoto and Kyowa representatives in Seoul demonstrate Sewon's skepticism (Tr. Ex. 125-T and 126-T). Another long internal Sewon memorandum written in December 1994 discusses difficulties caused by auditing of lysine sales volumes. Sewon was concerned about Ernst & Young displacing its local auditor and reporting volume levels that would be higher than Sewon wanted to report to cartel members (Tr. Ex. 136-T). A Sewon lysine manager suggested that hiding true volume would be difficult, but that volume could be "adjusted" by introducing "minor error by willful negligence." Sewon's position is strange, because estimates of its sales tonnage for 1992 presented to the cartel (Table 8.A.6) are accurate reflections of its true 1992 sales volume (Tr. Ex. 136-T). As far as is known, the third-party-auditing feature was never implemented. Although it withheld its monthly sales for a while in 1994, by early 1995 Sewon was again supplying data (Tr. Ex. 138-T).

Concerns About Antitrust Violations

Cartel members were aware that their discussions were antitrust violations. At a meeting in Seoul, Korea of all four Asian manufacturers in August 1992, Cheil objected to having future meetings in Korea because of "legal matters," presumably concerns about Korea's young but relatively rigorous antitrust agency (Tr. Ex. 126-T). Even in Tokyo fixing a domestic price "can cause trouble," but ". . . talking about 'fixing an international price' is alright" *(ibid.)*. Further evidence of the cartel's consciousness of the antitrust illegality of their activities comes from a memorandum of its Hawaii meeting in March 1994 (Tr. Ex. 137-T). The Asian firms were reluctant to audit the sales data being sent monthly to Mimoto at the end of the year, claiming that replacing their regular auditors with a large international auditing firm might be illegal. Wilson demurred, saying that ". . . price negotiation is illegal, not the volume auditing." At their Atlanta meeting, participants made nervous jokes about the FTC knocking at their hotel room door.

Perhaps the best evidence that the group was aware of that they were violating the antitrust laws showed up in their consistent efforts to hide their activities from the antitrust authorities, especially those in the United States. The lysine association was intended to provide reasons for the members to travel to a central location for meetings; travel invoices and credit card charges could ostensibly be covered by travel to a legitimate industry association. The conspirators took pains to avoid meetings on U.S. territory until the 1993 gathering in Hawaii. At the FBI's prompting, Whitacre urged the group to meet there. When Whitacre proposed the Hawaiian venue, Mimoto expressed his concern about the severity of the U.S. antitrust laws. It was the conspirator's temptation to play golf at a luxurious course that overcame their fears (Eichenwald 2000). The mail was avoided in favor of telephone conversations that often times included code words and code names. Conspirators were urged to destroy written records of the meetings, but this dicturn was often ignored by the Asian companies' empolyees who typically kept diaries or wrote detailed memorandums for their supervisors, most of which became evidence later. Finally, ADM kept the number of employees knowledgeable about the conspiracy quite limited at the beginning, only three or four managers. However, by 1995 about a dozen employees were aware of lysine price fixing.[13]

ADM's Charm Campaign

ADM had a general reputation as a tough, indeed ruthless company. The other lysine producers had seen ADM bully its way into the industry in 1991-1992. However, in mid-1992 ADM tried to reassure its future partners in crime of its good will by displaying remarkable candor about many aspects of its technology of production, information that is normally treated as a trade secret by biotechnology enterprises. ADM twice gave complete tours of its Decatur plant, first to Sewon in June 1992 and second to Ajinomoto in April 1993. Ajinomoto's Mimoto later described a plant tour of this type as "very unusual." During the first tour, ADM revealed its lysine production capacity, its costs of manufacturing,[14] the employment size of the Bioproducts Division (120 persons), daily production capacities of six ADM products (dry corn, soybeans, sorbitol, dextrose, alcohol, and carbon dioxide), the name of the company supplying its MSG technology, the identity of its enzyme supplier, and future products in pilot production. It is doubtful that any of these facts were publicly known (Tr. Ex. 140-T). ADM also admitted that two former Ajinomoto employees had provided lots of technical information about Heartland's lysine operations to ADM.

At another general meeting of the cartel just three weeks before an agreement on volume allocation was reached, ADM again revealed a substantial amount of proprietary information about its Biotechnology Division to its Asian co-conspirators (Tr. Ex. 135-T). Partly this presentation was designed to boast about its size and prowess, but partly it was a demonstration of ADM's intention to be an open, candid, and reliable business partner in the price-fixing venture. ADM told the others of the location of its three domestic (Decatur, St. Louis, Atlanta) and six overseas sales offices (UK, Singapore, Sidney, Tokyo, Mexico, and Miami for South America). The group was told of the Division's present and future product portfolio.[15] Whitacre revealed technical details on its imminent entry into vitamin B2 production.[16] Specific information was shared on recent capital equipment purchased, such as the size of its largest fermentors (31 million liters per year). In general, ADM's reports of monthly dry lysine sales volumes were accurate. For example, at the 1992 Mexico City meeting, ADM reported that two recent month's sales were 5,000 and 5,700 tonnes (Tr. Ex. 4-T). A cross-check with ADM's own internal manufacturing records shows that these figures were exactly correct (Tr. Ex. 61).

ADM was particularly concerned about keeping good relations with Ajinomoto, the volume leader of the lysine cartel, because it relied on the company as a laison with the other three members. Ajinomoto's CEO Toba had been entertained in Decatur in a lavish fashion (Lieber 2000). At a dinner at the Four Seasons Hotel in Chicago in April 1994, Michael Andreas promised to take his father Dwayne to visit Ajinomoto's headquarters in Japan. Later, Andreas vowed to reduce ADM's output of monosodium glutamate (MSG) by 50 percent. This was good news to Yamada because MSG was one of Ajinomoto's major products and its price had been under pressure at the time. In the previous July, Ajinomoto had proposed that a cartel be launched for MSG (Eichenwald 2000: 164).[17]

ADM's charm campaign, though probably genuine, had only limited success in quelling an unruly group whose only glue was the glitter of profits.

Continuing Cartel Contentiousness

It was not easy for the five lysine producers to arrive at a consensus on prices and volume shares. Distrust and disagreements of many kinds permeated the discussions among the five from the beginning of their contacts in early 1992 until their last meetings in early 1995. The greatest number of complaints were directed by the four Asian companies against ADM, but complaints by both Japanese companies and ADM against the Korean companies were not far behind. There were relatively few criticisms made about Ajinomoto and Kyowa, who acted as buffers and liaisons between the two more assertive wings of the cartel.

In models of tacit oligopoly, cooperative relationships characterized by a willingness to sacrifice or compromise are not absolutely necessary. Oligopolies can function successfully through various "non-cooperative" modes of behavior. However, even non-cooperative behavior (also called "tacit" cooperation) require that leading firms be able to form fairly reliable expectations about the *reactions* of rivals to changes in the market, such as changes in prices, output levels, or product designs (see Chapter 2). Forming such expectations usually requires observations of rivals' actual market behaviors over several production periods. Economists call these conjectures. If conjectures free of uncertainty cannot be formed, then the likelihood of collusive behavior trumping a tacit oligopoly increases. Evidence of mistrust, misperceptions about facts, international obfuscation, guile, and so forth make overt conspiracies more likely to be formed in concentrated industries. However, relatively trustful relations *are* required for cartels to operate effectively.

The cultural gap between ADM and the other companies was significant at the beginning of this story. It narrowed over time, but never closed completely. ADM's two plant tours helped reduce Asian companies' skepticism about ADM's capacity, but even here Whitacre exaggerated how low ADM's costs of production were (Tr. Ex. 140-T). In late 1991, ADM claimed to have 113Kt capacity, but this was really the *plant's planned* capacity that would not be reached for about a year (Connor 2000: Table A5). Its Asian rivals were disbelieving, even in 1993 when the Decatur plant was fully built. Nevertheless, all the technical data ADM shared with its rivals must have raised the level of trust. At the cartel's first major meeting, ADM attempted to create trust by giving its best estimates of lysine capacities (Tr. Ex. 4-T). Ikeda's notes of that meeting indicated that he found ADM's figures for Ajinomoto so close to his company's actual figures that he speculated that ADM had a spy at Heartland Lysine. At a May 1993 "summit" meeting of the three largest Asian companies, Ajinomoto and Kyowa took the candid position that "Each company is lacking reliability . . . There is no measure against a contract violation" (Tr. Ex. 130-T). That is, the Japanese thought that the cartel had a problem of disciplining deviants from price or volume agreements. In June 1993, near the end of several months of dissension within the cartel, at a meeting of the four Asian producers in Tokyo Cheil raised concerns about ADM's misuse of the proposed lysine association. Paraphrasing the remarks by Cheil's representative J. M. Suh, minutes of the meeting say: "ADM's attitude is not clear: Are they not [going to] use this to get information and one day they betray?" (Tr. Ex. 131).

Five months later at the cartel's second Paris conclave, on the whole a friendly and businesslike meeting lubricated by a dinner at one of the city's temples of gastronomy, ADM and Kyowa clashed openly about one of the main episodes that led to a decline in the group's consensus in the spring of 1993 (Tr. Ex. 135-T). The dispute concerned ADM's aggressive drive into Latin American lysine markets, which Kyowa viewed as a threat to its perceived franchise in the area by virtue of its ownership of Latin America's only lysine plant in Mexico. "Latin American – this is the area over which the Japanese (especially Kyowa) and ADM disputed each other most strongly" noted Sewon's representative *(ibid.)*. Specific transactions in four major Latin American markets were held up as breaches of the price agreement. Acrimony over ADM's perceived aggressiveness practically disappeared at the cartel's meetings once the late-1993 volume-allocation agreement was successfully implemented. So long as members of the cartel made progress toward keeping to their global market shares, arguments over sales in particular regions became moot.[18] The reporting system on monthly regional volumes greatly reduced concerns about price cutting by their former rivals. Price cutting, if excessive (transaction prices were almost always a few cents below the target or list prices), became self-destructive because it lowered short-run profit margins and might require costly compensation of other cartel members at the end of the year.

The great majority of accusations of bad faith were aimed by ADM and the Japanese companies toward the two Korean firms. Both Sewon and Cheil Jedang were committed to an export-driven, high-growth global strategy. Even though Sewon seems to have cooperated somewhat more consistently with cartel demands for discipline, Sewon's larger capacity made it a more frequent object of criticism than the guiltier but smaller party, Cheil.

At Sewon's first contact with ADM (the June 1992 plant tour), Sewon's top officials had already been briefed about ADM's offer to fix prices by its Japanese rivals. Sewon expressed its unqualified desire to develop a fully cooperative understanding with ADM about soft competition in the lysine market (Tr. Ex. 140-T). At the same time, Sewon warned ADM that it was "an old company" in the industry and was committed to remaining an important player. Sewon had begun production of lysine in the 1970s (see Chapter 7).

Sewon was not invited to the cartel's first overtly collusive meeting in Mexico City a week later (Tr. Ex. 4-T). Ajinomoto and Kyowa agreed to inform the Koreans of the bad news of ADM's initial demand that all four Asian manufacturers would have to accept cuts in production to accommodate ADM. Sewon hosted two meetings with Ajinomoto and Kyowa in Seoul in June and August 1992 to try to hammer out a response to ADM's demand.

Significantly, Cheil was not invited, probably because it was viewed as the least likely to cooperate in any plan that restrained its sales. At these meetings Sewon was interested in a price agreement but highly skeptical that a volume-allocation agreement could be reached, implemented, or monitored (Tr. Ex. 125-T). If surveillance of such an agreement involved export statistics ". . . our company will be the most disadvantaged" said a Sewon internal memorandum. At the second Seoul meeting, a volume agreement was again discussed at length, but ". . . no one agreed. Especially we/our company cannot," said a Sewon document.

Sewon was often accused by the other lysine producers of aggressive sales increases. At a top-level meeting of the big three Asian producers in Tokyo a year later (May 1993), Sewon was accused by Kyowa of being primarily responsible for the on-going U.S. spring 1993 price declines. Kyowa's Managing Director Akita was blunt: ". . . it is Japan's view that the price drop this time was due to [Sewon]. Definitely it is because of [Sewon]" (Tr. Ex. 130-T). Sewon retorted that the Japanese dropped their export prices first. Neither could the three companies agree on how to coordinate any joint decisions reached. At the otherwise harmonious second meeting in Paris in October 1993, Sewon was accused of aggressively increasing exports to both the United States and Europe (Tr. Ex. 135-T). In its own memorandum of the meeting Sewon admits that its export volumes did increase 18 percent and 25 percent, respectively, from the previous year.

Shortly after the Irvine meeting that resulted in an ADM-Kyowa-Ajinomoto volume agreement, Sewon came under intense pressure from Ajinomoto to accept a 34,000-tonne allotment for 1994. An angry telex from Ajinomoto in mid-November shows that Sewon was trying to maneuver for a 37,000-tonne share (Tr. Ex. 28), after having previously agreed to the lower figure. The minutes of the December 1993 Tokyo meeting show that Sewon was eventually forced to accept the lower volume allocation (Tr. Ex. 142-T). In its internal assessment of the volume agreement, Sewon notes that the benefit of higher prices is traded-off by the cost of losing loyal customers, outside of Asia at least. One part of the volume plan Sewon could not stomach was the idea of faithfully reporting honest volume data to one of the big five international accounting firms (Tr. Ex. 136-T). In fact, during part of 1994, Sewon stopped sending its monthly volumes of sales to Mimoto, an action that threatened the unraveling of the cartel's consensus (Tr. Ex. 17-T). Somehow, later in 1994, Sewon wrangled a 3,000 tonne supplemental increase in its share. At the 1995, Atlanta meeting Sewon began agitating for a 46,000-tonne allocation for 1995, an extraordinary 25 percent increase at a time when general market growth was one-fourth that rate. It had to settle for a 39,000-tonne allocation in the end, but in its own minutes of the Atlanta meeting, Sewon noted that, "as in the previous case, all the competitors except for our company said they agree with the allocated volumes." Sewon's attitude presaged continuing friction with its cartel partners throughout 1995.

Cheil Jedang was close to being a maverick throughout the cartel's existence. The other four sellers consistently underestimated its production capacity and its stubborn desire to grab disproportional increases in market share. Cheil was the firm least likely to attend conspiracy meetings and the most likely to play hard-ball tactics to get sales increases. It rarely shared information with the others about its capacity and sales plans. Cheil's Indonesian plant opened in 1991 with a modest capacity of 9,000 tonnes, but expanded to at least 30,000 tonnes by 1995 (Connor 1998a)

Cheil's case was frequently discussed at the May 1993 meeting of the three other Asian manufacturers in Tokyo (Tr. Ex. 130-T). The Japanese were blunt: "[Cheil] is no less a trouble maker than ADM." Kyowa's Yamamoto said that ". . . the big worry is the attitude of Cheil Jedang." On the other hand, Cheil was viewed as the weakest and least important participant by the Japanese firms: "Cheil Jedang: It is nothing because of its small capacity. There is no big problem." (*ibid*). Moreover, having only two years of lysine production experience, Cheil was believed to be experiencing technical or financial problems.

Cheil finally sent a representative to a conspiracy meeting in Tokyo in June 1993 (Tr. Ex. 13 l-T). It expressed its concern about sharing proprietary sales information with ADM, but it did engage in sharing information with its three Asian competitors. That same month at the Vancouver meeting, Cheil was the only one of the five companies to refuse to join the proposed lysine association (Tr. Ex. 134-T). It had boycotted part of this meeting in order to extract a higher volume share than had been proposed earlier. At the Paris meeting of October 1993, Cheil claimed that its 1993 sales volume would reach 22,000 tonnes, which was a lot higher than the 14,000 tonnes it had claimed it sold in 1992 (Tr. Ex. 135-T). The other lysine companies were evidently incredulous at the large size of these purported sales volumes. Cheil boycotted the next meeting in Tokyo (December 1993) to demonstrate its unhappiness at the low volume share being offered to it (14,000 tonnes) which was 6,000 tonnes less that it demanded (Tr. Ex. 142-T). There was more discussion about Cheil at the Hawaii meetings in March 1994 (Tr. Ex. 137-T). The consensus was that Cheil's 1993 sales were about 17,000 tonnes and that 18,000 tonnes was a reasonable counter-offer to Cheil for its 1994 quota. Cheil apparently agreed to accept the offer, though its 1994 sales turned out to be slightly higher (about 1,200 tonnes or 7 percent) than its agreed target (Tr. Ex. 17-T and 138-T). In early 1995, Cheil apparently acceded to a quota that represented a slight decrease from actual 1994 sales volume. It had taken a long time for the maverick to be broken.

In general, it was Ajinomoto and Kyowa that acted as the glue that held the cartel together. They often had a moderating influence in the negotiations at several points. Although clearly concerned about their impending loss of industry leadership, eventually they came to a position of almost fatalistic acceptance regarding ADM's drive to become Ajinomoto's peer. At other times they bargained hard with Sewon and Cheil to get these two companies on board. In the end, it was the Japanese companies' acceptance of virtually no growth in the volume of sales that made the historic compromise in Irvine, California possible (see Table 8.A.6). ADM and Cheil were, in market-share terms, the biggest winners.

At the high-level meeting in Tokyo in May 1993, Ajinomoto and Kyowa presented a united front in order to win over Sewon to a volume agreement. They helped convince Sewon that ADM was fully capable of soon getting one-third of the world market. The Japanese firms argued that ADM had set up a plant much larger than necessary, would use its excess capacity to drive down prices, and was generally ". . . ruthless in terms of marketing" (Tr. Ex. 13 O-T). Although apparently agreeing to this view, Sewon still had the feeling that the volume agreement was a device to favor Ajinomoto: "AJI is trying to take the leadership position." Sewon detected a slight break in the Japanese united front when Kyowa took the position that: "Frankly speaking, . . . the lysine price has dropped suddenly because of the AJI/ADM fight over leadership . . ." However, these 1993 remarks aside, the record of the meetings provides few criticisms of Ajinomoto or Kyowa by the other companies, perhaps because the Korean firm had historically deferred to their leadership. More importantly, the others must have recognized that the two oldest firms in the industry were sacrificing some of the growth they could have had without an explicit agreement.

THE CARTEL IS UNMASKED

The little Corn Belt city of Decatur, Illinois had never seen anything like it. Later, they would call it "Gestapo Night" (Leiber 2000). Residents were used to seeing convoys of limousines conveying Washington big-shots or foreign dignitaries in town to meet the powerful Chairman of ADM. But the scores of federal cars filled with 70 to 100 FBI agents and Department of Justice lawyers who arrived in the evening of June 27, 1995 were something else.

The majority of the FBI agents headed off in pairs to interview virtually every ADM officer wherever they were that night. Around 5:30 p.m., Terrance Wilson, drink in hand, was found at a local country club. Simultaneously, Executive Vice President and heir-apparent Michael Andreas was interviewed in his home (Eichenwald 2000). During the taped interviews, all the officers were asked questions about their knowledge of price fixing by ADM in the markets for lysine, citric acid, and high fructose corn syrup. The interviews with Wilson and Michael Andreas went a little differently. For Andreas, the FBI played excerpts of meetings on a tape recorder on which they say incriminating things. The agents made a one-time offer to both men: if you agree to cooperate in our investigation, they said, the government will go easy on you (Tr. 3503-3508). Both Wilson and Andreas make the last of many mistaken decisions in this sorry affair: they refused to cooperate, and they lied repeatedly to the FBI agents about their involvement in the conspiracies (in itself a federal crime). Even worse in the end, the explanations of their activities they did give during their FBI interviews little resembled their lawyers' theories when they had to defend themselves in court three years later. As soon as Wilson and Andreas turned down the offers of cooperation, around 6 p.m. the largest contingent of FBI agents moved to ADM's rather spartan corporate headquarters building and, armed with subpoenas and search warrants, began to remove boxes and boxes of documents from the files of certain offices. The offices of Michael Andreas, Terrance Wilson, Barrie Cox, and Mark Whitacre were given particularly close scrutiny. The top floor offices of Dwayne Andreas and James Randall were not searched.

The scene in Decatur was repeated at the U.S. headquarters or sales offices of nine other companies. Investigators found a treasure trove of documents showing volume targets and actual volumes of lysine in the files of Heartland Lysine in Chicago, Biokyowa in St. Louis, and Sewon America in New Jersey. Eventually, more than 2 million documents would be cataloged and turned over to attorneys representing Wilson, Andreas, and Whitacre. However, on the night of the raid, interviews produced practically nothing of value. By 6:30 or 7:00 p.m., ADM's general counsel was calling all the ADM officers in Decatur and ordering them to say nothing to the FBI. The ADM employees proved to be a loyal bunch.[19] It would take the government more than a year to get any of them to cooperate, and then only under the protection of an immunity agreement.

ADM's immediate reaction was to contact one of their law firms, the Washington, DC firm of Akin Gump, whose governing partner was Robert Strauss. Strauss had held important federal government positions, including ambassador to Russia. He was a former director of the National Democratic Party, an old friend of Dwayne Andreas, and a member of ADM's Board of Directors. Akin Gump flew squadrons of lawyers to Decatur. One of those lawyers, John Dowd, began to interview top ADM executives. Michael Andreas suspected that a former employee named Brasser who had been fired when he refused to engage in price fixing had gone to the FBI and perhaps made the tape he had heard the FBI play. At one point Dwayne Andreas even suspected that President James Randall, his right-hand man for almost 30 years at ADM, was the FBI mole (Eichenwald 2000: 327). Despite being warned by his FBI handlers, on June 28th Whitacre confided to Dowd about his role as an informant to the FBI for the previous 32 months.[20] Dowd immediately informed ADM's management about Whitacre's role as a mole. When he heard about it, Dwayne Andreas said that Whitacre would "learn to regret the day he was born." The next day, Whitacre was ordered to leave ADM headquarters, and he was fired on August 7, 1995 for fraud and embezzlement (see Chapter 13).[21]

It is fairly safe to assume that the conspiracy ceased to function on that day, June 27, 1995. It had begun in Mexico City on June 23, 1992, almost exactly three years before.

Chapter 8 Endnotes

[1] In 1984, a price war had brought U.S. prices to $0.70 per pound, but adjusting for general inflation that previous record low was at least $0.80 when measured in 1992 dollars. The actual prices for June-August 1992 were $0.69, $0.64, and $0.79, respectively (Connor 2000: Appendix Table A2). The first price fixing occurred in late June 1992 with list price changes announced in early July. Prices declined in July because of the price-protection clauses in contracts but rose sharply thereafter.

[2] Quantity demanded in 1992 was up only 1 percent over 1991, partly because of cartel-induced high prices in late 1992. It was also likely that buyers built up their inventories in 1991 on the expectation that the price war would be shorter than 18 months.

[3] To dispel criticism of his ability to manage the lysine facility, Whitacre concocted a story about a mysterious Mr. Fujiwara who was sabotaging the Decatur plant and was demanding a $10 million ransom. The FBI was called in to investigate the allegation, which led to Whitacre being recruited as a mole for the FBI. See Chapter 13 for details.

[4] The word "men" is used in its strict gender sense. Price-fixing is a boys' game.

[5] A tape of Andeas, Wilson, and Whitacre at a meeting in Decatur on March 18, 1993 reveals that the Japanese numbers may have been understated. When ADM realized the total market was larger than they had formerly believed, they increased sales volume, thus precipitating the spring 1993 price war (Eichenwald 2000: 134-137).

[6] Of course peak demand in Australia, South Africa, and the Southern cone of Latin America would occur six months later, but this effect was slight compared to Northern hemisphere demand. The winter effect was verified for the U.S. market during 1990-1995 by Morse and Hyde (2000).

[7] Amylum was a joint venture between ADM and Eridania Beghin-Say, but sometime in the early 1990s, Tate & Lyle replaced Eridania.

[8] Soon after the Cargill/Degussa announcement, ADM issued a press release promising to build a second, larger lysine plant in Iowa, only a couple of hundred miles from the Cargill/Degussa joint venture.

[9] It is known that Kyowa paid a "consultant" with close ties to the head of ADM's lysine operations who revealed ADM's costs of production. (See the testimony of Yamamoto in Chapter 15 below).

[10] During the cartel's existence, ADM's lysine department paid from $0.15 to $0.25 per pound for dextrose. Cargill's costs of making dextrose were very similar. Thus, Cargill was making a gross profit of 20 to 33 percent on its sales to Heartland Lysine, which I believe is much higher than its opportunity cost.

[11] Apparently, the declining average fixed costs were offset by increasing average variable costs as production volume rose from 10 to about 20 million pounds per month. At high levels of output, ADM was required to sell a higher portion of lysine overseas where distribution and selling costs were higher.

Morse and Hyde (2000) attempted to estimate ADM's production function from monthly data during 1990-1995. Output was positively, significantly related to the quantity of dextrose, other variable inputs, and capital employed with strong scale effects in evidence.

[12] ADM itself, its major public corn wet milling rivals, and U.S. companies in the organic chemicals manufacturing industry earned pre-tax profits close to 6 percent of sales.

[13] Eventually at least eleven ADM employees would come to know about the lysine conspiracy, besides Andreas, Wilson, and Whitacre, four ADM sales executives were informed late in the conspiracy (Lassar, Klein, *et al.* 1999). ADM salesperson Shuji Tani was informed about the conspiracy in March 1994 by Mimoto of Ajinomoto. Marty Allison and John Ashley testified that they and six other lysine salespersons learned about the conspiracy in the fall of 1993 shortly after the Andreas-Yamada meeting in Irivne, California. Alfred Jansen also learned of the conspiracy after October 1993. Allison and another ADM employee met with co-

conspirators in Europe in order to coordinate the cartel's sales in that region (Eichenwald 2000). Dwayne Andreas and James Randall may have known early.

[14] Whitacre claimed that it was less than 60 cents, but the lowest previous monthly total cost was in fact 62 cents (Tr. Ex. 60). Variable costs of manufacturing had dipped to 49 cents per pound in May 1992.

[15] ADM was making at least two feed additives, the amino acids lysine and threonine, and had immediate plans for tryptophan (1994) and methionine (Rhône-Poulenc joint venture in West Virginia). ADM would shortly enter production of riboflavin (vitamin B2). Food additives included citric and lactic acids now and MSG and xanthan gum in late 1993.

[16] ADM purchased the proprietary production technology from Zeagan, the biotechnology division of Coors Corp. Further, ADM would lease the Zeagan factory to make B2 until early 1995 when production would be shifted to Decatur. Entry into vitamins was a major strategic move by ADM.

[17] ADM was not indicted in the U.S. for price fixing MSG but it has been sued in civil cases. ADM's criminal plea agreement in October 1996 probably immunized the company from prosecution for its MSG price fixing.

[18] After the second Paris meeting in October 1993, conspirators held at least ten more meetings (Appendix Table A3). The only time ADM was accused of serious bad faith was in reference to an ADM-Kyowa price war in China at the Atlanta meeting (Tr. Ex. 17-T). However, memorandums of only six of those ten meetings are part of the public record.

[19] Except for Mark Whitacre, only Howard Buffett talked openly to the FBI before ADM's guilty plea and agreement to cooperate. Buffett knew little of value (Eichenwald 2000: 308).

[20] Whitacre later claimed that he had been told or led to believe that his confession was a matter of attorney-client privilege. In fact, Dowd was hired by the *management* of ADM and represented its interest. Whitacre was explicitly warned by the FBI not to cooperate with ADM's lawyers and to get his own (Eichenwald 2000).

[21] It was reported that ADM President James Randall went to the offices of ADM's controller and ordered numerous records of contracts and invoices pulled from the company's files. These records showed that Whitacre had forged Randall's signature in order to embezzle $9 million from ADM. Randall's actions also provoked speculation by supporters of Whitacre that Randall removed documents that might have verified Whitacre's claim that many ADM officers engaged in illegal invoicing or kickbacks to obtain tax-free, hidden bonuses.

Table 8.A.1. U.S. Lysine Sales, Quarterly 1990-1998.

Period		Quantity Sold[a]				U.S. Market Share		ADM's Export Share
		ADM		Ajinomoto, Kyowa, and Sewon in U.S.	Cheil U.S. Imports	ADM	Others	
		Total	U.S.					
		Million pounds				*Percent*		
1990	Q1	0	0	21.1	0	0	100	--
	Q2	0	0	21.0	0	0	100	--
	Q3	0	0	24.0	0	0	100	--
	Q4	0	0	26.7	0	0	100	--
1991	Q1	0.7E	0.7	19.8	0	3	97	0
	Q2	3.5E	3.5	19.9	0	15	85	0
	Q3	10.9	8.6	18.1	0	32	68	21
	Q4	17.7	11.6	18.0	0	39	61	34
1992	Q1	24.3	11.9	9.0	0	56	43	51
	Q2	29.7	14.3	9.4	0	60	40	52
	Q3	38.5	19.4	7.8	0	71	29	50
	Q4	34.2	13.2	18.8	0	41	59	61
1993	Q1	29.7	12.5	25.2	0	33	67	58
	Q2	41.5	20.1	16.9	0	54	46	52
	Q3	44.2	18.8	23.6	0.3	45	55	57
	Q4	36.6	13.6	32.9	0.3	29	71	63
1994	Q1	40.2	15.7	24.8	0.1	39	61	61
	Q2	37.3	17.5	22.4	0.2	44	56	53
	Q3	47.1	19.3	25.9	0.1	43	57	59
	Q4	46.1	14.8	34.8	0.2	43	57	68

Period		Quantity Sold[a]				U.S. Market Share		ADM's Export Share
		ADM		Ajinomoto, Kyowa, and Sewon in U.S.	Cheil U.S. Imports	ADM	Others	
		Total	U.S.					
		Million pounds				*Percent*		
1995	Q1	46.1	15.2	25.6	0.5	38	62	67
	Q2	41.6	18.2	21.8	0.5	44	56	56
	Q3	52.0E	23.0E	26.1	0.5	47	53	56
	Q4	48.0E	22.8E	28.7	0.5	44	56	53
1996	Q1	52	19	30.5	1.5	38	62	63
	Q2	45	17	27.6	1.6	38	62	62
	Q3	58	19	30.4	1.4	38	62	67
	Q4	50	21	36.2	1.2	37	63	58
1997	Q1	60	13	34.9	2.9	27	73	78
	Q2	55	11	22.1	3.1	26	74	80
	Q3	70	13	34.8	2.8	27	73	81
	Q4	60	14	37.6	2.6	27	73	77
1998	Q1	70	24	31.7	4.7	43	57	66
	Q2	65	22	29.6	5.6	43	57	69
	Q3	70	24	31.2	4.2	43	57	66
	Q4	75	26	32.0	4.0	44	56	65

Sources: Connor (2000: Appendix Table A2), Connor (1999: Table 17).
E = Estimated by the author (see notes).
[a] For 1995 Q3 to 1998 Q4, estimated first Cheil sales with Indonesia imports (peak in Q2); then estimated Sewon sales with Korean exports to U.S.; then estimated ADM, Kyowa, and Ajinomoto U.S. sales from plant capacities times reasonable utilization rates (peak in Q4). Total U.S. sales of top 4 known up to 1996 Q2 (Table A2); from 1995 Q2, ADM's U.S. sales are estimated from the volume of U.S. exports (Table 17), of which ADM accounts for 90 percent in 1996-1998 and Ajinomoto and Kyowa for 10 percent.

Table 8.A.2. U.S. Sales Volume of Lysine, By Company, Annual 1990-1998.

	ADM			Ajinomoto			Kyowa Hakko					
Year	Total	U.S. Sales[h]	U.S. Exports	Total	U.S. Sales[f]	U.S. Exports	Total	U.S. Sales[f]	U.S. Exports	Sewon America[e]	Cheil Food & Chem.[e]	Total
						Million Pounds						
1990	0	0	0	45	42	3	32	30	2	20.8	0	92.7
1991	34.8[a]	24.0	10.8	41	35	6	30	25	5	19.3	0	103.2
1992	126.7	58.8	67.9	24	16	8	18	11	7	18.1	0	103.9
1993	152.0	65.0	87.0	55	50	5	36	31	5	16.5	0.6	162.9
1994	170.7	67.3	103.4	57	52	5	45	40	5	15.0	0.6	174.5
1995	187.7[b]	79.2[a]	108.5	51	51	0	35	35	0	14.8	0.2	181.9
1996	205.0[b]	64.0	141.0[d]	69	61	9	46	39	7	18.8	5.7	190.0[a]
1997	245.0[b]	51.0	194.0[d]	73	62	11	51	41	10	25.7	11.4	192.0[g]
1998	280.0[b]	95.0	185.0[d]	50	39	11	35	25	10	42.7	18.5	220.0[g]

Source: Table 8.A.1 and U.S. trade data.
[a] Projected from six months known production.
[b] Projected from ten months known production..
[c] Assumes 80% utilization.
[d] Assumes 90% of U.S. Exports by ADM (as in 1993-94).
[e] Based on import volumes by country.
[f] In 1990-91, assumed 55/45 split; in 1992-98, split by relative U.S. production capacities. In all years, a residual. Includes imports.
[g] Projections from 1996.
[h] Includes liquid lysine.

Table 8.A.3. Global Feed-Grade Lysine Production and Capacity, 1990-1996.

Year	Capacity[a]						Production[b]					
	Ajino-moto	ADM	Kyowa Hakko	Sewon	Cheil	Total[c]	Ajino-moto	ADM[d]	Kyowa Hakko	Sewon	Cheil	Total[c]
	Thousand metric tonnes											
1990	77	0	42	30	0	157	73^E	0	40^E	25^E	0	145
1991	88	60	53	36	9	254	78^E	15	46^E	29^E	7^E	180
1992	90	80	55	36	15	284	58^E	50	34^E	30^E	12^E	199
1993	105	113	58	50	20	354	72	67	42	34	16	236
1994	105	113	63	50	20	364	80	78	43	34	17	254
1995	130	113	70	80	40	458	85^E	86	39^E	40^E	20^E	270
1996	131	113	50	80	40	454	87^E	92^E	35^E	55^E	36^E	310
	Percent											
1990	49	0	27	19	0	100	50	0	28	17	0	100
1991	35	24	21	14	4	100	43	8	26	16	4	100
1992	32	28	19	13	5	100	29	30	17	15	4	100
1993	30	32	16	14	6	100	31	28	18	14	7	100
1994	29	31	17	14	5	100	32	31	17	13	7	100
1995	28	25	15	17	9	100	31	32	14	15	7	100
1996	29	25	11	18	9	100	28	30	11	18	12	100

[E] = Estimated

[a] From Tables 6 and 7 of Connor (1999).

[b] From known production allocations of the lysine cartel during 1993-95 (Eichenwald). Another source confirms that the world dry lysine market shares for the five cartel members in 1995 were: Ajinomoto 34.0%, ADM 26.4%, Kyowa 18.1%, Sewon 14.2%, and Cheil 6.3% according to the Department of Justice (*WSJ* 7/9/98: B10). Other years estimated from capacity utilization rates.

[c] Includes minor producers not shown separately.

[d] Includes liquid lysine (dry equivalent); from internal company records 1991-1995 in trial exhibits.

Table 8.A.4. Agreed Lysine Target Prices, by Region, Delivered or CIF, 1992-1995.

Area	Effective Dates								
	10/92[a]	10/92[b]	11/92[b]	12/92[a]	7/93[c]	10/93[d]	1/94[e]	4/94[f]	1/95[g]
	Currency unit/pound[h]								
North America	$1.05	$1.05	$1.05	$1.20	--	$1.20	$1.20	$1.16	--
USA	--	--	--	--	$0.85	--	--	--	$1.30
Canada	--	--	--	--	$0.85	--	--	--	C$1.75
Europe/Middle	$1.05	DM1.8	DM1.8	$1.18	DM1.45	DM2.4	DM2.4	DM2.4	DM2.2
East/Africa:									
South Africa		$1.04	$1.18	--	$0.85	--	--		--
Latin America:	--	$1.05	$1.13	--	$0.85	$1.22	$1.22	$1.18	$1.22
Mexico		--	--	--	P2.95	00	00	$1.20	$0.99
Asia/Oceania:	--	$1.04	$1.13	$1.15	$0.85	$1.22	$1.22	$1.22	--
Australia		A$1.54	A$1.68	--	A$1.36	A$1.90	--	$1.35	A$1.86
New Zealand		A$1.54	A$1.68	--	NZ$1.63	--	--	--	--
Taiwan		NT$32	NT$32	--	NT$28	--	--	$1.54	NT$42
Malaysia		--	--	--	--	--	--	$1.33	$1.33
Philippines		--	--	--	--	--	--	$1.59	$1.59
Thailand		--	--	--	B57	--	--	B36	B36
Indonesia		--	--	--	Rp4500	--	--	$1.47	$1.40
Japan		--	--	--	--	--	--	$1.43	$1.56
China		--	--	--	RNB19	--	--	--	$1.27

-- = Not available
[a] Mexico City agreement of 6/92 (Tr. Ex. 4-T).
[b] Paris meeting agreement of 10/92 (Tr. Ex. 10-T and 128-T).
[c] Vancouver meeting agreement of 6/93 (Tr. Ex. 134-T and 45).
[d] Paris meeting agreement of 10/93 (Tr. Ex. 135-T).
[e] Tokyo meeting agreement of 12/93 (Tr. Ex. 142-T).
[f] Hawaii meeting agreement of 3/94 (Tr. Ex. 137-T).
[g] Atlanta meeting agreement of 1/95 (Tr. Ex. 17-T and 138-T).
[h] U.S. dollar unless otherwise specified.
Note: This is not an exhaustive list of price agreements and dates. Many agreements were made in subsequent telephone calls. This is a complete list of prices shown in the trial exhibits.

Table 8.A.5. U.S. Feed-Grade Lysine Sales and Capacity, 1990-1996.

Year	North American Capacity and Imports[a]						U.S. Domestic Sales[b]						U.S. Exports
	Ajinomoto	ADM	Kyowa	Sewon	Cheil	Total	Ajinomoto	ADM	Kyowa	Sewon	Cheil	Total	All Companies
	Thousand metric tonnes						*Million dollars*						
1990	16	0	24	9	0	49	47.7	0	33.6	23.5	0	104.8[E]	5.0[E]
1991	21	60	31	8	0	120	35.0	21.0	35.0	19.1	0	110.0	6.2
1992	21	80	30	7	0	138	27.2	52.0	27.2	12.6	0	118.9	37.7
1993	23	113	32	7	0	175	26.7	82.9	21.8	13.1	0.7	145.2	43.7
1994	23	113	38	7	0	181	38.5	109.4	31.5	16.5	0.7	196.6	51.4
1995	40	113	41	7	1	202	36.5	106.2	29.8	10.5	1.9	184.9	49.2
1996	40	113	41	8	3	205	41.0	130.0[E]	33.6	17.3	8.1	230.0[E]	71.4
	Percent						*Percent*						
1990	33	0	49	18	0	100	46	0	32	22	0	100	5[c]
1991	18	50	26	7	0	100	32	19	32	17	0	100	6[c]
1992	15	58	22	5	0	100	23	44	23	11	0	100	32[c]
1993	31	65	18	4	0	100	18	57	15	9	0	100	30[c]
1994	13	62	21	4	0	100	20	56	16	8	0	100	26[c]
1995	20	56	20	3	0	100	20	57	16	6	1	100	27[c]
1996	20	55	20	4	1	100	18	57	15	8	4	100	31[c]

Source: Connor (1999) and Table 8.A.1.

[E] = Estimated.

[a] Tables 6 and 17 of Connor (1999). Includes Mexico, Sewon and Cheil from U.S. import data.

[b] From public antitrust litigation documents on ADM's volume and sales (monthly), four "settling defendants" monthly sales and prices, and imports valued at domestic prices.

[c] Exports as a proportion of total domestic sales.

Chapter 9

ECONOMIC EFFECTS OF THE LYSINE CARTEL

This chapter documents the economic effects of the operation of the lysine cartel on prices, production levels, international trade, and buyers' incomes. Monetary estimates of these effects typically play a key role in legal actions to punish cartels or compensate their victims. The legal ramifications of the lysine cartel are discussed in Chapters 13 to 16. Chapter 13 covers the U.S. government's criminal investigation that began in November 1992, Chapter 14 non-U.S. prosecutions, and Chapter 15 details the sentencing of three ADM officers in July 1999. Chapter 16 concentrates on the many parallel civil actions by parties seeking compensation for economic injuries they alleged they received at the hands of the lysine conspirators. The impacts on the companies themselves, the individual conspirators, and on the antitrust legal apparatus are reserved for the final chapter.

The principal objective of the lysine cartel was to raise selling prices around the world, thereby generating profits well in excess of the profits cartel members would have earned if the normal forces of demand and supply had been allowed to play out. For the participants the decision to collude or not to collude involves a weighing of benefits and costs. The corporate benefits are primarily the increases in company profits above normal levels adjusted for some subjective probability of the likelihood of success. Personal benefits may accrue to participants as well through enhanced job promotions or profit sharing. The costs are mostly some vague notion of the social and economic pain that might be imparted by prison time or fines for antitrust violations adjusted downward by the probability of being caught, indicted, and found guilty. The probability of discovery is certainly less than 100 percent (see Box).

PRICE EFFECTS

Civil antitrust proceedings and the criminal trial of Andreas, Wilson, and Whitacre released abundant information on prices charged for lysine from 1991 to 1995. Without these legal documents, the behavior of prices would remain hidden or cloudy to this day.

Weighing Benefits and Costs

Take, for example what might have gone on in Terrance Wilson's head. On the benefits side, Wilson was caught on tape asserting that the lysine industry was giving up $200 million in profits by not agreeing to raise their price to $1.20 per pound (Tr. 712-714). ADM's share would be about $60 million per year, and these extra profits would propel ADM's stock prices upwards, which would monetarily benefit nearly all ADM officers. Perhaps he guessed that price-fixing cartels last an average of four years. Wilson had helped get the citric acid cartel going the previous year, and it had been performing admirably well in his eyes. Even if the lysine conspiracy was going to be more of a challenge, perhaps Wilson thought that it had an 80 percent chance of success. This means that the probable benefits to his employer would be $192 million over four years.

The cost calculation is rather more difficult on which to put a dollar figure. It had been 35 years since a major price-fixing case had affected a major U.S. company, so it would be natural for Wilson to ignore the costs to ADM. At worst, if Wilson was sentenced to the full extent of the law, he would face three years in prison, and be fined $350,000 and pay legal defense costs. In fact, most conspirators spend no time in prison and pay smaller fines than the maximum. Wilson may have mused on his poor health (a serious heart condition) and the few years he had remaining until retirement. And the chances of being caught? Probably less than 10 percent. Pain and suffering? He was a Marine. Loss of his ADM pay? Less than $5 million for sure. Wilson might well have valued all these possible costs at no more than $10 million, of which 10 percent is $1 million. The net benefits are $192 – 1 = $191 million.

The decision is clear. Take the risk.

U.S. transaction prices for dry feed-grade lysine in 1991 to 1995 are shown in figure 9.1. This price series is the weighted average price received by the four largest suppliers of lysine, that is, all five members except Cheil, the smallest producer. Only sales to customers located in the United States are included, though a tiny share of those sales might have been purchased by U.S. wholesalers for export. These prices reflect all contract sales (and customer rebates) at prices below list as well as a small portion of spot sales at list prices. Without the compulsory legal process known as "discovery," there would be no practical alternative to the prices shown. During 1990-1995, the secretive nature of lysine dealing meant that trade magazines rarely reported transaction prices and that those reports were usually inaccurate.[1]

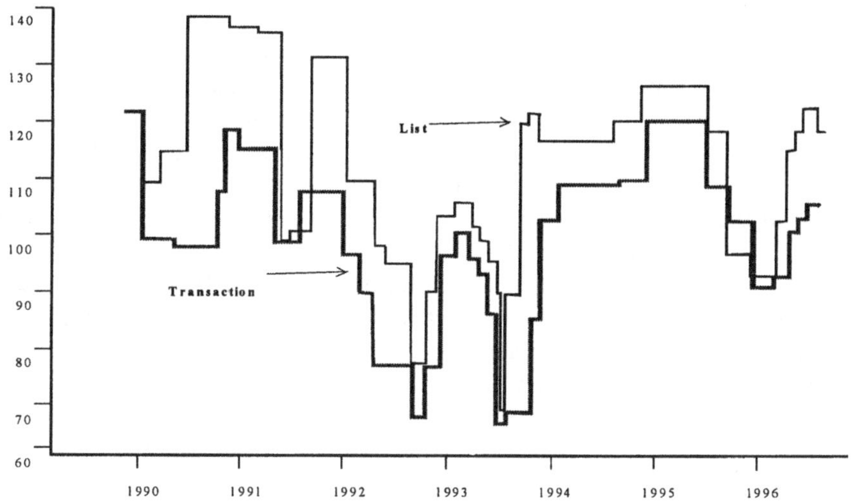

Figure 9.1. U.S. List and Transaction Prices of Feed-Grade Lysine 1990 – 1996.

Sources: Lysine transaction prices supplied by the three largest defendants in a notice to class-action members. List prices from buyers as reported to *Journal of Commerce.*

U.S. lysine prices averaged $1.12 per pound in 1990, the last year of the price-fixing by the three oldest manufacturers: Ajinomoto, Kyowa Hakko, and Sewon. Thereafter, prices fell three times (January 1990-July 1992, January-June 1993, and January-September 1995) and rose to plateaus twice (July-December 1992 and July 1993-December 1994). In all five phases, these price movements were primarily propelled by the actions of cartel members and were secondarily reinforced by regular seasonality in the demand for lysine.[2] Sometimes the pricing or output actions of cartel members were group decisions, and sometimes the actions were by ADM alone attempting to discipline the rest of the group. Specifically, transaction prices rose or fell within a month or two of comparable changes in the cartel's list prices. Transaction prices were nearly always below list. When the cartel was enjoying a period of discipline (lack of cheating and discounting off list), the two prices were only a few cents apart. The cartel set list prices as close as it could to the monopoly level (probably near $1.30 to $1.40 per pound) unless the shadow price pressed down so low as to make the monopoly price impossible. But when bickering was rife, disharmony led to a wide gap between list and transaction prices.

In the first phase, except for a brief uptick in prices peaking in October 1991, prices fell inexorably from late 1990 until reaching a trough in July 1992. Such a 20-month decline in prices of 48 percent was unprecedented.

The reduction in 1990 was due to the unilateral actions of ADM. In order to build its U.S. market share quickly ADM cut its prices below its three Asian rivals. In the last six months of 1991, ADM sold lysine at 4 cents per pound (4 percent) lower than its three market rivals.[3] As a result of its aggressive price cutting, ADM's 1991 growth in sales was extraordinary – quarter-over-quarter volume grew by an average of 194 percent (Table 8.A.1). At the same time, sales volume by the three established manufacturers stagnated. Because ADM poured so much lysine into the U.S. market, the increase in supply outstripped the long-run increase in demand, thus forcing down prices for all sellers.

In the first half of 1992, prices continued to fall, but not because of ADM's underbidding of prices offered by its three rivals. Generally, at this time ADM's domestic selling price was equal to that of its rivals or a penny or two higher. However, ADM continued its aggressive increases in output. In the first three quarters of 1992, ADM sold on average 19 percent more pounds of lysine than in the previous quarter. Because overall demand shrank in the spring quarter for seasonal reasons, the three Asian producers suffered a huge decline in their collective market share (Figure 9.2). This slippage continued through the third quarter of 1992 when the three firms' share hit a rock-bottom 29 percent of the U.S. market. ADM's success in moving from zero to 70 percent of the market continued in the face of desperate price cutting by the Asian firms.[4]

The plight of the three Asian companies set the stage for the second phase of price movements, the rapid rise and plateau of July 1992 to January 1993. ADM lost money on its lysine operations for four months in mid 1992. Because their costs were higher, most of the Asian companies had negative earnings for six or seven months in 1992.[5] All the evidence points to the Mexico City agreement as the primary reason for the late 1992 price rise of 53 percent. Moreover, the November-January plateau immediately followed the first full-scale meeting of the lysine association in Paris on November 1,1992. Ajinomoto's global sales manager testified explicitly that prices responded to the agreement made in Mexico City and to all subsequent meetings (Tr. 1468-1666). The CEO of Eurolysine said the same thing, explaining further that the one-month lag in price response was due to price protection clauses in lysine supply contracts (Tr. 2198-99). It is true that the plateau price of $0.98 fell short of the $1.05 (and later $1.20) price objective, but the 50 percent increase in price from July to November must have seemed highly satisfactory to cartel members who had seen only a downward trend for one and one-half years.[6]

One competitive factor seems to explain part of the variation in prices of lysine over time. Figure 9.2 shows that quarterly quantities of lysine sold peaked in the fourth quarter of the year (in five out of six years). This suggests that the late 1992 price increase was caused by seasonality of demand. Even with modern confinement methods of raising hogs and poultry, colder temperatures increase overall feed use in the winter months, creating a peak in derived manufacturing demand in the late fall of the previous year, followed by a relaxation of lysine demand in mid-winter.[7] An examination of monthly lysine volume by the four leading U.S. lysine sellers during the years 1990-1995 shows a December peak followed by a March trough. Moreover, there is an intra-annual price peak between October and January each year; the price trough is usually in June or July. Excluding 1992 and 1993, the average peak-to-trough price increases ranged from 4 to 23 percent and averaged 13 percent. Therefore, it is likely that about one-fourth of the late 1992 price increase could be attributed to regular seasonality. Put another way, an ideal time to initiate a price agreement is in mid-summer when a seasonal surge in prices is normally expected by buyers. The cartel in fact implemented its first price agreement in July 1992 and reconstituted its consensus on prices in June and July 1993.

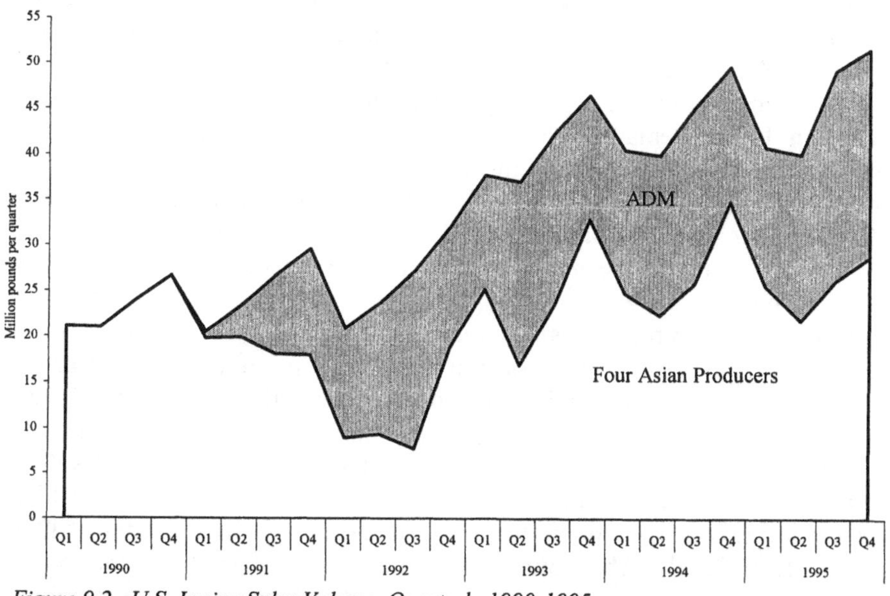

Figure 9.2. U.S. Lysine Sales Volume, Quarterly 1990-1995.

Source: Table 8.A.1.
Note: The average annual compounded rate of growth in U.S. sales from 1990 Q1 to 1995 Q5 was 14.3%.

The third price phase was a tumble in U.S. lysine prices from $0.98 per pound in January 1993 to $0.62 in June. Although aided by the seasonal relaxation in demand, bickering among the cartel members seems to have been the primary cause of the early 1993 price decline. ADM's demand for a market share equal to Ajinomoto's caused a good deal of friction, as did ADM's rapid expansion into regions long dominated by Ajinomoto or Kyowa Hakko.

Three bilateral meetings were held in Illinois in April to try to patch things up between ADM and Ajinomoto. At the regular, full-scale meetings of the cartel (in early 1993), ADM's push for a market share agreement was repeatedly thwarted. ADM exports invaded many markets previously considered Asian hegemonies. The two Korean firms pressed hard for volume shares well above their historical levels. Ajinomoto's executives believed that Wilson had promised that ADM would limit its production to 9 million pounds per month during 1993. In fact, ADM's 1993 monthly production had averaged 13.2 million pounds through October and was rising. Total U.S. volume of sales of the top four lysine manufacturers had reached a new peak of 138 million pounds per year by mid-1993, pushing prices down again to unprofitable levels of $0.62 to $0.78 per pound late in the spring of 1993.

The crisis was resolved at a summit meeting in Irvine, California in October 1993 between ADM's Executive V.P. Michael Andreas and his counterpart at Ajinomoto. This meeting, caught on video by the FBI and shown in public at the Chicago trial, restored harmony to the lysine cartel. For the second time, prices rose quickly, aided at first by the normal seasonal increase in lysine demand. Moreover, the serious Midwest flood caused soybean prices to rise to very high levels, which lifted the ceiling price of lysine well above actual lysine prices in late 1993. ADM restrained its plant production then and throughout 1994 to adhere to the Irvine volume agreement, thus ceding the major part of the U.S. market to its rivals once again (Figure 9.2).

During the fourth phase from November 1993 to August 1994, U.S. lysine prices varied by at most a penny or two from $1.11 per pound. Lysine prices later reached an apogee of $1.22 per pound for several months in late 1994, but began a slow decline of a few cents per month in February or March of 1995. Clearly, the period November 1993 to June 1995 was the cartel's most effective in raising transaction prices very close to the list prices. The high prices caused U.S. sales volume to fall by 10 percent in first quarter of l994 from late 1993 levels. The volume agreement had ushered in a period of exceptional harmony for the cartel, and the shadow price of lysine remained high.

The fifth and final price phase was a decline in prices from January to September 1995. This reduction coincided with weakening seasonal demand. Yet, the cartel had avoided such a decline in early 1994 when it was enjoying its most effective collusive discipline. Kanji Mimoto attributed the decline in prices to an increase in ADM production in early 1995, a reaction of ADM's Whitacre to Ajinomoto's filing suit for patent infringement on two of ADM's amino acids. However, there is little evidence of an unusual increase in lysine production or sales in early 1995.[8] The most cogent explanation lies with the ceiling price for lysine. Because of large declines in the prices of soymeal and corn, the opportunity cost fell from almost $2.00 per pound in 1993 to about $1.00 in mid 1995 (Figure 9.1). This ceiling price dropped below the U.S.

transaction price in January 1995 and stayed below for five months. After a lag of a month or two, U.S. transactions prices followed. When the ceiling price rose in mid-1995, so did transaction prices a couple of months later.

Therefore, apart from the influence of seasonal demand fluctuations and one instance of a falling ceiling price, the cartel's decisions to fix list prices controlled transactions prices during the conspiracy period. The lysine cartel was successful in raising market prices in six out of eight attempts. Price-fixing agreements made in June 1992, October 1992, July 1993, October 1993, January 1994, and April 1994 were in each case followed by actual price increases one to three months later. On average, the U.S. list prices decreed by the cartel resulted in market prices about 90 percent as high as the target price. However, two list price increases implemented in December 1992 and January 1995 were not effective in raising transaction prices (Connor 1990: Table A8). In general, when the conspirators were cooperating, transaction prices were 3 to 5 cents below list, but the gap widened in early 1993 and early 1995 when there was more contentiousness.

PRODUCTION EFFECTS

The cartel had profound effects on the production levels and capacity investments of the world's leading lysine producers. The increase in price caused consumption and, hence, production to decline. Moreover, the advent of the cartel had the effect of freezing the relative positions of the leading firms in comparison to what had been a very fluid situation prior to the conspiracy. This solidifying of the structure of production was especially evident from late 1993 to 1995 when the conspirators had finally arrived at a workable agreement on global production shares.

As was just discussed, the price of lysine at the peak of the cartel's effectiveness in 1994 reached about $1.20 per pound, which was about $0.50 above the long-run competitive price of lysine. With information on the elasticity of demand (see Chapter 8), it is possible to apply a formula to calculate the value of lost production due to the monopoly pricing (Connor and Peterson 1996:208). Taking the quantity consumed in 1991 as the base year, this loss to U.S. consumers and producers (the dead-weight loss) in 1994 was between $9 and $17 million.[9] This dollar loss implies that the 1994 quantity sold was from 37 to 66 million pounds lower than a competitive U.S. market would have generated. Using the same assumptions, global sales volume was suppressed by 120 to 230 million pounds because of cartel pricing and volume allocation. Put another way, the lysine industry produced at least 20 percent less in 1994 than it would have made had there been perfect competition. In the other years of the conspiracy, the price effects were weaker and, hence, the production losses were smaller.

Figuring out the loss to final consumers of pork and chicken is a difficult exercise. Feed manufacturers might have increased the proportion of corn (which contains lysine) in their feeds. Swine producers would cut back on their purchases of balanced feeds or feed premixes, thereby marketing fewer and smaller hogs for slaughter, or would require a higher price per pound for their slaughter hogs. Poultry producers would react in a similar fashion. Faced with higher pork and chicken prices, consumers would cut back on the quantities they purchased, which in turn would diminish the demand for slaughter animals, their feeds, and finally lysine. When all these forces have had time to work themselves out, a 20 percent reduction in lysine output would ultimately result in a small (less than 1 percent) but measurable reduction in retail sales volume.

Global capacity and production volumes may be found in Table 8.A.3. Prior to the volume-allocation agreement, ADM's capacity grew from nothing to one-third of global capacity in 1993. ADM's capacity grew at the expense of the three established Asian manufacturers. Only little Cheil was able to increase its capacity share in the face of ADM's onslaught. Production shares followed capacity shares except in 1991 when ADM's plant was new.

From 1993 (the year in which the cartel agreed to allocate global volume of production) to 1995, both capacity shares and production shares were quite stable. ADM's production share was about 5 percentage points above the cartel's agreement on 26.4 percent primarily because Table 8.A.3 includes ADM's sales of liquid lysine.[10] ADM's share of dry lysine conformed closely to the agreement. The cartel did not include liquid lysine in its deliberations, but ADM's expectation of substantial liquid sales probably made it easier to accept what was by agreement second place to Ajinomoto (which was allocated a 34 percent share of dry lysine). In 1994-1995, ADM achieved its primary strategic goal of global parity with the leader when both kinds of lysine are counted.

After the cartel broke up in late 1995, notable changes in global shares can be observed (Table 8.A.3). The shares of the top three companies declined in 1996, collectively losing 7 percent of world production. The aggressors were the two South Korean companies, Sewon and Cheil. These two had chaffed at their volume restrictions mightily during the conspiracy. As soon as those chains were removed, they returned to their old strategy of building new lysine capacity as fast as possible on borrowed money. Even during the conspiracy, Cheil had been the cartel's biggest cheater, selling at least 10 percent more dry lysine than its share allowed.

The production story is just about the same in the U.S. lysine market as it was worldwide (Figure 9.3). In 1990, Ajinomoto, Kyowa Hakko, and Sewon were a triopoly; Ajinomoto controlled nearly half and Kyowa nearly one-third of U.S. sales. As ADM's production ramped up in 1991 and 1992, the two former leaders saw their sales displaced by the intruder. By 1992, the three established Asian sellers saw their collective U.S. sales volume drop from 100 percent to 43 percent. This loss of market share is one of the main reasons the Asian companies were eventually persuaded to join the cartel.

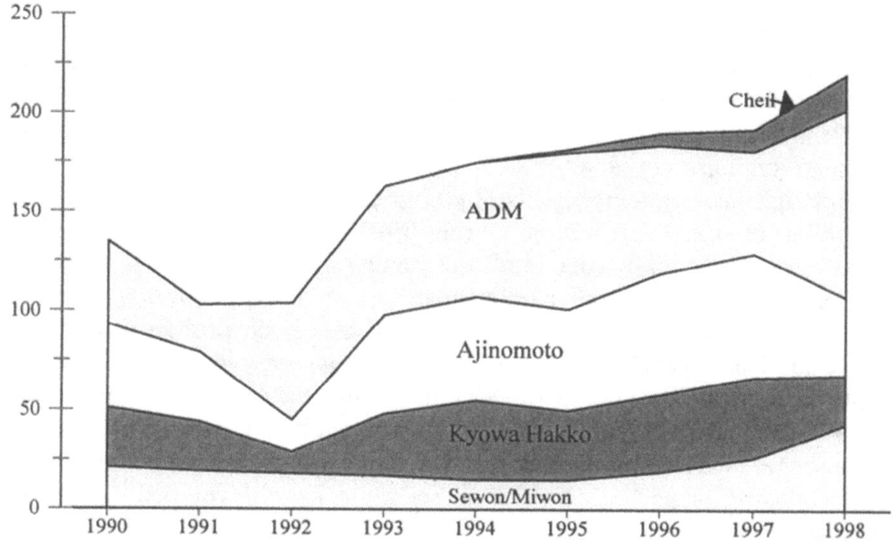

Figure 9.3. U.S. Lysine Sales Volume, By Company, 1990-1998.

Source: Table 8.A.2 in Appendix.

As soon as a price agreement was reached in late 1992, ADM reduced its U.S. sales and made room for its Asian co-conspirators. In the fourth quarter of 1992, ADM's sales volume declined by 6 million pounds from the previous quarter, and the Asian producers' rose by 11 million pounds (Table 8.A.1).[11] During 1993-1994, Ajinomoto and Kyowa had their pre-ADM sales volumes restored; ADM essentially held a share of the market based on *growth* in the U.S. market since 1990. During the conspiracy, ADM shifted its massive production toward export sales, which averaged about 60 percent of ADM's total lysine sales during 1993-1995. Immediately after the cartel broke up, market shares started shifting once again.

EFFECTS ON INTERNATIONAL TRADE

The lysine cartel fixed the shares of sales volumes in 1993 on a global basis. No formal agreement was reached on national or regional market shares. Yet, as mentioned above, Ajinomoto, Kyowa Hakko, and Sewon had in the 1980s created regional spheres of influence. Ajinomoto had pioneered production in Western Europe at an early stage in the industry's history;

during the 1980s it had prevented Sewon from importing more than 10 percent of the continent's supply. Kyowa Hakko was the first to establish lysine production in the New World, first in Mexico and soon afterwards in the United States. Kyowa Hakko believed that it had special rights to the Latin American market. In the late 1980s, Kyowa got Ajinomoto to agree to restrain exports to Mexico; in return, Kyowa agreed to avoid exporting to Thailand where Ajinomoto had a plant. Ajinomoto and Kyowa colluded to divide the U.S. market in the late 1980s. Most of Sewon's exports were destined for Asian countries.

International trade patterns shifted radically before, during, and after the lysine cartel was in operation. From 1991 on, U.S. exports and ADM's exports are practically one and the same.[12] As part of its strategy to aggressively seek a global market share equal to Ajinomoto's, before the cartel was formed ADM cut prices worldwide, set up foreign sales offices, and established beachheads abroad. This phase of cut-throat competition approximates the ideal competitive market. During the high point of the cartel in 1994-1995, trade would be affected by monopoly behavior. What happened a year or two later was a blend of the two situations; a form of behavior called tacit collusion or partial cooperation seems to have developed.[13] The years 1993 and 1996 are transitional.

U.S. Export Volume

What happened to U.S. lysine exports during the three competitive periods? First, after a brief burst of growth in 1990-1992, the cartel restrained ADM's exports. From 1992 to 1997, the volume of exports rose an average of about 23 percent per year (Figure 9.4). During the peak cartel years of 1994-95, export growth fell below the trend. When the cartel ended, export volume doubled, far above the average growth rate.

Second, the cartel restricted U.S. exports to the "home countries" of Ajinomoto and Kyowa (i.e., countries in which they owned plants making lysine). During the period of aggressive price cutting, the share of U.S. exports rose to Mexico, France, Italy, Thailand, and Japan and rose faster than average growth in each home market (Figure 9.5). ADM was behaving quite aggressively toward its future co-conspirators. During the cartel's high period, 1994-1995, the share of ADM's exports to Ajinomoto's and Kyowa's home countries was cut in half.[14] After the cartel broke up ADM resumed exporting to the countries in which Ajinomoto and Kyowa dominated production.

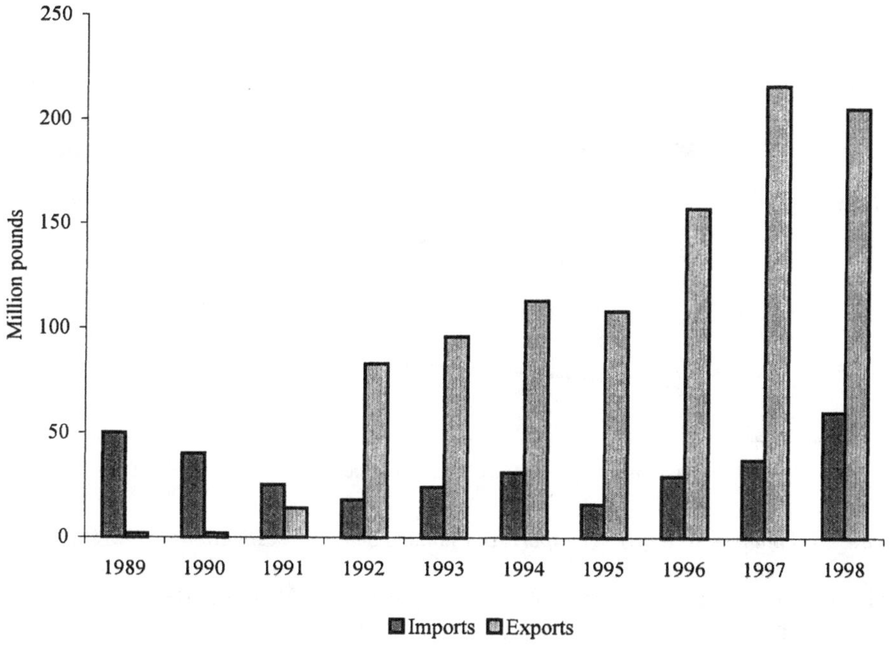

Figure 9.4. Volume of U.S. Lysine Exports and Imports, 1990-1995.

Source: Tables 9.A.2 and 9.A.3 from STAT-USA on-line data service of U.S. Dept. of Commerce. HTS Code No. 292241000.
Imports include food and feed grade.

Third, ADM shifted its exports toward two areas during the cartel's most efficient period. It's share of exports to the Netherlands rose from 25 percent in 1992 to 35 percent in 1994-1995. When the cartel ceased operating, the share of exports to the Netherlands dropped. A similar pattern on a smaller scale can be observed in major South American markets and in selected markets in East Asia (Malaysia, Singapore, Indonesia, Philippines, and Taiwan). While there is no public information on the cartel's regional allocation decisions, ADM's actual export behavior conforms to a pattern of restraint to Ajinomoto's and Kyowa's key markets complemented by a pattern of aggressive sales in the Netherlands, South America, and certain Asian markets.

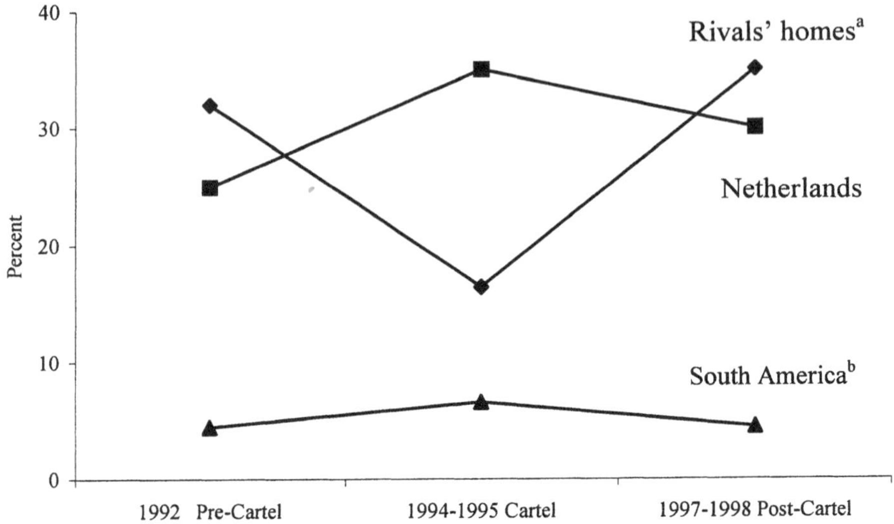

Figure 9.5. Volume of U.S. (ADM) Exports of Lysine to Selected Destinations, 1992-1998.

[a] "Home" countries of Ajinomoto and Kyowa are Mexico, Belgium, France, Germany, Spain, Italy, Thailand, Hong Kong, and Japan.
[b] Columbia, Venezuela, Brazil, Argentina.

U.S. Export Prices

Trade data offer one more possible insight into the lysine cartel's behavior, and that is geographic price discrimination. Feed-grade lysine is a homogeneous product. If nondiscriminatory pricing is followed, prices would not be expected to vary systematically according to county of destination *prior* to the time the product leaves U.S. ports. (The only exceptions are that small shipments and shipments being routed through West Coast ports to Pacific destinations may be priced 3 to 5 percent higher because of greater domestic transactions or transportation costs). However, ADM was in a position to discriminate among recipient countries on the basis of their price or income elasticities, or what is called pricing-to-market (PTM) behavior.

Lysine prices of exports "free alongside ship" (f.a.s.) are shown in Table 9.A.5. One clear feature of these prices is the very large variability across countries during the pre-cartel year 1992 and narrowing over time until 1995.[15] The high variation in export prices in 1992 is not unexpected because the vast majority of the countries being served in 1992 were not destinations for U.S.- made lysine prior to 1991. The jump in price variability in 1995 is consistent with the disarray that accompanied the exposure of the cartel. The

1997 prices are surprisingly close across many nearby countries; for example, 12 of the 13 South American destinations had lysine prices between $1.27 and $1.28 – less than 1 percent apart!

During 1992-93, ADM was aggressively invading many overseas markets that had been served for many years by plants in Japan, Korea, and France. Ajinomoto's Italian and French plants were nearly the sole suppliers to most of Europe in the 1980s; Sewon's Korean plant was the major source of supplies in countries near the Pacific Ocean, with smaller amounts exported from Indonesia and Japan; and Kyowa's small Mexican plant might have exported some lysine to other Latin American markets. During 1992-1993, ADM used low prices to signal its world rivals that it intended to build market share quickly in many of the world's largest markets for lysine.

ADM immediately began exporting to all parts of the world, but *Europe* seems to have been an especially important target, accounting for almost 45 percent of total lysine exports in 1992 (Table 9.A.3). That ADM was courting customers in Europe is revealed by the relatively low prices offered in the Netherlands, UK, Germany, and even France in both 1992 and 1993. In only a few smaller European markets did ADM set lysine prices well above world levels (Norway, Spain, Italy, and Switzerland). ADM's *Canadian* pricing strategy was different: even though Canadian demand approached 20 percent of U.S. exports for the first three years, lysine prices were kept almost precisely at the global average selling price. In the early years, the *Asian* market accounted for about one-quarter of total U.S. lysine exports. Despite its growth potential, ADM kept prices relatively high to most Asian destinations for the first two or three years (Table 9.A.5). There were three very instructive exceptions: Thailand, Korea, and Indonesia, where lysine was priced about 13 percent lower than the average (despite higher U.S. transport costs of lysine from West Coast ports). Exports were priced so low to these countries that it is easy to entertain the idea that ADM was predating on Sewon and Cheil. Only Japan itself was spared ADM's aggressive pricing among the four Asian lysine-producing countries, perhaps a signal to Ajinomoto and Kyowa of ADM's friendly intentions. Finally, the *South American* lysine market accounted for about 10 percent of total U.S. export sales. Here, ADM kept prices quite high in nearly all markets in the first three years: as a rule the large "southern cone" countries (Brazil, Argentina) were priced 3 to 8 percent higher and most other countries on the continent, which were 10 to 30 percent higher than the world average during 1992-1994. Again, there is one telling exception: Mexico, where Kyowa's plant was located, was treated to *below* average prices in 1993 and especially 1994.

The effects of the lysine cartel on U.S. export prices are revealed most vividly during 1995-1996. Recall that export price differences widened markedly from 1994 to 1995 and narrowed considerably in 1997. In its later stages the cartel set prices for several importing regions. In 1995, U.S. lysine exports were allocated by volume as follows: Europe 45 percent, Canada 14 percent, Asia and Oceania almost 30 percent, and Latin America not quite 10 percent. Since 1992, there had been a slight shift in export volumes away from Canada and towards Asian destinations.

Within *Europe* during 1995-96, U.S./ADM exports to the Netherlands and Spain about doubled, while exports to nearly all other European countries withered. Except for the UK, lysine exports were zero or negligible to France, Belgium, Italy, Germany, Switzerland, and Scandinavia. Prices to the Netherlands, UK, and Spain were set on average (simple average of five country-year observations) 6.5 percent *below* the U.S. average export price. On the other hand, for the remaining European countries prices averaged 13.3 percent *above* the U.S. average. Rather than refusing to deal with customers in countries close to Ajinomoto's plants in France and Italy, ADM simply used higher prices to discourage imports into what appears to be Ajinomoto's cartel-designated "exclusive sales territory." Put another way, ADM was adhering to a price increase of about 25 percent to Ajinomoto's historical European customers above ADM's average export prices in 1992-93 (about $1.10 per pound compared to $0.89 earlier). In either case, the effect was the same: ADM dominated the UK, Dutch, and Spanish markets and priced lysine relatively low to achieve that dominance, whereas the rest of Europe was ceded to Ajinomoto. It is perhaps no accident that the three countries apparently given to ADM were those geographically closest to eastern U.S. export ports.

Canadian export volume fell absolutely and relatively in 1995-96 compared to 1992-93 (Table 9.A.2). Prices are responsible for this singular departure from prior and world trends. During 1992-95, U.S. export prices to Canada hewed closely to the world average. However, in 1995-96 prices were raised to $1.15 (16 percent above average) from $0.89 in 1992-93 (a 29 percent increase). Prior to ADM's entry, Canada was provided lysine either from Japan-Korea through British Columbia or from France through Atlantic ports. Later, the cartel assigned Canada mostly to ADM.

In general, ADM set relatively high prices on exports to *Asia* in 1995-96. Excluding the home-production countries (Thailand, Indonesia, Korea, and Japan), a couple of newly penetrated markets (e.g., Vietnam), and Australia-New Zealand, U.S. prices to Asian destinations averaged 9.8 percent above the world average. However, before the cartel's formation, ADM already sold lysine at above-average prices (5.6 percent above average). Thus, the effects of the cartel on Asian prices were positive (a 15-percent increase in prices) but not as dramatic as in Canada and Europe. Australia and New Zealand became ADM-dominated markets as ADM dropped its prices compared to the 1992-93 levels. The pricing of U.S. exports to the home countries of the four Asian cartel members is quite curious. On average, prices in 1995-96 were 5.7 percent higher than the global average (the same as the rest of Asia), but these prices were significantly higher than the competitive phase (3.2 percent below global). That is, ADM went from about $0.86 per pound pre-cartel to $1.05

during the cartel; the *direction* is what would be expected, but the *degree* is less than what was seen in Europe.

Latin America was forced to pay the largest price premium for ADM's lysine. Excluding the one home country of Mexico, lysine prices in 13 other countries of the region averaged 21.2 percent above global prices in 1995, falling to 6.7 percent in 1996, with very little variation across countries. During 1992-93, Latin American lysine prices averaged 11.6 percent above the $0.89 global price. The $1.16 export price in 1995 ($1.09 in 1996) represented a 17-percent increase (10-percent increase) over 1992-93 levels. Thus, the 1995 observed export prices conform closely to what was seen in Canada and Continental Europe, but in 1996 ADM was charging more moderate prices, especially in the two biggest markets, Brazil and Mexico. The trend toward price moderation continued in 1997. The best guess is that (except for Brazil and Mexico), ADM was pricing itself out of the Latin American market in 1995. The volume response to the large 1994-95 price increase was very small, so perhaps the cartel changed its allocations regarding Latin America in 1996.

The final time period to be examined is when the formal overt cartel was abandoned. Because the cartel was publicly exposed in June 1995, it might be considered that 1996 and 1997 both belong to whatever new pricing regime developed. However, it is possible that the cartel's territorial allocations and price agreements may have persisted for several months following July 1995. It is safer to regard 1996 as a transitional year and focus on 1997 as more likely to be a new post-cartel equilibrium.

The volume of lysine exports increased considerably in 1997, doubling from 1995 and tripling from 1992, in accordance with expectations (Table 9.A.2). Prices rose, as did the ceiling price, and became far more uniform across countries. Pricing in *Canada* returned to only average levels (just like 1992-93), but unlike the early 1990s. Pricing to *Latin America* became extremely close to the average and almost completely uniform. It appears that ADM is using low prices to consolidate a dominant position in the Western Hemisphere. In *Europe,* ADM has essentially withdrawn from almost every national market except the three countries where it used low prices to expand its share in 1994-95: the UK, Netherlands, and Spain. (Italy is an inexplicable exception). In these three markets, ADM has returned to an average-price policy. *Asia* is the one area where some variability in export prices can be found. In all four "home countries" in Asia, ADM was selling at relatively low prices (6.7 percent below global average). Despite the relatively low prices, ADM's export share slipped in all four countries in 1997 compared with its share during the cartel phase. Thus, ADM's volume and pricing of lysine exports in 1997 supports a continuation of the international "spheres of influence" established by the cartel for North America, South America, and Europe.

U.S. Imports

Because there were relatively few countries in which lysine was produced, the effects of the lysine cartel on U.S. imports are much simpler to analyze. Import volume in 1997 doubled over 1992-93 levels and tripled from 1995, directly parallel to the export pattern (Table 9.A.6).

Sewon in Korea was the dominant source of imported lysine up to 1993, but its share of total U.S. imports eroded somewhat as plants in other countries matured and expanded (Table 9.A.7). Kyowa and Ajinomoto exported very little feed-grade lysine from Japan throughout the 1990s, consistent with information that their Japanese plants were becoming less efficient over time. However, Kyowa did export lysine from its Mexican plant irregularly to the United States, reaching second place among imports in 1992 and 1993. Of Ajinomoto's three locations outside Japan, only exports from its plant in France ever reached high levels and then only in one year, 1994. After 1995, Ajinomoto directed European exports to the United States solely from its newer Italian lysine plant. Its Thai plant exported only once to the United States.

Finally, Cheil Jedang's Indonesian plant made its first exports of lysine to the United States in late 1993. During 1993-1994 Cheil Jedang accounted for less than 3 percent of U.S. imports. Cheil Jedang must have had substantial export capacity during the cartel phase; its Indonesian plant was the sixth largest in the world in 1995 and was adding capacity that came on stream in 1996 (Table 8.A.2). Cheil grabbed a very large increase in U.S. sales of lysine in 1995: U.S. import volume quadrupled from 1993-94 levels and, because imports were severely reduced, its U.S. import share rose to 14 percent. Cheil's share of U.S. consumption in 1995 was only 1.2 percent; for the three years that the lysine cartel may have operated, Cheil accounted for only 0.7 percent of U.S. sales. Cheil joined the cartel only at its later stages, so its share of U.S. sales when it was a conspirator might have been as low as 0.4 percent of the cartel's total sales during 1992-95. At any rate, Cheil was forced to pay a $1.25 million criminal fine for its role in the lysine conspiracy in the United States. This fine represented 1.4 percent of the total paid by the five co-conspirators.

When the full effects of the lysine conspiracy were felt in 1995, U.S. imports of lysine fell 33 percent below the volume of the previous three years. However, imports from Thailand and Indonesia are not consistent with supply contraction directed by a cartel. Cheil increased its imports by more than 200 percent in 1995. Either Cheil had bargained hard for a larger share of the U.S. market or it was a maverick company. The reduction in imports is not quite as dramatic when calculated in *value* of lysine imports because prices rose during the conspiracy period (Table 9.A.8). Imports were priced at the border (including insurance and freight charges) some 15 to 19 percent below the average domestic sales price. This mark-up is close to a normal wholesale margin to cover transportation and other handling charges for lysine between the port of import and the customers in internal U.S. locations.

When the price-fixing conspiracy began to have effects on market prices, lysine import prices also began to move up. The implicit domestic margin fell to 10 percent in 1994 and 1995. The cartel brought about a large and permanent charge in the composition of U.S. lysine imports. Prior to 1991, feed-grade imports comprised more than 90 percent of total lysine import volume. By 1995, imports accounted for less than 9 percent of U.S. consumption (Table 9.A.7).

EFFECTS ON PROFITS

Exhibits presented at the criminal price-fixing trial of three ADM executives provide a rare glimpse into the profitability of the lysine conspiracy for ADM. Internal documents prepared for the president of ADM's Biotechnology Division reveal with great precision how various phases of the cartel's activities benefited ADM's bottom line. Operating profits were calculated monthly for lysine, lactic acid, and the other "departments" of the Division.[16] For each product sales were calculated and product-specific production and marketing costs. Production costs subtracted were of three types: variable costs internal to the department (energy, labor, and chemicals), variable costs of inputs transferred from other parts of ADM (dextrose, other intermediate materials), and fixed costs. When the manufacturing operations were mature and running at planned output levels, total manufacturing costs averaged about 62 cents per pound; distribution, storage, and selling costs averaged 11 cents per pound. Manufacturing costs averaged 10 cents per pound for fixed costs, 20 cents for dextrose, and 32 cents for other variable costs. The major sources of monthly variation in costs were the price of dextrose (ranged from 16 to 25 cents per pound) and the yield of lysine per pound of dextrose (clustered near 36 percent, but ranged from 26 to 41 percent). Yields below 30 percent signaled that a batch of lysine had become contaminated, causing average monthly production costs to soar above $1.00 per pound. These types of production glitches pretty nearly ended after the first year of production.

ADM's lysine profit rates are shown in Figure 9.6. In late 1991 the company was still experiencing low yields, so even average selling prices of $0.98 to $1.06 per pound resulted in losses. In the first eight months of 1992, ADM's costs were under control but selling prices fell by 30 percent or more from late 1991 levels, so the lysine department continued to experience very low or negative profits.

The big turn-around in profitability came in September 1992. The cartel's late June 1992 agreement to raise list prices began to affect U.S. market prices in August and export prices in September. By the end of the year, domestic prices had risen 62 percent from their July nadir and export prices by about half that amount. As a result, the profit rate in the fourth quarter of 1992 soared to 25 percent of sales. After the brief second price war in mid-1993, profits once again took off. In the six quarters shown in 1994-95, ADM's lysine profits averaged 33 percent of sales, or more than six times ADM's historical pre-tax profits. It is likely that Ajinomoto and Kyowa Hakko were earning similar profit rates on their U.S.-made lysine.

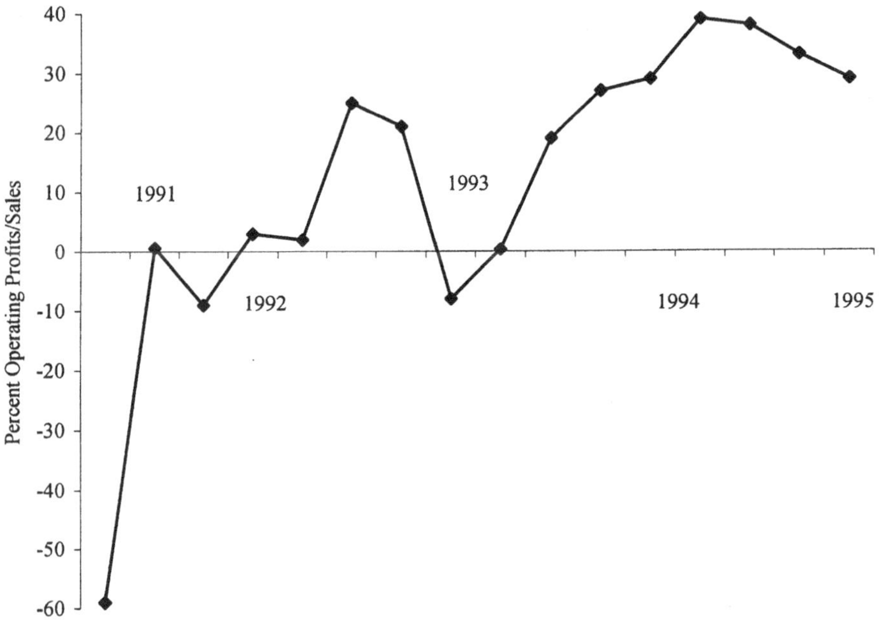

Figure 9.6. Pre-Tax Profit Margin of ADM's Lysine Department, Quarterly, July 1991-June 1995.

Source: ADM Bioproducts Division, *Operations Statistical Reports.*

Figure 9.7 demonstrates the impacts of the price conspiracy on ADM's dollar lysine profits. At the peak of the conspiracy in late 1994 operating profits reached as high as $6.3 million per month. During the cartel's most effective nine quarters, ADM's lysine profits totaled about $104 million. The cost of punishing the other cartel members in mid-1993 so that they would join the deal on market shares was a modest $4 million. It is likely that not all of the $104 million represents pure monopoly profits. Some of these profits may have compensated ADM for the costs of learning how to produce and sell lysine and how to improve its manufacturing processes. Moreover, some of the operating profits may reflect a normal return to investors that they would rightfully expect to receive from any similar industry investment.[17] Despite these caveats, the vast majority of ADM's $104 million in profits represents a return to illegal price fixing, say, at least $80 million.

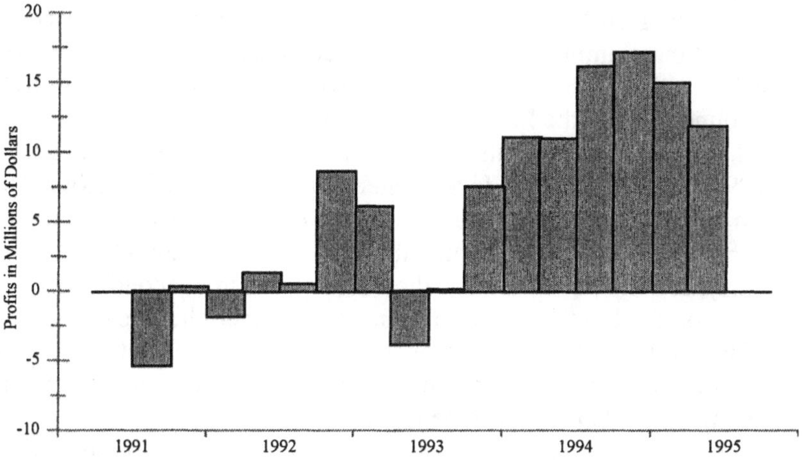

Figure 9.7. Operating Profits of ADM's Lysine Department, Quarterly, July 1991 - June 1995.

Source: ADM Bioproducts Division, *Operations Statistical Reports*.

In Chapters 13 to 16 below, details are given on the financial costs to ADM of various legal sanctions levied on the company. Fines paid to the governments of the United States, Canada, Mexico, and the EU amounted to $125 million; ADM paid a further $37 million to settle private antitrust suits by U.S. buyers. Other civil suits and legal-defense costs were at least $80 million. Thus, ADM's financial costs seem to be about double its profits from price fixing.

THE CUSTOMER OVERCHARGE

Direct buyers of lysine are injured two ways by an effective seller's cartel. They pay more for each unit purchased and, because the price is higher than it would have been absent the cartel, there is a reduction in quantity purchased. The first loss is called the overcharge. Under U.S. law customers that were overcharged may seek triple the damages they sustained. The second source of injury is called the dead weight loss. Although it is recognized as a compensable harm in some federal court districts actionable, this section focuses solely on the lysine overcharge to direct buyers.[18]

Two legal developments provide minimal indicators of the size of the lysine overcharge imposed by the cartel on buyers located in the United States. First, in April 1996 the law firm representing the federal class of lysine buyers negotiated a settlement of $45 million to be paid by the four largest members of the cartel. Because this amount theoretically represents triple the overcharge, ADM *et al.* implicitly were asserting an overcharge of $15 million. Depending on how long the conspiracy affected market prices, this overcharge estimate implies an average price increase of only 2.6 to 3.1 percent of U.S. sales (Table 8.A.4). Alternatively, it implies a but-for price of $1.10 per pound. This is the lowest of the estimates.

Second, the $70 million fine paid by ADM when it pleaded guilty in October 1996 was based on the U.S. Sentencing Guidelines for felons. Under one section of the Guidelines, the fine could be assessed as 20 percent of ADM's U.S. dry lysine sales during the conspiracy, or about $40 million (Table 9.A.1). As this is far below the actual fine, the second section that bases the fine on double the overcharge must have been the one employed by the DOJ. Thus, given ADM's share of the U.S. market, the total overcharge must have been at least $65 million. If ADM received a discount for its cooperation, the overcharge would be higher.[19]

Besides these two legal indicators, direct economic facts revealed about the lysine cartel can be used to make a third estimate the overcharge. The calculation of the overcharge rectangle is in principle a simple arithmetic exercise (see Chapter 2). One requires actual transactions prices charged by the conspirators, the quantities sold during the conspiracy (or, more precisely, the period during which prices were affected by the conspiracy), the dates of the conspiracy-effects period, and the price that sellers would have charged but for the conspiracy. The overcharge is the revenues of the members of the cartel during the conspiracy-effects period less revenues that would have accrued at the but-for price.[20]

During the discovery phase of the civil case, four of the lysine defendants made public their average monthly lysine transactions prices for the years 1991-1995. Annual sales to customers located in the United States were also given, so reasonable estimates of monthly quantities sold by the four companies could also be calculated (see Connor 2000: Table A2). In addition to market prices and quantities, there was essential agreement among experts on the market structure of the U.S. lysine market in the early 1990s. Seller concentration was very high, the product was homogeneous, and barriers to entry were substantial.[21]

It is at this point that a consensus ended. Disagreement about the dates of the conspiracy-effects period, the but-for price, and the type of industry conduct absent collusion produced disagreement about the estimate of the lysine overcharge.[22] Assuming a conspiracy-effects period of 36 months and a but-for price of $0.70 per pound, the overcharge was $155-166 million, or at least ten times the defendants' implicit overcharge estimate (Table 9.A.1).

The Time Period

Reasonable persons might well differ about the conspiracy-effects period. The high and curiously stable monthly prices observed during the period November 1993 through March 1995 makes this period the least controversial one (17 months). It is clear that prices began to rise a month or two after the Mexico City meeting in June 1992. While the cartel's consensus broke down in the spring of 1993, there is little to be gained by excluding this period because the prices were so low that the overcharge estimate will hardly be affected. In early 1995, prices began trending downward, but this decline was in response to a lower corn-soybean ceiling price that limited the effects of the agreement but did not destroy it. July 1995 seems to be the earliest the effects period could have terminated, which brings the conspiracy-effects period up to 36 months. Out of consideration for lags in raising production and exports to the United States, the rest of 1995 might be included as well (44 months).

The But-For Price

There are four analytical approaches to estimating the appropriate non-conspiracy price (Page 1996). First and most common in court proceedings is the before-and-after approach. In this instance the analyst uses information on industry conduct to identify a period or periods free of collusive conduct. The reigning price(s) during that (those) period(s) becomes the basis of comparison, that is, the elusive but-for price. Second, given information on industry concentration, marginal costs of production, the own-price elasticity of demand, and an assumed mode of pricing behavior, a theoretical model of oligopoly can be employed to predict the but-for price. This approach is rarely used in antitrust trials. Third, consonant with the definition of the Lerner index, defendants could provide proprietary information on capacity utilization, fixed costs, and variable costs in order to construct a proxy for a but-for price. Cost and capacity data often supplement the before-and-after price analysis in courts. Fourth, a time-series econometric model[23] that would estimate industry demand and supply relationships could then include a qualitative variable for the alleged conspiracy period that should capture the collusive effect on price.

The Before-and-After Method

Employing the before-and-after method, two periods of three or four months each were identified as apparently highly competitive ones, namely, May-July 1992 and April-July 1993.[24] During both periods, U.S. transactions prices of lysine averaged $0.70 per pound.

The two periods seem to exhibit the kind of cutthroat price rivalry described by the economist's model of pure competition. The two periods correspond to the months just prior to two key meetings of the lysine conspirators: Mexico City in late June 1992 and Irvine, California in October 1993. Prior to Mexico City there was no oligopolistic consensus, and ADM was behaving very aggressively in expanding output. Prior to the California meeting the fragile consensus had broken down over a dispute about ADM's promise to restrain production.[25] During May-July 1993, it appears that ADM was also attempting to signal its unhappiness to its co-conspirators about the cartel's failure to reach an accord on volume allocations. However, $0.70 may be too low to be considered a long run competitive price. After all, the most efficient firm, ADM, was suffering operating losses in lysine during July-August 1992, losses that turned to profits in September when the market price rose above $0.70 per pound. Internal ADM documents verify that its average total costs (including a normal profit) $0.70 in the short run and $0.80 per pound in the long run.[26] If the but-for prices are $0.70 or $0.80 per pound, the overcharges are $141 and $78 million, respectively.

The Cournot Method

ADM's expert Warren-Boulton took the oligopoly-model approach to develop a but-for price. He asserted that the homogeneous Cournot model was the appropriate model to generate a predicted but-for price. Even if one agrees with the Cournot assumption, the predicted price is highly sensitive to assumed parametric values. The choice of the Herfindahl index of concentration (3500 or a little lower) is uncontroversial for the lysine industry, but identifying long run marginal costs and the elasticity of demand are difficult.[27] If, as appears to be the case, lysine is mixed in fixed proportions with grains and feed supplements, then the farm level demand for hog or poultry feed is likely to be quite inelastic. Consequently, lysine demand by feed manufacturers for species-specific feeds will also be inelastic. However, because many buyers purchased lysine for a range of feed products, it is more likely that their demand elasticity was even more inelastic, perhaps approximating the demand for all meat and poultry rather than one meat.[28] No matter what the costs of production, a demand elasticity less than -0.35 for all meats results in Cournot equilibrium prices that are negative. Put another way, if marginal costs were anywhere near $0.70 per pound, then at optimal Cournot price of lysine between $0.76- $0.82 per pound, demand must be almost infinitely elastic.[29]

There are also structural reasons that cast doubt on the idea that the Cournot model is appropriate for long-run pricing in the lysine industry in the early 1990s. First, entry barriers created by production technology (scale economies, fermentation secrets) may not have been as formidable during the cartel's existence as was believed by the experts writing in 1996. Information has come to light that substantial supply flexibility may exist among fermentation finishing units.[30] Producers making lysine, sweeteners, ethanol, monosodium glutamate, and other fermentation products from a common starch source may be able to alter the mix of products with a few weeks of conversion time. Moreover, trade publications subsequently reported more *actual* entry during the conspiracy than was known to have existed in 1996. Thus, during the later phase of the conspiracy the Cournot assumption of barricaded entry may no longer have been tenable.

Second, the type of passive-non-aggressive behavior envisioned by the Cournot model was unlikely to be attainable, during 1992-1994 at least. While it is true that the two Japanese manufacturers had a long history of cooperative behavior, Sewon had not previously agreed to limit production. Like most Korean manufacturers, Sewon had displayed a strategy of aggressive market-share enhancement throughout the 1980s.[31] When the lysine cartel came to light, Sewon complained publicly that it had been coerced by Ajinomoto and Kyowa into joining. The small fine assessed by the DOJ tends to confirm that Sewon was the most cooperative of the Asian conspirators in settling the criminal case. Even less likely to behave in a passive manner were the two 1991 entrants, ADM and Cheil. Cheil acted like a maverick during most of the cartel's existence. Besides the absence of strategic interaction, the chasm in business cultures between ADM and the rest of the cartel was profound.[32]

The Cost-Based Method

In early 1999 during the sentencing phase of the criminal trial of three ADM executives, the size of the U.S. overcharge became an issue because the prosecution asked for fines above the statutory amount. The government requested and received detailed information on the costs of production and distribution of all the lysine plants in the world owned by the five members of the cartel. An analysis by the government's expert economist determined that ADM's Decatur plant had the lowest costs of production of any that supplied the U.S. market and that average total costs were constant during the conspiracy period.[33] Allowing for a generous expected rate of return for investors in the industry, the government's uncontested estimate of U.S. overcharges was $78 million. By an eerie coincidence, $78 million is the midpoint between the defendants' estimate of $15 million and the federal class' estimate adjusted for seasonality of the $141 million (Table 9.A.1). Moreover, the $78 million is nearly identical to a more complex, multiple-equation econometric model developed and tested by Morse and Hyde (2000).[34]

Summary

All four known methods of estimating overcharges due to price fixing have been applied to the lysine cartel. I have argued above that the approach that assumes some model of oligopoly pricing, such as the Cournot model, is inappropriate for the lysine industry in the early 1990s. The remaining three techniques (before-and-after, cost-based, and econometric) yield a set of estimates from $15 to $141 million. However, the two most recent and scientifically satisfying analysis came up with a $78 million overcharge estimate for the U.S. market during July 1992-June 1995. The U.S. sales of dry lysine during the conspiracy period were $460 million, therefore direct buyers of lysine overpaid by 17 percent on average. Although no formal analysis of non-U.S. overcharges are available, the higher prices in Western Europe suggest an overcharge of around $100 million to European customers; the lower prices in Asia suggest overcharges in the rest of the world were lower than those in the United States. A reasonable projection of the global overcharge by the lysine cartel would be in the $200 to $250 million range.

CONCLUSIONS

The lysine cartel was successful in raising prices worldwide for most of its three years of operation. Although aided in small part by a regular seasonal increase in the demand for lysine, the lion's share of the 50 to 70-percent increases in prices can be traced to the cartel's collusive agreements. As a result, the cartel's direct U.S. customers, feed manufacturers, were overcharged between $200 and $250 million for the lysine they added to their products. It is likely that most, if not all, of this monopoly overcharge was passed on eventually to consumers in the form of higher pork and chicken prices.

A second negative affect on buyers of lysine was a contraction in output of lysine and in small subsequent lysine-containing products: animal feeds, marketed swine and poultry, and processed pork and poultry products. In the cartel's peak year 1994, lysine volume sold was at least 20 percent below the volume a competitive industry would have sold. However, because lysine is such a small portion of the total weight of balanced animal feeds, the effect on retail volumes of pork and chicken were less than one percent.

There were several effects on the cartel members' sales as well. What had been a tumultuous industry structure in 1991-1992 suddenly became frozen for two or three years. The aggressive newer lysine producers were tamed, and the two industry pioneers saw their slide in market share halted. Investment in new capacity by the cartel members slowed. Before and after the cartel, the total volume of trade followed a steep growth path, and there was little evidence of price discrimination. During the collusive period, U.S. lysine imports declined, the rapid increase in exports stopped, and there is evidence of geographic price discrimination in U.S. exports.

Chapter 9 Endnotes

[1] Only four public price reports could be found. Three averaged 4 percent above true prices. One report said prices in 1995-1996 were "just above $1.00," which was wrong most months.

[2] Peak demand for feeds in the winter caused peak demand for lysine in the late fall. It is noteworthy that during the period of greatest cartel discipline (late 1993 and all of 1994) these natural demand forces were suppressed by the strong force of cartel collective action.

[3] ADM's prices in the first five months of 1991 are not publicly available, but its rate of growth in market share was so high that even larger discounting by ADM was likely. It was suggested in the trade press that ADM was engaging in predatory pricing against the weakest Asian supplier, Sewon. Sewon had no U.S. plants and may have had the highest costs in the U.S. lysine market, but it held on anyway. In fact, Sewon's share of the U.S. market would not have satisfied ADM by 1992.

[4] One reason for ADM's leaps in quantity was that it had become the sole U.S. seller of liquid lysine (Ajinomoto sold liquid lysine in Japan only). Liquid lysine was sold at a dry-equivalent price several cents below dry lysine in most months (23 cents lower in one month). Liquid lysine accounted for 10 to 30 percent of ADM's total U.S. volume in 1991-1992. It was slightly cheaper to produce and could be shipped to nearby buyers equipped to handle the liquid version at considerable savings over dry.

[5] In 1991-1992, Ajinomoto's U.S. total costs were only 2 to 5 percent higher than ADM's costs, but Ajinomoto's biggest plant in France was 35 percent more costly than the Decatur plant. Kyowa, Sewon, and Cheil had higher average total costs in 1991-1992 than Ajinomoto.

[6] It has been suggested that the late 1992 price rise has alternative competitive explanations (White 2000). It is widely accepted that the prices of natural sources of lysine provide a ceiling on the price of lysine made by fermentation. During late 1992, these ceiling prices were at least $0.68 higher than observed lysine prices, so this cannot have acted as a constraint on monopoly pricing (Connor 2000: Table A2).

[7] The conspirators themselves called this the "winter effect," which began mid-winter and extended through most of the spring as feed manufacturers anticipated lower feed demand with the approach of warmer weather.

[8] ADM's output increased by 10 and zero percent in the first and second quarters of 1995 compared with the fourth quarter of 1994. Sales in those 1996 quarters barely changed from the same quarters in 1995.

[9] U.S. sales volume in 1991 was 104 million pounds; world volume was 397 million pounds. The own-price elasticity was assumed to be between 0.9 and 1.6. In 1995, U.S. and global volumes were 174 and 560 million pounds, respectively.

[10] In 1994, ADM sold about 12 million pounds of liquid lysine measured in a dry-substance-equivalent basis, or 7 percent of sales by weight. In earlier years the liquid ratio was a little higher. Ajinomoto also sold a little liquid lysine.

[11] Somewhat surprising is the constancy of Sewon America's volume of sales throughout the 1990-1996 period.

[12] During almost every year of the 1990-1995 period, both Ajinomoto and Kyowa had to import lysine to the United States to supplement their U.S. production.

[13] During 1996-1997, unlike any previous period, price changes lagged a month or two behind changes in the lysine shadow price. This suggests that the shadow price had become a barometer for price followership.

[14] ADM did not cut exports to Chiel's and Sewon's home markets (Indonesia and Korea) during the cartel period.

[15] The absolute percentage-point difference in prices averaged 16.6 percentage points in 1992 (across 39 destinations), but declined to 12.5 percentage points in 1993 (45 countries) and to 7.8 percentage point in 1994 (41 countries). The variation in prices widened again to 17.5 percentage points in 1995 (42 countries), settled down to an average 8.8 point spread in 1996,

and reached its nadir in 1997 at 4.0 points across 38 countries. These spreads are similar when calculated for a constant sample of countries.

[16] The Division also made AMG, riboflavin, and nematodes, but these were minor products throughout 1991-1995.

[17] It is not clear whether the fixed costs charged to the lysine department include a component to cover this "normal return" to investors. Certain other central-office expenses may also not be included in operating profits. Corporate income taxes are not netted.

[18] Indirect buyers of lysine, such as hog farmers or consumers of pork may seek treble damages in some state courts. Their injuries depend on the size of the direct buyers' overcharges

[19] Because ADM was the last of the cartel participants to settle with the government and because ADM was viewed as the cartel's ringleader, any discount must have been fairly modest. The fines paid by ADM's co-conspirators were based on the $10 million statutory limit, not on the "double the harm" rule, because they cooperated earlier.

[20] In some federal districts conspirators are also responsible for the overcharges imposed by firms that remained outside the conspiracy but that raise price to the level of the cartel. The extent of non-conspiratorial overcharges was *de minimis* in the lysine market.

[21] The top four lysine companies supplied more than 95 percent of the U.S. market. The Herfindahl index was between 3000 and 3500.

[22] Although information on meetings, price announcements and demand and supply factors are often used to distinguish the noncollusive ("before") periods from the collusive ("after") periods, time-series price data can be analyzed econometrically using a dummy variable to measure price effects during a conspiracy.

[23] The econometric-modeling approach was infeasible to apply in the case of the lysine class-action decision. The two months available was insufficient, the technique requires a significant portion of nonconspiracy time periods, and certain necessary data (capacity utilization, for example) are near to impossible to measure without the full cooperation of the defendants. Plaintiffs' demands for production and cost information were not honored.

[24] I was employed by a law firm representing buyers of lysine who were contemplating opting out of the federal class of private plaintiffs. I performed this analysis during April-July 1996, a time during which the lysine defendants had offered to settle the private suit for $45 million but before they had pleaded guilty to criminal price fixing.

[25] In May-July 1993, ADM's lysine output averaged 10.3 million pounds per month, an increase of 88 percent above the first quarter of 1993 and 22 percent above the August-October quarter. The May-July surge in production cannot be attributed to the industry's seasonal peak in demand (usually December but always very late in the year), and except for 1993 ADM also had peak production later in the year. In both mid-1992 and mid-1993, ADM's U.S. production share rose well above 80 percent, a level it did not reach at any other time.

[26] To average costs of manufacturing of $0.62 per pound should be added U.S. distribution costs (about $0.11 per pound) and normal profits (about $0.06) to get average total costs. Average variable costs of production would be $0.10 lower because corn wet milling is a capital-intensive industry. Costs were constant over the relevant range during the conspiracy, thus short run marginal costs were about $0.70 and long run marginal costs about $0.80 per pound. Werden (2000) argues that the long-run (higher) price is the most appropriate measure of the legal concept of monopoly power (a "high degree" of market power).

[27] Perhaps uncontroversial is too strong because the 3500 HHI refers solely to the U.S. market. If the cartel viewed the world market as the appropriate competitive space, then the HHI was 2100. Observed cartel prices are then compatible with elasticities less than -0.8. However, trial evidence shows that the cartel set discriminatory prices in up to nine regions during 1994-1995, suggesting that regional HHI is the appropriate choice.

[28] My review of the literature on hog and pork demand found elasticities in the -0.2 to -0.4 range. Poultry elasticities were far more variable, roughly in -0.15 to -0.50 range. For all high protein products, demand is even more inelastic, probably in the range -0.10 to -0.25.

[29] These improbable prices are partly an artifact of assuming a linear demand function. Linear demand may be a reasonable assumption during periods of steady output growth like 1994, but other demand-curve shapes may not predict such unlikely prices. Another possibility is that ADM employed Cournot pricing behavior to set its own price, expecting the other U.S. sellers to follow its commanding lead in the market. However, this approach produces "reasonable" prices (in the $0.90 to $1.20 range) only if the absolute value of the elasticity is too high, viz., $1.10 to $4.95, for a likely range of long run marginal costs.

[30] Flexibility was unlikely to be so high as to permit ADM or any other supplier to be able to supply the entire world with lysine. This is another necessary condition of the Cournot model.

[31] When the East Asian financial crisis hit Korea in 1997, Sewon was by Western accounting standards bankrupt. Sewon's urge to grow led it to acquire a debt load that was three or four times its net assets. Sewon sold its lysine business to BASF in 1998.

[32] It is possible that by late 1995, cartel members had developed the degree of historical interaction necessary to form the conjectures necessary for a tacit understanding to develop, and this may account for the price increases observed from late 1995 to early 1997. However, even if one concedes that some form of noncooperative oligopoly became feasible in 1994 or 1995, the fundamental arbitrariness of the choice of the Cournot model over all others remains. I believe the profession agrees with Kwoka and White (1989:11) that the popularity of the Cournot model is mainly a result of its mathematical tractability. Equally viable oligopoly candidates are the many varieties of the price-leadership model and the homogeneous Bertrand. Of course, with five players in the lysine industry, the latter model brings us back to a predicted competitive price.

[33] The present author was the government's expert. ADM's lysine production and distribution costs are in the public record.

[34] Morse and Hyde (2000) estimate the U.S. market demand for lysine and ADM's cost of production using monthly data from January 1990 to June 1995. Then they estimate ADM's conjectural variation, that is, the responsiveness of the sales volume of ADM's rivals to changes in ADM's sales volume. The econometric results are good-fitting and reasonable. Industry behavior becomes progressively less competitive from October 1992 to the 1994-95 period. Their model predicts a competitive but-for price for each month during the conspiracy. The total overcharge to U.S. buyers was $80 to $83 million.

Table 9.A.1. Alternative Estimates of the Monopoly Overcharge to U.S. Lysine Buyers.

Source	Method, Period, and But-For Price (P_{BF})	Overcharge, All Members of the Cartel
		Million dollars
A. Defendants ADM *et al.* in federal class action	Unknown, but probably before-and-after analysis probably September 1994-June 1995, and P_{BF} = $1.10	15
B. ADM's criminal U.S. antitrust fine	Department of Justice confidential analysis, July 1992-June 1995, P_{BF} unknown	65+
C. Plaintiffs' estimate in federal class action, price data only	Before-and-after, July 1992-June 1995, P_{BF} = $0.70/lb	156
D. Plaintiffs' estimate in federal class action	Same as C. above, adjusted for seasonality of lysine sales	141
E. Prosecution's estimate based on detailed ADM cost information in U.S. v. Michael Andreas *et al.*	Average costs or production, distribution, and selling, July 1992-June 1995, P_{BF} = $0.81/lb	78
F. Same as E.	Econometric modeling with qualitative conspiracy-period variable, June 1992-June 1995, no P_{BF} assumption	80

Sources: Connor (2000a, 2000b), redacted DOJ memoranda, Morse and Hyde (2000).

Table 9.A.2. U.S. Lysine Exports, by Country, 1992-1997.

Country of Destination[a]	1992	1993	1994	1995	1996	1997	1998
			Metric tonnes[b]				
Canada	6781	8469	8625	7010	7410	12992	9083
Mexico	1111	1765	3576	2250	3004	6148	4939
Columbia	364	544	512	524	505	254	159
Venezuela	412	305	297	274	189	455	708
Brazil	720	1553	2440	1899	2718	3027	3021
Argentina	205	362	352	304	404	375	371
United Kingdom	1302	1255	832	933	862	1280	2724
Netherlands	9452	9772	15644	19235	25582	26502	31383
Belgium	685	340	0	0	0	17	48
France	856	984	283	2	69	50	167
Germany	2779	1420	342	17	46	6	367
Spain	382	369	556	1055	5432	8141	6647
Italy	102	336	315	0	480	2715	2282
Israel	61	0	0	1	424	932	664
Thailand	1227	1981	1115	1821	3075	2262	210
Malaysia	713	1094	1178	1641	2671	2334	1600
Singapore	73	324	259	476	1515	885	628
Indonesia	0	1069	953	1108	1106	1456	98
Philippines	0	656	767	540	1207	1702	743
China	41	750	3316	878	0	0	127
Korea	0	300	784	578	860	1340	1043
Hong Kong	2902	1174	962	1622	2594	11487	15158
China-Taiwan	810	1473	741	1204	2818	2760	1480
Japan	203	416	421	439	587	806	644
Australia	2793	3636	2450	2315	2372	3919	2753
New Zealand	380	485	291	457	701	591	581
S. Africa	349	308	1210	958	2326	2133	2125
Total	37708	43655	51446	49212	71359	97796	92994

Source: STAT-USA.

[a] All countries whose exports accounted for 1 percent or more of total exports in any one year are listed.

[b] The year 1989 is the first that the U.S. Commerce Department (Bureau of the Census) reports data on "lysine and its esters and salts" separately from all other organic acids. However, U.S. lysine exports for 1991 were only 6,200 tonnes. Nearly all exports are feed-grade in this period.

Table 9.A.3. U.S. Lysine Exports, by Country, 1992-1999.

Country of Destination[a] (hypothesis classification)	1992	1993	1994	1995	1996	1997	1998
				Percent of volume[b]			
Canada (U.S. hegemony)	18.0	19.4	16.8	14.2	10.4	13.2	9.8
Mexico (home)	3.0	4.0	7.0	4.6	4.2	6.3	5.3
Columbia (U.S. hegemony)	1.0	1.3	1.0	1.1	0.7	0.3	0.2
Venezuela (U.S. hegemony)	1.1	0.7	0.6	0.6	0.3	0.5	0.8
Brazil (U.S. hegemony)[d]	1.9	3.6	4.7	3.9	3.8	3.1	3.3
Argentina (U.S. hegemony)	0.5	0.8	0.7	0.6	0.6	0.4	0.4
United Kingdom	3.5	2.9	1.6	1.9	1.2	1.3	2.9
Netherlands (U.S. hegemony)	25.1	22.4	30.4	39.1	35.9	27.1	33.8
Belgium (Ajinomoto hegemony)	1.8	0.8	0.0	0.0	0.0	0.0	0.1
France (home)	2.3	2.3	0.6	0.0	0.1	0.0	0.2
Germany	7.4	3.3	0.7	0.0	0.1	0.0	0.4
Spain	1.8	0.9	1.1	2.1	7.6	8.3	7.2
Italy (home)	0.3	0.8	0.6	0.0	0.7	2.8	2.5
Israel	0.2	0.0	0.0	0.0	0.6	1.0	0.7
Thailand (home)	3.3	4.5	2.2	3.7	4.3	2.4	0.2
Malaysia	1.9	2.5	2.3	3.3	3.7	2.4	1.7
Singapore (Cheil hegemony)	0.2	0.7	0.5	1.0	2.1	0.9	0.7
Indonesia (home)	0.0	2.5	1.9	2.3	1.6	1.5	0.1
Philippines (U.S. hegemony)	0.0	1.5	1.5	1.1	1.7	1.7	0.8
China (home: 1996-97)	0.1	1.7	6.4	1.8	0.0	0.0	0.1
Korea (home)	0.0	0.7	1.5	1.2	1.2	1.4	1.1
Hong Kong	7.7	2.7	1.9	3.3	3.6	11.8	16.3
China-Taiwan (U.S. hegemony)	2.2	3.4	1.4	2.5	4.0	2.8	1.6
Japan (home)	0.5	1.0	0.8	0.9	0.7	0.8	0.7
Australia	7.4	6.0	4.8	4.7	3.3	4.0	3.0
New Zealand	1.0	1.1	0.6	0.9	1.0	0.6	0.6
So. Africa	0.9	0.7	2.4	2.0	3.3	2.2	2.3
Total	100.0	100.0	100.0	100.0	100.0	100.0	100.0

Source: STAT-USA.

[a] All countries whose exports accounted for 1 percent or more of total exports in any one year are listed.

[b] The year 1989 is the first that the U.S. Commerce Department (Bureau of the Census) reports data on "lysine and its esters and salts" separately from all other organic acids. However, U.S. lysine exports for 1991 were only 6,200 tonnes. Nearly all exports are feed-grade in this period.

Table 9.A.4. Countries Classified by 1992-1997 Patterns of U.S. Lysine Exports.

Observed Trade Pattern[a] (1993-94/1995-96)	Conform to Trade Pattern	Come Close to Hypothesized Trade Pattern
Home or hegemonic markets, ADM rivals (low/low-medium)	Thailand Indonesia Taiwan	France Belgium Germany Italy Japan China (1996-)
U.S. neighbor/hegemony (high/high-medium)	Mexico Brazil Netherlands Korea*	Maylasia* Philippines
Neutral/distant markets (medium/high-medium)	Argentina Spain	(no examples)
Other patterns: (high/higher)	Singapore South Africa	(no examples)
(low/lower)	Canada UK	Columbia* Australia

Source: Table 9.A.3.

[a] High, medium, and low are based on percentage of volume relative to the 1992-93 base years. Generally two-year averages, sometimes greater weight given to years 1992, 1994, and 1997.

* Results do not conform to prior expectations.

Table 9.A.5. Implicit Prices of Feed-Grade-Lysine Exports from the United States, by Country, 1992-1997.

Country [Plants Owned By]	1992	1993	1994	1995	1996	1997	1998
			Dollars per pound (f.a.s.)				
Canada	0.911	0.874	1.016	1.108	1.195	1.150	0.891
Mexico [Kyowa]	1.148	0.856	0.830	1.002	0.947	1.230	0.860
Brazil [Ajinomoto, 1997]	0.962	0.900	1.105	1.130	1.014	1.230	0.936
Columbia	1.028	0.825	1.054	1.136	1.095	1.237	0.867
Venezuela	1.034	0.842	1.018	1.016	1.164	1.158	0.912
Argentina	0.959	0.921	1.083	1.109	1.134	1.233	0.918
Germany	0.722	0.830	1.052	1.272	1.271	1.249	0.771
Netherlands	0.800	0.871	1.008	0.823	1.004	1.144	0.892
United Kingdom	0.702	0.819	1.350	0.783	0.957	1.085	0.904
France [Ajinomoto]	0.911	0.758	1.002	1.152	1.268	0.733	0.864
Spain	0.995	0.985	0.989	0.751	1.016	1.101	0.887
Italy [Ajinomoto]	1.084	0.935	1.244	--	1.015	1.057	0.809
Belgium	3.256	1.865	--	1.219	--	1.254	1.194
Australia	1.031	1.045	1.237	0994	0.854	1.116	0.916
New Zealand	2.295	0.955	0.947	0.962	1.064	1.095	0.852
Malaysia	1.033	0.990	1.161	1.149	1.035	1.138	0.872
Hong Kong	1.018	0.967	1.061	0.838	0.879	1.086	0.875
Thailand [Ajinomoto]	0.967	0.775	0.851	0.945	1.036	1.092	0.734
Indonesia [Cheil]	--	0.734	0.995	1.090	1.025	1.115	1.064
Japan [Ajinomoto, Kyowa]	5.388	1.039	1.124	1.130	1.114	1.186	0.835
Korea [Sewon]	--	0.749	0.838	0.882	0.922	1.009	0.727
Philippines	--	0.725	1.016	1.005	1.021	1.196	0.811
South Africa	1.149	0.893	1.124	1.060	1.007	1.184	0.843
U.S. Total Exports	0.916	0.871	1.028	0.957	1.026	1.133	0.881
U.S. Total Imports (c.i.f.)[a]	0.66	0.74	1.02	0.91	1.14	1.63	0.73

Source: STAT-USA.
-- = Not available, no trade
[a] From Table 9.A.8. Feed grade.

Table 9.A.6. U.S. Imports of Feed-Grade Lysine, 1992-1997.

Country	1992	1993	1994	1995	1996	1997	1998
	Metric tonnes[a]						
Mexico	207	2072	3472	96	0	52	0
Europe:	0	351	3016	60	267	772	391
France	0	348	3016	60	24	11	309
Italy	0	0	0	0	243	761	82
Thailand	0	0	0	0	820	0	720
Indonesia	0	255	272	845	2575	5187	8406
Korea	7018	6786	4151	4080	6428	8805	14622
Japan	0	0	771	821	605	217	46
India[b]	1	16	10	10	19	0	0
Total U.S.	7226	9477	10691	6152	11048	15138	24521
Proportion feed grade[c]	87	85	77	84	85	88	90

Source: National Trade Data Bank, STAT-USA.

[a] Adjusts for misclassification of feed-grade and food-grade using prices as a guideline.

[b] Country has no known lysine fermentation capacity; product is probably food-grade of a low quality.

[c] Proportion of total lysine volume that is feed-grade in percentage.

Table 9.A.7. U.S. Feed-Grade Import Shares, 1992-1997.

Country	1992	1993	1994	1995	1996	1997	1998
				Percent of volume			
Mexico	2.9	21.9	23.1	1.6	0.0	0.3	0.0
Europe:	0.0	3.7	28.2	1.0	2.4	5.1	1.6
France	0.0	3.7	28.2	1.0	0.2	0.1	1.3
Italy	0.0	0.0	0.0	0.0	2.2	5.0	0.3
India	0.0	0.2	0.1	0.2	0.2	0.0	0.0
Thailand	0.0	0.0	0.0	0.0	7.4	0.0	2.9
Indonesia	0.0	2.7	2.5	13.7	23.3	34.3	34.3
Korea	97.1	71.6	38.8	66.3	58.2	58.2	59.6
Japan	0.0	0.0	7.2	13.4	5.5	1.4	0.2
Total imports	100.0	100.0	100.0	100.0	100.0	100.0	100.0
Imports/consumption	13.1	15.8	16.5	8.8	15.1	17.4	26.6

Sources: Tables 9.A.5 and 9.A.6.

Table 9.A.8. Prices of Imported Feed-Grade Lysine, 1992-1997.

Country	1992	1993	1994	1995	1996	1997	1998
			Dollars per pound (c.i.f.)				
Mexico	0.80	0.76	1.02	1.40	--	1.34	--
Europe:							
France	--	0.56	1.00	1.79	4.08	12.60	--
Italy	--	--	--	--	1.14	2.19	0.86
India	2.00	2.02	2.09	1.99	1.99	3.02	3.02
Thailand	--	--	--	--	1.04	--	0.65
Indonesia	--	1.00	1.06	0.89	1.11	1.73	0.72
Korea	0.66	0.73	1.03	0.86	1.09	1.44	0.68
Japan	--	--	1.03	0.95	1.56	4.33	10.22
Total food-grade imports	5.89	5.63	3.11	2.17	1.69	1.79	1.35
Total U.S. feed-grade imports	0.66	0.74	1.02	0.92[a]	1.14	1.63	0.73
U.S. Domestic price	0.81	0.87	1.13	1.01	1.11[b]	--	--

-- = Not available

[a] Eliminating the small and questionable Mexican, French and Indian imports reduces the price to $0.905, including all six

[b] First six months only but price was rising throughout 1996.

Chapter 10

THE GLOBAL VITAMINS INDUSTRY[1]

Basel, Switzerland is an historic city of about a half million population located at the intersection of the French, German, and Swiss borders. Home to Switzerland's first university established in 1460, the city played a pivotal part in the Protestant Reformation. Although the city houses many architecturally important medieval buildings, manuscript and art collections, and a pretty late-Gothic Rathaus fronting the central market place, Basel does not receive nearly as many tourists as it does business visitors. Aided by its fortuitous location on the Rhine River, Basel was the Swiss city most affected by the 19th century forces of industrialization. By the turn of the century, it had become the center of Switzerland's, indeed Europe's, chemical and pharmaceutical industry. Basel pharmacist Felix Hoffmann-La Roche was the founder of a pharmaceutical manufacturing partnership that would become a global leader in medicinal products. Its corporate successor, Roche Holdings, remains headquartered in the city of its birth and is still controlled by the founding families.

Basel became an important focus for both the citric acid cartel (Chapter 5) and the vitamins cartels. By virtue of Hoffmann-La Roche's headquarters and that of other conspirators, Basel may well be able to lay claim to the title of World Capital of Global Cartels.[2]

To paraphrase an Iranian propaganda slogan, the vitamins cartel was the "Mother of All Global Cartels." It was the first, the biggest, most elaborate, most complete, longest lasting, and most influential of the cartel pandemics of the 1990s. Moreover, the success in vitamins inspired the formation of the citric acid cartel. The initial steps in establishing global conspiracies in vitamins took place in 1988 and 1989. By 1990 the early signs of financial success in price fixing were so convincing to the participants that it inspired them to explore the feasibility of forming more feed or food ingredient cartels. Memoranda have come to light that show the citric acid cartel was joined in 1991 by Hoffman-La Roche explicitly because of its profitable prior experience in vitamins. Then the cartel contagion spread within Archer Daniels Midland (ADM) from citric acid to lysine in 1992.

The vitamins conspirators erected a mechanism of customer exploitation that exhibited almost every technique of cartel organization that had ever been employed. These exploitive techniques created pressures that extracted historically unprecedented monopoly overcharges from customers. These overcharges later appeared on the profit statements of the vitamin manufacturers. Eventually, the number of manufacturers that joined the cartel and the number of markets infected by price fixing would grow to more than double that of any comparable conspiracies. Virtually addicted to the flow of monopoly profits, the conspirators continued their activities for up to eleven years, one of the longest lasting of the conspiracies discovered in the 1990s. These activities persisted in the face of multiple public prosecutions of parallel conspiracies, mounting economic sanctions by antitrust authorities, and warnings to stop from the conspirators own lawyers. The conspirators simply burrowed deeper and developed more elaborate methods of subterfuge.

ORIGINS OF THE INDUSTRY

The discovery and commercialization of vitamins typically evolved through five stages (Kiple and Ornelas 2000). First, physicians would describe and name a disease of unknown etiology. Second, a dietary cure would be identified empirically, but the active ingredient responsible for the cure is not understood. Third, scientific researchers isolate a compound that is known to be curative. Sometime an unused letter of the alphabet was provisionally assigned to the vitamin at this time. Fourth, usually within a few years the chemical structure of the vitamin would be identified. The vitamin's chemical name would sometimes require its letter to be redesignated. Fifth, chemists would find a method of synthesizing the vitamin. At this point, patents could be issued and commercial production would begin on a small scale. Engineering improvements would subsequently permit cost reductions, and the falling price would stimulate mass-market demand. Sometimes demand would spurt well before dietary deficiencies were identified for the vitamin or all a vitamin's curative powers understood.

Companies with experience in making organic chemicals and marketing human health products were the best positioned to be pioneers in vitamins. The early manufacturers of vitamins started by extracting them from plant or animal materials relatively rich in the vitamins of interest. However, the greatest period of growth for the vitamins industry occurred in the 1930s when the techniques of synthetic chemistry began to be applied. Long in use for dyestuffs and certain pharmaceuticals, synthetic chemistry permitted manufacturers to substitute less expensive raw materials, to achieve economies of scale in production, and to make final products of greater purity than extraction methods allowed.

Uses of Vitamins

The value of certain foods in maintaining health was enshrined in customary culinary practices that predate written history (Tannahill 1988).

Moreover, premodern medical texts make it clear physicians with no notions of vitamins prescribed dietary cures for diseases now known to be caused by vitamin deficiencies. For example, night blindness was diagnosed by Egyptian physicians, and in texts dating from 1520 BC beef liver was prescribed as a cure (Kiple and Ornelas 2000). Classical Greek medical manuscripts repeat the diagnosis and cure. Published European medical experiments verified the cure from 1861 onwards, long before it was known that animal livers are rich in vitamin A that can overcome a deficiency in ocular retinol. However, long before nutritional experiments justified the practice, fish-liver oils had been administered as a folk remedy in Northern Europe for certain deficiency diseases. By the 1840s, cod-liver oil had become a common dietary supplement in North America and Western Europe, demand was met by supplies out of fisheries in Newfoundland and Norway.

Scientists in the late 18th century demonstrated that the addition of citrus fruits to the diet would prevent the onset of scurvy. In the late 19th century, the cause of a rising incidence of beriberi in the Indonesian population was discovered. The introduction of polished white rice had removed some then unknown substance in the germ and coating of brown rice that prevented beriberi in rice-based starchy diets. Another important step in scientific understanding was research published in 1906 by British biochemist Frederick Hopkins. He showed that many foods had substances that could not be classified as carbohydrates, proteins, fats, or minerals. Then, in 1912, chemist Casimir Funk identified the antiberiberi substance to be an amine (a compound containing nitrogen). Thus, he proposed that it be named "vitamine" a neologism that combined the Latin word *vita* ("life") with "amine." Later, when scientists determined that many vitamins do not contain nitrogen, the final "e" was dropped.

In 1912, Hopkins and Funk proposed the vitamin-deficiency theory of nutrition. This theory postulates that minimal amounts of vitamins must be ingested in order to avoid the appearance of certain diseases or functional impairments. Among the diseases they believed were caused by vitamin deficiency were scurvy, beriberi, pellagra, and rickets. Over the next three decades or so, this theory would be verified for more than 20 vitamins, popularly known by their letters or letter-number combinations (e.g., B12).[3] Research showed that minute quantities of vitamins are necessary for the regulation of metabolic functions in humans, animals, and even some bacteria and yeast. Technically, most vitamins act as enzymes, coenzymes, or precursors of coenzymes; many vitamins undergo chemical changes after being ingested in order to arrive at their functional (coenzyme) stage and may further chemically change before reaching an active (enzyme) stage. The enzymes then become catalysts in regulating various metabolic processes. Unlike minerals and the macronutrients (proteins, carbohydrates, and fats), vitamins are not converted into energy or building materials for tissues.

The need for specific vitamins varies across species. A compound that is a vitamin for one species is not necessarily a vitamin for another. Levels of vitamins required also vary by the gender and growth phase of the species. For example, in humans one type of vitamin D is synthesized in the skin tissue when it is exposed to sunlight. The enzyme produced by vitamin D regulates the conversion of calcium into bone. However, children deprived of adequate sunlight may require dietary supplements of vitamin D during phases of rapid skeletal growth to avoid arrested or deformed bone development.

Today, many vitamins are purchased primarily or exclusively for inclusion in animal feeds. The principal components of animal feeds are pasture grasses, hay or silage crops, or the so-called rough grains (maize, millet, sorghum, and the like). Surplus food grains or byproducts of food processing are also incorporated into animal feeds. Under more intensive modern farming practices, animals are fed supplements containing proteins, minerals, and vitamins. These relatively costly ingredients are called concentrates or premixes. Mature cattle, sheep, and other ruminants are able to synthesize vitamins in the first of their stomachs (the rumen) from grains or roughage. However, like humans, animals with single stomachs will benefit from supplementary vitamins to enhance the rate or type of growth or to increase production of eggs. Swine, poultry, fish, and immature ruminants use large amounts of most vitamins produced today (Table 10.1). Except for vitamins C, B1, and B6, the major part of the world sales of the 13 other major vitamins are purchased for animal feed. Besides dietary supplementation, a small amount of vitamins are included in cosmetics or skin creams.

Pharmaceutical and Vitamin Manufacturing

Drug production is a branch of the chemical manufacturing industry group. Pharmaceutical raw materials may be plants, animal byproducts, or other biologic products; inorganic elements and compounds; or organic compounds. Allowable raw materials and purity standards are usually specified by a national formulary or pharmacopoeia.[4] The oldest drugs, now called crude drugs, were obtained from biologics that were cured, ground, and dried or preserved in solutions. Modern industrial methods of production can also involve extraction from natural sources, but preparation from biotechnologies or chemical synthesis is now more typical.

Table 10.1. Relative Size of the Feed, Food, and Pharmaceutical Channels for Vitamins.

	World, Circa 1995			U.S., 1990-1998		
Product	Feed	Food	Pharma	Feed	Food	Pharma
	Percent[a]					
E	50	9	40	58	8	34
C	18	40	43	10	60	30
A	80	10	10	83	8	9
B4 Choline chloride	100	0	0	100	0	0
B5 Cal Pan[b]	58	6	36	61	6	33
B2 Ribo-flavin	70	18	12	60	15	25
B3 Niacin	70	20	10	--	--	--
B6	44	15	42	--	--	--
H Biotin	87	6	4	--	--	--
B12	68	4	28	--	--	--
B1	46	22	32	--	--	--
D	81	5	14	--	--	--
K	84	0	16	--	--	--
Folic acid	85	9	5	--	--	--
Carotenoids	--	--	--	2	47	52
Total	55	16	29	--	--	--

-- = Not available

[a] Percent of value of sales. Feed includes pet food. Some percentages may not add to 100% because of technical uses.

[b] Calcium pantothenate.

In the case of extraction methods, a material containing the drug is placed in water or a solvent, and then the active ingredient is separated by distillation, skimming, pressing, filtering, or centrifuging. For example, cod livers can be suspended in warm water until their oil rises to the surface. The oil that is skimmed off is rich in vitamins A and E. In the case of vaccines, bacteria or viruses are incubated on a medium, which is later separated from the vaccine.

When vitamins were first produced commercially, various extraction methods were employed, but today chemical synthesis is the predominant method.

Synthesis is a less expensive process and generally produces a purer product. Synthetic organic compounds are produced from chemical reactions that rearrange the molecular structures of two or more chemical elements or compounds, at least one of which must contain carbon. The reactions are caused by heat, pressure, acids, or other catalysts. Many different types of reactions are used to synthesize vitamins. Sometimes the same vitamins will be synthesized by different pathways depending on a manufacturers raw materials, equipment, or access to proprietary technologies. The expertise required to master synthetic processes comprised of multiple stages of reactions may take decades for a manufacturer to acquire (März 1996). That is, there are formidable technological barriers to entry in many bulk vitamins industries.

Biotechnologies are quite different. They harness the metabolism of microbes in biological systems using generally inexpensive carbohydrates (dextrose, sucrose, starches, etc.) as the source of carbon. Except for the final separation and purification, the fermentation process is a single-stage operation during which cascades of chemical reactions occur within the microorganism. In principle, the simplicity of these biotechnologies allows them to be commercialized at modest scales of production. Advantages in production efficiencies will accrue to manufacturers that select the most productive microorganisms and improve their productivity through genetic manipulation. Genetically improved microorganisms can be patented. Almost 100 biotechnologies for the production of vitamins were patented from 1985 to 1995 (März 1996:31). By the mid 1990s, a significant amount of vitamins E, B2, B5, H (biotin), and D3 were being made via biosynthesis. The major raw material for vitamin C, 2-ketogluconic acid, is made from biosynthesis, and then it is converted to ascorbic acid (vitamin C) by a final stage of synthetic chemistry. The Archer Daniels Midland Company has made a strong commitment to producing vitamins from fermentation of corn sweeteners. It already makes and markets vitamins E and B2 and produces biotin for captive use by means of various fermentation technologies. However, harnessing biotechnology for vitamin production still faces many technical hurdles. For example, ADM's 1996 annual report featured its new world-class vitamin C plant, yet even two years later trade magazines could find no evidence that sales had begun.[5]

Early Development of the Industry

Hoffmann-La Roche (now organized under Roche Holdings) was the first company to learn how to synthesize most of the vitamins. Its first success was synthetic vitamin C (ascorbic acid) in 1933. Soon after, Roche learned how to manufacture vitamins A and E through synthetic chemistry (Connor 2000:

Appendix E). By the early 1970s, Roche had become the dominant supplier of synthetic vitamins, with a global market share of 50 to 60 percent. The big German chemical firm Badische Anilin-und Soda-Fabrik (now called BASF) was successful in imitating Roche in several vitamin-product lines. By the early 1970s, Roche and BASF controlled more than 75 percent of global vitamin production. Another big German chemical company, Hoechst, also entered a couple of lines of vitamin manufacturing that have small sales.

Despite the worldwide depression of the early 1930s, this was the decade of the most dramatic growth for the chemical industry in general and the pharmaceutical branch in particular (Henahan 1976). The rapid pace of scientific discoveries in vitamins and pharmaceuticals that began just before World War I fed a speedy adoption into commercial production by chemical companies in Europe, the United States, and Japan. Roche, Lilly, Merck, Upjohn, and many other drug makers expanded their research laboratories and developed close relationships with university chemistry departments. Pain killers, antibiotics, sedatives, hormones, and germicides of many kinds were introduced to world markets in the 1930s.

Vitamins became an important segment of the pharmaceutical industry's boom period. Vitamin C was first isolated and its chemical structure identified in 1932. One year later, Merck and Co. was manufacturing synthetic vitamin C from a process that used sorbitol as the primary starting material. Roche's production in Switzerland began around the same time, and Pfizer soon followed with a different synthetic chemical process. When vitamin C was first sold commercially in 1933, its wholesale price was $7,515 per kilogram. Competition and process improvements brought its price down to $97 per kilogram five years later. By the late 1970s, further technological progress had dropped the wholesale price of bulk vitamin C to $10 per kilogram.

Vitamin B1 followed a similar course. A scientist at Bell Laboratories patented a method for making vitamin B1 from bran in 1934. Merck and Co. scientists developed an improved synthetic method two years later; when sold that year by Merck, its price was $300,000 per kilogram. Five years later, the flour industry was able to begin fortification of flour because the price of B1 had fallen to $1,750 per kilogram. By the late 1970s, vitamin B1 could be procured in bulk for merely $30 per kilogram. Some other vitamins took longer to reach commercial production. Vitamin E was discovered by Herbert Evans and colleagues around 1922. However, it was not until 1936 that the chemical structure of one of its four forms, alpha-tocopherol, was identified. Two years later, Paul Karrer, working in Hoffmann-La Roche's Swiss laboratories, first synthesized vitamin E. Demand grew slowly at first because the physiological functions of vitamin E were not understood until the 1970s. By the end of the

1930s, synthetic chemistry had also made possible the commercial introduction of vitamins A, D, B2 and B5.

COMPANIES

Prior to World War II Roche and BASF dominated the global production of most vitamins.[6] Rhône-Poulenc, Takeda Chemicals, Hoechst, and a number of smaller European and Japanese chemical companies entered in the post-World War II period. By the late 1980s, the "Big Three" manufacturers of vitamins (Roche, BASF, and Rhône-Poulenc) would control 60 percent of world production. Adding Takeda, Eisai, and Daiichi to the list brings control of the "Big Six" to more than 70 percent of global sales. This section provides brief sketches of some of the major players in the vitamins cartel, some early episodes of cartel behavior, and the structure of the vitamins markets.

Hoffmann-La Roche

The company began as a partnership founded in Basel, Switzerland in the late 19th century to manufacture medicines. By the advent of World War I, Roche had developed a successful portfolio of products like cough medicines, heart treatments, and pain killers that were sold on four continents. During World War I, both the Germans and the Allies suspected that Roche was selling its products to both sides of the conflict, so the company's sales slumped. It was forced to raise capital by incorporating and selling shares to the public in 1919. However, even today the majority of the company's stock has been retained by the heirs of the five founding families. One of them, the late Paul Sacher, owned at least 49 percent of Roche from 1930 to the late 1990s.

Roche invested heavily in research and development from the beginning. As a result, it was the first company to develop feasible synthetic techniques for making many vitamins. Roche also began to invest abroad quite early in its history. Its first U.S. branch was opened in 1905.[7]

In the 1960s, Roche began marketing two important tranquilizers, Librium and Valium, which became a major source of profits. Around 1973 a British employee of Roche revealed an extraordinary level of geographic price discrimination across Europe for its tranquillizers.[8] Further investigation by the UK Monopolies Commission determined that Roche's UK subsidiary was required to pay $2,500 per kilogram, while in Italy where there was no patent protection for drugs, a generic version of Valium sold for $50 per kilogram. Despite Roche's public pronouncements that such prices were necessary to pay for research and development costs, the Monopolies Commission ruled against Roche. The company was required to reduce its UK wholesale price by 60 percent and to compensate UK buyers of Valium. Other European countries held investigations of Roche's tranquilizer pricing, keeping the company tied up in litigation until 1980.

Roche's patents on the two tranquilizers expired in 1985, and its failure to find any exceptional new drugs in the 1980s began to place pressure on the company's profits. Adding to the company's woes were losses in market shares in two other major product lines: vitamins and citric acid. Chinese manufacturers were making significant inroads into these industries in the late 1980s, a trend that accelerated in the 1990s. Moreover, the biotechnology divisions of ADM and Cargill entered the citric acid industries in 1989-1990.

However, Roche remained a large, strong company in the late 1990s. In 1997, Roche had global sales of $12.9 billion, of which almost two-thirds is pharmaceuticals. Including the sales of its Roche Bioscience Division (formerly the California biotech firm Syntex, purchased in 1995 for $5.3 billion), Roche is the fourth largest drug company in the world. The remaining third of its sales is spread across flavors and fragrances (Givaudin-Roure), vitamins, carotenoids, citric acid, enzymes, and genetic-engineered products. Roche employs 51,000 people.

In fiscal 1997, Roche was very profitable. Its net income was 22.8 percent of sales. Bloated by two as yet uncovered price fixing conspiracies, Roche's Vitamins and Fine Chemicals Division had an operating profit of 18.5 percent of sales. Vitamins and citric acid accounted for about 85 percent of the Division's sales.

BASF AG

BASF was founded in 1865. Its first successful products were dyes produced synthetically from coal tar, a messy and nearly worthless byproduct of petroleum distillation. BASF grew quickly in the early 20th century. In 1910, the company employed 8,000 workers at its huge complex at Ludwigshafen near Hanover. By 1926, the plant covered 2,787 acres and employed 26,000 people. This plant was very likely the largest chemical manufacturing site in the world at the time, a title it still retains.

In 1904, BASF joined with the huge chemical company Bayer and many smaller German chemical companies to form a full-blown cartel in numerous lines of chemicals. The BASF-Bayer cartel did much more than set prices. It set production quotas for each of its members, forced vertical integration among its members, engaged in predation and full-line forcing against rivals outside

Germany, and pooled its profits.[9] In the same year, Germany's largest chemical company, Hoechst, and most of the rest of Germany's chemical companies formed a second similar cartel. In 1924-1925, the two German chemical cartels extended their dominance of the world's chemical industries by merging into one giant cartel called I.G. Farben. This new cartel continued and refined the monopolistic practices of its predecessor cartels. I.G. Farben was larger than the three largest chemical companies outside Germany combined: DuPont, Imperial Chemical Industries, and Rhône-Poulenc. Beginning in the early 1930s, I.G. Farben began secretly helping Germany re-arm, a violation of the Versailles Treaty that ended World War I. As early as 1931, Farben's directors began to make secret contributions to the Nazi party, an activity that was repaid by the huge profits Farben was allowed to make during World War II.[10] As a result of active collaboration with the German war effort, I.G. Farben's directors were indicted, tried, and found guilty of war crimes at the Nuremberg trials in 1946. In 1947, I.G. Farben was dismantled by the Allied occupation authorities. However, BASF, Bayer and Hoechst were essentially recreated in their pre-war images.

Because so many of its physical assets were concentrated at the highly visible Ludwigshafen site, more than 60 percent of BASF's productive capacity was destroyed by wartime bombing. Nevertheless, BASF made a rapid recovery. By the 1960s, BASF had become a world leader in dyes, petrochemicals, plastics, synthetic fibers, coatings and agricultural chemicals (including vitamins). Beginning in the late 1960s, BASF invested heavily abroad, mainly in the United States. By the late 1980s, more than 20 percent of BASF's sales were being made in the United States.

BASF's rapid growth continued up to 1989. In that year, BASF earned a pre-tax income of DM 4.4 billion on sales of DM 46.1 billion – a profit rate of 9.5 percent. However, 1989 proved to be a peak year, with sales and profits falling each year for four years thereafter. Employment, which had reached 137,000 in 1989, contracted to 104,000 by 1994. Besides massive layoffs, BASF divested itself of many operations (primarily in Europe), directed most of its new investments to East Asia, and made biotechnologies a high priority. In 1995, BASF gave new prominence to its health and nutrition products by placing pharmaceuticals, vitamins, agricultural chemicals, and other fine chemicals in a new division. In 1999, BASF became the fourth largest manufacturer of lysine in the world when it purchased the lysine business of South Korea's Daesang Corporation (formerly named Sewon).

From 1994, things began to improve at BASF. Sales, profits, and profit rates rose once again. By 1997, sales had reached $31 billion, and profits were back up to about 8 percent of sales. Indeed, in 1997 BASF had edged slightly ahead of its two historically bigger rivals, Bayer and Hoechst.

Rhône-Poulenc SA

This company traces its roots to two French companies. Ets. Poulenc-Frères began in Paris in 1858 as a maker of household cleansers, but turned to pharmaceuticals in the late 19th century. Rhône was started in Lyon in 1895 as a manufacturer of dyes and fragrances. Aggressive behavior by the German dyestuffs cartel forced Rhône to leave the dyes industry, but in the early 20th century it had successes in aspirin, cellophane, and perfumes. The two firms merged and took their present name in 1928. During the second World War, Rhône-Poulenc became a leader in nylon and penicillin. Rapid post-war growth made the company France's largest industrial enterprise by the late 1960s.

A number of poor business decisions in the 1970s combined with the poor performance of the French economy brought Rhône-Poulenc to the brink of bankruptcy in 1980-82. The French government nationalized the company in 1983 and sold off its assets in petrochemicals and agricultural chemicals. Armed with funds supplied by the government's treasury, Rhône-Poulenc went on a buying spree. From 1986 to 1992, it spent $7 billion on U.S. acquisitions. One of its purchases was the agricultural-chemicals division of Union Carbide. Rhône-Poulenc purchased subsidiaries in 15 other countries in the late 1980s and set up at least 26 foreign joint ventures. By 1993, when Rhône-Poulenc was privatized once again, it was drawing on foreign markets for 75 percent of its sales. During the late 1990s, Rhône-Poulenc was described as a company undergoing constant reorganization.

By the 1990s, Rhône-Poulenc had become a big, diversified chemical manufacturer that made moderate profits in most years (pre-tax profits of 5 to 7 percent of sales). However, overall sales in the decade stagnated at around $15 billion per year. The company employs 68,000 workers to operate more than 200 chemical plants around the world. The life sciences division (pharmaceuticals and agricultural chemicals) has been among the fastest growing in the company. In 1998, Rhône-Poulenc and Hoechst announced plans to merge into a new entity called Aventis. This new company with its general headquarters in Strasbourg, France became a reality in December 1999. Aventis' life-sciences division is the largest in the world.

Hoechst AG

From its founding through the early 20th century, Hoechst (in German Höchst or "supreme") was specialized in dyes. However, chemical similarities of dyes with many pharmaceuticals led its researchers to discover many powerful new drugs. By 1923, Hoechst had introduced novocaine, salvarsan (for syphilis), adrenaline, insulin, and many other medicines. As mentioned above, from 1924 to 1947, Hoechst, BASF, and Bayer were the three leading units of the egregious chemical cartel I.G. Farben.

After being released from Allied supervision in 1952, Hoechst grew even faster than the rest of the German chemical industry, in part because its plants were less affected by bombing than its major German rivals. By the late 1960s, Hoechst was growing at a rate of 15 percent per year, partly because of a vast diversification program into synthetic fibers, petrochemicals, and many other products. In 1980, Hoechst surpassed DuPont to become the world's largest chemical company. Hoechst also began to invest heavily outside Germany.

However, like most other European chemical companies, Hoechst's growth reached a peak around 1989. Sales and profits began to decline for four years thereafter. From a 1989 level of 179,000, Hoechst's employment fell to 118,000 by 1998. Besides ruthless layoffs, the company divested many lines of business and tried to enhance its core businesses through some major acquisitions, such as the U.S. pharmaceutical firm Merrell Dow in 1995. Although Hoechst's restructuring efforts led to a modest turn-around by the mid 1990s, the company was still dissatisfied with the results. It therefore put an even more radical restructuring plan in place in the late 1990s – the giant merger with Rhône-Poulenc into the new combined entity called Aventis.

To get itself ready for the merger Hoechst spun off major parts of its businesses: basic chemicals (Hoechst Celanese) and technical polymers (Ticova) were sold off as Celanese AG; its paints and coatings division was sold to DuPont. What remained in 1999 was its huge drug business (Hoechst Marion Roussel), its animal health unit (Hoechst Roussel Vet), and its plant-protection division (Schering AgrEvo). The European Commission's antitrust directorate required Hoechst to sell off its animal health division as a condition of its merger with Rhône-Poulenc.[11] Other smaller divestitures of drug and herbicide subsidiaries were also required. One 1999 sale of a U.S. generic drug maker was made at a price 80 percent below what Hoechst paid for the company in 1993.

Aventis officially came into being on December 15, 1999. It is now the world's largest life-sciences company. Aventis is the global leader in vitamin B12; is third in rank in the vitamins A, E, and B2; and co-markets vitamins B1, B5, B6, B9, D3, H, and K3.

MARKET STRUCTURE

Because of its early technological lead and continuing improvements in the synthetic chemistry of vitamins manufacturing, Hoffmann-La Roche quickly became the dominant producer in the 1930s and retained its premier position throughout the 1990s. When news began to leak out about the U.S. government's vitamins antitrust investigation in 1997, Roche's average global share of the markets for 14 major vitamins was reported in the business press to be between 45 and 50 percent. BASF and Rhône-Poulenc were widely reported to be second and third in the world, with market shares of 15 to 20 percent and 10 to 15 percent, respectively. That is, these big three companies allegedly supplied as much as 70 to 85 percent of the global market for vitamins sold in bulk. In late 1999, after the three had been fined, Roche, BASF, and Rhône-Poulenc were reputed to hold 60, 28, and 7 percent of the U.S. market for bulk vitamins, or 95 percent in total. In retrospect, these figures were either terribly out of date or exaggerated.

It is inappropriate to view all vitamins as a single market at the manufacturers' level. True, when consumers buy multivitamins at retail or when feed manufacturers purchase vitamin premixes, these items contain blends of many vitamins. However, when the multivitamin supplement makers or feed premix companies buy vitamins, it is done on a vitamin-by-vitamin basis so that they can tailor the blends to the needs of the specific target group of end users. Whether speaking of human or animal populations, the metabolic functions for each vitamin are unique. One vitamin cannot be substituted for another with the expectation of avoiding some specific health or growth problem in a given species. Moreover, the manufacturing techniques used to make one vitamin will not work to make another. The factories, machines, raw materials, and other supply factors are unique to each vitamin.

Thus, differences in demand and supply characteristics assure that each vitamin falls into its own separate market. Moreover, because the major channels of distribution for each vitamin vary so much, it is likely that each of these also comprises a separate market as well. There is a sharp distinction between bulk vitamins destined for consumption by humans and those made for animal-feed market. Human-grade vitamins must meet higher standards of purity, must be packaged in containers affording greater protection from contamination, and typically are sold in lower strengths so as to avoid toxic effects. In some cases, food-grade, pharmaceutical-grade, and cosmetic vitamins may form separate markets. For example, vitamin powders would be preferred for tablets or dry food applications, whereas liquids would be needed for capsules, beverages, or skin creams. Of course, in a pinch human-grade vitamins might be substituted for feed-grade, but the typically higher prices of the former (on an active-ingredient or 100%-basis) would generally rule this out as a regular practice. Finally, within the human grades of vitamins, a distinction may be made between natural and synthetic versions, which is important for marketing purposes. Many consumers, especially those who shop in health-food outlets, will be willing to pay more for the natural version. In vitamin E, natural versions may be made with old-fashioned extraction methods or with newer fermentation techniques. In the United States, three manufacturers are specialized in the production of natural vitamin E (ADM, Eisai, and Henkel). Although only 20 percent of total vitamin E demand, the natural segment has been growing considerably faster than the synthetic version.

The significance of these market features is that the number of suppliers will be fewer for one vitamin type than all types of vitamins in the aggregate.[12] That is, seller concentration will be higher for natural human-grade vitamin E than for all grades and types of vitamin E. Thus, in general market shares for all types of a vitamin will understate the shares held by companies in the market for one type of that vitamin.

The sum of the squares of the market shares of the top 20 manufacturers of bulk vitamins. Table 10.2 contains some rough 1995 estimates of the global sales shares of the six largest vitamin producers. The average share held in 14 vitamin markets by the Big Three companies was 59 percent, which is somewhat below the lower end of the range reported in the business press. Adding the shares of the next three largest producers brings the average share of the Big Six to 70 percent of these world markets. As Table 10.2 demonstrates, higher company average shares are associated with participation in a large number of vitamin industries. Roche and BASF are significantly more diversified than other vitamin manufacturers. Rhône and Takeda make only four or five vitamins, Eisai and Daiichi only one or two. Smaller companies below the top six (not shown) typically make only one vitamin. However, some of the more specialized companies have large shares in the few product markets in which they participate. Daiichi, for example, has stronger positions in its two markets than Roche.[13]

Looking at the individual vitamins, it is clear that the typical product market is dominated by at most three or four firms. Only in vitamins B6 and folic acid does the share of the top four drop below the 50-percent mark. The markets for vitamins A, E, B3, B5, D, and carotenoids are especially highly concentrated. A Herfindahl index of 1800 or higher is often used by economists as a rule of thumb as a threshold point above which oligopolistic behavior is likely to be observed.[14] Eleven of the 14 markets are highly concentrated by that standard, and vitamin C is the only large vitamin market with moderate sales concentration. Vitamin C is among the few industries in which manufacturers from China have increased their global shares during the 1990s.

Table 10.2. Global Market Shares, 14 Vitamins, Circa 1995.

Company[a]	A	C	E	B1	B2	B3	B4	B5	B6	B12	Folic Acid	D	H	Carto-tenoids	Share of World Market
									Percent						
Roche	40	30	40	40	39	-	-	35	25	-	31	40	40	70	33
BASF	32	4	24	-	26	-	15	20	-	-	-	18	-	30	17
Rhône-Poulenc	23	-	12	-	5	-	-	-	-	80	-	-	-	-	9
Takeda	-	18	-	22	15	-	-	-	10	-	13	-	-	-	5
Eisai	-	-	11	-	-	-	-	-	-	-	-	-	-	-	3
Daiichi	-	-	-	-	-	-	-	35	10	-	-	-	-	-	2
Share of the Top Six	95	53	87	62	85	0	15	89	45	80	44	58	40	100	70
Herfindahl Index of Concentration[a]	3162	1260	2458	2063	2434	4220	1387	2815	713	6514	1133	3666	2720	5771	-

– = None or not available
Source: Connor (2000a).
[a] The sum of the squares of the market shares of the top 20 manufacturers of bulk vitamins.

Getting access to the sophisticated synthetic chemistry needed to produce most vitamins is difficult. That and mastering the implementation of large scale manufacturing of vitamins appear to be the major barriers to entry. Technological impediments vary somewhat across vitamins (Table 10.3). Producing vitamins A, B3, D, and E seems to present the greatest difficulties for entry because they are still in the hands of the original producers, Roche, BASF, and Rhône-Poulenc; the same appears to be true for the carotenoids (beta carotene and canthaxanthin). A somewhat lower degree of technological barriers to entry is revealed by production by Japanese chemical companies. Although evidence is spotty, Takeda, Eisai, and Daiichi seem to have begun producing vitamins B1, B2, B5, folic acid, and biotin a decade or two later than the big three European pioneers.[15] The more moderate barriers for these B type vitamins can be inferred by the less advanced state of Japanese pharmaceutical and organic-chemicals R&D up to the 1950s; however, by the 1970s the general scientific prowess of Japanese research had caught up to U.S./Western European levels in most fields.

Table 10.3. Evidence of Technological Barriers to Market Entry into Vitamins, 1990s.

High Barriers: Big Three Pioneers Still Dominate Global Production[a]	Moderate Barriers: Pioneers No Longer Dominate, but Little Chinese Entry	Low Barriers: Chinese Exports to U.S. Market High or Increasing[b] (1996 % of imports)
A	B4	C (54)
E	B5	B1 (12)
B3	Biotin	B2 (8)
D		B6 (8)
K		B12 (27)
Beta carotene		Folic Acid (13)

[a] For A and E pioneers appear to be Roche, BASF, and Rhône-Poulenc; for B3 Lonza and Degussa; for D, Roche, BASF, and Solvay; and for K, Vanetta and Heterochemicals.
[b] In every case, there was earlier entry by Japanese chemical companies as well; moreover, cartels established in the early 1990s disbanded in late 1994 or late 1995.

Finally, there are a few cases of vitamins where more recent entry has occurred on a large scale in newly industrializing countries with relatively backward scientific infrastructures. The case of China in the 1980s and 1990s is particularly instructive, because the Chinese government has made investment in chemical industries with high export potential a high priority. Rapid rates of growth in Chinese exports of certain vitamins may be taken as an indicator that *technological* barriers to industry entry are fairly modest, especially access to knowledge about the synthetic chemistry required to implement feasible manufacturing methods. Thus, in those cases where Chinese vitamin exports were becoming competitive in the same markets to which the major European producers also exported, one can safely assume that patents or technological secrecy no longer protect the primacy of the established pioneer firms. There were six vitamin markets with large or growing Chinese exports to the United States in the 1990s: vitamins C, B1, B2, B6, B12, and folic acid. China's vitamin C imports were especially large, accounting for 54 percent of the value of total U.S. imports in 1996; B12 was next with 27 percent. The other four B vitamins were in the 8 to 13 percent import-penetration range, but growing. It is noteworthy that these are almost the same vitamins with significant Japanese production (B12 is the exception). However, there is little evidence of large-scale Chinese entry into synthetic production of vitamins A, E, B3, D, K, or carotenoids – all markets supplied nearly exclusively by the pioneering, mostly European manufacturers. Therefore, technological barriers to entry appear to remain high for this last set of vitamins.

The major significance of these suggestions about technological barriers in understanding the evolution of vitamin price fixing is the fact that the Chinese exporters were spoilers for the cartels. The Chinese vitamin companies were too small, too numerous, and too inclined to be aggressive about exporting – all characteristics that made them unsuitable candidates to recruit to the vitamins cartels. Whenever Chinese chemical companies could adopt production methods that made their vitamin production price-competitive (assisted by Chinese government export subsidies), they aggressively captured U.S. market shares that in some cases were so large that the cartels affected were unable to sustain their conspiracies. This certainly happened in the case of vitamin C around 1995. Chinese incursion into the U.S. market was also one factor for the early demise of the cartels established in vitamins B1, B2, B6, B12, and folic acid.

MARKET SIZE AND GROWTH

The sizes of the major vitamins markets varied considerably, but in the aggregate their sales were far larger than the lysine and citric acid cases discussed in previous chapters (Chapters 3 and 4 above). Indeed, the sales of the 15 vitamins and carotenoids that were affected by cartels were far greater than any of the price-fixing conspiracies uncovered by antitrust authorities in the 1990s.

Estimates of annual vitamin sales centered on 1995 are shown for the U.S. and the world in Table 10.4. Global sales approached \$3.7 billion per year, and the U.S. market accounted for nearly one-quarter of the global total. Western Europe probably accounted for another one-fourth of global sales and Asian countries for the majority of the remainder. One reason for the large global shares of Europe and North America is the fact that more than half of the value of vitamins are sold for animal-feed use, and meat, poultry, and aquaculture production are especially intense on those continents (see Table 10.1 above). It is likely that vitamins sold for food and pharmaceutical uses follow human populations more closely. That is, relative to feed-grade, human-grade vitamins have higher geographic shares in Asia, Africa, and Latin America. Vitamins A, C, and E are by far the largest of the individual vitamins markets, accounting for an estimated 66 percent of total vitamin sales worldwide and 60 percent of U.S. sales.[16] Five more vitamins and carotenoids have sales of at least $100 million per year around the world. The smallest global vitamin market is for folic acid.

Vitamin markets in the 1990s could be described as mature. The most rapid era for growth in vitamin production was from the early 1930s to the late 1940s. By the 1950s, all vitamins had been isolated and commercially produced for some time. The average rate of volume growth worldwide for all vitamins in the mid-1990s was 2.4 percent per year. Only vitamins E and B5 (Cal Pan) could be described as growing rapidly, and this might be due to temporary factors such as recent publicity about the health benefits of antioxidants (including E and C).[17] Most vitamin markets displayed negative or nearly zero volume growth in the 1990s. Rates varied across marketing channels as well, with cosmetic use of vitamins the fastest growing.

Mark-ups in vitamins sold for human use tend to be very high. Thus, there is often a great discrepancy between vitamin sales at the manufacturers' "bulk" level as shown in Table 10.4 and sales at retail. Vitamins sold for feed use are incorporated into premixes sold to feed manufacturers or farmers that raise animals. The price of feed-grade vitamins is eventually reflected in the prices paid by consumers for meat, poultry, eggs, milk, and farm-raised seafood. A similar mark-up from bulk vitamin prices occurs in the case of fortified foods (milk, flour, pasta, etc.). The mark-ups for feed- and food-grade vitamins are fairly modest in comparison to pharmaceutical grades. In the late 1990s one reliable study placed the size of the *retail* U.S. consumer market for vitamins at $5.8 billion. Now, bulk pharmaceutical-grade vitamin sales at that time cannot have been more than $330 million (see Tables 10.1 and 10.4). Therefore, by the time consumers bought packaged vitamins in their grocery and drug stores, the mark-up on manufacturers' prices was an astounding 1,600 percent. Put another way, only about 5 to 6 percent of the retail purchase price of vitamins by consumers can be attributed to the cost of the raw vitamins, the rest being accounted for by advertising, packaging, assembly, and distribution costs.[18]

Table 10.4. Estimated Size and Growth of the World and U.S. Bulk Vitamins Industries, 1990s.

Product	Sales per Year[a]		Volume Growth[b]		
	World, ca. 1995	U.S., ca. 1995	World 1995-2000	U.S. Late Conspiracy	U.S. 1990-1998
	Million dollars			*Percent per year*	
E	1,087	187	4.8	3.4	9.2
C	800	242	2.4	0.2	0.8
A	574	98	-0.8	0.0	-6.4
B4 Choline chloride	255	56	1.9	--	--
B5 Calcium pantothenate	161	26	4.2	1.3	11.8
B2 Riboflavin	139	35	0.7	--	1.9
B3 Niacin	121	40	-0.5	--	--
B6	89	25	1.7	-1.3	4.7
H Biotin	87	22	0.4	--	--
B12	81	30	-0.5	--	--
B1	68	15	-1.2	4.8	-16.1
D[c]	65	22	0.8	--	--
K[c]	37	12	-1.2	--	--
Folic Acid	16	12	-1.6	--	-9.8
Carotenoids[d]	130	55	--	5.7	12.2
Total	3,707	877	2.4	1.7	3.0

Source: März (1996), Connor (1999, 2000), STAT-USA.

-- = Not available

[a] U.S. estimates more accurate than world .

[b] World rates are projections. Late conspiracy is the second half when prices were steadier; "1990-1998" is actually full conspiracy period.

[c] There is no evidence of any price fixing in the market for vitamin K; vitamin D may have been sold mixed with vitamin E, but no separate conspiracy has been alleged for vitamin D alone.

[d] Two carotenoids are beta carotene (by far the largest) and canthaxanthin.

TRADE AND LOCATION O F PRODUCTION

In the 1930s and 1940s, Merck, Squibb, Pfizer, Lilly, and other large U.S. pharmaceutical firms were early entrants into vitamin manufacturing. However, a recently discontinued annual survey of the U.S. International Trade Commission reveals that by the early 1990s there was virtually no global production of most vitamins by U.S. companies (see box). The modest U.S. production remaining was limited to vitamins B3 and B4 or came from three non-U.S. chemical companies (Roche, BASF, and Takeda). As a result, most bulk vitamins sold in the U.S. market in the 1990s originated offshore. Most imports came from Europe, Japan, or China – the home countries of the world's leading vitamin manufacturers.

The United Sates International Trade Commission

The USITC and its predecessor agencies began to survey the organic chemicals industry annually in 1917. The mandatory survey resulted in a report that listed virtually every organic chemical manufactured in the United States and usually gave the names of the companies that made each chemical. Prior to 1992, the report gave sales and prices for aggregated classes of organic chemicals, including vitamins. Beginning in 1992, the USITC began to publish more detail on prices and quantities of individual vitamins and provitamins.

In 1994, the USITC, a nominally independent agency, was ordered to cease publication of its organic-chemicals reports by the powerful Chairman of the Ways and Means Committee of the U.S. House of Representatives, Mr. Bill Archer. The reason given by Mr. Archer in his letter was to save costs and to avoid competing with private sector companies that would like to produce similar reports themselves. Neither of these reasons rings true. Several years later no comparable private-sector survey yet has developed, and a uniquely detailed primary data source has disappeared after 89 years of continuous publication.

A more likely explanation is that Mr. Archer, a very conservative Republican, was lobbied by the chemical companies appearing in the report. Perhaps unwittingly, Mr. Archer played into the hands of the members of the vitamin cartel by removing a data set that might have assisted in investigating the vitamin price conspiracy.

Table 10.5 shows the sources of geographic supply for most of the vitamins and carotenoids sold in bulk in the U.S. market for the year 1996. Seven vitamins are manufactured in the United States; domestic production accounted for 45 percent of U.S. demand in that year. Roche is by far the largest producer of vitamins in the United States. It makes vitamins A, C, E, H, and beta carotene in plants that it operates in New Jersey and Texas.[19] Moreover, Roche also imported about 11 percent of the U.S. supply of vitamins from plants that it owns in Switzerland, Scotland, and Germany. Altogether, Roche's two domestic and three foreign plants manufacture every major vitamin except B3 and B4..

Besides Roche, Takeda is the only large producer of vitamin C in the United States. Takeda also imports vitamins C, B1, B2, B6, and folic acid in quantity from Japan. In 1999, ADM began manufacturing vitamin C at its Illinois plant by fermentation. Large imports of vitamin C came from China in 1996, but trade sources say that many Chinese companies failed when prices plunged after 1995. Vitamin E is made synthetically by Roche in New Jersey and BASF in Michigan. Besides these two large producers, smaller amounts of natural vitamin E are being made by ADM in Illinois (since 1995), Henkel in Illinois, Eisai in Texas (since 1997), and by a Roche/Cargill joint venture in Iowa (since 1997). Large amounts of vitamin E are exported to the United States from Europe (BASF and Rhône-Poulenc) and from Japan (Eisai).

The structure of U.S. supply for vitamins B3 and B4 is quite different than the other vitamins markets. Most B3 is manufactured by Nepera in New York and an Indiana joint venture controlled by the German chemical company Degussa. However, the largest supplier of B3 is Lonza from its Swiss plant. Lonza controls about 60 percent of the global market. Choline chloride (sometimes called B4) is manufactured in the United States by DuCoa in a Missouri plant and by Bioproducts (a subsidiary of Mitsui) in Kentucky. Almost half of the U.S. market of B4 comes from Chinook in Canada, with smaller imports from China. In the 1990s, none of the four big European manufacturers of B4 (BASF, ICI, Akzo Nobeland ICI) exported to North America even though they account for half of global production. B3 and B4 are unique in having no U.S. sales by the Big Three vitamin makers.

Carotenoids are a global monopoly of Roche and Rhône-Poulenc. The dominant carotenoid is beta carotene, a provitamin of vitamin A. The U.S. market is supplied almost entirely by domestic production from Roche-owned plants.

All the B vitamins (B1, B2, B6, B12, H, and folic acid) are supplied solely by U.S. imports. U.S. purchases for each of the B vitamins is relatively small ($12 to $55 million per year in 1996), so scale economies may dictate the construction of only a few plants in the world. Each of these B vitamins is mainly supplied by plants in Europe or Japan owned by the Big Six producers (see Table 10.5). With the exception of vitamin B5, Chinese imports are significant for these vitamins; in 1996, they accounted for an average of 12 percent of the U.S. supply.

Table 10.5. Estimated U.S. Sources of Bulk Vitamins, ca. 1996.

Product	Domestic Production[a]	Principal Imports									Total[b]
		Roche Europe	BASF Europe	Rhône Europe	Takeda Japan	Eisai Japan	Daiichi Japan	Other Europe	Canada	China	
					Percent of U.S. Sales						
A	21	31	18	29	0	0	0	0	0	2	100
C	66	1	5	0	5	0	0	0	0	20	100
E	66	3	2	14	0	12	0	0	0	1	100
B1	0	65	0	0	20	0	0	0	0	15	100
B2	0	27	15	24	22	0	0	0	0	9	100
B3 Niacin	64	0	0	0	0	0	0	34[c]	0	0	100
B4 Choline	47	0	0	0	0	0	0	0	47[g]	5	100
B5 Cal pan	0	29	10	0	0	0	52	8[d]	0	0	100
B6	0	60	0	0	12	0	12	0	0	10	100
B12	0	0	0	35	0	0	0	20[e]	0	25	100
D	0	41	9	0	0	0	0	49[f]	0	1	100
Folic acid	0	58	0	0	25	0	0	0	0	17	100
Carotenoids	65	2	33	0	0	0	0	0	0	0	100
Other	40	0	0	0	0	0	0	15[c]	15	0	100
Total	45	11	6	9	35	3	2	4	3	7	100

Sources: USITC (1996), STAT-USA, Connor (1999-2000), Table 4.

[a] Vitamin C Roche and Takeda, vitamin E Roche and BASF, and all other Roche except B3 and B4.

[b] Percentages often add to less than 100 because of other imports not shown.

[c] Lonza

[d] Unknown Israeli firm

[e] Hoechst

[f] Solvay Duphar

[g] Chinook Group

Despite the fairly complete picture that can be constructed of the ownership and location structures of the global vitamins industries, information on costs of production is jealously guarded. In general, it appears that the real costs of manufacturing vitamins synthetically has declined significantly since the 1950s, but the rate of decline may have slowed in the 1980s and 1990s. Conversion from synthetic to biotechnological methods typically results in steep cost reductions.

Chapter 10 Endnotes

[1] Dates and other facts about the vitamins cartels can be found in Appendixes D and E of Connor (2000) and Table 10.A.1.
[2] Switzerland is also the operational headquarters of the global cartel for gem diamonds, De Beers Centenary AG. In July 2000, De Beers announced that it would be abandoning its monopoly of rough gem diamonds that began in 1934. De Beers control of supply had dipped from 90% in the 1980s to 63% in 1999 (*Wall Street Journal* July 13, 2000).
[3] The urgency of research into the causes of malnutrition was spurred by the discovery that fully two-fifths of all young men called for military conscription in the UK in 1917-1918 were medically unfit because of diseases traced to vitamin deficiencies.
[4] In the United States, the acronym "USP" is used to signify products that meet the standards required by the *U.S. Pharmacopoeia*.
[5] The *Chemical Market Reporter* (February 23, 1998) speculated that the collapse of vitamin prices after 1995 – the year the vitamin C cartel disbanded – might have made sales unprofitable.
[6] They were not significant producers of vitamins B3 and choline chloride (B4). Four or five U.S. pharmaceutical companies were major players just before and after the War, but withdrew by the 1970s.
[7] Its foreign investments came in handy during World War II. Like some other Swiss multinationals, such as Nestlé, Roche transferred most of its assets to a North American holding company in case Switzerland was overrun. Roche's CEO moved to its U.S. headquarters in Nutley, New Jersey during the war to direct the company's operations not already in the hands of the Axis Powers.
[8] The whistle-blower's name was Stanley Adams. He was jailed by Swiss authorities for revealing Roche's trade secrets. Adams (1984) wrote a book about this episode. However, Adams, like Whitacre, came to a bad end. In 1994, he was convicted of conspiring to murder his wife for the insurance money (Barboza 1999).
[9] Predation is the use of irrationally low prices to force companies to leave the industry. Full-line forcing is a practice that required buyers to buy all the cartel's products the buyer can use or get none at all.
[10] When Germany occupied Czechoslovakia, the country's chemical assets were given to Farben. This scenario was repeated in Poland, Holland, Belgium, France, and other overrun countries. I.G. Farben built at least two chemical plants that were staffed with slave labor from concentration camps.
[11] Akzo Nobel won the auction of Hoechst Roussel Vet in August 1999 by paying $712 million. Akzo Nobel vaulted from 9th to 3rd place in the world in this market.
[12] This assumes that at least one company making a particular vitamin is more specialized in one type than the average firm.
[13] Below the top six, Lonza of Switzerland holds 60 percent of the B3 market.
[14] The Herfindahl index takes the market shares of each seller in an industry, squares it, and sums the squared shares. A monopoly has an index value of 10,000.
[15] In the case of vitamin H (biotin), the Japanese entrants were Tanabe and Sumitomo, each with about 20 percent of the world market.
[16] The U.S. sales are slightly more accurate than the global figures.
[17] Epidemiological studies released in the 1980s appeared to demonstrate reductions in heart disease and certain types of cancer associated with consumption of vitamins A,C,E, and B3; but controlled experiments with human subjects a decade later failed to find any positive health benefits (Table 10.A.1).

[18] During the vitamins conspiracies of the 1990s, which lasted four to eleven years, consumers probably spent $35 to $40 billion directly on vitamins at retail. However, assuming an overcharge on bulk vitamins of 30 percent and a 100 percent pass-through, consumers were overcharged about $350 million, but that is only 0.9 to 1.1 percent of the value of retail purchases.

[19] The USITC survey records U.S. production of vitamins B1, B2, B3, B5, and B6 by Roche in New Jersey, but the amounts seem to be small experimental or pilot production.

Table 10.A.1. Mileposts in the Discovery and Use of Vitamins, 1795-1994.

Year	Event
1795	British Admiralty decrees a daily ration of lemon juice for all seamen on long voyages to prevent scurvy.
1846	Justus von Liebig demonstrated that all living things were composed primarily of carbohydrates, fats, and proteins.
1861	An Austrian physician publishes a controlled experiment that demonstrated that night blindness can be cured by dietary liver extracts.
1886	The Dutch dispatch a medical team to discover the cause of beriberi in Indonesia.
1889	The team discovers that unpolished rice will prevent beriberi.
1905	German biochemist Stepp proves the existence of the class of fat-soluble vitamins.
1911	Polish biochemist Casimir Funk coins the term “vitamins.”
1912	Japanese biochemists extract a compound from rice hulls that prevents beriberi. U.S. biochemists discover a fat-soluble nutrient in butter and egg yolks whose absence causes mice to die prematurely. Funk proposes the vitamin-deficiency theory of certain diseases.
1915	The fat-soluble nutrient is named vitamin A by E.V. McCollum of the University of Wisconsin.
1916	A group of water-soluble vitamins (later named B) is isolated by U.S. chemist E.V. McCollum.
1918	English researcher Edward Mellanby demonstrates that cod liver oil cures rickets, long a folk remedy in the North Sea area. Yale biochemists L.B. Mendel and B. Cohen show that ascorbic acid deficiency causes scurvy in guinea pigs.
1919	Mellanby shows that rickets is caused by a vitamin deficiency.
1920	British biochemist J.C. Drummond names vitamins A, B, and C; he also discovers that carotene can be converted to vitamin A by the human liver.
1921	U.S. embryologist finds the first evidence that a vitamin plays a role in animal reproduction.
1922	E.V. McCollum isolates vitamin D and successfully treats rickets. Vitamin E is discovered.

Year	Event
1923	Univ. of Wisconsin biochemist Harry Steenbock discovers that ultraviolet light can increase the vitamin D in foods.
1924	Boston physicians show that eating liver prevents pernicious anemia.
1926	Research begins to establish that the B vitamin is actually several. Animal experiments find a relationship between pellagra and a vitamin B deficiency.
1927	Steenbock assigns his patent concerning vitamin D irradiation to the Wisconsin Alumni Research Foundation.
1928	Vitamin C is isolated from capsicum peppers at a Cambridge, England laboratory. Eli Lilly Co. introduces a commercial vitamin extract from livers to treat anemia.
1929	T. Moore proves that yellow carotene is the precursor of retinol in the eyes of animals. Five years later, researchers would establish that retinol (vitamin A) is essential to vision.
1930	A crystalline form of vitamin D is isolated and within three years is being used to fortify butter, margarine, and milk products.
1931	Swiss chemist Paul Karrer isolates vitamin A.
1932	University of Pittsburgh biochemist C. G. King synthesizes vitamin C.
1933	Cambridge University biochemist P. György discovers vitamin B6, a coenzyme that cures dermatitis. Vitamin C is named ascorbic acid and is chemically synthesized one year later.
1935	Researchers at Germany's Kaiser Wilhelm Institute, building on research published in 1932, isolate and synthesize vitamin B2 (riboflavin). University of California at Berkeley biochemist H. Evans isolates Vitamin E from wheat germ oil. St. Louis researchers isolate vitamin K, which is essential for blood coagulation.
1936	University of Wisconsin biochemist C. A. Elvehjem isolates vitamin B3 (niacin) and shows that it cures pellagra. R.R. Williams synthesizes vitamin B1 (thiamin). Vitamin A is synthesized, and New York entrepreneurs found a company to market Vitamins Plus, the first commercial vitamin-mineral dietary supplement.

Year	Event
1937	German biochemists K. Lohmann and P. Schuster discover the biological process whereby vitamin B1 prevents beriberi. U.S. and Swiss manufacturers introduce synthetic vitamin B1 to the market at about $450 per pound.
1938	U.S. biochemist R.J. Williams synthesizes vitamin B5 (pantothenic acid). P. Karrer, working at Hoffmann-La Roche, synthesizes vitamin E and finds it to be an antioxidant. Scientists propose enrichment of bread with vitamin B1; by 1941, 30 percent is being enriched.
1940	U.S. biochemist V. Vigneaud isolates biotin (sometimes vitamin H).
1942	H. Dam in the Netherlands identifies the chemical structure of vitamin K. One form of vitamin K is synthesized one year later.
1943	The Food and Nutrition Board of the National Academy of Sciences publishes Recommended Daily Allowances (RDAs) of various nutrients (including vitamins) for the first time.
1944	U.S. biochemists H. Mitchell and E. Snell isolate folic acid, later found to cure macrocytic anemia. The U.S. War Food Administration mandates vitamin B enrichment of bread and pastries.
1948	Vitamin B12 is isolated, but understanding its chemistry will take eight years of research. This is the last of the 13 vitamins considered to be essential for human health to be isolated.
1953	Researchers at Basel, Switzerland synthesize beta carotene.
1970	Nobel prize winner Linus Pauling writes a popular book that recommends megadoses of vitamin C to cure the common cold, joining a lengthening list of popular writers who make unsupported claims about the health benefits of excessive vitamin consumption. The FDA begins to develop rules to regulate megadoses of vitamins, but in 1973 Sen. William Proximire spearheads a new law that frees dietary supplements from government regulation.
1994	Three major scientific studies of vitamins-health relationships are published. They found that large doses of vitamins A, B3, C, and E were either toxic or ineffective in reducing cancer or heart disease.

Sources: Tannahill (1988), Hui (1992), Trager (1995), and Kiple and Ornelas (2000).

Chapter 11

THE VITAMINS CONSPIRACIES

FORMATION OF THE CARTELS

The vitamins cartels were remarkably complicated. There were wheels within wheels. At least 18 manufacturers joined one or more of the eight conspiratorial groups that met to agree on prices and to enforce those agreements.[1] Price fixing was arranged for at least 13 products, 11 vitamins and two carotenoids (or provitamins). There were six groups of conspirators that carried out price fixing for 11 of the 13 vitamins. In these six groups, each of which deserves to be called a cartel, Roche, BASF, or Rhône-Poulenc took the lead in initiating the conspiracy; the six cartels began and ended their illegal activities on a unique pair of dates; and membership in the six groups was comprised of unique combinations of companies. Some of the companies belonged to only one cartel, while others joined up to five of the cartels. However, two more vitamin cartels were unique groups of companies that virtually did not overlap with the membership of any of the other conspiratorial groups. The members of the B3 cartel were exclusively members of that cartel and no other. The same can be said for the vitamin B4 cartel. These two cartels operated independently from the other six cartels.

The Roche Cartels

The anatomy of the eight vitamin cartels is displayed in Table 11.1. In six of the eight groups, Hoffmann-La Roche was the largest seller and probably took the lead in managing the conspiracies. These are named the "Roche Cartels."

The first and by far the largest in terms of estimated North American sales affected by price fixing is the vitamin A and E cartel group. It was reported that Roche and BASF met in late 1989 to start the conspiracy in motion; they began raising prices worldwide in 1990, but only very slowly during the first year, and they divided the world into exclusive sales territories for each firm (Barboza 1999). With more than 70 percent of the world market between them and no threat of entry, Roche and BASF should have been able to make the higher prices stick. However, with a cartel, the greater the market shares of its members, the closer it can come to charging the maximum rational price, that is, the monopoly price. So, later in 1990, the two instigators invited the last remaining producers of vitamins A and E of any consequence, Rhône-Poulenc and Eisai. From early 1991 to February 1999, these four companies accounted for nearly all the world's production of the two vitamins. As will be shown below, list prices of A and E started rising precipitously in early 1991, and transaction prices followed soon after. This one cartel would account for nearly half of the sales of cartel-influenced markets and more than half the economic damages to vitamin buyers in North America (and very likely the rest of the world as well).

The second cartel monopolized the global market for vitamin B12. In terms of timing, the B12 cartel was virtually coterminous with the A and E cartel. Only two firms accounted for almost 90 percent of the global supply, Rhône-Poulenc (80 percent) and its much smaller German rival, Hoechst (9 percent). The vitamin B12 cartel was in effect a merger ten years in advance of the late 1999 formal merger of the two companies into the firm now called Aventis. Although B12 is one of the smaller vitamin markets in annual sales, its longevity caused its affected sales to mount to the highest of the B vitamins.

The first two cartels made such promising starts in 1990, that Roche, BASF, and Rhône-Poulenc spread their net wider still. In addition to attracting Eisai to the vitamin E conspiracy, three more companies were persuaded to join the Big Three: Takeda and Daiichi from Japan and the small German pharmaceutical firm E. Merck. Together with Roche, Takeda and Daiichi were able to reach a critical mass of supply control in the three B vitamins B1, B6 and folic acid that allowed price fixing to begin in January 1991. The three conspirators controlled from 45 to 60 percent of the production of vitamins B1, B6, and folic acid. Unfortunately for the cartel, all three of these markets were experiencing an upsurge in Chinese production. Consequently, this third cartel folded by late 1994, after only four years of operation. For this reason, the affected sales in these markets were only half of that in B12.

The vitamin C and B2 cartel involved Roche, BASF, Takeda and E. Merck. This group also got together relatively early and in the face of a rising tide of Chinese competition. However, because of the large size of the vitamin C market, the cartel-affected sales over five years of conspiracy were the second largest, accounting for nearly one-fourth of total affected sales in North America.

The last two cartels in the Roche group monopolized the markets for vitamin B5 and beta carotene. Roche, BASF, and Daiichi began conspiring in January 1991 but were forced to cease in February 1999, after eight full years of conspiring, only because their conspiracy was discovered by U.S. antitrust authorities. Neither product market was challenged by Chinese supplies, and the cartel members controlled about 90 percent of global output.

Table 11.1. Eighteen Conspirators Formed Eight Global Groups to Fix Prices of Thirteen Vitamins, 1990-1999.

	Groups							
	A	B12	B1	C	B5	Carotenoids	B3	B4
Dates:	1990-1999	1990-1999	1991-1994	1991-1995	1991-1998	1991-1998	1989-1998	1989-1996
Products:[d]	A & E	B12	B1,B6 & Folic	C & B2	B5	Beta Carotene[b]	Niacin	Choline Chloride
Cartel Members:	Roche BASF Rhône[c] Eisai	Rhône[c] Hoechst[c]	Roche Takeda Daiichi	Roche BASF Takeda E. Merck	Roche BASF Daiichi	Roche BASF	Degussa[c] Lonza Napera	Chinook Mitsui DuCoa BASF Akzo UCB
	Million dollars							
Affected U.S. sales:[a]	2,544	258	124	1,252	182	82	375	600

[a] Sales in million U.S. dollars during the conspiracies in Canada and the United States. Global sales were at least double those in North America and approached triple in some cases. In millions of U.S. dollars. Total of all groups is $5,417 million.

[b] Also canthaxanthin.

[c] Merged in late 1999 to form Aventis.

[d] Roche and BASF also organized a cartel for animal-feed vitamin premixes. Each of the vitamins shown were incorporated as ingredients in these premixes, but relatively little is known about this cartel. The premix conspiracy dates are January 1991 to December 1997.

[e] Degussa (now Degussa Hüls) was until 1995 the dominant partner in a U.S. joint manufacturing venture named Vitachem. The junior partner was Reilly Industries, Inc. of Indianapolis, Indiana. Degussa conspired "as early as" January 1992 until July 1995, Nepera from January 1991 to July 1995, Reilly from September 1994 to March 1998, and Lonza from about January 1992 to March 1998. Other unindicted co-conspirators are unnamed.

Niacin and Choline Chloride

The last two cartels were different from the first six in several ways. The participants in the niacin (B3) and choline chloride (B4) conspiracies were a completely different set of nine companies from those in the "Roche groups."[2] Moreover, these conspiracies were initiated in January 1988 and early 1989 – a year or two earlier than the six others. The niacin cartel lasted 11 years and the choline chloride conspiracy about eight years. The leaders of the niacin cartel were the Swiss firm Lonza, which is loosely part of the Alusuisse conglomerate, and the German chemical company Degussa. Two U.S. companies joined the B3 cartel in early 1991. The B3 cartel was protected by technological barriers and was more concentrated (the three known B3 conspirators controlled more than 90 percent of global supply) than B4.[3] The latter had six members (two more than the next largest cartel) and some small Asian rivals to contend with. The B3 and B4 cartels ended up affecting almost one-fifth of the sales subject to vitamin price fixing.

Although the dates and identities of the cartels are known, why eight cartels had their origins in meetings held during the two years 1988-1989 is something of a puzzle. One possibility is that decelerating growth rates and standardization of quality standards had caused the vitamin business to evolve from its former specialty-chemical status to one more like a mature, commodity-type industry in which buyers focused solely on price during purchase negotiations.[4] Such an evolution would have squeezed profit margins for the producers, but ironically a movement towards greater homogeneity of quality would have made price fixing easier.

Another hypothesis about the timing of the vitamins cartels may be derived from the general financial conditions facing the prime movers of the conspiracies. Recall what conditions were like in 1989-1991 from the review in Chapter 10 of the major chemical companies involved (Roche, BASF, Rhône-Poulenc, and Hoechst). In each case, these companies faced a financial crisis in the late 1980s that became public knowledge when their financial results were later reported for fiscal years 1990 to 1994. However, internal projections of sales and profitability would have been known to top managers of the companies in the 1988-1989 period. The poor financial prospects were the result of overstaffing, overcapacity, and unprofitable diversifications, particularly in the companies' core Western European operations. Compounding the companies' woes was the onset of a global recession in 1990, a downturn that lingered for several years longer in Western Europe than in other regions of the world. In Japan too, the miraculous growth that had characterized the post-war period had burst. Japan experienced a nearly zero-growth phase that was to persist throughout the 1990s. Desperate times produce desperate men, and the top managers of the world's great vitamins concerns would not be immune to desperate measures to restore profitability. Price fixing, though illegal for pharmacists to dispense, was a tonic that restored the financial health of these companies' anemic vitamin divisions.

Major price increases announced by leading companies are usually faithfully reported by the chemical trade press. *Chemical Week*, *The Journal of Commerce*, and *Chemical Marketing Reporter* are the major sources. The decade of the 1980s was generally a period of modest inflation for the U.S. economy; there were very few price increases announced for vitamins during that time, and the evidence suggests that many of the increases did not stick. In any case, the announcements concerned only list prices. While smaller buyers might sometimes pay list for spot purchases, the largest companies sought bids for their purchases or negotiated annual supply contacts at prices well below list.

However, rounds of list price increases announced in late 1989 (effective January 1990) and early 1990 caused vitamin buyers to sit up and take notice. Market demand for many vitamins was described as flat and in early 1990 the first signs of a recession were appearing, so the timing of the price increases was curious. Rhône-Poulenc made the first "official" public announcement in November 1989, but other European producers were doing the same informally to their customers. The most publicized list-price changes came from Roche and BASF in early March 1990. Roche *raised* its list prices on both human-grade and feed-grade vitamins A and E, while BASF simultaneously *lowered* its list prices. The important result was that both leading producers' prices now exactly matched. The March 1990 round was the first change in list prices since 1988. The two companies admitted that during 1989 market transaction prices had hovered 20 percent below their list prices, but they promised that the gap would close during 1990. Indeed, the major purposes in the March 1990 changes were to close the gap and to increase margins. A more forthright, if brazen, statement can hardly be imagined.

In August 1990, Roche and BASF announced a second round of price increases for vitamins A and E. This time movements in foreign currency exchange rates were given as the main reason. The decline in the value of the U.S. dollar relative to the Deutsche mark and Swiss frank made imported bulk vitamins more costly. Currency movements would not affect the cost of producing vitamins A and E in the United States where both Roche and BASF had major plants. The ferment in vitamin pricing in 1990 prompted *The Journal of Commerce* to begin reporting on list and spot prices on an almost weekly basis. The magazine queried a number of bulk vitamin buyers in the New York City area about these prices. Most vitamin sales occur in bids or annual supply contracts, but it is believed that transaction prices track movements in the list and spot prices fairly closely.[6] Graphs of vitamin price movements are shown in Chapter 12.

GLOBAL CARTEL CONNECTIONS

The previous section showed how the initial financial success in raising the prices of vitamins A and E prompted the formation of several more cartels to fix the prices of vitamin C and vitamins belonging to the B complex. However, there is considerable evidence to suggest that the effectiveness of the vitamin cartels inspired the formation of the citric acid cartel a year later. Moreover, there is irrefutable evidence that it was ADM's satisfaction with its citric acid scheme that incited an ADM officer to work hard to start the lysine cartel less than a year later. Not only is there enough information on which cartel spread the infection that caused cartel fever elsewhere, but also there is a fair degree of certainty about which companies and which persons were the carriers.

The causal chain of events linking the three global cartels is sketched in Figure 11.1. The time line begins with Hoffmann-La Roche and BASF getting together in late 1989 to begin colluding on the prices of vitamins A and E. The first price increases take effect in January 1990. Around this time, Kuno Sommer, head of Roche's Vitamins and Fine Chemicals Division, wrote an internal memorandum suggesting that Roche's experience with these two vitamins is so satisfactory that cartels should be explored for other products in his division. By late 1990, several other vitamin manufacturers had joined Roche and BASF in forming more vitamin cartels that are launched in January 1991.

More to the point, Sommer's colleague Andreas Hauri, Roche's marketing manager for citric acid, received an unexpected visit from top officers of the world's newest manufacturer of citric acid, ADM. The timing could not have been better. Roche and Hauri are primed to accept the emissaries' overtures to form a global cartel for citric acid. Within two months, the four largest global suppliers of citric acid came to a durable agreement to raise prices worldwide.

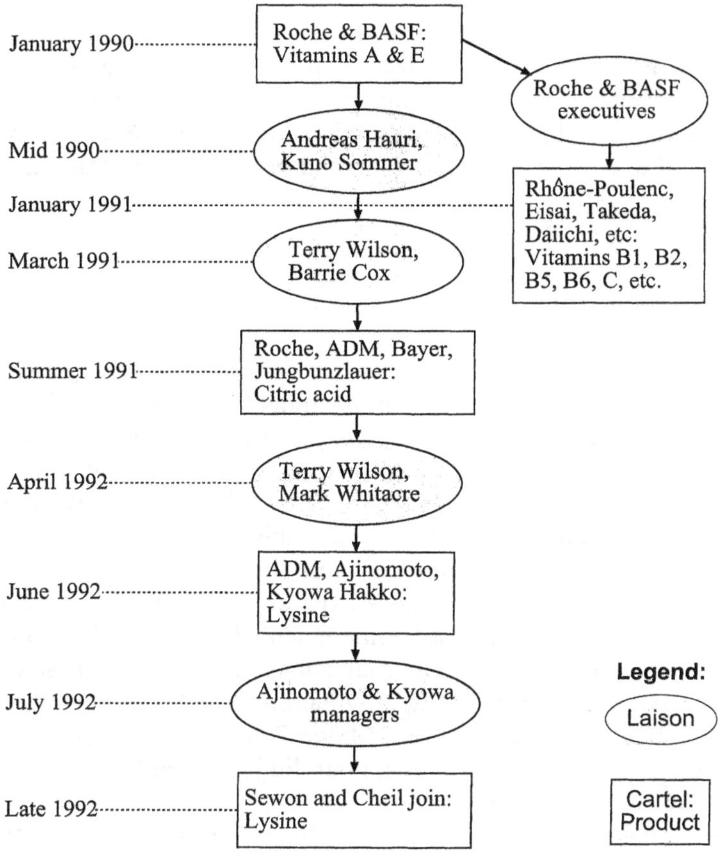

Figure 11.1. Linkages Among the Lysine, Citric Acid, and Vitamins Cartels.

One of the two ADM officers was Terrance Wilson, and he almost immediately began the search for cartels for other ADM products. Although Wilson considered some other food-and-feed ingredients to be good candidates for price fixing, lysine was one that has all the necessary characteristics.[7] In April 1992, Wilson took the young Mark Whitacre to Tokyo to meet with the largest suppliers of lysine (Ajinomoto and Kyowa Hakko) and began to mentor Whitacre in the craft of price fixing.

HOW THE CONSPIRACIES WERE ORGANIZED

Because the vitamin conspirators pleaded guilty and settled out of court with private plaintiffs, there are fewer details available on the vitamins cartel than the lysine and citric acid cases discussed in previous chapters. Nevertheless, many hard facts came to light in the U.S. and Canadian plea agreements, government press releases, and investigative press reports. The huge settlements made by the leading cartel members with private plaintiffs in the United States brought to bear exceptionally intense press scrutiny. Enough has come out to be able to construct a broad-brush portrait of the cartels' inner workings.

The Roche Cartels

As mentioned above, there were wheels within wheels. Working groups organized around various combinations of vitamins and their principal suppliers were formed, each of which can rightly be identified as cartels themselves. The vitamin B3 and B4 cartels discussed below were operating on separate tracks from their start in 1989, but the other six working groups were overlapping and interconnected (see Table 11.1 above).

Roche and BASF vitamin managers first met in late 1989, probably in Basel, Switzerland. Swiss cartel laws exist on the books, but they are rarely enforced and in any case cannot be implemented retroactively.[8] Germany, on the other hand, has had fairly vigorous anticartel enforcement since the late 1940s. The success of price fixing on vitamins A and E prompted Roche and BASF to extend invitations to Rhône-Poulenc and several Japanese manufacturers to join the conspiracy. Four did join in early 1991.[9]

Like the I.G. Farben cartel in the 1930s, the vitamins cartels employed almost every trick in the price-fixer's book. Enormous managerial resources were expanded on the complex price-fixing structures that were created. Unlike the previous cartels described in this book, the vitamins conspiracies were affected using three types of meetings, each of which involved different managerial levels. First, the cartel held what were called "top-notch" or "summit" conferences for a couple of days once a year in August or September. These meetings were restricted to corporate officials on the companies' management committees, officers just one-half step below the company's Chief Executive Officer (the U.S. equivalent of corporate Executive Vice President).[10] These top business leaders met to make grand strategic decisions and to formulate the cartel's "budget." The budget specified the prices to be charged and the market shares to be allocated to each participant for the following calendar year.[11] These corporate chiefs pampered themselves by choosing to meet in luxury hotels, mostly in Switzerland, France, or Germany. They also met in the historic Bottminger castle near Basel, the wine cellar maintained by BASF at its corporate headquarters, and a hot springs resort outside Tokyo (Spratling 1999).

Second, the summit meetings were followed four months later by managers one level lower in the companies. In December or January each year, the vitamin division presidents and their global marketing managers would gather to formally adopt the budget for the coming year. They were called "Shareholders' Meetings." Within the group of conspirators, their venture was referred to as "Vitamins, Inc.," not an inappropriate moniker for what was in effect an illegal merger. In addition, these second-tier officers would review the profitability of their schemes for the previous year. Finally, it was at these meetings that members who overshot or undershot their quotas would be required to redress the imbalances. Just as in the citric acid cartel, members that sold too much were required to compensate the underachievers by selling their product at cost.

Third, the cartel members' regional managers met each quarter. At the quarterly meetings, prices and sales volumes would be reported to each other and the information passed up to the global sales managers. At these meetings, participants were reminded that paper records were to be destroyed. To further avoid discovery, the cartel meetings were held outside the United States. The regional managers' meetings were primarily held to monitor and enforce compliance with the budget goals set at the summit meetings. These managers frequently conferred by telephone between meetings.

On the day the first guilty pleas were announced, Joel Klein, Assistant Attorney General for Antitrust stated:

> "The vitamin cartel is the most pervasive and harmful criminal antitrust conspiracy ever uncovered . . . The enormous effort that went into maintaining the conspiracy reflects the magnitude of the illegal revenues it generated . . . These cartels . . . are powerful and sophisticated and, without intervention by antitrust authorities, will often go on indefinitely."

Of course, some of the vitamin conspiracies ended in 1994 to 1996 because producers outside the cartel cut prices and captured large shares of the market. However, most of the cartels were operating smoothly up to the end, despite increasing signals to outsiders that collusion was afoot. According to one source, U.S. investigators first got wind of the vitamins cartel and Roche's role in it in late 1996 from sources at ADM cooperating with the DOJ in its investigation of the citric acid cartel. At that time ADM was making biotin and was soon to enter production of vitamins E and C. Perhaps Barrie Cox had learned about the vitamin price fixing from one of his contacts at Hoffmann-La Roche.[12] Another possibility is that ADM had learned of rumors of price fixing when it studied the new vitamin markets it was entering. As a result of the tip, the FBI interviewed Dr. Kuno Sommer in March 1997 (Barboza 1999). Sommer was at the time president of Roche's vitamin and fine chemicals division. Sommer had to agree to the interview because of Roche's promise to the DOJ to cooperate in the citric acid case. During the FBI interviews Sommer denied the existence of any vitamin cartel, and the DOJ apparently decided to wind down its investigation for the meanwhile. What the investigators did not know at the time is that Sommer had pre-arranged his denial by agreement with his co-conspirators at Roche. This agreement constitutes obstruction of justice, a very serious offense under U.S. law.

In late 1997 or early 1998, lawyers working for Roche heard allegations that some managers in the company were fixing vitamin prices (Barboza 1999). Apparently, they discovered some corroborating evidence because a top Roche official issued a directive specifically ordering that the conspiracy stop. This directive was defied. The only effect was to move the cartel's meetings from hotels and other public places to the homes of the vitamins executives. This subterfuge extended the cartel's life by another year.

More evidence of illegal price fixing began to appear. In late 1997, a partner of the law firm Boies & Schiller with experience in representing class-action plaintiffs claims to have discovered evidence of vitamin price fixing when working on a patent-infringement suit. Soon after Roche dropped a counter-claim in the case, he began hearing many complaints from Roche customers. Vitamin buyers reported several instances of inexplicable behavior. Customers who habitually purchased from Roche would not be able to get price quotes from BASF or other suppliers, and vice versa. Buyers of vitamin C were threatened with unspecified retaliation should they try to resell purchased products. A manager of a small vitamin premix company in Little Rock, Arkansas quoted a BASF executive as threatening his company with the following words: "You need to remove yourself [from the premix business] or you'll be forced out of the business" (Barboza 1999). The Little Rock company and many others did in fact fail.

Boies & Schiller filed a civil price-fixing suit in U.S. District Court in Dallas, Texas on behalf of several direct purchasers of bulk vitamins in March 1998. It would be more than one year before the government indicted Hoffmann-La Roche, BASF, and others for the same crimes. Plaintiffs in civil suits against Roche and BASF alleged that predatory pricing forced many premix companies to fold; the vitamins sold to feed manufacturers as a premix were priced below cost at the same time bulk vitamins sold to premix companies were sold at monopoly prices.

Perhaps these and other allegations were forwarded to the DOJ because a grand jury was established in Dallas, Texas in November 1997 to investigate vitamin price fixing. The FBI interviewed officers of animal-feeds firms, but little progress was made for the first year. In the summer of 1999, one of the vitamin manufacturers, the Swiss firm Lonza, began to negotiate a guilty plea agreement with the DOJ. Although signed in secret in September, the size of Lonza's fine shows that it could not provide much useful information about the "Roche Group" conspiracies. The DOJ's big break in its investigation came in January 1999. Following brief negotiations, the third largest vitamin manufacturer, Rhône-Poulenc was admitted to the Department's leniency program. As the first of the conspirators to come forward and admit its culpability, Rhône-Poulenc probably had an automatic right to full amnesty.[13] Conditional upon satisfactory cooperation with the DOJ's vitamin price-fixing probe, Rhône-Poulenc would receive a tangible benefit: no U.S. government fine would be levied on the company. Although Rhône-Poulenc's compensation was substantial, the DOJ's demands were likewise. Rumor has it that Rhône-Poulenc's managers were required to attend a conspiracy meeting in February 1999 and tape record it. In effect, Rhône-Poulenc took up Mark Whitacre's mantle, becoming an FBI mole.

Whatever the evidence provided by Rhône-Poulenc, it must have been highly incriminating. Within two months both Roche and BASF had agreed to plead guilty and pay record-setting U.S. fines of $725 million. Within two years, 24 criminal convictions would be obtained (Chapter 13). Like Whitacre, Rhône-Poulenc's motives were hardly pure. Not only did it save more than $100 million in U.S. fines, the company was now free to carry out its long-planned merger with Hoechst. In the end, it was the urge to merge that broke the vitamin cartel's cover.

Niacin and Choline Chloride

Very little has surfaced publicly about the operation and discovery of the niacin and choline chloride price-fixing conspiracies. What little is known must be pieced together from court documents containing only minimal facts filed in U.S. and Canadian courts.

Lonza dominates the world market for vitamin B3 (niacin or niacinamide) from its single plant in Switzerland. Degussa was the second largest in Europe in the late 1980s. They made roughly 60 and 20 percent of the world's vitamin B3. It is possible that the two began colluding on European sales and exports to North America in the late 1980s (the U.S. guilty plea agreement is vague on this point). Although the small New York chemical manufacturer Nepera had only 10 percent of the global market, its 30 percent share of the U.S. market meant that it was big enough to spoil the price fixing agreement of Lonza and Degussa alone. List prices of vitamin B3 in the United States began to rise in mid 1990; transaction prices showed a corresponding rise in 1991. From the U.S. guilty pleas, it is clear that Nepera had a leading role in the conspiracy beginning by at least January 1992. Lonza and Degussa began to coordinate their vitamin B3 conspiracy with the main group of vitamin price fixers associated with Hoffmann-La Roche (Barboza 1999).[14]

Degussa formed a joint venture with Indiana chemical company Reilly Industries in the early 1990s. Until late 1994, the pricing of vitamin B3 was Degussa's responsibility while Reilly's management confined itself to production decisions. However, in September 1994, Degussa involved Reilly in the conspiracy, which persisted until March 1998. In July 1995, about the time it was acquired by Cambrex Industries, Nepera withdrew from the U.S. conspiracy. Cambrex was never charged with any wrongdoing. So, from July 1995 to March 1998, Lonza and Reilly continued with U.S. price fixing on their own.

The choline chloride (B4) cartel began even earlier at a meeting in Toronto, Canada in January 1988. There the longtime vitamin B4 sales manager for Chinook, Ltd. (Russell E. Cosburn, employed from 1967-1992) hosted a meeting of the other two manufacturers of the vitamin in North America, the Ohio firm Bioproducts (owned by Mitsui of Japan) and DuCoa of Illinois, at the time a joint venture of DuPont and ConAgra. The three companies agreed to raise the North American price of choline chloride, to allocate specific customers, and to share the market equally. By the winter of 1989, market prices of choline chloride began to rise.

However, the higher North American prices attracted imports, mostly from Western Europe. The three big exporters were BASF (Germany), Akzo Nobel (the Netherlands), and UCB (Belgium). To address this problem, the three North American producers met with their three European counterparts in Mexico City in October 1992. A month later, the six met again at the headquarters of BASF in Ludwigshafen, Germany. There they agreed to stop exporting to each other's continents, to further allocate exclusive world sales territories, and to further raise the price of choline chloride all over the world. The six continued to meet regularly until April 1994 as a group. The last bilateral agreements ceased after June 1995, just about the time that DuCoa was acquired by another company. Neither DuCoa's old parents nor its new one were charged for price-fixing violations.

Chapter 11 Endnotes

[1] The European Union has charged several more companies with vitamin price fixing bringing the total to 23 (see Chapter 14).
[2] One small exception is the choline chloride (B4) cartel. BASF colluded in B4 in the European market and agreed not to sell B4 in North America.
[3] Guilty plea agreements of Lonza, Degussa, and Nepera state that their participation began "as early as January 1991." Nepera left the cartel in July 1995, about the time it was sold to Cambrex Corp. Degussa turned over its price fixing to its U.S. partner, Reilly Industries, at the same time. This cartel had more unindicted co-conspirators.
[4] The biggest vitamin sellers maintain lists of scores of varieties of one vitamin, while smaller companies tend to have narrower lines. Some are available in liquid or dry forms, and most come in human and feed grades; these are significant functional differences. Some varieties differ according to the strength of the active ingredient, type of inactive ingredients if any, and packaging. Despite this apparent heterogeneity, from the point of view of pricing, there tends to be one most common product form for which price quotes are made. All other varieties are then priced off this model product form by means of conventional, customary premia or discounts.
[5] This price round was reported to have been initiated by a smaller manufacturer of dry vitamin A from Denmark, DanoChemo.
[6] Based upon a private communication from a vitamin defendant's expert economist, who stated that sellers' transaction prices closely tracked list prices before and during the conspiracy.
[7] It is known that Wilson explored establishing a cartel in lactic acid, a food acidulant similar to citric acid. Other products believed to have cartelized by ADM include monosodium glutamate (MSG) and sodium gluconate. Corn sweeteners and methionine are other possibilities.
[8] Limiting fines only to future violations of prohibition orders strikes this author as one of the stranger handicaps facing a national antitrust authority.
[9] Some major Japanese vitamin companies that were not charged with conspiracy by U.S. antitrust authorities include Tanabe and Sumitomo. Mitsui had joined the B3 cartel in1989.
[10] These were the individuals indicted by the U.S. DOJ and forced to pay stiff fines or serve prison sentences. The Roche officers indicted were Kuno Sommer and Roland Brönnimann.
[11] Prices were fixed to the penny per kilogram and market shares were set to the nearest 0.5 percentage point.
[12] Andreas Hauri was global sales manager for both vitamins and citric acid (See chapter 5 above).
[13] Given the on-going grand jury investigation, it seems likely that one of the conditions for automatic amnesty was not met, so the amnesty was negotiated by its lawyers.
[14] Roche and Lonza both make the vitamin biotin.

Chapter 12

EFFECTS OF THE VITAMINS CARTELS

Like many pharmaceutical products, the consuming public has a high regard for the benefits and efficacy of vitamins. There is something particularly reprehensible about price-fixing schemes that affect products destined for vulnerable populations. Children, pregnant or lactating mothers, the sick, and the elderly often need supplementary vitamins to achieve full health. These groups, as well as meat eaters, ultimately paid the price of price fixing in vitamins. The purpose of this section is to document as precisely as possible the extent of these economic injuries.

PRICE EFFECTS

Bulk vitamins are homogeneous products with highly inelastic demand. Given the high concentration of sales in the hands of the cartel and the cartel's elaborate methods for detecting cheating, the ability to raise buyer's prices would be expected to be very high. DOJ officials who had seen the price data submitted by the cartel members were impressed with how cautious the sellers were in raising prices at the beginning of the conspiracy. Prices were increased slowly and in stages, rather than the sharp escalation seen in the lysine and citric acid cartels. By the time the cartels reached their peak pricing, U.S. transaction prices mostly were 24 to 40 percent higher than in the immediate pre-conspiracy period. However, the transaction price of one type of vitamin A experienced a 71-percent increase from February 1990 to November 1998 (Barboza 1999). Even more impressive was the decline in vitamin prices observed after the government announced the guilty pleas in May 1999. An analyst at SRI Consulting, which follows the chemicals industries closely, stated that the vast majority of vitamins prices had collapsed by 50 percent within two months, causing sellers' margins to approach zero. If true, the post-conspiracy price reductions brought vitamin prices to a level 30 to 40 percent *lower* than pre-conspiracy levels. This suggests that the post-conspiracy period was far more competitive than the pre-conspiracy period. That is, the competitive regimes in most global vitamins markets went through three phases from 1989 to 1999. They switched from oligopoly pricing (probably non-cooperative or tacit) to monopoly to highly competitive.

The price changes just discussed were measured in U.S. dollars. Multinational companies generally seek to maximize the company's global profits.[1] Because the principal members of the cartel were based in Europe or

Japan, they would want to set local prices from the point of view of their home-country's currency. Moreover, more than half of the bulk vitamins sold in the United States in the 1990s were imported from Europe, Japan, and China. Because the U.S. dollar strengthened against the home-country currencies of the cartel participants, higher vitamin prices observed in the U.S. market could be due to two independent causes: collusion and currency-rate changes. For example, if a cartelized U.S. vitamin price rose by 70 percent and if the product was imported from Switzerland, a rise in the value of the Swiss frank of 20 percent over the same period would imply that collusion was responsible for raising the U.S. price by only 42 percent. An increase in Swiss manufacturing costs would also moderate the collusive effect on U.S. prices.

The *Journal of Commerce* price surveys provide useful illustrations of the beginning of a conspiracy and its most effective period up to the end of formal conspiring. Although these data cover only list prices quoted to buyers and buyers' actual spot prices, the effects on contract prices should be seen after a delay of six to 12 months. However, list and spot prices seem to take two or three years to fall after a significant drop in contract prices. That is, the lag between list and transaction prices is relatively brief when list prices rise, but quite long after the point when large discounts begin to appear on transaction prices.

The U.S. price effects of the vitamin cartels are shown in several figures on the next few pages. For simplicity, we begin with the prices for the longest lasting of the conspiracies: vitamins A, E, B5, and B12. These four conspiracies share three common characteristics. Each of these began in the first quarter of 1990 or 1991 and lasted for eight to ten years. Each was instigated by Roche and BASF, but grew to encompass four more conspirators (Rhône-Poulenc, Eisai, Daiichi, and Hoechst). Finally, none of these products was affected by significant imports from China or other areas of the world with non participants.

Figures 12.1 and 12.2 illustrate the movement of prices for the two main types of vitamin A, a liquid or oil version and a dry powder. From early 1990 until the end of 1997, the prices for liquid oil and dry vitamin A followed closely parallel paths. Both started out with a pre-conspiracy price in the low $30 per kg. area, and both remained at the $60 plateau for two years. In both cases, the price increases in the first conspiracy year of 1990 were modest compared to the late 1991-late 1992 price increases; the main reason is that the cartel initially controlled only 72 percent of global output in 1990, but after Rhône-Poulenc joined, the three controlled 95 percent.

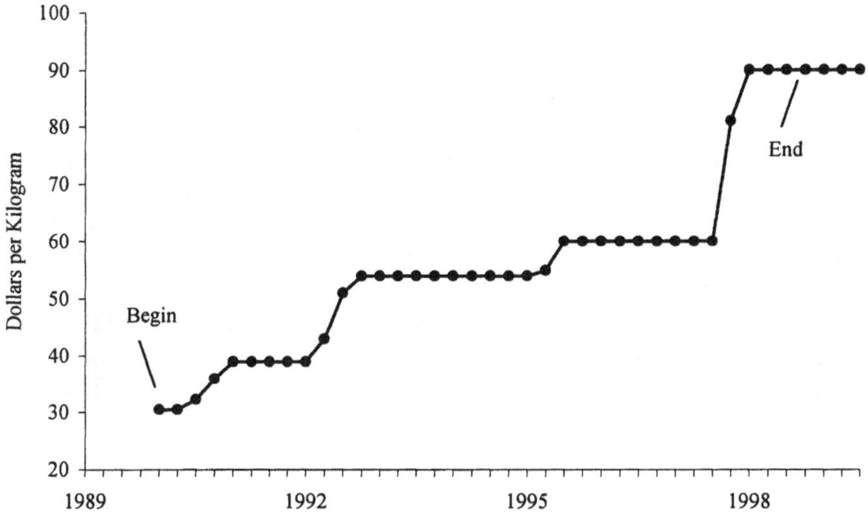

Figure 12.1. List and Spot Prices of Liquid Vitamin A, 1990-1999.

Source: *Journal of Commerce*, quarterly average of 1.7 million international units per gram vitamin A in oil.

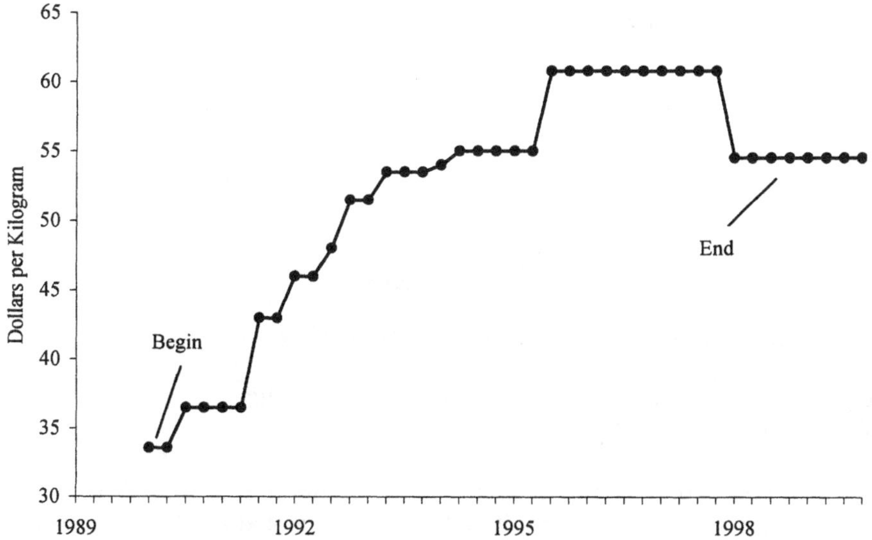

Figure 12.2. List and Spot Prices of Dry Vitamin A, 1990-1999.

Source: *Journal of Commerce*, quarterly average prices of vitamin A acetate, type 500 (5000,000 international units/gram).

A puzzling divergence between liquid vitamin A and dry vitamin A prices is evidenced in late 1997. List and spot prices of the liquid version *rise* another $30, whereas dry vitamin A prices are *cut* by 10 percent. At the end of the cartel's life, list prices for liquid vitamin A were almost *triple* their pre-conspiracy levels. Even after the penultimate-year price cut, dry vitamin A was 62 percent above the pre-conspiracy price. Liquid vitamin A is used primarily in food and pharmaceutical applications, but this is dwarfed by the much greater volume of vitamin A being purchased for feed use (almost all of it dry powder). Thus, the dry prices are more representative of spot market transactions for vitamin A as a whole. Nevertheless, what was behind the cartel's end game in vitamin A pricing remains a mystery.

The pattern of price increases in the U.S. market for vitamin E is very similar to that of dry vitamin A (Figure 12.3).

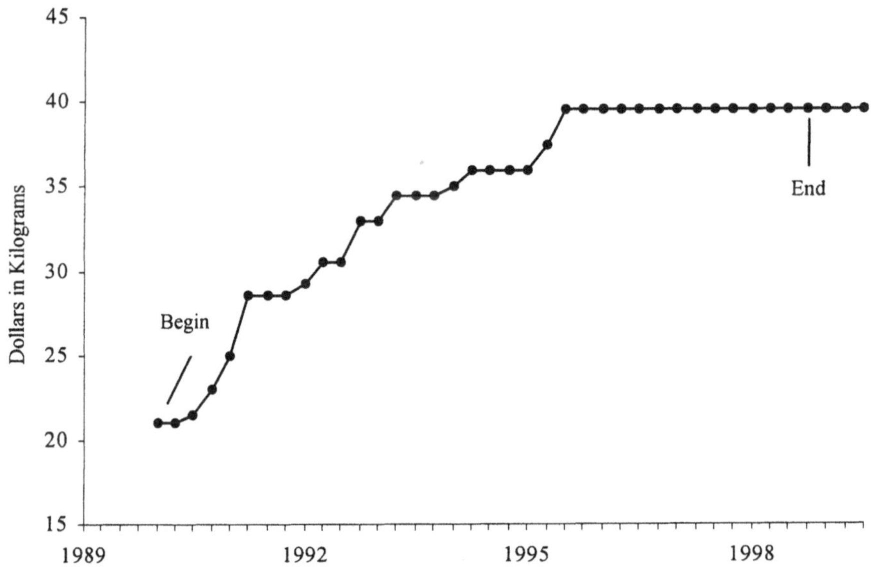

Figure 12.3. List and Spot Prices of Bulk Vitamin E, 1990-1999.

Source: *Journal of Commerce*, quarterly average prices of liquid, USP-grade, di-α-tocopherol acetate.

List and spot vitamin E prices rise after the middle of 1991 (when there were only two conspirators with 64 percent of global production), pause a bit in 1992, continue their steep rise until the third quarter of 1995 (at that time with four members that controlled 87 percent of the industry), and then flatten out. After twelve quarterly price increases, the price comes to rest 88 percent above its pre-conspiracy starting point. Because sales of vitamin E are the largest of all, these price increases will translate into the greatest of the consumer overcharges in absolute dollar terms. Although vitamin D was not a product for which U.S. or Canadian prosecutors brought price-fixing charges, it is often sold mixed with vitamin E for fortification of dairy products. Roche and BASF controlled nearly 60 percent of vitamin D production, and the French firm Solvay-Duphar supplies most of the rest. Collusion on the price of vitamin D by Roche and BASF alone could have been just possible, but Solvay's passive participation would have helped to firm prices. Whatever the degree of Solvay's cooperation, what is obvious is that vitamin D prices moved in tandem with those of vitamin E (compare Figures 12.3 and 12.4). Again, both rise after the quarter of 1990, pause a bit in 1991, and after seven upward movements vitamin D prices come to rest 47 percent above their starting point. These parallel price movements do not in any sense provide more than circumstantial evidence of a conspiracy in vitamin D, but the circumstances do seem compelling.

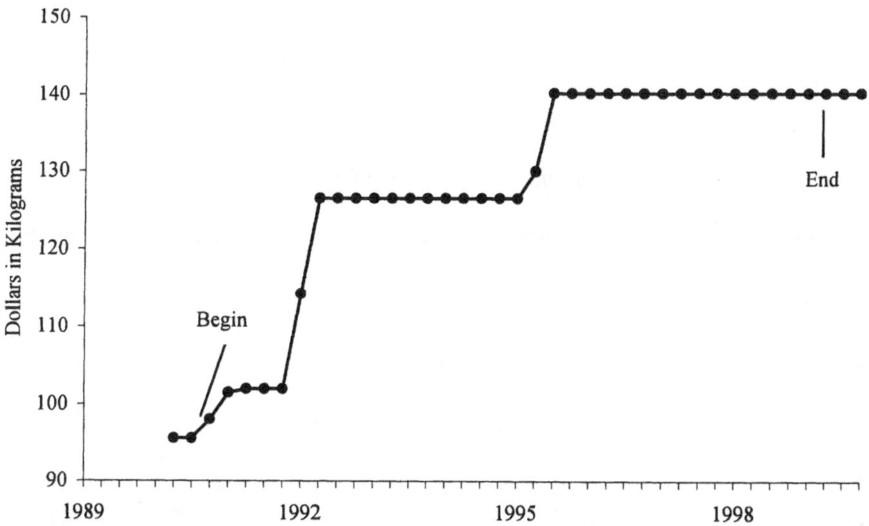

Figure 12.4. List and Spot Prices of Bulk Vitamin D-3, 1989-1999.

Source: *Journal of Commerce*, quarterly average spot prices of grade 850 vitamin D-3.

In the next two cases, companies began colluding in January 1991 (a year later than A and E), yet the list prices of B5 and B12 show a large number of similarities (Figures 12.5 and 12.6). Price increases moved up soon after the talks began. After five to seven steps upward, both vitamins settle on a long-lasting plane in the third quarter of 1995. (Vitamin A and E prices also plateaued in the same quarter). The price plateaus from 1995 to 1998 were 61 to 54 percent above their respective pre-conspiracy levels. All in all, the strong similarities in the list and spot price movements for vitamins A, E, D, B5, and B12 are remarkable. Given the different mix of raw materials and composition of demand for each vitamin, the chances that these prices were driven by competitive market forces in the 1990s are dim indeed.

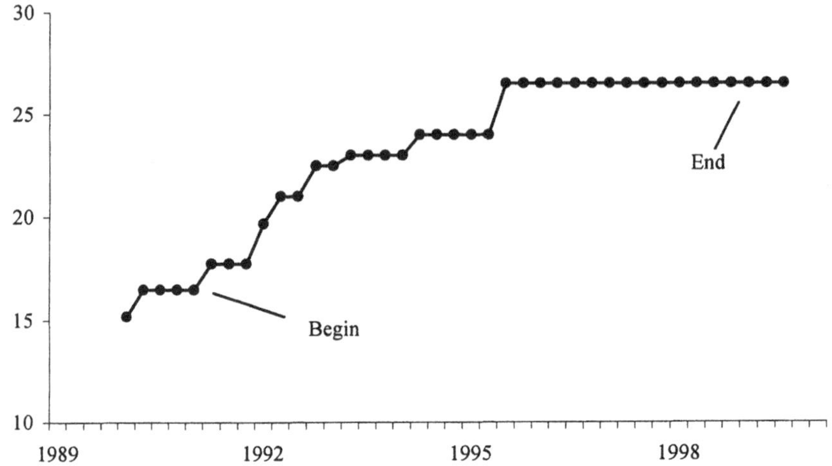

Figure 12.5. List and Spot Prices of Vitamin B-5, 1990-1999.

Source: *Journal of Commerce*, quarterly average prices of calcium pantotheonate, USP grade.

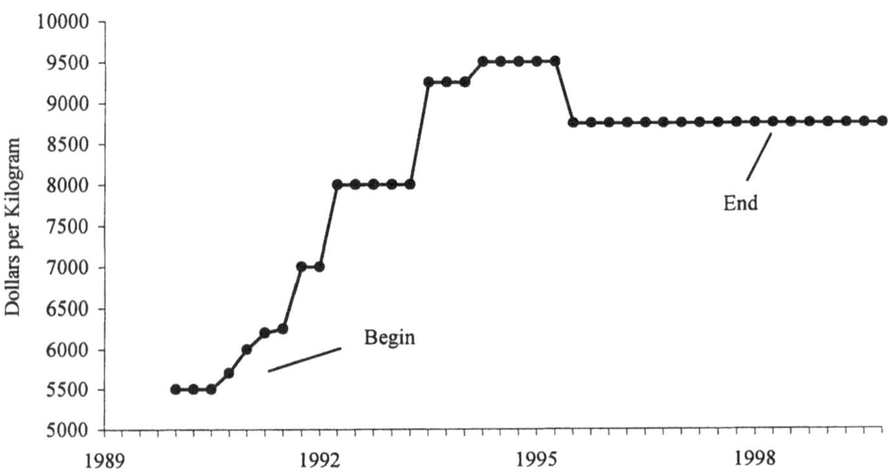

Figure 12.6. List and Spot Prices of Bulk Vitamin B-12, 1990-1999.

Source: *Journal of Commerce*, quarterly average prices of crystallized B-12, cyanocobalamin.

The second group of vitamins (C, B1, B2, B6, and folic acid) display price movements quite different from A, E, D, B5 and B12. The second group was beset by a declining cartel share of the world market in the mid 1990s. Chinese producers in particular were aggressively seeking increases in shares of world sales, a trend that intensified in the mid 1990s. Consequently, these conspiracies ended earlier than the others. They all started in 1991 but lasted only four or five full years. Another common feature of these five product markets was the participation of Takeda or Daiichi in at least one of the industries; perhaps these companies were less committed to the cartels, but more likely the cartels disbanded by mutual agreement when their abilities to control supply eroded.

List and spot prices for vitamins C, B1, B2, B6, and folic acid are shown in Figures 12.7 to 12.11. In each case, prices rose after the first agreement was made in early 1991. However, it appears that B1 and B6 prices rose only slightly above pre-conspiracy prices. For the other three, when prices reached a plateau after the first year or two, the increases were in the 22 to 38 percent range – roughly half the increases seen in the first group of vitamins. This weaker ability to raise prices is not unexpected. The top six vitamin makers in these cartels controlled a mere 58 percent of global output (versus 82 percent for the first group). Thus, even without the Chinese challenge, this latter group had less market control from the beginning of the conspiracies. Another notable feature of Figures 12.7 to 12.11 is that list prices collapsed after the cartels were abandoned in all but the folic acid case. On average the price breaks took almost 18 months.

The vitamins B3 (niacin) and B4 (choline chloride) cases are so different from the first two groups that they are treated separately. Besides list prices, there are reasonable proxies for transaction prices available, so plotting both together is possible and gives additional insight.

The vitamin B3 cartel was the first to be prosecuted by U.S. antitrust authorities (see Chapter 13). The world's leading manufacturer of vitamin B3, Lonza, pleaded guilty in September 1998, but the company's plea was kept under seal until March 1999. Lonza's guilty plea was vague on the dates of the vitamin B3 conspiracy, merely noting that it began as early as January 1992 and ended sometime around March 1998. Although Lonza's cooperation was secured for the B3 investigation, delays in announcing further guilty pleas suggested that the probe had run into roadblocks. However, it seems clear from press leaks and the structure of the industry that Lonza's co-conspirators were the New York manufacturer Napera and the Indiana manufacturer Vitachem or its joint owners. Vitachem is a joint venture between the large German chemical firm Degussa and a smaller Indiana firm, Reilly Industries. The locus of the price-fixing decisions may be one factor complicating the investigation. However, the three firms controlled more than 90 percent of the global market for niacin, with Lonza accounting for two-thirds of the presumptive cartel's sales. In the U.S. market the three producers had more equal shares, but they totaled more than 90 percent. The U.S. vitamin B3 market was not affected by large Chinese imports.[2]

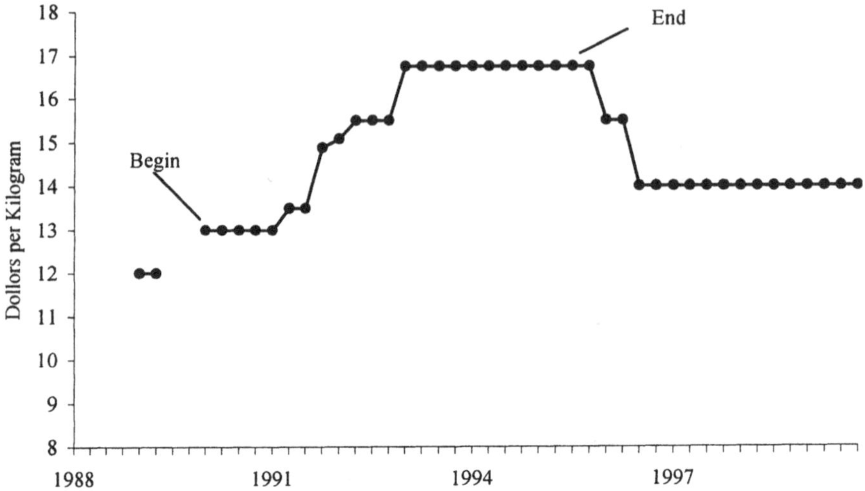

Figure 12.7. List and Spot Prices of Bulk Vitamin C, 1989-1999.

Source: *Journal of Commerce*, quarterly average prices of l-ascorbic acid, USP-grade, f.o.b. plant. No price data available for 3rd quarter 1989 to 1st quarter 1990.

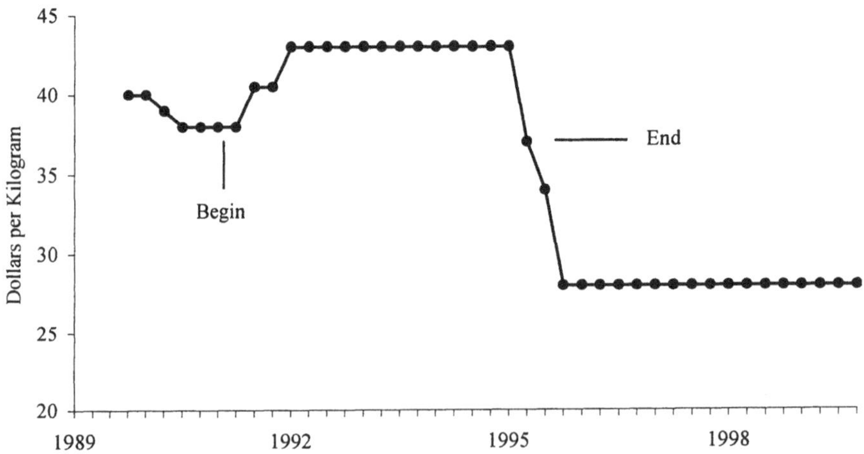

Figure 12.8. List and Spot Prices of Bulk Vitamin B-1, 1989-1999.

Source: *Journal of Commerce*, quarterly average spot prices of thiamin hydrochloride.

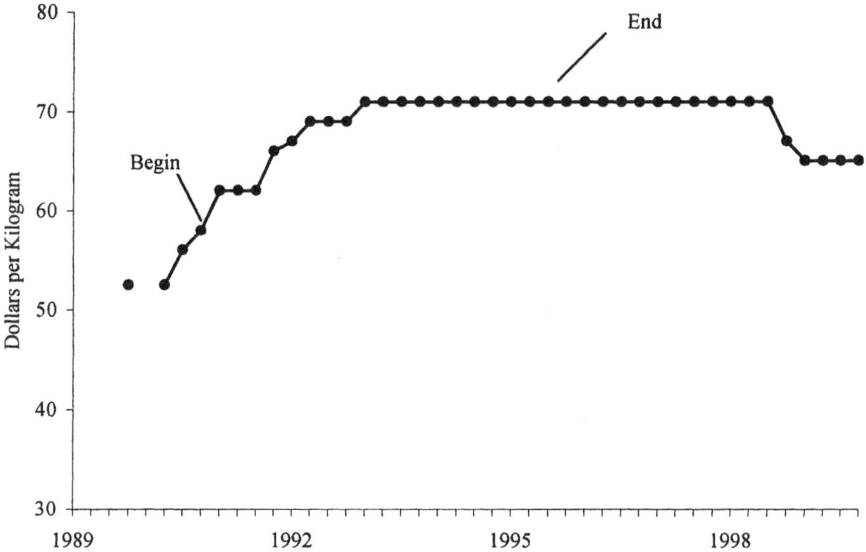

Figure 12.9. List Prices of Vitamin B-2, 1989-1999.

Source: *Journal of Commerce*, quarterly average prices of USP-grade riboflavin. No prices available for 1st quarter 1990.

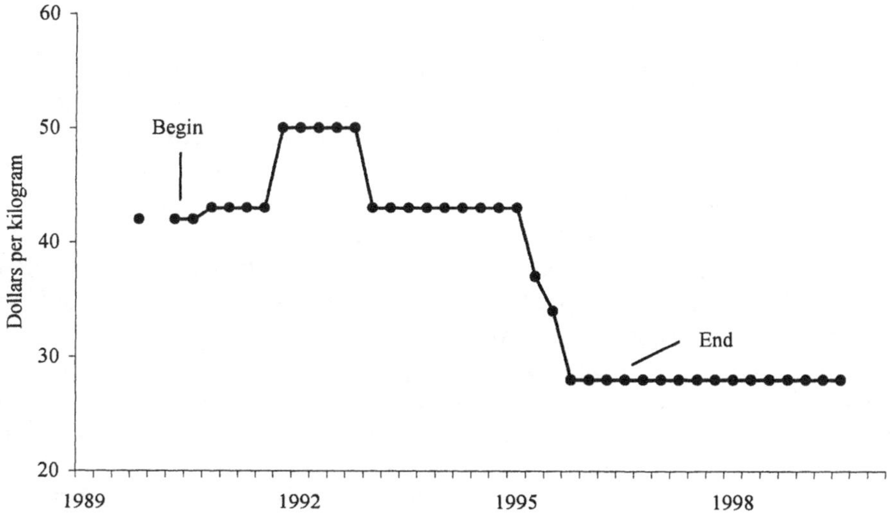

Figure 12.10. List and Spot Prices of Bulk Vitamin B-6, 1989-1999.

Source: *Journal of Commerce*, quarterly average prices of pyridoxine hydorchloride. No price available 1st quarter 1990.

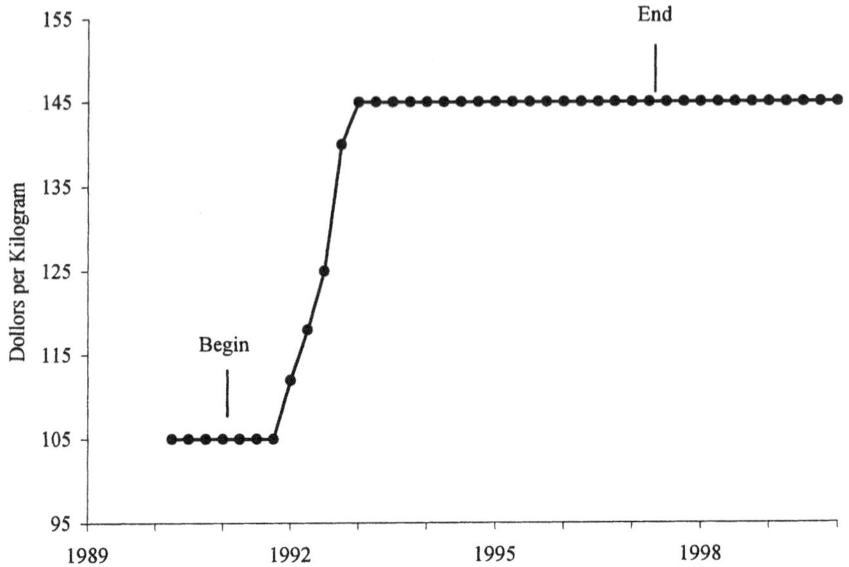

Figure 12.11. List Prices of Bulk Folic Acid, 1990-1999.

Source: *Journal of Commerce*, quarterly average spot prices of USP-grade folic acid.

The list price data traced for bulk vitamin B3 are consistent with a price-fixing conspiracy that began as early as 1988 but probably no later than the end of 1990 (Figure 12.12). After some minor fluctuations in list and spot prices in 1990, including a 9 percent blip in the third quarter of the year that had to be withdrawn. However, the large price increases in 1991 of 32 percent do stick. Prices reached at the end of 1991 remain fairly constant for more than five years. After one final attempt to raise prices to a yet higher plane in mid 1997, list prices collapsed throughout 1998 back to their original pre-conspiracy or early conspiracy levels.

Trade data provide a fairly good proxy for U.S. transaction prices for vitamin B3.[3] It is known that Lonza's main production facility was located in Switzerland, though it may have also operated a small Texas plant for making some vitamin B3. U.S. import prices from Switzerland are shown in Figure 12.13 as transaction prices. A modest but distinct rise in transaction prices of 33 to 37 percent occurred between 1990 and 1992-1995. (If the conspiracy began in 1998, the maximum price increase was an immodest 70 percent). Transaction prices of B3 fell in 1996 and 1997, which suggests that the cartel's collusive power began to erode two years before the formal end of the conspiracy in March 1998 or thereabouts. In other words, the vitamin B3 cartel began to lose its ability to prevent cheating in its last two years of formal collusion. The large gap between announced list prices and transaction prices also hints at problems that made B3 one of the less effective cartels.

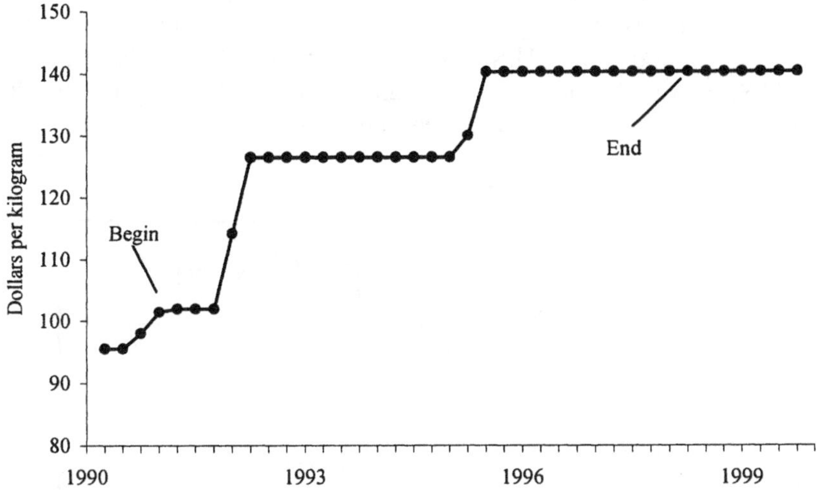

Figure 12.12. List and Spot Prices of Bulk Niacinamide ("B-3"), 1989-1999.

Source: *Journal of Commerce*, quarterly average prices of feed-grade niacinamide, 100% dry-substance basis 5Kt delivered. For 1988 and 1989, prices were \$5.60 and \$6.10, respectively, from *Chemical Market Report*.

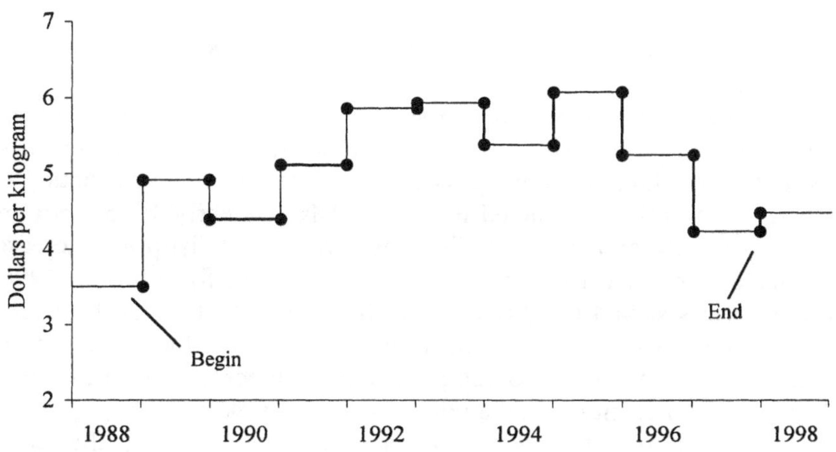

Figure 12.13. Estimated Transaction Prices of Bulk Niacin and Niacinamide ("B-3"), 1988-1999.

Sources: STAT-USA average annual prices from Switzerland, almost all from Lonza, an admitted price conspirator; 5 cents per kg. added for transportation.

In contrast, transaction prices of choline chloride (B4) pulled up close to list prices during this cartel's middle and late stages (Figure 12.14). The vitamin B4 conspiracy lasted from January 1988 to September 29, 1998; at nearly 11 years, it was the longest of the vitamin cartels. Top officers of the Canadian firm Chinook and a U.S. manufacturer named DuCoa have pleaded guilty in U.S. courts. A third large U.S. maker of B4, the Bioproducts, Inc. subsidiary of Mitsui Co., may be indicted in the future.[4]

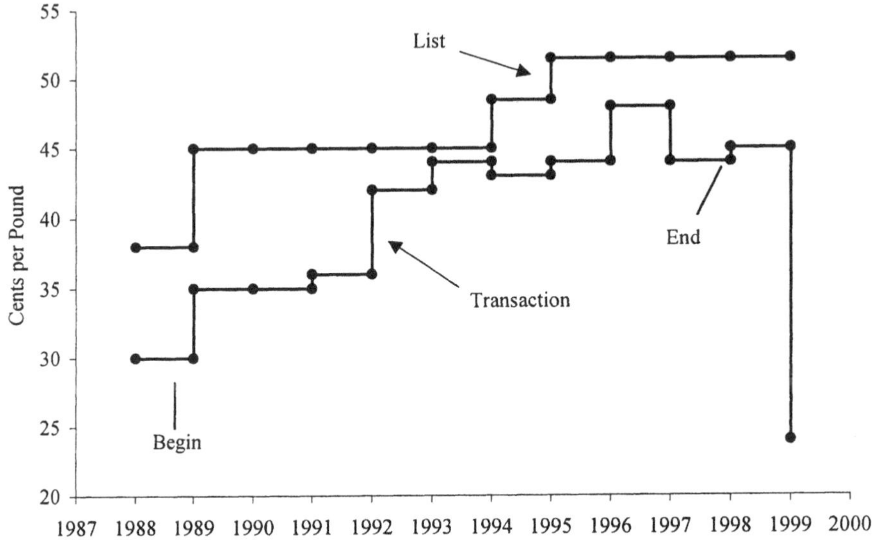

Figure 12.14. U.S. List and Transaction Prices of Choline Chloride ("B-4"), 1988-2000.

Both the list and transaction prices of vitamin B4 responded quickly to the initiation of price fixing. Both prices jumped 17 to 18 percent in the cartel's first year, 1990. While list prices held constant at $0.45 per pound for five years, selling prices ratcheted up relentlessly. By early 1995, spot and contract prices were almost equal. Two more rounds of list-price increases failed to have much effect on transaction prices (except for a blip in 1996). Transaction prices stayed roughly constant from 1995 to 1998 at 45 percent above their preconspiracy levels. In 1999, a year after the cartel ceased operating, B4 prices plunged to $0.24 per pound B 20 percent lower than their 1988 level and 50 percent lower than their cartel-era peak in 1996.

To summarize, the price increases achieved during the cartel compared to pre- or post-conspiracy prices were high. For the long-lasting cartels, average price mark-ups achieved were between 35 and 75 percent; peak price elevations were in the 60 to 100 percent range (Table 12.1). The briefer cartels, which had less market control, exhibited monopoly prices 12 to 45 percent above more competitive levels – lower but still impressive.

Table 12. 1. Summary of Vitamins Cartels' Price Impacts.

Product	Types of Prices	Price Increases[a]			
		Average During Conspiracy		Maximum During Conspiracy	
		Mark-up	Margin	Mark-up	Margin
		Percent			
Long Lasting Cartels:					
Vitamin A	List & spot	60-70	25-30	80	45
Vitamin E	List & spot	55-65	30-40	90	95
Vitamin D	List & spot	30-35	20-25	45	30
Vitamin B3	Transaction	13-30	15-35	40-79	37-70
Vitamin B5	List & spot	35-45	20-30	60	38
Vitamin B12	List & spot	40-50	30-35	78	42
Vitamin B4	Transaction	35-50	25-30	60-100	38-50
Shorter Cartels:					
Vitamin C	List & spot	15-20	10-20	28	25
Vitamin B1	List & spot	8-10	8-12	12	36
Vitamin B2	List & spot	8-18	10-20	34	25
Vitamin B6	List & spot	4-30	5-40	15-50	13-44
Folic acid	List & spot	15-20	20-25	38	28

Sources: Figures 12.2 and 12.13.
[a] Average price during conspiracy less the pre-conspiracy price (or in the case of vitamins B1, B4, and B6 post-conspiracy also) divided by the selling price.

PROFITS

Price increases of the type just described were bound to increase seller profits to extraordinary levels. What profit rates were prior to collusion is impossible to learn with any precision because the cartel members did not report operating profits separately for their vitamins lines of business. Vitamins were usually part of some broader corporate division called specialty or fine chemicals. Whole-company profits are not particularly useful indicators because they were affected by the high profits normally found in pharmaceutical businesses or the lower profit rates associated with other bulk organic chemicals. However, as a rough guess, pretax profits on vitamins prior to cartel formation were probably in the range of 5 to 15 percent of sales (Connor 2000:Appendix F). Because the additional management costs of operating "Vitamins, Inc." were small relative to the increase in sales, even a minimal cartel price elevation would double a conspirator's profit rate on sales.[5] During the long-lasting cartels' most effective years, vitamin profit rates will have increased by a factor of six to ten times pre-conspiracy rates.

The true test of the cartels' effects on company profits will come during fiscal years 2000 to 2005 when the monopoly profits have disappeared and the impacts of the large U.S. and Canadian fines no longer distort profit statements. Stock analysts have spent considerable effort in calculating the effects of the fines on defendants' earnings. Hoffmann-La Roche paid the biggest U.S. fine, $500 million (see Chapter 13). The fine represented 17 percent of the company's FY 1998 net income from all lines of business and 20 percent of its sales of vitamins and fine chemicals division. It is quite likely that this fine wiped out Roche's total profits from vitamins for 1998 as Roche's CEO claimed in a 1999 interview and possibly 1997 as well, but it is well to recall that Roche's illegal activities generated excess profits for *nine* years, not just one or two. However, in considering whether the vitamins conspiracy may yet yield net profits for Roche, other post-cartel costs must be added. Fines imposed by Canada, the EU, and other jurisdictions will likely amount to $125 million; civil suits in the United States and Canada will cost Roche at least $750 million (see Chapter 16); and Roche is bearing legal defense costs of several tens of millions of dollars.[6] If, as expected, Roche's antitrust outlays reach $1.4 to $1.6 billion, then there is a chance that the company may have been forced to disgorge most or all of its illegal profits. The next section tries to address this question.

CUSTOMER OVERCHARGES

Profits generated by price fixing are a transfer of income from customers to the stockholders of the companies in the cartel (see Chapter 2). Vitamin buyers who had no choice but to continue making purchases at the cartel-inflated prices simply overpaid. The amount of this overpayment is called the customer overcharge. The size of the vitamin overcharges is vitally important information for assessing felony fines in the United States and for judging the adequacy of civil antitrust settlements. Calculating the overcharge requires knowledge about the prices actually charged, the volume purchased during the conspiracy period, and the price that would have reigned in the market absent collusion, which is called the but-for price. Usually buyers or sellers can assemble accounting data on transaction prices and quantities purchased in the appropriate market period. Occasionally, the appropriate dates of the affected period are a matter of contention between plaintiffs and defendants, though a prior guilty plea usually provides *prima facie* evidence on the conspiracy dates. Lags in implementing a price agreement may delay price effects early in a conspiracy. Price lags following the termination of a conspiracy will generate overcharges, but defendants will rarely wish to acknowledge responsibility for these carry-over effects. Most of the disagreement between plaintiffs and defendants will focus on the but-for price. Alternative methods of economic analysis can be used to arrive at the but-for price, several of which require information that defendants will be reluctant to provide to plaintiffs.

Overcharges are estimated as a routine matter by economists assisting prosecutors at the antitrust agencies as they weigh the seriousness of price-fixing charges, which concessions to offer to defendants in order to extract a guilty-plea agreement, and the size of fines or prison sentences to seek from the courts (see Chapter 3). U.S. fines that are determined under the new U.S. Sentencing Guidelines require the government to calculate and reveal the "base fine," which is either 20 percent of affected sales or double the defendants' price-fixing overcharges. Overcharges are also central to both parties in civil antitrust suits. Lawyers representing plaintiffs must present fair and reasonable claims in class action suits, and these are often revealed in briefs submitted to the courts. Lawyers representing defendants often have their own estimates, but rarely make these public, except implicitly when making an offer to settle a treble-damages case. Plaintiffs' counsel tend to exaggerate the seriousness of their clients' case by making various assumptions that lead to generous estimates of the overcharges, though this is not always the case.

On May 20, 1999, the U.S. DOJ announced the guilty pleas it had obtained from the three leading price fixers, Roche, BASF, and Rhône-Poulenc. Joel Klein, head of the DOJ's Antitrust Division, was asked how large the U.S. overcharges were on vitamins, but this question only elicited the vague response that they were "hundreds of millions of dollars." At the sentencing hearing in federal court in Dallas, Texas the same day, the DOJ was required to be more precise when it explained the basis for its proposed fines on Roche and BASF. The government's indictments specified price fixing on seven vitamin products and the conspiracy periods.[7] The U.S. overcharges implied for Roche alone were in the range of $350 to $550 million. With information on Roche's U.S. market shares for these vitamins during the conspiracy period and the sales of other vitamin products for which guilty pleas were later made, it is possible to extrapolate Roche's overcharges to the broader markets for vitamins. The total U.S. vitamins overcharges implied by Roche's is estimated to be $850 to $1,350 million. As the affected sales during the conspiracy claimed by sources within the DOJ were $5 to $6 billion, the percentage overcharge on bulk vitamin purchases becomes 15 to 25 percent.[8]

The size of the vitamin overcharges came up again during and after settlement talks between the Big Six defendants and private plaintiffs. In November 1999, these defendants offered to pay members of the federal class $1.17 billion to settle the treble-damages suit brought as a federal class action. There were some differences of opinion between the class counsel, who ended up representing mostly smaller claimants, and attorneys for the larger buyers in the class. The first group of lawyers consistently represented the settlement as a generous one. Robert Silver of the lead counsel firm Boies & Schiller opined that the recovery amounted to about 20 percent of U.S. purchases of vitamins during the affected periods. He stated that the $1.17 billion "somewhat exceeds" the overcharges paid by direct buyers on roughly $5.5 billion of vitamin purchases. However, Kenneth Adams of Dickstein Shapiro, who represented almost 100 of the larger buyers of vitamins, believed that the vitamins overcharges were considerably larger. His economic experts were working with a somewhat larger affected sales of about $7 billion.[9] Adams asserted that the average percentage overcharge was 33 percent on the seven products sold by the Big Six defendants, or $2.3 billion. Extrapolating plaintiffs' counsel estimates to defendants beyond the Big Six (which accounted for 86 percent of sales) and beyond the seven products, the total U.S. overcharges amount to $1.6 billion (Silver's estimate) or $3.1 billion (Adams' estimate). The methods used to obtain these estimates were not revealed, but most likely they were based on the before-and-after approach. In sum, both the government's and the plaintiffs' estimates of the U.S. overcharges fell within the range of 15 to 33 percent of the affected sales!

These broad estimates can be broken down by market. Global and U.S. sales were shown above in Table 10.2. These can be converted to affected sales with the growth rates shown in Table 10.4 and by identifying the conspiracy dates. Finally, the average overcharge margins (not the mark-ups) shown in Table 12.1 can be multiplied into the estimated affected sales. This approach assumes that the cartels were able to achieve the price effects seen in U.S. markets to their sales all over the world.

The overcharges estimated by the author are shown for each vitamin market in Table 12.2.[10] For the U.S. market, which accounts for about one-fifth of global sales of vitamins, the overcharges totaled $1.2 to $1.5 billion for the twelve products shown (Connor 2001). As a proportion of affected sales, the price fixing overcharges were 25 to 28 percent, which is close to the middle of the rates suggested by the prosecutors and plaintiffs' counsel.

The three biggest vitamin markets accounted for 75 percent of the U.S. dollar overcharge. Vitamin E is both the largest market in terms of sales and the largest in terms of overcharge rate. Vitamins A and C are correspondingly lower in affected sales and percentage overcharge. The remaining products are all over the map. By construction, the global overcharges have the same percentages as the U.S. estimates, but the large sales outside the United States boost the overcharge to the $7 to $8 billion range. The global estimates may not be as accurate as those for the United States because U.S. prices were employed to calculate the global percentage overcharges. Nevertheless, these estimates suggest that the 17 participating conspirators made at least $7 billion in monopoly profits from their 1988-1999 conspiracies. Moreover, Roche alone was responsible for nearly half of the affected sales, so the company's profits were in all likelihood at least $3 billion and possibly as high as $4 billion. Recall that Roche's antitrust outlays were estimated to be $1.4 to $1.6 billion. Thus, purely from a benefit/cost perspective Hoffmann-La Roche profited mightily from its role in the vitamins cartel.

Table 12.2. Estimated U.S. and Global Vitamins Overcharges, 1989-1999.

Product Market	Conspiracy Dates	Affected Global Sales[a]	U.S. Average Overcharge	Dollar Overcharges	
				U.S.	World
		$ millions	*Percent*	*Million dollars*	
Vitamin A	Jan.1990-Feb.1999	5,740	25-30	207-248	1,435-1,722
Vitamin E	Jan.1990-Feb.1999	10,840	35	584	3,794
Vitamin C	Jan.1991-Dec.1995	4,000	11-23	120-295	440-920
Vitamin B1	Jan.1991-Dec.1994	272	9-10	8-9	24-27
Vitamin B2	Jan.1991-Dec.1995	695	12-19	19-31	83-132
Vitamin B3	Jan.1992-Mar.1998[c]	847	33	83	280
Vitamin B4	Jan.1988-Dec.1998	2,805	9-10	55-61	252-281
Vitamin B5	Jan.1991-Dec.1998	1,288	25	43	322
Vitamin B6	Jan.1991-Dec.1994	356	4-40	4-36	14-142
Vitamin B12	Jan.1991-Dec.1994	32	33	4	11
Folic acid	Jan.1991-Dec.1994	64	23	6	15
Beta carotene	Jan.1991-Dec.1998	1,080	25-30[b]	87-105	270-324
Total		28,019	25-28	1,220-1,505	6,940-7,970

Sources: Connor (2001b)

[a] 1995 sales projected to cartel period. Does not include premixes.

[b] Assumed to be the same as vitamin A.

[c] Might have started two years earlier.

Chapter 12 Endnotes

[1] In the simplest cases, a multinational's stockholders and its listing stock market will be located in the company's headquarters country. For Roche that is Switzerland, and thus Roche would aim to maximize profits calculated in Swiss franks.
[2] China's 1996 U.S. imports were less than 2 percent of U.S. supply. All other imports were from conspirator's home countries: Switzerland, Germany, and Belgium.
[3] Import prices include freight charges to the port of import, but do not include delivery costs to U.S. customers. Although illegal, Lonza could have misreported the value of its U.S. imports, especially those to its own U.S. sales branch. Low U.S. tariffs make this scenario unlikely.
[4] In Canada, Chinook, DuCoa, and Bioproducts were indicted and pleaded guilty. Also, the four leading European producers of B4 (BASF, Akzo Nobel, and UCB) pleaded guilty to restraining exports to Canada for three years. The latter charge was not part of the U.S. indictments.
[5] Profit rates on investment or net assets would increase more than proportionately.
[6] There may be substantial losses of intangible, goodwill capital as well. Disruption of investment plans is also a possible outcome. These are more difficult to quantify.
[7] The products were vitamins A, E, C, B2, B5, beta carotene, and premixes. The conspiracies began in January 1990 or January 1991 and mostly ended around December 1998, except for C and B2, which ended in late 1995. See Chapter 6 for details.
[8] The affected U.S. sales apparently exclude premix sales. Including such sales might involve a double counting of overcharges on some vitamins manufactured by the premix sellers. Sales were reported by Barboza (1999).
[9] The $7 billion probably includes the sales of premixes by the defendants, which one can infer was in the neighborhood of $2 billion. However, these sales exclude sales of vitamins B1, B3, B4, B6, B12, biotin, and folic acid, which would add slightly more than $1 billion in sales.
[10] These estimates were prepared by the author and extrapolated to cover sales of vitamin manufactures smaller than the Big Six. The estimates are built upon several conservative assumptions using the before-and-after method.

Chapter 13

U.S. GOVERNMENT PROSECUTION OF THE CARTELS

The United States Department of Justice (DOJ) began investigating allegations of price fixing in the market for lysine in late 1992.[1] Tape recordings made by an informant of conversations among the lysine conspirators contained language that suggested that parallel conspiracies were ongoing in the citric acid and corn sweeteners industries. Separately, information about possible price fixing in the markets for bulk vitamins came to the attention of the DOJ. In 1995 and 1997, four grand juries were formed to consider the evidence held by the DOJ. Three of the four grand juries determined that there was probable cause for indicting certain companies and individuals for criminal violations of the Sherman Antitrust Act. The DOJ negotiated guilty pleas with a large number of companies and key managers of those companies. However, three executives who refused to such a plea bargain were tried and found guilty in a 1998 federal court. In the late 1990s, officials in an unprecedented number of countries piggybacked on the DOJ's indictments and brought charges against many of the same defendants for violations of their competition laws.

The purpose of this chapter is to recount and assess the investigations and prosecutions of four alleged price fixing schemes by the DOJ and its investigative arm, the FBI. The following chapters 14 and 15 will consider enforcement actions overseas and civil suits, respectively, against the same set of defendants. The latter suits are usually termed "private" civil actions. Unlike the cases brought by public prosecutors, the private suits are mostly class actions. The two types of suits involve different legal powers, strategies, standards of proof, and consequences.

THE ANTITRUST DIVISION

The Antitrust Division is an agency of the U.S. Department of Justice. The head of the division, the Assistant Attorney General for Antitrust, is nominated by the President, confirmed by the Senate, and reports directly to the Attorney General. The Division is relatively small as federal agencies go, with less than 1000 employees, but it has formidable legal powers to enforce the Sherman and Clayton Acts.[2] It is in effect the sole federal agency empowered to bring criminal indictments for alleged antitrust violations.[3] The Antitrust Division has a cadre of experienced career lawyers and economists serving in positions just below the political appointees, aided by a select group of younger attorneys who spend a number of years with the Division before leaving for positions at private law firms. When a possible criminal violation of the nation's antitrust laws come to its attention, the Federal Bureau of Investigation (FBI) assists the Division by collecting information from witnesses and other sources. The decision about whether to indict violators is left to the lawyers if they and a grand jury believe there is probable cause.

Beginning in the early 1980s, the Antitrust Division experienced deep cuts in the size of its professional staff of lawyers and economists and in the real size of its budget (Preston and Connor 1992). Although none of the formal authority of the Antitrust Division was diminished, the cuts imposed by the Reagan administration were concrete indicators of a desire for less aggressive enforcement of many areas of the federal antitrust laws. By the late 1980s during the Bush administration, the Division's resources had stabilized and the pace of enforcement had quickened somewhat since the early part of the decade. While the DOJ had never departed from its formal commitment to rigorous enforcement of the price fixing laws, relatively few important cartel cases had been launched since the electrical-equipment conspiracy cases of 1960.

In August 1992, Anne K. Bingaman was appointed Assistant Attorney General for Antitrust in the new Clinton Administration. Bingaman often said that she wanted to restore respect for the antitrust laws. She was perceived as more populist and activist than her two immediate predecessors and more prone to pursue difficult prosecutions. In retrospect, Bingaman's tenure may be seen as a watershed in antitrust enforcement. As pointed out by Eleanor Fox of New York University's law school, the main shift in priorities in the 1990s was a greater emphasis in global antitrust enforcement (*Washington Post* March 30, 1997: C1).

However, as the DOJ learned to its dismay in 1994, the prosecution of global cartels is fraught with practical difficulties. One of Bingaman's first decisions was to approve the indictment of General Electric and De Beers Consolidated for global price fixing in the market for industrial diamonds. De Beers, a South African company, did not show up for the trial that began in November 1994. Moreover, key witnesses in France and important documents located abroad were beyond the reach of U.S. subpoenas. General Electric's internal memoranda were ambiguous, the credibility of the government's star witness was punctured during cross-examination, and other GE employees' testimony only weakly supported the government's case. For all these reasons, after five weeks of trial the presiding judge dismissed the case. Analyses by legal trade magazines later took the position that prosecutors were outspent, outnumbered, and outlawyered. GE had spent \$20 to \$60 million in legal fees for 25 top litigators and scores of junior lawyers from several prestigious law firms; by contrast, the DOJ's team had a total of seven lawyers (*American Lawyer* January 1995:57).

Another challenge to global cartel prosecutions was some legal uncertainty about conspiracies that took place entirely offshore. U.S. legal authorities had always maintained that offshore conspiracies were actionable if they affected U.S. trade and commerce. However, this extraterritoriality theory was placed in doubt in the Japanese thermal fax paper case (Daniel *et al.* 1997). One of the defendants was dismissed from the case because none of the conspiratorial acts occurred on U.S. territory. It was only after the diamond-cartel case was dismissed in March 1997 that this decision was overturned re-affirming the offshore reach of the Sherman Act.

Thus, when the lysine investigation turned up solid evidence of international price fixing, the DOJ may well have had some trepidation about leaping forward into another risky global venture. After the major and humiliating loss of the industrial diamonds case, it would be vitally important to win lysine convictions in order to restore the Division's reputation.

THE BIGGEST MOLE EVER SEEN

The lysine investigation was the result of serendipity.

More than a year after ADM's Decatur plant had begun manufacturing lysine, the company continued to experience production problems. Large vats in which the dextrose mixture was being fermented became contaminated from time to time. Each time a vat was dumped, ADM incurred unrecoverable costs of millions of dollars. These episodes had been more frequent in the first year of operation but had continued sporadically in the summer of 1992. In late October 1992, Mark Whitacre went to Michael Andreas and told him that he suspected that an ADM employee was sabotaging the fermentors. Moreover, Whitacre further claimed that a Mr. Fujiwara, an employee of Ajinomoto, had telephoned him to inform him that Ajinomoto had placed a mole inside ADM's plant. The mole would continue to sabotage the lysine production process unless $6 to $10 million was wired to Fujiwara's Swiss bank account. In return for the money, the saboteur would stop the mole and provide ADM with Ajinomoto microbes that were resistant to contamination (Eichenwald 1996).[4]

It is revealing that Michael Andreas believed this cock-and-bull story and indeed acted upon it. (That Andreas readily believed that its arch rival Ajinomoto was capable of such wicked industrial espionage is rather revealing of ADM's perception of business methods in the industry). Andreas acted decisively. After seeking his father's counsel, Michael almost immediately telephoned ADM's representative in Europe, his cousin G. Allen Andreas, and asked the executive to inform a CIA acquaintance in London about the international extortion demand (Eichenwald 2000). Andreas later explained that he believed that if he had the cooperation of the CIA, then ADM would be able to make a payment legally to the extortionist.[5] The CIA rightly recognized that counter-espionage is the responsibility of the FBI. In early November, the extortion allegation was turned over to FBI Agent Bria Shepard.

Shepard, 43, had served more than 20 years in the FBI and had bee in charge of the small three-person FBI office in Decatur, Illinois since 198. (Tr. 2805-2837). Investigations of sabotage and price fixing allegations woul be far from run-of-the-mill activities for the FBI in a small Midwestern tow like Decatur. Indeed, Shepard initially had no idea whether price fixing was a federal crime or whether the FBI should ever get involved (Eichenwald 2000) Shepard reported to his supervisor in the FBI's Springfield, Illinois office Eventually, Shepard would be able to rely on a large team of additional agents and attorneys from the DOJ for guidance, but at the beginning some of the investigative techniques were improvised. In the end not all FBI investigative guidelines would be followed to the letter.

On November 4, 1992, at Michael Andreas' suggestion, Shepard and two other FBI agents interviewed Andreas at this home. Although because of past cooperation with the FBI Andreas might have expected nothing but help from the agents, it is likely that Andreas would have preferred not to deal with the FBI because of the danger that the agents might discover the lysine conspiracy that had started four months earlier.[6] During the interview, Andreas confirmed that he had indirectly alerted the CIA to the so-called Fujiwara extortion attempt. Andreas had also contacted a lawyer in Europe who knew experts in industrial sabotage (Tr. 2805-2810). In fact, one of those specialists had already been in contact with ADM's director of security, Mark Cheviron. At one point during the interview Andreas volunteered that ADM had been meeting with some Japanese lysine manufacturers because ADM was trying to break into the industry.

On the same day, Agent Shepard interviewed Mark Whitacre in the FBI's Decatur office. In a departure from normal procedures, Mark Cheviron was also allowed to be present. During the interview, Whitacre confirmed the details of the Fujiwara extortion demand, which he said had been made in a telephone call to his Decatur home. Whitacre did not mention his role in the ongoing lysine conspiracy. [7]

Whitacre's motives for concocting the sabotage/extortion tale have been the subject of much speculation. One leading candidate suggests that Whitacre, who was depressed at times and habitually loose with the truth, made up the story in order to draw attention away from his own incompetence. However, this explanation is at variance with a number of facts. First, in October 1992, Whitacre was about to get a raise and promotion to corporate vice president at ADM (officially took place on November 1, 1992). Whitacre was well regarded by ADM's management. Dwayne Andreas would later say: "We trusted him completely – a good man, a good salesman for us" (Carlson 1996). Second, the frequency of contamination incidents had slowed significantly since 1991. In fact, the Bioproduct's Division's own internal reports show that the lysine/dextrose yields were nearly ideal from May to October 1992. ADM's President James Randall, an experienced builder of fermentation plants, advised that the occasional episodes of contamination were simply the result of inadequate sterilization and were preventable. In fact, Mark Cheviron would later testify that he had been informed by Randall on November 5th that the contamination episodes were entirely normal (Lieber 2000). All in all, the contaminations were generally viewed as regrettable but inevitable in the early stages of production of a new product.

A second explanation seems more cogent. Whitacre was both ambitious for further promotion and greedy. He had already begun embezzling funds from ADM, and the extortion payment would fit in well with those plans. He could take the money, claim to pay the extortionist, and pretend to install the stolen technology. The contamination incidents would appear to disappear, because they were already under control anyway. Prosecutors would later suggest that Whitacre could count on Michael Andreas' behavior to further Whitacre's embezzlement plans (Tr. 5637-5638). He knew that Andreas would not call in the FBI because of Andreas' personal involvement in price fixing, and he knew that Andreas would have no compunctions about spending at least $6 million for an improved lysine technology. What neither of them counted on was the CIA's decision to call in the FBI.

At about 8:00 p.m. on November 5, 1992, Brian Shepard showed up at Whitacre's home, a large estate with a six-car garage and horse barns. Whitacre had purchased the house from Dwayne Andreas. Shepard had come to install a device on Whitacre's telephone that would record the origin of incoming calls, a fancy version of "caller ID." Instead of a quick visit, Whitacre asked to talk to Shepard in his car. For the next five hours, Shepard would listen to a series of the most incredible and bizarre tales in his long career. Mark Whitacre was about to become the highest-ranking executive mole in the history of the FBI (Tr. 2813-2817).

Mark Whitacre

Mark Whitacre was only 35 years old when he began confessing to Brian Shepard. He had grown up in comfortable middle-class circumstances in a small town north of Cincinnati, Ohio where his father owned an automobile dealership. He was president of his senior class in high school where he dated his future wife Ginger (Leiber 2000). By all accounts, Whitacre was talkative, engaging, brilliant, hard working, and prone to exaggeration and to gratuitous departures from the truth. He earned a bachelor's degree and a master's degree in animal science from Ohio State University in just four years. He required only two more years to complete a Ph.D. in nutritional biotechnology at Cornell University in the early 1980s.

Whitacre's first job was with Ralston Purina in St. Louis, but in less than a year he moved to the German firm Degussa, the world's leading manufacturer of amino acids. From his initial position as a technical sales representative in Germany in 1985, he rose within three years to vice president at Degussa's U.S. headquarters in New Jersey. When ADM decided to enter the lysine business in early 1989, the company followed its usual practice of trying to interest Degussa in forming a joint venture. When the negotiations stalled in 1989, ADM instead hired Degussa's chief negotiator, Whitacre, to become manager of its fledgling Bioproducts Division, for which ADM was already building a state-of-the-art lysine manufacturing plant.

Whitacre's job would be to oversee the plant's startup, work out its initial production bugs, and market the lysine. Large investments – more than $1 billion – that would be made by ADM to expand into additional biotechnology products in the early 1990s. By 1995, Whitacre had been named President of the Bioproducts Division and ADM corporate Vice President, would be earning a salary of $320,000 per year, and would be supervising more than 120 employees in Decatur and around the world. Whitacre was a rising star at ADM. In March 1995, Dwayne Andreas circulated among ADM management a highly laudatory report prepared by the investment firm Dain Bosworth that mentions Whitacre as the likely next President of ADM.

Like many whistle-blowers, Whitacre would turn out to be an unreliable witness. While many of his allegations of unethical behavior at ADM would be corroborated, he also had a tendency to spin tales that were pure fantasy. One of his counterparts at ADM gave credible court testimony about some of these stories. Whitacre had claimed that his parents were dead, that he had been raised in a Cincinnati orphanage, and that his adoptive parents owned the well known King's Island amusement park in Cincinnati – none of which was true. It is obvious that Whitacre relished the role of secret agent. During 1993, Whitacre sent or revealed several of ADM's trade secrets to an international business consultant by the name of David Hoech, who was not employed by ADM; the secrets included lysine production targets, production costs, customer lists, and division earnings reports (Tr. 4360-4375). [8] After becoming an undercover agent for the FBI, he revealed his role to his gardener, showed a briefcase with a hidden tape recorder, and boasted that he should be called "Agent 014" because he was twice as smart as James Bond. Whitacre himself stated that he was a victim of bipolar disease (formerly termed manic-depression), which might explain some of his bizarre behavior. Yet, in September 1998 when he was asked about his mental health, he told a federal judge that he felt fine and that he was no longer receiving medication for bipolar disease (Tr. 4705-4715).

Whitacre Becomes a Mole

November 1992 was a pivotal month in Mark Whitacre's life. On November 1st, he was officially appointed President of ADM's Bioproducts

Division and thereby became a corporate officer. During the first few days of November, his boss Michael Andreas was taking action to set up a payment of millions of dollars to an extortionist that would end the sabotage of ADM's lysine production processes. On November 4th, local FBI agent Brian Shepard and two other agents visited ADM headquarters during the day and Michael Andreas' home that night to begin the extortion investigation (Tr. 715-716). Mark Whitacre, with ADM's security chief present, was interviewed in Shepard's Decatur office, where he confirmed the outlines of the Fujiwara extortion demand.

On November 5, 1992, Mark Whitacre was confronted at work by ADM's general counsel and its security chief Mark Cheviron about inconsistencies in Whitacre's Fujiwara extortion tale. As Whitacre knew, ADM had installed sophisticated security devices on both of Whitacre's home phone lines, part of a company-wide system thought to be necessary to prevent rival grain-trading companies from gaining illegal access to commercially important information. It is likely that Cheviron had been unable to find any incoming calls from the phantom Fujiwara. Moreover, Whitacre as usual had spiced up his story by claiming that a foreign-sounding man had called and threatened his daughter who was studying at Culver Academy in Indiana; presumably, there was no record of a frantic call from Indiana on the right days. Faced with this evidence, Whitacre recanted (Tr. 5640-5650). For more than a month afterwards, ADM did not inform the FBI that the suspected extortion was a hoax. Indeed, ADM ceased cooperating with the FBI's investigation, on orders from the two Andreases (Lieber 2000). Of course, Michael Andreas was informed about Whitacre's flip-flop, yet for three years he did nothing to punish Whitacre.[9] He did nothing because he could not. Whitacre knew too much.

That same night Whitacre spilled the beans about the lysine conspiracy to FBI Agent Shepard. With the agreement of ADM and Whitacre, Shepard went to Whitacre's house around 8 p.m. on the night of November 5th to install a telephone monitoring device that would record the source of incoming calls and point to the location of the extortionist. Whitacre, fearing that his house was bugged and perhaps realizing that no telephone evidence of the extortion story will be forthcoming, went to Shepard's car and unloaded a series of accusations that were scarcely believable to the agent (Tr. 2813-2817). This was to be the first of many installments in two and a half-year saga of Whitacre's life as a mole for the FBI (Whitacre 1995).

Over the course of the five-hour confession, Whitacre laid out a long list of illegal activities and practices at ADM. Among the allegations that have proven accurate were the lysine cartel, the citric acid cartel, and the attempted theft of a lysine biotechnology by ADM officers. However, many of Whitacre's allegations about illegal or unethical behavior by the Andreas' or other ADM officers have not been corroborated. For example, Whitacre charged that ADM president James Randall had paid $50,000 to steal a microorganism that could have been used to make the amino acid bacitracin

(Tr. 5638). He also claimed that Michael Andreas, acting in his capacity as Whitacre's informal mentor, had advised him on how to carry out multiple kickback schemes for the purpose of obtaining routine off-the-books bonuses. Whitacre alleged that ADM routinely sold toxic animal feed ingredients by, for example, spraying active biomass waste on corn gluten that would fraudulently increase protein levels. ADM corporate jets were alleged to have been frequently diverted to personal use by ADM executives. He described the bribery of Indonesian politicians to obtain environmental permits and suitcases full of ADM cash to bribe Russian politicians. Finally, in 1996 when the full extent of Whitacre's embezzlement was not yet known, he stated that he had taped a conversation in ADM's executive dining room in which Michael Andreas updated his father on all the details of ADM's price fixing activities. "Dwayne heard all those details – on tape. He didn't comment much – just 'Uh-huh, uh-huh.' But he definitely got updated. Definitely." (Carlson 1996).

No indictments were ever made on Whitacre's more colorful allegations, though in some cases the FBI may have been prevented from doing so because the statute of limitations had been exceeded.[10] Whitacre's tendency to mix facts with fantasy called into question his motivation for cooperating with the FBI. Creating diversions to cover up his embezzlements seems likely to have been one of his motives. At various times he demanded money from the FBI for his services, once suggesting ten times his salary as an appropriate benchmark, but in the end he received only $270 for alteration of a suit to accommodate a hidden tape recorder (Tr. 3389).[11]

Whitacre's unreliability became an issue at his Chicago criminal trial. Michael Andreas' personal lawyer went so far as to accuse the absent Whitacre of intending to frame Andreas. In a radio interview, John Bray said, "It is for Mr. Whitacre to eliminate his chief competition as the next potential president of ADM . . ." (National Public Radio 9/18/98). This accusation seems far-fetched because at the time Whitacre was a government agent, Andreas was a shoe-in for his father's post of Chairman of ADM, not president. Whitacre was still in running for Randall's job when it would open in a few years' time. Indeed, several commentators have suggested that Whitacre was naive and out of his depth at ADM, that it was he who was subtly drawn into an existing web of dishonesty at the higher echelons of the company.

In the end, Mark Whitacre's motivations remain a mystery wrapped in controversy. In the view of one *Chicago Tribune* columnist who closely followed the case:

> "Mark Whitacre . . . streaked across the business world like a meteor – spectacular and mysterious but ultimately crashing and burning" (9/17/98).

Meteors at their core are a bundle of dirt – an appropriate metaphor.

ENTER THE FBI

Naturally, the FBI wanted proof that ADM was engaging in illegal price fixing with three Asian manufacturers of lysine.[12] Three nights later, Shepard and another agent interviewed Whitacre about the price fixing allegations. For the first time, the FBI got some verifiable facts from Whitacre. He gave them specific dates of four meetings between ADM and its Asian rivals in the lysine market.[13] Moreover, Whitacre handed over copies of expense reports that supported the dates, and he showed the agents the lysine department's profit statements that confirmed the increase in lysine prices and profits in September and October. Finally, Whitacre made a telephone call to Masuru Yamamoto, a co-conspirator in Tokyo, discussing their lysine price fixing, with Shepard recording the conversation on tape (Tr. 2834-2835 and 716-718). With this evidence, the FBI must have concluded that there was sufficient probable cause to open an official investigation.

The lysine investigation, later dubbed "Harvest King," did not at first go smoothly.[14] The next day, ADM's security chief telephoned Shepard that ADM would no longer cooperate with the FBI in the extortion investigation. Cheviron gave as the reason the fact that a normal security check by ADM had turned up monitoring devices on *two* of Whitacre's home telephone lines, whereas ADM had agreed to only one line. This rationale seems flimsy. It is highly unusual for the victim of a crime to cease cooperating with a police investigation. Fear about discovery of the lysine conspiracy may well have driven this curious behavior. By this date Whitacre had had to recant his story about the Fujiwara extortion to Cheviron and ADM's legal counsel, and within days Whitacre too had ceased to cooperate with the FBI, giving a number of patently incredible excuses. Strangely, a month later, even though they knew the whole extortion story to be phony, ADM employees again began to cooperate with the FBI by preparing a list of possible saboteurs in their lysine factory.[15]

For four months after the November 9th interview and taping session, Whitacre became increasingly agitated about his role. Perhaps he was being pressured to break off contacts with the FBI by people at ADM, but the latter did not know that he had already admitted to participating in a felony. That admission gave the FBI considerable leverage over Whitacre. On the night of November 16th, Whitacre called Shepard and complained that the FBI was "destroying him," that the investigation was going to hurt Michael Andreas and "other innocent people," and that he wanted to end his role as an FBI mole (Eichenwald 1996). On November 18th, he again called Shepard saying that his supervisors at ADM were "turning against him" and that he was becoming depressed and suicidal. He stated that he "could not figure a way to win in this situation" (*ibid.*).

By this time the FBI too had begun to doubt that there was an extortionist asking for $6 million, so on December 21, 1992 Whitacre was required to take a polygraph test. Whitacre failed the test miserably. He admitted that day that the whole extortion story was a hoax intended to explain away the start-up contamination episodes (Tr. 2864-2866). To again confirm the truth of his allegations, Whitacre made a telephone call that same day to Wayne Brasser, a former ADM executive. With the FBI listening, Whitacre and Brasser talked about the reason for his firing: Brasser had refused to help Terrance Wilson fix prices of citric acid and sodium gluconate. Brasser also confirmed that Wilson had tried to form a conspiracy in lactic acid (Eichenwald 2000:109-111). [16]

Despite Whitacre's unsteadiness, the FBI had Whitacre sign a contract in January 1993 to serve as a "cooperating witness" in the lysine investigation. Signing that agreement would prove to be a major blunder for Whitacre, who naively did not hire a personal attorney until July 1995. Although the agreement granted him conditional immunity from prosecution for some past and all future price fixing actions, any lawyer worth his salt could have spotted a highly disadvantageous feature of the agreement. Whitacre was immunized only from November 5th onwards. Because the FBI knew of illegal meetings prior to that date, even if Whitacre turned out to be a model whistle-blower, the FBI had a powerful tool to force Whitacre's continuing cooperation.[17] Perhaps offering agreements to moles containing loopholes favorable to the investigating agency is standard practice, but it does suggest manipulative bad faith on the part of the FBI. The presiding judge at Whitacre's criminal trial would gratuitously highlight the government's "hardball" tactics in handling Whitacre. On the other hand, Whitacre had begun embezzling from ADM prior to signing his cooperating-witness agreement with the FBI and continued to embezzle shortly thereafter.[18] These actions were sufficient to abrogate Whitacre's contract no matter haw valuable his cooperation.

In early 1993, the FBI had increasing doubts about Whitacre's truthfulness and degree of cooperation. By early March, he had been telling the FBI that ADM had abandoned the lysine price fixing scheme and that he had no personal involvement in it in any case. In fact, Whitacre had hidden from the FBI a January 1993 conspiracy meeting with two Japanese lysine makers, a fact that was revealed when he was given and failed a second polygraph test on March 10th. As a result, Whitacre agreed once again to begin taping conspiracy-related events. After a hiatus of five months, Whitacre began making audio tapes on March 12, 1993.

FBI Taping Procedures

Mark Whitacre turned in to the FBI 120 to 130 audio tapes that he personally recorded from March 1993 to mid-1995. Many of these were telephone conversations with Japanese, Korean, or French co-conspirators. Others were made at formal price fixing meetings around the world or at informal meetings of fellow ADM employees. In addition, where local laws allowed, four formal meetings of the lysine cartel were videotaped in hotels by FBI agents in adjacent quarters.[19] All these recordings would become the "smoking gun" evidence that secured guilty pleas and convictions of the lysine conspirators, both corporate and individual.

Whitacre was given two tape recorders. One was hidden in a briefcase and was of a type only available to law-enforcement agencies. The second was a commercial-type micro cassette recorder. Whenever a filled tape was returned, Whitacre would fill out and sign a consent form, and the tape would be numbered, labeled, and catalogued. Whitacre was instructed to record any conversations likely to refer to price fixing, but otherwise had a great deal of discretion. Not all conversations about the lysine conspiracy were recorded, and in the case of the micro-cassette recorder the FBI could not guarantee that Whitacre had not used purchased cassettes to make recordings that he did not turn in. The possibility of unlogged tapes became an issue in the legal battles to follow. At one time Whitacre claimed he had incriminating tapes of Michael Andreas and Brian Shepard. However, Whitacre retracted his claim about Shepard in a March 1998 affidavit. Defense attorneys attempted to suppress all tapes made by Whitacre because he had too much discretion. In a ruling on their admissibility in court, a federal judge termed the FBI handling of taping negligent, inconsistent with DOJ rules for cooperating witnesses, and improper but not intentional.

Whitacre's own taping was consensual, and no court order was required even when it was the FBI doing the video taping. However, when Whitacre left the room, taping had to stop.[20] Despite advanced requests by the FBI through diplomatic channels, meetings in France and Canada could not be taped even by Whitacre himself.[21] In Japan, Whitacre was allowed to tape meetings, but had to use a locally purchased machine. In all, 239 tapes were presented in evidence at the 1998 trial (Tr. 3736). By the end of 1993, the FBI judged that there was sufficient evidence to prosecute ADM, its officers, and others for fixing the price of lysine. However, Whitacre's taping continued for more than a year longer because from time to time there were statements about price fixing in other markets, notably citric acid and corn sweeteners. Whitacre had alleged price fixing by ADM in all three of these markets (and two more besides) as early as December 1992 (Tr. 2906-2908). Other than lysine, the taped evidence was strongest for citric acid.

Other than the vide tapes made by FBI agents who controlled the camera in an adjacent room, investigators had to rely totally on Whitacre's taping efforts. They tried several methods of electronic surveillance, but were repeatedly frustrated by ADM's world-class security equipment. The agency got legal authorization to tape Michael Andreas' telephones, but ADM's security system defeated the attempt (Eichenwald 2000:241). Experiments with listening devices that would broadcast signals by radio from ADM's headquarters also failed to work.

Embezzlement

Besides Whitacre's propensity for manufacturing stories, his embezzlement of ADM funds made him highly unsuitable as a witness for prosecutors. Most of the embezzlement occurred by means of cash kickbacks from vendors to ADM's Bioproducts Division. In some cases, Whitacre forged the signature of ADM president James Randall. It is surprising that a company with such a good reputation for management quality would have such loose accounting controls. Whitacre's fear of being discovered might explain some of his overreactions to events. For example, a patent-infringement suit filed in early 1995 concerning ADM's lysine production technology was very upsetting to Whitacre because he knew that a suit would reveal that he had used technology licensing agreements as vehicles for fraud.

Whitacre's embezzlement of ADM began in April 1991. To facilitate the theft, he opened two bank accounts on the Cayman Islands in August 1991 and a Swiss account in January 1993 (Tr. 4872). The schemes involved phony invoices for new fermentation technologies for the Bioproducts Division or kickbacks from vendors for legitimate services. In October 1993, Whitacre received $2.5 million for a bogus contract for a technology purchased from a Swedish agricultural company. In February 1995, he got $3.75 million in ADM funds that were sent to a nonexistent Ukrainian company. All told, Whitacre stole almost $10 million, with some help from three salesmen in the Bioproducts Division working in Mexico, Germany, and Atlanta.

The FBI first became aware of the fraud by Whitacre in August 1995, the same month Whitacre and his three associates in crime were fired by ADM (Tr. 721). That same month, prosecutors met with Whitacre and his attorney to inform him that his immunity for prosecution for price fixing was being withdrawn because of his failing to disclose fraud. ADM immediately filed a civil suit to recover the money stolen. Whitacre claimed in 1995 and still claims that what ADM calls fraud was the standard method for rewarding favored ADM officers with tax-free bonuses. Nevertheless, on October 10, 1997 Whitacre pleaded guilty to fraud, embezzlement, and tax evasion. On March 4, 1998 Mark Whitacre was sentenced to nine years in federal prison and required to pay $11.4 million in restitution. Judge Baker in Urbana, Illinois excoriated Whitacre for his "socio-pathic behavior" and opined that he was motivated by "garden-variety venality and greed."

Because Whitacre lost his federal immunity, he was made a defendant together with Michael Andreas and Terrance Wilson in the 1998 criminal trial in Chicago. This was a stroke of luck for prosecutors because Whitacre could not be compelled to testify for the prosecutors, and ultimately he declined to be present in court at all. His absence made it more difficult for defense lawyers to pin the whole guilt on him. Prosecutors had realized for some time that he would be unconvincing on the stand, but his embezzlement made him useless as a prosecution witness. In his opening statement, the DOJ's chief prosecutor said, ". . . never will we ask you to rely on the truth of anything that Mark Whitacre says" (Tr. 744).

The government's star whistle-blower was convicted and sentenced to 30 months in prison for lysine price fixing. During the trial prosecutors hardly mention Whitacre's two price fixing meetings held before November 5, 1992, yet his sentence was harsher than that of his supervisors at ADM. One cannot but draw the conclusion that Whitacre was being punished more for hiding his thefts from the FBI while he was a mole than for two relatively minor instances of conspiracy. It is true that Whitacre's perfidy jeopardized the government's case against the ring leaders at ADM, but federal whistle blowers beware. Only those willing to keep their whistles clean need apply.

THE GRAND JURIES

Criminal federal trials are heard by "petit juries" of twelve citizens in open court. However, grand juries, so-called because they have up to 23 citizens, operate under different rules. Although loosely supervised by judges, they are formed by federal prosecutors to assist in bringing indictments. In the presence of jurors, prosecutors interview witnesses under oath who may have incriminating information. Witnesses may include investigators, or experts with direct knowledge of the alleged crime. Jury members are also shown documents in the hands of prosecutors. Possible defendants or targets of the investigation do not usually testify. Grand jury proceedings are completely secret in principle, and that principle seems to be followed rather closely in practice in order to protect targets who are not indicted for lack of evidence and witnesses who, without the promise of confidentiality, might not be forthcoming with inculpatory information.[22] After hearing the evidence of possible illegalities, the grand jury considers whether there is "probable cause" of a violation and votes on whether to indict and on which counts. The grand jury system has been part of common law procedures since the 13th century. It was designed primarily to protect citizens from over-zealous prosecutors, but it is also useful as a formal investigative tool for gathering of facts from witnesses under oath. Moreover, the existence of an active grand jury puts pressure of targets to plea guilty prior to trial. Alone among the federal antitrust agencies, the Department of Justice is authorized to use grand juries.

Federal grand juries were empanelled in major cities around the United States where the Department of Justice has field offices established for its Antitrust Division. The lysine grand jury was established in Chicago, the closest field office to the headquarters of the three U.S. manufacturers of lysine: ADM in Decatur, Illinois; Ajinomoto's Heartland Lysine in Chicago; and Kyowa's Biokyowa in St. Louis. It was reported that this grand jury was formed in early June 1995, just a few weeks before the FBI raided the headquarters of the lysine sellers and companies selling citric acid and corn sweeteners. Around the same time, grand juries were established for citric acid in San Francisco and for corn sweeteners in Atlanta. The grand jury investigating vitamins was set up in November 1997 in Houston.

The government's lysine investigation was initially headed by James M. Griffin, chief of the DOJ's regional office for antitrust, who became the lead attorney for the prosecution. By March 1996, Deputy Attorney General Jamie Gorelick, the second-ranking official of the Justice Department, had assumed overall supervision of the three ADM-related grand juries and the criminal investigation of Whitacre. Gorelick worked closely with the Assistant Attorney General for Antitrust, Anne K. Bingaman.[23] These supervisory arrangements indicated the high priority given to prosecution of the alleged lysine, citric acid, and corn-sweeteners cartels by the Clinton administration. Not only was special care being taken to ensure aggressive prosecution, but the arrangements signaled the political sensitivity of prosecuting Dwayne Andreas' company.

Late in the summer of 1995, Gorelick invited Scott Lassar to become co-lead prosecutor with Griffin in the lysine case. Lassar, first assistant U.S. District Attorney for the Northern District of Illinois, was a highly regarded and experienced prosecutor.[24] Lassar and Griffin worked together in the negotiations with the five companies in the lysine cartel until the end of 1996 when the last of them pleaded guilty. It was after an August 1995 meeting with Lassar that the government decided to prosecute Whitacre for fraud and price fixing. Griffin and Lassar also shared prosecutorial duties in the criminal trial of Andreas, Wilson, and Whitacre in 1998. DOJ officials believe that this pairing of resources was unique in the history of U.S. antitrust prosecutions, but because it worked so well probably not the last.[25]

In the spring of 1996, another individual was assigned to the Washington, DC group in overall charge of the ADM-related cartel cases. Joel I. Klein was transferred from a position in the White House to work closely with Gorelick at the Justice Department. Gorelick resigned from the DOJ a few months after Klein arrived, and when Assistant Attorney General Bingaman also resigned in October 1996, Klein was appointed to act in her place. Joel Klein was confirmed by the U.S. Senate in mid-1997. Like Bingaman, Klein would become identified with a more assertive posture in enforcement of federal antitrust laws.

The lysine grand jury in Chicago never had to vote to indict the five companies in the cartel because prosecutors arrived at a negotiated settlement (see below). However, four individuals failed to arrive at such a settlement. On December 3, 1996, the jury handed down criminal indictments for price fixing against four men: Michael Andreas, Terrance Wilson, Mark Whitacre, and Kazutoski Yamada. Although a warrant was issued for his arrest, Yamada, a managing director of Ajinomoto, did not appear in the United States to have it served. One of the puzzling aspects of the lysine story is why the DOJ never requested extradition of Yamada.[26]

THE FBI RAIDS

Shortly after the three ADM-related grand juries were formed, the FBI was granted search warrants by an Illinois magistrate to search parts of the offices of many agribusiness companies that made or sold lysine, citric acid, or corn sweeteners. Subpoenas were also issued to be served to knowledgeable individuals to compel them to testify about possible price fixing in the three markets.

The multiple raids were carefully planned well in advance of the chosen night. Mark Whitacre had snooped around to find a night when all the principal targets would not be traveling on business (Eichenwald 2000). On the night of June 27, 1995, in a massive show of force some 70 FBI agents arrived at ADM's corporate headquarters in Decatur and began removing evidence in the offices of Michael Andreas, Terrance Wilson, Mark Whitacre, and several of their lieutenants.[27] The top floor where Dwayne Andreas and James Randall worked was not searched.[28] Other agents went to the homes of most of the ADM officers who had anything to do with the three products, served the subpoenas, and began interviewing the executives on the spot. Local residents of Decatur took to referring to the episode as "Gestapo Night."

From the audio and video tapes in the hands of the FBI, Michael Andreas and Terrence Wilson had already been identified as the chief perpetrators of ADM's price fixing activities, so they received special treatment that night. For Andreas at his home that evening and Wilson at his country club, the FBI played excerpts of incriminating taped conversations. Andreas listened calmly to the recordings but responded that they didn't prove anything. The FBI offered Andreas a chance to reduce his sentence by cooperating, but that offer was summarily rejected.

The many ADM executives that were interviewed that night remained tight-lipped, yielding no useful information for the prosecution. However, the files in ADM's headquarters did yield documents that contained useful information. Besides travel and telephone records that would confirm attendance at conspiracy meetings, ADM's files contain the conspirator's "score sheets" kept by the lysine and citric acid associations. The score sheets display monthly sales data, both "budgeted" (i.e., goals of the conspirators) and actual, for each of the members of the cartel. These score sheets were the primary decision-making aid for the conspirators at their quarterly meetings. They provided confirmation that the cartels attempted to monitor their volume agreements and gathered the information necessary to implement year-end compensation schemes. Sharing information in this way may in itself constitute a crime, but shared for the purpose of detecting cheating makes it clearly a violation.[29]

FBI raids continued that night and over the following days. The U.S. offices of at least nine other multinational agribusiness companies were affected: Cargill, Heartland Lysine Ajinomoto, Biokyowa, Sewon America, Cheil/Samsung, Bayer, Hoffmann-La Roche, Tate & Lyle's A.E. Staley, and CPC International. Many cartons of documents were removed, duplicated, stamped, catalogued, and copies returned to the companies. In addition, depositions taken by prosecutors or defense lawyers, press clippings, reports, and other documents were exchanged. In the lysine criminal trial alone, the DOJ turned over more than two million documents to defense counsel prior to the start of the trial.[30]

U.S. subpoenas were useless for obtaining documents from the files of companies that had their headquarters abroad. Indeed, when it was learned at Ajinomoto's Tokyo headquarters that their Chicago office had been raided, the company's legal department immediately ordered the destruction of all incriminating documents on lysine.[31] Under U.S. law, this would be considered obstruction of justice and would receive harsh sanctions by a judge. However, most of the participants in the lysine meetings other than ADM took copious notes at the meetings and prepared memoranda that were circulated to their supervisors. These minutes were highly damaging to the defendants, and might have proved sufficient to convict the price fixers even without the taped evidence. They clearly indicated the target prices, dates, places, and market shares agreed upon.

As the FBI raids became known a great deal of unfavorable publicity was generated for ADM and the other companies. On June 29th and following days, virtually all major newspapers and news organizations reported the news. Within a month leaks from the investigation suggested that suspicious documents had been obtained by the FBI that supported the existence of a lysine cartel. For ADM, the most prominent of the firms under suspicion, the immediate financial impact was enormous. From the day of the raid until October 1995 as the unfavorable speculation mounted, its stock market price fell by 24 percent, or by a market value of $1.4 billion. The stock market was clearly overreacting if only lysine was at stake, because the Bioproducts Division accounted for only a few percentage points of ADM's total revenues. The major concern of investors probably centered on high fructose corn syrup, which was a far larger share of its sales and was believed to generate almost half of the company's net revenues.

The response of ADM and most of the affected companies to the searches was similar. They remained silent or issued brief press releases denying guilt and immediately hired lots of legal help. ADM's press release was two sentences long. Several law firms were hired for the company's management and for individual executives. Later, even the boards of directors hired separate legal representation. At ADM, John Dowd of Akin Gump headed up a large team of top-flight lawyers to assess the company's position and develop a defense strategy. Akin Gump is a prestigious Washington D.C. law firm governed by Washington insider Robert Strauss, an ADM board member and close friend of chairman Dwayne Andreas. Soon afterwards, ADM's management hired a second law firm headquartered in Washington

D.C. Williams & Connelly had developed over the years a reputation as Washington's

> ". . . premier purveyor of hardball litigation tactics . . . famous for gaining outstanding results for notorious clients in desperate jams" (Leiber 2000:7).

The law firm's founder, Edward Bennett Williams, had represented Dwayne Andreas in 1964 in a criminal case that alleged that Andreas had made illegal payments to persons involved in the infamous Watergate scandal. Senior partner Aubrey Daniels soon became ADM's chief strategist and negotiator with the Department of Justice where he was well known and perhaps even deferred to (Eichenwald 2000). The Antitrust Division prosecutors in Chicago would grow to dislike the Williams and Connelly lawyers because they felt that the firm was seeking to solve ADM's problems through lobbying rather than the justice system. What is undeniable is the fact that ADM's mole hill was thrusting upward to volcanic proportions. By September, more than 20 civil suits had been filed against ADM seeking compensation for buyers of lysine, citric acid, and corn sweeteners.

The Akin Gump legal team began interviewing company employees the day after the FBI raid. Mark Whitacre was interviewed by John Dowd. Thinking that he was protected by the lawyer-client privilege of confidentiality, Whitacre told Dowd everything about his role as a FBI mole, and Dowd immediately informed ADM's management.[31] Within days Whitacre was banned from the ADM premises, and within a month ADM's law firm had assembled a pile of invoices and travel records that proved Whitacre's embezzlement. The speed with which the company located these company records, as well as suggestions that ADM's president James Randall was intimately involved in finding them almost immediately, raised strong suspicions that ADM was fully aware of his off-the-books income for years. It also supports Whitacre's steadfast assertion that the practice was a form of tax-free bonus system available to a favored few top officers of ADM (Leiber 2000).

By the first week of August, information about Whitacre's fraud had become known to DOJ prosecutors, who immediately turned on their star mole. By late September, the fraud section of the DOJ's Criminal Division had taken charge of the fraud investigation having the antitrust attorneys in Chicago in charge of the lysine price fixing probe. Whitacre's apparent attempted suicide at the time ADM made his probable embezzlement publicly known (August 7, 1995) confused the hoards of journalists covering the dramatic lysine-cartel events. For a month, the story had been presented to the public as an epic struggle between a saintly David and a corrupt Goliath. When the simplicity of the stark good vs. bad theme was replaced by a messier reality, the mass of reporters departed (Leiber 2000: Preface). A story that would take another four years to play out would have been lost had it not been for a couple of wire services and three dedicated newspapers: the *New York Times*, the *Wall Street Journal*, and the *Chicago Tribune*.

In the weeks after the raid, only one company failed to follow the standard scenario. Sewon America issued a statement saying that it had been coerced by its much larger Japanese rivals in the lysine business. This was the first tiny crack in the dam of solidarity that had been erected by the five lysine conspirators.

THE LYSINE GUILTY PLEAS

After the FBI searched the offices of ADM and three other lysine sellers in June 1995, prosecutors from the U.S. District Attorney's office and the DOJ's Antitrust Division office presented the evidence obtained to the lysine grand jury in Chicago. While the evidence from the tapes was strong and the conspiracy documents provided useful corroboration, for well over a year the prosecutors had grave difficulties assembling sufficient evidence to bring *criminal* price fixing indictments against the five companies and key executives who operated the cartel. Criminal price fixing charges require that the prosecution prove "beyond a reasonable doubt" that the defendants knowingly and intentionally conspired to fix or control prices.[33] That is by design a heavy burden of proof. A jury must arrive at a consensus that there is no other reasonable alternative explanation for the lysine discussion other than an intent to raise prices, fix market shares, and enforce those decisions on wavering members of the cartel.

After Mark Whitacre's embezzlement came to light in late July, he was swiftly fired from ADM and was sued by his former employer. That month, he made the first of two attempts at suicide.[34] Juries tend to place insiders to a crime who turn state's evidence in roughly the same category as Mafia stool pigeons. Their testimony is treated with skepticism because they are viewed by juries as trying to save their own skin. Whitacre's fraud made things worse for the prosecutors. Without Whitacre's availability to testify, the government's case was hurt in two ways. First, the tapes he made, while graphic and convincing, would be regarded as potentially tainted. Whitacre had an opportunity to turn in tapes that would be damaging to the conspirators, but could have withheld tapes that might exonerate them (Daniel *et al.* 1997). Second, the government absolutely needed at least one credible participant who was prepared to testify that they knew that the purpose of their meetings and agreements was illegal market manipulation. Otherwise, defendants could claim that even the video tapes (these were made directly by the FBI, not by Whitacre) showed play-acting, management training, or some such innocent activity. For more than a year, no participant came forth to corroborate the intent of the meetings, phone calls, and documents. At ADM at most four or five men had detailed knowledge about the lysine conspiracy.[35] Dozens of executives knew at the other four companies, but nearly all of them resided outside the United States, giving them personally a measure of immunity from U.S. prosecutors.

Plea bargaining between prosecutors and the lawyers representing the lysine makers began soon after the FBI raid. Negotiations were made difficult by the fact that the companies' counsel knew that the government's chief witness was a fallen star. Cooperation among the target companies' law firms during the first nine or ten months of this phase meant that they knew that none of their executives had agreed to cooperate with prosecutors. ADM hired one of the best known Washington law firms, Williams & Connelly, to defend itself in the lysine antitrust case and help coordinate a public relations lobbying effort that would restore some of ADM's former reputation. ADM spent lavishly on its legal defense; its filings with the Securities and Exchanges Commission (SEC) admit to legal costs of at least $40 million for the first year alone. At a minimum, these costs include payments to retained law firms for their presentation of the company's management in antitrust matters. Legal expenses paid by the company for its executives, notably Michael Andreas and Terrance Wilson, and for its board of directors may not be included as legal costs in its financial statements, nor is the time spent by its executives in dealing with its lawyers, time spent in depositions, or renegotiating contracts in hopes of repairing customer relations hurt by the alleged conspiracy.

Negotiating a guilty plea agreement is a tricky business. In the agreement, the guilty party must admit to one or more specific acts that violated the antitrust laws, the dates of the violations, a fine to be paid, and cooperation in providing evidence against other guilty companies or individuals, including possibly a company's cooperation against its own culpable employees. The prosecution must follow the U.S. Sentencing Guidelines in arriving at the size of the fine, but the DOJ has an important source of negotiating leverage: it may request a "downward departure" from the Guidelines fine range if the degree of cooperation of a company or individual is large. It may also offer immunity from prosecution for cooperating witnesses, extend immunity to other indictable employees, reduce the number of counts in the indictment, or agree to phrase the dates of the conspiracy in a plea agreement in ways that are favorable to the guilty parties.[36] The latter concession would reduce a company's exposure to what can be sought as settlements by civil plaintiffs. In order to offer immunities or other concessions, the DOJ must know in advance the quantity and quality of cooperation to be expected in future depositions or testimonies. This is formalized in pre-plea-agreement negotiations through a proffer letter from the charged parties that details the purpose and conditions of the depositions and immunities to be given. A time-honored practice of prosecutors is to try to identify and focus on the parties to a conspiracy that are most likely to cooperate and break ranks with the other conspirators. In the lysine case, the company least able to withstand the financial consequences of a large fine was debt-burdened Sewon.[37]

Behind the scenes, about three weeks after the FBI raid at its regular quarterly meeting, the ADM board of directors formed a special committee to advise the management on the criminal and legal suits arising from the price fixing allegations.[38] It is normal practice for boards to form such committees for such sensitive matters, but normally it would include only outside directors. This antitrust committee of nine (later six) members had at most one outside director on it, using the strictest definition of an outside director.[39] The ADM board also hired a law firm to advise it, a firm different from the one advising ADM's management. M. Brian Mulroney, former prime minister of Canada, was chair of the antitrust committee and became chief negotiator of the ADM board with the prosecutors (Nicol and Ferguson 1999). Mr. Mulroney's law firm represented ADM in Canada. Harvard Professor of agribusiness Ray Goldberg also took a leadership role in this matter. Goldberg and his father were long time family friends with Dwayne Andreas. Presumably, the four other companies in the lysine cartel had similar committees of officers or board members monitoring legal developments and offering strategic advice to their companies' management.

ADM's antitrust committee was permitted to hear some of the tape recordings made by Mark Whitacre that the DOJ considered to be incriminating. It is likely that some of its members became convinced that it was in ADM's interest to settle as early as possible with the government and private parties, but these directors faced one powerful obstacle. Dwayne Andreas (and his confidants who likely reflected his views) took the position that the now undeniable meetings with lysine competitors were innocent affairs intended to collect information from their rivals about the lysine market. Indeed, ADM's management put an additional positive spin on the meetings: Andreas and Wilson were attempting to break the grip of a pre-existing Asian cartel in the global lysine industry. It quickly became clear that Andreas' son Michael was the chief target of the DOJ, so attempting to resist a settlement that would turn the company into an accomplice in Michael's prosecution would only be natural. It was in the Andreas family's interest that ADM delay settling and stonewall the government's investigation.[40] There was also a great deal of residual loyalty to the Andreas family among ADM executives and many board members. For whatever reason, no ADM employee was willing to cooperate with prosecutors until at least September 1996, some 14 months after the FBI raid. Perhaps in anxious to induce such cooperation, the DOJ made a very unusual move in March 1996. It announced that Dwayne Andreas was not the target of its price fixing investigations.[37] If this was intended to shake loose an ADM employee, it did not work. However, the announcement may have emboldened the ADM board to press harder for a deal.

Meanwhile, prosecutors continued to apply pressure elsewhere in the wall of silence surrounding the lysine cartel. Cracks in its solidarity began to appear fairly early. In July 1995, an unidentified source inside Kyowa Hakko told a reported at the *Wall Street Journal* that it viewed itself as a "minor player" in setting lysine prices; moreover, Kyowa blamed its bigger rival Ajinomoto for coercing it into colluding. Sewon too considered itself pressured into joining the cartel by its bigger Asian co-conspirator. As the largest of the five companies, Ajinomoto knew that unless it confessed early and was granted leniency, it potentially faced the largest criminal fines.

Ajinomoto, Kyowa, and Sewon had caved in to prosecutors' demands for guilty pleas by July 1996. According to one source, the first manager to agree to cooperate with the government was Masaru Yamamoto, Kyowa's long-time lysine sales director (Lieber 2000). A letter written by ADM critic David Hoech and sent to Yamamoto in January 1996 may have prompted Yamamoto to cooperate with the DOJ (*ibid.* p. 30). Eichenwald (2000) gives a greater role to Sewon in cracking the case. As early as December 1995, Sewon began plea negotiations by offering the testimony of its chief conspirator as well as a large number of documents about the 1986-1990 price fixing conspiracy and the 1992-1995 cartel. Ajinomoto offered its busiest conspirator (Kanji Mimoto) also, but refused to compel its top official involved (Kazutoshi Yamada) to testify. Eventually, Ajinomoto would agree to require both Mimoto and his predecessor to pay fines and testify. In any case, by June 1996, the DOJ and the three Asian lysine cartel members had arrived at mutually acceptable deals on the three companies' guilty pleas.

The incentive offered by the DOJ for corporate cooperation was a generous offer to apply only the statutory maximum fine of $10 million for the two Japanese companies and even less for Sewon. Moreover, except for two Ajinomoto officers, only one officer from each of the other two companies would be required to plead guilty and pay modest fines; all of the scores of other employees who assisted in the lysine conspiracy were to be immunized. Except for Yamada, who may have left Ajinomoto by this time, no employees would face time in prison.

The reductions offered by the DOJ in monetary damages were indeed a bargain. Under U.S. Sentencing Guidelines, Ajinomoto could have been required to pay from $80 to $231 million in fines had they been based on Ajinomoto's U.S. sales only (Table 13.1). Had the DOJ chosen to base the fines on Ajinomoto's global sales, the company's liability could have been as high as $1 billion, a fact that may well have been mentioned in the company's negotiations with prosecutors. Instead, the DOJ offered Ajinomoto the statutory fine of $10 million, which is only 4 to 12 percent of Ajinomoto's liability under the Guidelines. Moreover, only one Ajinomoto manager, Kanji Mimoto, was fined, and the fine of $75,000 was less than the $350,000 statutory maximum. Both Kyowa Hakko and Sewon also received huge discounts on the maximum possible fines, but the extremely small fine paid by Sewon ($1,250,000) suggests that it was probably the first to crack of the three Asian firms.

Table 13.1. Potential and Actual U.S. Sanctions Applied to the Lysine Conspirators, 1996.

Company Name	Corporate Fines			Individual Sanctions					
	Maximum under Guidelines[a]		Actual	Number[b]		Prison Time		Fines	
	20% Sales Rule	Twice the Harm		Max.	Actual	Max.	Actual	Max.	Actual
	Million dollars					*Months*		*Thousand dollars*	
ADM	54-108	156	70	8	3	288	78	2,800	700
Ajinomoto	80-160	231	10 [c]	14	2	504	0	4,900	75
Kyowa	45-90	129	10 [c]	5	1	180	0	1,750	75
Sewon	32-65	94	1.25 [c]	7	1	252	0	2,450	50
Cheil	15-30	43	1.25	6	0	216	0	2,100	0
Total	225-448	559	92.5	40	7	1,440	78	14,000	900

Source: Connor (2000: Appendix A and Tables A4, A7, 4 and 7).

[a] From the U.S. Sentencing Guidelines based on 20% of sales during 6/92-6/95 with culpability score of 9 and multipliers 1.8 to 3.6; or twice the U.S. overcharge on buyers using ADM ($78 million) as the base (see Chapter 4).

[b] The maximum is the number of named conspirators in the government's proffer (Griffin and Lassar 1998). The "actual" number is the number of persons who were fined. Besides the three defendants at ADM, the proffer alleges that five more employees in the Bioproducts Division knew about and implemented the price fixing, viz., John Ashley, Alfred Jansen, Suji Tani, Martin Allison, and Sidney Hulse.

[c] Known to be a "downward departure" from the range of fines mandated by the U.S. Sentencing Guidelines. Typically, prosecutors recommend such reductions when the defendant has been accepted into its leniency program, has been one of the first of several defendants to cooperate with prosecutors, or provided prosecutors with essential information for the prosecution of bigger violators or violators in other industries.

Although agreed upon in principle through proffer letters in early July, the DOJ held off making the guilty pleas public until August 1996. Before that happened, the good faith of the three companies was tested. On July 17, 1996 Hirozaku Ikeda, recently retired general manager of Ajinomoto's Feed Division, and his successor Kanji Mimoto were interviewed in Hong Kong about their roles in the lysine conspiracy by the FBI (Tr. 1759-1765). Kyowa's Yamamoto was interviewed at the same time. Sewon's Kim was deposed in New York City in August. Their memories were sufficiently clear and consistent that the DOJ believed they would make good prosecution witnesses in any possible trial of ADM or uncooperative individual conspirators. With several potential witnesses now available to corroborate the intentions of the conspirators and interpret the taped evidence, prosecutors were able to pressure ADM itself. In August, they leaked the fact that the DOJ would seek a $400 million fine from ADM.

The guilty pleas of the three Asian firms were formally announced and presented in federal court in Chicago on August 27, 1996. Ajinomoto, Kyowa Hakko, and Sewon America and one officer from each company admitted their guilt to one count of criminal price fixing in the U.S. market for lysine.[41] The officers testified that their companies did not contest the facts mentioned in the plea agreements. However, they agreed to pay fines and cooperate with prosecutors in their investigation of the remaining cartel members, ADM and Cheil. Subject to court approval, the three voluntarily yielded their rights to jury trials.

The guilty pleas of the Asian firms must have been a shocking setback for ADM. It was now in a completely untenable legal position. Should it refuse to plead guilty also, the government had overwhelming evidence of the conspiracy and a dozen participants in the cartel willing and able to testify as to intent. Worse, as the last holdout, ADM had no additional information about the lysine cartel to offer to the prosecutors.

Not surprisingly, ADM furiously negotiated a guilty plea agreement over the next couple of weeks. Eichenwald (2000) provides a detailed account of the bargaining between DOJ official Gary Spratling and ADM's attorney Aubrey Daniel (pp. 508-511). By September 10th, the government was demanding a $125-million fine and no immunity for four ADM officers: Dwayne Andreas, Michael Andreas, Terrance Wilson, and James Randall. A week later, Williams & Connelly countered with a $35-million fine for ADM and indictments for only two officers. On September 17th, the government agreed to give up indicting Dwayne Andreas and James Randall in return for an additional $65-million on the fine. The ADM board agreed to the $100-million fine as the price of avoiding a court trial for the company and its two most senior officers. While such prosecutorial horse-trading may not be pretty, it is probably necessary in order to conserve judicial resources.

By late September, all ADM employees except Michael Andreas and Terrance Wilson were presenting prosecutors with details of the lysine and citric acid conspiracies that satisfied prosecutors as to ADM's good faith.

Prosecutors were especially pleased with Barrie Cox's deposition on October 12th, which was full of rich details about the citric acid cartel (Lieber 2000). Thus, on October 15, 1996, news of ADM's guilty plea covering lysine and citric acid were announced in three venues: Washington, D.C.; Chicago, IL; and Decatur, IL. In Washington, a press conference was held attended by Attorney General Janet Reno, Joel Klein, Gary Spratling (deputy to Klein), Jim Burns (U.S. Attorney, Chicago), and William Esposito (Assistant Director, FBI). These government officials emphasize the precedent-shattering fine of $100 million placed on ADM. Reno said that the fine should "send a message worldwide" about the "tough, tough penalties" now likely for criminal price fixing. Klein called ADM's behavior "shameful" and motivated by "simple greed." Burns praised the work of the two lawyers in his office (Lassar and Guentert) who worked well and closely with the DOJ's Chicago field office. Esposito recalled how the investigation began with just one agent and ended with almost a dozen fully assigned to the case.[42]

ADM paid a fine of $70 million for its lysine infractions and $30 million for citric acid. The citric acid fine for ADM could have been $112 to $224 million had ADM not received a 73 to 86 percent discount for its cooperation on the case (Lieber 2000:37). The $70 million was only the second to exceed the statutory $10 million fine, the first for $15 million imposed the year before in an unheralded dynamite price fixing case. For its cooperation in the citric acid investigation (it had nothing to give in lysine), ADM received a number of important concessions, not all of which were revealed in the government's press release or plea agreement. Both ADM's public-relations effort and the DOJ's press conference tended to gloss over these substantial concessions to ADM. First, the deal granted immunity from prosecution of all ADM employees for price fixing except Michael Andreas and Terrance Wilson. Although most employees were required to be interviewed or to testify, an exception was made for the company's top two officers, Dwayne Andreas and James Randall. Second, the government agreed to drop a federal grand jury investigation in Springfield, Illinois that was charged with an investigation of allegations of theft of technology and trade secrets by ADM. Third, in a deal proposed by ADM's Washington law firm and worked out between the DOJ's Joel Klein and Dan Glickman the Secretary of Agriculture but not revealed until years later, ADM would be allowed to continue signing sales contracts with USDA.[43] Previously, companies guilty of felony violations had been disbarred for a number of years from government sales. Suspicions remain that Klein also agreed to quash the investigation by the fraud division into the many allegations made about ADM by Mark Whitacre (Leiber 2000). Finally, and potentially the most valuable concession, the government agreed to drop its investigation of price fixing in the corn sweeteners market. The huge size of the market implied that even modest overcharge percentages would generate huge liabilities for ADM and any co-conspirators. Dwayne Andreas and James Randall were not required to testify before the fructose grand jury. Mick

Andreas and Terrance Wilson were deposed in the private suit but refused to answer substantive questions.

At the Washington, D.C. press conference, Gary Spratling was forced to field a number of pointed questions by the press. He disagreed that ADM's fine was small relative to its exposure. He denied that there was politics involved in the special treatment accorded D. Andreas and J. Randall. He defended the granting of immunity to ADM in the corn sweeteners markets, but described the basis of the decision as one of ". . . a great complexity of factors and prosecutorial discretion." In other words, ADM was not granted immunity from prosecution because it was innocent of the charges, but because the DOJ judged that successful prosecution would be a challenging one with an uncertain outcome.

Virtually simultaneously with the D.C. press conference, ADM's guilty plea agreement was being presented to Judge Ruben Castillo in U.S. District Court in Chicago. At that hearing prosecutors presented the terms of the agreement and outlined the evidence that supported the price fixing conspiracy. Steven Mills, ADM's controller and a corporate officer, testified that the company accepted the terms of the agreement, waived its right to a jury trial, and did not dispute the facts about the conspiracy that were presented by the government. Mills pleaded guilty for the company, and Castillo accepted the plea. In his closing comments, Judge Castillo said:

> "It's not a good day for corporate America. I'm hopeful that this black day will be overcome by the new behavior of the Archer Daniel Midland Co. . . Some will say that this fine is not high enough . . . no American company is above the law, and if a hundred million dollars doesn't send that message, I don't think there is a number on God's earth that I can set that would send that message."

At the hearing, DOJ prosecutor James Griffin had been interrogated by Castillo concerning the appropriateness of ADM's fines, $70 million for the lysine and $30 million for the citric acid conspiracies. At the DOJ's press conference that day it was erroneously stated that ADM was the first of many price fixers that would be forced to pay fines based on the "two-times rule" contained in the U.S. Sentencing Guidelines. In fact, as Griffin explained to Judge Castillo in Chicago, ADM's fine was based on a much more favorable alternative allowed under the guidelines. One method of calculating the fine allows a base fine of 20 percent of the sales of the company in the affected market to be adjusted by a multiplier based on the felon's culpability score. ADM's U.S. sales of dry lysine were about $150 million, the base fine was $30 million, and the multipliers raised the base fine to a final figure of $54 to $108 million.[44] Of course, $70 million lies within that range. However, the DOJ could have presented its estimates of ADM's actual overcharge. Indeed, under the guidelines, if there was evidence that the overcharge was significantly higher than 10 percent, the government was obligated to use the alternative method that was based on twice the actual harm to buyers. When the DOJ presented such an analysis in a federal sentencing hearing two years later, the overcharge to be doubled was calculated to be $78 million (52 percent of sales). Thus, ADM's actual fine was less than half the fine calculated under the "two-times rule."

To summarize, as high as the fines on the lysine conspirators appear to be, they were still less than what could have been applied (Table 13.1). The three larger Asian companies received the largest discounts because they were the first to cooperate with the government. ADM's fine, while a record for the time and within one of the two guidelines ranges, also received a relatively favorable fine, one well below twice the harm caused to buyers of lysine. Of the 40 named conspirators who worked at the five companies, three paid modest fines only and three were handed down prison sentences. Corporations paid as little as one-eighth and individuals 7 percent of the maximum fines that could have been imposed by the courts.

THE CITRIC ACID PROSECUTIONS

The Investigation Phase

A grand jury was empanelled around June 1995 in San Francisco to investigate allegations of price fixing in the global market for citric acid. The grand jury worked with prosecutors from the local field office of the DOJ's Antitrust Division and the U.S. Attorney for the Northern District of California. Based on tape recordings of the lysine conspirators that contained fairly clear references to an ongoing conspiracy in citric acid, and on the deposition of ADM's chief sales manager in citric acid, the grand jury issued subpoenas and obtained search warrants directed at five firms: ADM, Cargill, Haarmann & Reimer (a U.S. subsidiary of the German Bayer Corp.), the Austrian firm Jungbunzlauer, and the Swiss firm Hoffmann-La Roche.

The FBI first learned about price fixing of citric acid on December 10, 1992 from ADM's Mark Whitacre. ADM's involvement was confirmed by a tape recording made by Whitacre on December 21, 1992 of ADM manager Brasser. On that tape Brasser said that Terrance Wilson told him not to worry about going to jail for price fixing in citric acid (Tr. 2868-2873). Soon afterwards, Brasser was fired because he refused to become involved in the conspiracy. Other sound recordings contained references about how well the citric acid cartel was organized. Wilson frequently extolled its ability to agree on volume allocations and monitor the agreement through the trade association that the cartel members belonged to. However, because Whitacre had no managerial responsibility for citric acid and did not know about the cartel's meeting dates, the FBI was unable to make video tapes of the conspirators in action. While the June 1995 FBI raids turned up some incriminating evidence of monthly production targets and sales figures, without a witness to corroborate the purposes of the meetings and documents, such evidence remained circumstantial.

The government's big break came on October 12-13, 1996. Behind the scenes, ADM and the DOJ had made a deal on a plea bargain that covered both lysine and citric acid. Solid evidence on the citric acid cartel was the most valuable bargaining chip ADM had to offer the prosecutors. Although the last to settle in lysine, ADM was the first member of the citric acid cartel to offer to cooperate with the DOJ and, therefore, could expect to receive leniency for its help. Within ADM, the citric acid conspiracy had been managed by Terrance Wilson and his head of citric acid marketing, Barrie Cox. Wilson would not cooperate, but on October 12th Barrie Cox began to tell all to prosecutors in San Francisco.[45] As part of the ADM plea agreement, Cox would be immunized from prosecution for price fixing so long as he told the truth. Later, Cox would become in many ways the government's star witness in the criminal antitrust trial against Terrance Wilson. Cox presumably had ADM's blessing at this point because without his full cooperation, ADM could be indicted for price fixing in corn sweeteners and Dwayne Andreas might be held accountable as well.

The Guilty Pleas

Cox divulged all the details of the conspiracy by the "G-4." The DOJ later said publicly that Cox "did cooperate and it is substantial." A couple of days later, ADM paid a $30 million fine for its role in price fixing in the market for citric acid, an amount that reflected a hefty discount for its cooperation with prosecutors. At the October 15, 1996 hearing in federal court in Chicago, prosecutors explained to Judge Castillo the amount of U.S. commerce in citric acid affected by the cartel from June 1992 to June 1995 was $350 million. The "base fine" under the U.S. Sentencing Guidelines is therefore $70 million. A "culpability score" of 8 for ADM implies a fine range of $112 to $224 million. However, the government requested that the judge grant a downward departure because of ADM's "substantial cooperation." Thus, the $30 million fine represents a 73 to 87 percent discount from the fine normally required by the Sentencing Guidelines.

However, if the DOJ had prepared estimates of the cartel's overcharge on U.S. buyers of citric acid (which the agency almost always does), then prosecutors could have requested even a larger fine based on double the overcharge. Because there was no trial for the citric acid conspiracy, no details on costs of production were made public. While estimating the but-for price depends on the dates of the conspiracy, for the period June 1992-June 1995 the U.S. overcharge by the cartel was in the range of $250 to $550 million, of which ADM accounted for $75 to $165. Thus, this method implies that ADM's actual fine was 9 to 20 percent of its liability (Table 13.2). No ADM officers were fined or imprisoned for their role in citric acid.

Table 13.2. Potential and Actual U.S. Sanctions Applied to the Citric Acid Conspirators, 1996- 1997.

Company Name	Corporate Fines			Individual Sanctions					
	Maximum under Guidelines[a]		Actual	Number[b]		Prison Time		Fines[c]	
	20% Sales Rule	Twice the Harm		Max.	Actual	Max.	Actual	Max.	Actual
	Million dollars					*Months*		*$ thousands*	
ADM	112-224	150-330	30	4	0[d]	144	0	1,400	0
H&R/Bayer	34-68	120-264	50	2	1	72	0	700	150
Hoffmann-La Roche	18-36	24-53	14	3	1	108	0	1,050	150
Jungbunzlauer	24-48	32-71	11	2	1	72	0	700	150
Cerestar	1-2	1-3	0.4	1	1	36	0	350	40
Total	189-378	327-721	105.4	12	4	432	0	4,200	790

Source: Connor (2000: Tables 7 and Appendix B).

[a] From the U.S. Sentencing Guidelines based on 20% of U.S. sales affected by the cartel (for ADM $350 million) during 6/92-6/95 with a culpability score of 8 and multipliers 1.6 to 3.2. Using U.S. sales is conservative because global sales may be used. Twice the harm is double the best estimate of the U.S. overcharge made by the author (see Chapter 3).

[b] An undercount of persons mentioned by name in trial transcripts or reliable press accounts as conspirators.

[c] Maximum statutory fine is $350,000 per person; however, this is conservative because the U.S. Sentencing Guidelines allow fines up to $25 million or 5 percent of the effected sales.

[d] Michael Andreas and Terrance Wilson were convicted for their roles in lysine price fixing but were not tried for citric acid; Barrie Cox was given immunity; Cox's friend Roger Dawson knew of the conspiracy.

On January 29, 1997, the second of the citric acid conspirators entered a guilty plea in federal court in San Francisco. The defendants were Haarmann & Reimer Corp., a subsidiary of Bayer AG, and Hans Hartmann its president. The company paid a fine of $50 million, at the time the second largest in antitrust history. At its press conference, DOJ officials called the conspiracy "one of the largest, if not the largest, conspiracies ever prosecuted by the Department of Justice." They also asserted that Bayer's fine would have been larger had it not agreed to cooperate in prosecuting the remaining conspirators, but they declined to specify the actual overcharges. Private antitrust lawyers called the new higher fine structures "a staggering development for business." Haarmann & Reimer held about 24 percent of the U.S. market during the conspiracy, thus a fine based on double the overcharge would have amounted to $120 to $264 million. Bayer too was granted a substantial discount for its cooperation (58 to 81 percent), but not nearly as large a discount as ADM received.

Hans Hartmann and Terrance Wilson were clearly regarded by prosecutors as the ringleaders of the cartel. Under the Sentencing Guidelines, Hartmann's offense rated a culpability score of 17.[46] This score implies a prison sentence of 24 to 30 months and a fine of $0.8 to $3.5 million. Instead, because of his cooperation in providing information on the remaining members of the G-4, Hartmann received no prison sentence and a downward departure on his fine to $150,000.

Two months later, the remaining two members of the G-4 signed and submitted guilty pleas for price fixing. Hoffmann-La Roche and Jungbunzlauer agreed to pay $14 and $11 million respectively. Udo Haas, former managing director of Citrique Belge, the Belgian subsidiary of Roche that manufactured citric acid, agreed to pay a $150,000 fine, as did Rainer Bilchbauer, Chairman and President of Jungbunzlauer. Neither will serve time in prison. At this point in the prosecution, neither company had much to offer by way of cooperation, so in a relative sense their sentences were more severe.[47] That is, the actual corporate and individual fines were larger percentages of the maximum possible fines they faced given the size of their overcharges (Table 13.2).

One of the more curious aspects of the pleas was the time period in the agreements. The conspiracy was stated to have begun "as early as January 1993." Why the DOJ chose such a patently late date is unknown. As mentioned above in Chapter 4, the conspirators met to set prices in March 1991. Moreover, the Statement of Facts given to Canada's Federal Court by the Attorney General (and co-signed by the defendants) gives July 1991 as the beginning date for the citric acid conspiracy. By suggesting that ADM's illegal activity might have begun almost two years later, prosecutors severely disadvantaged private plaintiffs who were in the midst of negotiations with the citric acid defendants in October 1996. The criminal plea bargains are *prima facie* evidence in civil antitrust cases, so a longer conspiracy period would have significantly increased the damages claimed by plaintiffs.

PROSECUTION OF THE VITAMINS CARTELS

For government trust-busters, the vitamins conspiracies were the greatest catch in antitrust history. Lysine and citric acid pale in comparison to the vitamins case in scope, size, complexity, longevity, or nearly any other conceivable measuring stick. At least 17 chemical manufacturers fixed the prices of 12 vitamin products for up to 11 years. The cartels' global sales during the conspiracies mounted to grand total of $28 billion, of which $5.5 billion occurred in the United States (Table 12.2 above). Illicit profits made by the cartels totaled $7 to $8 billion. Two dozen corporations or individuals would be judged guilty of price fixing felonies.

The Investigation Phase

The U.S. DOJ had been busy prosecuting the lysine and citric acid cases throughout 1996 and early 1997. However, in early 1997 the FBI had received information about a possible price fixing conspiracy in the vitamins industry. In March of that year, FBI agents interviewed Dr. Kuno Sommer about the matter. Sommer was the global head of vitamins marketing for Hoffmann-La Roche, the world's leading manufacturer of vitamins. Roche made at least 11 vitamins in plants located in Germany, Scotland, Japan, and the United States. The company was widely reported to enjoy a 45 to 50 percent share of the global markets for bulk vitamins.[48] Sommer also served on Roche's small management committee that formed the pinnacle of the company's management structure. If anyone should have known about vitamins price fixing within Roche, it was Sommer.

Sommer denied that Roche was involved in any such illegal activity. He was interviewed under the January 1997 citric acid plea agreement in which Roche had promised full cooperation from its employees in any antitrust investigations, so Sommer's denial would have serious legal consequences if he did not answer truthfully. Later it came to light that Sommer had prearranged with others at Roche to lie about the cartel's existence. However, because Roche was the only vitamin co-conspirator with a cooperation pledge, Sommer's denials must have slowed the FBI's investigation considerably.

In November 1997, the DOJ investigation picked up speed again. Press reports revealed that numerous executives responsible for procuring vitamins for animal-feeds manufacturers were being interviewed about possible price fixing activities in the industry. Moreover, word leaked out that a grand jury had been opened in Dallas, Texas to assist the DOJ in its vitamins investigation. This grand jury would toil away in secret for 16 months before the first fruits of the investigation would become public. By mid-summer 1999 strong and persistent rumors had begun circulating among Washington antitrust lawyers that indictments were likely in the case of vitamins A, C, E, and riboflavin; Roche and BASF were mentioned as targets of the vitamin probe.[49] In March 1998, it would become known that the Dallas grand jury had made considerable progress in two product markets, vitamins B3 (niacin) and B4 (choline chloride), both of which have their main applications in animal nutrition. In fact, in September 1998, the dominant manufacturer of vitamin B3, the Swiss firm Lonza, had been indicted and had agreed to plead guilty for criminal price fixing. However, in an unusual move, Lonza's indictment and guilty plea were kept secret under a court seal for six months. The most likely explanation for the secrecy is that knowledge about Lonza's cooperation would have alerted other, bigger targets in the vitamin industry and thereby imperiled the DOJ's investigation.

Lonza Pleads Guilty

In retrospect, it seems that Lonza itself or one of Lonza's smaller rivals (and co-conspirators) in the B3 market must have cracked sometime in early or mid 1998 and agreed to provide evidence about Lonza's role in the conspiracy. Lonza's cooperation was secured by a fairly small fine (only $10.5 million) and by the DOJ's agreement not to seek criminal charges against any of Lonza's executives.[50] None of the big fish in the world's vitamins industry make vitamin B3, but Lonza does manufacture one other vitamin, biotin (vitamin H). Lonza, together with two other Japanese manufacturers, share the top spots in the world biotin market. The dominant world producer of biotin with about 40 percent of the market is none other than Hoffmann-La Roche. Although this is rather speculative, biotin may have provided the route from the B3 conspiracy to Roche's wider involvement.[51]

Another possibility as to how the DOJ first cracked the silence of the vitamin cartel is a small detail noted by investigative reporter David Barboza in a major *New York Times* article on the cartel. Barboza (1999) notes that three companies joined the main collusive group of the Big Six in 1992. They were Lonza, the dominant maker of vitamin B3, and Chinook and DuCoa, the dominant producers of choline chloride (B4) in North America. The vitamin B4 cartel in North America may have started before Roche and BASF launched their vitamin A and E conspiracies in January 1990. However, it is known from documents released by the Canadian Ministry of Justice that the nature of the vitamin B4 conspiracy changed in 1992; at that time BASF (a member of the main cartel group since early 1991) agreed to stop exporting B4 from Europe to North America and in return the North American manufacturers stopped exporting B4 to Europe. Moreover, Lonza's guilty plea states that its collusion in vitamin B3 began "as early as January 1992." Thus, the evidence is consistent that Lonza, Chinook, and DuCoa joined the main cartel of six firms in January 1992, meeting with them mostly in Germany and Switzerland. Lonza's vitamin B3 managers had plenty of detailed information to give DOJ investigators about the Big Six vitamin makers' roles in the cartel, and the five officers of Chinook and DuCoa indicted in September 1998 could have easily corroborated the allegations.

Convictions in Vitamin B3

More information about the vitamin B3 cartel came to light in May 2000 when three companies and two individuals pleaded guilty to criminal price fixing. The three vitamin B3 manufacturers convicted were Degussa-Hüls of Frankfurt am Main, Germany; Reilly Chemicals, Inc. of Indianapolis, Indiana; and Nepera, Inc. of Harriman, New York. Degussa and Reilly owned a joint venture that made B3 in the United States; in addition, Degussa probably exported B3 to the United States from one of its European plants. Nepera was a relatively small U.S. manufacturer of B3, but the fact that Nepera's President and Vice President for sales were the only two persons convicted in this cartel suggests that Nepera was one of the leaders and initiators of the conspiracy.

The plea agreements for Lonza, Degussa, and Nepera admit that each of the companies began conspiring "as early as January 1992," which is consistent with information on transaction prices shows a suspicious jump in B3 prices in 1989. Both Nepera and Degussa seem to have resigned from the cartel in July 1995, but in Degussa's case it handed on its conspiratorial role to its joint-venture partner, Reilly Industries.[52] When the conspiracy ended in March 1998, the two largest U.S. sellers of B3, Lonza and Reilly, were still conspiring.[53] In addition, the DOJ stated that there were unnamed co-

conspirators that were not indicted. By May 2000, four companies had paid $33.5 billion in criminal fines, and two Nepera executives were to be sentenced to a total of 20 months in prison (Table 6.A.1). Degussa seems to have paid the largest fine relative to its sales during the conspiracy, a sign that it was the most culpable of the corporate cartel members.

The Big Three Plead Guilty

With fairly solid evidence of a broad conspiracy in several vitamins markets in the hands of government investigators by mid-1998, in the time-honored fashion of prosecutors everywhere, they turned the screws tighter on the smaller vitamins manufacturers. Rhône-Poulenc was a vulnerable target. It was the smallest of the Big Three vitamin manufacturers, holding about 9 percent of the global market. Rhône-Poulenc was amenable to a deal because it had previously announced its intention to merge with Hoechst, and such a merger could not be consummated if the uncertainty of severe price fixing sanctions hung over their heads. Whatever Rhône-Poulenc's motives, it agreed in late 1998 to cooperate with the DOJ's broader vitamins investigation. In fact, Rhône-Poulenc was formally admitted into the DOJ's amnesty program after it provided crucial evidence for prosecutors. Not only did its executives, who were deeply involved in colluding on vitamins A, E, B2, and B12 begin to provide incriminating details, but also its vitamins managers gave the DOJ the kind of evidence that is most persuasive with juries – tape recordings of an actual cartel meeting.[54] The meeting in February 1999 was one of "Vitamins Inc.'s" top-flight occasions, with all of the companies' top officers present. The cartel had by now gone into deep cover, so this last meeting was probably held in one of the participant's private homes in Switzerland or Germany.[55] When the DOJ approached the lawyers representing Roche and BASF with the overwhelming evidence provided by their former co-conspirator Rhône-Poulenc, the two leaders quickly agreed to plead guilty. The DOJ would later praise Roche and BASF for their exemplary cooperation.

DOJ negotiations in March to May of 1999 mainly involved the size of the fines to be paid by Roche and BASF. Under the twice-the-harm rule for sentencing of corporate felons, Roche was presented with the doubtless astounding news that their company was facing U.S. fines of $1.3 to $2.6 billion (not to mention untold millions in tag-along civil penalties). However, Roche and BASF were fortunate in being the third and fourth companies to settle with the DOJ.[56] The DOJ prosecutors likely pointed out the material benefits of a downward departure in their ultimate fines if only they too would cooperate. The decision to pay even the greatly reduced fines offered by the DOJ was obviously not an easy one to make for Roche and BASF. There is a revealing detail in the plea agreement signed by BASF, an appended letter from its general counsel to the DOJ dated May 18, 1999 committing BASF to plead guilty under the DOJ's terms: the meeting of BASF's Executive Committee at its Ludwigshafen headquarters to approve the deal took seven and one-half hours.

On May 19, 1999 the *Wall Street Journal* announced to the world that momentous guilty pleas of price fixing in the vitamins industry would be made public the next day. The announcement day itself was full of dozens of coordinated events. In the morning of May 20th, a press conference was held at the headquarters of the Department of Justice in Washington, attended by the Attorney General Janet Reno, the Assistant Attorney General for Antitrust Joel Klein, and many other top officials of the DOJ and FBI. At about the same time, officers of Roche and BASF appeared with DOJ prosecutors in U.S. District Court in Dallas, Texas to file their guilty pleas and explain to the Court how the fines and jail sentences were arrived at. The DOJ and the Big Three vitamins makers also released statements to the press. Rhône-Poulenc's statement admitted that it had engaged in criminal price fixing and would face harsh civil penalties in the future for its crimes; it also pointed out that it had been admitted to the DOJ's amnesty program and thereby would save tens of millions of dollars in potential U.S. penalties. Joel Klein spent much of the day being interviewed about the plea agreements. The world's business press would be filled with news of the deal the next day.

The deals involved an almost unimaginable stepping up of price fixing sanctions. Hoffmann-La Roche agreed to pay $500 million in fines, almost five times the previous record antitrust fine. BASF paid $225 million (Table 13.3). These fines were proportional to the each companies' U.S. and global market shares. (Had Rhône-Poulenc been fined proportionately, it would have paid $120 to $135 million). As huge as they were, both fines reflected discounts of 45 to 80 percent from what could have been obtained had the DOJ gone to court and won in trial. As the second firms to confess, they were entitled to great leniency (Spratling 2000). Prosecutors could easily have argued that the sentencing guidelines would have required using the twice-the-harm standard to calculate the base fine.[57] Twice the harm is twice the overcharges; from Chapter 12 above, twice the U.S. overcharges would yield a base fine of $2.5 to $3.0 billion. Then the base fine would be multiplied by two to four because of numerous aggravating factors (Roche and BASF were ringleaders, and Roche was a repeat offender). With possible future fines of up to $12 billion for all the participants (including $4 billion for Roche and $2 billion for BASF), settling for a mere $725 million eventually was seen by the defendants to be a reasonable compromise.[58]

More detailed information on how the DOJ's newest leniency program works in practice was revealed in a speech by retired DOJ official Gary Spratling (2000). Amnesty is granted to the first firm to confess to its role in a criminal antitrust conspiracy, but only if the DOJ was unaware of the cartel and the first-comer was not a leader or enforcer in the cartel. That is, the first to offer this valuable information and to agree to cooperate automatically receives a 100-percent discount on the fine specified by the U.S. Sentencing

Guidelines. However, the second firm to confess also receives a substantial break as well, typically 50 to 80-percent discount from what is specified by the Guidelines or 10 to 25-percent of the affected sales by the company. Attracting a second cartel member to the prosecutors' side is important if the other conspirators decide to go to trial. If a cartel is large enough to have third and fourth firms, they too may apply for leniency. Their fines will be successfully larger percentage of their sales during the cartel era. The degree of leniency will increase for these late-arrivals if they are quick to confess, relatively small players in the cartel, offer valuable information, created modest overcharges, or can show that the conspiracy was not condoned by top management (Spratling 2000).

Table 13.3. Potential and Actual U.S. Sanctions Imposed on the Vitamins Conspirators, 1998- 2000.

Name/Subsidiary	Corporate			Individual					
	Maximum[a]		Actual	Number[b]		Prison Time		Fines[c]	
	20% Rule	Twice the Harm		Max.	Actual	Max.	Actual	Max.	Actual
	Million dollars					*Months*		*$ thousands*	
Hoffmann-La Roche Ltd.	440-460	2050-4640	500	9	4	324	13	3150	600
BASF AG	150-160	770-1600	225	9	3	324	9.5	3150	275
Rhône-Poulenc	95-105	465-1090	0[d]	9E	0[d]	324	0	3150	0
Takeda Chemical Industries	85-90	265-735	72	2E	0	72	0	700	0
Eisai Co.	35-40	175-415	40	2E	0	72	0	700	0
Daiichi Pharmaceutical	20-25	55-225	25	2E	0	72	0	700	0
Alusuisse/Lonza AG	20-30	40-160	10.5	2E	0	72	0	700	0
Chinook Group	50-60	95-335	5	2E	2	72	0[e]	700	0[e]
DuCoa, LP[f]	16-20	30-112	pending	3	3	108	0[e]	1050	0[e]
Mitsui/Bioproducts, Inc.	35-40	70-225	pending	2E	0	72	0	700	0
Degussa/Vitachem	11-15	22-85	13	2E	0	72	0	700	0
Reilly/Vitachem	11-15	22-85	2	2E	0	72	0	700	0
Hoechst AG	0-1	1-6	pending	2E	0	72	0	700	0
E. Merck	8-10	16-60	14	2E	0	72	0	700	0
Nepera/Cambrex	18-20	35-112	pending	2E	0	72	0	700	0
TOTAL	994-1091	4100-9850	908.5	52	13	1872	22.5	18200	875

Source: Table 13.A.1.
E = Estimate by author.
[a] From the U.S. Sentencing Guidelines based on 20% of U.S. sales affected by the cartel (for ADM $350 million) during 6/92-6/95 with a culpability score of 8 and multipliers 1.6 to 3.2. Using U.S. sales is conservative because global sales may be used. Twice the harm is double the best estimate of the U.S. overcharge made by the author (see Chapter 3).
[b] An undercount of persons mentioned by name in trial transcripts or reliable press accounts as conspirators.
[c] Maximum statutory fine is $350,000 per person; however, this is conservative because the U.S. Sentencing Guidelines allow fines up to $25 million or 5 percent of the effected sales.
[d] Granted amnesty by the DOJ.
[e] Indicted but not yet sentenced.
[f] Began colluding when jointly owned by DuPont and Conagra.

Specific numerical examples are provided from two of the largest global cartel cases prosecuted by the DOJ in table 13.4. It is difficult to reconcile all of Spratling's criteria with the actual outcomes of these two cases. For example, Roche and BASF were tied for second place in the race for leniency in vitamins, yet the second largest ringleader (BASF) got a smaller percentage discount than the number-one ringleader. The later arrivals in this populous cartel also received discounts that put the them below the presumptive ranges. In the graphite electrodes case, the discounts decline with rank as expected, but again the discounts are excessive when compared to the percentages of affected sales the companies were supposed to be fined. In sum, compared to its discount in principle, the DOJ seems to be too lenient in practice.

Besides the corporate fines eight senior executives of Roche and BASF were indicted for criminal price fixing. The four Roche officials were Dr. Kuno Sommer (former head of global vitamins marketing, promoted to President of Roche's fragrances and flavoring division), Dr. Hugo Brönnimann (President of the vitamins division), Andreas Hauri (head of global vitamin marketing), and a former Roche executive whose name is secret.[59] At BASF, four officers with similar positions were indicted: Reinhard Steinmetz, Dieter Suter, Dietz Kaminski, and Hugo Strotmann. In addition to these eight, ten more managers were listed by name as unindicted co-conspirators. While all eight top executives were fined, the DOJ saved its harshest treatment for Kuno Sommer. He had not only fixed prices but also made false statements to DOJ investigators in March 1997. In addition to a $100,000 personal fine, Sommer had to agree to a four-month prison sentence. This was the first time in U.S. antitrust history that a European had agreed to serve prison time for price fixing.

Table 13.4. Two Examples of the U.S. Department of Justice's Leniency Program for Corporate Price Fixers.

CASE: Company	U.S. Sentencing Guideline's Fine Range	Normal Leniency		Actual Fines Paid		
		Amount	Proportion of Affected Sales	Amount	Proportion of Affected Sales	Discount from Guidelines
Vitamins[a]:	*Million Dollars*		*Percent*	*$ million*	*Percent*	
First to plea (Rhône-Poulenc	120-240E	120-240 E	0	0	0	100
Second to plea (Roche)	1312-2624	360-900	10-25	500	14	62-81
Second to plea (BASF)	409-818	160-420	10-25	225	14	45-72
Third to plea (Daiichi)	80-180E	25-40	25-35	25	24	69-86
Fourth to plea (Eisai)	150-320E	55+	30+	40	22	73-88
Graphite Electrodes[b]:						
First to plea (Carbide/Graphite)	90-250E	0	0	0	0	100
Second to plea (Showa Denko)	65-135	32-82	10-25	325	10	50-76
Third to plea (UCAR Intl.)	125-275E	175-250	25-35	110	15-18	12-60
Last to plea (SGL Carbon)	100-240E	150+	30+	135	24-28	0-44

Source: Connor (2000), Spratling (2000)
E = Estimated by the author.
[a] Includes vitamins A, E, B1, B2, B5, B6, beta carotene, and vitamin premixes. The dates of the guilty plea agreements were February 1998 (amnesty), May 1999 (Roche and BASF, the cartel's leaders, were tied for second), and the rest September 1999. Lonza pleaded guilty in September 1999, but was not indicted for any of the vitamins cited above. U.S. affected sales were about $6.4 billion.
[b] The dates of the three guilty pleas were February, April, and May 1998. Carbide/Graphite applied for amnesty some time in early 1997. U.S. affected sales were $1.5 billion to $1.75 billion. SGL AG of Germany was the cartel's leader, but SGL Carbon Inc., its U.S. subsidiary, paid the fine; because SGL Carbon was small, its fine was below the normal leniency level because it "could not afford to pay."

At its press conference, DOJ officials were grave and scolding. Janet Reno began by saying that the $500 million fine was,

> ". . . the highest fine the Justice Department has ever obtained in any criminal case. We mean business."

Joel Klein elaborated on the DOJ's view:

> "The vitamin cartel is the most pervasive and harmful criminal antitrust conspiracy ever uncovered . . . The enormous effort that went into maintaining the conspiracy reflects the magnitude of the illegal revenues it generated . . . These cartels . . . are powerful and sophisticated and, without intervention by antitrust authorities, will often go on indefinitely."

Klein's assistant Gary Spratling provided the most pithy characterization:

> "Simply put, the vitamin cartel was as bad as they get."

When asked by a reporter why he thought the vitamin cartel lasted so long, Spratling gave three reasons. First, the Antitrust Division had only stepped up its efforts directed at global price fixing since the 1995 ADM case. Second, the conspirators had gone to great lengths to cover up their conspiracy. Third, the DOJ's newly revised leniency program had been very useful in attracting Rhône-Poulenc's cooperation.

A day after the DOJ press conference, the Chairman of Roche, Franz Humer, and the company's CEO met with the press. He said:

> "I am personally absolutely shocked at what has happened. You will understand that this was not part of our responsibility. We really don't know what [the Roche price fixers] did."

He claimed to have learned of the conspiracy only in February 1999; two previous internal investigations by the company in 1997 and 1998 (in response to civil suits brought against Roche by vitamin buyers in the United States) had failed to uncover any skullduggery. Huber said that he would take steps to avoid a repetition of antitrust offenses, but his plan was rather vague. The only concrete step taken was firing Kuno Sommer and Hugo Brönnimann; the six other managers mentioned in Roche's guilty plea agreement were left in their jobs.

Humer's performance at this press conference raised a chorus of critical comments. In an article laced with acid language, *New York Times* writer Edmund Andrews derided Humer's statements:

> "... the chairman and chief executive of Roche Holdings AG pronounced themselves blameless and clueless ... "

An article appearing in the *Financial Times* of London commented that:

> "The fine is a severe blow to the reputation of Roche, one of the world's oldest and most conservative pharmaceutical companies."

Industry analysts were not long in issuing glum prediction about the financial implications for Roche *et al.* By June 1999, they were speculating that the total antitrust costs for the defendants would be at least $2 billion. Although promptly denied by Roche, one chemical-industry analyst estimated that Roche alone would face antitrust liabilities of $1 billion or more and might want to sell its vitamins/fine chemicals division.

In October 1999, a Roche spokesperson was interviewed about the vitamin conspiracy. In a statement that is quite revealing about the company's continuing attitude of myopic self- deception, she said:

> "We can't dispute the facts and we've decided it is of no value to unravel it. The situation is behind us. We've paid dearly for it."

Public-relations specialists often see their role as putting a positive spin on any adverse news facing their employers or clients. The truth is that Roche and its fellow conspirators in vitamins still faced a bewildering and unprecedently broad array of legal problems. The civil suits in the United States and Canada were still being filed or negotiated (see Chapter 16). More to the point, Roche *et al.* were besieged by investigations by antitrust officials of many nations, and several of these actions were at early stages in late 1999.

Smaller Firms Plead Guilty

Many more corporate and individual guilty plea agreements followed those of Roche and BASF. This time it was *USA Today* that broke the news about further indictments in its June 17th edition. Seven companies and the vitamins they made were specifically mentioned. An official announcement about three of them, all from Japan, came on September 9, 1999. Takeda Chemical Industries, Eisai Co., and Daiichi Pharmaceutical paid fines of $72, $40, and $25 million, respectively, for price fixing in vitamins E, C, B2, and B5. It is typical for conspirators that take longer to admit their guilt to be fined at a higher rate than companies that settle early and cooperate. However, the fines paid by the Japanese firms were less than proportional to those paid by Roche and BASF, perhaps because the former were not considered ringleaders in the cartel.[60] Also, the Japanese vitamin conspirators sold products that had lower overcharges than the other members of the cartel.

The large U.S. fines paid by the three Japanese chemical companies were widely reported in the companies' home country. Perhaps to counter the adverse publicity, the companies imposed on themselves additional sanctions. At Takeda Chemical Industries all employees were to be required to take new training in antitrust principles. The company's president, Kuno Takeda, took a 15 percent pay cut for three months, and all members of the board of directors imposed a 5-percent, three-month pay cut on themselves. Moreover, Kuno Takeda resigned his post as Chairman of the Japan Federation of Pharmaceutical Manufacturers. Daiichi and Eisai announced very similar sanctions for their boards, presidents, and employees on the same day. Although there is a certain ritualistic flavor to their public self-flagellation, at least it makes the point that the companies' entire governance structures accept some of the burden of responsibility for the companies' criminal behavior. In any case, the Japanese companies' responses stand in stark contrast to the "clueless and blameless" stance of Roche's top officials.

While possibly not the last guilty pleas in the far-ranging vitamins case, the DOJ seemed to be winding down its investigation by mid 2000. In May, four corporate and two personal price fixing convictions were announced that seemed to be tidying up the slate. The Darmstadt, Germany-based pharmaceutical firm E. Merck pleaded guilty to fixing the price of vitamin C and agreed to pay a $14 million fine. Roche, BASF, and Takeda had previously admitted their guilt in the vitamin C case, but the DOJ announcement hinted that other unnamed firms might well be added to the roster in the future. Three companies were convicted in the vitamin B3 cartel: Degussa-Hüls (Germany), Nepera (a subsidiary of the U.S. firm Cambrex Corp.), and Reilly Industries (a privately owned Indiana firm). The distribution of the $19 million in fines suggested that Degussa was a leader of the cartel, but its high fine may have been due to recalcitrance in settling with the government. Degussa's guilty plea came 18 months after the largest member of the B3 cartel (Lonza) had capitulated and agreed to supply the DOJ with information. Both of the men convicted and given prison sentences were Nepera executives. As with vitamin C, the government's press releases hinted darkly at further punishments of additional unnamed co-conspirators who had not yet settled.

In September 1999, Chinook Group Ltd. of Canada became the 14th prosecution in the vitamins scandal. It agreed to pay a $5 million criminal fine for its role in the price fixing of choline chloride (B4). Previously, two of its officers pleaded guilty for the same crime. Interestingly, one of its partners in crime, DuCoa, was not required to plead guilty, though three of DuCoa's sales managers did so. It appears from this turn of events that the top managers at DuCoa might not have been aware of the price fixing going on in the company's vitamin sales department. DuCoa's case is unique in that the company was sold to a new owner, DCV Corp., during the middle of the conspiracy in vitamin B4. DCV maintains that it knew nothing of the price fixing. Indeed, DCV has sued DuCoa's former owners, DuPont and ConAgra, for failing to reveal a material fact prior to the acquisition of DuCoa. The absence of a fine imposed by the DOJ on DuCoa lends credence to the notion that the company's new owners had no knowledge of the conspiracy.

By the end of the year 2000, about 20 chemical companies had been indicted or convicted for international price fixing in the markets for bulk vitamins. Fines imposed by competition-law agencies would approach $2 billion worldwide, half of that accounted for by the U.S. government (see Chapter 19). The most injurious cartels in modern history also became the most expensive in terms of fines.

HIGH FRUCTOSE CORN SYRUP: THE FORGOTTEN CARTEL?

High fructose corn syrup (HFCS) is the outstanding example of a new industry created by the application of advanced biotechnologies. Produced mainly in North America, HFCS was unknown before 1970 but had achieved global sales of $3 billion by 1995. It has become an indispensable ingredient for the U.S. soft drink industry, which buys nearly three-fourths of U.S. output. Moreover, HFCS by the 1990s had become the principal product of the U.S. corn wet milling (starch) industry and its largest single source of profits.

Ordinary corn syrup is a viscous liquid containing mostly the sweetener glucose. This low-intensity corn sweetener has been made since the mid-19th century and is still widely used in the bakery and confectionary industries. The manufacture of glucose corn syrup and dextrose, another corn-derived sweetener, were dominated by the Corn Products Refining Co (CPR) from its formation by merger in 1906 to the 1950s. During that period CPR was the target of many antitrust suits that accused the company of monopolistic or conspiratorial behavior. Basic enzyme research in the 1950s, by scientists employed by the company, later called Corn Products Co. (CPC), marked the beginning of the development of commercial methods for making fructose. Improvements patented by scientists working in the Japanese Ministry of Agriculture were purchased by Clinton Corn Processing Co. in 1965. Clinton began manufacturing a form of HFCS that was almost as sweet as sucrose (ordinary sugar) in 1968 or 1969. A few years later Clinton was acquired by ADM, which surpassed CPC in the 1970s to become the leading seller of HFCS in the world.

The market for HFCS enjoyed spectacular growth of 20 to 40 percent p.a. until 1986 or 1987, supplanting crystalline and liquid sucrose in many uses. One of Dwayne Andreas' greatest accomplishments was persuading the cola drink industry to convert to HFCS in the mid 1980s, but once that conversion was complete, volume growth slowed markedly because major substitution possibilities were exhausted. By the early 1990s, HFCS had become a mature industry growing only as fast as the food and beverage industries it supplied, about 4 percent per year. Even though HFCS had become a commodity, profitability remained fairly high because there were few suppliers and because the U.S. sugar program kept the price of sucrose high.

In 1992, nearly all corn wet milling output was accounted for by nine companies, but only six or seven made HFCS. The top four producers of HFCS controlled 85 to 90 percent of HFCS capacity: ADM was the leader with about one-third of the market; A.E. Staley (also headquartered in Decatur, Illinois and owned by Tate & Lyle) about one-fourth; Cargill about 20 percent; and CPC with 10 to 15 percent. A small amount of HFCS was made in Canada and Mexico, but exports to the U.S. market were minimal. Although HFCS accounted for only a small portion of ADM's total sales (about 7 percent in 1992-1995), the product line was a cash cow for the company. One respected industry analyst estimated that nearly 40 percent of ADM's total profits derived from its HFCS sales.

Like CPC, ADM had been involved in an antitrust suit over HFCS. In 1981, the DOJ brought a civil antitrust suit against ADM concerning its acquisition of two HFCS plants from Nabisco Brands, Inc. located in Iowa and New York.[62] The Department of Justice alleged that the increased market share acquired by ADM tended to create a monopoly in the U.S. market for HFCS. The outcome of the case, like many such merger cases, depended on the scope of the market accepted by the court. ADM for its part argued that HFCS, other corn sweeteners, and sugar were in the same market and that ADM therefore controlled only 10 percent of the market. If HFCS was a separate market, ADM's share was closer to 40 percent and likelihood that it would gain market power from the merger was high. In 1991, the case was dismissed because the judge hearing the case in Des Moines, Iowa accepted the broader market definition.[63] However, in December 1998, the 8th Circuit Court reversed on appeal the dismissal of the District Court; the Circuit Court decided that HFCS and sugar were not in the same market because the U.S. sugar program keeps the price of sugar 20 to 30 percent above an equivalent amount of HFCS.

In July 1995, the DOJ revealed that it had empanelled a grand jury to investigate ADM, A.E. Staley, Cargill, and CPC International for criminal price fixing in the HFCS market.[64] Early the next year, leaks from the investigation revealed that HFCS prices were discussed at meetings of the lysine cartel and were caught on tape. An example is a conversation recorded in ADM's headquarters in Decatur, Illinois in the fall of 1993. Present were Michael Andreas, his cousin Martin Andreas, Terrance Wilson, and Mark Whitacre. The topic was raising the price of high fructose corn syrup. Knowing that ADM's principal customer Coca Cola Co. would be angry if ADM went through with it, Terry Wilson asks:

> "What are you gonna tell [Coke]...that we got to deal with two, our two biggest customers, to fuck ya over?" (Leiber 2000: 320).

Martin Andreas and Terry Wilson laughed heartily at the joke (*ibid.*). The tapes also show that Terrance Wilson held up the industry's trade association, the Corn Refiners Association, as an example for the lysine conspirators to emulate.

Another piece of evidence comes from a deposition made in October 1997 by James House, a Kraft executive in charge or purchasing corn sweeteners. He told about how a few years before Dwayne Andreas had offered money to a farmers' cooperative president if the cooperative would stop building a new corn sweetener plant. In addition, House reported on a refusal to deal in HFCS by A.E. Staley, ADM's cross-town neighbor and second in the industry.

> "We made an overture to Staley and offered them significantly increased volume. Our assumption was that Staley would be very happy to have that increased volume. But we were shocked that they took no increased volume" (Leiber 2000: 321).

The DOJ officials met twice with Kraft about these changes, but oddly House was never invited to give grand jury testimony.

Soon after the government's investigation became known, private plaintiffs began filing treble-damages suits against the HFCS manufacturers. By November 1995, ADM was a defendant in more than 20 such suits. One of the defendants, CPC, smallest of the big four, settled with plaintiffs for $7 million in September 1996, but developments since then tend to support the idea that CPC may not have settled because it thought it would lose in a trial.[65] Nevertheless, most of the major HFCS companies remain defendants in what is now a federal class action lawsuit that is asking for billions of dollars in compensation.[66] Indirect buyer suits have also been filed in several states.

As mentioned above, ADM's plea agreement in October 1996 granted immunity from prosecution for price fixing in the market for HFCS.[67] However, the government's investigation of price fixing by the other leading producers of HFCS continued for two years after the ADM deal. In August 1999, the DOJ announced that it had closed its criminal investigation of price fixing sometime during the first half of the year. Termination of the criminal case might strengthen the hands of the four defendants in the civil treble-damages case. Cargill was delighted that they would not be indicted by the government. A company spokesperson said:

> "We're proud of our reputation for integrity. Our commitment to ethical behavior paid off with the conclusion of the sweetener investigation."

Perhaps Cargill's statement will prove to be too optimistic. The DOJ's abandonment of the criminal investigation may have been a pragmatic decision based on having only circumstantial evidence insufficient to prove price fixing beyond a reasonable doubt in a jury trial. The FBI's sound and video tapes contain incriminating statements by Michael Andreas and Terrance Wilson, both of whom reportedly exercised their rights against self-incrimination during their civil depositions in the HFCS case.[68] With an absence of direct testimony by company insiders, the DOJ would not have testimony about intention, which is helpful in criminal convictions. Written evidence of meetings and agreements may be weak or absent. Plaintiffs in the civil case believe that they have compelling economic evidence of substantial price increases in corn sweeteners for a six-year period, 1989-1994, that cannot be explained by the normal competitive market forces. Given the very large sales of corn sweeteners, even a relatively small overcharge (say 5 to 10 percent) would result in treble-damage liabilities of $2 to $4 billion. The defendants have hired battalions of lawyers and squads of economic experts that greatly outnumber the resources that the DOJ could marshal for a trial, resources that had many alternative uses in the numerous global conspiracies discovered. Moreover, the chances of winning high-profile guilty pleas in these other industries were probably much higher than winning a long, drawn-out, messy trial in HFCS. Diverting constrained professional resources from costly battles enhances the total deterrence effect of the antitrust laws and improves managerial efficiency of the antitrust agencies (Preston and Connor 1992).

IMPACT ON CIVIL CASES

Guilty pleas in criminal antitrust proceedings can have a substantial impact on formally distinct civil antitrust cases. Historically, civil damages were sought after the government indicted alleged violators and were concluded after guilty pleas or guilty verdicts were obtained. Indeed, this timing was enshrined by Congress in Section 4 of the Clayton Act, which specifies that guilt determined in a criminal proceeding provides *prima facie* evidence for civil trials.[69] Therefore, the scope and wording of the guilty plea agreement is crucial to the outcome of follow-up civil cases (see Chapter 16). The shape and content of these agreements are the result of careful negotiations between DOJ prosecutors, and counsel for the defendants will press for wording that will be favorable to their clients in any anticipated civil damages actions (Victor 1998).

Antitrust plea agreements negotiated by the DOJ tend to be terse and formulaic. They usually outline the nature of the product, legal name and abode of the defendants, the nature of the conspiracy in restraint of trade, conspiracy dates, and sometimes the size of the market's sales during the conspiracy. By the time the guilty pleas are composed, the government usually has assembled a good deal of evidence: subpoenaed documents, depositions, tape recordings, and public information on the structure of the market and business practices in the industry. This body of evidence will have been analyzed for sentencing purposes. In particular, DOJ economists typically will have done at least preliminary estimates of the size of the affected market, the market shares of the defendants or major sellers, and the overcharges generated by the conspiracy. When guilty plea agreements are entered, much of this evidence and all of the economic analysis will be unavailable to private plaintiffs.[70]

The U.S. Sentencing Guidelines (USSG) and the 1994 alternative felony provisions should have made things easier for civil plaintiffs. The USSG requires the DOJ to estimate a base fine for corporations that represents 20 percent of the company's sales on the *assumption* that the conspiracy had caused approximately a 10 percent overcharge. Because this is an assumption used to set fines, the size of the fine provides no useful evidence for subsequent civil actions. However, if the government believes the overcharge is significantly greater than 10 percent of sales, it is obligated to calculate a higher base fine. The size of the base fine, when revealed at a sentencing hearing, could be useful for private plaintiffs. Moreover, if the government chooses to use the 1994 alternative sentencing provisions, private plaintiffs can be greatly assisted because the fines are supposed to be equal to twice the economic damages caused by the defendant. Thus, the two times rule is a reliable guide to the damages that should be awarded to private plaintiffs.[71]

Private plaintiffs should be consciously assisted by government plea bargaining because, just as is the case of government fines, one of the purposes of treble damages is to deter future violations. The greater the public *and private* punishment, the greater the deterrence effect. Regrettably, public prosecutors in the global price fixing cases studied in this book often made compromises that disadvantaged piggyback private suitors. In the citric acid case, plea agreements were vague on the initial date of the conspiracy, placing it as much as two years later than the actual date. This concession to the defendants greatly reduce the estimated overcharges. One prominent private plaintiff's lawyer attributed this failure to the DOJ's haste to clinch a big fine:

> "The Justice Department has allowed the facts to be covered up . . . It is clear what ADM and DOJ got out of the deal – reduced civil liability for Archer Daniels and a record settlement for the Justice Department."

A more serious disadvantage occurs when private plaintiffs are offered settlements before criminal-guilty pleas are made public. When the government is still negotiating a plea with defendants (or has sealed an agreement), plaintiffs are at a severe informational disadvantage. Not only is economic intelligence difficult to come by, but also there is great uncertainty about the guilt of the defendants themselves. In the lysine and citric acid cases, defendants dangled relatively cheap settlements in front of the federal class of plaintiffs months before the guilty pleas were announced. Hold-outs from the federal class were rewarded for their patience, but the smaller companies remaining in the class paid for theirs.

WERE THE FINES HIGH ENOUGH?

U.S. Government investigations of global price fixing begun between 1992 and 1997 yielded a striking number of guilty pleas and convictions in the late 1990s. At least 40 large corporations have pleaded guilty in U.S. federal courts to criminal violations of the Sherman Act, three of them in two separate markets (Table 13.A.1). In addition, 29 officers of those companies have pleaded their personal guilt to antitrust infractions and have paid fines ranging from $50,000 to $10,000,000 (*ibid.*). As of early 2000, five of those convicted have had prison sentences imposed of up to two and one-half years. Several other participants in global price fixing conspiracies have had arrest warrants issued by U.S. courts, but because they are foreign nationals residing abroad, most may never be extradited to face charges.

The increase in penalties imposed by U.S. authorities for criminal price fixing is striking (Figure 13.1). Starting with the lysine case in October 1996 (fiscal 1997), the size of the fines to be paid by corporations skyrocketed in the late 1990s. In fact, the average corporate antitrust fine in 1999 was *more than 100 times higher* than the fines collected in the early 1990s. Fines paid prior to fiscal 1997 were minuscule, but during the four years 1996-1999 defendants indicted for global price fixing promised to pay nearly $1.6 billion to the U.S. Treasury.[72] The DOJ has set new records for corporate Sherman Act fines no less than six times the 1990s (Figure 13.2). The three cases covered in depth in this volume – lysine, citric acid, and vitamins – accounted for 70 percent of the fines levied on the defendants (Figure 13.3).

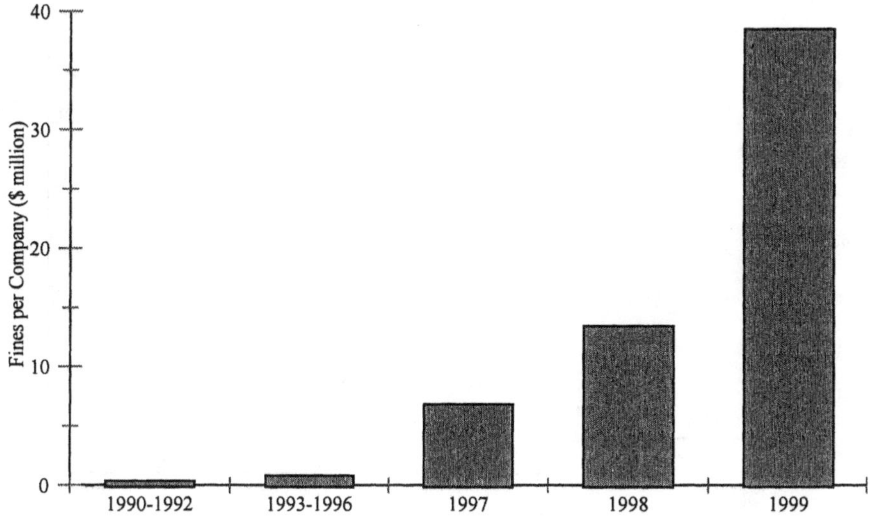

Figure 13.1. Average Corporate Fines Paid for U.S. Antitrust Violations, Fiscal Years 1990-1999.

Note: Nearly all of these fines were paid for price-fixing violations. Fiscal year 1997 includes ADM's $100-million fine, and 1999 includes most of the vitamin-cartel fines.

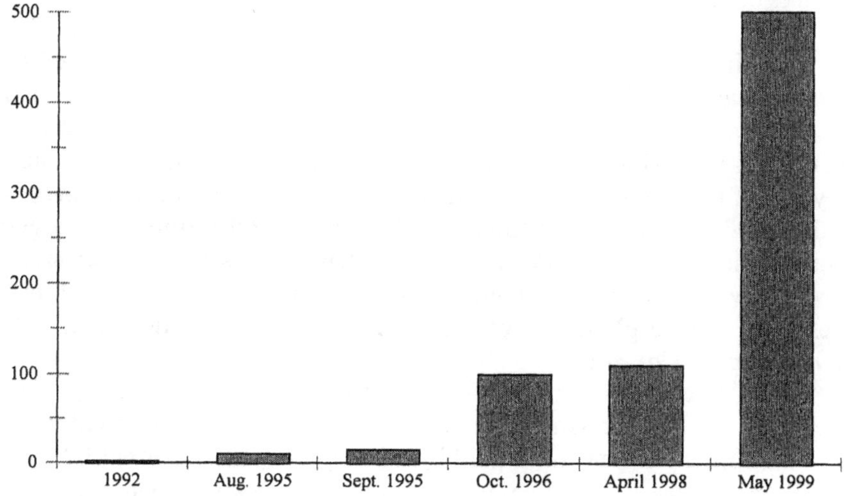

Figure 13.2. Record Corporate Criminal Fines Imposed on Price Fixers, 1992-1999.

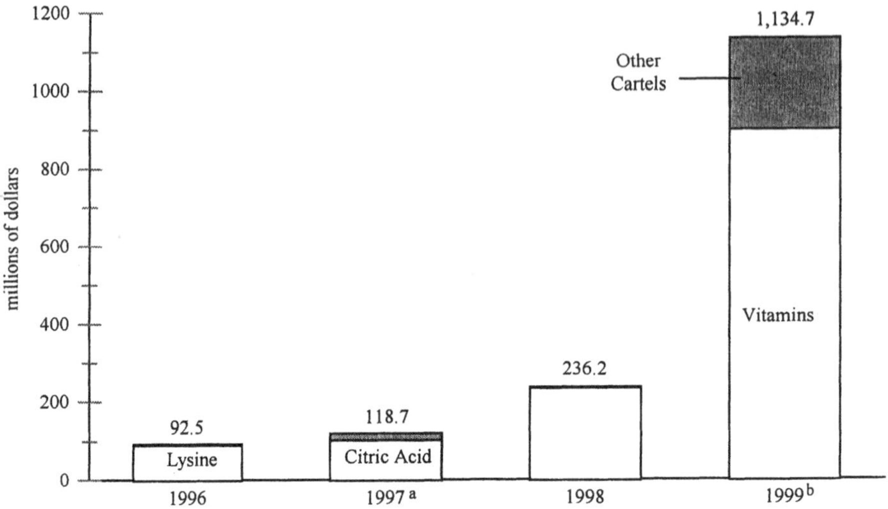

Figure 13.3. Global Price-Fixing Fines Collected by the U.S. Department of Justice, 1996-1999 Calendar Years.

Source: Table 13.A.1.
[a] Includes one late-1996 citric-acid fine. Shaded area is non-citric cartel fines of $12.8 million.
[b] Includes one late-1998 vitamin fine revealed in 1999. Shaded area is non-vitamins cartel fines of $231.9 million.

In all cases these fines were the result of efforts by one rather small government agency, the Antitrust Division of the U.S. Department of Justice. With some investigative assistance of the Federal Bureau of Investigation, the Division has been able to conclude eleven global cartel cases during the last four years of the 1990s. This is a remarkable performance for an agency with less than 900 authorized positions and less than $100 million in budgetary resources, many of these spread over enforcement of several other areas of antitrust law.[73] It is also a concrete vindication of the DOJ's thrust to aggressively pursue global cartels in the wake of its 1994 defeat in *U.S. v. General Electric Co., et al.*.

The fines paid by antitrust violators do not, of course, become revenues for the DOJ nor any other agency of the federal government. Rather, together with the criminal fines paid by all corporate and personal felons, the $1.6 billion in price fixing fines were paid into a specially ear-marked Crime Victims Fund administered by the U.S. Treasury Department. Since 1994, these federal criminal fines have been dispersed to the states annually on the basis of the state's population. The states in turn award compensation to victims of violent crimes, such as those injured or killed in the infamous Oklahoma City bombing of its federal office building. In 1996, this fund distributed $529 million to victimized citizens.[74] Since 1996, the major source of funds has been the perpetrators of global price fixing, and by far the lion's share has come from companies registered and headquartered outside the United States. This detail on the disposition of criminal antitrust fines is important because some conservative political writers have railed against the DOJ's newfound assertiveness as simply one more federal government scheme to raise taxes on corporations. For example, Holman W. Jenkins, in an op-ed opinion column in the *Wall Street Journal*, wrote that antitrust fines are just another way to raise taxes (August 5, 1998).

It is not possible to know all of the factors that went into the decisions to reduce the fines of guilty late-settling firms below the maximum allowed. Prosecutorial resources are limited and the evidence available for successful litigation is rarely iron-clad. However, in their zeal to cut deals with price fixers, DOJ prosecutors may in hindsight have given away too much. After all, the twin purposes of the criminal fines are to punish and to deter. As prosecutors fully recognized, it is difficult to inflict much fiscal pain on a company like ADM that had cash reserves of more than $1 billion. Moreover, deterrence is absent if companies expect their profits from price fixing to exceed the costs of being caught. A certain hubris has developed at the Antitrust Division concerning the large fines imposed on cartel participants. In 1999, the Division's web site initiated a page that kept a running account of the so-called Ten-Million Dollar Club, that is, all the companies that had been required to pay $10 million or more in fines. Perhaps such public gloating is understandable and may even build agency morale, but officials must know that $100 million was the equivalent of a mosquito bite to an elephant like ADM. Indeed, on the day that fine was announced, the stock market breathed a collective sigh of relief and rewarded ADM with a run-up in its stock price of more than 4 percent.

Not only did many politically savvy commentators judge ADM's fine a "bargain," but they correctly recognized that the grants of immunity and other concessions were too generous. An irate Robert Sherill writing in *The Nation* (he called ADM "super-briber to the world") was aghast that chairman Dwayne Andreas was not even interviewed by investigators of the lysine/citric acid scandal (April 7, 1997). "Andreas once again proved himself to be a masterful escape artist . . ." Sherill went on to suggest that Andreas' political largess in Washington was the reason he escaped untouched.[75] In addition to Andreas there is the puzzling treatment of ADM's President James Randall. During the Chicago lysine trial, FBI agent Brian Shepard was asked why Randall was not prosecuted for obviously self-incriminating statements caught during one of Whitacre's taping sessions (Tr. 3383-3388). Shepard rather incredibly responded that the statute of limitations had run out. Other tapes, and possibly some of the six placed under seal by the courts, suggest wider involvement of other ADM officers besides the three who were convicted (Eichenwald 1997, Mihm 1999). Sherill's parting thoughts on the inadequacy of the lysine punishments were:

> "The trouble is . . . most of the federal agencies with jurisdiction over the business world are woefully out manned by the huge array of corporate lawyers. It isn't a David-and-Goliath situation – it's more like Shirley Temple versus King Kong."

The DOJ's concessions to ADM may have been unnecessarily generous, but the fact is that the public does not yet know what all of them were. At the time of ADM's plea, the DOJ's plan to immunize ADM from alleged price fixing in corn sweeteners, to immunize all but three ADM officers from lysine and citric acid price fixing, and to end its probe of ADM's theft of technologies were known. But since then new concessions have come to light. ADM was given amnesty for its role in fixing the prices of sodium gluconate; also, the DOJ got USDA to promise to continue to permit ADM to bid for its commodity contracts, a right that normally would have been withdrawn because of its felony conviction. What other breaks ADM may have been dealt may never be known.

Other defendants received generous deals. Hans Hartmann, by all accounts the prime mover behind the big citric acid cartel, by USSG standards should have gotten 24 to 30 months in prison and paid a fine $350,000 because 1 percent of the affected commerce was quite high. Instead, because of his last-minute offer of cooperation (his employer, Bayer Corp., was one of the last to settle) Hartmann was granted enormous "downward adjustments" at the behest of the DOJ: no prison time and a fine of $150,000.[76] Moreover, other softer sanctions available to prosecutors were ignored, such options as restitution, probation, and home detention. The typically harsher 1994 alternative fine provisions for individuals have *never* been successfully litigated, though the government did try once in the case of Michael Andreas.

One of the problems with antitrust fines is that prosecutors may have excessive discretion to grant downward departures from the guidelines. Instead of being exceptions to the rule as envisioned by Congress, downward departures are sought by prosecutors for nearly all defendants, even the last to fold and the most culpable. Prosecutors seem to have almost unlimited discretion to chose among the USSG, the alternative provisions for felonies, and the weaker statutory limits. Moreover, prosecutors never seem to have to justify such huge decisions as which concept of "affected sales" to present in sentencing hearings. In lysine, ADM's fine was said by prosecutors to be based on the *company's* U.S. sales ($197 million), but prosecutors could have easily chosen the *cartel's* U.S. sales ($454 million) or even, as in some recent cases, the cartel's *world* sales (more than $1 billion). Each of these sales concepts is justifiable, but the difficulty is that experienced defense counsel know about these alternatives and realize that they are matters of negotiation. One of the simplest ways to improve the deterrence value of the antitrust statutes would be for Congress to tighten the conditions under which downward departures can be granted by the judiciary, to eliminate the tension between the two sentencing guidelines (USSG § 2R1.1 and 18 USC § 3571(d)), or to specify which sales concept ought to be used to calculate damages.[77]

Chapter 13 Endnotes

[1] Source citations can be found in Connor (2000).
[2] When the division was first active during President Teddy Roosevelt's administration, it had five lawyers. By 1943, it had 190.
[3] Technically, U.S. Attorneys are also empowered, but they almost always seek the Division's approval to bring criminal antitrust cases.
[4] In other variations on this story, Whitacre says that it was *Dwayne* Andreas that he approached (Whitacre 1995). It is noteworthy that an Ajinomoto engineer named Fujiwara had in fact toured the Decatur plant not long before as part of a group invited by ADM to the facility.
[5] In yet another of Whitacre's versions of this incident, Michael Andreas authorized Whitacre to offer a "finders fee" and a "couple of million dollars" to identify the saboteur and to steal Ajinomoto's secret lysine technology (Carlson 1996).
[6] Michael's father Dwayne had helped the FBI a few years before by training agents so that they could infiltrate the floor of the Chicago Board of Trade's Soybean Pit. On the other hand, the FBI had also recently investigated allegations that ADM had fixed the price of carbon dioxide.
[7] In a famous article he wrote for *Fortune* magazine in 1995, Whitacre claimed that *Dwayne*, not Michael, Andreas had made the call to the CIA in London. He described Michael as "pissed off" at his father's interference. Whitacre repeated this fabrication to Carlson (1996). Moreover, Whitacre alleged that Michael Andreas ordered him not to reveal anything about the lysine conspiracy. Andreas was never charged with obstruction of justice.
[8] Hoech promptly fed these secrets to a top Kyowa Hakko executive, for which Hoechst was paid a consultant's retainer.
[9] In a 1996 interview, Dwayne Andreas confirmed that the company had been aware of Whitacre's embezzlement of ADM for three years (Carlson 1996). Failing to inform the authorities about this federal crime is in itself a crime. Failing to stop it is gross mismanagement.
[10] The attempted thefts of technology (bacitracin and lysine) and obstruction of justice by ADM's director of security Mark Cheviron are three examples (Tr. 3383-3388).
[11] He also asked for ten percent of the ADM fines (Herndon).
[12] ADM was simultaneously being investigated for price fixing of carbon dioxide. Whitacre also divulged his suspicions of conspiracies in citric acid, sodium gluconate, and lactic acid (Tr. 2868-2873).
[13] Wilson and Whitacre met them in Tokyo (4/14/92), Hawaii (4/16 and 4/17/92), Mexico City (6/23/92), and Paris (10/1/92). The first two meetings might not have been illegal, but the other two definitely were.
[14] Identifying cases with obscure titles is standard practice in law enforcement so as to avoid revealing a secret investigation to other parties. Was Harvest King a sly reference to Dwayne Andreas? Defense attorneys suggested as much, hinting that Shepard and the FBI were biased against the powerful Chairman and his family. The FBI's behavior during its investigation would become of the bases of a defense appeal to reverse the conviction of Michael Andreas in 1998.
[15] Normal business practice would have dictated that Michael Andreas, Whitacre's boss, fire a deceptive employee. Clearly, Andreas did not want the FBI to know that the Fujiwara extortion story was concocted. One explanation is that Whitacre's intimate knowledge of ADM's three-month-old lysine cartel would endanger Andreas had Whitacre been fired.
[16] Wayne Brasser had worked for ADM for only five years when he was terminated, yet he was awarded a highly generous 18 months of severance pay, possibly to buy his silence.
[17] Whitacre would later claim that he was discouraged by Shepard from getting a lawyer to review his cooperation agreement. He would also complain that the FBI should have allowed him to seek psychiatric help for his depression, later diagnosed with bipolar disease.

[18] In late 1992, Whitacre already had a secret overseas bank account, but he may not have been asked or investigated about this until 1996. On February 21, 1993, Whitacre illegally authorized an ADM payment of $3.75 million to his personal Swiss bank account (Eichenwald 1996).

[19] Video tapes were made in Hawaii, Atlanta, Chicago, and Irvine, California.

[20] A gap of about an hour in the FBI's videotape of a critical meeting involving Michael Andreas in Irvine California was attributable to Whitacre's absence for lunch.

[21] In Paris at one of the cartel's regular meetings, the FBI whisked Whitacre off to the American Embassy. There he *was* able to record his fresh impressions of what transpired at the meeting.

[22] Transcripts of grand jury testimony are almost never publicly released, but witnesses are free to speak about their own testimony. Witnesses and their lawyers may exchange such information voluntarily among themselves. The release of grand jury transcripts by Congress related to the impeachment of President Bill Clinton was severely condemned by Posner (1999).

[21] Gorelick and Bingaman reported directly to Attorney General Janet Reno and probably kept her informed of developments in the four price-fixing investigations.

[22] He had had a successful private practice before returning to public service. In July 1998 in the midst of the Chicago lysine trial, Lassar was nominated to become the U.S. District Attorney by President Clinton.

[23] Personal communication of Antitrust Division employers. A similar pairing across DOJ divisions was arranged for the citric acid prosecution in San Francisco.

[24] One hypothesis is that the DOJ had reason to believe that the Japan Ministry of Justice would turn down the request or that it would harm evolving antitrust cooperation with Japan. Another guess is that prosecutors needed the enthusiastic testimony of two Ajinomoto executives who might have found it culturally difficult to confront their former superior.

[25] When interviewed later by the FBI, Howard Buffett said that he observed a box full of documents being removed out the back door of Dwayne Andreas' office the morning after the FBI raid (Leiber 2000: 326).

[26] The activity is akin to one of the functions of otherwise legitimate trade associations, some of which have been found guilty of antitrust violation by distributing to their members overly detailed sales information that was shown to have no competitive justification.

[27] The FBI had initially considered arresting the lysine conspirators in January 1995 as they met as a group in Atlanta, Georgia. An April 1995 date for the raid was dropped because of the massive FBI resources required to investigate the bombing of the Oklahoma City federal building.

[28] This from a comment made by John Bray during a sidebar conference at the Chicago trial. Probably a count of Bates Numbers (pages) that are affixed to all documents obtained during discovery.

[29] Some of Ajinomoto's cartel records in Tokyo escaped destruction because Kanji Mimoto had stored some in his house and turned them over to U.S. prosecutors after Ajinomoto reversed its policy.

[30] Whitacre had chosen the date of the raid so as to ensure that all the targets of the FBI's investigation were in Decatur. Whitacre had confided his undercover role to his best friend at ADM, Howard Buffett, in 1994. Whitacre also gave advanced warning of the raid to several of his own employees. The fact that none of them informed ADM's management speaks volumes about their loyalties to the company (Leiber 2000).

[31] Prosecutors probably had sufficient evidence to proceed with a civil case where the standard of proof is only the preponderance of the evidence, but civil prosecutions carry much weaker sanctions for defendants. Less than ten percent of all cases brought by the DOJ are civil matters.

[32] Some journalists and one ADM director have expressed the opinion that the suicides were staged (Lieber (2000) seems to agree.).

[33] Counting sales representatives with limited knowledge, the number rises to about 12.

[34] If there is the slightest doubts about whether a participant in a cartel joined in, say March 1991 or January 1992, the plea agreement may read "as early as January 1992." This phrasing will have the effect of reducing a corporate defendant's civil liability.

[35] In common with most South Korean conglomerates, Sewon had by Western accounting standards was a dangerously high ratio of debt to equity. By 1996, the first signs of the 1997-98 Asian financial crisis would add to Sewon's worries (Connor 2000: Appendix F).

[36] The existence and the composition of the special committee would be revealed at the late October 1995 stockholders meeting.

[37] Current and retired officers of the company are considered inside directors, as would relatives of officers. Directors who are consultants or are on retainers with the company are probably insiders too. Close friends of top officers might also be so classified.

[38] At this stage in his career, Dwayne Andreas was somewhat removed from ADM's day-to-day operations yet was well enough informed to be part of most strategic decisions that the company made. ADM critics harbor the suspicion that the announcement was some sort of political payback. More likely, there were no tape recordings made that were incriminating because Andreas had long ago learned how to keep his shirts clean.

[39] The fact that Sewon America, a small U.S. sales subsidiary, was indicted rather than its parent company (Sewon Korea or Samsung) is significant. The lower assets of the subsidiary assured the courts would approve a small fine, because the DOJ recommended no particular level and judges are loath to impose fines that would bankrupt a defendant. This is further evidence that Sewon was the first of the three to cooperate.

[40] The ADM board and its management were represented by different law firms. Eichenwald (2000) shows a number of areas in which the company's law firm, Williams & Connelly, seemed to act as though it represented the Andreas family rather than the company.

[41] Hollis states that the date of the Washington, D.C. press conference was hurriedly moved forward by a day because ADM had begun leaking the news of the settlement and emphasizing the large size of the fine it would be paying. News of the settlement did appear in the October 14th edition of the *Wall Street Journal*. ADM apparently believed that the $100 million fine, which was less than 10 percent of its cash reserves, would help convince investors that the worst was over and that the costs of the legal sanctions would be easily absorbed by the asset-rich company.

[42] Scott Lasser "convincingly denied" that the Chicago prosecutors had negotiated forgiveness on USDA disbarment. He called back-channel deals not mentioned in the written plea agreement "dirty-pool" (Leiber 2000: 317-318). Others suggest that it might constitute contempt of court.

[43] The culpability score was 9 and the multipliers 1.8 to 3.6. The 20 percent base score basically *assumes* an overcharge of 10 percent of sales.

[44] Barrie Cox flew from England to be interviewed on April 5, 1996. Cox had been transferred to ADM's office in Erith, Kent by Michael Andreas. He was given a raise and told he would be given expanded duties, but these expanded responsibilities never materialized (Tr. 2652-2654). Some observers speculated that Cox's transfer might have been arranged to take him out of reach of U.S. subpoenas. Cox also told the FBI about some inexplicable payments he had seen concerning technology to produce monosodium gluconate (MSG), but so far the DOJ has failed to act on the information (Leiber 2000: 316-317).

[45] Price fixing is a level 10 offense. Seven points were added because of the size of Bayer's sales, three more were added because he was a leader, and three subtracted because he accepted responsibility. Fines for individuals at this offense level are based on 1 to 5 percent of sales of affected commerce.

[46] The last to be indicted were Cerestar Bioproducts, NV, a Dutch subsidiary for the French agribusiness giant Eridania Beghin-Say, and Silvio Kluzer, its managing director. They were fined $400,000 and $40,000, respectively. The company was part of the conspiracy for only 17 months (11/92 to 4/94) and had a small U.S. market share.

[47] This information may have been accurate in the 1970s or 1980s, but by 1995 Roche's shares in its 11 vitamin lines averaged close to 40 percent. Moreover Roche had no sales in three more vitamins; counting these, Roche's global shares averaged about 33 percent.

[48] While grand jury proceedings are almost always secret, those who testify are free to talk about their own testimony, and it is often in the interest of those testifying to pool their information.

[49] The figure of $10.5 million is above the statutory limit, so Lonza was assessed a fine on the basis of the felony guidelines. However, it is far less than 20 percent of Lonza's U.S. sales during the cartel.

[50] Biotin is a small world market with less than $100 million in annual sales. While no price-fixing indictments have yet been issued, it is likely that Roche tried to initiate a biotin cartel with Lonza.

[51] There may have been a change in ownership or management of the joint venture, Vitachem, Inc. Reilly's participation began in September 1994. It paid the lowest fine of the four conspirators ($2 million). Nepera's exit may also be explained by its take over in 1995 by Cambrex Corp., which was not charged by the DOJ.

[52] The existence of such tapes has not been formally acknowledged by the DOJ, but when asked about it at a press conference, Gary Spratling artfully avoided denying it. Barboza (1999) accepts the story.

[53] It is not clear if the unnamed co-conspirators might be corporations or individuals. No executives from either Degussa or Reilly were required to plead guilty, so some of them may have been granted immunity.

[54] In the European Union, European Commission investigators can only search places of business for documents, not private homes.

[55] The 20-percent-of-sales rule was inappropriate because the overcharge clearly exceeded the 10-percent-overcharge level. The 20-percent rule would have implied a $600-$650 mil. fine.

[56] Spratling (2000) would later assert that Roche and BASF were "tied for second place" after Rhône-Poulenc, but he is not counting Lonza for some reason.

[57] The DOJ might even have argued that the *global* sales affected by Roche and BASF were more appropriate than U.S. affected sales. On this basis, Roche and BASF could have been threatened with fines as high as $26 billion!

[58] The unnamed executive is probably a retired predecessor of Sommer or Brönnimann who will be apprehended if he tries to enter U.S. territory. The name Hauri has appeared earlier in this book. He was one of the Roche officials first contacted by ADM's Terrance Wilson and Barrie Cox when they first traveled to Europe to launch the citric acid cartel (see Chapter 5). Hauri paid the maximum monetary fine for his recidivism.

[59] At the same time Lonza's indictment was announced on March 2, 1999, five executives in the choline chloride (B4) industry were indicted. Two were employed by Chinook and three by DuCoa. Chinook pleaded guilty in December 1999, but it appears that DuCoa will not be indicted

[60] Roche and BASF paid fines that represented about 25 percent of their U.S. sales of vitamins during the conspiracy periods. For the Japanese producers, their fines were a little under 20 percent of affected sales.

[61] Technically, ADM obtained the plants from Nabisco under a long-term lease, but the lease was viewed as similar to ownership.

[62] Given that the judge was dealing with facts that preceded 1981, a period of intense substitution of HFCS for sugar, this was not an unreasonable interpretation of market boundaries.

[63] CPC underwent a major restructuring in 1997. The part of CPC that made consumer food products became Best Foods, and the assets devoted to corn wet milling became Corn Products International. An unresolved antitrust suit might have hindered the restructuring.

[64] One of the many uncorroborated allegations of Mark Whitacre made to the FBI on November 8, 1992, was that Michael Andreas and Terrance Wilson had gone to a Corn Refiners Association meeting in Florida where they would set prices on fructose at evening meetings (Eichenwald 2000).

[65] The case is named *In Re High Fructose Corn Syrup Antitrust Litigation* (MDL No. 1087). In 1999, plaintiffs got the FBI's lysine tapes. See Chapter 7 for details.

[66] However, ADM may still be indictable for price fixing in the markets for corn syrup and dextrose. There is a civil treble-damages suit against ADM *et al.* alleging price fixing of corn syrup.

[67] On the other hand, one tape made by Whitacre reportedly has Michael Andreas saying that his counterpart at Cargill would not participate with ADM in overt price fixing. All of Whitacre's tape recordings were ordered to be released to civil plaintiffs by the Appeals Court of the 7th Circuit Court on June 19, 2000. ADM, James Randall, and other ADM employees had resisted their release for years.

[68] On the other hand, failure of the government to prevail in a criminal trial does not prevent a civil case from moving forward, because the standard of proof is lower.

[69] If a case goes to open court, then all this evidence, including the economic analyses, is discoverable.

[70] Of course the government fines are frequently refused by prosecutors because defendants have cooperated, but these downward departures are explained in sentence hearings.

[71] Some payments were being made on an installment basis over several years.

[72] In 1998, the Division had 831 positions authorized from clerks to political appointees and an annual budget of $93 million. Corrected for inflation, the budgets of the Antitrust Division and the Federal Trade Commission declined by 7 percent from 1977 to 1997. The Clinton administration has proposed increases slightly higher than the rate of inflation, but the House of Representatives has shaved these requests.

[73] In that year the principal source of reserves was a fine of $340 million paid by Daiwa Bank for fraudulently covering up huge bond-trading losses.

[74] During President Clinton's 1992 political campaign, Andreas co-hosted a dinner that raised $35 million for Clinton's campaign fund.

[75] The USSG state that in the great majority of cases of criminal price fixers, prison sentences of at least six months are called for.

[76] Other ways to regularize sentencing decisions would be to make parent firms bear the risk of price fixing by their subsidiaries. In the lysine case, Sewon America was deemed "too poor" to pay more than $1.25 million, whereas, its parent in South Korea was rich in assets. Permitting fines that exceed a company's ability to pay – as sort of a corporate penalty – could be an alternative worthy of consideration. Why prosecutors and jurists find the prospect of deadly fines is puzzling to an economist. The roaring market for companies means that takeovers need not disrupt economic viability of the acquired firms. There are several instances in the global cartel cases examined in this book where companies showed reckless disregard for the viability of their victims.

Table 13.A.1. Criminal Fines Paid by Global Price Fixers in the United States, 1996-2000.

Product	Defendant/Subsidiary	Date Announced	Amount
			Dollars
1. LYSINE	Archer Daniels Midland Co:	October 1996	$70,000,000
	Exec. V.P. Michael Andreas[d]	July 1999	350,000
	V.P. Terrance Wilson[d]	July 1999	350,000
	V.P. Mark Whitacre[d]	July 1999	350,000
	Ajinomoto Co., Inc./Heartland Lysine:	November 1996	10,000,000[a]
	Div. Mgr. Kanji Mimoto	November 1996	75,000[a]
	Div. Mgr. Hirozaku Ikeda	November 1996	0
	Director Kazutoshi Yamada	pending	--
	Kyowa Hakko Kogyu Co., Ltd.:	October 1996	10,000,000[a]
	Div. Mgr. Masaru Yamamoto	October 1996	50,000[a]
	Sewon America, Inc.:	December 1996	1,250,000[a]
	Pres. Jhom Su Kim	December 1996	75,000
	Cheil Jedang, Ltd.	December 1996	1,250,000[b]
2. CITRIC ACID	Archer Daniels Midland Co.:	October 1996	30,000,000[a]
	V.P. Barrie Cox	October 1996	0
	Bayer AG/Haarmann & Reimer:	January 1997	50,000,000
	H&R Pres. Hans Hartmann	January 1997	150,000[a]
	Hoffmann-La Roche, Ltd./Citrique Belge NV:	March 1997	14,000,000
	Mgr. Dir. Udo Haas	March 1997	150,000[a]
	Jungbunzlauer International AG:	March 1997	11,000,000
	Pres. Rainer Bilchbauer	March 1997	150,000[a]
	Eridania Beghin-Say/Cerestar Bioproducts NV:	June 1998	400,000
	Mgr. Dir. Silvio Kluzer	June 1998	40,000
3. VITAMINS	Alusuisse/Lonza AG	September 1998[b]	10,500,000[a]
	DCV, Inc./DuCoa LP:	March 1999	
	Pres. Lindell Hilling	March1999	Indicted
	Div. Pres. J.L. Fisher	March 1999	Indicted
	Div. V.P. Antonio Felix	March 1999	Indicted
	Chinook Group Ltd./Chinook Group Inc.:	March 1999	5,000,000
	V.P. John Kennedy	March 1999	Indicted
	Sales Mgr. Robert Samuelson	March 1999	Indicted
	Hoffmann-La Roche, Ltd:	May 1999	500,000,000[a]
	Managing Dir. Kuno Sommer[d]	May 1999	100,000
	Div. Pres. Roland Brönnimann	August 1999	150,000
	Mktg. Dir. Andres Hauri	April 2000	350,000
	BASF AG	May 1999	225,000,000[a]
	Div. Pres. Reinhardt Steinmetz	April 2000	125,000
	Div. Pres. Dieter Suter	" "	75,000
	Group V.P.. Hugo Strotmann	" "	75,000
	Rhône-Poulenc [amnesty]	May 1999	0[a]
	Takeda Chemical Industries	September 1999	72,000,000
	Eisai Co.	September 1999	40,000,000

	Daiichi Pharmaceutical	September 1999	25,000,000
	Hoechst AG/Roussel	Pending	--
	Nepera/Cambrex Corp.	Pending	--
	Mitsui Co./Bioproducts Inc.	pending	--
	Degussa/Vitachem Inc.	May 2000	13,000,000
	Reilly/ Vitachem Inc.	May 2000	2,000,000
	E. Merck KGaA	May 2000	14,000,000
4. SODIUM GLUCONATE	Akzo Nobel Chemicals NV/ Glucona v.o.f.	September 1997	--
	Avebe BA/Glucona v.o.f./ Glucona America:	September 1997	10,000,000
	Mgr. Dir. Cornelius R. Nederveen	September 1977	100,000
	Mgr. Dir. Marcel L. van Eekhout	September 1997	100,000
	Roquette Frères SA:	December 1997	2,500,000
	Bertrand Dufour	December 1997	100,000
	Fujisawa Pharmaceutical Co./ PMP Fermentation Inc.:	February 1998	20,000,000
	Asso. Div. Dir. Akira Nakao	February 1998	200,000
	Unindicted co-conspirator [probably ADM]	December 1997	0[a]
5. HEAVY-LIFT MARINE CONSTRUCTION	Heere Mac v.o.f.:	January 1998	49,000,000[a]
	Director Jan Meek	January 1998	100,000
	Unindicted co-conspirators [leniency program]	January 1998	0[a]
6. HEAVY-LIFT MARINE TRANSPORT	Dockwise NV:	January 1998	15,000,000[c]
	Christiaan Bernadus van der Zwan	January 1998	150,000
	Bastiaan Albertus de Jong	January 1998	75,000
	Dockwise U.S.A.	January 1998	1,000,000[c]
7. GRAPHITE ELECTRODES	Showa Financing/Showa Denko Carbon Inc.	February 1998	29,000,000[a]
	UCAR International, Inc.:	April 1998	110,000,000[a]
	Pres. & CEO Robert Krass[d]	September 1999	1,250,000
	COO Robert J. Hart	September 1999	1,000,000
	SGL Carbon AG:	May 1999	135,000,000
	CEO Robert J. Koehler	May 1999	10,000,000
	Carbide/Graphite Group, Inc. [amnesty]	February 1998	0[a]
	Tokai Carbon Co.	April 1999	6,000,000
8. SORBATES	Eastman Chemical Co.	October 1998	11,000,000

	Hoechst AG:	May 1999	36,000,000
	Mktg. Mgr. Bernd Romahn	May 1999	250,000
	Nippon Gohsei:	July 1999	21,000,000
	Hiromi Ito	July 1999	350,000
9. BROMINES	Great Lakes Chemical Group [amnesty]	June 1999	0[a]
	Dead Sea Bromine Group	July 2000	7,000,000
	Albermarle Corp.	pending	--
10. SODIUM ERYTHORBATE	Pfizer Corp.	July 1999	10,000,000
	Fujisawa Pharmaceutical/PMP Fermentation	pending	--
11. MALTOL	Pfizer Corp.	July 1999	10,000,000

E = Estimated by author.

-- = Not available or not yet announced in late 2000.

[a] This fine represents a substantial downward departure from the range of fines called for under the U.S. Sentencing Guidelines (USSG). Discounts were requested by the U.S. Department of Justice because the defendant was one of the first to admit guilt or because it/he agreed to cooperate with the DOJ in providing information about other guilty parties. For example, ADM's sales of citric acid and its culpability score implied a fine of $112 to $224 million, but it was granted a discount of 73 to 87 percent. Ajinomoto, Kyowa, Cheil, and Sewon each were required to pay the "statutory" maximum fines of $10 million in place of much larger felony-guideline fines; furthermore; the DOJ made the specious argument that Sewon America was "too poor" to pay even the $10 million, even though its parent company was very rich.

Hans Hartmann's offense under the USSG requires a prison term of 24 to 30 months (reduced to zero) and fine of $0.8 to 17.5 million (reduced to $150,000).

In graphite electrodes, Carbide/Graphite Group was admitted to the DOJ's leniency program. Showa Denko was the second to confess and cooperate, so it got a 61% discount. UCAR, third, also cooperated.

In vitamins, the USSG fine for Roche was $1.3-$2.6 billion but it received a DOJ discount of 62 to 81%.

[b] Kept under seal until March 1999.

[c] Fines based on affected *global* sales, not just U.S. market.

[d] These individuals also were required to serve prison sentences.

Table 13.A.2 Record Criminal Fines Imposed on Corporate Price Fixers, United States, 1995-2000.

Date Offered	Company	Industry	Amount
			$ million
1992	Premdor	Metal	2.0
August 1995	ICI Explosives USA	Explosives	10.0[a]
September 1995	Dyno Nobel	Explosives	15.0[b]
October 1996	Archer Daniel Midland	Lysine and citric acid	100.0[c]
April 1998	UCAR International	Graphite electrodes	115.0
May 1999	BASF AG	Bulk vitamins	225.0
May 1999	Hoffmann-La Roche	Bulk vitamins	500.0

Source: www.usdoj.gov/atr.

[a] This was the first application of the maximum "statutory" Sherman Act fine.

[b] The first application of the federal felony statute that permits fines based on twice the harm. In addition to the $15 million paid by Dyno Nobel, a wholly-owned subsidiary of Nobel Industries of Norway, a joint venture 50%-owned by Dyno was fined $1.9 million.

[c] $70 million for lysine and $30 million for citric acid.

Chapter 14

ANTITRUST PROSECUTIONS BY FOREIGN GOVERNMENTS

The Sherman Act was 110 years old in the year 2000. Although not quite the oldest national antitrust law in the world, the United States has the richest body of legal decisions of any jurisdiction in the world.[1] One of the greatest movements in international law is the widespread adoption of competition laws outside of North America since the end of World War II. Some of these laws were instituted by countries that were under Allied occupation; Germany and Japan are examples. It was Germany that pressed hard to have competition laws included in the 1958 Treaty of Rome that established the then six-nation European Economic Community. The competition laws of the European Union (EU) are enforced for cross-national trade within the EU by Competition Directorate of the European Commission in Brussels. EU member states have also adopted national competition laws that apply to intra-national commerce. Indeed, all recent entrants and many aspiring entrants to the EU such as Poland and Hungary have been required to form effective national antitrust agencies as a condition of membership in the EU. Mexico formed its competition agency upon joining the North American Free Trade Agreement area. Many other countries (e.g., South Korea, Russia, Chile, and Argentina) adopted competition laws as part of a package of institutional innovations that replaced centralized economic planning or enhanced the development of democratic institutions to serve civil society. Today, countries representing more than 80 percent of the world's Gross Domestic Product have antitrust laws on their books, though enforcement remains weak in Japan and many low-income nations.

No sooner did the existence of the U.S. investigations of the food-and-feed-ingredient cartels become public than the antitrust agencies in some countries began their own investigations. In other countries, these agencies had to wait for complaints to be lodged from buyers in their jurisdictions. In some cases, U.S. defendants themselves scurried to be first to admit their guilt with antitrust officials so as to obtain leniency in sentencing. With the notable exception of Canada, only public authorities can seek sanctions against alleged cartel members because there is no statutory basis for private parties bringing civil suits to seek compensation for antitrust injuries. Even in countries with statutory authority for civil antitrust actions, no tradition has developed, because the relief offered by the courts provides inadequate incentives for the plaintiffs.

This section summarizes the non-U.S. antitrust investigations as they had evolved to late 2000 in the cases of the lysine, citric acid, and vitamins conspiracies.[2] More is known about Canadian enforcement than the slower, more secretive processes in the EU.

LYSINE

Canada and Mexico

Recall that guilty pleas by the four largest members of the lysine cartel were entered in the U.S. courts in August and October 1996. An investigation of lysine price fixing began in Canada in the summer of 1995. In an interview with the Canadian official who headed the government investigation of the lysine cartel, Nicol and Ferguson (1999) reported that Canada worked closely with U.S. antitrust investigators under an existing protocol. By October 1996, Kyowa Hakko agreed to assist the Canadian investigation in return for immunity from prosecution; Sewon soon followed in Kyowa's footsteps. Officials from both companies met with investigators to be interviewed for ten days in Hong Kong in October 1997. Later that year, the Ministry of Justice sent letters to ADM and Ajinomoto informing them that they were targets in the lysine investigation.

In May 1998 ADM pleaded guilty to fixing the prices of lysine exports to Canada. The Competition Bureau proposed and ADM accepted a penalty of about Canadian $11.4 million (U.S. $7.9 million), which was six times the previous record Canadian antitrust fine (Figure 14.1).[3] ADM's fine represented 23.8 percent of its 1992-1995 sales of lysine in Canada. In July 1998, Ajinomoto, Kyowa Hakko, and Sewon America also pleaded guilty to fixing export prices of lysine in Canada. Ajinomoto was penalized C$3.5 million and Sewon America C$70,000. However, Kyowa paid no fine because of its previous grant of immunity by Canada's Attorney General; Sewon also received a steep discount for its early cooperation. All four lysine producers had "prohibition orders" imposed on them by the federal court, which forbid the companies from any further price fixing. Measured by fines levied, Canada too has been getting increasingly tougher with global price fixers.

The next lysine investigation was opened in Mexico in February 1997. The only U.S. source for this information was ADM's annual financial report released in September 1997. Two years later, ADM reported to its stockholders that it had been fined $125,000 by Mexico's Federal Competition Commission.[4]

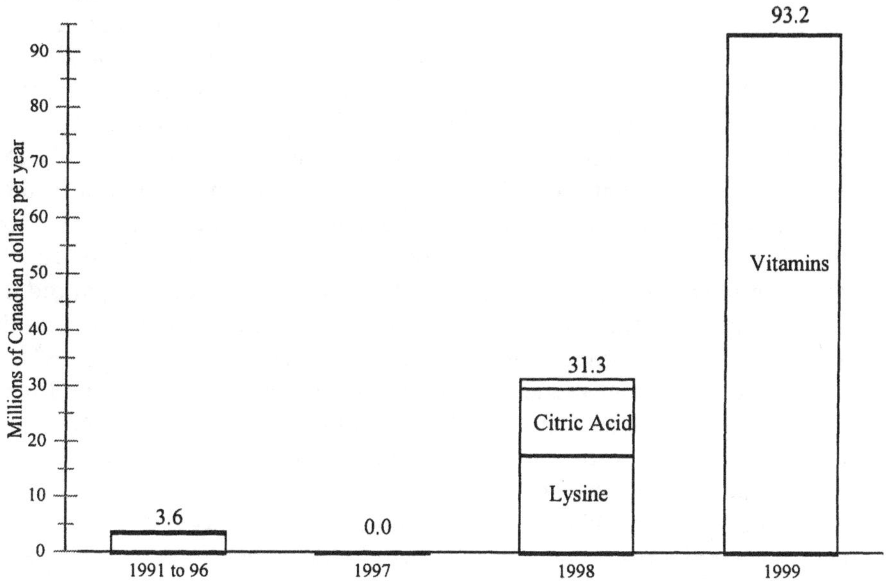

Figure 14.1.Global Price-Fixing Fines, Canadian Ministry of Justice, 1991-1999.

Source: Table 14.A.1.

The European Union

Directorate General IV of the Commission of the European Economic Communities began investigating the lysine cartel in July 1996, one year after the U.S. investigation became public knowledge. According to the European Commission's (EC) press release of June 7, 2000 that announced the conclusion of the EC's investigation, Ajinomoto approached the EC in July 1996 seeking leniency for its cooperation.[5] As the first to inform the Commission about the cartel, Ajinomoto was entitled to a 50 percent reduction in the fines to be levied on members of the cartel on the basis of each company's sales.

Although most investment analysts who follow ADM and the lysine industry should easily have surmised that a quiet EC investigation was under way, when that quiet was shattered the stock markets once again reacted adversely to the news. On June 12, 1997, the EC's investigation of the lysine cartel was confirmed when investigators raided ADM's sales offices in Kent, England and Wiesbaden, Germany as well as Kyowa Hakko's offices in Dusseldorf. On that day, the price of ADM's stock fell 4 percent. A source within the EC confirmed that Ajinomoto was cooperating with the European competition law authorities. Later, it would be announced that the other three

Asian members of the cartel also cooperated with the EC investigation. The second to approach the DG-IV was Sewon. Because Ajinomoto had failed to mention the lysine cartel that Ajinomoto, Kyowa, and Sewon had operated in the late 1980s, Sewon too was awarded the maximum 50-percent discount on its fine for its information on the earlier price-fixing. Kyowa and Cheil could only confirm certain details of what Ajinomoto and Sewon had already told the EC, so their cooperation was worth only a 30-percent reduction in their fines. Strangely, ADM made no effort to cooperate with the EC investigation, despite the obvious monetary incentives to do so. However, when the Commission later laid out its case in a Statement of Objections, ADM did not contest the facts contained in the Statement, nor did the company contest the EC's final decision of guilt. For this minimal degree of cooperation, ADM was granted a 10 percent reduction on the maximum fine the EC could levy. In 2000, ADM announced that it would appeal the size of the EU fine.

The EC's fines for the five corporate members of the global lysine cartel were announced in June 2000. The five were required to pay 109.9 million euros or U.S $105.4 million, which reflected an average discount of 33 percent from the maximum fines that could have been imposed. The basis of the EC's maximum fines for price fixing is 10 percent of sales of each guilty company in the year prior to the violation. While this standard seems quite precise on the surface, in fact the EC has a great deal of discretion because of the flexibility of the definition of "sales." A fine can be calculated using either the global sales of the convicted firm or just its sales within the European Economic Area; moreover, sales can refer to the company's total in all lines of business or just the line of business that was cartelized. In the case of lysine, the existence of two successive cartels in 1986-1990 and 1992-1995 further muddies the clarity of the basis for the fines.

Adjusting for the discounts given to the lysine conspirators, it is apparent that the Competition Directorate had concluded that the appropriate fines that it could collect from the five participants totaled 163 million euros or $155 million (Table 14.1). Therefore, the annual sales basis employed by the Commission can be inferred to be at least $1,580 million. This figure is considerably less than 10 percent of the global sales of the five companies (more than $20 billion), but it is well above the sales of lysine in Western Europe (about $240 million in the early 1990s).[6] In the past, the EC has most often used the narrowest definition of sales – the cartelized product sold in the EU only – to assess price fixing fines. Clearly, the Commission had decided that the seriousness of the lysine cartel's crime warranted punishment stiffer than that ordinarily meted out because the actual fines were almost eight times higher than precedent would suggest.[7]

Table 14.1. European Commission Fines for the Lysine Cartel.

Company (Group)	Global Sales			Lysine Sales 1994		EC Fines 1999	
	1992 Group	1992 Company	1995 Company	Global	EU	Full	Discounted[f]
	Million euros[a]						
Archer Daniels Midland	10,154[b]	10,154	13,940	218	55E	52.6	47.3
Ajinomoto	4,645	4,645	5,444	223	115E	56.6	28.3
Kyowa Hakko	2,750	2,750	2,860	120	30E	18.9	13.2
Sewon (Miwon Group)	625[c]	625	845[c]	95	25E	17.8	8.9
Cheil Jedang (Samsung)	44,000[d]	1,432[e]	2,016	45	15E	17.4	12.2
Total	62,174	19,606	25,105	708	240E	163.3	109.9
Maximum Fines	6,217	1,961	2,511	71	24	--	--

Source: Connor (2000) especially Appendixes D and E; Chapter 4.
E = Estimated
[a] At the time the fines were announced (May 2000) the euro was worth \$0.95. In 1992-1994, the euro's predecessor was worth about \$1.10.
[b] Excludes sales of a large number of joint ventures.
[c] Miwon Group was split into two operating companies (Miwon Co., Sewon Co.) in 1994, but were reunited in 1997. Sales are for the whole group.
[d] Approximate sales of the exceedingly complex Samsung *chaebol*, which controlled Cheil until a 1993 divestiture.
[e] The lysine subsidiary in Indonesia (Cheil Samsung Astra, CSA) had 1992 sales of less than 10 million euros and 1998 sales of \$154 million.
[f] Discounts of 50 percent, 30 percent, or 10 percent based on the degree of cooperation with EC authorities.

The EC's fines on the lysine cartel were high by the EC's historical standards. For example, ADM's fine of 47 million euros was the fourth highest ever imposed by the EC. With nearly equal lysine sales in the United States and the EU, perhaps it is surprising that the EC fines were higher than the U.S. government's fines imposed on the same five companies (\$73 million). However, seven top managers were convicted of criminal price fixing in the United States, whereas the EC rules do not permit imposing individual penalties.

The EC has been opaque in the past in its standards for setting fines (Korah 1997). An interview with the EC's competition law commissioner verifies that there are no rigid rules for imposing fines; in fact the lack of transparency is considered a virtue by the DG-IV (Alchin 1999). However, one can *infer* the standards for fines by comparing the actual lysine fines with five possible sales bases. The "full" fines (those not discounted for cooperation with the EC's investigation) are most highly correlated with the 1994 *global* sales of lysine by the five cartel members (the correlation was r = +0.95). Although global lysine sales were too low to justify the full fines, the EC acted as if the harm caused by each firm worldwide was the basis of the relative sizes of the corporate fines. Note that 1994 data are employed – the year before the last year of the cartel's violations. The year before the cartel was formed could not have been the basis of the lysine fines, because sales of ADM and Cheil were insignificant in 1992. Unless the EC was not aware that Cheil Jadang was part of one of South Korea's biggest conglomerates, it did not asses fines on the basis of the ultimate parent's sales; neither the full nor discounted fines are correlated with group sales.

One final observation is that the discounted fines actually imposed are almost perfectly correlated (r = +0.99) with 1992 company sales. It appears that the size of the discounts may have been influenced by the company's ability to pay, not just their degree of cooperation. Ability to pay is not an explicit standard for EC fine setting, though it is explicit in U.S. practice.

Meanwhile, some other non-U.S. national antitrust authorities were taking action. For example in July 1999, the UK's Office of Fair Trading (OFT) announced that it would bring ADM and Cheil to court for price fixing of lysine and would seek a consent decree forbidding the two companies from future price fixing. This was at the time the maximum sanction the OFT could impose. The OFT will not have the authority to levy fines for antitrust violations until March 2000. Of the five cartel members, ADM and Cheil were singled out because the others had no assets in the UK.

CITRIC ACID

Enforcement actions against the four members of the citric acid cartel followed a pattern similar to that of lysine. In Canada, the Competition Bureau imposed a fine of U.S.$3.1 million on ADM in May 1998 (Figure 14.1). During the 1992-1995 conspiracy ADM sold $11.6 million of citric acid out of a total of $70 million sold in Canada. Thus, the fine represented 27 percent of ADM's citric acid sales during the conspiracy. Six months later, the remaining three "Swiss" companies in the cartel were fined $6.7 million, or about 11 percent of their sales during the conspiracy. The Canadian fines imposed on the citric acid cartel were relatively lighter than those in lysine, given the larger Canadian market for citric acid and the higher percentage overcharge imposed on citric acid sales.

In Mexico, the Federal Competition Commission began an investigation of ADM and other members of the citric acid cartel on February 11, 1999, three and one-half years after the U.S. investigation became public. It is likely that because of the large size of the Mexican soft-drink market that the fine faced by ADM *et al.* will be larger than for lysine.

The EU's investigation into citric acid began in September 1997. As of late 2000 no further steps had been announced by the DG-IV. The maximum fines that can be imposed are about $60 million, but Ajinomoto will probably be given a substantial discount for its early cooperation.

VITAMINS

Of the three cartels examine in this chapter, the global bulk vitamins markets had by far the greatest sales and attracted the most enforcement activity outside the United States. By late 2000, at least seven jurisdictions launched formal antitrust investigations of price fixing in the vitamins markets: Canada, the European Union, Switzerland, Japan, Australia, Brazil, and Mexico.

The Canadian Competition Bureau (CCB) began its investigation sometime before early 1999 and had the cooperation of the U.S. DOJ. The CCB recommended precedent-setting corporate fines for five vitamin manufacturers, and the Federal Court of Canada agreed to accept its recommendation. On September 22, 1999, fines of Canadian $88.4 million were imposed on Roche Holdings, BASF, Rhône-Poulenc, Eisai, and Daiichi (see Figure 14.1 above). These were the largest criminal fines in Canadian legal history. One officer of Chinook Ltd. was sentenced to nine months of community service. The fines accounted for 12.8 percent of Canadian sales of nine products: vitamins A, C, E, B2, B4, B5, B6, beta carotene, and vitamin premixes. Prices of vitamins were pushed as high as 30 percent above competitive levels. The federal prosecutor stated that these fines "were big enough to eliminate most illicit profit" made by the cartel in Canada, but he admitted that the defendants were given a discount below what could have been imposed by the Court, mainly because the guilty pleas spared the Crown the expense of litigating a conviction. He noted that the defendants still faced monetary penalties from civil suits; class-action suits have been permitted in Canada since 1992 but rarely have been litigated.

By late 1999, official investigations of vitamins price fixing had begun in the European Union, Switzerland, Australia, Brazil, and Mexico. In May 1999, the EU's antitrust chief, Karel van Miert, stated that Roche, BASF, and Rhône-Poulenc were cooperating with its investigation. Van Miert also prepared the European public for lower fines than those imposed by the United States. In July 2000, the European Commission sent legal warnings, which are similar to target letters in the United States, to 13 vitamin manufacturers informing the companies that they were the objects of a price-fixing probe. The next step is for the targeted companies to respond to the Commission's preliminary findings, either in writing or at a confidential oral hearing.

Seven of the targeted companies (two of which were merged in 1999) were the same companies that had pleaded guilty in the United Sates and Canada (Table 14.2). However, one European manufacturer (Solvay) and four Japanese companies (Sumitomo, Sumika, Tanabe, and Congo) had not been previously charged in North America possibly because the five sold vitamins in Europe but not in North America. On the other hand, except for the Swiss firm Lonza, the EC charged none of the other vitamin B3 or B4 cartel members; moreover, the German chemical firm Hoechst is absent from the EC's initial target list.

Table 14.2. Targets of the EU Vitamin Cartel Investigation, July 2000.

Previously Convicted in the United States	Not Previously Convicted
Hoffmann-La Roche	Solvay Pharmaceuticals
BASF	Sumitomo Chemical
Rhône-Poulenc	Sumika Fine Chemicals
Lonza	Tanabe Seiyaku
Merck KGaA	Congo Chemical
Takeda Chemical	
Eisai Pharmaceutical	
Daiichi	

Source: *Wall Street Journal,* July 12, 2000: A21.

Penalties in the EU are not likely to be as harsh as in the United States. On the other hand, the EU does not impose prison sentences on individuals for price-fixing violations, and its ability to impose fines on companies is limited by a cap of 10 percent of annual sales of a corporate violator in the year prior to a violation. Although the sales basis of the EU's fines can be global sales, in the past DG-IV has recommended fines that did not exceed 10 percent of sales solely in the European Union. Sales affected by the cartel in the EU were likely to be about the same size as those in the United States, that is, approximately \$7 to \$8 billion dollars. However, the *annual* sales of vitamins and premixes in the year prior to the start of the conspiracies is only about \$500 to \$700 million. On the other hand, the EU is trying to impose monetary fines as high as those in the U.S. Indeed, the EU's lysine fines were significantly higher than those obtained by the U.S. DOJ. One way to get around the 10-percent cap is to impose a fine for *each year* prior to a violation in one year. For example, if a cartel in vitamin A operated in the EU from January 1990 to March 1999, then sales for the years 1989 through 1998 could be used as the basis of the fine. Combining this procedure with global company sales could result in very high fines indeed.[8]

In early December 2000, the Australian Competition and Consumer Commission announced a proposed settlement with three vitamin suppliers that admitted fixing prices of bulk vitamins A and E sold to animal-feed companies (*M2 Presswire* December 5, 2000). The three Australian subsidiaries of Hoffmann-La Roche, BASF, and Rhône-Poulenc (now

Aventis) agreed to pay penalties of Australian $26 million, a record amount under the 1974 Trade Practices Act.[9] In fact, the A$15 million to be paid by the Roche subsidiary was more than double the previous record amount. The Commission Chairman stated that the settlement was a lenient one because of the defendants' cooperation in avoiding a costly trial. Price fixing allegations concerning human vitamins were still under investigation.

One of the more surprising developments concerned Swiss reactions to the vitamin cartel. In early May 2000, the Swiss competition-law agency WEKO came to the fairly obvious conclusion that the global vitamin cartel had affected vitamin prices in Switzerland. Therefore, WEKO issued an injunction against its national champion Hoffmann-La Roche and its co-conspirators to cease price fixing. This is in fact the maximum sanction WEKO can impose for a first-time price fixer. Only if Roche or its co-conspirators *repeat* their crime can they be fined under current Swiss law. With the weakness of Swiss sanctions so fully revealed to the world, to avoid the appearance of a cover-up for Roche both houses of the Swiss parliament passed motions in late May supporting the imposition of fines for first-time offenders. Presumably, if the law is changed it will not be applied retroactively to Hoffmann-La Roche.

Among the jurisdictions with well established antitrust laws, Japan is notable for the absence of any official actions taken publicly against foreign conspirators or the two lysine or six vitamins companies headquartered in Japan.[10] The two Japanese lysine companies (Ajinomoto and Kyowa Hakko) issued press releases apologizing for their actions, but did not fire any of its employees.[11] However, the three Japanese vitamin manufacturers imposed a number of sanctions upon themselves immediately after their guilty pleas in the United States. The presidents and all board members of the three companies voluntarily took fairly significant pay cuts; their presidents resigned from honorary positions in various Japanese trade associations. Although newspapers were reporting in July 2000 that Japanese authorities were going to bring charges against the global cartel in vitamins, it is unlikely that the fines will be severe by U.S. standards.

Chapter 14 Endnotes

[1] Several states of the United States adopted antitrust statues prior to 1890, but these proved ineffective in prosecuting multi-state companies. The first price-fixing legislation was passed in France in 1789, but was never enforced. Canada's federal government adopted its first competition law in 1889 (Connor 1997). All 50 states of the United States have antitrust laws that apply to markets that fail the "interstate commerce" test. Moreover, about half of the state Attorneys General frequently join civil litigation that seeks compensation for their citizens who were indirect buyers of products sold by national or international cartels. On the other hand, Pennsylvania and a few other U.S. states have statutes that are very limited in scope or are allocated few resources by the state attorney general's office.

[2] Although the text covers only three products, jurisdictions in Europe and elsewhere are investigating and prosecuting alleged global food-and-feed cartels in other product areas.

In July 1999, Degussa-Hüls confirmed that it was the target of an EU investigation into price fixing of the amino acid *methionine*. Rhône-Poulenc (now Aventis) is the other leader in the industry. It is rumored that the DOJ had a grand jury investigation going on about methionine in the late 1990s.

Just a couple of months after similar U.S. convictions in the summer of 2000, three corporations were fined by the Canadian courts for price fixing in the market for the food preservatives called *sorbates*. These convictions followed by about a year the Canadian guilty pleas of five corporations for price fixing in the *sodium gluconate* industry.

[3] ADM actually paid a fine of C$16.5 million for both lysine and citric acid. The C$11.4 for lysine is a prorated amount for a general price-fixing penalty and a lysine-specific fine. The plea agreement granted ADM immunity from prosecution for price fixing of sodium gluconate.

[4] It is probable that Kyowa Hakko, which dominated lysine sales in Mexico, had an even larger fine imposed upon it by Mexico. Major Spanish-language newspapers have been silent on these developments.

[5] Ajinomoto, Kyowa Hakko, and Sewon were to announce their capitulation to the U.S. DOJ's demands for guilty pleas in August 1996. It is probable that Ajinomoto had made this decision in June 1996.

[6] For information on the size of ADM, Ajinomoto, Kyowa Hakko, Sewon, and Cheil, see Appendix F in Connor (2000).

[7] Of the two remaining alternative sales bases, total EU sales of the five companies in all their fines of business seems like the most reasonable one. Global sales of lysine in the early 1990s were about $600 million, which is less than half of the inferred sales basis of $1,580 million.

[8] Highly conjectural estimates of possible EU fines for vitamin cartel members are shown below in Table 19.3. Injured parties in Europe generally have no legal recourse to seek monetary compensation through the European Court system, and only a few national courts permit civil compensation to be awarded to buyers injured by price fixing.

[9] The proposed settlement must be approved by a federal court.

[10] There is one lone exception. The German newspaper *Berliner Zeitung* reported in July 2000 that the Japan Fair Trade Commission was planning on indicting members of the global vitamins cartel.

[11] Kazutoshi Yamada, the chief conspirator at Ajinomoto, was relieved of his duties as a managing director after the company's guilty plea. One Kyowa manager may have been slightly demoted. If additional sanctions were imposed on managers, there were not made public in the major Japanese newspapers or chemical-industry magazines.

Table 14.A.1. Canadian Global Price-Fixing Convictions and Fines, 1991-1999.

Year	Product:	Company (Ultimate Parent)	Fine
			C$ million
1991-96	Various:	12 Companies	21.80
1998	Lysine:	ADM	14.00
		Ajinomoto	3.50
		Sewon America	0.07[a]
		Kyowa Hakko	0.00[a]
1998	Citric acid:	Jungbunzlauer	1.90[a]
		Haarmann & Reimer (Bayer Corp.)	4.70
		Hoffmann-La Roche	2.90
		ADM	2.00
		Cerestar Bioproducts (Eridania)	0.70
1998	Sodium gluconate:	Jungbunzlauer	0.10[a]
		ADM	0.00[a]
		Roquette Frères	0.70
		Fujisawa Pharmaceuticals	0.36
		Glucona (Akzo Nobel)	0.35
1999	Vitamins[b]	Hoffmann-La Roche	50.90
		BASF	19.00
		Rhône-Poulenc	14.00
		Daiichi	2.50
		Eisai	2.00
		Chinook International	2.25
		Roussel (Höchst)	2.50

Source: Canada Department of Justice, Fines Chart dated November 23, 1999; News Releases; and Statements of Fact.

[a] Discounted because of early cooperation with the Ministry

[b] Investigations continuing as of early 2000. Two individuals were fined C$250,000 each (not shown).

Chapter 15

THE CHICAGO CRIMINAL TRIAL

On the night of the Decatur, Illinois raid of ADM's headquarters, ADM Executive Vice President Michael Andreas and Corn Products Division President Terrance Wilson were offered a chance to cooperate with the government, but to no one's surprise they refused the offer. On the expectation that Andreas and Wilson would continue to deny their culpability, DOJ prosecutors formed a prosecutorial team under the initial leadership of James M. Griffin, Chief of the Antitrust Division's regional office in Chicago.[1] About five weeks later, Mark Whitacre's embezzlement of ADM became known to the DOJ and his immunity from prosecution was revoked.[2] Under the terms of his cooperation agreement, Whitacre's fraud made his indictment for price fixing practically automatic in the view of the DOJ. Whitacre's perfidy made him unsuitable as a government witness and greatly complicated the government's burden of proof in its prosecution of Andreas and Wilson. By indicting Whitacre on the same charge as Andreas and Wilson, the prosecution was counting on the likelihood that Whitacre would not take the stand in his own defense. More importantly, it made it impossible for the defendants to call Whitacre as a witness and thereby paint him as the chief price fixer.[3] Successful prosecution could not rely simply on the audio and video tapes in the hands of the prosecution, because witnesses were needed to authenticate the tapes and documents to be introduced as trial exhibits. Moreover, the testimony of the conspirators would help confirm that the conspirators knowingly and intentionally engaged in price fixing. Even before his fraud was discovered, Whitacre's testimony was tainted by the fact that he was a government informant. As a result, prosecutors would have to rely on a diverse group of foreign-born lysine executives whose credibility before a Chicago jury would be uncertain.[4]

In August 1995, Scott Lassar, first assistant U.S. Attorney in Chicago, was appointed to co-direct the prosecution of Andreas, Wilson, and Whitacre. Prosecutorial teamwork across divisions of the DOJ is highly unusual, but Lassar was a highly regarded and experienced prosecutor who would rise to the occasion. Griffin and Lassar requested that Whitacre be tried alongside his former bosses at ADM. The decision to prosecute their own cooperating witness was possibly unprecedented, but made exquisite tactical sense. This decision proved highly advantageous to the prosecution because Whitacre, as a defendant, could not be compelled to testify at his own trial. Indeed, the prosecutors could *assume* he would not testify, but as a defendant the jury would be instructed not to interpret his silence as guilt. Unable to call Whitacre to the stand, defense counsel for Andreas and Wilson were hobbled in their attempt to portray Whitacre as an ambitious, vengeful employee who became the tool of the FBI's plan to entrap Andreas and Wilson. In such situations, defense lawyers have the option to request that separate trials be conducted, but strangely Whitacre's lawyer never petitioned the court for separation. Pre-trial motions by Andreas and Wilson for separation were denied.

The fourth defendant in the Chicago trial was Kazutoshi Yamada, managing director of Ajinomoto. Yamada supervised the lysine department at Ajinomoto and took part in at least six meetings of the lysine conspirators. Moreover, he took a leading role in negotiating the market-share agreement with Michael Andreas in Irvine, California that was so decisive in cementing the lysine cartel. Along with the other three defendants, a U.S. subpoena was issued for Yamada's arrest in December 1996, but as Yamada was beyond the reach of U.S. law in Japan, he never appeared at the Chicago trial. At one point, Yamada had agreed to stand trial, but he later reneged (Leiber 2000). As his was a criminal offense, the U.S. DOJ could have tried to have him extradited from Japan. However, according to some legal authorities, extradition has never been sought by the U.S. government for antitrust violations. In the end, the Japan Ministry of Justice stated that it had never received such a request from U.S. authorities. Quite possibly, the Ministry might have ruled against such a request, because antitrust has only recently become criminalized in Japan. It is also possible that prosecutors decided that obtaining the full cooperation of its Ajinomoto witnesses might become easier if Yamada was not sitting in court as a defendant. In any case, Yamada is unlikely to show up in the United States to be tried for price fixing. With an outstanding federal warrant for his arrest, Yamada is effectively barred from entering U.S. territory for the rest of his life.

Arrayed against the eight-person team of government prosecutors was a formidable group of defense attorneys. The chief defense attorney for Michael Andreas was John M. Bray of the Washington, DC firm King & Spalding. Heading Terrance Wilson's defense was Reid H. Weingarten of the Washington, D.C. firm Steptoe & Johnson.[5] Both of these lawyers were highly experienced litigators who had handled the cases of numerous white-collar celebrity-defendants in the past.[6] Their firms had outstanding reputations and resources, all paid for by ADM's deep pockets. In sum, Andreas and Wilson got the best legal defense that money could buy.

The same cannot be said for Mark Whitacre's legal defense. Whitacre had parted ways with a previous attorney and was represented throughout the trial by Bill T. Walker, who is apparently a sole practitioner from tiny Granite City, Illinois. By the time the trial began, Whitacre was bankrupt with poor prospects for future employment, so his attorney was effectively working *pro bono*.[7]

Before the end of 1997, U.S. District Court Judge Blanche Manning had been assigned to preside in the case, officially designated as *United States of America versus Michael D. Andreas, et al.*, case number 96 CR 762 of the

U.S. District Court, Northern District of Illinois, Eastern Division. This case was one of the first to be handled by Judge Manning and very likely her first antitrust case. Manning had started out in her professional life as a high school English teacher, and her written opinions at times reflect a style imbued by a familiarity with classic English literature. In 1967, Manning was admitted to the Illinois bar. She served as a judge in Cook County Circuit Court from 1979 and became an appellate judge in 1987. After running unsuccessfully for a seat on the Illinois Supreme Court in 1992, Manning was nominated for her federal appointment by both of Illinois, U.S. Senators and sworn in to her position in 1994.

Judge Manning was chosen to preside at the trial by lottery. When the DOJ prosecutors heard about their selection, they attempted to undo the assignment and substitute Judge Rueben Costillo, who had somewhat more background in complex corporate litigation. Leiber (2000) called this "blatant judge-shopping." As was her right, Manning refused to be removed from the case. Leiber believes that Manning harbored no resentment against the prosecutors for their lack of confidence in her, but he also notes that ". . . at times she seemed indulgent to the high powered defense lawyers" (p. 46). She developed a special rapport during the trial for John Bray, whom Leiber termed "a consummate professional." Nevertheless, both sides early in the trial had a chance to remove Manning when she voluntarily revealed a potential conflict of interest that could have justified recusal. At that point at least, neither side wanted to file a motion to remove her from the case. Despite the often-contentious behavior of opposing counsel, she displayed outstanding courtesy to both sides and was solicitous to the needs of the jury members.

Manning was inundated by a flood of motions before, during, and after the trial that required rulings on close or often unprecedented issues, many of them relating to the use of the plethora of audio and video tapes displayed at the trial and summarized in various ways by both sides for the jury. She worked hard to produce opinions on the motions so as not to hold up progress of the trial. However, skeptical perhaps because of her previous experiences in the local courts, Manning frequently lashed out at what she perceived as heavy-handed tactics by the prosecutors. She also displayed a certain amount of unsureness and inconsistency in her rulings on the complex U.S. Sentencing Guidelines during the sentencing phase of the trial. The one guiding principle most often seen in her decisions was to give great latitude to both sides to introduce evidence, trusting in the wisdom of the jury's considerations.

THE MAIN ISSUES

In the grand-jury indictment handed down in December 1996, the three defendants were charged with only one count: conspiracy in restraint of trade in the U.S. market for dry lysine made by fermentation during the period June 1992-June 1995.[8] The allegation was a violation of Section 1 of the Sherman Act of 1890. One of the puzzling aspects of this case is why prosecutors did not push for additional criminal counts (Lieber and Boyer 1999). At least three more criminal indictments would have been possible given the evidence presented during the trial: mail fraud, wire fraud, and price fixing by Andreas and Wilson in the market for citric acid. Perhaps the last is understandable because of the many additional witnesses that would have been necessary to convict. Federal mail and wire fraud convictions would have added substantially to potential sentences with relatively little additional prosecutorial effort.[9] A ruling of the appeals court of the 7th Circuit Court a few years earlier seemed to rule out an indictment for wire fraud that merely furthered a price-fixing conspiracy. On the other hand, "surgical charging" by the prosecution carried at least one big advantage. It would force the jury to choose between guilt and innocence on the one charge. With multiple charges, the jury could compromise by finding a defendant guilty of one of the lesser charges but not guilty of the main charge. As for charging Andreas and Wilson for citric acid price fixing, this would have required prosecutors to hold a separate trial for the third defendant, Mark Whitacre, which would have removed an important tactical advantage for the prosecutors.

Antitrust scholars and lawyers, political analysts, and journalists considered this trial the most important U.S. prosecution ever undertaken of an international price-fixing conspiracy. The trial would illustrate in vivid detail how the cartel was managed and how cozy once hostile rivals had become by the end of the conspiracy. Antitrust lawyers interviewed by the *Chicago Tribune* believed that convictions in the case would have a strong influence on private business practices by demonstrating that the Sherman Act once again had real teeth in it. The mere fact that the government had opted for a criminal indictment, with its much higher standard of proof compared to a civil case, was in itself a strong signal of prosecutorial toughness in dealing with price fixing in general.

The most difficult task facing the government prosecutors was to prove beyond a reasonable doubt to the jury that Andreas, Wilson, and Whitacre "knowingly and intentionally" engaged in price fixing. That is, in their meetings with rival lysine makers, they agreed to set their list prices at equally high levels in specific markets with the purpose of transacting future sales at significantly higher prices than would have occurred had no conspiracy taken place. Whether actual prices moved in concert was irrelevant for such a proof. Moreover, the prosecution was going to have to assemble the evidence of intent without the help of their discredited former agent Mark Whitacre and on the assumption that neither Andreas nor Wilson would be available for grilling on the witness stand. To prove intent, the government had to rely on taped and written accounts of the conspirator's meetings and telephone calls and the testimony of other participants whose credibility with the jury was uncertain. All of the lysine conspirators who would testify had pleaded guilty to criminal price fixing, but the low fines they had paid might make it appear to the jury that they had been given sweetheart deals by the DOJ in return for testimony favorable to the prosecution's case. There were even problems with the audio tapes. The words "price fixing" never appear, though similar phrases were on them. More important was the possibility that the audio tapes were tainted by Whitacre's actions, such as his ability to withhold tapes that might exonerate Andreas, Wilson, or others at ADM. Whitacre's fall from grace also would allow the defense to argue that he plotted against his superiors at ADM by trying to entrap them.

However, there were four types of evidence that the jury would probably view as unimpeachable. First, there was one current officer of ADM who had not pleaded guilty and who was willing to testify against Andreas and Wilson. His name was Barrie Cox. Second, there were numerous written memorandums of lysine meetings that clearly established that the group's object was to fix prices. Third, there was evidence that the co-conspirators knew that their actions were illegal because they warned each other and took steps to cover up their meetings. Fourth, the video tapes of four conspiratorial meetings were made directly by the FBI and could not be manipulated by Whitacre.

The defense's principal theory was that this evidence was consistent with perfectly legal information-gathering. Indeed, the defense sought to portray Andreas and Wilson as patriotic heroes whose intent was to smash an evil Asian cartel that had been ripping off U.S. consumers for years. By collecting sufficient market intelligence from their Asian rivals, ADM would become a formidable force in the industry, thereby lowering prices and driving the invaders out of the U.S. market. Although a fairly disparate invention on the face of it, with no evidence to be presented showing ADM tried to match their rivals' prices to be presented, this defense theory had a chance of carrying the day.[10]

PRE-TRIAL MOTIONS

Starting nine months before the trial began, both sides began submitting numerous motions to Judge Manning that might yield tactical advantages later on. Her decisions would determine the fairness of the trial. One of the early skirmishes concerned defense allegations that Whitacre had sent exculpatory audio tapes to a friend of his, business consultant David Hoech. Whitacre had leaked confidential information to Hoech about ADM's lysine operations, though he may not have been aware that Hoech was receiving a large retainer from Kyowa Hakko to pass that secret information on to one of ADM's rivals. Since the lysine cartel had become public, Hoech had become a thorn in ADM's side, sending the press numerous letters unfavorable to the company and spreading Whitacre's views on ADM's unethical behavior. He continued his anti-ADM campaign up to and after the

1998 trial.[11] Hoech had refused to answer questions when subpoenaed by the defense.

At a December 1997 hearing, Manning expressed her frustration at the government's failure to help the defendants find the missing tapes; she chastised the FBI for its failure to request immunity for Hoech in order to elicit his full cooperation. The government stated that Hoech had no credible evidence to offer.[12] Nevertheless, in a March 1998 pre-trial hearing, defense attorneys moved that all tapes made by Whitacre be ruled inadmissible. Judge Manning eventually allowed them to be presented. A month later, she again ruled in the government's favor by denying defense motions to grant testimonial immunity to Hoech, Whitacre's former lawyer, and Whitacre's wife Ginger Whitacre.[13] At the same time, Manning took the occasion to chide the FBI for giving Whitacre too much discretion in his taping decisions and for violating its own procedures for handling cooperating witnesses. The FBI conduct "borders on gross negligence," she said, but because it was unintentional it was not grounds for suppressing the tapes.

The most important pre-trial rulings occurred just before the trial was to get underway. Manning again ruled against a defense motion to suppress Whitacre's tapes. The defense had argued that Whitacre's decision not to testify would make authentication impossible, but the prosecution said that the testimony of other participants and experts would allow the jury to decide on their authenticity. She also ruled against deletion of offensive language on the tapes by Andreas and Wilson. Finally, Manning decided to allow Barrie Cox to testify on Wilson's role in the citric acid cartel; the idea was to permit the jury to make inferences about Wilson' intent in lysine and to show parallelism in conduct. This last ruling would prove to be of immense advantage to the prosecution.

However, Manning also handed the defense three important favorable rulings. First, the defense would be allowed to raise the issue of selective taping and tape destruction by Whitacre. Second, they could pursue the question of FBI misconduct, specifically whether it was biased against the Andreas family or had mishandled its informant Whitacre.[14] Third, she ruled that references in court to ADM's criminal guilty plea would be too prejudicial to the defendants, who after all were ADM employees. She believed that to mention the ADM plea in court would be equivalent to a court directed verdict. The prosecution naturally viewed this decision as a great handicap, about which they groused frequently. Leiber (2000) judges that the law was on the prosecutor's side, because matters that relate to pretrial deals can affect the credibility of a witness that benefited from a deal. What the jury later inferred about the company's guilt after listening to Barrie Cox can only be imagined. Besides Cox, there were four other witnesses who would admit in court their personal guilty pleas or that the Asian companies they worked for had pleaded guilty to price fixing.[15]

THE TRIAL OPENS

Jury selection (*voir dire*) began on Thursday, July 9, 1998 and ended the following Wednesday. The questioning of potential jurors took three days and required 700 pages of trial transcript to be recorded. There were virtually no restrictions on questions that potential jurors could be asked. Spending so many days selecting a jury is unusual these days. The result was a representative cross-section of Chicago's demographics. The jury and its alternate members were balanced by gender, age, and ethnic background. Such pluralism tended to blunt the appeal of the defense's xenophobic, yellow-peril arguments during the trial.[16]

As befits a proceeding in the Electronic Age, the courtroom was crowded with audio-visual equipment (Leiber 2000). There were eight computers, four giant TV monitors, and an Elmo machine for translated texts. The room was also bursting with dozens of Decatur residents, friends and well-wishers of Michael Andreas and Terrance Wilson, brought to Chicago in chartered buses arranged by ADM. Whitacre looked physically fit, Wilson pale and sickly.

DOJ prosecutor James Griffin opened the trial proper on July 15th, but he faced only two of the three defendants on the other side of the courtroom. The day before, Mark Whitacre had requested to return to his federal prison in North Carolina. He told Judge Manning that he feared for his safety after two weeks in Chicago's Metropolitan Correctional Center because it had become known that he was a government snitch. Over the objections of defense counsel, Manning agreed to have him moved back to his federal prison. Lieber (2000), who attended most of the Chicago trial, believes that the trial was fairer because of his absence. With Whitacre elsewhere, lawyers representing Andreas and Wilson would find it more difficult to act as prosecutors against him, which was their firm intention.[17]

Griffin's opening remarks (Tr. 703-746) contained few surprises, and indeed echoed the evidence assembled in the government's proffer submitted to the Court in May (Griffin and Lassar 1998). Andreas and Wilson were identified as the chief architects of ADM's price-fixing scheme. Keeping his boss Andreas informed at all times, Wilson instructed Whitacre on the mechanisms of price fixing. Once the cartel was operating smoothly (after about 18 months of operation), he withdrew from active management of the lysine cartel, leaving Whitacre to make most decisions. Whitacre eventually got the help of five sales managers in his division to carry out the conspiracy. Although the most distant from the day-to-day operations of the cartel, Andreas attended four conspiratorial meetings, was frequently briefed by Wilson or Whitacre on the cartel's progress, and made several tactical and strategic decisions about ADM's role in the cartel.

Griffin emphasized that the government would supply numerous documents,[18] tapes, and witnesses to the jury to confirm its assertions. Most important, it would not rely on any statements made by Whitacre (Tr. 744).

Rather, Griffin promised that four direct participants in the conspiracy meetings would testify about the group's pricing intentions. Equally important, taped conversations by Andreas and Wilson will be self-incriminating, he promised, including evidence of threats to use ADM's formidable lysine production capacity that were meant to intimidate the Asian companies.

Next, John Bray made his opening statement for his client, Michael Andreas (Tr. 755-801). He tried to minimize the importance of the taped evidence of Andreas' statements by asserting that they contain no explicit language, that many exculpatory tapes were destroyed by Whitacre, and that the crafty ambitious Whitacre had every reason to selectively tape his client. Andreas, he asserted, was candid with the FBI about ADM's contacts with its Asian rivals, which were made simply to get market sales data to allow ADM to help America fight a predatory Asian lysine cartel. In his opening, Bray introduced a fancy chart of lysine prices that showed them rising a few months after the cartel disbanded. Despite prosecutors' objections that this was a *per se* case in which economic evidence was irrelevant, Manning gave Bray a favorable ruling that allowed the chart to be introduced. Finally he excoriated the FBI for its stupidity and dishonesty; in particular, it coached Whitacre to "plant words in Mick Andreas' mouth" (Tr. 791).

Reid Weingarten took a similar tact in opening his defense of Terrance Wilson, who was portrayed as merely bluffing in his dealings with his Asian counterparts in order to assist ADM's cartel-busting goals. Whitacre was again assigned a Machiavellian role, scheming to topple Wilson for his own private advantage. Weingarten also tried to anticipate the jury's reaction to hearing Wilson on tape by describing his client as uneducated, gruff, and given to using "salty" language. He urged the jury not to believe what they saw and heard on the tapes because the conspirators were always lying to each other, *except* the so-called "locker-room chats" at ADM headquarters. This exhortation was a blunder. Trying to create sympathy for his client, Weingarten described Wilson as a life-long employee of ADM, utterly loyal to the ruling Andreas family, and blindly following Michael Andreas' orders as a good soldier should. Finally, Weingarten also injected an irrelevant economic line of defense, namely, that the lysine market could not have been manipulated even if ADM had tried to do so.[19]

Opening statements ended with brief, half-hearted speech by the absent Whitacre's lawyer, Bill Walker. He noted the short period for which Whitacre is being charged for conspiring and correctly points out to the jury that Whitacre is being prosecuted not only by the government but also by his fellow defendants. Throughout the trial, Walker seemed to be a lonely, sad figure struggling on without the benefit of client, lavish charts, or backroom support (Leiber 2000).

WITNESSES FOR THE PROSECUTION

The prosecution opened its case on Thursday, July 16th and it did not rest its case until September 1st, 48 days later. Normally, testimony in front of the jury were held only on the first four days of the week. Nevertheless, 27 full days of such testimony is an extraordinarily long period to question only 12 witnesses, several of which spoke only for a few hours.[20] While a few days were lost to illnesses of one defendant and a juror, the major reason for the lengthy prosecution phase was the defense's legal strategy. The defense phase of the trial lasted for only about one hour on September 2nd. Despite repeated statements to Judge Manning in chambers that several defense witnesses would be called, only one minor and ineffectual defense witness was called.[21] In effect, the defense of Andreas and Wilson was mounted almost exclusively during extensive cross-examinations intended to discredit nearly all of the prosecution's witnesses. Moreover, Manning even allowed the defense to introduce their exhibits during the prosecution phase. This irregular tactic was a source of great frustration to the prosecution, though the government was generally able to repair any damage to their case during the re-direct examinations. Yet, the tactic may have been the best course to take when the defendants fail to testify and there are no witnesses ready to verify the defense's theory.

The prosecution put 12 witnesses on the stand. Four of the witnesses were senior managers of the two largest Asian companies in the cartel: Mimoto, Ikeda, Crouy, and Yamamoto. In each case, these men had faithfully attended nearly all of the general meetings of the cartel from June 1992 to April 1995.[22] The fifth key witness was Barrie Cox, a corporate vice president of ADM who testified on his and Wilson's role in managing ADM's participation in the parallel citric acid conspiracy. Finally, FBI agent Brian Shepard was called upon to explain the FBI's 44-month investigation of the lysine cartel and especially its handling of its undercover mole Mark Whitacre.[23]

Kanji Mimoto

Kanji Mimoto was a middle-aged senior manager of Ajinomoto who had spent his entire business career with the company. He was a specialist in selling lysine for Ajinomoto for at least 25 years, beginning in 1970. He must have been pretty good at his job because in 1976 he was promoted to sales manager of Eurolysine, the Ajinomoto subsidiary that operated the company's largest plant and produced more than one-fourth of its global sales of lysine. Transferred back to Japan in the mid-1980s, Mimoto was promoted again to section manager for Ajinomoto's feed additives division and by 1992 was being groomed to replace his boss as division manager.[24] After he pleaded guilty and paid a $75,000 fine for his role in lysine price fixing, he was appointed president of Ajinomoto Indonesia, a manufacturer of monosodium glutamate (MSG) with 3000 employees.

As a witness, Mimoto's clear memory and good English made him a credible advocate for the prosecution's case. Observers noted that his body language conveyed deep shame (Leiber 2000). He confirmed that raising prices worldwide was the purpose of the meetings of the lysine cartel, that an agreement on volume shares took a year or more to arrange, and that the group experienced quarrels and cheating but at a level that was tolerable. Mimoto testified that documents were prepared to cover up the true purpose of the lysine meetings: "It was camouflage . . . There was a fake agenda . . ." (Tr. 941-947). He admitted being surprised at being allowed an open tour of ADM's lysine plant and also confessed to trying to gather microbes while on the tour to see if ADM might have stolen Ajinomoto's technology. Most interesting was his revelation that Ajinomoto had conspired to fix lysine prices on at least three occasions prior to ADM's entry in 1991. However, a distinction that would prove quite helpful to the prosecution was that the earlier price-fixing episodes had not involved volume allocations.

Tapes played during Mimoto's testimony were quite revealing about ADM's regular business tactics and attitudes. At the lysine cartel's March 1994 meeting in Hawaii, Wilson explained that while having Cheil join the group was going to be quite troublesome, because of the company's tendency to cheat, it was preferable to having no opportunity to try to educate them on the benefits of cooperation. He also threatened the other lysine managers that ". . . we would hire some mafia . . ." if they lied about their monthly volumes.

To demonstrate ADM's good faith, he boasted to the Asians that he had just fired ADM's best lysine salesman, an eleven-year veteran, for selling lysine at $1.13 per pound instead of the fixed price of $1.16. At another taped meeting in October of that year, Mick Andreas was overheard promising Ajinomoto's Yamada to reduce ADM's output of monosodium glutamate to only 50 percent of capacity as a favor for Ajinomoto's continued cooperation in the lysine market. He proposed their companies should establish a joint venture – any old product would do – just to have "a good excuse to get together" (Leiber 2000: 153). He also suggested that to cement their friendly relations, ADM and Ajinomoto should buy stock in each other (just as ADM had done with A.E. Staley). Some of the tapes made on this day Manning refused to allow to be played in court because of their inflammatory nature.[25]

After two and one-half days of convincing direct testimony, Mimoto was subjected to another two and one-half days of cross examination. He proved to be a stubborn sparring partner for defense counsel, who were somewhat successful in painting him as an experienced price-fixer long before ADM's entry. He admitted that ADM's entry into lysine worried Ajinomoto and caused it to lose money, but did not agree that ADM ever had a chance of driving his company out of the industry. Yes, Ajinomoto did try to withhold initially some of its superior market information from ADM, but only because ADM's lower estimate of global sales led ADM to believe it had a larger market share than it actually did. He stubbornly maintained that Ajinomoto's sales figures submitted to the cartel were accurate, that the price agreements were substantially honored by the participants, and that the cartel was the principal force accounting for lysine price increases in late 1992 and 1993. Most importantly, Mimoto verified that Wilson talked and behaved in a manner consistent with the group's price-fixing goals and that Michael Andreas seemed well informed about the cartel on every occasion that they met.

Press coverage of Mimoto's testimony was extensive and elicited little skepticism.

Hirozaku Ikeda

Hirozaku Ikeda had retired as manager of Ajinomoto's feed-products division in 1994 just six months before the lysine cartel was exposed publicly. He had worked for Ajinomoto for 34 years. During his last ten years with the company he had reported directly to Kazutoshi Yamada, a managing director of Ajinomoto and absent defendant, and had directly supervised Kanji Mimoto, who succeeded him in 1994. Two years after he retired, Ikeda was essentially instructed to sign his guilty plea agreement by the legal office of his former employer. He claimed to be unaware that his guilty plea was a condition for all but three Ajinomoto officers being extended immunity from prosecution. Leiber (2000), who observed his testimony, described him as a tiny, wizened man who looked older than his advanced age. In general, Ikeda's excellent memory allowed him to reinforce Mimoto's testimony in all particulars.

It was during Ikeda's direct examination by prosecutors that a devastating 82-minute portion of the videotape of the October 1993 Andreas-Yamada meeting in Irvine, California was played. It was at this meeting that Andreas proposed a market-share plan that came to be adopted by the cartel a few months later. Ikeda testified that Andreas had agreed to limit ADM's production to a level well below its capacity in return for the adoption of volume allocations by all the producers.

On the tape Andreas is caught saying that senior management at ADM kept a close handle on its many businesses, especially ones like its Bioproducts Division:

> "Myself and my father and Mr. Randall, we know all the time what is going on, especially with new businesses that need our attention."

Andreas told Yamada that ADM's management was so centralized that top officers were responsible for pricing decisions, not the sales managers as at Ajinomoto and most other companies. Sales persons at ADM were viewed as:

> ". . . agents for the customer . . . We pay them, but they're not our friends. They're friends with the customer."

The main point of Andreas' lecture on ADM's management philosophy seemed to be that tight control over information was superior for organizing a cartel than Ajinomoto's more dispersed system.

Another audio tape was played in court, this one of an April 1993 meeting between Ikeda, Yamada, Michael Andreas, Wilson, Randall, and Whitacre in Decatur. The ADM party again offered to form joint ventures with Ajinomoto. Yamada urged the ADM representatives to come to Tokyo soon, an event that Randall described as "getting laid and fixing prices" (Leiber 2000:166). Later, at a locker-room conversation among themselves just after the larger meeting, the ADM executives agreed that Ajinomoto appeared to be a reliable partner in crime. However, Mick Andreas was concerned about the three smaller lysine producers: ". . . well OK, I'm gonna talk to Dad about it, and see what he thinks" (*ibid.* p. 167).

After a day of direct examination, defense counsel spent three more days attempting to discredit Ikeda's major points, but largely to no avail.[26] Ikeda was mostly able to parry a number of defense theories: that Ajinomoto was afraid of going out of business after 1991, that Ajinomoto hid substantial lysine sales, that Ajinomoto tried to intimidate ADM's Asian sales representative, that he was prepped and coached for his testimony by the FBI, and that he was compensated for his pro-prosecution testimony by the DOJ's decision not to seek a fine for him. Ikeda does such a good job of holding on to his original positions that John Bray betrays his irritation at one point:

> "You seem to have a greater ability to respond to the government's questions than you do to our questions" (Tr. 2131).

Perhaps the one area in which the defense scores is in getting Ikeda to admit that Andreas and Yamada frequently state their intention to comply with the antitrust laws governing mergers. The jury may have been left with the impression that they also meant to comply with the price-fixing laws as well.

Alain B. Crouy

Alain Crouy is a French citizen with an articulate command of English and a skillful way of explaining the economics of the lysine market. He had worked at Eurolysine, Ajinomoto's French subsidiary, during 1990-

1993. From the spring of 1991 to the fall of 1993, he was the CEO of Eurolysine, leaving when promoted to a greater position within Eurolysine's minority French owner, Lafarge Industries.

A key portion of Crouy's testimony was his rendition of his meticulous and detailed notes that he made during the first of the lysine cartels general meetings in Mexico City in October 1992. He explained the clear intent of the group to raise prices worldwide and to establish a lysine trade association as a cover organization. Crouy laid out the reasons why it was so difficult to develop a consensus on market shares. Later, he gave a cogent explanation of the mechanics of the cartel's operation and their economic rationales. For example, he noted that 30-day or 45-day price-protection clauses were common in the annual contracts the manufacturers signed with their customers. Thus, when the cartel announced a price increase, clients could buy a portion of their contracted annual volume at the pre-announcement price; that is why domestic transaction prices took a month or two to respond to announcements of price increases. On international shipments the lags were even lengthier. Crouy also testified as to the necessity of keeping lysine prices close together across the major regions of the world. Otherwise, wholesale distributors with stockpiles of lysine could resell their product in the high-priced region and undermine any wide gap in prices.

Finally, Crouy provided the logic for a cartel agreement on volumes to be sold by each company, and using a percentage basis in particular. An effective agreement on the upper limits each firm could sell over a year's time would eliminate the incentive of some of its members cheating on the agreed price; moreover, a volume monitoring method would prevent members from cheating by making extra sales. A percentage agreement on global sales was greatly preferable to an agreement that divided sales territories or specific customers among the manufacturers. At a 1993 meeting of the cartel in Tokyo, Terrance Wilson had warned the group against implementing a "don't touch [each other's] customers" policy because of the increased risk of "legal problems" (Tr. 2239). Crouy elaborated on Wilson's dictum. Refusal to deal is an antitrust violation in itself and "second, the customer will say: Why is he not giving me an offer?" (Tr. 2239). That is, customers will immediately suspect the presence of a price-fixing agreement and may make formal complaints to the competition-law authorities.

Defense counsel did their best to undermine Crouy's direct testimony by quizzing him on how unlikely the cartel's success would be, but Crouy easily withstood their attacks. Crouy denied or failed to confirm that Ajinomoto gave ADM false information on market size or shares, spied on ADM, feared and loathed Terry Wilson, or that the lysine price increases in 1992 and 1993 were due to natural market forces (Tr. 2357-2428). They also continued their strategy of presenting their case during cross-examination.[27] At one point, Crouy was closely questioned about a remark made by Michael Andreas that the defense repeatedly tried to spin as exculpatory. In a May 1993 meeting, Andreas said:

> "We don't do deals. We can tell you what we want to do without any *quid pro quo*, but [one] has to be very careful . . "
> (Tr. 2242).

This remark, taken in isolation, might well be interpreted as a sign that Andreas intended to interact with his Asian rivals in an arguably legal fashion. However, Crouy's response punctured the defense's interpretation. He said that this remark was obscure and puzzling. Furthermore, in the context of the discussions on volume allocations that preceded and followed Andreas' remark, it made no sense to Crouy whatsoever.

Masaru Yamamoto

Along with Mark Whitacre and Kanji Mimoto, Masaru Yamamoto was the most faithful attendee at the lysine cartel's general meetings. He was also involved in many meetings with Ajinomoto and Sewon during 1991-1993 as those companies tried to develop a plan to thwart ADM's successful entry into the global lysine industry and later wrestled with whether to accept ADM's offer to form a cartel to set prices and volume shares. Like the three Ajinomoto managers who preceded him, Yamamoto was highly experienced in the lysine industry, had excellent recall of the events, and stoutly defended a view of the cartel's activities that strongly favored the prosecution's case. However, his testimony helped the defense to score points by supporting somewhat their theory that ADM was a white knight doing battle with rapacious Asian conspirators. On balance, Yamamoto's testimony, coming almost at the end of the trial might have muddled the government's case more than it helped. But the prosecutors were in a bind. Without his testimony, all the witnesses to the lysine meetings would have drawn from only one company.[28] In the end, Yamamoto's testimony provided one of the most sordid peeks into the rough-and-tumble of clashing titans of global business.

From 1964 Masaru Yamamoto was a career-long employee of Kyowa Hakko. He began selling lysine for his company in 1971, when the industry was barely ten years old. At first assisting in Kyowa's lysine export office in Tokyo, he eventually worked his way up through the company's hierarchy to become head of the worldwide lysine division in the early 1990s. Yamamoto had lived and worked in the United States for eleven years, first from 1978 to 1983 in New York to sell imported lysine and then from 1983 to 1989 in St. Louis in charge of Biokyowa's new Missouri lysine plant. In 1996, he pleaded guilty to lysine price fixing, personally paid a $50,000 fine, and was demoted by his employer Kyowa Hakko.[29]

Yamamoto's brief direct testimony (three hours) reaffirmed the government's view that the lysine cartel was indeed organized for the purpose of raising prices. He rendered in detail the meetings and telephone calls that led to the rise in lysine prices in late 1992. Audio tapes, video tapes, and his personal notes recounted the conspiracy in all its particulars. At the Vancouver meeting, it was Yamamoto that proposed fine-tuning the cartel's operations by setting up regional meetings among local sales managers. Although some of these meetings were in fact held, Wilson objected to the proposal because he said that only he, Andreas, and Whitacre were fully informed about the conspiracy inside ADM. In 1993, Wilson had his plan of a lysine cover association established as well as monthly reporting of company sales of lysine. By 1994, their lysine association had become affiliated with a quasi-official organization of feed-additives manufacturers that was sponsored by the European Union.

In two days of brutal cross-examination, defense counsel did their best to portray Yamamoto as one of the fearsome Asian predators on U.S. lysine buyers. Much of his testimony fit this scenario, but the additional part of the story that sees ADM as the buyers' savior did not come off as well. Yamamoto was forced to admit that the first three manufacturers of lysine did form a cartel from 1986 to 1990 and that a territorial division of the U.S. market was made by Kyowa and Ajinomoto. He also testified that the three established producers were anxious about ADM just before and after ADM's entry in 1991, which precipitated a serious price war. However, Yamamoto was steadfast in his view that it was ADM that initiated the contacts that led to the formation of the new lysine cartel in 1992.

The first year or so of the cartel's operation was rocky, replete with mistrust and mutual recriminations. Yamamoto himself seems to have hired Whitacre's good friend David Hoech to spy on ADM's lysine operations. Kyowa paid Hoech $175,000 during 1992-1995 to obtain numerous trade secrets, though getting the garrulous Whitacre to talk hardly took the skills of a Matahari. While Yamamoto tried to downplay the value of the information he received, Kyowa's espionage must have looked nefarious to the jury. Indeed, though he denied it, defense counsel planted the idea that Yamamoto was in fact bribing Whitacre and using Hoech as an intermediary for the bribe. Yamamoto also admitted that many personal tensions existed in the cartel, some of which originated from Western/Eastern cultural differences. Wilson' behavior was particularly insulting at times.[30] ADM's aggressive build-up of market share in 1991-1993 was distressing to middle-level Kyowa employees, as many documents showed, but Yamamoto maintained that stealing customers was acceptable to Kyowa as long as the price and market-share agreements held, as they pretty much did in 1994-1995. His interpretation of the second lysine price war in early 1993 was not favorable to the defense who wanted it to be seen as ADM aggression; according to Yamamoto it was simply ADM's way of concretely signaling its unhappiness over the lack of a volume agreement (Tr. 4430). Yamamoto also recounted the cartel's general pricing rule for lysine adopted at its first meeting in Mexico City (Tr. 4590-4592). The cartel would adjust its lysine price to a level 5 to 10 cents below the corn-soybean shadow price.[31]

Barrie Cox

Barrie Cox was an ADM vice president with no direct knowledge of lysine price fixing, yet his testimony was in all likelihood the most effective of all the prosecution's major witnesses. Unlike his former counterpart Mark Whitacre, Cox had all the appearance of a truth teller. Indeed, because what he said placed him and the company he still worked for in a most invidious light, his testimony was all the more believable. Defense attorneys knew that Cox's testimony would be devastating, particularly to Wilson, and did their best to exclude him from the courtroom, but in this case Judge Manning's propensity to allow everything to be laid in front of the jury worked against them.[32]

Cox's testimony dealt exclusively with ADM's participation in the global citric acid conspiracy (see Chapter 3). Cox, British-born and well educated, had spent nearly his entire career in the citric acid business. From 1969 to 1990, he had been working in Europe, Canada, and New York for the giant pharmaceutical firm Pfizer selling citric acid, an industry that Pfizer had pioneered in the early 1920s. As a result, he was well acquainted with the managers of all the leading European producers. Pfizer's citric acid assets were sold to ADM in late 1990, and Cox was one of a handful of managers hired by ADM to continue marketing the product. Cox moved to Decatur in early 1991 to become ADM Vice President of the Food Additives Division, reporting directly to Terrance Wilson. He had been promoted to President of that division in 1993. What the jury made of Cox testifying against his boss is difficult to say, because he was never permitted to mention the fact that two years before his company had pleaded guilty to price fixing the global market for lysine. Nor could the defendants' attorneys try to smear his motives for fear to calling attention to ADM's guilt.

The citric acid conspiracy had begun more than a year before the lysine conspiracy was fashioned. Of course, the nature of the products and the composition of the two cartels differed, but Cox's testimony revealed a vast number of parallels in how the two cartels were organized. The two cartels began by invitation of ADM; both began with four members and added a fifth seller mid-way through; both markets had been cartelized in the 1980s; meetings were held quarterly to review sales and reset prices, with numerous telephone calls to iron out problems between meetings; both had a trade association with legitimate business objectives, but which behind the scenes facilitated illegal meetings; association members reported their monthly global sales to a secretary-general who compiled regular reports for all members; once ADM's participation had become routinized, Wilson withdrew personally to concentrate on other business; global market shares were adhered to, obviating the need for territorial splits or exclusive customer assignments; and steps were taken to destroy evidence of price fixing (Connor 1999). Of all his direct testimony, perhaps the most damaging to the defense concerned an episode in ADM headquarters a month or two after the FBI raid.

Wilson, Cox reports, said that the lysine tapes made by Whitacre contained "bad stuff" (Tr. 2683-2685). No wonder that during Cox's day on the witness stand, Wilson studiously avoided gazing at Cox.

The cross-examination of Cox was gentle by comparison to all the other major witnesses. It focused on the personality of Mark Whitacre and Cox's managerial discretion with respect to price fixing. Cox disliked Whitacre, because he was boastful, prone to lying about his background, and nosey about the citric acid business. Defense lawyers spent a great deal of time trying to demonstrate that Cox had run the conspiracy for ADM with little or no help from Wilson, but on redirect he clarifies his subservient role vis-a-vis Wilson. Defense attorney Hulkower's cross examination of Cox was somewhat disorganized. He led Cox into several seemingly purposeless digressions, including a number of questions on Cox's conversations with citric acid executives at Cargill, whose relevance would never be explained to the jury. By the end, "[Cox's] testimony was virtually unimpeached. It had been devastating to Wilson" (Leiber 2000:193).

Brian Shepard

Brian Shepard was the local Decatur, Illinois FBI agent who opened the lysine price-fixing investigation in November 1992 when Mark Whitacre unexpectedly confessed to his role. His role as a witness was to relate the FBI's investigative techniques, his handling of their mole Whitacre, and defend the Agency's tape-handling techniques. Discrediting the Bureau's methods was essential for the defense's theory that Mark Whitacre had malevolently manipulated the tapes to fabricate an indictment against Wilson and Andreas. They wanted to show that Whitacre was driven by his ambition to become President of ADM. In the end, the FBI's reputation may have been tarnished by sloppy procedures, but the few mistakes that were made were not sufficient to overturn the government's case. Besides, the FBI's own video tapes were untainted by the half-believable image of Whitacre constructed by defense lawyers. Prosecutors were successful in creating a great deal of sympathy from the jury for Shepard when he described how he and his family were shunned by the citizens of Decatur after his investigation of ADM became known.

Whitacre was issued two types of tape recorders, a small one that recorded on standard commercial microcassettes and a special reel-to-reel machine available only to law enforcement agencies. As defense lawyers were able to establish, the commercial recorder was open to abuse by a manipulative mole. Inadequate cataloging and identification of the microcassettes meant that Whitacre could have failed to return some of the cassettes issued to him or purchased extra tapes that he kept for himself. The defense made much of this during Shepard's four grueling days of cross-examination.[33]

Many of the government's most persuasive tape excerpts were not allowed to be played for the jury for procedural reasons. One tape had a conversation among Whitacre, Wilson, and ADM sales manager Wayne Brasser. On the tape, Brasser expresses his anxiety about his price-fixing activities in the global market for sodium gluconate.[33] Wilson offers the following comfort to Brasser:

> "You don't have to worry Mr. Brasser, because if anyone goes to jail, it's gonna be either Mr. Cox or myself [for citric acid]" (Tr. 3544-3545).

A more self-incriminating statement can hardly be imagined, but the comfort was to no avail because Brasser was fired for failing to continue price fixing as ordered by Wilson. The FBI interviewed Brasser, who confirmed Whitacre's account of Brasser's firing. Interestingly, a few days after the FBI raid of ADM headquarters, Whitacre made a tape of Michael Andreas in which he falsely assumed that it was the fired Wayne Brasser who had become the FBI's informant. Because this tape excerpt showed Andreas' awareness of sodium-gluconate price fixing by ADM, and not lysine, Judge Manning disallowed its presentation to the jury. At least two other taped conversations that were highly self-incriminating were similarly disallowed.[35]

Weingarten's cross-examination of Shepard was flawed. At one point, he asked Shepard why Whitacre's "lies" about ADM using prostitutes to wrest secrets about Ajinomoto's lysine production in its Iowa plant and ADM's theft of a bacitracin mircoorganism were not investigated by the FBI. Weingarten was "stopped in his tracks" by Shepards unexpected answer (Leiber 2000). In fact, said Shepard, they had tapes of ADM's Randall and Cheviron admitting that they had carried out the theft. Moreover, the FBI had interviewed the prostitutes and they had confirmed the story. The FBI had even recovered lists of the technical questions prepared by an ADM employee for them to ask Ajinomoto's employees. Shepard even talked about how Whitacre believed that ADM was price fixing ten of its product lines. Thus, inadvertently, Weingarten's attempt to make a point about Whitacre's greed and unreliability backfired. The jury now knew that ADM was a world champion of price fixing.

THE END GAME

After a tape expert and a couple of accountants testified briefly, the government rested its case on the morning of September 2, 1998. Not unexpectedly, the defense moved for acquittal. Both sides argue their cases for and against acquittal away from the jury. In most cases, the arguments repeat what was heard already in open court. The one defense point that was new was their theory that what defense lawyers termed the "second charge" of volume allocation is not a *per se* violation, but rather a "rule of reason" violation. If the judge were to accept this original view of the Sherman Act, then the defense could have introduced *economic* evidence about cheating on market shares to the jury. Whether indicative of defense counsel's pessimism about their case or their disregard for the judge's experience with antitrust law, this argument did not have much merit.

Despite several statements to the contrary, the defense stunned the judge and Whitacre's lawyer by calling only one very minor witness to testify (Lieber 2000).[36] This paralegal presented an ineffectual analysis of telephone calls, travel records, and meeting dates. Promised experts on audio tapes and economics never materialized.[37] The defense had intimated that they would also call retired FBI agents, David Hoech, Whitacre's parents, and even Michael Andreas himself.

After the defense rested its case, an amazing amount of time was spent discussing jury preparation. The tapes presented problems because in some cases only small portions had been played in court. Paper transcripts had been prepared, and even the video tapes had electronic scrolls to provide a text of what was being said on screen. Most of the time was expended on jury instructions: the better part of four days was spent contesting each word of a statement that ended up being only a couple of pages long.

On September 8th, U.S. Attorney Scott Lassar gave the prosecution's closing argument, and in most respects it was exemplary. He first laid out the three elements required for the prosecution to prove the defendants guilty in simple, easily understood terms. Assuming that the jury was convinced that price agreements were made and the lysine clearly involved interstate commerce, he focused almost exclusively on the third element: did the defendants knowingly, willingly, and intentionally participate in the scheme?

Lassar listed for the jury what he believes to be the six types of evidence supporting guilt: video tapes, audio tapes, four co-conspirators' testimony, the defendants' own notes, the citric acid parallels, and the defendants' lies when confronted by the FBI. Lassar suggested that:

> ". . . the case presented here by the government is one of the most compelling and powerful that has ever been presented in an American courtroom" (Tr. 5605).[38]

Moreover, he pointed out, all six types of evidence were consistent and self-reinforcing.

Lassar then began an extended chronological summary of the events that very likely helped the jury synthesize the various bits and pieces of evidence presented. First, ". . . the lysine conspiracy was explicitly modeled after the citric acid conspiracy in almost every way" (Tr. 5609). Defense attorneys could not question Barrie Cox's testimony because ". . . he is one of them. He still works for ADM . . . They couldn't suggest he was lying" (*ibid.*). Lassar even went as far as to suggest that Andreas and Wilson transferred Cox to England before the trial in order to make him unavailable for testimony.[39] Second, Lassar reminded the jury of the many "smoking guns" presented by the prosecution, such as the contemporaneous notes of conspiracy meetings. Many similar records were destroyed to cover up illegal activities.

Lassar recalled for the jury the many statements that proved that Andreas knew of and directed the lysine conspiracy. In the spring of 1993, Andreas was taped instructing Wilson and Whitacre to blame the Japanese for the on-going price war. Just after meeting with Kyowa representatives, Andreas complained that ". . . we raise the price, they cut. What did they say about that?" (Tr. 5634). The way in which Andreas handled the fake extortion threat in 1992 also revealed his complicity. When Whitacre confessed to the ploy, why didn't Andreas fire him, Lassar asks? On other tapes, Andreas says that ADM will cut production to assist its rivals (Tr. 5560) and also orders Whitacre to raise the price 5 cents. Just before Andreas met to set up a market share deal he said ". . . maybe we ought to come to an agreement" (Tr. 5638). After a dinner with top lysine managers of Ajinomoto, Andreas parting words were: "We hope you make a lot of money, and if you do, we will too" (Tr. 5712). These and many other statements of Andreas were assembled for the jury during Lassar's closing in order to counter any impression jurors may have had that Andreas was uninformed or remote from the conspiracy.

Lassar spent relatively little time reminding the jury of Wilson's pivotal role in the lysine cartel. It is fairly evident that prosecutors thought that the abundance of evidence presented against Wilson had already convinced the jury of his culpability. The U.S. Attorney's closing remarks on Whitacre were brief in the extreme. He simply mentioned that Whitacre's guilt was based on a couple of conversations Whitacre had with Mimoto and Yamamoto at the first two general meetings of the lysine cartel prior to November 5, 1992. Lassar's calculated neglect or minimizing of Whitacre's role as a conspirator almost seems to be an invitation to the jury to acquit their whistle-blower.

Lawyers are allowed a great deal of latitude in their summary statements to the jury, and Andreas' lawyer John Bray took every advantage of the Court's permissiveness in his closing statement. Bray asserted that all the conduct observed during 1992-1995 – collecting information on prices and volumes, forming a trade association, hiring Cox because of his personal connections with the Swiss citric acid makers – was perfectly legal. He implored the jury to ignore the defendants' statements, and instead to focus only on their actions as a guide to their intentions. Bray also spent much of his summing up in trying to discredit Whitacre and the government's witnesses. Whitacre, Bray claimed, framed Andreas; moreover he manufactured "ADM's lies" on lysine production just as he manipulated the audio tapes he made for the FBI (Tr. 5759). All the government's witnesses "except two" paid no fines so their testimony should be discounted.[40] Bray even ridiculed Ikeda's heavily accented English, suggesting that Ikeda's language skills were too poor to understand Andreas' words. Finally, Bray asserted that Andreas never knew about the lysine association and that his threats to flood the lysine market were perfectly legal.

Bill Walker, Whitacre's lawyer, made a short and unexciting closing statement.[41] He did his best to point out inconsistencies in the few testimonies that refer to the first four months of the conspiracy. At the first general meeting of the conspirators in Mexico City, Walker made a convincing case that the price agreements there were "tentative" and tried to discount the definitiveness of Whitacre's follow-up telephone calls to his contacts at Ajinomoto and Kyowa. He also tries to sow seeds of doubt about the certainty of the price agreements made at the cartel's second meeting in Paris in October 1992. It is doubtful that Walker swayed the jury on this second point.

The last closing statement was by Wilson's counsel, Reid Weingarten. It was an extraordinary performance that extended far beyond the allotted three hours given to each lawyer. Weingarten relentlessly spun interpretations of the tape and memo evidence that strain one's credulity. He was in fact, putting Wilson's defense case before the jury almost for the first time, including the playing of many tape excerpts. His delivery was plodding, ponderous, and confusing to the jurors, two of whom fell asleep in its midst. The one statement he made that cannot be contested is: "I don't want to summarize" (Tr. 5986).

Weingarten expended most of his energy on his xenophobic "Asian peril" theory. It was a fervent speech laced with half truths and littered with canards. Of course, the long history of price fixing by Ajinomoto and Kyowa gave a certain superficial validity to this scenario. ADM, he asserted, fought the Asian cartel with two punishing price wars, and another was in progress at the time of the FBI raid (Tr. 5904). While there was no evidence presented of a third price war, Weingarten seems to imply that planned price wars could not possibly occur in a market controlled by a cartel.[42] Not only did Yamamoto's testimony contradict Weingarten's view, economic thinking is pretty clear that international price wars frequently are devices to enforce cooperative or collusive business behavior.

Weingarten charged the FBI with dereliction of its duty because it "never looked at the marketplace" (Tr. 5905). He pointed out that no evidence was presented that ADM's prices were synchronize with those of the other firms in the cartel. These statements overlook the fact that price fixing is *per se* illegal, which means that the effects of an agreement on market prices is irrelevant to the prosecution's burden of proof. Weingarten harped mightily on the fear, distrust, and terror the Asian conspirators' felt for ADM and his client, Wilson. Of course the documents he cites are nearly all from the pre-conspiracy or early formative period of the cartel (Tr. 5919-5925). The last two years of the cartel's operation were ones of exemplary harmony. He drew a picture of a wide cultural gap between ADM and its Asian rivals, which he hinted was the reason that ADM was able to meet regularly with cartel members without the Asians ever being suspicious of ADM's true aim – the collection of market intelligence. Subsequent interviews of the jury verified that this jingoistic, chauvinistic theme did not go over well and indeed probably backfired (Lieber 2000).[43] His rather hokey, hammy peroration probably didn't help either.

Scott Lassar got the last extemporaneous word in a final rebuttal, and it was right on target. He pointed out numerous logical inconsistencies in the closing statements of Bray and Weingarten and asked many unanswerable questions. Why did ADM spend more than $100 million building a lysine plant if they didn't have a good idea of market demand? Why was Wilson attending overseas meetings on lysine, a division that he did not even supervise? Why didn't Andreas complain to the FBI about an Asian lysine cartel when he was first interviewed? Why so much effort to cover up the cartel meetings if they were thought to be legal? Why did ADM supply honest sales data to the Asians if they believed the latter were being dishonest? Why did Wilson consistently push for outside auditors if he didn't want the agreement on volume to work?

THE VERDICT

Lassar's rebuttal ended on Thursday, September 10th. After being trained in the use of a personal computer to retrieve documents, the jury was sequestered on Friday the 11th.

Leiber (2000) interviewed two of the jurors immediately after the trial ended, so we have a good idea about the jury's thinking. Wilson's guilt was the clearest to the jury and a consensus quickly developed on that point soon in their deliberations. Their discussion about Andreas' guilt took a bit longer, but the video tape made in Irvine, California tipped the balance against him. The vast majority of the jury's deliberations concerned Whitacre. "We thought he was crazy [to become a mole] when he had that kind of a position and salary," said one juror (Leiber 2000: 278). While the jurors disliked Whitacre because of his disloyalty, they realized that the FBI had no choice but to use him to make the tapes. The jury's attitude toward the three Japanese witnesses was similar because of the light punishment they had received in return for their testimony. Despite their dismay at some aspects of the FBI's investigation, the jury never lost sight of the fact that "price fixing is a serious matter" (*ibid.* p. 279).

Shortly after noon on Thursday the 17th, after more than four days of deliberation, the jury foreperson sent a message to Judge Manning that they had arrived at a consensus. At 2:25 that day, with all the parties assembled in the courtroom, the jury's verdict was announced. Michael Andreas, Terrance Wilson, and Mark Whitacre were found guilty as charged. After serving for ten weeks, the jurists were thanked by Judge Manning and were discharged.

All the major news wires flashed the verdict to their customers within the hour. That evening and the next day, there was extensive coverage by radio and television news shows and scores of newspapers. Especially detailed retrospective pieces appeared in the *Chicago Tribune, New York Times, Wall Street Journal,* and *Financial Times* of London, all of which had sent reporters to follow the trial on a daily basis.

The *Washington Post* quoted a longtime writer on agribusiness that: "This is probably the best documented case of corporate crime in history . . . It shows how corporations operate behind the scenes . . ." The *New York Times* said that the verdict ". . . marks a sweeping victory for Federal prosecutors." The article noted that the use of video evidence was unprecedented at an antitrust trial. Finally, the newspaper found some satisfaction in the fact that Dwayne Andreas, despite his unmatched political power in Washington, was unable to prevent ". . . the weight of the judicial system from falling on his son and one-time heir apparent . . ." Michael Andreas was identified as the ". . . most prominent American executive ever convicted for international price fixing" by the *Wall Street Journal* reporters. Perhaps surprisingly, there were no regrets for the loss of a key ADM manager expressed by business analysts. Indeed, the widespread assumption was that the leadership of the Andreas family as a whole was at an end. Sam Peltzman, a professor at the University of Chicago Business School, opined that the "family fiefdom" model of management at ADM could not continue. John McMillin, perhaps the most widely quoted financial analyst on agribusiness companies, said that ". . . some people want less Andreas involved in the boardroom." McMillin's assessment seemed to be widespread, because ADM's stock price did not move in the wake of the verdict's announcement.[44]

In the days following the verdict, Terrance Wilson's attorney promised an appeal. Defense counsel had filed dozens of objections and made several motions that could have become the basis of a retrial if Judge Manning's decisions were found wanting by the Seventh Circuit Court of Appeals. One of the defense's most impassioned pleas occurred on the last day of arguments when they alleged prosecutorial misconduct by Scott Lassar during his highly effective closing speech. They alleged that Lassar had improperly called attention to the defendants' exercise of the "fifth amendment" rights to decline to testify in their own defense.[45] In her decision on the day jury deliberations began, Judge Manning stated that she almost called for a mistrial were it not for the curative jury instructions she had given. Procedural issues were very likely the only basis on which an appeal could be made, because defense counsel interviews of the members of the jury surely revealed that they considered the evidence overwhelming against Andreas and Wilson. Jurors stated after the trial that they were surprised at the brevity of the defense's case (it covered less than 1 percent of the trial transcript); moreover, partly because of the way the FBI handled him, their only difficulties were in convicting the hapless Mark Whitacre.

THE SENTENCING PHASE

Judge Manning set January 7, 1999 as the date for the sentencing hearing, but ceaseless maneuvering by defense counsel eventually pushed that date back another seven months. Numerous motions made by the defense over the 10 months following the verdict severely tested Judge Manning's ability to analyze the applicability of the various laws on antitrust sanctions.

Under the Sherman Act (15 USC §1) as amended by Congress in 1974, criminal convictions became felonies for the first time (Connor 1997). The practical effect of this change in the law was to raise the maximum length of the prison sentence that federal prosecutors could seek from one year to three years. Before 1974, when violations were merely misdemeanors, convicted price fixers rarely received sentences of more than 30 days, many of the sentences were suspended, and most got no jail time whatsoever.[46] After 1974, about half of the individuals convicted for criminal price fixing had received prison sentences; the average sentence imposed was about ten months.

Congress further raised sanctions for price fixing in 1990 when the maximum statutory fines for individuals were increased from $100,000 to $350,000. It is the uncontested right of any federal prosecutor to seek fines up to this amount for any conspirator who pleas guilty or is found guilty by trial. However, when in 1987 Congress passed the U.S. Sentencing Guidelines (USSG) for individuals guilty of felonies under federal laws, things became much more complicated for judges (U.S. Sentencing Commission).[47] First, the USSG placed constraints upon federal judges as to the range of fines or prison time they could impose on felons. A numerical point system was developed that required judges to be quite explicit about a long list of aggravating or mitigating factors when composing their sentencing decisions. Aggravating factors include the size of the commerce affected by the conspiracy and whether a conspirator was a "manager" (ring-leader) of the conspiracy. Mitigating factors allow for downward adjustments if the individual recognizes his responsibility for the crime, cooperated with prosecutors, withdrew early from the scheme, is in poor health, and so forth. The final culpability score is equal to the base level (10 for conspiracies in restraint of trade) plus the aggravating factors' points less the mitigating factors' points. For each culpability score, a range of fines and prison terms is specified by the USSG.

Second, the judge must choose between two alternative fine rules. Section 2R1.1 of the USSG just described above *must* be used to calculate prison terms, but for fines since 1994 there have been two possibilities: the USSG standards or an alternative provision under 18 USC 3571(a)(d) that has been in the law for all federal felonies not specifically exempted. The first, USSG, alternative is much simpler in principle to apply: "For an individual, the guideline fine range shall be from one to five percent of the volume of commerce" (U.S. Sentencing Commission 1997: 226).[48] The definition of the term "affected commerce" is subject to differing interpretations in the context of price fixing. It could be as narrow as the sales of an individual's employer to U.S. customers only (or even some smaller region); or it could be as wide as the cartel's aggregate sales in all regions of the world for which prices were set. Judges are instructed to set fines within this guideline range depending on the extent of the defendants' roles and their importance within the conspiratorial group, subject to the statutory upper limit of $350,000. By contrast, the 1994 alternative sentencing provision is based on the size of the economic damages caused by the violation. The maximum fine is determined by a sliding scale that rises with the economic harm done to the injured parties, which is the sum of the monopoly overcharge and the dead-weight loss caused by the cartel.[49] The 1994 alternative provision is more burdensome to the courts because it would require expert testimony by economists at pre-sentencing hearings (just as in the case of civil antitrust proceedings), whereas the USSG approach requires only sales figure readily available from company financial records.

Pre-Sentencing Skirmishes

When prosecutors spoke anonymously to journalists a few days before the verdict, they announced that they would be seeking unprecedentedly high fines for Andreas, Wilson, and Whitacre. In fact they speculated that the three fines based on the twice-the-harm standard could total as much as $90 million. As the lysine case was the first large price-fixing episode to be litigated since the 1994 felony law was enacted, seeking to implement the alternative fine provision would be a first in the history of the antitrust laws for individuals. For reasons that are not clear, the DOJ apparently did not officially inform defendants or Judge Manning about their intent in this regard until early January, slightly before the sentencing hearing was originally scheduled to occur.

The defense became alarmed when they learned that the prosecution intended to invoke the 1994 alternative fine provision. The prosecution wanted a $25-million fine for Andreas and lesser amounts for the others. The defendants argued in a brief that the Court should use the USSG guidelines because it would be less time consuming, and would avoid evidentiary hearings on an "elusive" damages calculation. The much greater size of the maximum fines under USSG option ($92 million per defendant) was certainly one motive for the defendants' position. The prospect of making a precedent-setting decision of such a magnitude must have been daunting to Judge Manning. As a relatively new federal judge, she would be concerned about being overruled on appeal. Journalistic reports indicated that prosecutors would seek sentences of three years in prison and a $25-million for Andreas because he was unrepentant about his role in the cartel.

In February 1999, Judge Manning ruled against the defendants; that is, the 1994 alternative fine provisions based on damage estimates would govern. Both sides immediately secured economists who could testify on the damages caused by the lysine cartel.[50] In a pre-sentencing hearing Andreas' lawyer John Bray again warned Manning that no court has ever applied these provisions in litigation.

After an exchange of briefs and expert opinions, Judge Manning announced her decision on June 2, 1999. For reasons that are difficult to understand she reversed herself by declaring that the 1994 alternative fine provisions were inappropriate. In crisp language that betrayed personal exasperation, the decision to revert to the low statutory fine levels was justified on the following grounds. First, there is a "serious conflict" between the USSG and alternative 1994 guidelines, which she felt was beyond her power to resolve. Of course, this was precisely the issue she ruled on in February 1999. Nevertheless, it may indeed require Congressional attention. Second, Manning believed that the government showed "bad faith" by "sandbagging" the defendants with its late announcement of its intent to seek the alternative fine and by employing an economist to estimate damages far in advance of its announcement.[51] Third, the government dragged its feet when asked to compel documents from lysine producers located outside the United States. The DOJ's position that it was unsure when first asked that extraterritorial authority to seek the documents she termed "ludicrous." "The government played hard ball with Mark Whitacre and presumably could have done the same here," Manning wrote (1999:4). Leiber (2000) reports that the U.S. Attorney's office categorically denied that the overseas producers withheld production data. Finally, although adequate overseas data were in fact produced, Manning allocated the majority of her order listing all of its many flaws, points that were evidently adopted wholesale from the defendants' briefs. Defendants' experts used alleged imperfections in the non-U.S. lysine data as their major excuse for providing no overcharge estimate at all. Judge Manning concluded that somehow the more limited foreign plant information placed the defendants at a disadvantage, even though both sides had previously stipulated to the United States as the relevant market. Unfortunately, the documents exchanged by both sides for sentencing purposes remain sealed (Leiber 2000).

Although clothed in the rationalizations just listed, the main reason for Manning's decision to reject both guidelines seems to be fear to explore virgin territory.[52] "By all accounts the potential fines . . . would be staggering to the individual defendants" (Manning 1999:3). It appears that Judge Manning believed that personal bankruptcy is too high a price to ask from miscreants who caused buyers $78 million in financial losses.

The Sentencing Hearing

On the morning of July 9, 1999, in Chicago's Federal Building, Judge Manning presided over the final chapter of a story set in motion seven years earlier. Michael Andreas, Terrance Wilson, members of their families and their lawyers were present, but Mark Whitacre remained by choice in his federal prison in Edgefield, South Carolina.[53] Prior to the hearing, the Andreas family had organized a letter-writing campaign in support of Andreas and Wilson.

The hearing lasted four hours. Both Andreas and Wilson remained calm and silent until their sentences were read. Only one witness was heard, Wilson's wife. She appealed for home detention for her husband in lieu of prison, mentioning his frail health (excessive smoking, drinking, and a poor heart) and the presence of their disabled child at home. Only Whitacre took the opportunity to speak in his own defense prior to sentencing, over a speaker phone:

> "[The government] would have no case without me, against ADM and its executives. I risked my life and career for them, and I have yet to see anything."

Instead of the normal lecture chastening the guilty defendants, Judge Manning said she was impressed by the letters of support for Andreas and Wilson, which she said described them as "wonderful" family men and members of the community. Yet both received jail terms: two years each, the *minimum* allowed under the federal guidelines. In addition each was fined the maximum statutory amount of $350,000.[54] As described by a *Chicago Tribune* reporter who was present:

> "Wilson and his wife sat stone-faced as Manning issued his sentence. Andreas reddened when his was pronounced, staring down and touching his mouth with a finger."

In his response in court, Michael Andreas sounded an unrepentant note:

> "I love this country, your honor, and I thought I knew its rules. I did not want to commit a crime and did not think I had committed one."

Andreas' statement, presumably one he had prepared with some care, was absurdly imprudent (Leiber 2000). The remark clearly showed that he still believed himself innocent. Moreover, by suggesting that the world's rules had changed, he implied that there were other crimes he had committed that fit his personal rules.

Ever the stalwart soldier, Wilson's response was dignified and proper:

"I accept total and complete responsibility for my actions."

Finally, the courtroom once again heard Whitacre's disembodied voice on a speaker phone amplified for all to hear. His statement coaxed a small smile from Michael Andreas:

> "I was both young and stupid to play the risky and unethical games of the ADM elite. Life in prison has been better than life at ADM."

Judge Manning imposed an even stiffer prison sentence on Mark Whitacre: 30 months.[55] Many observers were dumbfounded as to why Manning would place a higher sentence on a whistle-blower who had conspired for at most four months than on the other defendants who conspired for 36 months. Leiber (2000) wrote that Whitacre's lawyer Bill Walker was stunned and speechless because:

> "It is extraordinary for a judge to mete out more time than a prosecutor is fighting for and unheard of when the defendant is a cooperating witness" (p.287).

The only explanation prosecutors could make for Manning's unprecedented harshness was that she might have concluded that Whitacre's cooperation was offered solely to cover up his on-going theft.

The reasons given for Whitacre's harsh sentence were that he was a "repeat offender" because of his prior conviction for embezzlement and that he alone was identified as a "manager" (leader) of the conspiracy. According to Manning, Andreas and Wilson did not qualify as managers. The principal reason for the seemingly paradoxical determination lies in Manning's reading of the USSG. A "manager" is explicitly identified for sentencing purposes as one who directs at least five employees to carry out the conspiracy. Manning had information that Whitacre directed at least five willing lysine salesmen as part of the scheme. Andreas and Wilson each directed fewer "willing" employees at ADM who helped them to conspire, and the Asian companies' managers in the cartel did not count because they were peers.[56] Besides, briefs for Andreas and Wilson denied they were managers, whereas Whitacre's counsel appeared to blunder again by making no objection to his being categorized as a manager.

As odd as it sounds, Whitacre's sentencing has a certain strained logic to it, but the signal it sends to future antitrust whistle-blowers is a chilling one.

The Appeals Court Decision

With nearly unlimited funds from ADM to pay for their legal defense, Michael Andreas and Terrance Wilson had nothing to lose by appealing their sentence, or so they thought. At about the time that Andreas and Wilson began serving their sentences in a federal prison in Illinois, their lawyers submitted a brief to the U.S. Court of Appeals for the Seventh Circuit.[57] The government responded with its own lengthy brief in October 1999 (Lassar *et al.* 1999).

The defendants tried to overturn the guilty verdict by making several arguments. One point of appeal was the government's offer of use-immunity to Barrie Cox and other ADM employees in return for ADM's cooperation with the DOJ. The defense argued that the immunity also applied to Andreas and Wilson. The defense also argued that Whitacre had destroyed exculpatory tapes and that prosecutor Lassar had improperly misled the jury when he said that the evidence presented at trial was the "most powerful" ever seen in a price-fixing case. Finally, the defendants asked for a reduced sentence because agreeing to volume shares is not a *per se* violation, and they should have been allowed to introduce economic evidence on the weak effects of the lysine cartel. Prosecutors rebutted all these points of appeal vigorously; moreover, they asked for a longer sentence because Andreas and Wilson were ringleaders of the cartel.

A three-judge panel of the Court of Appeals issued its 103-page opinion in June 2000 (Kanne *et. al.* 2000).[58] The immunity question was dismissed with derision because the prosecution had informed the defendants in writing of their intent to indict them in December 1996. The Court noted that the "no-defense" strategy had resulted in virtually no evidence being presented in court of tampering with or withholding taped conversations. As for Lassar's statement vouching for the power of the evidence, the Appeals Court dryly noted that ". . . the evidence [was] overwhelming" (*ibid.* p.78). In any case, Judge Manning's instructions to the jury were curative of this and all other procedural flaws. On the question of whether setting market volume shares is a *per se* or a rule-of-reason violation, the Appeals Court was definitive: tonnage allocations for each company were *in effect* a restriction on total output, which is clearly a *per se* violation of the Sherman Act (*ibid.* pp. 54-63).

The appeals decision contains a long and subtle discussion on two points concerning the application of the U.S. Sentencing Guidelines that are likely to be read with great interest by antitrust lawyers (*ibid.* pp.88-102). These are at least three concepts of "affected commerce" used in various circuit court decisions. In some, only sales that occur at prices *at or above* the agreed conspiracy price can be counted for sentencing purposes. In the lysine case, which set list prices, this concept of affected sales may well have resulted in a zero figure; in any case, significant economic testimony would be required. In some other circuits the courts have used the total sales of the participating company during the conspiracy period in all lines of business.[59]

The Seventh Circuit will take the middle ground on the issue. Admitting that interim price wars should perhaps be subtracted, the Court ruled that only ADM's lysine sales during the conspiracy are the "affected sales" for sentencing purposes. (This implies a seven-point enhancement of the defendant's culpability score). Second, the Appeals Court found "clear error" in Judge Manning's interpretation of the defendants' leadership roles in the cartel. Andreas and Wilson were part of the "collective leadership" of the lysine cartel, and they invited the cartel's discussions as well. Andreas was the chief of six conspirators at ADM. For all these reasons, Judge Manning was ordered to give a three or four point enhancement to the defendants, which implied an addition of six to nine months to their 24-month sentences.

On September 22, 2000, Andreas and Wilson listened silently from their federal prison as Judge Manning increased their sentences. Michael Andreas was given the maximum of 36 months and Terrance Wilson 33 months. They are expected to be released in mid-to-late 2002.

Chapter 15 Endnotes

[1] Assisting Griffin were DOJ lawyers Marvin N. Price, James Mutchnik, Robin Mann, Susan Walcoff Booker, and Kevin C. Culum. From the U.S. Attorneys Office was Lassar's assistant Phillip A. Guentert.

[2] More precisely, Whitacre would be prosecuted for his price fixing activities prior to November 5, 1992, the night he confessed his role to the FBI. Once Whitacre became a cooperating witness for the government, he was no longer indictable for his price fixing activities. Had Whitacre consulted a lawyer to examine the FBI cooperation agreement he signed in January 1993, he in all likelihood would never have been indicted for lysine price fixing. Rather, he would have been advised to seek immunity for all such activities prior to November 5, 1992, a concession that the FBI would have readily granted as soon as the quality of Whitacre's information became apparent. Of course, Whitacre's indictment for embezzlement under the noses of the FBI would never have gone unpunished, because by August 1995 Whitacre had no more bargaining chips.

[3] A year later, the presiding judge would cite this move by prosecutors as an example of how the government "played hardball" with Whitacre. Whitacre was poorly served by his lawyer on this issue. He would have had a much greater chance of acquittal had he moved to be tried separately, but no such motion was made to the Court.

[4] Another factor that probably weighted in the prosecutors' tactics was the English-language abilities of possible foreign-born witnesses. All the cartel's transnational meetings were conducted in English. Nevertheless, translators were available in the court room whenever Japanese witnesses were on the stand. In the end, one French and two of the three Japanese managers testified in Chicago without the use of translators.

[5] Bray was assisted in court by Kevin Dinan, James Phalen, and local counsel Joseph J. Duffy. Weingarten's co-counsel were Mark Hulkower, Monica Selter, and local counsel Kristina Anderson. Behind the scenes dozens of other junior lawyers and experts toiled for the litigators. It is a fair guess that Bray and Weingarten's hourly fees were more than ten times the hourly pay of the best paid government lawyer.

[6] Weingarten, age 48, had been a trial attorney for the DOJ for ten years. He had also served as counsel for several high-profile Congressional investigations such as the Iran-Contra scandal. Perhaps his best known client was former Secretary of Agriculture Mike Espy, whom he successfully defended from bribery charges.

[7] Whitacre had been well paid at ADM (he had received $1.2 million in compensation from 1989 to 1995) and had stolen $9 million from ADM, but was forced to disgorge the stolen money plus interest in early 1997. He filed for bankruptcy in September 1997, listing $1.25 million in unpayable debts.

[8] Note that this market definition excluded two types of lysine: liquid lysine, which was sold only to a few animal-feed manufacturers specially equipped to handle the liquid form, and extracted natural lysine sold exclusively for pharmaceutical uses. ADM's total dry lysine sales were $454 million during the conspiracy, of which $197 million were to customers in the United States.

[9] Later, in a separate criminal prosecution of Mark Whitacre for fraud and embezzlement, the indictment would list no less than 45 counts against its former undercover witness, including several counts of mail and wire fraud (see Chapter 16). Whitacre's prosecution was held in a federal district court in central Illinois that is part of the 7th Circuit in 1997 before the Chicago trial commenced.

[10] A similar theory had been successful for some defendants in the *Thermal Fax Paper* antitrust case.

[11] Asked why he had expended so much energy to harassing ADM in this matter, Hoech replied: "Because Dwayne [Andreas] is no better than a street pimp" (Leiber 2000:32). Apparently, Hoech was referring to stories that ADM was willing to entertain visiting clients or business executives by procuring prostitutes. At least one instance of this ADM practice was tape recorded (Eichenwald 2000).

[12] In late February, 1998, Whitacre signed an affidavit retracting his former allegation that the FBI had instructed him to destroy tapes favorable to ADM (the tapes he had earlier claimed to have sent to Hoech). Hoech told the FBI that he heard such a tape played but did not have it in his possession.

[13] The government said that it would be improper to immunize Ginger Whitacre because she was involved with her husband in the embezzlement of ADM.

[14] Technically, Whitacre was a "cooperative witness" and therefore subject to slightly different handling rules than those for an informant or undercover agent.

[15] In a sense, Manning's decision to delay her decision on whether to allow economic evidence was helpful to the defense. It meant that the defense might be permitted a "rule of reason" defense that prosecutors were unprepared for.

[16] Judge Manning repeatedly warned defense counsel about connotations of this type, but they continually tested the limits of the Court's tolerance. Defense attorney Mark Hulkower clearly breached her orders on at least one occasion.

[17] Worse from the prosecutors' point of view was the possibility that Whitacre might forego his 5th Amendment right and testify at the trial, however ruinous to his own chances. As a defendant he could not be compelled to testify.

[18] More than 200 government exhibits were presented. They included notes of minutes, interoffice memos, notes from diaries or date books, tabulations, price lists, letters, agendas, travel records, and FBI interviews.

[19] This issue was irrelevant because as a *per se* violation, the effects of an agreement to control price cannot provide evidence about the existence of an agreement. However, the tactic may have succeeded in sowing confusion among the jurors when they were shown a price chart in which the price of lysine was quite high just before and just after the conspiracy period. In other words, the defense hoped that their clients might be held blameless because the jury perceived them to be incompetent price fixers.

[20] The other weekdays were filled with judge-lawyer conferences at the bar or in chambers without the jury present.

[21] Judges need to be informed in advance by counsel for both sides about witnesses for scheduling purposes. Moreover, opposing counsel must be told 48 hours in advance about upcoming witnesses. Technically, the defense called two witnesses because it was permitted to conduct direct testimony of Ikeda during the prosecution's phase.

[22] There were many bilateral contacts, but by "general" meetings is meant those attended by ADM, Ajinomoto, and at least one of the three remaining Asian companies in the cartel. There were 11 general meetings, the last seven scheduled on a regular quarterly basis. Witnesses Mimoto, Ikeda, Crouy, and Yamamoto attended ten, seven, two, and 11 meetings, respectively. Crouy stopped attending because of a promotion. For details see Connor (2000:Table A4).

[23] More details of the testimony of the six key witnesses and six minor ones can be found in Connor (2000: Appendix A) and Lieber (2000).

[24] Large Japanese companies typically are organized in a manner similar to German companies. Besides the usual broad-based board of directors, the company has a management committee chaired by the CEO. Five to seven "managing directors" also serve on the committee; they correspond to senior vice presidents or division presidents in a U.S. corporation. Most managing directors supervise one or more broad product groups or divisions of the company. Each division contains several sections or departments that are responsible for a product or group of closely related products. Departments typically are profit centers.

[25] On the way back to Decatur from Chicago, a "locker-room" conversation dwelled on the availability of certain women in their office for sexual favors. Also, Andreas bragged that he had been able to persuade Ajinomoto's Chairman Toba to visit Decatur by offering and later delivering a prostitute.

[26] It is at the beginning of Ikeda's cross-examination that Bray pulls off his "evidentiary coup" that would bedevil prosecutors for the rest of the trial. Contrary to federal courtroom procedures, Manning ruled that the *defense* could introduce their documents during the prosecution phase of the trial (Lieber 2000).

[27] Judge Manning displayed an abundance of permissiveness in allowing new topics to be introduced that had not, strictly interpreted, been covered during direct examination.
[28] Mimoto and Ikeda worked for Ajinomoto proper, and Crouy was employed at the time by Eurolysine, a joint venture in which Ajinomoto held a supra majority of the shares. The government did not call any managers from Sewon or Cheil, the smallest participants, except for brief technical testimony by a Sewon treasurer.
[29] Taking his interpretation of his career move at face value, Yamamoto was the only employee of a lysine manufacturer to be punished in this manner. However, K. Yamada of Ajinomoto appears to have been quietly let go by Ajinomoto. Yamamoto's plea secured immunity for six other Kyowa employees (Tr. 4245).
[30] When the conspirators met, business etiquette dictated that the senior local host is the unofficial chairperson. Wilson was prone to interrupting others he judged to be long-winded, including the chairperson's welcoming speech. Wilson appeared to relish reminding the others of ADM's intention to become equal in size to the largest producer, and he showed no respect for the pioneer roles of Ajinomoto and Kyowa in the lysine industry. In comments made in private, Wilson frequently expressed his antipathy for the Japanese.
[31] The shadow price is a combination of corn and soybean meal prices that would make a mixture of the two functionally perfect substitutes for pure lysine from fermentation. Low soybean and high corn prices do form a *ceiling* to raising lysine prices. However, costs of making lysine and other factors sometimes prevent a cartel from following this rule; that is, the monopoly price can be more than 10 cents below a high shadow price. See Chapter 7.
[32] Cox's testimony was required by his plea agreement. He was allowed to talk about the citric acid cartel only because it explained Wilson's motivation in lysine and because the methods used by both of the cartels were so similar.
[33] Shepard's younger colleague, Robert Herndon, also testified for three days on several of the same topics as Shepard. Perhaps the most interesting new fact revealed by Herndon was that Dwayne Andreas' personal assistant was present during part of a telephone call from Whitacre to Andreas in which they discuss Kyowa Hakko's role in the lysine cartel (Leiber 2000:223). The prosecution's eminent tape expert later testified that some of the cassettes had been erased and re-recorded in places.
[34] Not to be confused with monosodium glutamate (MSG). Sodium gluconate is used primarily as a safe cleaning chemical for stainless steel and glass used in the food industry, safe because it can be ingested without harm to humans. Though not made public, this fermentation product was cartelized by ADM and two European firms, yet ADM was immunized from government prosecution in the United States. Canada prosecuted ADM.
[35] One tape contained a reference to ADM's price fixing activities in the market for lactic acid (Tr. 3547). (That makes a total of four conspiracies involving ADM). Another tape caught James Randall, ADM's president, admitting to buying illegally a microorganism to make the amino acid bacitracin and to hiring prostitutes in Iowa to steal information from Ajinomoto employees about its lysine technology (Tr. 3549).
[36] Technically, Ikeda was briefly a defense witness but called out of order so that he could return early to Japan.
[37] Defense counsel had submitted many charts and computer analyses to the prosecutors near the end of the trial prepared by Dr. Donald Martin. In retrospect, Martin's presence may have been simply to keep prosecutors off balance.
[38] Lassar was upbraided for this statement, which Judge Manning termed improper. If confined to antitrust price fixing trials, Lassar may have been on firm ground for his assertion.
[39] Barrie Cox was given a raise and told that he would have expanded responsibilities abroad. When the promotion proved empty, he resigned on October 15, 1998 – exactly two years after ADM pleaded guilty. The message seems hard to miss. In 1999, Cox moved back to the United States to a town near Decatur, Illinois. Since resigning from ADM, he was on retainer as a consultant at $17,000 per month; moreover, he had become a sales agent for ADM's xanthan gum production.
[40] This is a blatant distortion of the facts and highly misleading. The prosecution put on the stand 12 witnesses. Two of the four lysine co-conspirators had paid personal fines, two were

ADM employees, two were paid experts, two were FBI agents, and two were accountants for ADM and Sewon.

[41] Two members of the jury fell asleep during Walker's summary, requiring an unplanned adjournment.

[42] Recall that a graph of lysine price trends showed a slight decline in the early summer of 1995. The most likely factor responsible was a drop in the corn-soybean shadow price (see Figure 8.2).

[43] Perhaps Weingarten's most bizarre argument during his closing was his feeble attempt to denigrate Barrie Cox's testimony. He charged it was Cox who ". . . brought this [citric acid] price fixing to ADM" (Tr. 6042). Moreover, ". . . the real issue here is if the Government has problems with Terry Wilson in citric, they should charge him" (*ibid.*).

[44] Either stockholders no longer cared about the loss of its future CEO, or they had already correctly predicted the outcome of the trial.

[45] According to defense counsel this occurred twice, first when Lassar said that the defendants had not even tried to rebut Barrie Cox's testimony, and second when he pointed out that both defendants had failed to confess when confronted by the FBI in June 1995.

[46] The most serious price fixing prosecutions up to 1996 were the electrical equipment cases of 1960. Forty-five high ranking executives of 29 corporations were indicted, and 35 of those pleaded guilty. All paid at least small fines, but only seven officers actually spent time in jail, and they were short sentences.

[47] These guidelines apply only to bid-rigging, price fixing proper, and market allocation, which are the only antitrust offenses prosecuted as criminal felonies. It appears that Congress intended the USSGs to be mandatory for judges when their use is requested by the federal prosecutors. Prosecutors seem to regard the USSGs as simply one more optional tool in their arsenal to squeeze defendants.

[48] In *U.S. v. Michael Andreas* the two sides stipulated in advance that the affected commerce was U.S. sales of dry feed-grade lysine from July 1992 to June 1995, which was $460 million. Thus, the fines for the three convicted men ought to have been in the range of $4.6 to $23 million were it not for the $350,000 statutory cap.

[49] Under the 1994 law, the fine is greater of either double the harm (actual damages) or double the gain (profits) from the felonious activity. But because damages from price fixing include the dead-weight loss, the harm will always be greater than the gain. If twice the harm exceeds $100 million, then the maximum personal fine is $25 million.

[50] I was asked to prepare overcharge estimates for the U.S. Department of Justice. The defense had engaged the Washington D.C. consulting firm of Glassman Oliver well before the trial began.

[51] Judge Manning seems to have confused my overcharge analysis prepared for the federal class-action suit in early 1996 with an entirely new analysis based on cost data largely revealed in public exhibits prepared for the 1998 trial.

[52] In 1999, the DOJ negotiated price fixing fines for individuals far above the statutory $350,000 limit, as high as $10 million in one case. Nevertheless, as late as 2000 no $350,000-plus fines had been litigated.

[53] Michael's father Dwayne Andreas and his mother had attended many days of the trial one year earlier, but they were absent at this hearing.

[54] Most observers were struck by the harshness of the sentences because they were high relative to the average sentences imposed in the past. However, Wilson's lawyer, Weingarten, was "ecstatic" about his client's sentence. He called the single Sherman Act charge "a tremendous gift" (Lieber 2000).

[55] Of which 10 months was to run concurrently with his nine-year sentence for embezzlement. The government had requested a fully concurrent sentence, and before the hearing Whitacre's lawyer had fully expected the same. Thus, 20 months was added to his previous sentence. Judge Manning showed that she too could play hardball with Whitacre.

[56] The point about the Asian companies is defensible, but the undeniable fact that Whitacre and all his willing accomplices were subservient to Michael Andreas makes the first point debatable.

[57] The two surrendered to the Federal Bureau of Prisons on October 5, 1999.
[58] The Appeals Court decision is final because the U.S. Supreme Court denied certiorari to Andreas and Wilson's further appeal.
[59] In the case of ADM, its total sales for the three fiscal years 1993-1995 were at least $33.9 billion (or more than $65 billion counting some unconsolidated ventures). Lysine sales were 0.5 percent (or less) of total sales.

Chapter 16

THE CIVIL SUITS

INTRODUCTION

Earlier chapters have recounted how low antitrust fines were prior to 1990 and how these fines have grown in the 1990's in the case of price fixing. This chapter will demonstrate that civil settlements for price fixing have grown apace. In part, the increased size of criminal and civil financial sanctions reflects the growth in the size of corporations and the markets that they exploited. In order to deter managers from contemplating the formation of future price fixing conspiracies, the penalties must rise at least proportionately with the size of the injuries that would be caused. However, there is evidence that the severity of the price fixing infractions has increased. Not only have most of the cartels prosecuted since 1995 been international cases (whereas most were national or regional in prior years), but also the percentage overcharges appear to have risen. Combined with the newly assertive stance of the federal antitrust agencies and the expanded opportunities for private suits, fines and settlements have both increased faster than the size of the affected markets.[1]

Private antitrust suits provide deterrence complementary to public prosecutions. Civil class-action suits are a vehicle especially suitable for permitting small buyers – small firms or consumers – to win relief against price fixing conspirators. The conspirators in cases brought in the late 1990s were mainly large, powerful corporations in highly concentrated industries. Their great wealth and access to legal resources generally brings a David-and-Goliath aspect to antitrust class actions. Yet, there are many legal commentators that have disparaged their use in treble damage cases.

In part, the debate over the desirability of class-action treble-damages suits reflects a wider debate on the social benefits of treble damages themselves. Some believe triple damages to be unnecessarily high to deter (Easterbrook 1986), while others argue that plaintiffs often receive closer to single damages (Lande 1993). From a financial benefit/cost perspective, companies will be deterred only if the expected financial losses (the total fines and settlements multiplied by the expected probability of conviction) exceed the financial gains from price fixing (see Chapter 2). If plaintiffs really do get closer to single damages, then civil settlements alone provide virtually no deterrence because only a small portion of all conspiracies are discovered and prosecuted.[2] Moreover, buyers who had to exit a market because of cartel-elevated prices are rarely compensated (Page 1996). Another issue that troubles critics of class-action suits is the large size of the legal fees and the incentives they might give for lawyers to file frivolous suits. Calkins (1997:441) suggests that the rise in successful government prosecutions make the need for supplemental deterrence from civil cases much less justifiable. However, in Chapter 13, it was shown that the typical criminal fine imposed was one-fifth to one-half of the best estimate of actual overcharges, so the need for "supplemental" civil punishment would appear to be still strong. This is particularly true in cases that relied on subtle or innovative methods of price fixing that fall short of the naked cartels documented in this book.[3]

This chapter examines the civil cases generated by the lysine, citric acid, and vitamins cartels.[4] Federal class-action suits were filed by direct buyers in each case and are fairly well documented. Some of the members of the federal class opted out of the purposed settlements, and many of them settled by means of private negotiation. Much less is known about the opt-out settlements because terms of the settlements typically include non-disclosure clauses. Indirect buyers of these products launched suits in several states and Canadian provinces with varying degrees of success. At least one *parens patriae* action by large number of state attorneys general was initiated. Finally, related suits for fraud and mismanagement were decided in the lysine case. The global cartels chosen for inclusion in this book will allow the full panoply of civil actions to be illustrated.

THE FEDERAL LYSINE CASE[5]

The FBI raid on ADM's headquarters on the night of June 27, 1995 alerted buyers of lysine and law firms to the possibility of a treble-damages suit. Some feed manufacturers contacted their retained law firms, and in other cases law firms contacted lysine buyers to offer their services. The identity of two of ADM's co-conspirators soon became known through pithy press releases by Heartland Lysine in Chicago and Biokyowa in St. Louis that denied wrongdoing and pledged cooperation with government investigators. ADM's management immediately hired the large, well known Washington, DC law firm Akin Gump. The governing partner of the firm is Robert Strauss, long a personal friend of Dwayne Andreas and a lawyer with an extensive network of contacts in the Washington power structure. By the next day a squadron of Akin Gump lawyers had arrived in Decatur to assess the company's legal situation. The team was headed by John Dowd

On June 28th the Akin Gump attorneys began interviewing ADM employees about what they knew. That morning the *Wall Street Journal* had already reported on its front page that subpoenaed and seized documents found at ADM's offices showed "score sheets" of "sales targets" and the actual monthly sales of the world's three largest producers of lysine. Dowd personally interviewed Mark Whitacre on that day. Naively assuming that Dowd represented him as an ADM officer, Whitacre told all about his role as an FBI informant. It is doubtful that Dowd would have explicitly promised personal attorney-client confidentiality to Whitacre. (Later, ADM would provide attorneys from unrelated law firms for most of its officers who came under suspicion). In any case, Dowd that day informed ADM's top management of Whitacre's undercover activities. Dwayne Andreas' response to this information was that Whitacre would "regret the day that he was born." The Andreases began to realize the seriousness of their legal positions quite early. On the next day, June 29th, Mark Whitacre was ordered to leave ADM headquarters. ADM President James Randall personally began examining Whitacre's files for anything that could be used against him.

Whitacre was formally fired on August 7th and was soon charged for fraud and embezzlement of at least $3.5 million, an amount later raised to more than $9 million. ADM showed the financial records of Whitacre's theft to DOJ prosecutors. After a couple of meetings with Whitacre in the first week in August with U.S. Attorney Scott Lassar and other prosecutors, the DOJ became convinced that ADM's claims had merit and Whitacre's immunity from prosecution was revoked. In late August, Whitacre made an attempt to commit suicide.[6] It is perhaps more than a curious coincidence that the next regularly scheduled general meeting of the lysine conspirators was to have occurred in July in the Cayman Islands. Whitacre maintained secret accounts at a bank in the Cayman Islands that held much of his stolen money.

Meanwhile ADM's troubles with civil litigants began quickly to mount. The combined effects of a possible criminal indictment and actual civil suits had a horrendous impact on ADM's stock price. Over the three months following the FBI raid, in the near absence of unfavorable economic trends for the company's markets, ADM's stock fell by 24 percent wiping out $2.4 billion in the company's capitalization. Naturally, the board of directors became alarmed. At its regular quarterly meeting in mid July, the board appointed nine of its 17 members to a special *ad hoc* committee charged with advising management on the suits arising from the alleged price fixing in the market for lysine. Co-chairmen of the special committee (later reduced in size) were M. Brian Mulroney and John H. Daniels. Mulroney, former Prime Minister of Canada and a lawyer by training, would eventually play the leading role in negotiating settlements proposed by plaintiffs with ADM's management, which was notably reluctant to cave in to such pressures. Daniels was the retired former Chairman of ADM and an heir of one of the company's founding families. Later, he would be replaced as co-chair of the committee by Harvard professor Ray Goldberg, whose father had been

Dwayne Andreas' mentor decades ago when Andreas first learned how to become a grain trader. Normal practice when special committees are established to handle sensitive matters is to choose at least a majority from among the board's "outside" or independent members. The problem faced by ADM's board is there really weren't any.[7]

By November 1995, ADM was facing 11 private treble-damages suits by lysine buyers. In addition, more than 30 stockholders' suits were filed against ADM officers and directors for "material mismanagement" of the company. Counting antitrust suits by buyers of citric acid or corn sweeteners, ADM was grappling with a total of 70 private suits. Several of the shareholders' suits sought structural reforms of ADM's governance structure. Among the demands were a smaller board and more board members that meet a stricter definition of outsiders. The board as it was constituted in 1995 was described by the *Washington Post* as ". . . handcuffed by company insiders, family members, cronies, and friends of the powerful chairman." Also open to criticism was the advanced age of many board members; nine of the 17 were 69 years or older in January 1996.[8] By February 1996, the number of private suits against ADM alleging price fixing or related management failures had risen to 85.

In early 1996, the many plaintiffs in the lysine treble-damages suits were certified as a single federal class. U.S. Judge Milton Shadur in Chicago was assigned the task of certifying the class, arranging for its representation, managing pre-trial discovery, and approving of any pre-trial settlement deals offered to class members. Judge Shadur had many original ideas about how to expedite antitrust class-action suits. In February, he told the law firms representing plaintiffs that he had decided to *auction* the right to act as lead counsel for the class. The low bidder would be the winner. In order to further minimize the size of class counsel's fees, Shadur refused to accept bids based on the traditional percentage contingency fee. The winner of the unprecedented auction was the Philadelphia law firm of Kohn Swift and Graf. The firm's bid was a sliding scale capped at $3.5 million for any settlement agreement equal to or above $25 million for class members.

During the period February to April 1996, there was little movement discernable in the government's criminal case against ADM and the other alleged members of the cartel. At this point, Michael Andreas and Terrance Wilson had been informed by the DOJ that they would be indicted, but no formal filing had been made and both men were refusing to plea bargain. No ADM insider except the discredited Mark Whitacre was willing to provide useful information to the government. The officers of the Asian cartel members were similarly tight-lipped, and besides most of them could not be deposed because they resided in Japan or South Korea. Although ADM hired the top-notch Washington law firm of Williams & Connelly to defend it against criminal charges in March, there was very little movement visible in the criminal case either. Even with a couple of resignations, the board was still very much the creature of Dwayne Andreas who was resisting settlement. Without a resolution of the criminal case, a civil settlement seemed less likely.

However, there were some signs that ADM was less resolute in opposing a civil settlement. In February, ADM stated publicly that it was willing to consider settling out of court. At about the same time, it became known that ADM had created a special reserve fund to pay suitors should the need arise. A key factor from ADM's point of view was the fact that a civil settlement requires no admission of guilt, nor can it be used as evidence in a criminal trial. From Dwayne Andreas' point of view, compared with a criminal guilty plea approving a civil deal was by far the lesser of the two evils. Besides, it might help repair his eroding support of ADM's Board of Directors.[8]

The likelihood of a deal on the lysine treble-damages suddenly increased in April 1996. On the 12th of that month, ADM, Ajinomoto, and Kyowa Hakko jointly announced that they had offered to pay the federal class of lysine buyers the sum of $45 million ($25 million from ADM and $10 million each from the other two). The law firm of Kohn Swift and Graf had spent only two or three months in negotiations for their 150 plaintiffs. Of course, any settlement above $25 million was equally lucrative to class counsel because of the cap on their fees. The fixed fee brought about the result Judge Shadur had wanted: a swift settlement with a minimum of fuss. Costs for class counsel were extremely low by historical standards.[10] No economic experts had been hired and no depositions taken of ADM officials – all standard procedure in civil negotiations. Legal experts considered a settlement offer at this early stage of discovery almost unprecedented. A major gap in the plaintiffs' knowledge was created by the too-early settlement: plaintiffs could not listen to the tapes. Even more critical a factor for the plaintiffs' decisions to consider an early deal was the uncertainty in early 1996 as to whether ADM would plead guilty, be indicted by the DOJ for criminal price fixing, or if indicted be found guilty. In other words, despite the mounting evidence that the DOJ intended to convict ADM, many plaintiffs calculated that there was a good chance they would get nothing in the future.

Judge Shadur set a "fairness hearing" for July 15, 1996. The purpose of the hearing was to hear arguments about whether the proposed settlement amount was fair and reasonable for the plaintiffs. The defendants' offer implied an estimated overcharge on lysine of $15 million of the "affected period." Defendants proposed that purchases for 1994 and the first half of 1995 would be the criterion for distributing the damages awards. As U.S. sales of dry lysine were about $250 million during that 18-month period, the three largest members were suggesting that lysine prices had risen by only about 6 percent during the apogee of the cartel's power. This overcharge percentage is relatively low by historical standards.[11] Moreover, two months later these defendants would plead guilty to price fixing for a period of almost three years. The additional sales implied by the longer conspiracy period means that the overcharge rate was a pitifully low 3 percent of purchases.

A split developed within the federal class. The larger lysine customers generally reacted negatively to what they believed was a small offer. In some cases, these firms had prepared overcharge estimates in hours. Several of them took the advice of their own counsel and had an independent estimate of the overcharge prepared by a professional economist.[12] The smaller members of the class were generally satisfied or at least tempted by the offer. Also, smaller companies often have to worry more about keeping smooth relations with big suppliers of a hot product like lysine; accepting the defendant's first offer would be seen as more courteous than demanding more.

Working under great time pressure and with very limited information, the plaintiffs' expert calculated that the lysine overcharge was closer to $150 million than the $15 million proposed by ADM *et al.* There were several reasons for the larger plaintiffs' estimate. They believed that the conspiracy began at the Mexico City meeting in October 1992 (a position that would be taken by the DOJ in its criminal indictments later in the year). The earlier starting date than the one preferred by the defendants implied a lower pre-conspiracy price (Connor 2000, White 2000). Anecdotal evidence on lysine costs of production also suggested a non-conspiracy price of $0.66 to $0.70 per pound.[13] The longer time period also increased the affected sales totals for the cartel. Despite its flaws, this analysis was probably the best that could be done with monthly average selling prices as the sole available information from the defendants.

The yawning disparity in overcharge estimates had little effect on Judge Shadur's inexorable drive for a tidy settlement process. At the July fairness hearing, he signaled his intention to approve the $45 million settlement for the federal class, and that decision was made final on July 19, 1996. However, on that day 33 companies, convinced that the amount was too low, opted out of the class. Although only about one-fifth of the number of class plaintiffs, the 33 represented a greater share of lysine purchases. Most, if not all, went ahead and settled through private negotiations over the next year.

The amounts that the opt-outs received may never be known because all parties are generally sworn to secrecy. Moreover, the one defendant with a fiduciary responsibility to tell its shareholders how much it had to pay, ADM, decided that the small size of the settlement was not "material." However, enterprising farm reporter Alan Guebert did get one plaintiff's lawyer to talk off the record in a March 1997 piece. The opt-outs that pursued their damages later reportedly received about $20 million. This lawyer also characterized the lysine plaintiffs who remained in the class as "dumb as rocks," which may be taken to mean that the opt-outs did significantly better in their compensation than those that remained in the class. The major factor that explains the superior recovery by the opt-outs is that they settled after the lysine defendants pleaded guilty.

More than a year later the wisdom of the lysine settlements was still being debated in the pages of *The National Law Journal*. Noted columnist, Columbia Law School professor John C. Coffee, cited the lysine case as the egregious example of the flaws in allowing law firms to bid for the right to represent class-action plaintiffs. The biggest problem is that of perverse financial incentives. Auctions for fixed fees leaves the winner ". . . with little incentive to maximize the recovery for the class." Coffee cites four pieces of evidence supporting his contention that the lysine settlement was "a study in class action pathology." (1) As a rule, private settlements vastly exceed the criminal fines, but in lysine just the opposite happened. (2) The rapidity of "the race to settlement . . . was unusual and did little to benefit the class." That is, patience would have been rewarded. (3) The recovery rate (claimed to be 7 percent by class counsel but closer to 3 percent in reality) cannot be meaningfully compared to the averages of all antitrust class actions "because most private settlements do not have the opportunity to piggyback on a criminal conviction." (4) Although the legal fees were modest (about 7 percent of recovery) in the lysine case, class members do not want to minimize fees, they want to maximize recovery.[14] In a retrospective assessment of the lysine civil settlement after the conclusion of the Chicago criminal trial, the *Illinois Legal Times* (October 1998) called the $45 million "unreasonable."

How class counsel should be appointed by a supervising judge is still an issue. Often, a judge appoints the first law firm to file if the judge deems the firm competent to handle several, sometimes thousands of plaintiffs. Alternatively, the competing plaintiffs' counsel may negotiate one of their number to become lead counsel for the class prior to certification, a sort of nomination process. Both of these methods may be criticized for failing to match the best possible firm to the task at hand, and neither addresses the perceived problem of excessive legal fees. Auctioning the right to represent is not in itself a bad idea, so long as the firm or group of firms bidding is well qualified. Rather, the main problem is one of incentives for the winning firm. An auction that awards the lead-counsel position to the firm offering the lowest *percentage* fee makes much more sense because it forces firms to calculate their costs relative to expected revenues; winners will tend to be low-cost firms or those willing to accept lower profits. The monetary incentive to get the greatest recovery for their clients remains, as does an incentive to compromise to save time.

Derivative Shareholders' Suits

ADM was hit with two sets of shareholders' suits, one directed at the management of the company and the other at the board of directors. Shareholders claimed that they were injured by gross mismanagement and failure to reveal information that would have a material effect on profits. In other words, under U.S. law if managers know about a secret cartel and later that information is the basis of unexpected expenses for the company, shareholders can seek civil compensation or other remedies. At first blush, asking for compensation seems self defeating because the company's payments to the shareholders, should they win such a suit, would reduce the value of the company by more than the payments received because legal defense costs must be borne by the company. However, most large companies like ADM have insurance plans that pay the cost of lost shareholders' suits, so in effect shareholders in all insured firms are the losers. The major benefit of shareholders' suits would seem to be in changes in corporate governance rules.

ADM's management settled its shareholders' suit in April 1997 for $30 million. In June of that year the board of directors offered to pay $8 million to the plaintiffs who had asked for $190 million. It also agreed to a number of changes in the board's structure, though most of them had been implemented by the board more than a year earlier. The board was reduced in size and a greater portion of "outside" directors were to be appointed. Compensation of board members was reduced to less than half its 1995-1996 levels. All inside directors and those on the board prior to June 1995 were forbidden to serve on the board's audit committee. In addition, all pre-June 1995 board members were excluded from nominating new board members. No specific individuals were made to resign, as in some previous cases.

Controversy erupted over the $8 million settlement when it became known by some major pension funds that half the money sent to "vulture firms" representing minor shareholders and that the rest was returned to ADM to cover the boards "expenses" in implementing the reforms. Shareholders got no monetary compensation because their lawyers valued the ADM reforms at $158 million. It is results like these that give law firms a bad name and that reinforce the image of America as a hyper-litigious society (Mullenix 1999).

Whitacre's Embezzlement

In August 1995, Mark Whitacre was fired for stealing from ADM. He had begun embezzling in November 1992, a few months before being signed up as an FBI agent, and continued through early 1995 (Eichenwald 2000). He had some help from at least three employees he supervised in the Bioproducts Division. In September 1995, ADM fired these three employees as well.[15]

Both the government and ADM went after Whitacre, seeking vengeance as well as justice. The government's criminal case against Whitacre was resolved in October 1997. Whitacre pleaded guilty in U.S. district court in Urbana, Illinois to 37 counts of wire fraud, conspiracy to defraud the United States, money laundering, and tax evasion. He was sentenced to 108 months in prison and ordered to pay $11.4 million in restitution to be paid to ADM. The previous month Whitacre had filed for bankruptcy, so the fine was largely symbolic.

Although ADM did everything it could to prosecute Whitacre, including intense lobbying of the fraud section of the DOJ by its Washington law firm, ADM also labored mightily to oppose the FBI's Chicago-based investigation of fraud by all other ADM employees (Eichenwald 2000). This was true even in the case of the three ADM employees who were convicted of criminal fraud (Sidney Hulse, Reinhart Richter, and Marty Allison) (Lieber 2000). Unindicted individuals include Ronald Ferrari, who parked some of Whitacre's money for a while; Milos Covert, an ADM consultant; Whitacre's Swiss banker, Burt Schweitzer; and David Page, an acquaintance who agreed to become an ADM "ghost employee." Eichenwald (2000) uncovered the fact that ADM has a long track record of trying to cover up embezzlement by its employees. In 1991, ADM's treasurer defrauded the company of more than $14 million through commodity trading, yet the FBI had to close its criminal probe of the affair because ADM refused to hand over relevant documents (*ibid.* pp. 27-28).

ADM's parallel civil suit against Whitacre was settled with a summary judgment in August 1999 (McCuskey 1999). By that time Whitacre had served almost two years of the ten years or so he will be in prison. He seemed to be unable to react in a timely or effective manner to ADM's motion for summary judgment. The judge called his reply totally inadequate. Partly as a result, the court granted most of what ADM wished. Whitacre must return all of his ADM salary for breach of duty and pay additional restitution for his theft and fraud, some $6.3 million in all.[16]

THE FEDERAL CITRIC ACID CASE

The government's investigation of the citric acid cartel moved more slowly than the lysine investigation (see Chapter 3). Since June 1995, the DOJ's Antitrust Division office in San Francisco handled the probe, but it did not have nearly as much evidence as had been collected for lysine. Some suspicious documents on "target sales" had been obtained in the files at ADM's and Cargill's headquarters, and brief references to a citric cartel had been picked up in Whitacre's tapes of the lysine meetings. However, Terrance Wilson and Barrie Cox, who had handled the citric acid conspiracy for ADM, said nothing of value to investigators for more than a year. It was only when ADM's cooperation was secured by August 1996 that depositions started producing solid evidence of the conspiracy. Unlike lysine, ADM was the first member of the citric acid cartel to crack, and its co-conspirators took months to cave into prosecutors' demands.

In the lysine case, ADM, Ajinomoto, and Kyowa negotiated on a common front with counsel for the federal class; talks began in February 1996 and came to fruition in April. However, in citric acid, the first references to efforts to negotiate a settlement appear only in May 1996. Moreover, it seems that ADM was moving ahead in talks with plaintiffs with little coordination with its Swiss co-conspirators.

Fewer civil suits were filed against ADM *et al.* in citric acid than in the lysine case. In November 1995 there were seven. Movement in consolidating the scattered suits into one federal class was slow. The class was not certified in San Francisco until late 1996. Thus, it came as a surprise when ADM suddenly announced that it had reached a settlement with U.S. citric acid buyers on September 27, 1996. Changes within ADM may have contributed to its *volte-face*. Just two weeks before, ADM's board had undergone its second shake-up, bringing the total resignations to eight since June 1995. ADM proposed to pay $35 million to the federal class when the class was certified. It would take several more months for the European members of the cartel to make their offers. About four weeks later, ADM and the DOJ announced ADM's guilty plea and a greatly reduced fine of $30 million for its role in the citric acid cartel. Barrie Cox's substantial cooperation with the DOJ and the fact that ADM was the first to confess were key elements in the discount.

As in the lysine case, a split soon developed between large and small buyers of citric acid. Kenneth Adams, an attorney representing four of the largest users of citric acid, paid defense attorneys an indirect compliment when he slammed the DOJ's wording of ADM's guilty plea. In Chapter 5, evidence was presented that the citric acid conspiracy began during the first half of 1991. However, after tough negotiations by defense attorneys, the government's wording of the October plea agreement vaguely stated that the cartel began operating only "at least as early as" January 1993. Not only did this shorten the collusive period by 18 to 24 months, but the later date also implied that the "pre-conspiracy" price was arguably much higher than that implied by an earlier initial date. What may have appeared to DOJ negotiators as a trivial detail in the plea agreement had a great impact on the estimated overcharge and, therefore, on ADM's civil liability.

If the cartel began to raise citric acid prices as late as January 1993 as the defendants claimed, then the cartel's sales volume was about 2.6 billion pounds through 1995, and the but-for-price could have been as high as $0.74 per pound (the average price in the year 1992). This scenario results in a global monopoly overcharge by the citric acid cartel of approximately $105 million during 1993-1995 (Figure 16.1). If, on the other hand as the evidence suggests, the cartel began to raise prices around July 1991, then the volume it sold was about 3.7 billion pounds and the but-for price was close to $0.62 per pound (the price in early 1991). Under this scenario, the global overcharge rises to $573 million – more than quintuple the overcharge implied by the later date.[17]

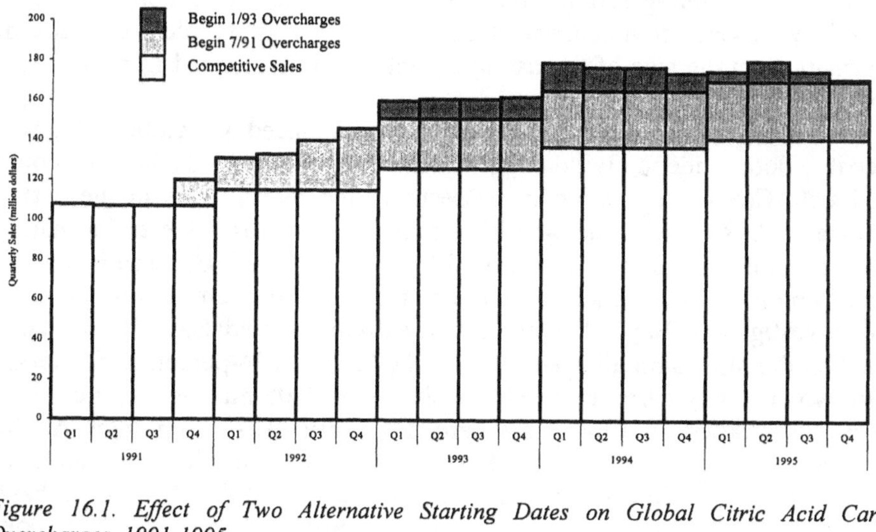

Figure 16.1. Effect of Two Alternative Starting Dates on Global Citric Acid Cartel Overcharges, 1991-1995.

Sources: Connor (1998: Table 1) and Table 4.A.1.
Note: Capacity of the five members of the cartel is adjusted by global capacity utilization to get volume of production for the year. Quarterly production is one-fourth annual. Prices are U.S. transaction prices. Cargill is not included. Corresponds to a $0.741 but-for price per pound and a $106 million global overcharge.

U.S. buyers of citric acid accounted for just about one-third of global purchases of citric acid during the affected period. Thus, if the plea agreement date of January 1993 is accepted, they suffered injuries of $35 million and could claim treble damages of $105 million from the cartel. On the other hand, the better supported commencement date of July 1991 yields U.S. price fixing injuries of about $191 million and treble damages of $573 million. Because ADM held approximately 29 percent of the U.S. market, its settlement offer in September was based upon an implied U.S. cartel overcharge of about $40 million (very close to the $35 million low estimate).

On December 9, 1996, the other large members of the citric acid cartel offered to settle with the plaintiffs. The amounts offered were proportional to ADM's offer and their share of U.S. sales. Haarmann & Reimer Corp., the New Jersey-based subsidiary of Germany's Bayer AG, offered to pay $46 million. The two Swiss chemical firms that exported to the United States, Hoffmann-La Roche and Jungbunzlauer International, agreed to pay $5.7 million and $7.6 million, respectively.[18] Taking a page out of ADM's book, none of the three "Swiss" firms had as yet pleaded guilty. Such pleas would not be entered until January or March 1997. Meanwhile, plaintiffs in the class were mightily tempted to take what seemed like a generous offer totaling $96 million. However, the plaintiffs not only would be misled by the late commencement date in ADM's guilty plea, but lack of information on the size of the damages that could be inferred from the fines imposed by the DOJ.

ADM's $30 million government fine announced in October 1996 was a terribly poor guide to civil damages because it had received a huge discount for Barrie Cox's cooperation in prosecuting the Swiss firms in the cartel. Haarmann & Reimer's fine was higher ($50 million) relative to its market share, but this was not announced until late January 1997. Because it was the second company to settle with the DOJ and its U.S. president was cooperating with investigators, Bayer too got a hefty discount. Had Bayer's fine been based on the maximum allowed of twice the harm, its 24-percent U.S. market share would imply cartel-induced overcharge of $105 million (Figure 16.2). Since it was based on a lower standard, $105 million is a minimum. As the last major members of the cartel to admit their guilt, the fines paid by Jungbunzlauer and Roche that were announced in March 1997 would have been somewhat better indicators for the plaintiffs of the U.S. monopoly overcharge. The two exporters agreed to pay fines of $25 million. As the last to settle, their fines are much more likely to approach the twice-the-harm standard mandated by the U.S. Sentencing Guidelines. With only 5.5 percent of the U.S. market between them in the early 1990s, the U.S. overcharge implied by their fines must be at least $227 million.[19]

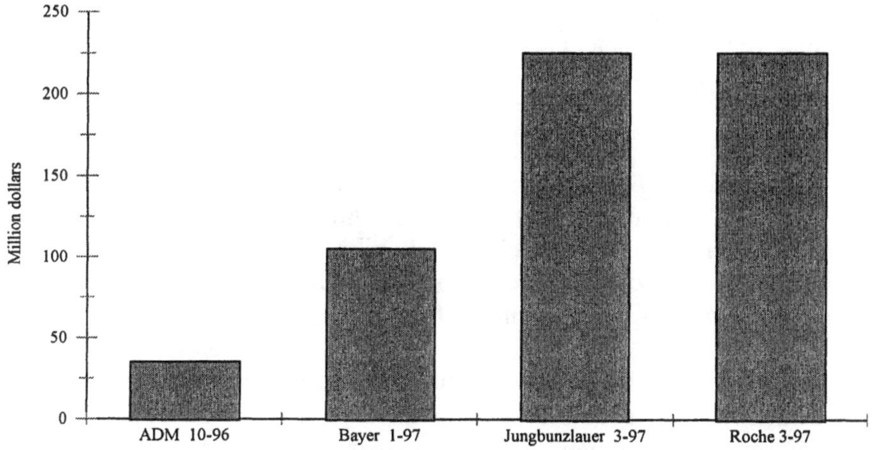

Figure 16.2. The Minimum U.S. Overcharge in Citric Acid Implied by the Government Fines, 1991-1995.

Source: Chapter 6.

Thus, the evidence points to a minimum overcharge on citric acid buyers of at least $227 million; under alternative conspiracy periods and but-for prices, the estimated overcharge rises to well over $300 million. This is not quite the $400 million claimed by lawyers representing federal class plaintiffs, but it is much larger than the overcharge implied by the settlement finally approved for class plaintiffs. In July 1997, Judge Fern Smith of the U.S. District Court in San Francisco approved a settlement of $86.2 million for the remaining members of the federal class. The total was slightly reduced from the four companies' initial offer because five large buyers had opted out of the class.[20] Nevertheless, the striking fact is that class plaintiffs received compensation that is at most *one-third* of the overcharges imposed on them by the citric acid cartel. More amazing still is that the class agreed to this paltry settlement four months after two members of the cartel handed the plaintiffs *prima facie* evidence that the overcharge was at least $224 million. So much for treble damages.

The Citric Acid Opt-Outs

Five companies withdrew from the federal class settlement in July 1997. Procter & Gamble, Kraft Foods, Quaker Oats, Unilever, and Schreiber Foods had purchased $350 million in citric acid from 1991 to 1995. All but

Unilever were represented by Kenneth Adams of Dickstein Shapiro. Back in November 1996, Adams had reacted with pique to ADM's offer to his clients and the poor guidance the DOJ had provided plaintiffs with the wording of ADM's guilty plea:

> "The Justice Department has allowed the facts to be covered up . . . It is clear what ADM and the DOJ got out of the [criminal] deal – reduced civil liability for Archer Daniels and a record settlement for the Justice Department." (*Bloomberg News* November 28, 1996).

A year and a half later, Adams announced that ADM and the three Swiss companies in the citric acid cartel had settled with his clients. While the terms of privately settled treble damages claims are normally kept confidential, some subsequent press reports allow reasonable inferences to be made as to their size. ADM as a public company is required to report developments that materially affect its profits. Civil settlements previously made by ADM in lysine were deemed nonmaterial, but it did report the amount it paid to P&G, Kraft, Quaker, and Schreiber. The payment was $36 million. Assuming that ADM paid in proportion to its U.S. market share, all four conspirators must have ponied up about $89 million. Given that these four opt-outs purchased 15 to 20 percent of all U.S. citric acid during the conspiracy period, the recovery rate for the opt-outs was three to five times higher than that for the federal class. More importantly, the opt-outs received a settlement that was definitely above single damages and probably close to double damages.

Confirmation of high recovery rates for the opt-outs came in a statement made at a 1998 press conference by the CEO of Roche Holdings, Franz B. Humer. He said that Roche had paid $10 million to settle U.S. civil suits in citric acid. It is public knowledge that of that $10 million $5.7 million was paid to the federal class. By subtraction, $4.3 million was paid to the opt-outs. Given their relative shares of U.S. market purchases, it is clear that from Humer's statement the opt-outs settled at a rate three to four times higher than the federal class.

Finally, a settlement with indirect buyers of citric acid in California was announced in July 1999. Most of the buyers were small food processors who purchased citric acid from chemical wholesalers. The plaintiffs' lawyer stated that the overcharge by sellers was 10 to 17 percent of sales; his clients were compensated at the rate of 27 percent of the value of their purchases, or about double the overcharge. Again, these plaintiffs got a settlement rate that was five or six times better than the federal class, though like the opt-outs they had to wait a couple of years longer to get paid.

THE FEDERAL CORN-SWEETENERS CASES

The large size of the markets for corn sweeteners makes these cases potentially much more important in terms of award sizes than either lysine or citric acid. However, the progress in the two civil cases against ADM, *et al.* has been disappointingly slow for the plaintiffs.[21] Unlike the earlier civil cases that were filed when federal investigations were known and indictments were forthcoming, corn sweeteners plaintiffs did not have the full advantages that such government activity can bring. In fact, the largest alleged conspirator (ADM) was offered immunity from indictment by the DOJ in the high fructose corn syrup market, which ADM readily accepted as part of the deal for its lysine/citric guilty plea in October 1996. Although ADM's deep involvement in citric acid price fixing was key evidence, the DOJ did not introduce evidence of any parallel activity by ADM in fixing the price of corn in the 1998 lysine criminal prosecution in Chicago (see Chapter 15). Had such evidence been presented in open court, the testimony and documents submitted in *U.S. v. Michael Andreas et al.* would have become *prima facie* evidence of price fixing in the civil treble-damages cases. Moreover, the DOJ closed its criminal investigation of corn-syrup price fixing sometime in early 1999. Without the advantage of prior criminal convictions, the burden of proof is greater for the civil plaintiffs. These developments forced plaintiffs to rely mostly on depositions, company documents, and market information that might be considered mainly circumstantial in a court of law. In their civil depositions in the corn syrup case, the two most knowledgeable ADM officials, Michael Andreas and Terrance Wilson, exercised their right against self-incrimination.

The second impediment to the rapid resolution of the civil cases was the resistance on the part of the defendants and certain ADM employees to the release of the audio and video tapes made by Mark Whitacre and the FBI. It is obvious that discussions occurred during the lysine conspiracy meetings or among ADM managers about price fixing in the corn-sweeteners market, otherwise the DOJ would not have obtained subpoenas seeking documents from all the leading U.S. corn starch manufacturers about their high fructose corn syrup businesses. After the conclusion of the Chicago lysine trial, all audio and video tapes used in evidence were released in their entirety by the Court. However, up until November 2000, motions and appeals by ADM, other defendants, and interested parties held up the release of the bulk of the recordings. In that month, the U.S. Supreme Court denied certiorari to the parties opposing the release of the tapes, thus allowing the corn-syrup civil case to go to trial in 2001.

Shortly after the dramatic FBI raid on ADM's headquarters in June 1995, the DOJ revealed that a Chicago grand jury was investigating allegations of price fixing in corn sweeteners. This investigation was later moved to the Atlanta field office of the Antitrust Division and a new grand jury was set up. Private antitrust suits against ADM and four other manufacturers were filed by buyers all over the country in the fall of 1995. By November, the number of treble-damages suits against ADM, A.E. Staley, Cargill, CPC International, and American Maize had reached 28. The federal suits were consolidated in U.S. District Court in Peoria, Illinois, yet as late as June 1999 ADM still had 41 civil suits filed against it alleging price fixing in corn sweeteners (some in combination with lysine or citric acid). Most of the 41 suits were state-level suits brought by indirect purchasers.

The evidence of price fixing in corn sweeteners was less direct than that in lysine and citric acid. In early 1996 press reports indicted that the tapes in the possession of government prosecutors refer to discussions about price fixing in corn sweeteners, but there are no tapes of any conspiratorial meetings by corn-sweetener makers. DOJ prosecutors, it was reported, considered the evidence in corn sweeteners distinctly weaker than that in lysine and citric acid. Moreover, the two largest U.S. direct buyers of high fructose corn syrup, Coca Cola and Pepsico, did not join the private suits. This was a curious development because Coke and Pepsi bottling operations reportedly accounted for about 70 percent of that sweeteners' U.S. sales. It may reflect a general company policy of refusing to join class actions, which some conservatively managed companies still regard with distaste. This older view has largely given away to the attitude that joining such suits, however unseemly, is required by the overriding principle of serving stockholders' pecuniary interests.[22]

In September 1996, the plaintiffs got a small break. CPC International agreed to settle for $7 million. As is typical of negotiated settlements, the first company to settle is often not one of the leaders (CPC was third or fourth in the industry), and plaintiffs are willing to settle for relatively low rates. An early settlement also helps finance continuing legal fees of plaintiffs' counsel. However, CPC's motive for settling may have been rather mundane. In December 1997, CPC International underwent the fashionable route of dismemberment and refocusing. CPC split itself into a consumer-products food company renamed Best Foods and an industrial-ingredients unit called Corn Products International. Settlement was a precondition for this restructuring plan to meet with investor approval.

Plaintiffs were handed access to the FBI's tape recordings played in the Chicago trial, according to a ruling made by presiding U.S. Judge Michael Mihm in March 1997. Thus, plaintiffs have had partial success in getting the tapes that they had subpoenaed from the DOJ in October 1996. Early on, the

DOJ resisted complying with the subpoena for the tapes because its grand jury on corn sweeteners' price fixing was still sitting. In February 1997, Judge Mihm ruled that virtually all the tapes should be turned over to the corn-sweeteners plaintiffs, but he was overruled on appeal by the 7th Circuit for "invading the law enforcement investigation privilege." In November 1998 after the Chicago trial ended, plaintiffs renewed their subpoena for the remaining 200-odd audio tapes not played at trial. ADM and seven unindicted ADM employees moved to quash delivery of the tapes. In April 1999, Judge Mihm made a Solomanic ruling that is unfathomable to a layman in the law. He found that the tapes made by Whitacre of face-to-face conversations do not meet the legal definition of an "oral communication," hence, these tapes ought to be released to the plaintiffs. However, tapes made of telephone calls are protected by privacy rules and will not be turned over. Mihm's ruling was of course appealed by ADM, all the way to the U.S. Supreme Court. The appeal was denied in November 2000. Plaintiffs expect that the tapes contain incriminating passages or hints of where the bodies are buried. The strong effort made by ADM may simply be a stalling tactic designed to wear down the plaintiffs, or the company may be concerned that the tapes may further hurt its reputation. In any case, even four years after being filed, no resolution of the corn-sweeteners civil actions is imminent.

THE VITAMINS CASES

Private antitrust actions in the United States proceeded quite rapidly, more or less in tandem with the government's investigation and indictments. Concrete information about the existence of a vitamins cartel first came to the attention of a partner in the law firm Boies and Schiller in late 1997. Schiller says that he discovered the cartel when working on a patent-infringement suit in which Hoffmann-La Roche was a defendant. When Roche dropped its counter-claim suit, the vitamin buyers felt free to allege a price fixing conspiracy in vitamins to Schiller. Vitamin buyers reported numerous instances of odd behavior in the market. Roche customers were refused price quotes by BASF and vice versa. Buyers of vitamin C were threatened with retaliation if they were to try to resell their purchases. Behavior consistent with bid-rigging was observed in the market for animal-feed vitamin concentrates. As a result of these complaints, Boies and Schiller filed a civil treble-damages suit in March 1998 in U.S. District Court in Washington, D.C. against the major bulk vitamins manufacturers.

By the end of May 1999, 27 law firms had filed similar suits for their clients who had purchased bulk vitamins. Well known class-action lawyers from Dickstein Shapiro, Cohen Millstein, Susman Godfrey, and others joined Boies & Schiller in a conference in Washington, D.C. on May 17th. David Boies II, who had become a celebrity for his role as a government prosecutor in the DOJ's prosecution of the Microsoft Corporation, was credited with helping engineer a plan for consolidating the many suits into a class action.[23] Some plaintiffs' lawyers were alleging that the price fixing damages to U.S. buyers were about $1.5 billion, an amount that appears to be within a credible range of estimates (see Chapter 12). If true, the vitamin manufacturers were in theory facing settlement costs of $4.5 billion, an amount many times higher than the previous record antitrust settlements. Just three days after the Washington meeting, the DOJ announced its success in obtaining guilty pleas from Roche and BASF (see chapter 13). As happened in the citric acid case, the DOJ's guilty plea agreements contained concessions in the wording that made negotiating civil settlements more difficult. In the criminal agreements only seven vitamin products were mentioned whereas in the civil case the defendants ended up paying for damages in 14 product markets.[24]

The 25 class actions filed around the country against the vitamins cartel were consolidated into one federal class in Washington, D.C. district court on June 7, 1999. Around that time, press reports began to divulge the step-by-step negotiations between the vitamin manufacturers and class plaintiffs. The defendants were reported eager to settle. In June, Roche, BASF, and Rhône-Poulenc had proposed settlement amounts of $500, $250, and $85 million, respectively; the first two figures were about equal to the amounts that Roche and BASF had promised to pay the government just two weeks earlier. The day after this proposal became known, Roche's shares fell by 3 percent or $3 billion. Apparently stockholders had not realized that Roche faced such high liabilities, or they believed that the settlement amounts would rise well above $500 million. On June 11th, plaintiffs lawyers did indeed ask for more, but not much more; an "agreement in principle" was signed that required Roche, BASF, and Rhône-Poulenc to pay $950 million, which was about 14 percent higher than the defendants initially offered.

Part of the agreement was an unusual clause, one that may be unique in the history of private antitrust class actions. It is sometimes described as akin to the "most favored nation" clauses often used in international trade treaties. The clause stated that the defendants agreed for a period of two years not to pay any opt-out firms *more* than members of the class would receive on a prorate basis. This clause was ultimately designed to prevent plaintiffs from opting out of the class since it reduced the chances they could win a larger settlement by doing so. This clause was a sign that the plaintiffs' class was disunified. Attorneys for some plaintiffs were alleging average overcharges in the 24 to 40 percent range, but the proposed $950 million settlement was far below that range adjusted for treble damages.

Late in the summer, the three largest Japanese vitamin manufacturers in the global vitamins cartel joined the negotiations over civil damages. By early September a recovery of $1.1 billion was being mentioned in press reports. The greatest point of dispute remaining was the size of the legal fees. However, a split was developing between some of the largest vitamin buyers and the smaller plaintiffs. Kenneth Adams, who represented a large number of the biggest purchasers, began to complain publicly that the proposed settlement was too low by at least $500 million. He said:

> "I would be surprised if large purchasers participated in a settlement that returns less than single damages, particularly when the defendants have admitted to criminal liability."

In early October some large buyers of vitamins (e.g., Procter and Gamble, Kellogg, and Bayer) filed suits against the major vitamin makers, thus putting additional pressure to bear on the defendants to raise their offer.

A "final agreement" was announced by the Big Six vitamin makers on November 4, 1999. Attorneys representing the federal class agreed to a recovery for their 4000 clients of $1.17 billion. Roche was to be responsible for 60 percent of the settlement. Attorneys' fees were fixed at $122 million or about 10 percent of the proposed recovery amount. Disagreement among the parties had focused on the so-called most-favored-nation clause that would require the defendants to pay premiums to plaintiffs that remain in the class if opt-outs negotiate a higher settlement rate in the next two years. The size of the proposed settlement is the largest for a private treble-damages award in U.S. antitrust history. However, it is likely to grow in the future as other cartel participants negotiate payments. Certainly, Lonza, Chinook, and DuCoa will be added to the list of payees. Other companies that may negotiate additional settlements with U.S. vitamin buyers include Nepera (vitamin B3, a U.S. company), Degussa-Hüls (B3, Germany), Bioproducts (B4, U.S. subsidiary of Mitsui of Japan), E. Merck (C, Germany), Hoechst (B12, Germany), Akzo Nobel (A, D, E, and B4, Netherlands), and UCB (B4, Belgium).[25] If the cartel participants below the top six pay in proportion to their U.S. sales during the affected period, the total settlement may reach $1.46 billion.

The size of the settlement by the Big Six is somewhat in doubt. Preliminary approval of the $1.17 billion agreement was given by U.S. District Court Judge Tomas Hogan the day after a lengthy hearing in Washington, D.C. on November 22, 1999. At this point, the defendants begin paying interest on the approved amount to the federal class at the annual rate of about 6.25 percent ($200,000 per day). Judge Hogan listened to the arguments about the reasonableness of the settlement and the fairness of the "most favored nation" clause but approved the proposed settlement at a hearing held on March 28, 2000. Despite the approval, the defendants continued throughout 2000 to use a number of legal tactics to delay the settlement.

Approval came despite the fact that about 225 dissatisfied larger buyers, representing 77 percent of the value of the purchases, opted out of the settlement before March 2000.[26] The main issue for the opt-outs was the reasonableness of the proposed settlement. Plainly put, their best economic estimates point to an overcharge by the Big Six of $1.5 to $2.7 billion, so the law specifies that treble damages of $4.5 to $8 billion should go to the injured parties. To be offered $1.2 billion – less than *single* damages – was viewed as an insult. There are no extenuating circumstances. Unlike the low civil settlements in lysine and citric acid, in this case all six defendants have admitted their guilt in sworn statements, and their abilities to pay are not in question.

Outside the United States, there were scattered reports of civil suits being launched against members of the vitamin cartel. As of August 1999, three civil class-action antitrust suits had been filed in Canada, two in Ontario and one in British Columbia. The Ontario suits claim a hefty C$3 billion in damages were incurred by the plaintiffs. In Australia, a civil suit was filed against the local subsidiaries of Roche, BASF, Aventis and other vitamin sellers in July 2000. There the class is requesting A$100 million. Because suits of these types are relatively new in Canada and Australia, their ultimate success is difficult to gauge.

INDIRECT PURCHASERS' CASES

In a famous verdict in 1977 in the case called *Illinois Brick*, the U.S. Supreme Court decided that in federal price fixing cases indirect buyers of a cartelized product would have no standing. The principal reason for this decision was "conservation of judicial resources." The Court was concerned that with extensive chains of buying-selling relationships between manufacturers and the final consumers, the courts would be overwhelmed with damage claims by multiple categories of indirect buyers (farmers, wholesalers, retailers, consumers). Moreover, the Court doubted the feasibility of apportioning the direct overcharges among successive stages of a marketing channel because calculating the extent of pass-through by industries is not without economic uncertainties. The Court was also worried that multiple claimants for the same cartel overcharges might distort the Congressional intent that treble damages would deter the formation of future cartels. If direct buyers of some input did secure treble damages from a cartel, those who purchased from the direct buyers might argue that all or most of that first-stage overcharge was passed on in the form of higher prices to the next buyers. The possibility of direct buyers being sued by indirect buyers would lower the incentive for direct buyers to bring treble-damages suits in the first place, reasoned the Court, thus reducing cartel deterrence by private suits.

The economic models of pass-through do display some complexities. Under the simplest possible assumptions (constant returns to scale in production, a homogeneous product, and a linear demand schedule), buyers with no market power must pass on 100 percent of an increase in the price of an input (Harris and Sullivan 1979). Total pass-through of a cartel price increase will also occur in industries that sell according to a cost-plus contract (a possibility the Supreme Court acknowledged). On the other hand, if the direct buyer is a monopolist, it will pass on only 50 percent of the overcharge to its customers. Oligopolies will display pass-through rates between 50 and 100 percent, depending on their degree of market power. Finally, pass-through rates are affected by the degree of product differentiation (Cotterill *et al.* 2000). When an intermediate buyer has a brand with strong differentiation in the market (a high degree of consumer loyalty), the brand's demand curve is likely to have a sharply convex curvature rather than linear shape and the own-price elasticity of demand will be low. Under these conditions an intermediate buyer with market power will pass on *more than 100 percent* of the marked-up input.

A possible example of this situation is the purchase of citric acid as an ingredient for cola soft drinks. Cola beverage consumers are as a group notably loyal to their habitual brands. If for the purposes of illustration, cola makers require citric acid in the formula that accounts for 1 percent of manufacturing costs, when the citric acid cartel raised its prices by 80 percent the cola companies raised cola prices by 2 percent. In this example the pass-through rate is 250 percent (the increase in price divided by the increase in costs of 0.8 percent).[27]

Although indirect buyers of cartelized products have no standing in federal antitrust suits, the Supreme Court has consistently recognized the rights of the states to permit indirect-purchasers suits under their state antitrust laws. In the late 1990s, at least 16 states and the District of Columbia permitted such suits. They are usually class actions and sometimes are filed in one state for indirect buyers in several of the 16 states. Not all these states follow the treble-damages rule; some allow only single or double damages, and Alabama permits claims on the basis of $500 per transaction. In addition to private plaintiffs suits by buyers, the attorneys general of the states may seek compensation equal to triple damages for their citizens in federal court (see Chapter 16).

Indirect-purchaser antitrust suits are not widely reported by the mainstream press, perhaps because settlement amounts are often rather small. Also, many state-level suits are settled privately out of court before a class has been formed, and the terms of these deals are not public. Nevertheless, because ADM had an obligation to report such suits to its stockholders in its annual reports, it is known that ADM (and its co-conspirators in each cartel) in 1997 was a defendant in 35 state-level class actions alleging damages by indirect buyers. Of these 35, 11 concerned lysine, 23 citric acid, and 19 corn sweeteners.[28] By mid-1999, ADM was still fighting about 74 such suits, which in the aggregate might not involve large payments but which were significant distractions to the company's management.

Some of these many suits may have been initiated for frivolous reasons on the basis of flimsy evidence of damages, the plaintiffs hoping to fleece a rich target. Yet, some court cases have been decided on terms that were costly for the cartels. For example, a suit by 20 feed manufacturers in San Francisco County Superior Court netted the plaintiffs in 1997 a recovery of $50,000 each plus 17 percent of the value of purchased lysine. The 17-percent figure was considered by local lawyers who were interviewed to be very high by historical standards in the state; most such suits are settled for one third that recovery rate or lower. Another class-action suit brought by indirect buyers of lysine in Michigan was settled in April 1997 for $2.1 million. However, a suit brought by buyers of citric acid in Alabama went badly for the plaintiffs when appealed to the state's supreme court. The court decided that the mid 19th-century Alabama legislature's intent in passing the state's antitrust code was to permit damages to be assessed on only intrastate commerce; as the bulk of the acid was purchased out of state, damage awards in Alabama will be much smaller than formerly.[29]

In nearly every session of Congress since the 1977 *Illinois Brick* decision, bills have been introduced to allow for indirect-purchaser antitrust suits. Supporters have been unable to muster majorities in either house. Opponents of indirect-purchaser suits are in many cases concerned that the nation is overly litigious, that the prevalence of frivolous suits will escalate, or that antitrust suits are bad for American business interests. The practical impediments to estimating objectively the extent of pass-through of overcharges are probably overstated, but that would not hinder Congress from passing legislation that would include simple rules for recovery by consumers and intermediate firms in a distribution channel. These rules could be formulated in a way that preserved the principle of treble damages, but no more than treble. If a change in federal legislation included concessions to business that limited their antitrust exposure to state-level and *parens* suits, one can even imagine business trade groups lobbying for such a proposal (see Chapter 9). As it now stands, the direct-buyer-takes-all rule perpetuates a huge distributional disequity that can only be justified by a presumption of zero-percent pass-through. There is no economic logic and no justice in such a view.

The only recourse in federal courts for indirect buyers injured by price fixing conspiracies is for the attorney general of their state to bring a civil case for them. Where state laws permit them to act, attorneys general have standing to bring indirect-purchaser suits to seek compensation for their citizens (see chapter 13). In the case of the lysine and citric acid cartels, no such suits were filed, nor were any pre-trial negotiations announced. However, in 1999 a large group of attorneys general began negotiations with the six largest vitamin manufacturers seeking damages for indirect purchasers of bulk vitamins who were overcharged by cartelization.[30]

In early October 2000, a settlement between the Big Six vitamin makers and 24 attorneys general was widely publicized in the U.S. and European press. The six vitamin companies agreed to pay the 24 states $305 million. Commercial indirect buyers doing business in those states will file compensation claims and receive shares of a pool of $198 million. Because it is infeasible for households to file individual claims, they will be compensated indirectly by appropriate state programs. For example, New York State announced that it would use the consumer portion for grants to nonprofit organizations and local governments for programs related to prenatal care, child nutrition, and alleviation of hunger. These settlements were by far the largest ever made under state indirect-purchaser antitrust laws. However, persons doing business in or living in most states received no compensation. Moreover, the $305 million, while an impressive amount, is under the most conservative assumptions of pass-through at most one-third the trebled indirect overcharges.

THE EFFECTIVENESS OF CIVIL ANTITRUST PENALTIES

One of the recurring themes of this book is the great escalation in monetary sanctions faced by price fixers since 1995. Not only have public prosecutors secured ever-larger fines on cartel participants, but civil settlements have also become more costly for companies. The total recovery by direct buyers that joined federal classes in lysine, citric acid, and vitamins has reached at least $1.44 billion.[31] As government antitrust fines have risen, private treble-damages suits have generated proportionately bigger awards (Figure 16.3).

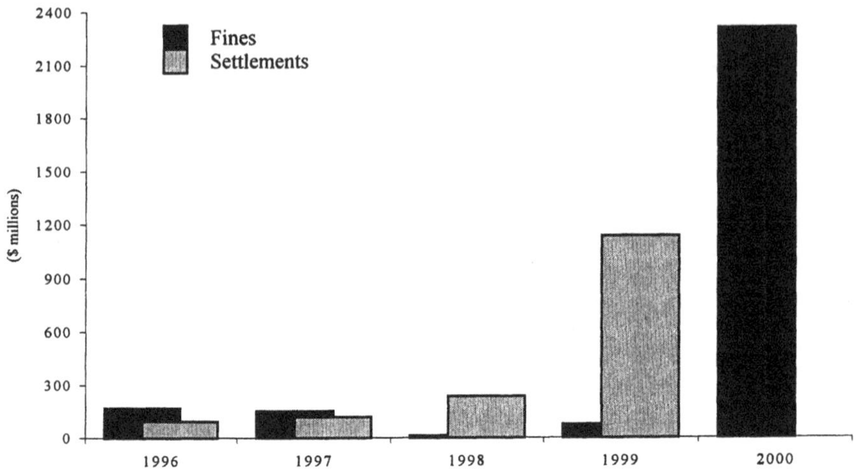

Figure 16.3. U.S. Global Price-Fixing Fines and Settlements, 1996-2000.

Sources: Appendixes of Chapter 13 and Chapter 16.
Note: Fines in year the plea agreement announced; settlements, in year defendants first proposed a settlement, except vitamins is placed in 2000.

Simply observed as a historical trend, these three cases have taken private price fixing settlements to a new, exalted plane. In their comprehensive study of federal private antitrust cases, Elzinga and Wood (1988) reported on the settlement amounts for a sample of 49 cases in a confidential survey with 285 usable responses. Their sample tended to include a high proportion of middle-sized law suits and spanned all categories of antitrust infractions. The average total settlement in these cases was $1.45 million, including a few awards made to defendants. Of this total, 93 percent represented the net recovery to the winners (i.e., the total settlement amount less attorneys' fees, sometimes called the cash settlement).[32]

Table 16.1 lists the largest private price fixing cases in which settlement awards were known. All but one of the cases, the famous *Heavy Electrical Equipment* case of the early 1960s, are class action suits settled since 1972. Although slightly incomplete, the list includes 23 cases with cash settlements (net recovery to the plaintiffs) of $50 million or more.[33] Two cases, *Brand Name Prescription Drugs* and *Vitamins* are not yet completed because of significant opt-outs, but these are so large already that they are worthy of being included. In terms of net recovery amounts, *Vitamins* for now ranks as the second-largest in history, not far behind the *NASDAQ* case, but is expected to surpass *NASDAQ* when fully settled.[34]

Table 16.1. Major U.S. Class-Action Price Fixing Awards. 1972-1999.

Name of Case	Total Settlement: Net Recovery[a]	Total Settlement: Legal Fees	Fees/ Recovery
	Million dollars		*Percent*
1. NASDAQ Market Makers (1999)	1,123	147	13.1
2. Vitamins (1999-2000)	1,170[e]	122	10.5
3. Brand Name Prescription Drugs (1999)	723	NA	NA
4. Corrugated Containers	550	44	8.0
5. Heavy Electrical Equipment (1961-64)[b]	405	41E	10.1
6. Lysine and Citric Acid (1966)	321	50E	15.6
7. Folding Carton[c]	218	14	6.6
8. Plywood (1983)	171	26	14.9
9. Petroleum Products	140	29	21.0
10. Infant Formula (1993, federal)[d]	126	33	26.3
11. Antibiotics	87	29	33.3
12. Travel Agency Commissions	90	22	28.3
13. New Mexico Natural Gas	81	11	14.0
14. Fine Paper	80	10	12.7
15. Gypsum	75	9	12.4
16. Sugar - Western Cases	60	10	17.1
17. Superior Beverage	58	18	31.2
18. Carbon Dioxide	53	10	18.0
19. Red Eagle Resources	53	19	35.9
20. Chlorine & Caustic Soda	53	12	22.8
21. Workers' Compensation	50	12	24.7
22. Cumberland Farms	50	14	27.2
23. Industrial Gas	50	12	24.5

Sources: Shepherd (1985); Class Action Reports, Inc. (1999) "Attorney Fee Study;" Table 4 and Lexis-Nexis.
E = Estimates, NA = Not Available.

[a] "Recovery" is the total amount of monetary damages paid by the antitrust defendants to the plaintiffs. Legal fees and costs go to the attorneys representing the class. It does not include settlements made by defendants with plaintiffs who opted out of the class. On average, costs represented 8% of legal fees and costs, but in some cases no costs were awarded.

[b] Estimate contained in Shepherd (1985) of the results of about 1,900 private suits, only some of which were class actions. The bidding ring consisted of 29 companies. Public prosecution netted $1.9 million in fines and conviction of 45 company officers. Collusion involved seven products over "decades."

[c] Collusion among 23 manufacturers during 1960-1974 in a market with $1 billion in sales in 1974. Public prosecution netted brief jail sentences for 15 of 48 convicted managers and fines of $5,000.
[d] In addition, the three formula manufacturers paid $200 million in a Florida class action suit (1993) and in 1996 paid $33 million to 17 states for overcharging state WIC programs. Several indirect-purchaser cases still in litigation.
[e] Amount announced November 1999. Until a formula for dispersal is agreed upon, interest will accrue, raising the eventual payout. In February 2000, some 200 members of the class accounting for 65-70% of purchases left the remaining 3800 class members.

Because they were settled almost simultaneously and initiated by the same defendant (ADM), the lysine and citric acid settlements are treated as a single event. Together, they rank sixth. Of course, these rankings depend mightily on the size of sales in the affected market.

To try to normalize the recovery rates so as to make them comparable across cases in Table 16.2, the recovery amounts are divided by the sales of the defendants during their respective conspiracies. The number of cases in Table 16.2 is smaller than the number in Table 16.1 because affected sales are unavailable for several cases. However, Table 16.2 makes clear the vital precedent set by the recoveries in the lysine, citric acid, and vitamins cases. Prior to 1996, recovery rates were typically quite low, mostly 4 percent of sales or less. However, recovery rates in the period 1996-1999 ranged from 11 to 22 percent. Taking into consideration the estimated additional recoveries of the opt-out firms (not available in the other cases), recovery rates rise in the late 1990s to the 16 to 35 percent range. Of course, it would be ideal to compare recoveries as a proportion of treble damages but such data are nearly impossible to come by.

The purpose of single damages is to provide monetary compensation for economic injuries. The purpose of treble damages is a dual one: to give private parties an incentive to search out for monopoly profits made by price fixers, thereby leveraging the powers of government antitrust prosecutors, and to deter future violations by inflicting memorable punishment on perpetrators. In practice, the punitive and leveraging functions of private settlements are not being served by class actions.

Table 16.2. Settlement Recovery Rates in Class-Action Price Fixing Litigation, Selected Cases.

Case	Number of Years of the Violation	Recovery Amt./ Defendants' U.S. Affected Sales
1. In re Vitamins Antitrust Litigation, MDL No. (District of D.C. 1999)	9	22[a]
2. In re Amino Acid Lysine Antitrust Litigation, MDL No. 1083 (No. District Ill. 1996)	2.6	11.3[a]
3. In re Citric Acid Antitrust Litigation, MDL No. 1092 (No. District California 1996)	3.5	15[a]
4. In re Catfish Antitrust Litigation, MDL No. 928 (No. Dist. Miss. 1996)	10	8.3
5. In re Folding Cartons Antitrust Litigation, MDL No. 250 (No. District Ill. 1980)	4	4.2
6. In re Eastern Sugar Antitrust Litigation, MDL No. 201a (East District Pa. 1976)	4	2.5
7. In re Chicken Antitrust Litigation, Civil A No. C74-24548 (No. District Ga. 1979)	2	1.0
8. Bagel Inn v. All Star Dairies, Civil Action No. 80-2645, (District of New Jersey 1982)	4	1.0+
9. In re Armored Car Antitrust Litigation, Civil Action No. 78-139A (No. District Ga. 1979)	2	3.9
10. In re Plastic Tableware Antitrust Litigation, Civil Action No. 94-3654 (East. District Pa. 1995)	NA	3.5
11. In re Anthracite Coal Antitrust Litigation, MDL No. 293 (Middle District Pa. 1978)	4	3.1
12. Fisher Bros. v. Phelps Dodge Industries, Inc., Civil Action No. 83-2457 (East. District Pa. 1985)	4	2.4
13. In re Domestic Air Transport Antitrust, MDL No. 681 (No. Dist. GA. 1994) Litigation	6	0.3[b]

Source: Court records of MDL No. 1083, Lexis-Nexis search and Calkins (1997).
[a]Including opt-outs' settlements' recovery, the recovery ratios for vitamins, lysine, and citric acid were an estimated 35%, 16%, and 32% of sales.
[b]This gargantuan case involved a certified class of at least 12 million individual and corporate plaintiffs against six of the largest U.S. airlines. The settlement awarded $50 million cash and coupons with a face value of $406 million, but many of these coupons have not yet and may never be exercised. Calkins (1997) estimated the value of coupons redeemed to be $200-300 million.

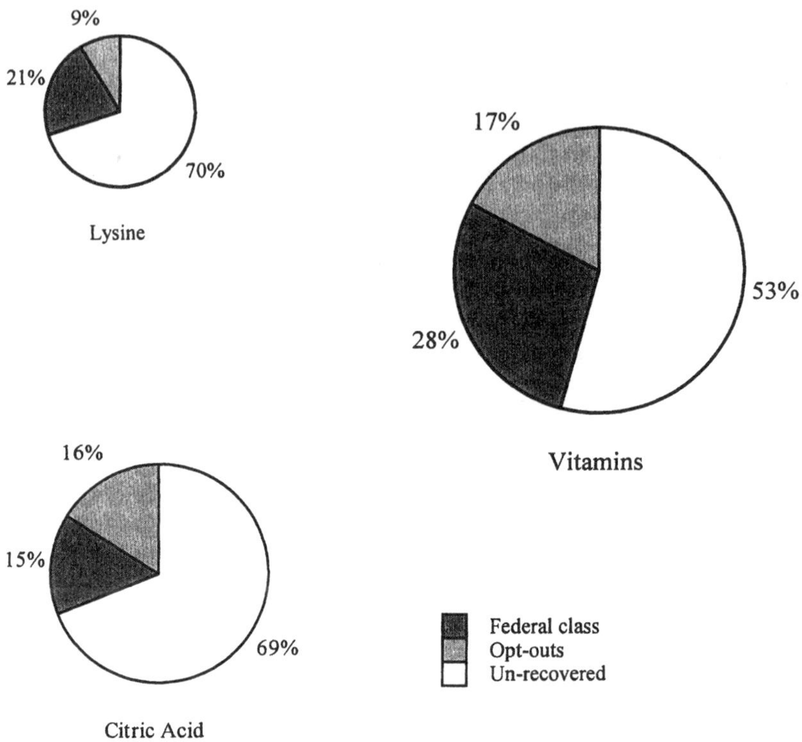

Figure 16.4. Proportion of Treble Damages Recovered by Plaintiffs.

Direct buyers of a cartel's overpriced product who joined federal class actions in the United States and Canada sometimes made large absolute dollar recoveries, but only rarely did the settlement amounts equal or exceed single damages (Figure 16.4). In the three cartels cases documented most fully in this book, the federal classes recovered about 21 percent of the treble damages created by the lysine cartel, 15 percent in citric acid, and 9 to 28 percent in the vitamins cases (Figure 16.4).[34] In no case were settlements as high as single damages made by the federal class. Indeed, members of the classes recovered on average only about 15 percent of treble damages. The opt-outs are believed to have done proportionately better on recovery, but adding both groups of direct buyers together brings the recovery rates to about 30 percent, 31 percent, and 45 percent of the legally mandated recoveries for lysine, citric acid, and vitamins, respectively. In other words, direct buyers got less than single damages in two of the three cases with final settlements. Even the amount of the vitamins settlement (somewhat speculative at this moment) is well under half the treble damages imposed on U.S. buyers.

These findings are important because there are arguments being advanced by thoughtful writers on the subject that treble-damage awards are passé. Rakoff (1992) argues that the entire concept of *corporate criminal* liability is a relatively new American concept in the law that is built on dubious logic. Prior to the 1980s, less than 1 percent of federal criminal indictments were charges against corporate defendants. The increasing use of corporate criminal indictments was largely a response to the necessity for punitive fines for large companies, levels that could not be attained with civil charges. Rakoff argues that the 1991 U.S. Sentencing Guidelines for organizations made civil treble damages unnecessary or excessive, given the harsh sentences mandated by the Guidelines. It should be noted that Rakoff was writing before there had been any experience with actual implementations of the Guidelines. Since then, the DOJ has habitually sought substantial downward departures from punishments suggested by the sentencing guidelines for the vast majority of price fixing defendants. The courts rarely second-guess these requests by prosecutors. Other commentators have noted the substantial flexibility in applying criminal sanctions (Jonas 1992). On the other hand, the DOJ has successfully appealed some sentences imposed by district judges in antitrust cases because they were too lenient compared to the Sentencing Guidelines ranges.

It is true that serious price fixing exposes corporations to highly punitive fines if the legal limits are adhered to literally. The government can impose felony fines up to *double* the overcharges on direct buyers; private plaintiffs can ask for *treble* those same overcharges; attorneys general can seek *treble* damages from price fixing; for their residents who were indirect buyers, and in 16 states indirect purchasers can request treble damages if not pre-empted by the attorneys general. In total, cartel defendants theoretically have liability for up to *eight* times their overcharges. This does sound excessive.

However, what a literal reading of the law implies and what actually has occurred in practice are quite different things. In the cases studied most closely in this book, most corporate conspirators paid well under single damages in government fines. Only the last to negotiate guilty pleas came close to double-overcharge fines. Plaintiffs who remained in federal class actions never received monetary recoveries above single damages. Even counting the more generous recoveries extracted later by class opt-outs, civil recoveries never exceeded half of the treble damages specified by the Sherman Act. As for consumers and intermediate buyers, *parens patriae* suits have been initiated by the attorneys general of less than half the states, and the few instances of state treble-damages awards to indirect buyers seem to involve mostly small settlements. In sum, because the burden of proof is on prosecutors and plaintiffs and because indirect buyers have no standing to sue in federal courts, most corporate price fixers in practice now face only about double damages, not the sextuple damages theoretically justified by law in felony cases. Only the most obdurate defendant who becomes the last to settle might expect to disgorge treble the illegal profits made from price fixing. Moreover, the courts will see to it that guilty parties will not be inconvenienced by fines or settlements which might cause bankruptcy.

In assessing the appropriateness of the size of private settlements, one has to keep in mind the fact that global cartels typically sell most of their overpriced products outside the United States and Canada. As a rough rule of thumb, the lysine, citric acid, and vitamins cartels did about 25 to 35 percent of their business in North America. Unless they maintain a buying office in the United States or Canada, offshore buyers of cartelized products seem to have no standing to join private plaintiffs.[35] Therefore, if a corporation is prosecuted for global price fixing and pays, for example, criminal and civil penalties equal to double the monopoly overcharge, these penalties may amount to only one-third of the conspirator's illicit profits. The U.S. DOJ has the authority to request fines equal to double the harm and to calculate those fines on the basis of *global sales*, but in all but one or two cases cartel overcharges are based conventionally on national sales. Injured buyers who made purchases outside of North America have no rights to seek compensation in civil legal proceedings, either by law or by custom. The vast geographical scope of global cartels severely undercuts the deterrence power of even harsh monetary sanctions in North American jurisdictions.

Finally, it must be remembered that the probability of being snared by antitrust officials in any jurisdiction is certainly less than 100 percent. Some antitrust scholars have hazarded that the historical probability of being detected and prosecuted for price fixing is around 10 percent.[36] The rebirth of global price fixing in the 1990s may have been influenced by the even smaller chances of being prosecuted outside North America. Global cartel managers often made a point of meeting as much as possible outside the United States. Not only are antitrust traditions not as well developed in Europe and Asia, the business cultures in those regions mean that buyers are likely to be less sensitive to or more resigned to collusive behavior on the part of their suppliers.

Chapter 16 Endnotes

[1] The U.S. DOJ has the authority under Section 6 of the Sherman Act to seek forfeiture of property transported in interstate commerce that was owned by a cartel. During 1992-1996, the DOJ exercised this penalty twice, obtaining $28 million in 1992 and $25 million in 1995 (Calkins 1997).

[2] A couple of writers of industrial-organization textbooks, themselves experienced forensic economists, have speculated that as few as 10 percent of all price-fixing conspiracies are investigated or prosecuted. An informal survey by Frederick Warren-Boulton (conveyed to the author) revealed that experienced antitrust defense counsel believed the same.

[3] Calkins (1997) cites the *Airlines*, *NASDAQ*, and *Infant Formula* cases as pertinent examples. Neither DOJ nor *parens patriae* cases were launched. They also required substantial economic analyses that class actions can afford to pay for.

[4] There are civil antitrust suits in some of the other product markets mentioned in Chapter 17 of this book, though many are at early stages or have been confidentially settled our of court.

A class action was consolidated in U.S. District Court in San Francisco in April 1998 for buyers of *sodium gluconate*. In October 1998, ADM offered the class $69,900 to settle the claims.

In July 1999, a class action suit was proceeding against several manufacturers of the amino acid *methionine*: Rhône-Poulenc, Degussa-Hüls, Mitusi, Nippon Soda, and Novus International. Although the lawsuit stems from federal investigations of lysine, it does not benefit, so far, from criminal indictments or convictions by the federal government. The global market for methionine, about $1 billion annually, is the largest of the amino acids.

In March 2000, six private antitrust lawsuits were consolidated in the Minneapolis District Court that charge price fixing in *monosodium glutamate* (MSG) and two related flavorings. Defendants are ADM, Ajinomoto USA, and Takeda Vitamins & Food USA. No criminal convictions preceed this civil case, but there is evidence on the lysine case that ADM at least planned to form a cartel for MSG (Eichenwald 2000: 164, 173).

Civil suits against members of a *bromine* cartel (Great Lakes Chemical, Dead Sea Bromine, and Albermarl) were being consolidated in late 2000. Two of the three cartel members have pleaded guilty.

[5] For an annotated list of sources for this section, see Connor (2000:Appendix A). A fuller description of the events of late June to August 1995 can be found in Chapter 13 above.

[6] Some commentators have expressed skepticism as to whether the attempt was genuine. Ross Johnson, an ADM director, ridiculed its sincerity in a public speech at a Georgia business school in which he also called the FBI investigators "scumbags." A couple of years later while in federal prison, Whitacre made another attempt that his wardens deemed staged.

[7] The other six members of the antitrust-advisory committee were Shreve Archer (heir of a founder), Ralph Bruce (retired ADM officer), Ross Johnson, Mrs. Nelson Rockerfeller, John Vanier (a farmer), O. Glenn Webb (Chairman of one of ADM's joint-venture partners). Vanier was the brother-in-law of ADM's Chairman of ADM Milling Co., and Archer was the father of ADM's treasurer. Rockerfeller was an old family friend of the Andreas family.

[8] Dwayne Andreas was himself 77 years old.

[9] By April, the *Wall Street Journal* reported that the board's special antitrust committee was urging ADM's management to plea-bargain with the DOJ. Shareholders' derivative suits were demanding a restructuring of the Board itself that would require the resignation of many of its members closest to Andreas.

[10] After two more defendants paid another $4 to $5 million, legal fees were only 7 percent of settlement amounts. For comparisons with other private antitrust settlements, see Chapter 8.

[11] Recall that the USSG suggests that 10 percent is a typical overcharge. The stock market was pleasantly surprised with the low proposal; ADM was rewarded with one-day price increases of 2 percent.

[12] The present author prepared such an analysis for the law firm of Dickstein Shapiro. Williams & Connelly hired two former chief economists of the DOJ to critique the analysis, Lawrence J. White and Frederick Warren-Boulton.

[13] Recall from Chapter 7's discussion of the 1999 sentencing hearings for *Michael Andreas et al.* the superior cost information resulted in a higher but-for price and, thus, a lower ($78 million) overcharge estimate.

[14] Robert Swift of Kohn Swift replied to Coffee's column by continuing to defend the "high" recovery rate and relating how tenacious his firm was in pursuing Sewon America for nine months after the others settled.

[15] Martin Allison sold lysine in ADM's German office; he pleaded guilty in early 1997. Reinhard Richter, based in Mexico City, pleaded guilty to income-tax evasion in 1997. Sidney Hulse was indicted for income-tax evasion in late 1997. Hulse operated Whitacre's secret bank accounts in Switzerland and the Cayman Island. He pleaded guilty in May 1998.

[16] Judge McCuskey rendered Whitacre a favorable opinion on two counts. He refused to extend ADM's nondisclosure agreement with Whitacre in perpetuity, and he protected Whitacre's ownership of stock options on ADM stock. However, ADM's many troubles have reduced the value of those options to very low levels.

[17] These overcharge estimates are conservative ones. They assume that Cargill was not a member of the cartel, that companies outside the collusive group did not opportunistically raise their prices (no umbrella effect), and that prices in Europe (where the cartel had a greater degree of market dominance) did not rise proportionately more than in the United States.

[18] The offers from Roche and Jungbunzlauer were first announced in late October. Bayer and Jungbunzlauer are owned by holding companies registered in Switzerland, thus all three are Swiss companies.

[19] As noted in Chapter 3, a fifth sporadic exporter pleaded guilty to fixing the price of citric acid. Cerestar Bioproducts, a subsidiary of Eridania Beghin-Say, paid $400,000 in June 1998. Roche and Jungbunzlauer may have received discounts for their help in investigating Cerestar.

[20] In January 1998, Judge Smith granted a summary judgment to Cargill that "no reasonable jury" would convict the company in a civil trial as a price fixer. His decision was later upheld on appeal to the Ninth Circuit Court.

[21] The larger of the cases is *In re High Fructose Corn Syrup Antitrust Litigation*, a class action (MDL No. 1087) consolidated in U.S. District Court in Peoria, Illinois. A "tag-along" case alleging collusion by the same defendants in two corn sweeteners is *Gray & Co. v. Archer Daniels Midland et al.* (Civil Action No. 97-1203). The author was a testifying expert in one of these cases.

[22] In the case of Coke and Pepsi, there is also the possibility that their huge procurement shares gave them sufficient buying power that they in fact suffered no overcharging.

[23] The Microsoft case was the biggest monopoly prosecution since the DOJ had filed cases against IBM and AT&T in 1969.

[24] The vitamins not covered by the criminal plea agreements of May 1999 are B1, B4, B6, B12, biotin, folic acid, and canthaxanthin. Vitamins B3 and B4 were covered by guilty pleas at later dates.

[25] Long shots include Tanabe (biotin, Japan), Sumitomo (biotin, Japan), and Solvay-Duphar (D, France).

[26] Thus, under the agreement, the remaining 3775 smaller vitamin buyers will share $242 million, or an average recovery of about $64,000 per firm on average purchases of $350,000 per firm.

[27] In this example, if the citric acid sold to cola beverage firms was overpriced by $10 million, the beverage firms would be entitled to $30 million in damages. However, the cola retailers or consumers would have suffered treble damages of $75 million.
[28] The sum of the parts is greater than the whole because some suits were brought by buyers of two or even three products.
[29] Plaintiffs believe that the plain wording of the Alabama law permits compensation for overcharges on out-of-state purchases by Alabama companies. In the spring of 2000, a bill was introduced to the Alabama legislature that would overturn the Supreme Court's decision retroactively. It is believed that there are sufficient votes to pass the bill (personal communication, Prof. Robert Taylor).
[30] The present author advised the attorneys general on the size of the overcharge and other economic matters.
[31] The vitamins opt-outs had yet to settle by mid-2000. I predict that their settlement may push the total to as high as $2.2 billion.
[32] Although only 7 percent of the total settlement represented legal fees (billings, contingency fees, and court awards for costs), plaintiffs' legal fees were very low (2.3 percent) while average defendants' legal costs were high (59 percent of the total).
[33] Inflation during the 1970s was high, so the amounts for the earlier cases are understated compared to more recent settlements. Adjusted for inflation, *Heavy Electrical Equipment* might just top *NASDAQ*.
[34] As interest payments mount or opt-outs secure higher recoveries than the class.
[35] In early 2000, vitamin buyers accounting for about two-thirds of sales of bulk vitamins by the cartel opted out of the $1.17 billion settlement. Those in the class will get $390 million. I expect the recovery rate to be about twice as high for the opt-outs, or about $1.5 billion.
[36] For a suggestion that there may be precedents to the contrary, see Adams and Bell (1999).
[37] It is difficult to be precise about that which cannot be observed. This figure seems to arise often in informal communications with forensic economists who have asked experienced antitrust lawyers to generalize about their clients' experiences.

Table 16.A.1. Civil Settlements Made by Global Price Fixers in the United States, 1996-April 2000.

Product	Plaintiffs[a]	Defendants	Date Offered	Amount
				Dollars
LYSINE	Federal Class	Archer Daniels Midland	April 1996	25,400,000
		Ajinomoto	April 1996	10,000,000
		Kyowa Hakko Kogyu	April 1996	10,000,000
		Sewon America	1997	4,000,000E
		Cheil Jedang	unknown[e]	1,000,000E
	Class opt-outs	ADM *et al.*	unknown[e]	20,000,000E
	State class	ADM *et al.*	unknown[e]	15,000,000E
	Shareholders	Archer Daniels Midland Management	September 1996	30,000,000
	Shareholders	ADM Board of Directors	June 1997	8,000,000
	ADM	Mark Whitacre	March 1998	12,600,000
CITRIC ACID	Federal Class	Archer Daniels Midland	September 1996	35,000,000[b]
		Bayer/Haarmann & Riemer	December 1996	46,000,000[b]
		Hoffmann-La Roche	October 1996	5,680,000[b]
		Jungbunzlauer Intl.	October 1996	7,570,000[b]
		Cargill	--	0[c]
	Class opt-outs	ADM *et al.*	1997	105,000,000E[d]
	State class	ADM *et al.*	1997-1999[f]	40,000,000
CORN SYRUP	Federal class	Corn Products Co., Intl.	September 1996	7,000,000
		Archer Daniels Midland	pending	
		Cargill	pending	
		Tate & Lyle/A.E. Staley	pending	
		American Fructose	pending	
VITAMINS	Federal class	Hoffmann-La Roche	March 2000	136,000,000E
		BASF	March 2000	47,500,000E
		Rhône-Poulenc	March 2000	41,500,000E
		Takeda	March 2000	24,200,000E
		Eisai	March 2000	11,000,000E
		Daiichi	March 2000	6,500,000E
		Hoechst	March 2000	90,000E

Product	Plaintiffs[a]	Defendants	Date Offered	Amount
				Dollars
		Lonza	2000	7,600,000E
		DCV/DuCoa	2000	5,500,000E
		Chinook	2000	16,400,000E
		Mitsui/Bioproducts	2000	11,100,000E
		E. Merck	2000	750,000E
		Degussa/Vitachem	2000	7,600,000E
		Nepera	2000	5,750,000E
	Class opt-outs	14 companies above	2000	800,000,000-1,500,000,000
SODIUM GLUCONATE	Federal class	Avebe BA and		
		Akzo Nobel Chemicals BV:		
		Glucona America Inc.	pending	350,000E
		Fujisawa Pharmaceutical Co.:		
		PMP Fermentation Products, Inc.	pending	700,000E
		Roquette Freres	pending	100,000E
		Archer Daniels Midland Co.	1999	69,900
		Jungbunzlauer Intl.	pending	300,000E
GRAPHITE ELECTRODES	Federal Class	UCAR International Inc.	2000	240,000,000E
		Showa Denko Carbon	pending 2000	
		SGL Carbon AG	December 1999	34,000,000E
		Carbide/Graphite Group	pending 2000	
		Tokai Carbon	pending 2000	
	Shareholders	UCAR Intl. management	October 1999	40,500,000
SORBATES	Federal Class	Eastman Chemical Co.	pending 2000	
		Hoechst AG Nutrovina	pending	
		Daicel	pending	
		Nippon Synthetic (Dohsei)	pending	
METHIONINE	Federal Class	Rhône-Poulenc/ADM	pending	
		Degussa-Hüls	pending	
		Mitsui & Co.	pending	

Product	Plaintiffs[a]	Defendants	Date Offered	Amount
				Dollars
		Nippon Soda Co.	pending	
		Novus International	pending	
MONOSODIUM GLUTOMATE	Federal Class	Ajinomoto	pending	
		Archer Daniels Midland	pending	
		Takeda Chemical	pending	

E = Estimated by the author.
-- Not available or undetermined.
[a] "Federal class" is direct buyers seeking compensation under the Sherman and Clayton Acts. "Class opt-outs" are companies that qualify as direct buyers to be members of the federal class but decided to opt out and seek compensation through negotiation. "State class" is indirect buyers in about 16 U.S. states that permit damages to be sought under their state antitrust laws.
[b] The original offer made by Bayer in 1996 was reduced to $38 million in 1997 by the presiding federal judge because several buyers opted out of the class.
[c] Refused to negotiate with buyers and was eventually dismissed from the case.
[d] Only ADM publicly announced its settlement amounts to opt-outs ($36 million). Roche later said that its fines and settlement were about $10 million. If all the citric-acid sellers paid settlement amounts proportional to ADM, then the four opt-outs received $53 million and Unilever possibly $25 million more (Connor 2000: Appendix B). Thus, the range is likely $95 to $114 million.
[e] Believed to have been offered mostly in 1997.
[f] Believed to have been offered mostly in 1998.
[g] Believed to have been offered mostly in 1999.

Chapter 17

MORE GLOBAL CARTELS

INTRODUCTION

The global price fixing cartels discovered and prosecuted in the late 1990s may be seen as the third great wave of such cartels in modern world economic history. While the history of ancient empires is replete with instances of state control over grain storage, long distance trade, and the distribution of food staples in urban areas, these took the form of state ownership or the regulation of private trade rather than unfettered private cartel behavior.[1] Medieval European guilds incorporated many of the features of a cartel, but the power of such labor organizations did not extend beyond a city's walls. The limited-liability companies that were given the task of exploiting areas of the world that were new to Europeans in the Age of Discovery did so with grants of monopoly by the state. However, these companies, far from forming joint ventures were usually at war with one another. It was not until the late 19th century that legal and economic conditions were ripe for the invention of private cartels that operated across national boundaries. Among those preconditions seems to be the limited-liability corporation, the establishment of foreign sales branches or subsidiaries, the telegraph and other electronic means of communication, modern methods of accounting and management controls, and the development of markets for homogeneous goods that are internationally tradable.

The first great wave of global cartels appeared very late in the 19th century and continued to build up to the outbreak of World War I. This period parallels the appearance of the first national "trusts" or monopolies in railroads, beef, tobacco, and many other product lines. Most of these early monopolies were concerned with knitting together regional businesses into a national concern, though a few did coordinate export sales or cooperated in foreign investment. The first era came to an end by antitrust actions in the United States or by the disruption of international trade during the Great War.

In Europe, many of the pre-war international cartels were re-established in the 1920s. Others were formed in the 1930s to cope with excess capacities that developed with the onset of the global depression. Unlike the previous war, during World War II the cartels operating within the Axis Powers thrived. These cartels became a key feature in the planning for and execution of the war economies of Germany, Japan, and Italy. Cartels were eminently compatible with fascist economic principles of authoritarian control over privately owned businesses. The second wave of global cartels ended with antitrust prosecutions in the United States and attempts by allied occupation authorities to fundamentally alter the legal environment that formerly supported cartel behavior. The imposition of anticartel laws was more successful in controlling German cartels that in preventing a resurgence of the *zaibatsu* in Japan.

The reappearance of global price fixing in the early 1990s took U.S. antitrust enforcers somewhat by surprise. When evidence began to mount of serious and widespread global conspiracies, the DOJ had no consensus on the definition what constituted an "international" matter (ICPAC 2000). International matters were so unusual that the agency did not bother to keep a separate data series for them until fiscal year 1997. By the end of the 1990s, the DOJ had prosecuted more than 80 corporate and 60 individual defendants for global price fixing.[2] The active prosecution of global cartels by the DOJ and its sister agencies abroad may well bring the third wave to a conclusion.

The prosecution of the lysine cartel in 1996 has often been compared to the tip of the iceberg, below which dozens of other cartels festered. Perhaps from a historical perspective it is better to compare lysine to a growler that presaged the appearance of a large field of large icebergs to come, fields that break off of their shelves every 50 years or so.

FOOD-AND-FEED INGREDIENTS

Lysine, citric acid, and vitamins had one functional characteristic in common – they all entered the global food supply either as food additives, nutritional supplements, or active ingredients in animal feeds. When sold in bulk by their manufacturers, these products were identified by quality grades that made the products essentially interchangeable across alternative manufacturers. This high degree of uniformity in product quality when combined with the structural conditions of few suppliers and many buyers proved to be ideal conditions for fostering global price fixing. In the period 1996 to 2000, a large share of the global cartels discovered by U.S. antitrust authorities fit a uniform profile: minor ingredients sold in bulk to tens of thousands of food and feed manufacturers. In other words, the lysine/citric/vitamins cases were in no sense isolated instances of global cartels. Rather, they were part of a broader phenomenon of cartelization of global industries with similar structural characteristics: homogeneous organic chemicals sold by a few dominant manufacturers to a vast number of atomistic purchasers. More importantly, these conditions are found today in scores of similar industries, many of them populated by one or more companies that have already been tainted by their admission of a history of price fixing. Unless the chilling effect of fines, imprisonment, and civil penalties for price fixing has reached the freezing point, more global cartels are likely to be discovered.

Sodium Gluconate

More generally known as gluconates, sodium gluconate is a salt form of gluconic acid.[3] Gluconates are sold in four commercial forms: 100% gluconic acid, a dry powder of 100% sodium gluconate, and liquid sodium gluconate in either a 40% or 60% concentration. Dry sodium gluconate is the most common product and apparently the form of which all other varieties are priced. A small amount of sodium gluconate is used in the curing of concrete, but it is principally purchased by food manufacturers for cleaning of glass bottles and steel food processing machinery. Sodium gluconate is unique among industrial cleansers in meeting pharmacopeia standards; that is, any residues that might enter food or beverage products are perfectly safe for consumers to ingest. Many of the alternative cleansers used for cleaning food machinery, such as benzene, are dangerous carcinogens. Microscopic traces of benzene detected in bottles of Perrier mineral water some years ago practically ruined the company's reputation, so a product like sodium gluconate is a godsend for food and beverage manufacturers.

Like lysine and citric acid, sodium gluconate is the product of a fermentation process. Some European manufacturers use potato starch as the feedstock, but in U.S. plants glucose or dextrose are converted into gluconic acid through microbial metabolism. Official documents describe the technology as complex and largely proprietary, a fact that implies that barriers to entry are high. Indeed, the global industry in the early 1990s was comprised of only five significant firms. They share global sales of only about $50 million per year. The largest global manufacturer was Glucona v.o.f., a joint venture between the large Dutch chemical firm Akzo Nobel BV and the smaller Dutch agribusiness concern Avebe BA. Glucona was majority owned by Akzo until about 1994, when it was sold entirely to Avebe. Glucona controlled about 28 percent of the global market for sodium gluconate from plants in the Netherlands and Wisconsin. Of equal size was the French agribusiness firm Roquette Frères. Roquette makes sodium gluconate in plants located in France and Italy. Slightly smaller (about 20 percent share) was the Japanese firm Fujisawa Pharmaceuticals Co., Ltd., which operates a fermentation plant in Illinois operated by its U.S. subsidiary PMP Fermentation Products, Inc.

The remaining one-fourth of global production was accounted for by two companies who were prominent participants in the citric acid cartel (see

Chapter 5).[4] The companies are ADM and Jungbunzlauer International. Both companies entered the sodium gluconate business through acquisitions of European companies in 1988-1991. ADM picked up sodium gluconate as part of the purchase of a fermentation products unit of Finnish Sugar Co., Ltd. in 1991.[5] Jungbunzlauer acquired its sodium gluconate facility in 1988 when it purchased a plant in Ladenburg, Germany in 1988 from Joh. Benckiser Gmbh as part of its strategy to expand into world leadership in citric acid. In 1997, Jungbunzlauer moved production of sodium gluconate from Ladenburg to a new vertically integrated plant in Marckolsheim, Alsace, France that makes the glucose feedstock on site. ADM and Jungbunzlauer each held about 12 percent of the world market.

The global sodium gluconate cartel was revealed by the U.S. Department of Justice in September 1997; more plentiful details were given a year later when the Canadian prosecutions were announced. Unsurprisingly, all five producers of sodium gluconate were involved in the conspiracy, which lasted from April 1987 to June 1995.[6] The early initial date is noteworthy because it suggests that the conspiracy began in Europe with the participation of Finnish Sugar and Joh. Benckiser before these two companies sold out to ADM and Jungbunzlauer. ADM and Fujisawa probably joined the cartel at a later date (August 1993) around the time that ADM got its new sodium gluconate plant started in Illinois. The termination date of June 1995 corresponds the month in which the FBI raided ADM's Decatur, Illinois headquarters looking for evidence of price fixing in lysine, citric acid, and corn sweeteners.

In the United States, only four manufacturers were indicted for price fixing, and only three of them pleaded guilty and paid fines (see Table 13.A.1). In Canada, five companies were participants in the conspiracy, but one of them, ADM, was not fined (Table 13.A.2). From these facts, one can infer that ADM was the "unindicted co-conspirator" in the sodium gluconate cartel mentioned in the DOJ's press release. That is, although never made public, as part of the deal for ADM's agreement to pay a $100 million price fixing fine in October 1996, ADM was granted an amnesty for its participation in the sodium gluconate conspiracy.[7] Moreover, ADM's early cooperation with the Canadian Competition Bureau in sodium gluconate also yielded an amnesty from Canadian fines.

After ADM confessed to the U.S. and Canadian antitrust authorities in late 1996, negotiations with the other sodium-gluconate cartel members dragged on for more than a year. In September 1997, the guilty pleas of Akzo Nobel Chemicals, its manufacturing subsidiary Glucona, and its U.S. distribution affiliate Glucona America were announced. Roquette and its U.S. sales subsidiary Roquette America pleaded guilty three months later. The largest fines were paid by Fujisawa and PMP Fermentation in February 1998, a sure sign that Fujisawa was the most recalcitrant defendant. Because Fujisawa paid a fine of more than $10 million, the two-times rule permits one to estimate that the overcharge rate was between 15 and 30 percent of affected sales. The Canadian fines were imposed on Jungbunzlauer, Roquette, Fujisawa, and Akzo in October 1998. As usual, the secretive and slow EEC authorities were moving ponderously against members of the cartel. Made public only through ADM's financial statements, the Commission informed the conspirators that it was formally opening an investigation only in November 1998. ADM and the others became defendants in civil treble-damages suits filed in the United States in late 1997. A year later ADM offered a small amount ($69,600) to the plaintiffs in the federal class to settle the civil damages.

The sodium gluconate conspiracy was a small cartel compared to others discussed in this book, but it had two notable features. First, four of the five members of the cartel were repeat offenders under the U.S. Sherman Act. Second, partly as a result of their recidivism, the defendants not given amnesty were hit with precedent-setting U.S. fines that dramatically expands the potential liability for future cartel participants.

ADM and Jungbunzlauer were both guilty of price fixing in citric acid, and admitted their culpability in federal court in October 1996 and March 1997, respectively. In addition, ADM pleaded guilty to price fixing in the market for lysine and became a defendant in civil suits alleging price fixing in corn sweeteners. Thus, for ADM, sodium gluconate marks its third or fourth known instance of criminal price fixing. Roquette America owns a major producer of corn wet milling products in the United States like ADM; it too is a defendant in the civil case alleging a conspiracy in the U.S. corn sweetener market. Finally, Akzo Nobel Chemicals is the Dutch member of the Nobel group, a large Norwegian chemical company with a long history of price fixing earlier in the 20th century; moreover, one of the Norwegian company's U.S. subsidiaries was convicted in 1996 of price fixing in the U.S. market for explosives. Indeed, Dyno Nobel bears the dubious distinction of having been the first price fixer to break the $10-million-fine barrier.

In terms of affected sales, the sodium gluconate market is the smallest discussed in this book, yet the three largest members of the cartel paid impressive total fines of $32.5 million (Table 13.A.1). In addition, four top managers were fined a total of $500,000. These are extraordinary levels when one considers that, according to the U.S. DOJ, U.S. sales during the 1993-1995 U.S. conspiracy amounted to less than $10 million.[8] That is, Fujisawa's fine of $20 million represented *fives times* its estimated U.S. sales or at least a 200 percent overcharge. However, the guilty firms in fact were assessed fines on the basis of their *global* sales, which is allowed under U.S. Sentencing Guidelines when the DOJ and the courts judge that fines based on domestic sales would fail to result in punitive sanctions. With global sales of $50 million annually, Fujisawa (the last firm to settle with the government) then paid a fine of 20 percent of the $100 million in sodium gluconate sold *worldwide* during the conspiracy period, *eight to 12 times* a fine based on only U.S. sales. This method of calculating fines represents a significant escalation in the potential exposure of global price fixers.

Sorbates

The sorbates market includes sorbitol, sorbic acid, and potassium sorbate. Sorbitol is often made by fermentation to serve as a chemical intermediate in the production of vitamin C. In their final forms, sorbates are frequently added to processed foods to preserve them or extend shelf life. In the mid-1990s global sales of sorbates amounted to about $200 million per year. Although the sorbates market is not especially large, the extraordinary 17-year life of the cartel meant that affected sales were quite high. Affected U.S. sales totaled $1 billion.

The existence of a global conspiracy to fix prices of sorbates was revealed in October 1998 when the Eastman Chemical Co. headquartered in Tennessee pleaded guilty in federal court and agreed to pay a fine of $11 million. Its executives were apparently granted immunity as a result of its early cooperation. Eastman, with more than 10,000 workers in the state, is Tennessee's largest private employer. The company accounted for about 10 percent of global output from a plant at Chocolate Bayou, near Alvin, Texas. Eastman was said to be cooperating with the DOJ in its investigation of the cartel. Immediately, speculation in chemical-industry trade magazines centered on Hoechst of Germany and a number of Japanese chemical firms, with Daicel and Nippon Synthetic Chemical heading the list.

The second company to plead guilty was indeed Hoechst AG, the leading world producer of sorbates. Hoechst paid $36 million fine, and the marketing manager of its Food Ingredients unit paid a $250,000 fine (Table 13.A.1). Hoechst's conviction in May 1999 came seven months after Eastman Chemical's, a lag indicating hard negotiations with the DOJ must have preceded its decision to plead guilty.[9] Hoechst's guilty plea completed a set: along with Bayer and BASF, Hoechst became the last of the three main successors of the infamous I.G. Farben chemical cartel to be convicted in the 1990s. Like ADM, Roche, and Jungbunzlauer, because of its conviction in the vitamins cartel Hoechst is a recidivist price fixer (Chapter 13).

Although additional firms may yet be added to the list of conspirators, two Japanese firms were convicted in the sorbates case in 1999-2000. The chemical manufacturer Nippon Gohsei became the third company to admit its participation in the sorbates cartel. In July 1999, the DOJ announced that Nippon Gohsei agreed to pay a $21 million criminal fine; in addition, one of its executives was fined the maximum statutory amount of $350,000, a sign that he had played a leadership role in the sorbates cartel. The fourth company to be convicted was Daicel Chemical Industries, Ltd. of Tokyo. Daicel agreed to pay a criminal fine of $53 million. Although the company admitted its guilt, it appears that no managers were willing to accept responsibility. Therefore, the DOJ indicted the company's three top executives for criminal price fixing; as of late 2000, they remained fugitives. The DOJ's press release promised more guilty pleas would follow.

The corporate fines paid to the U.S. government by the three sorbates cartel members totaled $121 million. The most remarkable aspect of the sorbates cartel was its longevity – 17 and one-half years. Also remarkable is the fact that Eastman Chemical joined the cartel only during its last two and one-half years, whereas Hoechst and Nippon Gohsei withdrew from the cartel 15 months before its U.S. operations ended.[10] Finally, a puzzling aspect of the sorbates cartel is the fact that the two largest U.S. manufacturers of sorbitol have not been indicted, even though both have a history of involvement in global chemical cartels. Until 1994, Pfizer was the leading U.S. producer of sorbitol, so perhaps the statute of limitations prevented Pfizer's conviction. In 1990, ADM built a sorbitol plant with its usual grandiose scale (100 million pounds capacity). Although ADM's entry caused sorbitol prices to fall and its production increased throughout the early 1990s, the expansion seems not to have had any impact on the ability of the sorbates cartel to continuing its collusive activity. Was ADM given immunity in the sorbates market in return for its $100-million fine?

Sodium Erythorbate and Maltol

The last example of a food-ingredient cartel centers on one company, Pfizer Inc., the fourth largest U.S. drug company. Pfizer conspired with one other chemical company spanning the period 1989-1995. Pfizer is one more example of a repeat offender in the price fixing area. Although not indicted because of the statute of limitations, Pfizer conspired with Bayer and other European manufacturers in the 1980s in the global market for citric acid. For its role in the sodium erythorbate and maltol conspiracies, Pfizer was fined $20 million in July 1999.

Sodium erythorbate is an antioxidant, a class of food additives that is increasingly popular with consumers because of perceived health benefits. Chemically it is quite close in its functional characteristics to ascorbic acid (vitamin C), yet has positive effects in preserving foods like cured meat products by slowing down changes in food colors and flavors. Maltol is a food additive widely used in dried fruits, candies, and beverages. Sometimes described as a sweetener, it is more accurate to say that maltol increases the perception of other sweeteners in the product. Besides its role as a flavor-enhancer, maltol increases the creamy mouthful and suppresses impressions of bitterness and acidity in foods. Maltol can be extracted from natural plant material, but in the mid 1970s, Pfizer had patented a synthetic chemical process for making maltol.

The U.S. sales of sodium erythorbate during the affected period (1992-1994) and maltol (1989-1995) were only $65 million. The size of Pfizer's fine suggests an overcharge of around 30 percent on the two products. The identity of the other participant in this conspiracy has not been announced, but there is only one other manufacturer of sodium erythorbate in the United States, PMP Fermentation Products, the U.S. subsidiary of Fujisawa Pharmaceutical Co. of Japan. PMP began making sodium erythorbate in its Peoria, Illinois plant in 1961; in 1996, PMP built a new erythorbate plant for $50 million. Fujisawa/PMP is the same company that pleaded guilty to price fixing of sodium gluconate in 1998.

Three years before Pfizer admitted its price fixing in the erythorbate and maltol markets, it sold its Food Science Group, the unit responsible for making these and other food additives. The Group operated four chemical factories in the United States and two in Europe The sale of the Group in January 1996 to the Finnish biotechnology company Cultor Oy effectively ended the price conspiracy. Cultor, which merged with the Danish sugar company Daniso in 1999, may well decide to sue Pfizer for damages because the $350 million it paid to Pfizer was very likely inflated by illegal profits in the early 1990s.

OTHER GLOBAL CARTELS

Not all the global cartels that were discovered and prosecuted in the 1990s were food or feed ingredients or even chemical products. Three examples of minor interest are marine services, bromines, and isostatic graphite. A fourth case, graphite electrodes, involved a number of novel features and will be recounted in some detail.

The heavy-lift marine-services cartel came to light in January 1998 when three firms agreed to pay a total of $65 million in fines for criminal price fixing during the period 1990-1997. The companies were registered in the Netherlands, Belgium, and the United States (Table 13.A.1); in addition, unnamed co-conspirators were granted amnesty and three executives of the Dutch and Belgian firms were fined a total of $325,000. The services in question were quite specialized: heavy lift marine barges used to construct offshore drilling platforms and heavy lift semi-submersible of marine transportation. The marine services cartel was an especially cozy arrangement; in a feature rarely seen since the I.G. Farben cartel, participants pooled their net revenues and later divided them according to a complex formula. The prosecution of these cartels is significant because for the first time the U.S. fines were assessed on the basis of *global* market sales rather than sales to U.S. customers only (Spratling 1998). Moreover, given the oceanic location of the services provided, this was an excellent test case for the U.S. DOJ to see whether a court would approve this new broader criterion for fines. However, it was not to be the last use of global sales to assess fines.

The DOJ's amnesty program has been progressively applied by the Antitrust Division to obtain reliable information about otherwise clandestine activities. Another example of the benefits of the program came to light in June 1999. Great Lakes Chemical Corp. announced from its headquarters in West Lafayette, Indiana that it had been accepted into the amnesty program after informing the DOJ about price fixing in the world bromine industry. Bromine and its derivatives is Great Lake's major product line, and the company is the world leader, with about one-third of the $800-million industry. According to press reports, Great Lake's role in the conspiracy was discovered soon after the company appointed a new CEO in April 1998. As yet unnamed, the co-conspirators are probably Albermarle Corp. of Richmond Virginia and Dead Sea Bromine Group in Israel. Dead Sea was convicted in July 2000.

The third small non-food cartel involved a specialized intermediate material called isostatic graphite. Cabone of America Industries and its French CEO pleaded guilty to criminal price fixing in March 2000. The fines so far total $7.25 million for the 1993-1998 conspiracy. Although a small industry, the list of restrictive practices followed by the cartel was almost exhaustive.

Graphite Electrodes

The graphite-electrodes cartel deserves considerable attention because of its size, complexity, and a new level of harshness in the sanctions meted out by the courts. This massive conspiracy involved eight or nine companies in Germany, Japan, and the United States. Some of the defendants have launched suits against one another for damages arising from withholding of material information about the conspiracy, and one firm's creative use of bankruptcy statutes has resulted in a clarification of bankruptcy law. Finally, this cartel was the first to spark raids by antitrust agencies simultaneously on three continents.

Like the marine-services and bromine cartels, the DOJ was alerted to the conspiracy in graphite electrodes by a company seeking amnesty. Because Carbide/Graphite Group, Inc. of Pittsburgh was the first firm to offer information on the cartel to a clueless DOJ, the company was automatically entitled to amnesty from government fines. Carbide/Graphite is the second largest U.S. manufacturer of graphite electrodes, instruments that transmit huge flows of electricity to scrap steel, which is then melted and turned into recycled steel. From as early as 1992 to January 1997 the eight companies in this cartel agreed on prices, sales volumes for each producer, exchange of sales information, and concealment of its illegal activities. In addition, the cartel designated one of its members to fix the *regional* prices to be charged by all the cartel participants. Finally, the cartel agreed to withhold certain advanced technologies from companies outside the cartel. The industry is quite large; in 1996 global sales were about $500 million, and 1992-1997 affected sales were $1.75 billion.

In early 1997, Carbide/Graphite went to the DOJ with its information. On June 5, 1997, antitrust officials from the Commission of the European Communities served subpoenas on the Paris office of the largest U.S. manufacturer (UCAR International) and the Wiebaden, Germany headquarters of Europe's largest company (SGL AG). Simultaneously U.S. investigators raided the offices of all the U.S., German, and Japanese companies that made graphite electrodes in the United States. Confronted with incriminating documents and the knowledge that Carbide/Graphite executives were prepared to testify about conspiracy meetings, Showa Denko Carbon, Inc. succumbed to the pressures exerted by prosecutors in February 1998. Showa Denko is the U.S. subsidiary of Showa Financing KK of Japan that manufactures graphite electrodes in a plant in Ridgefield, South Carolina. The company pleaded guilty and agreed to pay a fine of $29 million. In a speech a few months later, DOJ official Gary Spratling revealed that Showa Denko was offered a 60-percent discount from the $75-million fine specified under the U.S. Sentencing Guidelines. In fact, the range specified was from $65 to $135 million, so the discount may have been larger. Later in the year at a sentencing hearing in U.S. District Court in Philadelphia, the overseeing judge displayed a rare instance of judicial backbone in questioning prosecutorial discretion in the matter of Showa Denko's discount. In an even more rare event, Joel Klein appeared in court to argue the wisdom of the government's deal, but in the end the judge tacked on $3.5 million to Showa's fine.

Showa Denko was a small fish, but the big fish soon followed. In April 1998, UCAR International caved in and agreed to pay a fine of $110 million, a new record $10 million higher than ADM's fine imposed 18 months earlier.[11] UCAR's global market share of 31 percent made it the largest manufacturer of graphite electrodes in the world as well as the United States (41 percent share). All other things being the same, UCAR should have paid the largest fine, but because it cooperated earlier than the second-ranking member of the cartel, UCAR's record fine did not stand for long. Because of its recalcitrance and leadership in the cartel, SGL AG was fined even more – $135 million – in May 1999. By the end of the year three more small Japanese manufacturers of electrodes had pled guilty and paid fines. All told, six corporations were convicted and paid fines that totaled $291 million (Table 17.1). Although soon eclipsed by the sanctions on the vitamins cartel, the graphite electrodes case was the second most damaging conspiracy of the 1990s. The cartel overcharged its mini-steel-mill customers by at least 17%.[12] I estimate that the total U.S. fines paid in this case will reach about $400 million.

While the sanctions imposed on the corporate defendants were record-breaking, it is the sentences given to the individual conspirators that merit the most attention. Three executives were singled out by the DOJ for especially stiff sentences, very likely because they were the cartel's ringleaders. When SGL Carbon AG pleaded guilty in May 1999, its Chief Executive Officer Robert J. Koehler also pleaded guilty and agreed to pay a personal fine of $10 million. This fine was *29 times larger* than any previous personal U.S. fine for price fixing, and it is even more remarkable given that Koehler was a German citizen residing in Germany well beyond the reach of U.S. law.[13] Clearly Koehler had been fingered as the instigator and chief ringleader of the graphite electrodes cartel.

Table 17.1. Profile of the Graphite Electrode Market and Cartel.

Company (Country): Officers	Affected Sales 1992-1997				U.S. Antitrust Fines		Civil Penalties	
	Value		Shares					
	World	U.S.	World	U.S.	Double-the-Harm Guidelines[a]	Actually Paid	Paid to Buyers[b]	Derivative Suits[c]
	$ million		*Percent*		*Millions of dollars*			
UCAR International (U.S.):	543	300-450	31	41	250-500E	110.0	175.0E	40.5
Robert Krass						1.25		
Robert Hart						1.00		
SGL AG (Germany):	403	200-300	23	28	225-450E	135.0	174.2	0[f]
Robert Koehler						10.0		
Showa Denko (Japan)	150-200	100-150	8-10	10-15	65-135	32.5	32-48[h]	0[i]
Carbon/Graphite[d] (U.S)								
Tokai Carbon (Japan)								
SEC Corp. (Japan)	600-650	230-400	31-36	16-21	95-185E	13.3[f]	75-130E	5E
Nippon Carbon (Japan)								
Union Carbide (U.S.):[e]	--	--	--	--	75-150E	33-50E[g]	--	190E[g]
George Schwengler[e]						1-5E[g]		
Mitsubishi Corp. (Japan)[e]	--	--	--	--	75-150E	33-50E[g]	--	190E[g]
Total	1,750	700-1100	100	100	785-1,570	370-408	456-527	426

Sources: Tables 13.A.1 and 16.A.1.
E = Estimated by author.
-- = Not applicable.
[a] The U.S. overcharges were somewhere between 17 and 25 percent of affected sales, or $120 to $275 million. The U.S. Sentencing Guidelines would double the overcharge, multiply the result by 1.5 to 3.5 (depending on the degree of culpability), and prorate each company's fine range by its market share. SGL had the highest culpability score.
[b] Includes legal fees to class counsel of 22.5 percent of total settlement.
[c] Shareholders' suits for mismanagement (U.S. companies only).
[d] Carbon/Graphite was granted amnesty and paid no criminal fine.
[e] Indicted for criminal price fixing in January 2000 for years 1992-1995, when they controlled UCAR International.
[f] Paid by the Japanese firms only.
[g] Assumes that the three parties lose the criminal suit and are fined more than UCAR was per year; also assumes they lose the civil suit by plaintiff UCAR, which is expected to recover its fines and penalties.
[h] Showa will pay 25 percent of its $100 to $150 million in U.S. sales during the conspiracy.
[i] Derivative shareholders' suits are unlikely outside the U.S.

But Koehler could not have pulled off the conspiracy without the help of the number-one manufacturer in the world, UCAR International of Danbury, Connecticut. Just two weeks before UCAR International submitted its guilty plea to the courts, its two top executives suddenly resigned. They were Robert Krass, the company's President, CEO, and Chairman of the Board, and Robert J. Hart, UCAR's Chief Operating Officer. With UCAR fully cooperating with the DOJ's investigation, the two men finally agreed to plead guilty in September 1999 six months after their resignations. Not only did Krass and Hart receive long prison sentences (17 and nine months, respectively), but they also paid personal fines of $1.25 and $1.0 million. The fines paid by Koehler, Krass, and Hart were the first price fixing fines in history to surpass the $350,000 limit specified by the Sherman Act as amended in 1990. In other words, the DOJ had created a new precedent by implementing the federal felony guidelines for individuals rather than the lower statutory limit.[14] Now the DOJ has a much bigger stick to wield in its negotiations with individuals suspected of criminal price fixing violations.

As usual after criminal price fixing comes to light, private plaintiffs quickly organized civil suits seeking treble damages. The owners of mini steel mills were the principal buyers of graphite electrodes. Four days after UCAR International pleaded guilty, a civil damages suit was filed in federal court against the company. With affected U.S. sales of $700 to $1,100 million and overcharges of at least 17 percent, the treble damages created by the cartel were in the range of $350 to $825 million. UCAR, with 41 percent of the U.S. market had a liability of $145 to $340 million settlement; in fact, UCAR set aside a special antitrust contingency fund of $340 million. In less than four months UCAR announced agreements with about 75 percent of the private antitrust plaintiffs and a few buyers that chose not to sue. UCAR's proposed payment to these direct buyers was a relatively cheap $175 million. Six months later in December 1999, SGL announced that it had resolved nearly all U.S. civil antitrust claims against the company by offering to pay $135 million over a six year period to plaintiffs. (SGL's civil settlement was identical to its government fine). In addition, SGL said that it would pay $39.2 million immediately in legal fees (22.5 percent of the total settlement cost). Showa Denko Carbon (7 percent of market sales) became the second large electrode maker to settle with buyers in September 1998. It agreed to pay its steel-mill customers 25 percent of their 1992-1997 purchases or about $32 million. Thus, it appears from somewhat scattered information that the seven members of the cartel (including the amnestied Carbon/Graphite Group) will pay $400 to $527 million in civil damages to plaintiffs, or about 35 to 70 percent of their affected U.S. sales.[15]

SGL AG tried a legal maneuver to reduce its civil liability, but the tactic was unsuccessful. Although it was the German parent that accepted total responsibility for price fixing, it was SGL's U.S. subsidiary that became the defendant in the civil antitrust suits because it was SGL's U.S. sales that harmed U.S. buyers. SGL Carbon Corp. is a relatively small part of the global company. In early 1998, SGL filed for bankruptcy in Delaware, the state in which it is registered. SGL Carbon Corp. had only $124 million in assets at the time but was facing eventual claims in excess of its assets. While the District Court ruled initially in SGL's favor, in December 1999 the Third Circuit Court of Appeals overturned the decision. The appeals court said that SGL had acted in bad faith simply to get a quick, small settlement; SGL was in no imminent danger of failure. Thus, from now on antitrust defendants will have one less tactic to delay settlements.[16]

An interesting legal conflict developed between the government's prosecution of the electrodes cartel and civil litigants. In October 1998, the DOJ made a formal request of the supervising judge of the federal class to delay discovery in the civil suit. At this point, the three largest graphite-electrodes manufacturers had already pleaded guilty in the criminal case, but three more Japanese companies had yet to agree to plea. The DOJ argued that a delay in taking depositions for three and one-half months was necessary to avoid interference with grand jury testimony still to come. In particular, the DOJ argued that the civil depositions would witnesses the opportunity to tailor their subsequent criminal testimony to evidence revealed to them during the civil depositions.[17] This novel concern by the DOJ is certainly one argument for delaying civil discovery until completion of criminal grand jury investigations.

UCAR International has been strongly affected by events following the revelation of its leading role in the graphite-electrodes conspiracy. The loss of its top two officers has deprived the company of executive continuity. Derivative shareholders' suits were quite costly as well: $40.5 million was paid, of which UCAR's insurance policy covered only $25.5 million. Fines, settlements, and legal costs amounted to about $325 million. Smarting from these multiple blows, UCAR decided to take a novel legal path to restore its financial losses. UCAR is suing its two former parent companies to recover what it claims is $1.5 billion in damages, a figure that must include reputational as well as monetary losses.

The claim is made possible by a spin-off that occurred in 1994. UCAR International was a joint venture of Union Carbide and Mitsubishi Corporation in 1992 when the cartel is known to have begun fixing prices. In late 1994, UCAR was spun off as a separate entity, and after a period of ownership by a venture-capital firm went public in August 1995. UCAR also named as a defendant its CEO in 1992-1995 (a Union Carbide executive) and a Japanese executive of Mitsubishi who served on UCAR's board of directors as defendants. UCAR claims that the four defendants caused damages from initiating and carrying out the cartel scheme. Union Carbide responded that UCAR's suit was baseless extortion. However, a federal grand jury in January 2000 indicted Mitsubishi Corporation and one former UCAR executive for criminal price fixing, so UCAR's civil suit seemed to have some support. If the government prevails, total antitrust fines in the graphite-electrodes cases may mount to $408 million (Table 8.1). Moreover, if UCAR wins its suit, total civil settlements could easily reach $1 billion.

MORE CARTELS TO COME?

Perhaps the period 1995-2000 will be seen as an abnormal eruption of illegal activity followed by a return to normalcy, but that seem unlikely. The number of grand jury investigations was as high as ever in 2000. Moreover, the market conditions that in the past have given rise to the urge to conspire are as ripe as ever. Many homogeneous food-and-feed ingredients are made in industries with few sellers, many buyers, and selling conditions that obscure information about the terms of sale (prices, discounts, delivery terms, and so forth). Moreover, these industries are in many cases populated by companies with prior experience in illegally setting prices. If anything, the incidence of repeat offenders seems to be increasing over time. The chance of getting caught may have risen in the 1990s, but it is nowhere near zero and the monetary penalties in most cases are not large enough to overwhelm the probably profits. This section discusses some specific industries with a high likelihood of future cartel behavior.

Consider the five major commercially produced amino acids: lysine, methionine, monosodium gluconate (MSG), threonine, and tryptophan. All of these except the flavor-enhancer MSG are growth-regulating ingredients in animal feeds, and each of them is produced under economic conditions highly similar to lysine. ADM is reported to have begun production of threonine and tryptophan at its Decatur plant in the early 1990s. Ajinomoto is a leading producer of both amino acids and holds important patents on high yielding microorganisms used in making the two products. Another major manufacturer of these amino acids is Degussa. Although they are small industries compared with lysine, threonine and tryptophan consumption is reported to be growing faster than lysine. Given the conspiracy-prone behavior of the leading firms and the structure of these industries, conditions are ripe for cartels in the threonine and tryptophan markets.

Global demand for methionine is much larger. It is the first-limiting growth factor in poultry rations. World capacity is estimated to be more than 1 billion pounds in the late 1990s with nearly all world production in the hands of four companies. The leading manufacturer is Rhône-Poulenc (and ADM owns part of Rhône's U.S. facility), but Degussa is not far behind. Rhône-Poulenc and Degussa account for more than half of global capacity. Novus International, a U.S. subsidiary of Mitsui Co., has recently overtaken first place and is now in control of more than one-third of global production capacity. Sumitomo Chemical Co. of Japan makes about one-eighth of the world's methionine. ADM, Rhône-Poulenc, and Mitsui have each been convicted for price fixing in one or more food/feed ingredient cartel. List prices of methionine have in the 1990s ranged from about $1.30 to $1.80 per pound, but transaction prices seem to be closer to $1.00 to $1.20. Global demand in 1998 is estimated to be in the range of $750 to $1,000 million, with 35 to 40 percent of those sales in the United States. There is little or no reporting of methionine prices because most sales occur under bilateral private contracts.

These amino acids have competitive conditions strongly reminiscent of those in lysine. Indeed, in 1999 allegations surfaced of price fixing in methionine. In July 1999, a civil class action antitrust suit was filed in California with Rhône-Poulenc, Degussa, Mitsui, and Nippon Soda as defendants. Press reports suggest that an unannounced federal probe is under way. Finally, Degussa confirmed publicly that it was the subject of an EC Commission investigation into price fixing of methionine.

A product similar in functionality to citric acid is lactic acid. ADM announced that it was entering production of lactic acid in 1990; its 40-

million-pound plant came into production in 1993, narrowly beating to market a ConAgra-DuPont joint venture. Bayer's Haarmann & Reimer subsidiary made a small amount of lactic acid synthetically, but ADM's fermentation method allows it to claim to be the unique producer of natural lactic acid.[18] A pattern often observed in the corn wet milling industry is that of ADM and Cargill replicating each other's product lines. Lactic acid is no exception; Cargill entered this industry in the late 1990s.

Xanthan gum is another candidate for cartelization. It is widely used as a thickener in many processed foods as a substitute for natural gums that have unstable supply levels over time. In addition to feeds, xanthan gum has technical uses, including aiding petroleum companies in recovery of oil. The Nutrasweet unit of Monsanto is the world's dominant supplier, but two familiar companies also make xanthan: Jungbunzlauer and Rhône-Poulenc. In 1995, after years of technical production problems, ADM began making xanthan by fermentation, but its product is not yet pure enough to sell for food uses. Global demand in the late 1990s was around $250-350 million and growing quickly. In 1998, prices of xanthan gum rose almost 20 percent.

CORPORATE RECIDIVISM

This chapter completes the selective listing of global cartels discovered by antitrust prosecutors in the 1990s. The purpose of this chapter was to sketch the histories of cartels that were similar to those in lysine, citric acid, and vitamins. However, the selected conspiracies in this chapter brought forth one salient characteristic of global price fixing. When corporations with multiple lines of business enjoy the financial success that flows from a cartel in one line of business, it is likely to form or enter a cartel for another line of business.

Most of the companies convicted for global price fixing in the 1990s are diversified firms. Frequently, the cartelized product comprises only a tiny share of the company's total sales. As Table 17.2 shows, at least 13 multinational chemical or agribusiness companies engaged in multiple conspiracies. ADM, for example, was convicted for price fixing in two markets and was engaged in from two to five more conspiracies. The list of corporate "repeat-offenders" in Table 17.2 is hardly complete, but it does suggest the need for fine guidelines that explicitly raise fines in such cases.

Corporate conglomerization is a common feature on today's industrial landscape. Yet, an unfortunate side effect of diversification is the tendency for the price fixing disease to spread among a company's many organs.

Table 17.2. Corporate Recidivism in Global Price Fixing, 1990s.

Company	Cartel Membership	
	Convictions	Second Convictions, Targets, or Antitrust Defendants[a]
Archer Daniels Midland	Lysine	Citric acid Sodium gluconate Monosodium glutamate High fructose corn syrup? Methionine? Sorbates?
Hoffmann-La Roche	Citric acid	Several vitamins
Rhône-Poulenc	Vitamin A Vitamin E	Methionine
Degussa-Hüls	Vitamin B3	Methionine
Jungbunzlauer	Citric acid	Sodium gluconate
Roquette Freres	Citric acid	Sodium gluconate High fructose corn syrup?
Akzo Nobel	Dynamite	Sodium gluconate
Hoechst	Vitamin B12	Sorbates
Pfizer	Citric acid (1986-1990)	Sorbates? Sodium erythorbate Maltol
Ajinomoto	Lysine	Monosodium glutamate?
Cheil Jedang	Lysine	Monosodium glutamate?
Sewon/Miwon	Lysine	Monosodium glutamate?
Takeda Chemical	Vitamins	Monosodium glutamate?

[a] In some cases the companies are targets of an on-going government investigation, which indicates probable cause for price fixing. The entries with question marks are cases with civil complaints filed or inferences from guilty pleas.

Chapter 17 Endnotes

[1] However, it should be recognized that the distinction between the public and private spheres was not the bright line that it would become under constitutional monarchies or republics.
[2] The definition now used turns on the concept of an "involved party" – a potential or actual subject or target of any investigation or case. An international matter is one in which an involved party is a non-U.S. citizen or non-U.S. business, the alleged conduct occurred outside U.S. territory, relevant information is located outside the U.S., or substantive consultation with foreign agencies took place.
[3] Another minor salt of gluconic acid is potassium gluconate. The only known producer of potassium gluconate is Jungbunzlauer International made in its French plant.
[4] The market shares mentioned here are based on a Statement of Facts by the Canadian Ministry of Justice. Because Canada had no domestic production, the "global shares" may be more representative of North America and Europe than of the whole world. In the United States, trade sources estimated that PMP held 50% and Glucona 25% of the market.
[5] This private deal was not much mentioned in the trade press. In fact, the first reference to ADM's participation in sodium gluconate was a 1995 article in *Chemical Market Reporter* speculating that ADM "may enter" the business. ADM actually decided to *exit* in 1995.
[6] These are the dates given in the Canadian government's Statement of Facts. In the United States, the dates given are August 1993 to June 1995. The latter period seems to correspond to the dates of ADM's U.S. production. The small size of the industry coupled with the short time period accounts for the small size of ADM's civil settlement.
[7] The fact that Jungbunzlauer paid *no* U.S. fines but paid the *largest* Canadian fine is quite puzzling given the company's 12% world share.
[8] Trade magazines reported global demand in 1998 to be about 100 million pounds, of which 33 to 38% was sold in the U.S. market. However the U.S. DOJ's press release places U.S. sales at only 8% of 1996 global sales of $50 million. Canadian sales 1987-1995 averaged $0.6 million annually, suggesting that U.S. sales were $6 to $8 million in 1996.
[9] In October 1999, Hoechst and Eastman Chemical were fined C$2.25 and C$0.8 million, respectively, by the Canadian competition-law authorities.
[10] Eastman Chemical exited the sorbates industry in early 2000. In a statement that elicited skepticism in the trade press, Eastman said that its conviction played no role in the decision.
[11] UCAR's fine was the highest in nominal dollar terms, but its precarious financial condition forced it to request an installment payment. In real terms, ADM's was probably slightly higher.
[12] SGL clearly received the harshest fine ($135 million). With 23 percent of the U.S. market and affected sales of $1.75 billion, SGL's fine was 34 percent of affected sales. Thus, double the harm was the guideline used, not the alternative 20-percent standard.
[13] European Commission officials had raided SGL's headquarters in Wiesbaden, but it is not clear that they would have helped the U.S. Justice Department extradite Koehler. In the U.S., Koehler would face criminal charges, whereas under EU law no prison terms can be given for violating its competition law. It is noteworthy that SGL's U.S. subsidiary (SGL Carbon Corp. of North Carolina) was not charged, only the German parent company. This implies that the parent ran the conspiracy from Germany.
[14] The felony guidelines permit the government to seek individual fines of up to 5 percent of the affected sales of a conspiracy. UCAR's U.S. sales during the cartel were $718 million, so the maximum fine could have reached $36 million were it not for the $350,000 cap.
[15] The large range is the result of lack of knowledge about the size of the U.S. market. Also, the three smallest Japanese firms were U.S. importers with few U.S. assets, so civil plaintiffs may get little from them.

[16] Unfortunately, the appeals court decision came three weeks too late for all but three plaintiffs suing SGL.
[17] Two Japanese exporters did not plead guilty until 13 months later.
[18] Sold to Tate & Lyle in 1997.

Chapter 18

THE BUSINESS OF FIGHTING CARTELS

A BOON FOR LAW FIRMS

The proliferation of cartels in the 1990s has generated large fees for law firms with expertise in antitrust law. Large civil settlements mean large legal fees for plaintiffs' law firms. The antitrust revenues of major U.S. law firms reached historic highs (*The National Journal* July 15, 2000). At one leading firm with 120 antitrust lawyers, antitrust revenues were $64 million in 1999, up 13-fold from 1992. Five U.S. law firms employed from 100 to 150 antitrust lawyers each, most of them working in Washington, D.C. or New York City. Most of the work was generated by merger approvals; merger filings, of which there 5000 in 1999, cost the firms from $1 to $5 million in legal fees. Price fixing conspiracies probably rank second in antitrust revenues. The global scope of the cartels has stimulated U.S. law firms to expand abroad. Several U.S. firms now derive more than one-quarter of their revenues from work outside the United States.

Formerly derided for drumming up business in a manner akin to that of personal-injury lawyers, antitrust plaintiffs attorneys are now increasingly accorded somewhat greater respect for their skills and methods of operation. Instead of being pejoratively referred to as "ambulance-chasers," they are now more often described as entrepreneurial firms assisting social justice.

The elevated stature of antitrust plaintiffs' counsel is illustrated by a lengthy admiring profile of attorney Michael Hausfeld in the *Wall Street Journal* (January 4, 2000). His firm, Cohen Milstein, has been involved in high profile civil lawsuits against handgun manufacturers, German companies that enslaved workers during World War II, Swiss banks that did not return the assets of victims of the Nazi holocaust, and oil companies accused of causing pollution. Hausfeld calls these actions "social reform" class-action suits because they can mitigate injuries not being addressed by legislatures or regulatory agencies. More conservative publications refer to Hausfeld as a "corporate shakedown artist." Hausfeld, together with well known lawyers David Boies and Kenneth Adams, led the civil treble-damages lawsuit against the vitamin cartel. In that case, plaintiffs were represented by 18 law firms, while the six defendants had hired at least 42 firms.

Plaintiffs' law firms almost inevitably represent buyers on a contingency basis, which implies that the firms must bare the costs of prosecuting a case for up to three or four years for uncertain future rewards. Contingency fees may be negotiated by the clients, but most antitrust plaintiffs join a federal class whose legal fees will be determined by a supervising judge. The traditional system of contingency fees rewards plaintiffs' counsel with a fixed percentage of the settlement amounts won by the plaintiffs. This system encourages attorneys to settle for the highest amount that defendants can be persuaded to pay yet also provides incentives to economize by settling prior to a drawn out court battle.

Table 18.1 contains a list of civil antitrust price fixing cases for which information is available on attorney fees. In a sample of class-action suits from the 1970s and 1980s, Elzinga and Wood found that legal fees and costs[1] averaged $190,000 per case. While these fees may seem rather modest, so were the average value of the settlements – only $640,000 per case. That is, on average legal fees represented about 30 percent of the total awards made to private treble-damages recipients, or 42 percent of the net recovery to the plaintiffs. However, the rest of table 18.1 shows that the larger the size of a recovery, the smaller the ratio of legal costs to recovery amount. Moreover, the largest settlements tend to have been made in more recent years. Indeed, for the top eight settlements the legal-fees percentages are only one-sixth to one-half the rates found by Elzinga and Wood (1988). Thus, it appears that there are fixed costs in representing a civil treble-damages case, or at least some threshold level under which most law firms choose not to accept this type of legal action.

Many legal writers and federal judges have expressed concerns about excessive legal fees in class action cases. The decline in the percentage of settlement awards paid out as legal fees probably represents in part a reaction against perceived over-generous awards in the past. Some judges have tinkered with various methods of calculating fees and costs in order to develop fairer decision rules. Some years ago judges seem to favor the "loadstar" method, which required plaintiffs attorneys to submit timesheets and other cost documentation. However, the loadstar method cannot address the issues of fair hourly rates or reasonable profit rates.

In the lysine case, the supervising judge implemented a novel fixed-fee auction to keep legal costs low, but the perverse incentives introduced by a fixed-fee approach were fairly widely condemned (see Chapter 16). Overall, the tide seems to be turning back toward approving percentage contingency fees or fee amounts arrived at by negotiation with the parties to the suit. However, in a treble-damages price-fixing case settled in late 2000, customers of two New York City auction houses were represented by class counsel chosen by an auction operated by the supervising federal judge (*Wall Street Journal* December 6, 2000). Instead of bidding fixed fees, law firms submitted minimum amounts of recovery guaranteed to the plaintiffs; the amounts of the settlement above that minimum were used to generate legal fees at a rate of 25 percent. This type of auction preserves the incentive of class counsel to bargain for the highest possible recovery for the plaintiffs while simultaneously insuring relatively low percentages are paid to class counsel.[2]

There are free-rider issues in setting legal fees in class action suits generally. When a large number of geographically dispersed suits are consolidated and certified as a federal class, a "lead" firm or small number of firms is designated to represent the entire class. If the class is composed of a large number of small plaintiffs this arrangement works quite well. However, typically there is a wide range of sizes of buyers, and the interests of small and large buyers diverge. In nearly all the civil cartel cases examined in this book, many large plaintiffs opted out of the class because they wanted a larger recovery and they could afford to pay for high quality legal representation. In the most extreme case, buyers of bulk vitamins that accounted for three-fourths of purchases opted out of the federal class. As a result the opt-outs became free riders on the efforts of lead class counsel because the latter helped establish a floor on settlement rates. The plaintiffs who stayed in the class essentially ended up paying for legal services that the opt-outs benefited from.

The vitamins case illustrates a curious reversal of the usual free-rider phenomenon. In that class action, the federal judge overseeing the case approved legal fees of $122 million for about 60 law firms that represented direct buyers of bulk vitamins (Table 18.1). Those fees were a modest percentage of the recovery to be paid out to class plaintiffs. However, most of the larger plaintiffs became convinced that the settlement was far too low (about 20 percent of affected U.S. sales) compared to treble damages computed by their economist experts (about 100 percent of sales). In March 2000, some 200 plaintiffs representing 76 percent of vitamin purchases opted out. Because of an unusual *reverse* most-favored-nation clause in the settlement, the opt-ins will have their recovery increased if the opt-outs negotiate a more generous settlement rate.[3] Should this happen, the small plaintiffs who stayed in the class may become free riders on the legal costs of the opt-outs. Why the judge would approve legal fees for a rump class is most puzzling; the fees are likely to climb to about 45 percent of class recovery.

In examining the available data on legal fees, it must be kept in mind that not all treble-damages filings result in settlements of any kind. In these situations, the law firms obtain no revenue for their time and expenses. In addition, many cases are settled out of court before a class is approved, and on such cases virtually no information is available on legal fees.

Finally, legal costs are incurred by the defendants. By their very nature, defendants tend to be large companies with lots of experience in defending themselves from allegations of many kinds. Most have in-house counsel for routine matters, but when defending themselves on matters involving large liability tend to hire additional outside counsel. In the cartel cases examined in this book, defendants availed themselves of the most prominent and high priced U.S. antitrust law firms. Moreover, unless they were granted amnesty, defendants had to defend themselves in a legal war that had three fronts: prosecution by government antitrust agencies in as many as ten jurisdictions, civil suits by direct buyers in several nations, and civil suits by indirect buyers in up to 16 U.S. state courts.

Table 18.1. Legal Fees in Major U.S. Class-Action Price-Fixing Awards, 1972-1999.

Name of Case	Total Settlement Amounts		Fees as a percent of recovery
	Net Recovery	Legal Fees and Costs	
	Million dollars		*Percent*
1. NASDAQ Market Makers (1999)	1,123	147	13.1
2. Vitamins (1999-2000)	1,170[f]	122	10.5
3. Brand Name Prescription Drugs (1999)	723	NA	NA
4. Corrugated Containers	550	44	8.0
5. Heavy Electrical Equipment (1961-64)[b]	405	41E	10.1
6. Lysine and Citric Acid (1966)	321	50E	15.6
7. Folding Carton[c]	218	14	6.6
8. Plywood (1983)	171	26	14.9
9. Petroleum Products	140	29	21.0
10. Infant Formula (1993, federal)[d]	126	33	26.3
11. Antibiotics	87	29	33.3
12. Travel Agency Commissions	90	22	28.3
13. New Mexico Natural Gas	81	11	14.0
14. Fine Paper	80	10	12.7
15. Gypsum	75	9	12.4
16. Sugar - Western Cases	60	10	17.1
17. Superior Beverage	58	18	31.2
18. Carbon Dioxide	53	10	18.0
19. Red Eagle Resources	53	19	35.9
20. Chlorine & Caustic Soda	53	12	22.8
21. Workers' Compensation	50	12	24.7
22. Cumberland Farms	50	14	27.2
23. Industrial Gas	50	12	24.5
Average treble damages[e]	0.45	0.19	42.2

Sources: Shepherd (1985); Class Action Reports, Inc. (1999) "Attorney Fee Study;" Table 4 and Lexis-Nexis.

E = Estimates, NA = Not Available.

[a] "Recovery" is the total amount of monetary damages paid by the antitrust defendants to the plaintiffs. Legal fees and costs go to the attorneys representing the class. It does not include settlements made by defendants with plaintiffs who opted out of the class. On average, costs represented 8% of legal fees and costs, but in some cases no costs were awarded.

[b] Estimate contained in Shepherd (1985) of the results of about 1,900 private suits, only some of which were class actions. The bidding ring consisted of 29 companies. Public prosecution netted $1.9 million in fines and conviction of 45 company officers. Collusion involved seven products over "decades."
[c] Collusion among 23 manufacturers during 1960-1974 in a market with $1 billion in sales in 1974.
[d] In addition, the three formula manufacturers paid $200 million in a Florida class action suit (1993) and in 1996 paid $33 million to 17 states for overcharging state WIC programs.
[e] Average of 49 cases collected by Elzinga and Wood (1988).
[f] Amount announced November 1999. Until a formula for dispersal is agreed upon, interest will accrue, raising the eventual payout. In February 2000, some 225 members of the class accounting for 75% of purchases left the class.

Consequently, defendants' legal costs were often higher than the legal fees awarded plaintiffs' counsel. ADM, for example, had to retain multiple law firms to defend itself in the government's criminal cases (lysine and citric acid), two parallel federal civil cases, state-level indirect buyers' suits, and derivative shareholders' suits; ADM's executives were provided with separate counsel, as was its board of directors. ADM's total legal expenses for antitrust amounted to at least $50 million. If other defendants in the lysine, citric acid, and vitamins cases paid proportional amounts, scores of defendant's law firms benefited to the tune of about $180 million. Law firms representing private plaintiffs probably received 15 to 20 percent of the settlements in the same three global cartel cases, or $350 to $450 million. Therefore, not counting the modest costs of DOJ prosecution, these three cartel cases conservatively generated a total of $530 to $630 million in gross revenues for the U.S. law firms representing plaintiffs and defendants.

Doubtless many will regard such enormous sums as sad evidence of a hyper litigious society. They *are* wasteful expenditures in the sense that many were incurred simply to cancel the effects of expenditures by parties on the other side of the dispute. However, in the end most of the legal expenses were simply a necessary outgrowth of constitutionally guaranteed rights to due legal process. And as high as they were, these legal transactions costs may be low when compared to the economic costs of the alternatives: monopolistic distortions in affected markets or regulatory approach that requires regulatory commissions for price controls.

CAN THE ANTITRUST AGENCIES COPE?

The Antitrust Division of the U.S. Department of Justice is a small agency as federal agencies go. In federal fiscal year 1998, the Division had 831 positions authorized to be filled (51 fewer than in fiscal 1980) and a budget of $93 million. The Division's resources were cut mercilessly during the early years of the Reagan presidency but has recovered slowly during the

1990s. The Bush and Clinton administrations proposed modest but real increases for antitrust enforcement, and the Judiciary Committee of the U.S. Senate has typically endorsed the administrations' budget proposals. Support in the U.S. House of Representatives had typically been more tepid, but often for reasons related to overall budget considerations rather than lack of support for law enforcement.

The Antitrust Division's workload report for the federal fiscal years 1990-1999 demonstrates an increasing number of heavy tasks. The Division initiated an average of 88 new price fixing investigations each year in the 1990s.[4] At the same time the number of merger investigations rose to new heights throughout the decade, averaging nearly 250 per year during 1996-1999 (Antitrust Division 1999). When the preliminary evidence warrants it, the DOJ sets up grand juries to investigate the most serious price fixing cases. In the late 1990s, the Division set up about 20 to 30 new grand juries each year but because the grand juries often remained active for a few years, there were about 100 of them handling pending criminal investigations. On average in the late 1990s, these grand jury deliberations resulted in 40 to 60 criminal cases being filed annually against corporations or individuals. More than 90 percent of all criminal cases filed by the Division are price fixing cases,[5] and slightly less than 90 percent of all price fixing cases are filed as criminal rather than civil matters. While most price fixing cases are settled by plea agreements rather than formal bench trials, the negotiations leading to pleas are often lengthy and arduous.

The DOJ is the major bulwark against naked price fixing conspiracies, particularly the more intricate and challenging global conspiracies. There are several other federal agencies entrusted with enforcement of U.S. antitrust laws, the largest being the Federal Trade Commission. The FTC has a similar level of resources for antitrust work (it also has a mission for consumer protection), but suffers one great disadvantage in its formal legal powers compared to the DOJ. The FTC is a civil agency and cannot therefore file criminal indictments under the Sherman Act. The grand jury system, with its formidable prosecutorial and investigative powers, is available only to the DOJ among the federal antitrust agencies.[6] Each of the attorneys general of the 50 states has the legal authority to prosecute cartels, but as global cartels are almost inevitably engaged in interstate trade, federal authority trumps that of the states in criminal matters.

The Federal Trade Commission prosecuted only one major price fixing case in the 1990s, but the outcome of the case will have significant implications for the FTC's ability to seek monetary remedies. *FTC v. Mylan Laboratories Inc.*, filed in December 1998, charged Mylan with monopolization and restraint of trade in the market for two popular anti-anxiety medications. The FTC's complaint says that Mylan in 1997 signed exclusive ten-year contracts with two manufacturers of the active ingredients used in the drugs, one of which is made in Italy. The two suppliers are to receive percentages of Mylan's gross profits under the license contracts. A few months later Mylan increased the wholesale prices of the drugs by 1,935 to 3,200 percent. The FTC argues that Mylan was able to raise the prices so precipitously because other sellers were unable to obtain additional supplies of the active ingredients.

The principal legal issue is the type of relief being sought by the FTC. Normally, the agency seeks only injunctive relief (cease-and-desist orders) in antitrust cases, leaving restitution of monetary damages to the outcome of civil suits. However, in this case the FTC was also seeking monetary damages (technically disgorgement of illicit profits) of $120 million, an action nearly unprecedented in rule-of-reason price fixing prosecutions.[7] The FTC traditionally seeks restitution only in consumer-protection allegations, but in *Mylan Laboratories* argued that a 1975 amendment to the FTC Act permits seeking restitution for unfair acts that injure consumers. In July 1999, the presiding district judge agreed with the FTC, thus granting the agency a major new weapon in its fight against price fixing conspiracies that are more subtle than the naked cartels being pursued by the DOJ.

In the late 1990s, the DOJ faced what experienced legal experts were calling an "explosion of international criminal antitrust enforcement" (Adler and Laing 1997). During 1987-1990 *no* antitrust defendants were foreign companies or persons. In fiscal 1991, ten percent of all corporate antitrust defendants in cartel cases were foreign; by the late 1990s almost 50 percent of the corporate defendants in criminal cartel cases were foreign. At the beginning of 1998, Joel Klein testified that one-third of all the criminal investigations on-going at the Antitrust Division were international cartels (Klein 1998).[8] The more than 25 grand juries focused on global cartels had identified target companies in 20 countries. By all accounts, global price fixing cases are the most challenging type faced by the DOJ. Their offshore locations make their activities harder to detect and investigate than purely domestic cartels. In addition, once charges are brought, the typically large overcharges makes defendants more tenacious in defending themselves.

On the other hand, two developments in the 1990s have made prosecution of cartels somewhat easier for the DOJ. First, the 1993 revisions to its Leniency Program have borne fruit (ICPAC 2000). The global cartels in marine transportation services, graphite electrodes, bromines, and most importantly vitamins were brought to the attention of the DOJ by cartel participants that were granted amnesty for their cooperation. Other firms were granted lesser degrees of leniency for their early cooperation. The fact that amnesty for antitrust violators is automatic under certain conditions increased the number of applications for and grants of amnesty and thereby reduced the resources necessary to obtain convictions (see box). In 1998, more than 20 amnesty applications were received by the DOJ.

The U.S Antitrust Leniency Program

The present program was developed and put in place by the Antitrust Division in August 1993 under the leadership of Anne Bingaman. Amnesty will be granted to a company and all its employees if the company meets five conditions. The firm must (1) approach the DOJ before the agency has opened an investigation, (2) have stopped colluding, (3) confess to corporate guilt (rather than blame a rogue employee), (4) show that it was not the originator of the conspiracy and not the "enforcer" of cartel discipline, and (5) agree to full cooperation from all its employees. If condition (1) is not met, the firm may still be offered leniency but full amnesty is unlikely and a guilty plea will be necessary.

Automatic leniency is a powerful temptation for guilty price fixers to accept because it practically guarantees no fines. However, the DOJ cannot insulate an amnestied firm from civil damages or prosecution by overseas antitrust agencies. The DOJ program is unique in the federal government.

In 1999, the Leniency Program was further amended. In the late 1990s the DOJ noticed that more than half of its investigations into international cartels had been initiated by questioning a cooperating witness about cartel activities in unrelated industries. One example related in this book is the FBI's discovery of the citric acid conspiracy from statements made by its cooperating witness, Mark Whitacre in its lysine investigation (Chapter 5). The new policy, called "Amnesty Plus," tries to encourage amnesty applications from targets of ongoing investigations. If a corporate or individual target of an investigation into industry A does not qualify for amnesty (perhaps because it fails the "first in" test in industry A), the DOJ encourages the target to inform prosecutors about possible antitrust violations in industry B. If the target is the first to inform the DOJ about a cartel in industry B and meets certain other mandatory conditions, then the target will be guaranteed amnesty for its conduct in industry B and will also receive a substantial *additional* discount on a fine for its violation in industry A. This new policy appears to be a reasonable refinement of the amnesty program that has the potential for increasing the proportion of discovered caters and will substantially lower the costs of investigating global cartels. The Amnesty Program is understandably popular with members of the private antitrust bar (ICPAC 2000).

When full amnesty is not available, the DOJ has been successful in offering reduced sentences to targets in return for useful information about co-conspirators or for help in securing the guilty pleas of resisting cartel participants. One instance of the latter help occurred in the citric acid investigation. Bayer Corp.'s U.S. subsidiary Haarmann & Reimer was instrumental in persuading the two cartel members with the smallest sales (Jungbunzlauer and Hoffmann-La Roche) to negotiate guilty pleas with the

DOJ. As a consequence, Bayer was rewarded with a substantially reduced fine below U.S. Sentencing Guidelines levels. Another important concession that the DOJ can offer to targets of global cartel activity is to recommend to the Immigration and Naturalization Service that an executive convicted for price fixing be allowed continued freedom to cross U.S. borders; the DOJ will delay the individual's guilty plea until he receives positive assurances about his visa status. ICPAC (2000) notes that such concessions were

> ". . . instrumental in every international antitrust matter . . . [because] freedom to travel into and out of the United States [is] important to every foreign individual's decision to cooperate with the U.S. government . . ." (Chapter 4, p.12).

Besides the INS, the Antitrust Division has improved coordination with many other federal agencies in cartel investigations.

Second, the U.S. government has made substantial progress in signing protocols, cooperation agreements, and formal treaties that can facilitate international cooperation in antitrust matters between the DOJ and its sister organizations abroad. These new instruments supplement traditional international law mechanisms such as diplomatic channels. In 1994, the Antitrust Division secured evidence in the *Thermal Fax Paper* and *Industrial Diamonds* cases from Japanese and Belgian law-enforcement agencies, respectively. In addition to investigatory cooperation with EC authorities, the Japan Fair Trade Commission (JFTC) investigated six manufacturers of graphite electrodes for conspiring to cartelize the relevant Japanese market. In March 1999, the JFTC issued warnings to the six companies and probably issued an "administrative guidance" to discontinue the conduct (ICPAC 2000). The JFTC usually uses warnings when its investigation fails to turn up sufficient evidence to litigate a case but it believes that there is probable cause of a violation.

As of January 2000, the United States had signed 30 Mutual Legal Assistance Treaties (MLATs) that can be used for antitrust purposes.[9] There have been several instances in which MLATs have been used to conduct simultaneous executions of subpoenas, search warrants, or witness interviews in international cartel matters (ICPAC 2000). In addition, bilateral antitrust cooperation protocols have been signed by the DOJ with sister agencies in Canada, Brazil, Japan, Israel, Germany, and the EU that permit limited forms of enforcement cooperation. The biggest limitation to international antitrust cooperation has been in sharing confidential business information, particularly when such information has been obtained through compulsory legal processes. Other statutes typically block the DOJ from sharing such information with foreign competition-law agencies and *vice-versa*. A 1994 U.S. law does give the DOJ limited rights to share confidential information, but only where the offer can be reciprocated.

On balance, these new instruments have helped DOJ investigations of global cartels in precious few instances, and they rarely prove crucial to the outcome (ICPAC 2000). Indeed, compared to the number of matters in which international agreements have helped there are significantly more antitrust matters that have been stalled by the inability of the DOJ to access information or witnesses located abroad. However, there is a very positive interaction between the Division's Leniency Program and obtaining relevant overseas evidence. When a target of a global cartel investigation *voluntarily* agrees to cooperate, then the legal barriers tò obtaining relevant information abroad appear to melt away. Officials in foreign jurisdictions can and do cooperate without any offense to their sovereign rights. In sum, it is mostly the unilateral efforts of U.S. antitrust authorities that are succeeding in overcoming tradition barriers to international antitrust-law enforcement.

Although the leniency program and enhanced international cooperation has resulted in less effort in the investigatory phase of U.S. anti-cartel enforcement, these innovations are only a partial answer to serious under-funding of the Antitrust division. With record numbers of mergers being processed and big cases like that against Microsoft demanding attention, the Division's employees are in danger of being overworked or potential antitrust violations going uninvestigated. In 1999, the American public was treated to the unprecedented spectacle of the Department of Justice's own lawyers suing the Department because they were overworked and underpaid. Department managers seemed not to be wholly unsympathetic to their employees' plight.

If the two federal antitrust agencies in the United States seem starved for resources, the situation in the European Union is many times worse. In 2000, the European Commission's DG-IV had a mere 80 experts employed in Brussels. Yet, the EU covers an economic space that is just about the size of North America, and the Directorate must respond to almost as many merger proposals as do the two U.S. antitrust agencies. Moreover, the DG-IV is hobbled by legal rules that severely limit its powers to conduct investigations. Search warrants must be coordinated with the national courts, not the European Court of Justice. Moreover, the EC has no authority to search places that are not places of business, which may explain why the vitamin conspirators began meeting in private homes late in the cartel's life. Finally, the EC investigators can only ask questions about documents in their possession; they may not ask general questions about targeted individuals' behavior or whereabouts. In late 2000, the EC's Competition Commissioner, Mario Monti, asked for expanded staff and investigatory powers, but in an era when governments face rising "anti-globalization" sentiments, approval of these needed improvements is far from certain.

ARE NEW LAWS NEEDED?

The Sherman Act became 110 years old in the year 2000. Section One of the Act that governs cartel violations has remained virtually unchanged since 1890. Only the wording that refers to penalties having been adjusted over time. The U.S. penalties currently available for antitrust enforcement, particularly for criminal felony cases, are already the harshest in the world even though they are rarely applied to the fullest extent possible. In addition, civil penalties can be applied in treble damages cases that on paper are also the toughest in the world, though the settlements never seem to approach even half the levels authorized by the law. Although the DOJ investigates more allegations of global price fixing than it prosecutes, it can rightly point to a long string of successful prosecutions with quantitatively impressive sanctions. The Advisory Committee established by the DOJ to consider international competition policy made no recommendations for new laws or significant changes in anticartel enforcement procedures (ICPAC 2000).

There are perhaps a few proposals for improvement of U.S. anticartel enforcement that might require changes in the law. First, Joel I. Klein, head of the Antitrust Division, has proposed in testimony before the U.S. Senate Subcommittee on Antitrust that the *statutory* limit on corporate fines be raised from $10 million to $100 million. Since the DOJ has already obtained four fines of $100 million or more, why is it necessary? One reason is the fact that the prosecution of global cartels has revealed market sizes and monopoly overcharges that produce illegal gains far in excess of $10 million per firm in an alarming number of cases. The many fines above $10 million imposed on cartel participants have not been the result of litigation, rather, they have been the product of voluntary plea negotiations. Without the statutory authority to propose more than $10 million, in a full-blown court proceeding a judge might well bridle at the prospect of imposing a larger fine, even where a company's gains from the cartel exceeded $10 million. Raising the corporate fine limits to $100 million would give the DOJ greater leverage in plea negotiations, because at present many defendants are probably being advised that by going to court their monetary losses may be less. The same observation applies to the paltry $350,000 limit on the statutory personal antitrust fine. Despite the seriousness of the global cartels' infractions, executives engaged in price fixing have only in two cases negotiated fines above $350,000. In several cases, it is quite likely that cartel participants enjoyed stock options, bonuses, and promotions that had monetary values raised by their division's high, monopoly-induced profits.

An alternative to changing the statutory fines would be for Congress to clarify when the alternative sentencing provisions must override the statutory provisions. The first and so far only occasion on which the government sought personal fines for price fixing that exceeded the statutory level was in the lysine trial, *U.S. v Michael Andreas* (see Chapter 6). In that sentencing decision, the judge applied the U.S. Sentencing Guidelines to calculate the three defendants' prison sentences but declined to apply them to calculate the fine (Manning June 2, 1999). There are actually two alternative fine provisions provided in the law (Brown and Singhvi 1998: Section V). First, there is Section R of the U.S. Sentencing Guidelines, which states rather simply:

> "For an individual, the guideline fine range shall be from one to five percent of the volume of commerce, but not less than $20,000" (§R1.1(c)1).

Our purpose of the 1987 guidelines was to increase the penalties for antitrust violations to levels higher than those available under traditional sentencing when the size of the crime warranted it. Another purpose was to reduce judicial discretion in sentencing. In the lysine case, both sides had stipulated that the volume of commerce was $193 million, so the implied fine would have been $1.9 to $9.7 million for the two chief defendants, Andreas and Wilson. Congress can easily amend this section by raising the $350,000 cap on individuals to, say, $5 or $10 million.

Instead of using the sentencing guidelines, the government decided to make an example of Andreas and Wilson by seeking fines under the second alternative, the 1994 amendment to the Sherman Act that elevated criminal violations to felonies (18 U.S.C. § 3571(d)). According to Brown and Singhvi (1998):

> ". . . if the illegal conduct results in a pecuniary gain to the offender or a pecuniary loss to a person other than the offender, the fines may exceed the statutory limit to . . . twice the amount of the loss caused, unless such a provision would 'unduly complicate or prolong the sentencing process'" (p. 495).

Thus, this law as currently written seems to give *more* discretion to judges than they had before 1994 by allowing them to choose between the statutory range ($20,000 to $350,000) or the twice-the-harm amendment (in large industries up to $25,000,000).

The clear intent of Congress in the 1987 sentencing guidelines was to make federal sentencing more uniform and, for antitrust offenses at least, harsher. The intent of the 1994 amendment was clearly the same: make a "white-collar" crime like price fixing more similar to other felonies and to increase the penalties. Yet, at least two court decisions regarding the guidelines have interpreted the lower statutory fines as preempting higher fines calculated under Section R (*Edwards v. U.S.* and *U.S. v. Petty*). In *U.S. v. Michael Andreas* the judge first decided that §3571(d) was the controlling statute:

> "The alternative fines are intended to apply unless exempted by the governing statute . . . Congress saw fit not to exempt the Sherman Act . . . " (Manning Feb. 2, 1999:7).

Yet four months later the judge got cold feet. The major reason given for the reversal was the government's failure to produce uniform accounting records of production of lysine in every lysine factory in the world, data the defendants claimed was essential to their case.[10] Although that was given prominence in the opinion, the real reasons seem to be fear of economics, anger at the prosecutors, and anxiety about being the first judge to apply the alternative fines. Congress can correct the excessive discretionary power of judges by changing the word "may" to "shall" and listing narrow exemptions.

Another small, but useful expansion of U.S. antitrust-enforcement effectiveness could be effected by allowing the Federal Trade Commission to prosecute hard-core cartels as criminal matters. The FTC is at present not only restrained in its ability to sanction violators but also in the methods of investigation. As a civil-law agency, the FTC cannot make use of the grand-jury system and associated investigative powers. Excluding the FTC from pursuing global cartels is a pity because the agency has considerable expertise in many of the industries that have been cartelized in the 1990s, including most food-related industries.

A third improvement in anticartel enforcement involves the role of information. The DOJ tends to move more quickly than most other competition-law agencies around the world. The contrast with the secretive, lumbering investigative methods of the European Commission's competition directorate is particularly stark. Yet, compared to the detail offered by the Canadian Ministry of Justice, the DOJ is perhaps unnecessarily tight-lipped. The plea agreements, briefs, indictments, press releases, and other sources of information from the DOJ seem to be tailored to offer the absolute minimum of facts about the defendants or convicted parties in a global cartel. Briefs are often heavily redacted. Press meetings and interviews of prosecutors yield a similar dearth of details to the public, and penetrating questions are often evaded or unanswered completely in the name of on-going investigations. In many instances concerns about premature release of information that could jeopardize investigations or clandestine negotiations is well justified. Moreover, DOJ officials are bound by agreements not to release certain commercial trade secrets for firms that are targets of an investigation or defendants in antitrust cases.[11] As a result of this official reticence, parties unrelated to a global price fixing matter learn only about the bare bones of the living, breathing organism that was a cartel: names, titles, and residence of defendants; a list of generic illegal behaviors that hardly varies from one conspiracy to another; the identity of the product; and the minimal time spread of the conspiracy.

The Canadian model seems worthy of imitation. When a conviction has been secured, the Ministry of Justice issues a Statement of Facts about the case. In addition to the type of information released routinely by the U.S. DOJ, Canada's reports provide details about a defendant's sales, total Canadian sales, a description of the special role played by various participants, and more concrete descriptions of the illegal conduct. Unlike in the United States, unindicted co-conspirators are named. There is sometimes a justification provided about the size of fines extracted. All in all, these statements are more satisfying as public accounts of the Ministry's actions because they give citizens enough facts to make their own subjective evaluations of the justness of the punishments. The reports are a way to come to closure and provide definitive historical documents.

Revealing more information would recognize that convicted persons lose some of their rights to privacy. The U.S. practice of keeping secret the names of unindicted co-conspirators in cartels is particularly self-defeating because unindicted co-conspirators become named defendants in tag-along civil actions within a few months anyway. Plaintiff's attorneys must hire experts or investigators to find out the identities of unnamed conspirators and may at times wrongly do so. This observation raises the more general question of whether the DOJ has an obligation to assist private parties in their suits against cartel participants seeking compensatory and punitive damages. Injured parties suit under the Clayton Act treble damages clause are by Congressional design magnifying the deterrent effect of government prosecutions. Guilty plea agreements and guilty decisions by trial are by that law *prima facie* evidence in civil suits. Yet, the DOJ's habitual restraint in providing details in court documents hobbles the ability of private parties to obtain quick and full relief; it may also contribute to the dissent that emerges within federal classes. The DOJ does this by not revealing some participants names, company market shares, precise market sales during the affected period, minimizing the length of the collusive period, and the details of concessions given in guilty-plea deals. Details about concessions given to ADM to get it to agree to pay a $100-million fine have only dribbled out slowly from non-DOJ sources.[12] While the concessions to ADM may have been justified to avoid a lengthy court case, secrecy about most of them only adds to the public perception that ADM's deal was too sweet.

Private parties seeking damages under the Clayton Act typically reveal nothing about the terms of settlements reached before a federal class is certified. Moreover, normally nothing is revealed about settlement terms after a member of the class opts out of a proposed agreement. A change in federal court rules may be justified in the latter case. The vitamins case illustrates the problems of inadequate judicial oversight of class-action settlements. The low recovery proposed by the vitamins defendants led to the withdrawal of plaintiffs representing about 75 percent of the value of purchases. Yet the legal fees that were approved on the basis of total class purchases before the bigger buyers opted out remained unchanged. What were modest legal fees relative to recovery became extraordinarily high fees. Moreover, the confidential nature of settlements of opt outs means that the settlement rates may never by known.[13] Not only do late-settling plaintiffs fail to benefit from knowledge of earlier settlements, but also their secrecy greatly reduces the deterrent power of highly publicized recoveries. Because Congress intended the punitive component of private damages payments to deter, this would seem to justify an extended period of supervision of opt-out settlements in open court. Conservation of judicial resources seems to be the only rationale for the limited period of supervision now conventional.

A final procedural improvement concerns the standing of certain injured parties in treble-damages suits. At present, most federal courts permit only those buyers that took title to the cartelize product on U.S. territory to be qualified to sue price fixers. Thus, foreign companies that have their own buying offices in the United States can import cartelize products and get legal standing, but companies that buy abroad or that find hiring U.S. export agents more efficient become indirect buyers without federal antitrust standing.

From the standpoint of deterrence, the standing of foreign buyers is an important issue. In the lysine, citric acid, and vitamins cases, only about one-third of the sales of these cartels was in the form of direct purchases on U.S. territory. Putting aside government fines, even if private U.S. suits manage to result in settlements equal to actual treble damages, the deterrence effect is *zero* because two-thirds of the monopoly profits accrued in jurisdictions where private suits are not permitted. That is, treble damages disgorged by a cartel to U.S. buyers amount to only 100 percent of monopoly profits and no more; settlements become merely compensatory rather than punitive.[14] Given that private parties in the United Sates typically settle for something like single damages, the deterrence effect of private suits is less than zero unless government fines around the world are high enough.

Standing for foreign buyers in U.S. antitrust cases could remedy this imbalance. At least one analysis suggests that the courts already have the authority to grant standing to buyers of cartelize products purchased abroad. Adams and Bell (1999) cite the 1978 U.S. Supreme Court decision in *Pfizer Inc. v. Government of India* (434 U.S. 308) as a precedent. The Indian government purchased pharmaceuticals from Pfizer in India, yet the Court agreed that it had standing to seek price fixing damages caused by Pfizer's participation in a global cartel.

ANTITRUST SANCTIONS: AN OVERALL APPRAISAL

The severity and absolute size of both government fines and private-treble damages awards have increased throughout the 1990s to unprecedented levels. Although nearly all global price fixers were granted significant discounts from the maximum possible fines, the U.S. fines imposed on cartel participants steadily increased as a proportion of the economic injuries generated by cartel activities. From a maximum on a single company fine of only $2 million at the beginning of the decade, the record fine by 1999 had reached $500 million. The upward trend can be traced in part to an increase in the statutory fine from $1 million per count in 1989 to $10 million in 1990 and in part to the imposition of federal felony sentences that permit fines of up to twice the harm (double the overcharges and perhaps the dead-weight loss as well).[15] The huge fines on ADM ($100 million), UCAR ($110 million), BASF ($225 million), and Hoffmann-La Roche ($500 million) have certainly created enormous publicity that can only add to the deterrence effect of U.S. antitrust enforcement. Yet, the fines so far have fallen well short of the twice-the-harm upper limit. Moreover, by charging smaller subsidiaries of parent multinationals and by offering multi-year installment payments, the DOJ has signaled its reluctance to impose fines akin to corporate capital punishment. That is, the government has not imposed fines in excess of a defendant's ability to pay out of fear of creating a bankruptcy, a fear probably shared by the federal judiciary. While such a reluctance may be understandable from the point of view of anticipated popular reactions to perceived excessive judicial reach, there is little legal or economic support for bankruptcy-avoidance as a criterion for fines.[16] Nor have multiple counts been filed against defendants in the 1990s, though they were common in antitrust cases before the 1990s.

The Antitrust Division has since 1996 relied almost exclusively on large fines as the sole sanctions in criminal price fixing cases. There is no doubt that fines are among the most concrete sanctions that can be applied; also, once having been paid, they require no further government oversight. Yet, this book has recounted several cases of corporate recidivism in price fixing, which suggests that the earlier fines were too small or short-lived. There is a wide panoply of additional corporate sanctions that the government has the power request from the courts or could require in guilty plea agreements. Specific managers could be required to be fired or banned from the industry.[17] Boards of directors could be restructured to include more independent members on key committees. Tougher antitrust compliance programs could be required for convicted firms. In lieu of fines, assets can be seized. "Structural relief," i.e., the dissolution of corporate units, could be mandated for those businesses that are located in the United States.

The U.S. Government has been increasing the severity of the fines and prison sentences for executives directly involved in global price fixing. There is considerable scope for increasing the fines on convicted felons, and there will doubtless be higher amounts seen in the future. However, it is probably prison sentences that will ultimately make more of an impression on the individuals themselves and future potential violators. The two-year sentences placed on ADM's Michael Andreas and Terrance Wilson were clearly seminal events. The seven German and Swiss executives so far facing prison time in the vitamins cartel case is further evidence of the DOJ's intentions to seek tough penalties. Joel Klein's view regarding sanctions in the vitamins case is clear:

> "The [monetary] penalties coupled with the jail time I think is a far greater deterrent than structural relief. I'm confident we've nuked this cartel" (Barboza 1999).

And the tag-along investigations and actions by competition-law agencies in Canada, the European Union, Mexico, Brazil, Australia, New Zealand, and others cannot be discounted as a source of great discomfort to price fixers. U.S. actions are often only the first of numerous legal battles that must be at least a great distraction to management.

In the United States and a few other countries, private parties can add considerably to the woes of publicly prosecuted cartel participants. Combined with the double-the-harm fines, treble damages raise the potential legal liability to a theoretical level of *five times affected U.S. sales*. In fact, *parens patriae* suits by the states' attorneys general and indirect purchaser suits in 16 or so states raises the potential monetary liability for corporate price fixers to nearly *six* times affected sales. In practice, no cartel has been assessed fines or private payments as high as three times the relevant sales, but the potential is there.

In fact, most private antitrust actions in the cases examined in this book have resulted in civil settlements remarkably close in size to the criminal fines. Only a few patient, and relatively large opt-out firms have held out for recovery approaching that of double damages. This is not what the U.S. Congress of 1914 had in mind when it passed the Clayton Act, but private plaintiffs are typically at significant informational disadvantages compared to the defendants and to the DOJ itself. Quick discovery yields only very slim information on sales and prices for plaintiffs. Even extensive discovery with numerous depositions will not usually give plaintiffs all they need to compute an accurate overcharge estimate. Plant cost and capacity data are particularly hard to extract from defendants. Moreover, as we have seen in numerous cases in this book, the DOJ provides only minimally useful information in guilty plea agreements from the point of view of private plaintiffs.

Chapter 18 Endnotes

[1] Supervising judges sometimes reimburse plaintiffs' law firms for some of their costs separately from their fees.
[2] Boies Schiller, the winner of the judicial auction, guaranteed a minimum of $405 million to plaintiffs if they won at trial or settled out of court. Thus, their fee was zero up to $405 million and 25 percent for any winnings above the $405 million threshold. The settlement of about $535 million generated $27 million in fees for Boise Schiller, or 5 percent of the settlement amount.
[3] The clause expires in November 2001.
[4] Formally, these are Sherman Act Section 1 or restraint of trade cases. Although the number actually declined slightly in the late 1990s, the size and complexity of these cases increased markedly.
[5] The other criminal cases cover such crimes as perjury, fraud, false statements, contempt of court, or obstruction of justice. Non-price-fixing antitrust cases are almost always civil matters.
[6] Besides the DOJ and FTC, some of the smaller agencies with antitrust-like responsibilities include the Packers and Stockyards Administration of the U.S. Department of Agriculture (recently renamed GIPSA), and small agencies that govern mergers in banking, railroads, and airlines.
[7] The FTC did try once before in 1992 in *FTC v. Abbott Laboratories*. The judge allowed the FTC to seek disgorgement, but the FTC later lost the case.
[8] It is revealing that the Division had no standard definition to distinguish international cartels from domestic ones. In FY 1999, a definition of an "international matter" (i.e., a case or investigation) met one of these criteria: (1) the involved parties were foreign in a legal or geographic sense, (2) relevant information was outside the U.S., (3) illegal conduct took place outside the U.S. or (4) the matter involved foreign cooperation or consultation. A party is a subject or target of a matter (ICPAC fn. 15).
[9] Another 21 had been negotiated and would be coming into force in the near future.
[10] In fact, the lysine makers did provide at least annual data on 10 of the eleven facilities, but not at the same level of detail as ADM had provided.
[11] The accidental release of trade secrets of ADM during the trial of Michael Andreas *et al.* and in a sentencing document was one of the many prosecutorial actions that so irritated the presiding judge during the sentencing phase.
[12] An USDA agreement not to ban ADM from government contracts came out years later in a USDA official's speech. Further details came out during conversations at the bar during the Chicago trial. The DOJ never admitted that it would not indict ADM for fixing the price of sodium gluconate.
[13] Leaks are fairly rare, and the publicly traded defendants only have to report "significant" fines in their annual financial reports. The threshold for significance tend to be flexible and are often higher for non-U.S. companies.
[14] This scenario assumes that the monopoly overcharge rates are the same in regions outside the United States as they are inside the United States. The lysine cartel set higher prices in Western Europe but slightly lower prices in parts of Asia. However, costs of production and distribution of lysine in these areas were also higher, so the proportion of monopoly profits accruing from U.S. sales could have been slightly lower than one-third.
[15] Legal theory and the U.S. Sentencing Guidelines seem to support including the dead-weight loss as part of the total loss.
[16] A Florida prosecutor of an aircraft-maintenance firm responsible for a horrific crash of a Value Jet airliner in Florida intentionally sought fines that would cause the firm's bankruptcy.
[17] A good example is Andreas Hauri who was a key conspirator in the 1991-1995 citric acid cartel. He was moved by his employer, Hoffmann-La Roche, from citric acid marketing to vitamin marketing where he applied his price-fixing skills.

Chapter 19

GLOBAL PRICE FIXING: SUMMING UP

Awareness of antitrust enforcement matters has entered the U.S. public's consciousness to a degree that could hardly be imagined just a decade ago. Well-publicized mergers and the highly fascinating *Microsoft* case have certainly contributed to this heightened awareness. Important additional sources of public discussion were two books (Lieber 2000, Eichenwald 2000), extensive articles, and news shows on global cartels. The nation's leading newspapers have many times devoted prominent space to news about price-fixing fines, trials, and related enforcement activities. In the late 1990s, major investigative stories about global cartels could be found in the pages of *Newsweek*, *Business Week*, and *USA Today*. In March 2000, the largest demonstration by farmers and rural businessmen in Washington in more than 20 years lobbied Congress for tougher antitrust enforcement. Even during the early stages of the 2000 presidential campaign, George W. Bush and Albert Gore were being asked about their positions on the Microsoft prosecution or market power as a cause of high gasoline prices. Antitrust has not been as fashionable since the 1970s, if ever.

The ground swell of popular interest is partly a response to the scandalous behavior of the conspirators, whom Joel Klein skewered as "well dressed thieves." Their intrigues and deceptions are the stuff of racy mystery novels.[1] Yet, the story of the global cartels goes beyond mere fascination with aberrant behavior. It is also high drama pregnant with ethical lessons about contemporary business and politics.

This chapter focuses on the major impacts that the management and prosecution of these global cartels had on the corporate and individual conspirators, on stockholders and customers, on the antitrust agencies, and on the politics of antitrust. Specifically, the following section points out how the structure of the cartel's industries facilitated the formation and effective operation of global price-fixing behavior. Then the size of the corporate and personal penalties for price fixing are reviewed with four questions in mind. Will the corporate penalties deter future conspiracies? Is there evidence of reform of corporate governance structures that will be less hospitable to collusion? What were the ultimate impacts on individual conspirators? And how much did global price fixing cost society? Finally, the chapter assesses the effects of these global cartel cases on the enforcement methods, on the reputations of antitrust prosecutors, and on the degree of political support for such enforcement in the United States and abroad.

MARKET STRUCTURE MATTERS

The market environments for the lysine, citric acid, vitamins, and other global cartels discussed in this book made possible and indeed fostered collusive price-fixing behavior by the leading firms in the industry. Two industry features tower above all the others in importance because they are absolutely necessary conditions for cartels to be formed and flourish: high seller market sales concentration and product homogeneity. High barriers to market entry are icing on the cake: with them cartels will be durable, without them new sellers will enter the industry and in time make cooperation in pricing a thing of the past. Finally, the remaining structural features of markets shown in Table 19.1 may be called "plus factors." The plus factors are not necessary conditions for the formation of cartels, but they do facilitate the establishment of price agreements and increase the probability of serious price effects.

Concentration

There is no doubt that industry concentration – the share of sales or production capacity controlled by the leading suppliers – was high in every global-cartel case seen in this book. From information provided earlier, the share of global production accounted for by the four largest manufacturers of lysine, citric acid, and vitamin A was in excess of 80 percent in the early 1990s.[2] There is evidence that Western Europe, North America, South America, and Asia were viewed by the cartel members as geographically distinct markets. Except for citric acid in Asia, sales concentrations within the continents were even higher than global concentration (Table 19.1). Prices were set systematically higher in Europe and lower in most parts of Asia, yet never so far apart as to allow non-cartel firms to make profits through geographic arbitrage activities.

Exactly what threshold may be considered high enough to generate a measurable degree of market power is a matter of some debate in economics.[3] Moreover, the degree of industry concentration required for *monopoly* pricing behavior – the form of pricing to which cartels aspire – is likely to be higher than that needed to achieve significant market power. Finally, the critical concentration level for monopoly pricing may vary according to the type of industry and whether concentration had been historically rising or falling. Despite these uncertainties, empirical studies of manufacturing industries have variously identified the critical level of four-firm sales concentration at between 40 and 65 percent.[4]

Table 19.1. Economic Conditions Facilitating Global Price Fixing: Lysine, Citric Acid, and Vitamin A, Early 1990s.

Market Conditions	Lysine	Citric Acid	Synthetic Vitamin A
High seller concentration:			
Global market	CR4 > 95%	CR4 > 80%	CR4 > 95%
U.S. market	CR4 > 97%	CR4 = 90%	CR4 = 100%
Few cartel participants	4 or 5	4 or 5	3
High cartel supply control	95-99%	65-70%[b]	95-100%
Low buyer concentration	CR4 < 30%	CR4 < 40%	CR4 < 20%
Homogeneous product[a]	Perfect	High	High
High barriers to market entry:			
Large plant scales	$150 mil.+	$150 mil.	Probably
Sunk investment costs	Yes	Yes	Yes
Technology secret	Yes	Yes	Yes
Building new plants slow	3 years+	3 years+	3 years+
Transparency of market prices	None	Some	Little
Large, infrequent transactions	Yes	Yes	Yes
Major rivals have long history of strategic interaction	3 of 5	3 of 5	Yes[c]
Annual market growth	10%, steady	8%, steady	2-3%, steady
Cultural propinquity of cartel members	Low	Moderate	High

Sources: Chapters 4, 7, and 10.
CR4 = Sum of the market shares of the top four suppliers or buyers.
[a] Within well recognized industry grades when prices were at cartel-enhanced levels. There were no substitutes when prices were within a normal range.
[b] Control by formal members of the cartel. Cargill, a major supplier with up to 20 percent of U.S. capacity, provided passive support for the cartel's pricing decisions.
[c] The vitamin A conspirators were long time rivals from Western Europe, but in most of the other vitamin cartels Japanese or Northern American companies had to be recruited to the cartels.

Observed levels of seller concentration in the cartelized industries covered in this book exceeded the upper end of this range by a comfortable amount. In addition, in the few cases covered in this volume where entry caused industry concentration to dip below about 65 percent, cartel activity generally ceased.

Conceptually separate from the issue of overall industry concentration is the degree of control by the cartel itself. In every case except for citric acid the top four or five producers were all members of the cartel, so in practical terms industry control and cartel control of supply were one and the same. In the citric acid case the one missing leading firm – Cargill – appears to have followed the cartel's pricing decisions while refraining from active collusion. Another dimension of concentration is the fewness of company numbers. In every case examined in this book, the global cartel operated with three or four corporate conspirators; at times a fifth firm joined the lysine and citric acid cartels. Of course, a large number of vitamin makers admitted colluding on prices, but when one looks at the *individual* vitamin markets (A,C,E,B1, etc.) no more than five firms were members of the cartel. While there are historical examples of successful cartels with ten to 20 members, the fewness of firms observed in the present global cartels made formation and monitoring of a price agreement eminently feasible.

Finally, consistent with cartel theory, the degree of buyer concentration was low. In every instance, the top four direct purchasers accounted for less than 20 to 40 percent of the market, whether calculated at the global or regional level. Low buyer concentration makes it more difficult for purchasers to share credible information about transactions prices and prevents buyers from countervailing against the market power of sellers.

Homogeneity

Cartels can more easily agree on one price than on many and can more easily agree on a measurable market indicator like price rather than a fuzzier notion like superior product quality. Lysine, citric acid, and each of the vitamins are pure organic chemicals with unique chemical signatures. Within a recognized grade or type, each of the cartelized products was perfectly homogeneous. The presence of conventional grades in the market did not present the cartels with an insuperable challenge. In some cases, such as liquid lysine or natural human-grade lysine, the cartel simply agreed to ignore these relatively insignificant market niches. In some other cases, such as citric acid, the liquid product forms were simply priced off the 100-percent pure dry form, employing traditional industry rules of thumb for discounts. In some cases, such as vitamin A in oil and vitamin A in dry powder form, the two types flowed into such distinct marketing channels that two prices had to be agreed upon.

With few exceptions, the food-and-feed-ingredient cartels sold a somewhat more purified form to food processors or pharmaceutical firms and a less purified form to animal-feed manufacturers. As a rule the food/pharma version was sold at the highest price while the feed version sold at recognized conventional discounts. New entrants typically began selling the cheapest version first because the manufacturing standards were not as rigorous. Differences in technical standards prevented substitution of the lower priced grades for the high priced ones, thereby protecting the established sellers in the cartel from direct price competition.

In every case, when a cartel became successful in raising prices, participants had to take care not to raise them too high lest substitutes become price competitive. That is, product uniqueness and homogeneity is found only over a certain range of prices. For lysine, soybean or fish meal became an efficient substitute in animal feeds if the price of lysine made by the conspirators from dextrose rose above $2.00 per pound. Similarly, citric acid and vitamins can be extracted from natural vegetable matter, but only if the prices of the synthetic versions rose to well above the prices set by the cartel. The availability of substitutes at very high prices limited the ability of some cartels to charge the full monopoly price.

Barriers to Entry

Lysine, citric acid, and several vitamins are manufactured with fairly new fermentation technologies, many of which are still undergoing rapid improvements. Most processes are protected by patents or industrial secrecy. The finishing plants are usually dedicated to production of a unique product; while economies of scale for the finishing units are modest, there appear to be substantial economies from physical vertical integration with dextrose or other carbohydrate feedstocks. Even if an efficient technology is available, market entry is slow. The finishing plants require two or three years to be built and generally require a year or two more of learning-by-doing to reach optimal productivity levels. Thus, technological barriers of several kinds protect biotech industries making amino acids, food acids, and other organic chemicals.[5]

Several of the vitamins are made with traditional synthetic chemistry. While patents are unimportant, the synthesis is described as difficult to master and key intermediate chemicals are often made by only a couple of suppliers. In general, the cartels that were most protected by technological barriers had low rates of entry and the most durable agreements.

Other Plus Factors

There are five facilitating factors that are present to varying degrees in the cartel case studies presented above. First, collusion is difficult to maintain when frequent, accurate, public price reporting is available. For all these products nearly the only price data available are irregular announced list or spot prices from trade magazines. While these sources occasionally announce transaction prices, the relationship between the two types of prices tends to narrow considerably at the start of a price-fixing conspiracy. Thus, list price series would tend to underreport price changes due to collusion. Moreover, list prices typically do not drop when collusion ends, even though transaction prices plummet. International trade data can sometimes provide monthly implicit prices of imported product by country, but lags in sales and transportation costs interfere with developing reliable transaction prices. Only citric acid had a publicly available price series, a monthly survey of prices reportedly paid by purchasing managers.

Second, in all the cartelized markets examined, the lion's share of product was purchased under annually negotiated supply contracts. Reliable reporting of contract prices was rare. Illegal price agreements are easier to maintain when transactions tend to be large and infrequent because the opportunities for cheating by cartel members are fewer in number and harder to detect.

Third, a long history of rivalrous interaction among potential members of a cartel may tend to discourage overt price fixing. Predictability in the strategic behavior of one's rivals makes various forms of tacit, less risky cooperation more feasible for a firm. On the other hand, an industry with a history of price fixing is more likely to repeat that behavior again. In all the cartels examined in this book, some of the members of the cartel had engaged in price fixing in the 1980s or before. Also, in both lysine and citric acid, there were two new firms that had entered production only a year or two before the conspiracy was formed.[6] The new firms would not have had enough time in the industry to learn how to cooperate tacitly. In vitamins, a unique combination of firms had to form a multinational coalition for each product, so here too tacit cooperation would have been difficult to achieve. Overt price fixing was a faster route to supranormal pricing.

Fourth, rates of volume growth were quite robust for lysine and citric acid, but vitamin growth had decelerated greatly since the 1970s and 1980s. For the first two products there is little evidence of cyclic growth patterns that may have induced price wars. However, in examining the financial records of the major participants in the cartels examined, in the late 1980s nearly all of them showed signs of shrinking profitability in major lines of business other than the ones chosen for price fixing. Rather than seeking explanations for collusion in market growth patterns, the anxiety of a looming corporate slowdown in growth or profitability may provide a predictor of a willingness to collude.

Fifth, cultural or geographic closeness among conspirators has often been cited as a positive factor encouraging collusive schemes. These forms of propinquity are most often interpreted as proxies for lower conspiratorial transactions costs or the likelihood of developing group trust of a type likely to lower the tendency to cheat. While cultural similarities may have facilitated the cartels formed in Europe and Japan prior to the 1990s, one of the striking features of the global cartels of the 1990s is the cultural plurality of their membership. At times the South Korean firms seemed to be endangering the harmony of the lysine cartel, but in general the broad mix of national and business cultures observed in the case studies seems not to have inhibited cartel formation or longevity.[7] Cartels composed of companies drawn from all over the "triad" (East Asia, Western Europe, and North America) now seem eminently feasible.

Collusive Behavior

The main reason for focusing on the structure of markets is because imperfectly organized markets can give rise to oligopolistic behavior by sellers (see Chapter 2). In particular, the more closely an industry resembles a classic monopoly, the more likely it is that collusive behavior will be observed in a market. When two or more legally independent companies overtly agree to engage in coordinated actions with the intent of raising prices, a cartel is formed, and their actions are called restraints of trade.

There are many specific actions encompassed by the idea of restrictive business practices. The behaviors of the three global cartels featured in this book illustrate nearly all the 24 specific restraints of trade associated with cartels (Table 19.2). Under the category of setting common prices, all the techniques employed by historical cartels were practiced by the three food-and-feed-ingredient cartels except setting precise transaction prices. However, some transaction prices were indirectly set by the cartels because spot purchases were made at list prices. Only a few tactics were not tried by the cartels discussed in this book. Although no overt agreements were known to have been made on restricting plant investments, evidence in the lysine cartel indicates that expansion rates slowed markedly during the peak years of conspiracy as the higher prices choked off some demand growth. Under the enforcement methods category, none of the three cartels was reported to have employed a trigger-price mechanism or pooled their sales through a common agency.

Table 19.2. Restraints of Trade in the Lysine, Citric Acid, and Vitamins Cartels.

Types of Collusive Behavior	Lysine	Citric Acid	Vitamins[c]
Setting Common Prices:			
1. List price agreement	X	X	X
2. Transaction price agreement			
3. Agreement on customer discounts		X	
4. Agreement on price-protection clauses	X		
5. Rigging bids	X		X
Setting Company Market Shares:			
6. Global sales shares		X	
7. Global quantity shares	X		?
8. Regional or national shares	X		X
9. Allocating specific customers			X
Setting Production Limits:			
10. Global output reductions[a]	X		
11. On exports to specific destinations	X	X	X
12. On arbitrage by buyers	X		X
13. On production capacities			
Monitoring the Illegal Agreements:			
14. Reporting company production data[b]	X	X	X
15. Sales certification by third parties		X	?
16. Inspection of plant records or inventories on site		X	
Cartel Enforcement Methods:			
17. Trigger price mechanism			
18. Dominant firm threatened excess production	X	X	
19. Periodic compensation for under-share members	X	X	?
20. Marketing agency for pooling of sales			
21. Pooling and division of profits			X
Cover-up Efforts:			
22. Create or exploit an industry trade association	X	X	X
23. Hide evidence of travel, meetings, or communications	X	X	X
24. Employ code words or code names	X		

Source: Chapters 5, 8, and 11.

X = Behavior observed or highly probable in cartel above.
? = Some unconfirmed reports of such behavior.
[a] Production limits are set below historical rates of growth in the market.
[b] Frequent, detailed information on prices, production, sales, inventories, or costs of production.
[c] Because there was no trial conducted in this market, there is somewhat less detail available than for the lysine and citric acid cartels.

ESCALATING ANTI TRUST SANCTIONS AND DETERENCE

In the European Union, Canada, and several other countries, the example of the United States seems to have encouraged a significant stiffening of antitrust penalties for cartels. U.S. fines, prison sentences, and private settlements for price fixing escalated impressively in the 1990s as a result of changes in U.S. laws, the expansion of cartel injuries, and newfound vigor among both public and private prosecutors. In this section, the issue of the adequacy of the new penalty structures is addressed. Are they sufficient, too low, or too high? Most importantly, are the harsher penalties imposed on global price fixers in the 1990s likely to deter further future violations?

The two main purposes of monetary penalties for economic crimes are to *compensate* injured victims of the crime and to *punish* the perpetrators so as to prevent them from repeating the same crime in the future. In addition, penalties can serve to compensate professionals to detect, to investigate, or to provide legal advice concerning antitrust violations. The treble-damages provision for private plaintiffs in Sherman Act cases in the United States was designed specifically for all three purposes. Perhaps the goals could have been achieved with only double damages, but that would require a high share of all conspiracies are discovered and punished. If on the other hand only one-tenth of all conspiracies (more accurately one-tenth the compensable harm created by all such conspiracies are uncovered), then settlements of even ten times the damages are inadequate to deter repetitive crimes. On the assumption that civil plaintiffs actually receive amounts close to what the law permits, most legal scholars defend the treble-damages rule as a reasonable compromise (White 2001). However, if settlements fall well below treble damages or the chances of discovering a clandestine cartel are low, then the treble-damages rule is too lenient because it has no deterrence effect (that is, settlement costs for perpetrators are less than the expected monopoly profits).

Outside the United States, only a few countries permit buyers to sue for civil damages. Where they exist, such laws are new, nearly all permit plaintiffs to seek only single damages, and most seem to yield far less than actual damages in practice. When the ability to extract monopoly profits through civil suits is inadequate, then public prosecutors should be able to demand larger fines. The increases in financial penalties for price fixing violations in the United States that became law in 1987 and 1990 were partly in response to the perceived inadequacy of civil penalties. The toughening of the fine structure for cartel violations in the European Union in the late 1990s was partially a response to the lack of civil suits in national courts and to the absence of personal penalties for price fixing in most European jurisdictions.

Table 19.3 attempts to collect together all of the information on the financial costs imposed on the corporate participants in three global cartels: lysine, citric acid, and vitamins.[8] The data shown include both government-imposed fines and court-approved civil settlements, but they do not include the cost of legal services incurred by the companies for their defense. The total antitrust penalties amount to $4.6 billion for the 33 companies listed. More than four-fifths of the penalties arose from the vitamins cartels, and the largest single-company penalties also appear for the three largest vitamin manufacturers: Roche, BASF, and Aventis. Two firms, Roche and ADM, had penalties in two or more of the cartels. Several penalties represent historic new types as well as record amounts of payments.

The total U.S. criminal fines imposed on corporate lysine conspirators in 1996 were $91 million. In 1996-1997, the citric acid cartel members paid $105 million, and in 2000 fines paid by most of the participants in the vitamins cartels had climbed to $911 million. Each of these was a historic antitrust record. Canadian government fines on the same companies of $79 million were also the highest ever seen in Canada. The U.S. class-action settlement proposed for vitamins is just slightly below the number one U.S. settlement amount for price fixing; the civil penalties paid for lysine and citric acid rank sixth in size. Canadian class actions in lysine and citric acid were still being litigated in late 2000, but if successful they too will doubtless set new national records. Fines by the European Union may well exceed those imposed in the United States; if the fines for vitamins price fixing are even half the U.S. levels, they will represent the largest ever imposed for a competition-law violation. In short, the financial penalties for corporate conspirators were historically unprecedented. They are undeniably concrete indicators of increased prosecutorial toughness in the price-fixing arena.

The competition-law prosecutors are quite proud of their enhanced fine levels. U.S. prosecutors assert that in general their fines force firms to disgorge more than their illicit U.S. profits. The Canadian federal prosecutor, referring to the fines for vitamin cartel members stated that they ". . . were big enough to eliminate most illicit profit" and that the defendants ". . . still face huge legal fees and civil liability. . ." (*Toronto Star* September 23, 1999). Class counsel is quoted as being quite pleased at the size of the civil settlements. Counsel for the federal class of lysine plaintiffs defended the settlement of 7.2 percent of affected sales by asserting that it was among the highest percentage recoveries ever made in a civil price-fixing case (*National Law Journal* October 12, 1998). Yet, despite the higher fines, in 1998, DOJ officials stated that they would like to have greater powers to extract higher price-fixing fines. (Klein 1998).

Table 19.3. Summary of Corporate Fines and Settlements Paid for Global Price Fixing, 1996-2000.

Company/ Subsidiary[a]	Lysine	Citric Acid	Vitamins	Other[b]	Total
	Million dollars[c]				
Archer Daniels Midland Co.	176.3	133.8	0	58.0	368.1
Ajinomoto/Heartland Lysine	60.4	0	0	0	60.4
Kyowa Hakko Kogyo/Biokyowa	42.6	0	0	0	42.6
Sewon Group	19.0	0	0	0	19.0
Cheil Jedang, Ltd.	14.6	0	0	0	14.6
Bayer AG/Haarmann & Reimer	0	192.3	0	0	192.3
Hoffmann - La Roche	0	73.0	1966.0	0	2039.0
Jungbunzlauer International	0	73.0	0	0	73.0
Eridania/Cerestar Products	0	1.5	0	0	1.5
Cargill	0	0	0	15.0	15.0
CPC International	0	0	0	7.0	7.0
Tate and Lyle/ A.E. Staley	0	0	0	10.0	10.0
American Maize	0	0	0	5.0	5.0
Roquette Freres/ Hubinger	0	0	0	5.0	5.0
BASF AG	0	0	885.0	0	885.0
Alusuisse/ Lonza	0	0	41.0	0	41.0
Aventis/ Rhone-Poulenc	0	0	235.0	0	235.0
Aventis/ Hoechst	0	0	43.0	0	43.0
Takeda Chemical Industries	0	0	283.0	0	283.0
Eisai Co.	0	0	157.0	0	157.0
Daiichi Pharmaceutical	0	0	98.0	0	98.0
DuCoa, Inc.[d]	0	0	12.0	0	12.0
Chinook Group, Ltd.	0	0	20.0	0	20.0
Nepera	0	0	16.0	0	16.0
Reilly/ Vitachem	0	0	8.0	0	8.0
Degussa/ Vitachem	0	0	51.0	0	51.0
Mitsui/ Bioproducts	0	0	43.0	0	43.0
E. Merck KGaA	0	0	55.0	0	55.0
Solvay Phermaceuticals	0	0	43.0	0	43.0
Sumitomo Seiyaku	0	0	16.0	0	16.0
Tanabe Seiyaku	0	0	16.0	0	16.0
Sumika Fine Chemicals	0	0	16.0	0	16.0
Congo Chemical	0	0	16.0	0	16.0
Total	256.9	473.6	3,782.0	95.0	4,612.5

Sources: Tables 6.A.1 and 7.A.1, Connor 2000 (Tables 5 and 7).

[a] Subsidiaries that were indicted by U.S. or EU authorities are listed. Vitachem is listed twice because it was a joint venture controlled by Degussa until 1994 and Reilly after that. Aventis is the new parent firm (since 1999) of two former parent conspirators.

[b] Includes expected settlement amounts for high fructose corn syrup (civil suit in the United States), derivative shareholders' units, and rough estimates for cartels in MSG and methionine.

[c] Fines imposed and expected to be imposed by the U.S., EU, and Canadian antitrust authorities and estimated or actual private settlements in the United States and Canada. The largest predicted fines are these for citric acid and vitamins in the EU. Settlements for the U.S. opt-out buyers of vitamins are predicted.

[d] During the first few years of the vitamin B3 conspiracy, jointly owned by DuPont and ConAgra; then sold to DCV, Inc. None of the parent companies were charged.

Clearly, government fines and civil penalties (where they are permitted) are jointly determined. Yet, some legal commentators have argued that the penalties are too high, while others believe that they are too low. Even U.S. prosecutors realize that record-setting fines may be insufficient to deter. When announcing the plea bargains for the major vitamin manufacturers, Joel Klein noted that the $14 million fine paid by Hoffmann-La Roche in 1997 was insufficient to keep the company for continuing to fix prices in vitamins for another year. Perhaps the most detailed criticism of the new higher penalties for price fixing is given by Kelly and Sayyed (2000). The authors judge that the DOJ's double-the-harm fines (and the innovative 1999 FTC suit for disgorgement of illicit profits) when combined with treble damages "border on overkill." The *vitamins* cases, they say, illustrate the "unfortunate . . . scale and scope" of recent cartel litigation[9] They warn that double damages from fines when combined with treble civil damages may not be tolerated by the Supreme Court because the Court is opposed to "duplicate damages." Finally, the authors suggest that the treble-damages provision creates incentives for firms to harass rivals with frivolous suits, plays into the hands of greedy plaintiff's attorneys, and will drive some defendants into bankruptcy.

Kelly and Sayyed are long on passion but short on supportive facts for their arguments. ADM and Hoffmann-La Roche are given as examples of wronged defendants as though the excessiveness of their punishments were obvious. No instances of frivolous suits or bankrupt firms are provided. Indeed, courts appear to bend over backward to insure the economic viability of fined firms. As for the greed of plaintiffs' counsel, it is very likely the case that the defendants' firms garner more fees from their clients than formerly. Yet, no responsible commentator has suggested that defense counsel goad their clients into price fixing just to generate legal fees. Finally, one might ask why bankruptcy is not an appropriate sanction for egregious violations of the most serious type of corporate crime.[10]

Criticism that antitrust penalties are too low is much easier to find in the press. The 100-million-dollar fine on ADM was described as too generous, a "sweetheart deed," and a "bargain." However, the reasons for these descriptions are obscure or unexamined assumptions. The incompetence of government lawyers faced with attorneys that were the best that money could buy; Dwayne Andreas' political largess; reluctance to hobble a national business champion; and ADM's huge cash reserves were all cited as support. The positive reaction of the stock market to the announcement of ADM's fine does indicate that investors had speculated that it would be higher. In the case of private settlements there is abundant evidence that the smaller buyers of cartelized products received significantly lower payout rates than did the opt-out that settled later. However, none of these reasons seems to prove that the penalties were ineffective.

More trenchant are assertions that monetary sanctions extracted from cartel participants in the 1990s were lower than the monopoly profits earned (Barboza 1999). According to some critics, crime pays, and one of the main reasons it pays is that antitrust agencies only calculate harm to buyers within their jurisdiction when deciding on appropriate fines (Adams and Bell 1999). It is true that in the case of about 20 global cartels convicted by the U.S. government, only two rather small cartels were assessed fines on the basis of their affected global sales rather than the normal U.S. sales. Moreover, U.S. courts (among the few in the world that assess large civil penalties) do not generally permit overseas buyers to join local buyers as plaintiffs in treble-damages suits. Thus, in the era of global cartels that make large shares of their monopoly profits outside a given jurisdiction the chances that price fixing pays is quite large. Added to that is the fact that the secretiveness of cartels makes them difficult to discover. Deterrence can work only if the *probable* costs of prosecution exceed the *expected* monopoly profits. For example, assume that a cartel has two-thirds of its business outside the United States and that the chances of being caught are 20 percent. Then to deter cartel formation, the potential conspirators must guess that the probable U.S. criminal and civil penalties will be at least *fifteen times* their legal profits. Such high penalties are impossible under current U.S. law even as a theoretical proposition; in practice, the cartels of the 1990s only paid about double their illegal profits.[11]

Therefore, as impressive as the total dollar penalties imposed on global cartels may appear, by some yardsticks they are not particularly large. Three objective standards of severity suggest themselves: the actual penalties compared to the maximum legal liability, compared to the economic harm caused to customers, and compared to the monopoly profits generated by the cartel.

FINANCIAL IMPACTS OF ANTITRUST SANCTIONS

Companies will be deterred from repeating otherwise profitable price-fixing behavior if the financial costs incurred from antitrust sanctions are high enough. In several cases covered in this book, it is possible to chart the negative impacts of government fines, civil settlements, and related legal costs on the income and balance statements of the corporate conspirators. In addition, the major companies involved in global price fixing have suffered reputational losses that have persisted for years after their confessions of guilt. The reputational injuries show up as skepticism about the quality of a company's management and the sources of its financial performance during the conspiracy period as well as doubts about the management's ability to repair the company's profit-making potential in the years following a cartel's exposure and prosecution. The most dramatic and tangible evidence of loss of investor confidence are plunges in the stock prices of listed companies when antitrust investigations become known or when guilty pleas are publicized. In many cases, these share prices fail to recover for years after these events even though managers are replaced, capital expenditures continue, and sales or profits in the company's other lines of business show healthy growth. Perhaps in the long run the most important effect is not whether the conspirators themselves are deterred from repeating their crimes but whether their difficulties become a negative example to other firms in the industry. This broader industry deterrence effect is often hoped for by antitrust enforcers and explains why leading firms tend to be targeted for prosecution, yet it is difficult to detect or measure with any precision.

Archer Daniels Midland Co.

Among the companies involved in global price fixing in the 1990s, the best-documented example of financial and reputational losses is the Archer Daniels Midland Company (ADM). During the fiscal years ending June 30, 1992 to June 30, 1996, ADM's pre-tax profits were between 6.5 and 9.3 percent of sales. However, beginning in fiscal 1996, ADM's profit rate plunged each year as it incurred antitrust costs. During 1997-2000, pre-tax profits averaged only 3.5 percent of sales, or less than half the 1992-1996 period (Connor 2000:Table A.1). After-tax profits fell even more precipitously because companies are not permitted to offset part of the costs of fines and civil settlements by income-tax reductions; that is, ADM's effective tax rate rose by as much as 10 percentage points in 1997-1999 because antitrust payments are not tax deductible.[12] While other factors such as the 1997-1998 East Asian financial crisis and falling agricultural commodity prices have contributed to ADM's poor profit performance, direct antitrust costs accounted for 55 to 63 percent of ADM's profit declines in

1995-96 and 1996-97. Falling sales revenues from lysine and citric acid attributable to the breakup of the two cartels further added to ADM's poor financial performance in 1996 and 1997. These impacts on ADM's bottom line are all the more impressive in light of the fact that the two products accounted for less than five percent of the company's sales.

Abundant information on ADM's illegal profits from the lysine and citric acid cartels, together with fairly reliable information on the financial costs incurred for these infractions, permits one to develop an answer to the age-old question about crime: Does it pay? Table 19.4 attempts to gather evidence on this question from earlier chapters in this book, looking separately at ADM's U.S. business and its global lysine revenues.

The answer seems to be that ADM clearly bore more U.S. financial costs from antitrust legal actions against it than it earned in the form of monopoly profits from the lysine cartel. U.S. antitrust costs exceeded the extra profits from collusion by about \$70 million. However, ADM earned small positive returns from lysine price fixing on a non-U.S. accounting basis. In other words, because government fines were smaller and civil suits uncommon outside the United States, ADM has so far profited from its lysine price fixing outside the United States.[13] On a global basis, ADM did not make its crime pay, but the loss in net revenues was relatively small, about \$43 million.

An important lesson from this analysis is that the full force of the law could have vastly increased ADM's antitrust liabilities. Had the maximum legal sanctions been imposed, ADM's net losses from its participation in the lysine cartel could have reached \$490 million in the United States or \$1.6 billion worldwide. Note that this analysis of the costs and returns to price fixing does not include ADM's role in the citric acid cartel, which had global sales and monopoly overcharges twice the size of the lysine cartel. Given its market share, ADM's net legal exposure from citric acid price fixing probably approached another \$2 billion.

In addition to the adverse impacts on their income statements, some of the convicted cartel members faced losses in future revenues because government procurement rules required disbarment of suppliers with criminal convictions. ADM had contracts with the U.S. Department of Agriculture to sell agricultural commodities worth tens of millions of dollars each year that were placed in jeopardy by its criminal plea. It appears that ADM will continue to sell to the federal government because of a special deal arranged between the DOJ and USDA.

Table 19.4. Does Crime Pay? ADM and the Lysine Cartel, 1992-1995.

Income Statement	Actual Liability	Maximum Legal Liability
	Million dollars[c]	
United States:		
Revenues (Monopoly Profits)	80	80
Costs:		
U.S. government criminal fines	70	160
Federal civil settlements	45	240
Suits by attorneys general	0	120
State-level indirect buyers units[a]	15	30
Legal services	20	20
Total U.S. financial costs	150	530
Net U.S. revenues from price fixing	-70	-490
Rest of the World:		
Revenues[b]	100	100
Costs:		
European Union fines	45	1,200
Canadian government fines	8	10
Canadian civil suit	10E	25E
Other national agencies	10E	25E
Total non-U.S. financial costs	73	1,260
Net non-U.S. revenues from price fixing	27	-1,120
Global net revenues	-43	-1,610

Sources: Chapters 5, 6, 8, 9, 13, 14, and 16.
E = Estimated.
[a] Assumed half of U.S. sales in states that permit such suits and a 75% pass-through rate.
[b] Non-U.S. affected sales by ADM were $250 million. Assumed same overcharge rate as in U.S.
[c] ADM's global sales were about $12 billion in 1992. During the conspiracy, annual U.S. lysine sales were $200 million and global lysine sales about $450 million.

There is some evidence that the asset bases of some of the corporate price fixers have been hurt by the antitrust sanctions imposed on them. For example, in fiscal 1997 – the year with the greatest antitrust costs – ADM's liquid assets fell by $627 million from the previous year. This was the primary reason for a decline in ADM's stockholders' equity, the first such decline in many years. In the first quarter of fiscal 2000, ADM began selling some major physical assets, seemingly to boost quarterly earnings (ADM 2000). As a result of its weakened balance sheet, ADM does not appear as invulnerable to a takeover bid as it once did. One day in early June 1998, ADM's stock price jumped 14 percent in value when a rumor circulated that DuPont was about to make an offer to buy ADM. Some analysts welcomed the news because a takeover would remove the antitrust stigma that had depressed ADM's stock for almost two years. In fact, ADM's stock price was still near its ten-year low in late 2000, mainly because of the skepticism about the company's growth prospects that had been induced by the intense scrutiny of the firm since 1995 (Barboza 2000).

An intangible yet undisputable effect of antitrust conviction is its impact on the company's reputation. In some cases, a long held reputation for honesty and reliability may be lost. In other cases, an existing image for unethical behavior will be reinforced.

With ADM it appears to be the latter case. Prior to its conviction for price fixing, ADM was already perceived in the industry as an agile agribusiness giant that had cleverly exploited its political ties for profitable, government-sanctioned deals. For buyers and suppliers, ADM was known to be a tough negotiator willing to throw its weight around. To the broader public ADM's advertising featured sugar-coated themes of patriotism, ecology, and the relief of global famine that were barely indistinguishable from public service announcements; in fact, the spots were generally subtle appeals supporting public policies that benefited ADM.[14]

After its conviction, the perceptions about ADM's strengths took on a more sinister cast. The company's strategic success was attributed to "muscling into market position" thanks to "years of unashamed influence-peddling in Washington" (Carlson 1996). ADM's propensity to form joint ventures with natural rivals came to be seen as inimical to market competition. Its sponsorship of the most influential Washington news programs was interpreted as an effort to buy favorable publicity from key news organizations. When ADM paid a record $100-million antitrust fine, many journalists hinted that it was a sweetheart deal arranged by the White House as payback for years of extraordinary political contributions by ADM and the Andreas family.

Even years after ADM pleaded guilty to price fixing, the company was still being cited as one of the most egregious examples of poor management, corporate crime, and corporate welfare. In July 1997, the head of the U.S. Council of Institutional Investors said, "ADM is as good as a corporate villain as you can get." When three of its top officers were found guilty of price fixing in a jury trial in 1998, ADM's image slipped even lower. John McMillin, perhaps the most frequently cited stock analyst who follows ADM, spoke of the company's wearing a "scarlet letter" symbolic of its pariah status. In 1999, the *Chicago Tribune* called ADM "corporate America's black sheep" because of its habit of "flouting the law when it served its interests." Worse, the company's impressive record of growth in the early 1990s is now attributed to "criminal activity, corporate welfare, and other dubious sources."[15] By late 1999, with investor confidence at a new low, even ADM's decades-long strategy of diversifying into high valued agribusiness product lines was being called into question.

Perhaps the most common response of convicted corporate price fixers has been to increase their efforts to make dramatic acquisitions and publicize extensive plans for new product introductions. The large acquisitions seem to be designed to demonstrate that the companies still have ample liquid assets to remain major players in their industries and that management is not too distracted by antitrust suits that it is unable to act in the long-run strategic interests of the company. For example, ADM's 1999 shareholder's report trumpeted the fact that it had spent almost $1 billion per year from 1995 to 1999 on plant and equipment expenditures. ADM also surprised analysts by making several acquisitions of cocoa processing plants that almost overnight made the company the leader in this notoriously cyclical industry.[16] During the same period, ADM boasted that it had entered production of a score of new high valued products, many of them in the fast growing health and nutrition segment (vitamins, meat and dairy analogs, lecithin, isoflavones, antioxidants, etc.). Yet, through the end of the decade of the 1990s, the stock market continued to punish ADM's stock price. By October 1999, stockholders were voicing their dismay with ADM's corporate management and the company's financial performance. Analysts were questioning ADM's unprofitable move into the cocoa business and the wisdom of most of its investments in biotechnology products. Bond-rating agencies were threatening to lower the company's bond ratings because of its excessive investments in physical assets.

Hoffmann-La Roche

Most of the vitamin cartels collapsed in early 1998, and the U.S. guilty pleas of the major corporate conspirators came a year later. By late 1999, U.S. bulk vitamin prices had dropped about 50 percent from their cartel-induced peaks, and manufacturers' margins had hit rock bottom. Buyers reported that Hoffmann-La Roche, BASF, Rhône-Poulenc, and other manufacturers were cutting prices in order to mollify vexed customers and hold onto their historical market shares. Doubtless, these actions caused vitamin profits to decline from levels enjoyed in the mid 1990s, and the corporate fines paid in 1999 only added to financial stress of the conspirators' vitamins divisions.

However, for all cartel members, vitamins are a relatively minor portion of the companies' total sales, and the profitability of pharmaceuticals and other organic chemicals were quite high in fiscal years 1999 and 2000. Moreover, some of the companies reshuffled their assets in order to minimize the effects of poor vitamins profits. For example, in December 1999, Hoffmann-La Roche sold its flavors and fragrances division, which had previously generated ten percent of Roche's total sales. Around the same time, Roche sold $2.7 billion in stock it held in Genentech. The extraordinary gains from the sales were able to offset much of the $1.45 billion that Roche had set aside to cover antitrust charges. Together with high profits in pharmaceuticals and diagnostics, Roche was able to report an increase of 31 percent in its fiscal 1999 net income compared to 1998. Despite pulling off some other accounting tricks in early 2000, Roche's overall profitability was beginning to decline in late 2000.

Other convicted price fixers have had to contend with speculation that they will be forced to sell divisions of their companies in order to pay for the antitrust charges. In May 1999, a usually cautious trade journal, *Chemical Market Reporter*, suggested that Roche would be forced to sell its vitamin business in order to pay the fines likely to be imposed by the European Union. The same source repeated the rumor in June of that year. When in December Roche sold its flavors and fragrances division, the *Wall Street Journal* said that the vitamins division might be next. The uncertainties that such speculations create among customers that desire long-term relationships are bound to hurt business.

Hoffmann-La Roche has also suffered reputational loss and a decline in stock value as a result of its convictions for citric acid and vitamins price fixing. When the news broke of its participation in vitamin cartels, journalists reminded readers that Roche had a history of antitrust violations going back to the late 1960s (Barboza 1999). The immediate responses of Roche's CEO (who was not indicted for the conspiracy to raise prices) was derided in the business press as tepid and inept. He was aware of the necessity of repairing Roche's "broken image," and the *Financial Times* agreed:

> "The fine is a severe blow to the reputation of Roche, one of the world's oldest and most conservative pharmaceutical companies." (May 21, 1999).

At the CEO's first press conference after Roche pleaded guilty, he stated that:

> "You will understand that this was not part of our responsibility . . . We really don't know what [the four Roche conspirators] did" (*New York Times* May 22, 1999).

This statement, a *Times* columnist noted, meant that Roche's chairman considered himself "blameless and clueless."

When some financial analysts suggested that Roche would have to pay $1 billion in antitrust payments, Roche spokespersons immediately denied the possibility of such a large amount. In fact, such payments in the United States alone exceed $1 billion, and payments in the rest of the world could easily exceed the U.S. figure. Two billion dollars is about 20 percent more than Roche's global profits in fiscal 1999 and is equal to 50 percent of its 1998 sales of vitamins.

With such huge antitrust costs gaining credibility, investment analysts immediately began to speculate about divestitures of Roche divisions. As previously mentioned, Roche did sell its flavors and fragrances division (the world leader accounting for 10 percent of Roche's sales) and some stock in order to temporarily boost its fiscal 1999 profits by SF 4.5 billion. Roche's stock prices fell by 2 percent on the day these maneuvers were announced in March 2000.

In the first nine months of 2000, Roche's stock price fell by 32 percent during a period when the average drug company's price rose 23 percent. As a result, Roche dropped from first to eighth place in the world among the world's pharmaceutical companies in terms of market capitalization. A long analysis of the company by the *New York Times* (October 1, 2000) blamed the decline on the costs of price-fixing fines and the failure of many new drugs in testing trials. But behind these two strategic problems was investor doubts about the company's management practices, the perception that,

> ". . . the company was woven into an old-style corporate web in which family links and corporate cronyism counted for more than transparency and shareholder value" (*ibid.* p.3-1).

Another questionable practice was the maintenance of unusually large liquid reserves, some $17 billion in late 2000. These cash reserves were drawn down in 1999-2000 in order to boost flagging profits.

BASF

BASF was the member of the vitamins cartels that paid the second-highest U.S. antitrust fine, $225 million, and was facing additional fines in another six jurisdictions. The U.S. fine alone represented about 40 percent of BASF's fiscal 1998 operating profits from its Fine Chemicals division that made vitamins. In July 1999, BASF's leaders made tremendous efforts to reassure investors that no permanent harm would be done to BASF. They pointed out plans for large increases in R&D spending on life-sciences innovations and the introduction of more than 40 new chemical products soon. They predicted that BASF would have no trouble retaining customer loyalty and its 20-percent global share in vitamins. Optimistic sales growth predictions were offered, including a doubling of fine chemicals sales in five years. The Fine Chemicals Division of BASF would make $400 million new capital investment in the next five years, its president promised.

These optimistic pronouncements will prove difficult to realize. By late 1999, BASF's profits had begun to slide, primarily because of accounting provisions of more than $900 million for antitrust fines. Fiscal 1999 profits after taxes fell to 4.2 percent of sales, down from 6.1 percent in 1998. However, BASF *was* successful in maintaining its global share of the vitamins industry, though it did so by means of an expensive acquisition. In July 2000, BASF announced that Takeda Chemical Industries had agreed to sell all its vitamins assets to BASF. This combination of the second-largest and fourth-largest vitamins manufacturers would in fact raise BASF's market share to around 25 percent. The purported justifications for the merger were synergies that would lower the cost of manufacturing and being able to offer a complete line of vitamins to its customers, similar to what Roche already offers. The total investment required to achieve these goals would reach $600 million, the company said.

Another interpretation of BASF's strategy was that it intended to further strengthen its position in the vitamins premix market, which had been served by hundreds of small companies at the beginning of the 1990s. Premixes are custom-made blends suitable for finely targeted applications such as animal feeds optimized for genetic characteristics, gender, age, and life stage. Some of the premix companies had accused BASF of predatory tactics that had driven some of them out of business during the conspiracy period.

Rhône-Poulenc

The third largest vitamin manufacturer, Rhône-Poulenc, came out of the scandal relatively unscathed. Although the company still faces substantial antitrust penalties from several governments outside the United States and civil settlements to its customers, its role in the cartel is not often mentioned in periodical press reports about its financial performance. The fact that Rhône-Poulenc merged with Hoechst in late 1999 makes the effects of antitrust expenses more difficult to trace to their impacts on profits or investment plans of the successor firm, Aventis. Moreover, Rhône-Poulenc's critical assistance to the U.S. DOJ in collecting evidence against the other cartel participants is rarely remarked upon, except as an explanation for its amnesty from criminal antitrust penalties in the United States. Unlike individual whistle-blowers, who are typically reviled for their disloyalty, a neutral response to corporate whistle-blowers appears to be quite general. Companies like Great Lakes Chemical that were granted full amnesties for being the first to come forward and provide information about criminal cartel behavior have been neither praised nor condemned.[17]

CORPORATE GOVERNANCE STRUCTURES

As the previous section emphasized, firms can be deterred from violating the antitrust laws by judicially imposed sanctions. The greater the likelihood and severity of antitrust fines or civil settlements, the greater the deterrence effect. However, private-sector solutions to enhanced deterrence are also possible. That is, corporations and their trade associations may on their own institute structural reforms or compliance programs aimed at reducing the liability faced by corporations when their employees opt to violate the antitrust laws. There are four types of policies available to corporations. First, companies can develop personnel guidelines that would increase the degree of personal responsibility of executives guilty of contravening the antitrust laws. Second, firms can establish internal antitrust compliance programs and more aggressive financial accounting controls to detect violations at an earlier stage. Externally, corporations can press for antitrust safeguards for the trade associations in which they hold memberships. Third, corporate governance can be restructured in ways that make price fixing more difficult to hide.

Personnel Policies

Price-fixing schemes require managers to run them. One of the striking lessons of the global cartels examined in this book was how high ranking the chief conspirators were. At ADM the principal perpetrators of the lysine and citric acid conspiracies were the Vice Chairman and two presidents of the company's divisions. At Ajinomoto, the group's president blessed the lysine cartel and one other member of the company's management committee directed the conspiracy.[18] At Hoffmann-La Roche, two of the eight members of the company's management committee were deeply involved in fixing the prices of vitamins and citric acid. In five or six other companies, the Chief Executive Officers were the principal perpetrators of their company's price fixing agreement.

As far as can be determined only *one* corporate officer of the more than twenty five companies that pleaded guilty to lysine, citric acid, or vitamin price fixing voluntarily resigned in protest of their employer's illegal activities.[19] In a few cases, executives about to plead guilty for criminal price fixing were forced to resign their positions as officers. By resigning rather than being fired for cause, these executives for the most part retained their pensions, their vested rights to stock options, and their viability to seek employment at other companies. Only about five or six corporate officers guilty of price fixing were dismissed outright because of their antitrust violations. Presumably, these fired individuals incurred some losses of fringe benefits or customary severance payments. The most common sanctions imposed by companies on the top officers caught price fixing were mild reprimands and reassignments to positions that were lateral moves or slight demotions. However, for the vast majority, especially for lower level managers, companies did not formally punish these employees (or if they did, no public announcements were forthcoming). Possibly, for many of the unpunished price-fixing officers, a cloud hangs over their careers.

Some companies were extraordinarily supportive of the executives who devised and managed the cartels. ADM, for example, never fired any of the five or six officers who were actively engaged in price fixing. It did, however, fire Wayne Brasser when he refused to partake in the citric acid scheme. ADM permitted Michael Andreas to go on an extended paid leave when he was indicted in December 1996, 18 months after the FBI raid on ADM's headquarters. Moreover, Andreas was given a raise and immediately hired as a consultant to ADM up until at least the end of his trial in September 1998, and possibly for a year more. Terrance Wilson resigned in late 1996. Both Andreas and Terrance Wilson were provided with highly paid lawyers and an extensive support staff at company expense. Both men probably retained most of their retirement benefits.

The actions taken by the three largest Japanese vitamin manufacturers after their guilty pleas were quite different. After somewhat ritualized apologies featuring deep bows in public places, these companies took somewhat more tangible steps to symbolize shame and admit responsibility. The presidents of the three companies resigned their honorific positions as chairmen of regional or national trade associations. Many officers and members of the boards of directors voluntarily imposed on themselves significant, temporary reductions in their salaries or fees. Nothing similar has been seen outside of Japan.

When employees are being investigated for alleged antitrust violations and even after being indicted, companies must walk a fine line between the presumption of innocence and protecting the company's reputation for ethical behavior. An overly quick condemnation will redound badly on employees' morale, but doing nothing will signal the company's tolerance for unethical or indeed illegal behavior. It is well to be reminded of one of the principal lessons learned by the DOJ after years of prosecuting global cartels:

> ". . . in our experience, without exception, . . . foreign cartel members are fully aware that they are violating the law in the United States and elsewhere [and] show callous disregard for customer victims" (Spratling 1999: 9).

There are a number of steps that companies can take with regard to contractual conditions of employment for corporate officers that would raise the cost of engaging in price fixing. First, companies should have in place policies that would only protect employees that are innocent of price fixing.

Executives should continue to receive adequate legal counsel paid for by the company, but it would be a simple matter to make such legal costs reimbursable to the company should the employee plead guilty or be found guilty at trial. Second, employees should know that after being indicted for serious criminal offenses, being placed on leave is automatic. Third, being found guilty and having exhausted all appeals, it should be a corporate policy that dismissal for cause is automatic. Such dismissals should, by employment contract, require forfeiture of pension rights and stock options, lest such individuals materially benefit from their illegal activity.

Antitrust Compliance Programs

Many well-managed companies have antitrust compliance programs, but many do not. ADM, Roche, and BASF specifically announced after pleading guilty that such programs would be started or reinvigorated. These programs may be established or monitored by the company's office of the general counsel or by an outside law firm with antitrust experience.[22] Typically, antitrust compliance programs involve in-service training of officers and salespersons about legal principles and prohibited practices. Memoranda reminding employees of corporate ethics will be issued periodically by a top company executive. The general counsel's office will make known their availability to assess questionable pricing practices or to accompany officers when they confer with rival firms. ADM and other companies have set up "hotline" telephone systems so as to encourage employees to report anonymously on suspicious behavior by other employees. Some companies have an officer identified as an "ombudsman," a respected senior employee empowered to investigate allegations of improper behavior and to report findings to the Chairman or Board of Directors.

Compliance programs are complementary to traditional mentoring customs for corporate employees. Of course, if a company has a culture that positively encourages risky behavior that is ethically dubious, then an antitrust compliance program may not be able to overcome the effects of mentoring that teaches opposing standards. ADM in particular seems to have had a buccaneering spirit that inculcated disdain for laws like antitrust that by their very nature constrain firms from following many potentially profitable opportunities.

The antitrust compliance program of a company's general-counsel office should be supplemented by the checks and balances of a company's accountants. All the global cartels studied in this book were operated by a mulitfirm committee that met face-to-face on a regular, usually quarterly, schedule. Crosschecks of travel expenses and corporate telephone records could provide a company's top management with early warning of suspicious behavior. The controller's office should be authorized to make unannounced audits of suspicious travel and communications patterns.

However, none of these internal checks and balances will catch collusive behavior by employees if a cartel uses a legitimate trade association as a cover for illegal price fixing. Therefore, firms must satisfy themselves that the trade associations they belong to are unlikely to provide cover for collusive activity. Trained antitrust lawyers should be present at meetings to prevent illegal topics from being discussed. Regular meetings should be tightly scheduled so as to discourage side meetings of cartel participants.

Finally, the European Union should re-examine its policy of encouraging official trade associations comprised solely of private corporations. The lysine and citric acid cartels were facilitated by associations loosely affiliated by the European Commission's Agriculture Directorate. The European Union seems to have become aware that trade associations can have their dark side:

> ". . . in recent years, trade federations, an age-old tool for corporate networking, have become implicated in an increasing number of cartel investigations conducted by the [European] Commission's antitrust department" (*Wall Street Journal* August 28, 2000:A23).

Besides the European Citric Acid Manufactures' Association (ECAMA), the EU has investigated the anticompetitive roles industry associations in paperboard, cement, steel tubes, and banking. In some cases, the associations themselves have been fined for competition violations. For example the Product Group Paperboard was fined $117 million in 1994.

Boards of Directors

Boards of directors are ultimately responsible for ensuring the long run best interests of the stockholders of corporations. Directors must walk a fine line between skeptical oversight and intrusive meddling in major managerial decisions. Normally, they should be supportive of the many difficult decisions made by top executives, yet at the same time avoid becoming too complacent, even when financial results appear to be commendable. It is clear that investors value companies with good corporate governance policies. Valued policies include companies that have a majority of its board members independent from management, pay directors mostly in stock or stock options rather than cash, and have formal performance evaluations for directors. A McKinsey & Co. survey of 200 institutional investors in June 2000 reported that respondents were willing to pay 18 percent more for a U.S. company with such governance rules. Moreover, good governance rates equally high with financial performance when institutional investors rank potential investments.

ADM's Board of Directors bears a lot of blame for ignoring danger signs and acting too slowly once clear evidence of serious criminal price fixing had been presented to it. One major reason for the Board's inaction is that it was mesmerized by Chairman Dwayne Andreas' obvious talents and lulled by decades of extraordinary financial performance under his leadership. Contributing to the Board's indulgent view of management was the fact that it was too large (17 members), too old (average age over 70), and too close to the Chairman. Prior to 1996, at most three members could possibly be categorized as outsiders, and even these had been recruited for their prior personal ties to Dwayne Andreas. Friendship, loyalty to the company, and blood relationships made it nearly impossible for the Board to act quickly in the interests of reducing ADM's antitrust exposure when doing so meant throwing the Chairman's son and successor to the prosecutors. It is no wonder that the prestigious journal *Association Management* chose to highlight ADM's Board as an egregious example of failed governance.

By 1998, opinions favoring for reform of ADM's governance structure were universal. A well-known professor at the University of Chicago's Business School opined that ADM's "family fiefdom" model of management could not continue. An oft-quoted investment analyst said, ". . . some people want less Andreas involved in the boardroom." What is interesting about these comments is that they were made two years after the ADM board had made a number of structural improvements. Partly in response to a shareholders' suit against it, the board had decided in early 1996 to reduce its membership to 12 and increase the number of independent or outside directors. However, when three new board members were announced in April 1996, one turned out to be the niece of a remaining director and another some believed to be a crony of Andreas. By late 1996, after eight resignations from ADM's board, well over half of its members were still insiders by anyone's definition, a state of affairs that infuriated the company's largest institutional investors. In October 1996, a motion opposed by the board that was designed to tighten the definition of what constituted an outside director was narrowly defeated in a stockholders' vote.[20] In November 1996, a *Business Week* survey of management experts rated ADM's board as nearly the worst in the United States.

It is true that the board was able to secure Dwayne Andreas' approval to settle the civil suits quite early (mid-1996), but as the last cartel member to negotiate a guilty plea on the criminal charges with the DOJ, ADM could have got a better deal had the board been able to act more quickly. Moreover, the board has probably not served ADM well by praising the company and Dwayne Andreas to the skies since then. Directors Brian Muhoney, Andrew Young, and Robert Strauss have strained credibility by calling ADM "the cleanest company in America" and extolling Andreas' formerly anonymous philanthropy. No director of ADM has made a public statement suggesting that the board or ADM's management has any responsibility for price fixing in four or more product markets. Among the more controversial decision of the board was to replace Dwayne Andreas with his nephew G. Allen Andreas.[21] With G. Allen the only candidate interviewed for the job, the move had the appearance of a dynastic succession ordained by the discredited former Chairman.

THE FATE OF INDIVIDUAL CONSPIRATORS

The revelations of guilty pleas for criminal price fixing had no known effects on the professional careers of most of the conspirators. Moreover, the majority of businessmen who aided in the global cartels were simply cited in their company's guilty pleas as co-conspirators, but were not required to enter individual guilty pleas. These co-conspirators faced no sanctions from U.S. or Canadian courts. Outside of North America a small number of countries consider price fixing a criminal offense for individuals, but as far as is known no cartel conspirators were prosecuted as felons. Indeed, under EU law and the laws of two-thirds of its member states, price fixing is solely an enterprise offense. However, there were a small number of executives who played leading roles in global cartels in the 1990s, for whom U.S. criminal prosecution took a profound toll on their professional and personal lives.

Lysine

The three principal perpetrators of price fixing at ADM were the most severely punished individuals in the history of the Sherman Act. *Terrance Wilson*, who worked nearly his entire adult life for ADM, resigned in October 1996 about the time ADM pleaded guilty in the lysine case. He stood trial in U.S. District Court in Chicago in the summer of 1998 alongside his former boss, Michael Andreas. After being found guilty and exhausting all appeals up to the U.S. Supreme Court, he was fined $350,000 and sentenced to federal prison for 33 months. Commentators frequently noted that he had aged beyond his years, partly because of a couple of serious medical conditions. It is believed that Wilson's wealth and retirement benefits from ADM were left largely intact after prosecution.

Michael Andreas, who worked nearly his entire adult life for ADM, is "the most prominent American executive ever convicted for international price fixing" (*Wall Street Journal* September 18, 1998). But for his 1998 conviction at trial he would, in all probability, be the Chairman and CEO of ADM today. After being awarded a 15-percent pay raise, Andreas remained on leave from his position as Vice Chairman of ADM from October 1996 until sometime after his conviction, when he resigned his post. Andreas paid a $350,000 fine and was sentenced to 36 months in prison, which bestows on him the infamous distinction of being the first individual to pay the maximum penalties under the Sherman Act.[23] In a sense, Andreas' sentence was a light one because he almost became the first convicted price fixer to have been fined under sentencing guidelines that would have imposed a $25-million penalty. Thus, his fortune was largely preserved despite being convicted for his leading role in the lysine cartel. Although Michael Andreas would seem to have no future at ADM when he is released from prison in 2002, he still has three close relatives in top management positions at the company. In an interview in late 2000, ADM's Chairman refused to rule out Michael Andreas' reinstatement (Barboza 2000).

Andreas' counterpart at Ajinomoto, *Kazutoshi Yamada*, seems to have been forced to resign, but has otherwise escaped punishment. After agreeing earlier to surrender to U.S. authorities, Yamada failed to appear for the Chicago trial when it began in the summer of 1998. The United States has the authority to request extradition of Japanese citizens to face criminal price-fixing charges, and in December 1996 the Japan Ministry of Justice said that it was prepared to consider an official U.S. request. It appears that the extradition request was never made, even though it was known in advance that he would not appear for the trial voluntarily. It is fairly certain that Yamada's name appears on a "watch list" maintained by the U.S. Immigration and Naturalization Service thus effectively barring him from U.S. territory for the rest of his life.

Mark Whitacre, the FBI's informer in the lysine cartel case, was also found guilty of criminal price fixing at the 1998 Chicago trial. Given the brief period covered by the charge against Whitacre (about three months of the conspiracy's 36 months), Whitacre's 30-month prison sentence was surprisingly high to many observers.[24] A year earlier Whitacre had begun serving a nine-year criminal sentence for embezzlement of $10 million from ADM, so Whitacre may remain in prison until as late as 2008 at which time he will be about 50 years old. Besides restitution of the stolen money plus interest to ADM, Whitacre was further required to pay $6.3 million to ADM when his former employer won a civil suit for breach of duty and fraud. These judgments more than bankrupted Whitacre.

Just before he was fired from ADM, Whitacre seemed likely to replace James Randall as President of ADM sometime in the late 1990s when Michael Andreas would replace his father as Chairman. For a few years after his firing, Whitacre was a genuine American folk hero (Lieber 2000). Even after making scores of allegations about a wide range of illegal behavior at ADM, for many months he harbored the totally unrealistic dream that the ADM board would yet invite him back to lead ADM. This proclivity for self-destruction and tale spinning earned him the unenviable sobriquet "Pinocchio with a Ph.D."

Since being incarcerated Whitacre has made himself available for interviews by many writers (Nicol and Ferguson 1999, Lieber 2000, Eichenwald 2000). He seems to be relatively content with his prison life. He is taking correspondence courses, teaching fellow inmates, singing in the prison choir, and appears to be in a robust physical and mental shape. Other than those relating to price fixing, very few of his wilder accusations about widespread illegality at ADM have been verified. The most intriguing charge, that embezzlement was tolerated at ADM to reward favored executives with bonuses, was consistent with many facts in the case (Lieber 2000). Yet, finally Whitacre appears to have recanted this allegation (Eichenwald 2000).

Whitacre's fall from grace dragged many of his loyal subalterns down with him. Two of the Vice Presidents of Whitacre's Bioproducts Division were indicted and found guilty of aiding Whitacre in his fraud scheme. One, Sidney Hulse, went to jail for 10 months and paid a fine of nearly $1 million; the other, Marty Allison, was given probation. Reinhold Richter, and ADM consultant in Mexico, was fined $25,000 and given probation.

Warren Buffett, Secretary to ADM's board of directors, resigned "in protest" from ADM soon after the FBI raid on the company's headquarters. Except for providing inconsequential information to the FBI after his resignation, Buffett has said nothing publicly about the corruption he witnessed at ADM nor criticized his former boss, Dwayne Andreas. Formerly Whitacre's closest confidant while at ADM, they are now estranged. Buffett now owns and operates a small agribusiness.

ADM President *James Randall* and Chairman *Dwayne Andreas* have both retired. Both men had worked closely together at ADM for nearly 30 years, and both escaped indictment for price fixing only because of bargains made at the last hour. Several of Whitacre's undercover tapes made in ADM's offices provide evidence that Randall was aware of the price fixing meetings, but his lawyer claims that Randall was unaware of their illegal purpose (Eichenwald 2000). Randall's responsibility for the theft of one biotechnology and attempts to steal others is well established. The depth of Randall's involvement in antitrust violations may become better known because in late 2000 he lost a suit that had kept 200 of Whitacre's tapes out of the hands of private antitrust plaintiffs.

Neither Randall nor Dwayne Andreas were interviewed by U.S. investigators after ADM pleaded guilty in October 1996, which was a benefit granted by a clause in the company's guilty plea agreement. Neither were they called before grand juries that were investigating the citric acid and corn sweeteners cartel allegations. In Andreas' case, journalists have speculated that that this was evidence of special treatment by the DOJ for a politically exalted personality. However, by the time of ADM's October 1998 annual meeting, Andreas' stature had eroded greatly, so much so that the *Chicago Tribune* called him "the forgotten man." The conviction of his son and Wilson, both loyal acolytes, and the constant barrage of criticism of his secretive, ruthless, and shoot-from-the-hip management style had taken their toll.

Dwayne Andreas' retirement at the age of 80 in January 1999 took stock analysts by surprise. "Frankly, I thought he would die with his boots on," said John McMillan. Numerous profiles in the nation's leading business publications extol his visionary business decisions concerning soybeans and fructose, but inevitably end with references to ADM's continuing problems with antitrust matters and an uncertain future for its biotechnology ventures. On his last day as Chairman, several board members showered him with the most effulgent praise for his business acumen, great generosity, and contributions to international business diplomacy. His friend and fellow director, Robert Strauss, called Andreas "one of the greatest men that ever lived" (Lieber 2000:284). However, *Chicago Tribune* senior business writer David Greising expressed a different view of Andreas: the last of the "old-style corporate bosses," a "political heavyweight" who made ethically questionable political gifts, and a father "who looked the other way as his son . . . conducted a global price fixing scheme."

Citric Acid

One of the more curious stories concerns what happened to *Barrie Cox*, the ADM manager most actively involved with ADM's citric acid price fixing. Knowing that Cox had a great deal of damaging information about them, his immediate supervisors Terrance Wilson and Michael Andreas had Cox transferred to ADM's office in Kent, England about six months before ADM pleaded guilty. Ostensibly a promotion (he got a raise and was promised increased responsibilities), the new job was a disappointment. Prosecutors speculated that his move to England was engineered to place him beyond a U.S. subpoena. Nevertheless, Cox's testimony in the 1998 Chicago trial was probably the most damaging to Wilson in the trial. The defense never really rebutted any of it.

A few months after the trial and two years to the day after ADM pleaded guilty, Cox resigned at the age of 51 as president of ADM's Feed Additives Division. By this time G. Allen Andreas was the CEO of ADM and making big changes in the company's management structure. Perhaps G. Allen Andreas preferred not to have the witness who helped put his cousin Michael in prison around the company any longer. Cox was also a reminder that G. Allen Andreas was the head of ADM's European operations at the time that the lysine and citric acid cartels were operating there with ADM's full involvement. Curiously though, Cox maintained a consulting and sales-agent relationship with ADM for at least a couple of years after he quit ADM.

The first individual to be sentenced for the citric acid conspiracy was *Hans Hartmann*, head of Bayer's U.S. sales operations. In January 1997, Hartmann pleaded guilty and agreed to pay a fine of $150,000, which was about 60 percent lower than federal sentencing guidelines called for. No prison time was requested by the government, even though he was the acknowledged ringleader of the conspiracy and residing in the United States. In March 1997, Hartmann quietly retired from Bayer after 40 years of service to his company. Later that month the two chief conspirators in Hoffmann-La

Roche (Udo Haas) and Jungbunzlauer International (Rainer Bichlbauer) were handed down the same punishments. This was somewhat unusual because they were German and Austrian citizens, respectively.

Vitamins

The vitamin cartels were extraordinarily complex, comprehensive, lengthy, and injurious. More than a dozen companies each provided several managers to operate interlinked cartels for a dozen vitamin products. The seriousness of these crimes and the fact that the leading firm had been convicted of the same crime just two years earlier prompted prosecutors to seek heavy penalties for the individuals responsible.

Dr. Kuno Sommer, Hoffmann-La Roche's head of global marketing for vitamins and other fine chemicals, was interviewed by the FBI in the United States in March 1997. He admitted a minor role in the citric acid but by a pre-arranged agreement with other Roche executives he denied the existence of the vitamins cartel. In fact, he was deeply involved in both conspiracies, so his denial was a conspiracy to obstruct justice. When Roche's co-conspirator Rhône-Poulenc provided indisputable evidence of Sommer's crimes, he was forced to plead guilty for both criminal price fixing and making false statements. He agree to pay a $100,000 fine and go to prison for four months, the first European to be imprisoned for a Sherman Act violation in the law's 109-year history.

A few months later, the President of Roche's Vitamins and Fine Division, *Dr. Roland Brönnimann*, also pleaded guilty to criminal price fixing. Perhaps because he resisted coming to terms, he had to agree to a larger fine ($150,000) and longer prison sentence (five months) than his colleague Sommer. What is noteworthy in the vitamins case is that Roche immediately announced that both Sommer and Brönnimann were summarily fired from their jobs and were denied severance packages.[25] At the second largest company in the vitamins cartel, BASF, similar actions were taken. *Hugo Strotmann*, director of global vitamins marketing, and *Peter Suter*, head of the five chemicals division, were both forced to leave their company. Strotmann, Suter, and Suter's predecessor at BASF, *Reinhardt Steinmetz*, resisted settling with the DOJ for 15 months. All three eventually agreed to significant fines and prison sentences in April 2000. At the same time, an unnamed Roche executive was indicted and Roche's *Andreas Hauri* agreed to pay the maximum $350,000 statutory fine and spend four months in a U.S. prison. Thus, seven European executives of Roche and BASF accepted severe punishments for criminal price fixing,[26] an unprecedented development in the annals of antitrust enforcement. Numerous articles have begun to appear in law journals urging practitioners to warn their international business clients about the long reach of American antitrust law (e.g., *National Law Journal*, September 18, 2000: B11).

THE SOCIAL COSTS OF GLOBAL CARTELS

The previous sections above have attempted to make the case that discovered cartels typically result in profoundly unpleasant consequences for the corporate and individual conspirators. However, it is well to keep in mind that the costs incurred by buyers were also great. Indeed, in many cases the cartel prosecutions were unable to recover the full costs of the conspiracies to buyers. That is, the sellers in some cartels were able to reap rewards from their illegal behavior that exceeded the penalties imposed by antitrust judgments against them. This net gain from global cartel operations is more likely in jurisdictions outside North America where the government fines are low and where civil suits are either rare or yield low settlements for plaintiffs.

Customers of effective sellers' cartels are negatively affected in two ways. First, and quantitatively larger, purchasers of cartelized products overpay for the goods they continue to buy during the conspiracy period. This is the customer overcharge that was estimated for the lysine, citric acid, and vitamins cartels above (see chapters 6, 9, and 12). A customer overcharge is a transfer of income from buyers as a group to the sellers as a group.[27] That is, as a cartel's collusive behavior begins to raise prices above competitive levels, the joint profits of the cartel members rise roughly by the same amount that buyers' purchases fall. If a cartel is able to operate at peak efficacy, the sum of its members' profits will be almost as high as a monopolist would be able to extract in the same market. In equilibrium, the monopoly profits going to the conspirators will be equal to the sum of the lost revenues of direct and indirect buyers and the effective reduction in purchasing power by the ultimate consumers.

The second negative impact on buyers is the so-called "dead weight loss" or "social loss." This injury to buyers is an indirect consequence of higher prices. Under normal demand conditions, as a cartel is effective in raising market price, the quantity of sales will fall. The value of these lost sales is the dead-weight loss to customers. Because it represents both lost production as well as lost consumption, all social groups are injured: owners of the productive units, workers, intermediate buyers, and consumers. Consumers either must use the disposable income they would have spent on the overpriced good on some other good they regard as inferior or do without.[28] Of course, cartel participants do not make profits on sales they do not make.

Table 19.5 gathers information on the dollar losses to customers (direct buyers, indirect commercial buyers, and consumers) from the three cartels featured in this book. Unlike previous calculations, this table attempts to estimate the customer injuries worldwide by extrapolating comparable U.S. losses to a global scale.[29] The total losses incurred by buyers of lysine, citric acid, vitamins, and goods made from these ingredients amounted to $8.8 billion during the various conspiracy periods.

Table 19.5. Summary of Consumer Losses Due to Global Price Fixing, 1989-1999.

Affected Market			Losses to Consumers[a]		
Product	Period	Global Sales	Overcharge	Dead-Weight Loss	Total
			Million U.S. dollars		
Lysine	1992-95	1,660	330	33	363
Citric Acid	1991-95	3,950	690	60	750
Bulk Vitamins:					
A	1990-99	5,740	1,473	189	1,662
C	1991-95	4,000	460	26	486
E	1990-99	10,840	3,822	674	4,496
B group[b]	1989-98	3,483	668	64	732
Carotenoids	1991-98	1,004	267	36	303
Premixes	1990-98	9,094[c]	NA	NA	NA
Total	1989-99	39,771	7,710	1,082	8,792

Sources: Chapters 4, 6, 7, 9, 10, 12, and Connor (2001b).
NA = Not available.

[a] The overcharge is the increase in the cost of the product to buyers, both direct and indirect, due to the increase in the market price caused by the cartel (see Chapter 2). The consumer portion of the dead-weight loss is the reduction in purchases caused by the decrease in the quantity produced by the cartel during the affected period. In the absence of precise information, I assume that the own-price elasticity of demand is –1 when the price was at or close to the monopoly level; for the formula used, see Peterson and Connor (1996). The overcharge rate calculated for the United States was applied to global sales.

[b] The B complex of vitamins that were cartelized includes B1, B2, B3 (niacin), B4 (choline chloride), B5, B6, B12, and folic acid. The conspiracy period varies by vitamin: 1990-1999 (B3, B12), 1991-1995 (B2), 1991-1998 (B5), 1991-1994 (B1, B6, folic), and 1989-1998 (B4).

[c] As no reliable estimates of global sales are available, I simply doubled the U.S. sales estimates. Actual global sales could be 50 percent higher.

Some patterns jump out of the table. First, the sizes of the two losses are proportional to the amount of product sales during the affected time periods, but they are not exactly proportional. For example, the monetary injuries to customers of the citric acid cartel was more than twice that of the lysine cartel, primarily because annual global citric acid sales were about double those of lysine. Second, the size of the customer overcharge depends not only on sales during the affected period but also on the overcharge *rate*. The price increase for lysine was slightly higher than that for citric acid. The highest overcharge rate in Table 19.5 was 35 percent for vitamin E, the lowest for vitamin C (11.5 percent). Third, the size of the overcharge is directly related to the length of the conspiracy. All other things the same, more stable cartels extend the size of affected sales. As a rule, the vitamin cartels were more durable than the lysine and citric acid cartels and, therefore, caused more harm. Fourth, on average the social losses due to these cartels amounted to about one-eighth of the total losses. However, the ratio between the social loss and the overcharge varied slightly across products.[30] The social loss for vitamin E was a relatively high proportion of the total loss, but for vitamin C was relatively low.

It should be noted that the cartels that operated in the bulk vitamins markets accounted for nearly 90 percent of the customer losses generated by the three cases examined in this book. Indeed, this share is likely underestimated because there is no estimate of losses available for the huge vitamin premix market. The vitamin cartels raised the profits of vitamin manufactures by at least $6.7 billion and caused an additional $1 billion in lost production and consumption. Government fines and private antitrust suits in North America have recovered only one-third of these losses, and it is doubtful that European antitrust fines will raise the recovery rate above 50 percent.[31] The vitamins case appears to be one in which crime did pay.

ANTITRUST PROSECUTORS: METHODS AND REPUTATIONS

The worldwide convictions of global cartels elevated the reputations of prosecutors among nearly all groups of society. The widespread revelations of the cartels' insidious methods and the scope of their damage to global markets has reinforced the educated public's appreciation of the social benefits of the antitrust laws. Except for a minority ideologically opposed to the laws themselves, business leaders and their legal advisors have a renewed conviction about the importance of avoiding price fixing behavior. In the United States especially, markedly tougher investigatory techniques, substantially higher penalties, and a string of courtroom victories have deepened the image of the antitrust agencies as organizations armed with formidable legal powers. At the same time, the legal community has a heightened realization of the expanded powers of the enforcement agencies to dispense valuable concessions for clients under investigation. Finally, rapidly escalating international cooperation among the world's competition-law authorities has convinced multinational businesses and their executives that locations outside North America no longer provide shelter from criminal antitrust charges.

Positive Publicity

Dozens of press conferences and scores of press releases by the Department of Justice about their legal victories have had the effect of raising the public image of antitrust regulators to nearly heroic stature. Popular books like those by Lieber (2000) and Eichenwald (2000) have portrayed FBI agents and Antitrust Division lawyers as uncorruptable, dedicated public servants. Often, the defendants and their lawyers are drawn in contrast as power hungry, privileged, manipulative, shady characters. The crude amorality displayed on the lysine conspiracy tapes, shocking even to seasoned antitrust lawyers, has done much to justify treating price fixers like déclassé mafia types. The convictions of many prominent corporations for price fixing contributed significantly to the praise received by DOJ antitrust chief Joel Klein upon his retirement in late 2000 (*Washington Post* September 20, 2000).

The 1998 courtroom victory in Chicago against three ADM executives has had an especially strong impact. The convictions and harsh sentences meted out in *U.S. v. Michael Andreas et al.* had the effect of reversing the DOJ's image of incompetence (or at least being out-gunned) earned because of two embarrassing trial losses in the early 1990s (*U.S. v. General Electric and De Beers Consolidated, U.S. v. Appleton Papers*). Several of the prosecutors in the Chicago trial soon received important promotions. Scott Lassar was appointed U.S. Prosecutor in Chicago, and his co-chief prosecutor James Griffin was promoted to become a Deputy Assistant Attorney General in the Antitrust Division. Virtually the whole team was given a prestigious award by the Department of Justice, a sure sign of approbation by Attorney General Janet Reno and the White House. The trial victory was also important because it eased fears that someone so politically important as Dwayne Andreas could not prevent the wheels of justice form grinding to a halt. As the *New York Times* put it, the 1998 verdict ". . . marks a sweeping victory for Federal prosecutors . . ." and shows that Dwayne Andreas could not prevent ". . . the weight of the judicial system from falling on his son and one-time heir apparent . . ." (September 18, 1998). Antitrust lawyers interviewed by the *Chicago Tribune* just after the trial's conclusion said that the lysine and citric acid cartel convictions showed that the antitrust law "has teeth again" (September 20, 1998). A leading antitrust-law scholar, Professor Eleanor Fox, opined that the global cartel prosecutions marked the major direction of change in U.S. enforcement priorities in the 1990's and a vivid reversal of the lethargic pattern during the Reagan years.

There are tangible signals that the DOJ's "crusade against international price fixing" will persist well into the 21st century, because during 1998-2000 the number of grand juries investigating "foreign cartels" has remained at a historic peak above 30 (*National Law Journal* November 9, 1998). In a statement made in April 2000 by Joel Klein, head of the DOJ's Antitrust Division, on the day that seven high-ranking European pharmaceutical executives pleaded guilty, a determined and triumphant tone is apparent:

> "These cases represent a 'clean sweep' for the Division – we will have obtained convictions and U.S. prison terms of the high-level BASF and Hoffmann-La Roche business executives responsible for the vitamin conspiracy. The prison sentences that will be imposed against these foreign executives sends the strongest possible deterrent message – if you violate U.S. antitrust law businesses and consumers, we will hold you individually accountable and will seek tough sentences" (www.usdoj.gov).

Later that year, Klein's assistant James Griffin actually illustrated a speech before antitrust lawyers on the need for corporate antitrust compliance programs by showing video taped meetings of the lysine conspirators in action.[32]

The improved stature of public prosecutors in the United States has redounded on other prosecutors. In Canada, the Competition Bureau and prosecutors working with it in the Ministry of Justice, also have received positive press attention. Indeed, the only slight criticism heard, mostly from populist politicians, has been the Bureau's proclivity of replicating U.S. prosecutions some six to 18 months *after* parallel U.S. convictions. In the European Union, support for anticartel actions by the DG-IV, seems to be solid in the Commission and Parliament. In 2000, the competition-law commissioner was seizing on the moment by requesting significant new investigatory powers. Finally, in the United States where civil antitrust suits are the most effective in the world for compensating direct lawyers, private law firms representing plaintiffs have also experienced a positive alternation in their professional stature. Class action counsel were in the recent past typically described in the business press as opportunistic vultures who inveigled reluctant clients into suing corporations for huge legal fees. However, in the 1990s plaintiffs' counsel are more often portrayed as risk-takers seeking economic justice for exploited customers of cartels. Formerly tagged as "hustlers," class-action antitrust lawyers are now "entrepreneurs."

Perhaps the major reason for the renewed respect accorded antitrust prosecutors are the huge, newsworthy fines and settlements made in the late 1990s. The 100-million-dollar fine paid by ADM for its role in fixing the prices of lysine and citric acid was probably the seminal event among many (see chapter 13). Since 1996, new record judgments were entered against UCAR International and Hoffmann-La Roche by U.S. courts. Canada has similarly extracted record antitrust fines from members of the global food-and-feed-ingredient cartels (chapter 14). The EU's fines for lysine price fixing, while not quite the largest ever seen, were given extensive coverage in the European press. The punishments on individuals for global price fixing by

North American courts have been if anything more shocking to multinational businesspersons. Besides the lengthy prison sentences imposed by U.S. courts on dozens of violators, one German CEO paid a fine of $10 million for his role in fixing the global prices of graphite electrodes. Canadian courts for the first time imposed a prison sentence for price fixing in the case of a vitamin manufacturer.

Almost equally important in raising the public's consciousness about the seriousness of antitrust enforcers is the marked transformation in U.S. investigatory tactics. Prior to 1990, violations of the Sherman Act were misdemeanors. In common with other less serious white-collar crimes, the FBI employed a limited range of relatively gentle investigatory methods. However, since 1990, FBI probes into global price fixing have used the full range of "blue-collar" tools of the trade, methods long employed against drug dealers, kidnappers, and in counterintelligence: audio and video tapes, tapping telephones, undercover informants, and "flipping" small fish to get the big fish (Eichenwald 2000). To an old-fashioned lawyer like Robert Strauss, long accustomed to white-glove treatment for his corporate clients, the behavior of the FBI and DOJ in investigating the lysine cartel was "almost obscene and shocking" (*Business Week Online*: *www.businessweek.com*).[33] Another ADM director, Ross Johnson, in a public meeting at a southern university called the FBI "thugs." The use of large forces of agents to serve search warrants simultaneously at all the alleged cartel members' offices has the practical value of minimizing the destruction of evidence, but its psychological value may be even greater (*USA Today* July 10, 2000).

The third factor responsible for the perception of prosecutorial power in antitrust matters is the enhanced range of sentencing discretion available to public prosecutors. To obtain the cooperation of credible witnesses, prosecutors have long made deals for reduced sentences, but now that the potential fines and prison sentences are so much greater than before, the degree of downward departure is also ever so much greater. In only one instance did a judge fail to approve a reduction below the minimum guideline level that was recommended by the DOJ (and that involved only about a 5 percent increase in one firm's antitrust fine). Reduction of 50 to 90 percent in the amounts of the fines or prison sentences called for by U.S. Sentencing Guidelines are routinely approved. Moreover, to gain a company's cooperation, all but one or two of many potentially liable conspirators in the company are granted complete immunity from prosecution. For example, in the case of Ajinomoto, only two officers were fined, nine were granted immunity, and one remains a fugitive. In economic terms, perhaps the greatest grant of immunity was made to ADM in return for the company's rather spotty cooperation in the DOJ's citric acid prosecution. Among the most valuable of many favors showered on ADM was the DOJ's promise that it would not prosecute ADM for alleged price fixing in the market for corn fructose; indeed, the DOJ's criminal investigation was quietly ended three years later, much to the consternation of plaintiffs in civil suits involving fructose.[34]

Federal antitrust prosecutors also have great discretion in awarding leniency or amnesty to confessed corporate or individual price fixers. The latest leniency guidelines appear to be quite precise in print, but in practice prosecutors have a great deal of discretion in applying them to specific cases. A related concession of great interest to most businesspeople in global industries is the power of the DOJ to grant free entry to the United States to convicted price fixing conspirators, even those guilty of felonies.

The Limits of Power

The prosecutions of global cartels in the late 1990s also revealed some limitations in the powers of federal prosecutors. First, it is apparent that one reason for the successes in the lysine and citric acid cases was the active involvement of the highest-level officials during the investigation and plea-bargaining phases. From 1992 to 1996, the Antitrust Division's top official, Anne Bingaman, supervised the lysine investigation. Sometime in late 1995 or early 1996, direct supervision passed to Bingaman's chief assistant, Jamie Gorelick, who was joined unofficially by Joel Klein from the White House Office of the General Counsel around the same time. At the FBI, Director Louis Freeh was at times personally involved in decisions (Eichenwald 2000). In late 1995, Gorelick added Scott Lassar to the Chicago Antitrust Division's prosecutorial team. Later, when the lysine case led to evidence of cartel activity in other markets, the majority of the division's other regional offices would become involved (San Francisco, Dallas, Atlanta, and Philadelphia). Involvement of so many high officials was indicative of the high priority and extreme caution accorded to these cases, but it also demonstrated how thinly stretched were its human resources.[35] At the same time, the demands on the Division for merger clearances and other cases escalated.

Second, the antitrust agencies may have been hampered by other resource constraints. During the prosecution of the global conspiracies, the DOJ's antitrust resources were lower than in the 1980s. The Antitrust Division's annual budget in 1998 was only $98 million; it employed 363 attorneys, down from 456 in 1980. A record number of mergers required that large resources be devoted to monitoring corporate acquisitions. Moreover, the Division was pursuing the largest monopoly case since those against AT&T and IBM in 1969-1981. Those cases had required the agency to spend more than $37 million in 1982 dollars, and many outside observers thought that its case against Microsoft might require similar expenditures. Further evidence of budgetary strain was the surprising decision of a larger number of DOJ lawyers to sue the Department for its failure to pay them for overtime work.

The DOJ's October 1998 decision to indict Microsoft for monopolizing certain markets for personal computer software was a difficult and controversial one. Microsoft had first been investigated in the late 1980s during the Reagan and Bush administrations. It had signed a consent decree with the DOJ in 1995, but the DOJ alleged that Microsoft had violated terms of the decree. In its indictment, the DOJ was joined as plaintiff by the attorneys general of 19 states. The expedited trial began in federal court in the District of Columbia in late 1998, and after a few weeks of testimony, most commentators had concluded that Microsoft would lose the case. Yet, the Microsoft prosecution caused a third problem for the DOJ – a significant political backlash. Microsoft's response to its predicament is a revealing lesson about how rough Washington politics can get.

Until the late 1990s, Microsoft and its employees were distinctly apolitical. In 1994, they gave collectively only $106,000 in hard-money political contributions. By 1997-1998, political contributions, public relations expenditures, and lobbying costs had greatly expanded. During the 1997-1998 election cycle, their soft-money political contributions and lobbying costs rose six-fold over 1995-1996 levels to $3 million; hard-money contributions tripled. Microsoft and its employees became the largest single contributor to Washington State's Senator Slade Gorton. They also contributed to ostensibly broad-based citizens groups who supported the company's views. Furthermore, when in late 1998 the antitrust trial began to go badly for the company, it redoubled its efforts. Microsoft's Washington, D.C. lobbying office had ten employees by 1999; many other prominent lobbyists were hired.

The target of all these efforts was the Antitrust Division of the Department of Justice and Congressional and public opinion about the federal suit. One of Microsoft's lawyers contacted the newly appointed New York Attorney General and attempted to get the state to withdraw as a plaintiff in the Microsoft antitrust suit. The Attorney General's office called the action "crude and unsuccessful." However, Senator Gorton became Microsoft's main public critic of the DOJ. In 1998, he characterized the DOJ's antitrust chief's testimony about the need for assertive enforcement of the antitrust laws as "an endorsement of the very kind of socialist-style command and control economics embraced by the Soviet Union." A year later, in a meeting with Microsoft employees about the antitrust trial, he called the presiding federal judge "third-rate."

Potentially most damaging was Senator Gorton's well reported effort to cut the Antitrust Division's proposed fiscal 2000 budget. He and his allies were blunt about the reason: they estimated the DOJ was spending up to $60 million prosecuting Microsoft, and they wanted to cripple the Division's ability to continue the prosecution.[36] In March 1999, nine members of the Senate Judiciary Committee took the unusual step of sending a signed letter to the Senate Appropriations Committee saying the proposed budget cuts:

> ". . . may have the undesirable effect of opening the door to undue interference with ongoing Department of Justice litigation."

In other words, Senator Gorton's actions were unprecedented and tantamount to obstruction of justice. Even the Senator's hometown newspaper, the *Seattle Times,* debunked his quest in an editorial entitled "Gorton's Goofy Attack on the Justice Department."[37]

There is some danger that the antitrust triumphs over the cartels and Microsoft might lead to arrogance or hubris within the DOJ. One piece of evidence for this evolving posture is the Antitrust Division's "Ten Million Dollar Club," that is, its list of corporations that have paid $10 million or more in fines. Like stuffed animals in a hunter's trophy room, the list is prominently displayed on the agency's web page. Instead of somber references to such firms, DOJ official typically refer to the Club in gleeful terms. These and other references to the high fines the Division had garnered may place too high a weight on only one of many possible punishments for price fixers.

Although the Federal Government does not keep criminal fines as a sort of tax, the public is not aware of the fact. Critics of antitrust enforcement have sown some confusion on this point. Fines on a few violations are conflated into an attack on all businesses. In an editorial that focused on the impacts of the food-and-feed-ingredient cartel convictions, the writer asserts that:

> "There's one . . . place where business is still regarded as the enemy: The antitrust shop at Justice" (*Wall Street Journal* July 24, 2000).

The editorial then goes on to complain about how antitrust is an unacceptable intrusion on "shareholders' rights" by "unelected officials" like Joel Klein who are motivated only be "media attention and career visibility." While it is difficult to take such radical points of view seriously, it does show the desirability of the DOJ's avoiding the appearance of gleeful truimphantism.

Possible Antitrust Reforms

It is possible that the huge fines on corporations will have little long run effects on the largest multinational corporations. In most cases the fines are small percentages of the guilty company's liquid assets. Many antitrust observers believe that personal fines and prison sentences, when combined with sufficient social opprobrium, have greater long term deterrence effects. The "statutory" maximum fine for individual violators of the Sherman Act is $350,000 – an amount that is easily within the means of nearly all the top executives who were fined for international price fixing in the late 1990s. The U.S. Congress passed two alternative sentencing statutes that apply to antitrust felony convictions in 1987 and 1994 (Chapter 15). However, the first time that government prosecutors tried to obtain a significantly higher fine under the alternative statutes by litigation was unsuccessful. In 1998, prosecutors sought a fine of $25 million for Michael Andreas for his role in the lysine cartel; under another of the alternative statutes his lawyers calculated a personal liability of $92 million. Fines of these magnitudes would be more likely to deter all but the richest men from violation the laws against price fixing.

However painful such monetary penalties would be, the prospect of long prison sentences would probably be even more daunting. The present upper U.S. limit of 36 months is certainly a significant disincentive for would-be price fixers, but few have served anything close to the maximum sentence. Even the maximum prison sentence is low compared to many minimum sentences for non-violent federal crimes involving far less economic injury, such as the sale or possession of drugs. In general, there appears to be an imbalance between the prison sentences given out for "blue-collar" crimes and "white-collar" crimes like price fixing conspiracies. There is even a greater disparity between the U.S. willingness to impose significant criminal penalties and the absence of such powers in the EU and most of its member states.

The DOJ has been criticized for giving away too much when it negotiated guilty pleas for corporate and individual members of global cartels that were convicted in the late 1990s. In the case of ADM's lysine-citric acid fine, months before negotiations began prosecutors leaked to the press their intention to seek a $400 million fine. Perhaps this was just a bargaining ploy, but even as late as one month before ADM's plea bargain was made public, the DOJ wanted a fine of $125 million and the freedom to indict four officers (Dwayne Andreas, Michael Andreas, James Randall, and Terrance Wilson) (Eichenwald 2000: 508-511). The final compromise was $100 million and two current officers of ADM indictable. Doubtless most plea bargains involve compromises of this type between prosecutors and defense counsel. As distressing such a pragmatic process is to purists who value highly legal principles, the limited resources of the federal antitrust agencies makes avoiding all but a few trials each year virtually necessary. In deciding which penalties to concede to the defense and which to insist upon, a large number of competing factors must be weighed, including proportionality across crimes and the chances of losing through litigation or a failure to bring a foreign resident to trial.

The temptation is great to arrive speedily at a plea bargain that results in multimillion-dollar corporate fines of dubious punishment value, but it opens federal prosecutors to suspicions of political interference. At the press conference announcing ADM's fine, DOJ official Gary Spratling was peppered with aggressive questions from journalists about concessions made to ADM. He finally had to say: "There are no politics involved in this deal" (*Federal News Service* October 15, 1996). Nearly four years later Attorney General Janet Reno felt compelled to make a similarly defensive statement:

> "When news of our ADM investigation reached antitrust enforcers in other nations, some expressed skepticism that we would ever take action against such a powerful player in the U.S. market place . . . Not only were we ever pressured to stop . . . but we fully prosecuted that case . . ." (*Federal Document Clearing House* June 15, 2000).

While one might quibble about whether the DOJ *fully* prosecuted all culpable individuals at ADM, the statement of a popular Attorney General made near the end of her term in office must be accorded a large degree of credence. Moreover, given the fact that the great majority of the corporate conspirators in the lysine, citric acid, and vitamins industries were non-U.S. firms, demonstrating a willingness to seek severe punishments for the U.S. participants was a necessary adjunct to the movement towards convergence in international antitrust enforcement.

Although the Department of Justice conducted an independent and aggressive investigation of the lysine cartel, there are still a number of decisions that remain puzzling, the motives for which lie shrouded in official secrecy (Lieber 2000: 322-334). For example, it seems odd that in the 16 months prior to ADM's guilty plea, neither Dwayne Andreas nor James Randall were interviewed by the FBI or subpoenaed for grand-jury testimony about any of the five or more cartels in which ADM participated, nor were their offices searched. Another mysterious aspect of the prosecution is the DOJ's failure to seek the extradition of Ajinomoto's top conspirator, who may have had damaging information about Andreas and Randall. Doubts remain about why an affidavit from a major buyer of corn fructose about ADM's monopolistic behavior in that industry did not trigger grand-jury testimony. Williams & Connelly, ADM's principal law firm in antitrust matters, was granted an unusual degree of deference during the lysine investigation. It was allowed to have its lawyers present during FBI interviews, which had a chilling effect on ADM employees' responses.

Although the Antitrust Division and FBI did not succumb to Williams & Connelly's blandishments, the Washington, D.C.-based Fraud Section seems to have become a tool of the law firm. Except for Mark Whitacre, ADM did everything it could to resist the Fraud Section's investigation of all of its employees alleged to have embezzled the company, even five or six friends of Whitacre who assisted his theft.[38] Perhaps the most puzzling aspect of the case is why the DOJ joined the defense lawyers at trial in savaging their own highly productive whistle blower, Mark Whitacre, who received a sentence nearly as harsh as Terrance Wilson.[39] By charging Whitacre for about three months of price fixing behavior for which he was not immunized, his silence at the trial was virtually guaranteed. The DOJ's treatment of Whitacre may indeed be viewed as *sui generis*, as the agency believes, but it may serve to make recruitment of cooperating witnesses more difficult in future cartel cases.

Political Support for the Antitrust Laws

The United States' antitrust laws have generally received bipartisan support from the U.S. Congress. While the support of presidential administrations for antitrust enforcement has ebbed and waned over time, neither political party nor ideological orientation can explain such cycles.[40] This comment is especially true for the Sherman Act prohibition of conspiracies in restraint of trade. With respect to antimonopoly enforcement, there appears to be some tendency for major cases to be brought during the last year or two of a presidential administration.

The revelations about the global cartels in the late 1990s have reinforced political commitment to anticartel enforcement, and the relevant agencies have responded by shifting resources toward investigating and indicting international price fixing conspiracies. The U.S. shift has been further justified by a U.S. appeals-court ruling in 1997 that clarified the law on extraterritorial violations for the Sherman Act. At the state level, large monetary settlements involved in the global vitamins case prompted no less than 44 attorneys general to band together in 1999 to sue to recover price fixing injuries.[41] In the European Union, the commissioners in charge of the competition laws have sometimes come from political traditions antithetical to the antitrust philosophy of preserving the competitive process in markets, yet they have developed a zeal for their work typical of converts. In late 1999, the European Commission's DG-IV formed a new unit specifically focused on anticartel investigations.

The global cartels were also responsible for accelerating the trend evident since 1945 for countries outside North America to adopt new or more stringent anticartel legislation. Since 1996, countries as diverse as New Zealand, the United Kingdom, South Africa, Sweden, and the Netherlands have revised and strengthened their antitrust laws governing price fixing. The ADM case was cited as one reason for raising the maximum fine for cartel behavior in New Zealand in 1998. In 1999, South African legislation brought its fine structure in line with EU standards and permitted civil suits to seek private damage awards. Following the adoption of a set of recommendations on hard-core cartels by the Organization of Economic Cooperation and Development in 1999, at least four of its member states – Denmark, Sweden, the Netherlands, and the UK – significantly strengthened their competition laws in the area of price fixing. (*European Report* June 7, 2000).

A more recent set of OECD recommendations urges greater international cooperation in fighting global cartels, but the statement merely blesses a trend that has been strong since 1990. New bilateral agreements are being signed almost every month that make information-sharing and coordinated investigations possible. Cooperation among the U.S., EU, Canadian, and Australian antitrust agencies is already intense. A rather extraordinary example of such partnerships was the simultaneous raids by police agencies in Europe, the U.S., and Japan on the corporate offices of manufacturers of graphite electrodes. Whether enhanced international investigation might evolve into the establishment of a multilateral antitrust agency is uncertain. However, even though a distinguished advisory panel set up by the DOJ's Antitrust Division was split on the idea, public opinion in the United States seems to be shifting toward such an arrangement for limited areas of antitrust enforcement (ICPAC 2000). Smaller countries and the EU seem to favor centralization of antitrust authority in a body like the World Trade Organization.

AN ANTITRUST TRAGEDY

The story of the lysine cartel has all the elements of a tragedy in the tradition of Euripides or one of Shakespeare's darker historical plays.

Chairman Dwayne Andreas is the play's protagonist, the aged king of a city-state that he had raised from a position of weak obscurity to one of imperial dimensions. His character flaw is his monomaniacal urge to build an impregnable agribusiness empire that would serve as the foundation of a new dynasty. The means employed to refashion a provincial enterprise into a global powerhouse had all the hallmarks common to the warrior-kings of history.

The Harvest King created an extensive network of foreign alliances with powerful outsiders by giving valuable gifts, trading information known to only a few, or forming marriages that defanged potential rivals. The gifts were well placed political contributions, the information concerned global agribusiness markets and inscrutable foreign leaders, and the marriages were joint ventures. Within the little city, Andreas instilled unquestioned authority to his person with a combination of charm, cupidity, intimidation, charisma, and co-opting the council of elders. He taught his troops blitzkrieg marketing tactics based on cunning, guile, and casual disregard for the rules of war. He reinforced his position by creating the persona of a great statesman driven only by the highest goals of patriotism through careful cultivation of the organs of propaganda. The cult of personality and the unbroken string of strategic victories blinded ADM to the fact that its loose, informal, opportunistic, guerilla style of decision making – in itself a source of great pride – had become obsolete as its empire became more complex.

Michael Andreas is the crown prince, raised almost from the beginning to inherit the scepter of power. The prince inherited the paternal hubris and had learned his father's statecraft well, proudly repeating the old man's maxims, as did the chief lieutenants Randall and Wilson as well. They particularly cherished the paramount maxim:

> "Our competitors are our friends, our customers are the enemy."

But there was at least one skill that the prince failed to learn from the old king. He forgot to write down and cover up all his lies and indiscretions.

That left Michael vulnerable to the tragedy's triagonist, a brilliant lieutenant, driven by greed and ambition, who had a great deal of trouble telling anyone the truth. Mark Whitacre thrilled to the role of spy but found the role of double agent even more exciting. As a recent immigrant to the Andreas fiefdom, Whitacre never developed the blind loyalty to the royal family shared by most of the company's managers. Moreover, Whitacre quickly realized the great flaw in ADM's informal management methods – its lack of checks and balances. The unusually wide discretion accorded ADM managers worked well when the company was filled with men loyal to its chief and his vision. However, this thin, flexible management style, coupled with weak supervision by the board of directors, could easily be subverted by a determined deviant.

In the tragedy's background, obscured by the din and smoke of business battles, is a small band of guardians tending the fire of the old religion in a temple of classical proportions. Long ignored by the play's main characters, who ascribe the company/state's success to their own perspicacity, the guardians try to remind the citizens of the virtues of competition played freely and fairly. Throughout the first half of the play, the guardians stay near the back of the stage ignored by the chorus of citizens. As the play progresses and the main characters crimes are revealed, the guardians' warning began to be heard with greater prominence.

The curtain on this tragedy opened in the fall of 1989, when ADM hired a young Mark Whitacre to grow its new lysine business. The drama's denouement is reached in September 1998, when the guardians of the old religion are victorious in court, and a jury condemns Michael Andreas and Mark Whitacre to banishment. As the curtain falls in January 1999, the Harvest King abdicates as his fiefdom begins to crumble from within and the chorus chants "Shame. Shame."

Chapter 19 Endnotes

[1] *Business Week* (July 27, 1998) compared the global cartel stories to the plot of a "cheap paperback thriller-mystery" full of secret meetings, code names, and treaty negotiations. Eichenwald's (2000) account of the FBI's lysine probe borrows his style from this genre. Indeed, he suggests that some of Mark Whitacre's behavior was inspired by his reading of Grisham's novel *The Firm*. Life imitates art.

[2] Concentration was equally high for vitamin E and most of the B complex vitamins, but was lower for vitamin C.

[3] Indeed, most oligopoly models predict a continuous relationship between market share or industry concentration and the Lerner index of market power. These theoretical results have led some industry economists to dismiss the validity of a "critical" concentration level.

[4] The threshold employed by the DOJ for merger analysis (a monopoly power concept) is a Herfindahl index of 1800, which corresponds to a 60 to 65 percent four-firm concentration ratio. The critical concentration level identified in most studies appears to refer to a significant increase in market price above the purely competitive price. To achieve the monopoly (maximum rational) price, industry concentration would have to be higher than 40 or 50 percent.

[5] The methods for making most bulk vitamins use older methods of synthetic chemistry no longer protected by patents. Yet the production methods appear to be quite complex and difficult to master. Vitamin C is something of an exception.

[6] In the vitamins markets no previous cartels are known to have operated. Except for vitamin A, most of the cartels had non-European firms that were unaccustomed to cooperating with the major European vitamins manufacturers.

[7] A noteworthy exception is the behavior of Chinese chemical manufacturers. In the citric acid and several vitamin markets, Chinese companies were spoilers. Most Chinese suppliers were too small or technologically immature to be invited to join the cartels. None were ready to restrain their hunger for export growth.

[8] As of late 2000 not all governments had acted in all three cases. Estimates are provided for probable fines as well as some civil settlements not announced.

[9] The authors seem to be concerned about the large number of federal cases filed against the vitamins defendants (they claim 40 defendants faced 50 suits). However, the 4000 plaintiffs in vitamins were consolidated into one class until late 1999. Only after hundreds of firms rejected the low settlement offer did the opt-outs file suits. Therefore, it may be the low-ball settlement offered by the defendants that generated the suits.

[10] Of course, bankruptcy that reduces the number of viable firms in an industry to levels that endanger the competitiveness of the market itself would indeed be "overreacting" (Klawiter 1998). However, the market for firms is a highly liquid one, so valuable assets of bankrupt firms need not reduce capacity or company numbers in an industry.

[11] EU fines may add another layer of penalties about equal to actual damages, and the U.S. DOJ can use global sales as a fine-setting standard, though it rarely does. Allowing for these two factors, the theoretical maximum liability is about four times global profits.

[12] Other conventional profit rates such as profits/equity or profits/assets show comparable trends.

[13] Government fines for lysine price fixing, other than those by the EU and Canada, are not yet known, but are estimated to be small. At the end of 2000, the EU had not yet acted on the citric acid cartel, so an analysis of ADM's net revenues is not possible.

[14] Political writer, Michael Kinsey, excoriated ADM's ads in a 1990 magazine article as dishonest, cloying, offensive, and strange (*New Republic* June 18, 1990).

[15] ADM's dependence on political largess continues. In 1997, the federal subsidy for ethanol production was extended to the year 2007. The total subsidy is expected to reach $11 billion, with more than half going to ADM.

[16] BASF has also launched a number of major acquisitions in the late 1990s. Its largest purchase occurred in March 2000, when it agreed to pay $3.9 billion to Cyanamid Division of American Home Products after a six-week auction.

[17] Great Lakes confessed to the DOJ about its role in a global cartel in bromine products. Except for the guilty pleas of other members of the cartel, the business press has been silent since Great Lake's first press release in June 1999.

[18] It is quite possible that ADM's Chairman knew a little about the lysine cartel and it is probable that ADM's president was well informed. In Japanese and European companies, a management committee of five to nine executives form the top executive board.

[19] That official was Secretary to the Board of Directors of ADM, Howard Buffett, who has never been suspected of criminal antitrust violations. However, he has never publicly protested ADM's behavior. In a section below, the fate of many of the most prominent price fixers is described in more detail.

[20] Some other reforms included reducing directors' compensation from a minimum of $110,000 per year to about half of that level and changing the nominating committee's membership to include more outsiders. The company has at times tried to keep the identity of new directors secret from the stockholders because they continue to fail tests of independence.

[21] G. Allen Andreas' reputation was sullied by the fact that he had been in charge of ADM's European operations during the period when the company was conspiring on lysine and citric acid prices there. His decision to continue Michael Andreas' $1.3 million salary from October 1996 to late 1998 was questionable (Lieber 2000:42).

[22] The U.S. Department of Justice is encouraging companies to adopt antitrust compliance programs by making available a video tape of meetings of the lysine cartel for training purposes. The video tape is free to the public (Griffin 2000).

[23] This statement refers to the higher limits that became law in 1990. In any case, Andreas' penalties are the highest in the history of antitrust.

[24] Traditionally, whistle-blowers are given suspended sentences for illegal activity prior to signing on as an informant with the FBI, or they are not indicted at all (Lieber 2000). Only a minor portion of Whitacre's prison sentence was effectively suspended. On the other hand, Lieber (2000) suggests that Whitacre could have been found guilty of ghost employment, forgery, and witness tampering.

[25] All the details are not known. Whether the two employees were provided with legal assistance or retained retirement benefits is uncertain.

[26] One of the seven remained a fugitive in late 2000.

[27] When a cartel is able to recruit all the world's sellers into its folds, the sellers are of course equivalent to the cartel members. If some sellers do not join, their customers are still injured as non-cartel sellers benefit from the high prices caused by the cartel. Although principally an income transfer, Posner (1976) argues that much or all of the monopoly overcharge is a social cost. Many economists agree with this analysis.

[28] U.S. law is at present split on whether plaintiffs that suffer dead-weight losses can seek restitution or treble damages. Some U.S. circuits permit plaintiffs to seek such damages while others do not (Page 1996).

[29] The U.S. and EU portions of these monetary losses are approximately 25 to 30 percent of the global totals shown in Table 19.5. In the cases of citric acid and vitamin C, the global figures may be a bit too high because of strong price competition in Asia by Chinese manufacturers.

[30] The social loss depends on the size of the affected sales, the absolute value of the elasticity of demand, and the *square* of the overcharge rate. For simplicity, the elasticity was assumed to be the same for all products, thus the overcharge rate was the main determinant of this ratio.

[31] As of late 2000, the EU had not yet announced what fines it would seek for citric acid or vitamins. Suits in other countries would likely not be very large.

[32] His speech, a manual giving guidelines for such programs, and the videotape are now freely available to the public (www.usdoj.gov).

[33] Actually, the FBI found it impossible to tap telephones in ADM's headquarters and residential telephones linked to it because ADM's security system was state-of-the-art. The

agents were also defeated in their attempt to place radio transmitters inside ADM's office building (Tr. 4080-4081).

[34] The full extent of the concessions may not be known. ADM was not charged for criminal violations in the case of alleged cartel behavior in sodium glutonate, monosodium glutamate, methionine, and lactic acid.

[35] The degree of involvement by the Attorney General herself or other members of the White House General Counsel's Office is not know but is believed to be substantial.

[36] Later the DOJ released information that the Microsoft prosecution from October 1989 to October 1999 had cost $13.3 million, far less than the $17 and $20 million spent on the IBM and AT&T cases during 1969-1982.

[37] Among the more loony theories propounded by Gorton was that the DOJ suit was part of a White House conspiracy. Specifically, the plot was designed to boost Vice President Gore's presidential ambitions by benefiting corporate rivals of Microsoft located in California. The *Seattle Times* expressed concern that Senator Groton was getting "wiggy." In the 2000 election, Senator Gorton lost his seat in Congress to a Democratic Party challenger.

[38] However, Williams & Connelly's attempt to get two others charged failed: David Hoech, a shareholder-critic of ADM, and Bonnie Wittenburg, an investment analyst specializing in ADM.

[39] By the time the sentencing phase arrived, the Chicago-based prosecutors seem to have softened in their views about his culpability, though they did not request the usual suspended sentence.

[40] Companies like the ADM and Microsoft that are defending themselves from antitrust allegations tend to split their political contributions fairly equally between the two major parties.

[41] Only 24 claimed indirect purchaser injuries but all 44 represented their state governments as direct buyers. In October 2000, the states announced an agreement in principle that will require the six largest vitamin cartel members to pay the states $340 million.

REFERENCES

Abrue, D., D. Pearce and E. Stachetti. Optimal Cartel Equilibria with Imperfect Monitoring. *Journal of Economic Theory* 39(1986):251-269.

Achebe, Chinua. *Home and Exile*. Oxford: Oxford University Press (2000).

Adams, Kenneth and Anthony Bell. Overseas Victims of Price Fixing Should Be Welcomed into U.S. Courts. *Legal Times* (October 25, 1999):36.

Adams, Stanley, *Roche versus Adams*. London: J. Cape (1984).

Adler, Howard and David J. Laing. Explosion of International Criminal Antitrust Enforcement. *The Corporate Counselor* (March 1997):1.

ADM. *Annual Report to Stockholders*. Decatur, Illinois: Archer Daniels Midland (1997 and previous).

Alchin, Tim. Interview: Van Miert Sees EU Cartel Fines Exceeding U.S. Penalties. *Extel Examiner* (AFX) September 8, 1999.

Andretsch, David B. Legalized Cartels in Germany. *Antitrust Bulletin* 34 (1989): 579-600.

Antitrust Division. *10-year Workload Statistics Report*. Washington, DC: Antitrust Division, U.S. Department of Justice (1999) (www.usdoj.gov/atr/public).

Apple, Rima D. *Vitamania: Vitamins in American Culture*. New Brunswick, NJ: Rutgers University Press (1996).

Asch, Peter and Joseph J. Seneca. Characteristics of Collusive Firms. *Journal of Industrial Economics* 23 (1975):223-237.

Azzam, Azzedine and Dale Anderson. *Assessing Competition in Meat packing: Economic History, Theory, and Evidence*, GIPSA-RR 96-6. Washington, DC: Grain Inspection, Packers and Stockyards Administration, USDA (May 1996).

Bagwell, Kyle and Robert W. Staiger. Collusion Over the Business Cycle. *RAND Journal of Economics* 28 (1997): 82-106.

Bain, Joe S. Relation of Profit Rate to Industry Concentration: American Manufacturing, 1936-1940. *American Economic Review* 65 (1951):488-500.

Barbezat, Daniel. Cooperation and Rivalry in the International Steel Cartel, 1926-1933. *The Journal of Economic History* 49 (1989): 435-447.

Barbezat, Daniel. A Price for Every Product, Every Place: The International Steel Export Cartel, 1933-39 in *Coalitions and Collaboration in International Business*. Geoffrey Jones ed. International Library of Critical Writings in Business History, no. 7 (1993).

Barboza, David. "Tearing Down the Facade of 'Vitamins, Inc.'" *New York Times* (October 10, 1999): Section 3, page 1.

Barboza, David. New Sprouts, Old Doubts for ADM. *The New York Times* (December 24, 2000): Section 3, p. 1.

Barker, Ernest (ed.). *The Politics of Aristotle*. New York: Oxford University Press (1962).

BCC. *The Global Market for Vitamins in Food, Feed, Pharma, and Cosmetics*. Norwalk, CT: Business Communications Company, Inc. (November 1996).

Bell, Meridith and Elena Gaskin. Antitrust violations. *American Criminal Law Review* 36(Summer 1999):357-396.

Bingaman, Anne. K. International Cooperation and the Future of U.S. Antitrust Enforcement, American Law Institute meeting, Washington, DC (May 16, 1997).

Bingaman, Anne K. Change and Continuity in Antitrust Enforcement, speech at the Fordham Corporate Law Institute, Fordham Law School, New York (October 21, 1993).

Blair, Roger D. and David L. Kaserman. *Antitrust Economics*. Homewood, Illinois: Richard D. Irwin (1985).

Bork, Robert. *The Antitrust Paradox: A Policy at War with Itself*. New York: Basic Books (1978).

Bosch, J. and E. W. Eckard. The Profitability of Price Fixing: Evidence from Stock Market Reactions to Federal Indictments. *Review of Economics and Statistics* 73 (1991): 309-317.

Bovard, James. *Archer Daniels Midland: A Case Study in Corporate Welfare*, Policy Analysis No. 241. Washington, DC: The Cato Institute (September 1995).

Brewster, Kingman. *Antitrust and American Business Abroad.*

Brian-Simpson, A.W. English Common Law. *New Palgrave Dictionary of Economics and the Law.* London: MacMillan (1998).

Briggs, Hugh. Optimal Cartel Trigger Strategies and the Number of Firms. *Review of Industrial Organization* 11(1996):551-561.

Brock, W. A. and J. A. Scheinkman. Price-Setting Supergames with Capacity Constraints. *Review of Economic Studies* 52 (1985) 371-382.

Bryant, Peter G. and E. Woodrow Eckard. Price Fixing: The Probability of Getting Caught. *Review of Economics and Statistics* 73(1991):531-540.

Calkins, Stephen. An Enforcement Official's Reflections on Antitrust Class Actions. *Arizona Law Review* 39 (Summer 1997): 413-451.

Carlson, Peter. Chairman Across the Board. *Washington Post Sunday Magazine* (July 14, 1996):W13.

Caves, Richard E. *Multinational Enterprise and Economic Analysis (2nd Edition)*. Cambridge: Cambridge University Press (1996).

Christy, W. G., J. Harris, and P. Schultz. Why bid NASDAQ Market Makers Stop Avoiding Odd-Eighth Quotes? *Journal of Finance* 49 (1994): 1841-1860.

CMR. (Scores of articles on citric acid and other industrial organic chemicals produced by the wet-corn milling industry). *Chemical Marketing Reporter* (April 1990 to 1999).

Coate, Malcolm B. and F.S. McChesney. Empirical Evidence on FTC Enforcement of the Merger Guidelines. *Economic Inquiry* 30 (1992): 277-293.

Coate, Malcolm B. and Andrew N. Kleit (editors). *The Economics of the Antitrust Process.* Boston: Kluwer Academic (1996).

Connor, John M. *et. al. The Food Manufacturing Industries: Strategies, Structure, Performance, and Policies.* Lexington, Mass.: Lexington Books (1985).

Connor, John M. *The Cost to U.S. Animal-Feeds Manufacturers of an Alleged Price-Fixing Conspiracy by Lysine Manufacturers*, In Re Amino Acid Lysine Antitrust Litigation, July 1996a.

Connor, John M. *Expert Opinion on the Citric Acid Market*, confidential report to attorneys dated October 10, 1996b, 14 pp.

Connor, John M. *Report on the U.S. Corn Syrup Market*, confidential report to attorneys dated October 16, 1996c, 29 pp.

Connor, John M. International Convergence of Antitrust Laws and Enforcement. *Review of Antitrust Law and Economics* 28(1997):17-30 and 73-94.

Connor, John M. The Global Lysine Price-Fixing Conspiracy of 1992-1995. *Review of Agricultural Economics* (1997):19, 158-174.

Connor, John M. The Global Citric Acid Conspiracy: Legal-Economic Lessons. *Agribusiness: An International Journal* 14(1998):435-452.

Connor, John M. *Lysine Production, Trade, and the Effects of International Price Fixing* (Third Edition), Staff Paper 19-13. W. Lafayette, IN: Purdue University (October 1999).

Connor, John M. *Economic Analysis of the Markets for Vitamins B3 and B4*, confidential report to attorneys (June 9, 1999), 67 pp.

Connor, John M. *Archer Daniels Midland: Price-Fixer to the World (Fourth Edition)*, Staff Paper 00-14. W. Lafayette, IN: Department of Agricultural Economics, Purdue University (December 2000).

Connor, John M. "Our Customers Are Our Enemies:" The Lysine Cartel of 1992-1995. *Review of Industrial Organization* 18(2001):5-21.

Connor, John M. The Evolution of the Global Lysine Industry: 1960-2000. *Review of Agricultural Economics* (2001a).

Connor, John M. and Everett E. Peterson. New Estimates of Welfare Losses due to Imperfect Competition in U.S. Food Manufacturing, in *Contributions to Economic Analysis No. 234: Agricultural Markets: Mechanisms, Failures, Regulations*, David Martimort (editor). Amersterdam: Elsevier (1996).

Connor, John M. and William A. Schiek. *Food Processing: An Industrial Powerhouse in Transition* (Second Edition). New York: John Wiley & Sons (1997).

Cyrenne, Phillipe. On Antitrust Enforcement and the Deterrance of Collusive Behavior. *Review of Industrial Organization* 15 (1998): 257-272.

Daniel, John E., Mark F. Pomerantz, and Richard Wolfram. Japanese Companies Enter Pleas, Agree to Cooperate in Major U.S. Criminal Antitrust Investigation: How the Government Does It and Lessons To Be Learned. *Business Briefing Publishing Ltd.* (August 29, 1997): Lexis-Nexis, 4959 words.

Davidow, Joel. Cartels, Competition Laws, and the Regulation of International Trade. *Journal of International Law and Politics* 15 (1983): 351-376.

Davis, Audrey B. The Rise of the Vitamin-Medicinal as Illustrated by Vitamin D. *Pharmacy in History* 24 (1982): 59-72.

Decugis, Henri, *et al. Legal Aspects of Industrial Agreements*, report to the League of Nations (1930).

Dick, Andrew R. Are Export Cartels Efficiency-Enhancing or Monopoly-Promoting? *Research in Law and Economics* 15 (1992): 89-127.

Dick, Andrew R. Identifying Contracts, Combinations, and Conspiracies in Restraint of Trade. *Managerial and Decision Economics* 17 (1996): 203-216.

Dick, Andrew R. When Are Cartels Stable Contracts? *Journal of Law and Economics* 39 (1996):241-283.

Dick, Andrew R. If Cartels Were Legal, Would Firms Fix Prices? Unpublished manuscript (August 4, 1997).

Dick, Andrew R. ACartels" in *The New Palgrave Dictionary of Law and Economics*, John Eatwell (editor). London: Macmillan (1998).

Dick, Andrew R. Horizontal Antitrust Screens (www.antitrust.org/economics/pricefixing/screen) (1995).

Domowitz, Ian, Glenn R. Hubbard, and Bruce C. Peterson. *Business Cycles and Oligopoly Supergames: Some Empirical Evidence on Prices and Margins*, National Bureau of Economic Research Working Paper: 2057 (October 1986).

Domowitz, Ian, Glenn R. Hubbard and Bruce C. Peterson. *Business Cycles and Oligopoly Supergames: Some Empirical Evidence on Prices and Margins*, National Bureau of Economic Research Working Paper 2057 (October 1986).

Easterbrook, Frank H. Treble What? *Antitrust Law Journal.* 95 (1986):55.

Edwards, Corwin D. *Economic and Political Aspects of International Cartels* New York: Arno Press (1976). (U.S. Senate Subcommittee on War Mobilization study, 1944).

Edwards, Corwin D. *Big Business and the Policy of Competition.* Cleveland: The Press of Case Western Reserve (1956).

Edwards, Corwin D. *Control of Cartels and Monopolies: An International Comparison.* Dobbs Ferry, New York: Oceana Publications (1967).

Eichenwald, Kurt. "The Tale of the Secret Tapes: Bizarre and Mundane Mix at Archer Daniels." *New York Times* (November 16, 1997): 3-13.

Eichenwald, Kurt. Former Archer Daniels Midland Executives are Found Guilty of Price Fixing. *New York Times*, (September 18, 1998): A1.

Eichenwald, Kurt. *The Informant: A True Story*. New York: Broadway Books (2000).

Einhorn, Henry A. The Use of Economic Analysis in Establishing Market Collusion, in Robert J. Thornton and J. Richard Aronson (editors), *Litigation Economics*. Greenwich, Conn.: JAI Press (1993).

Ellison, Glenn. Theories of Cartel Stability and the Joint Executive Committee. *Rand Journal of Economics* 25(1):37-57 (Spring 1994).

Ely, Richard T. *Monopolies and Trusts*. New York: Macmillan (1900).

Elzinga, Kenneth G. and William C. Wood. "The Costs of the Legal System in Private Antitrust Enforcement," Chapter 3 in White (1988).

Epstein, Barbara and Richard Newfarmer. Imperfect International Markets and Monopolistic Prices to Developing Countries: A Case Study. *Cambridge Journal of Economics* 6 (1982): 33-52.

Feenstra, Robert C. Symmetric Pass-Through of Tariffs and Exchange Rates Under Imperfect Competition: An Empirical Test. *Journal of International Economics* 27 (August 1989): 25-45.

Feinberg, R.M. The Enforcement and Effects of European Competition Policy: A Survey of Legal Opinion. *Journal of Common Market Studies* 23 (1985): 373-384.

Feinberg, R.M. The Effects of European Competition Policy on Pricing and Profit Margins. *Kyklos* 39 (1986): 267-287.

Fog, Bjarke. *Industrial Pricing Policies: An Analysis of Pricing Policies of Danish Manufacturers*. Amsterdam: North-Holland (1960).

Fogt, Howard W. and Melinda F. Levitt. The Competitive Edge: Will Proposed Reform of EU Rules Undermine Antitrust Enforcement? *Legal Times* (May 15, 2000): 41.

Fraas, Arthur G. and Douglas F. Greer. Market Structure and Price Collusion: An Empirical Analysis. *Journal of Industrial Economics* 23 (1977): 21-44.

Friedman, J. A Non-Cooperative Equilibrium for Supergames. *Review of Economic Studies* 28(1971):1-12.

Fuller, John G. *The Gentlemen Conspirators: The Story of the Price Fixers in the Electrical Industry*. New York: Grove Press (1962).

Gallo, Joseph C. *et. al.* Criminal Penalties under the Sherman Act: A Study of Law and Economics. *Research in Law and Economics*. 16 (1994): 1-73.

Gallo, Joseph C. *et. al.* Department of Justice Antitrust Enforcement, 1955-1997: An Empirical Study. *Review of Industrial Organization* 17 (August 2000): 75-133.

Gellhorn, E. and W.E. Kovacic. *Antitrust Law and Economics in a Nutshell*. St. Paul, MN: West Publishing (1994).

Gertner, Robert H. and Andrew M. Rosenfeld. Agreement under the Sherman Act, in *The New Palgrave Dictionary of Economics and the Law*, edited by Peter Newman. London: MacMillan (1998).

Gilbert, Richard and Oliver Williamson. Antitrust Policy, in *The New Palgrave Dictionary of Economics and the Law*, edited by Peter Newman. London: Macmillan (1998).

Goodhue, Rachael E. Sustaining Collusion via a Fuzzy Trigger. *Review of Industrial Organization* 13(3):333-45 (June 1998).

Gordon - Ashworth, Fiona. *International Commodity Control: A Contemporary History and Appraisal*. New York: St. Martin's Press (1984).

Granitz, Elizabeth and Benjamin Klein. Monopolization by "Raising Rivals' Costs". *Journal of Law and Economics* 39 (1996): 1-47.

Green, E.J. and R.H. Porter. Non-Cooperative Collusion Under Imperfect Price Information. *Econometrica* 52(1984): 87-100.

Greer, Douglas F. *Industrial Organization and Public Policy* (Second Edition). New York: Macmillan (1992).

Griffin, James M. An Inside Look at a Cartel at Work: Common Characteristics of International Cartels, speech at American Bar Association, Antitrust Section, annual Spring meeting, Washington, D.C. (April 6, 2000).

Griffin, James M. OPEC Behavior: A Test of Alternative Hypotheses. *American Economic Review* 75 (1985): 954-963.

Grossman, Peter Z. The Dynamics of a Stable Cartel: The Railroad Express 1851-1913, *Economic Inquiry* 34(2): 220-36 (April 1996).

Guerrin, Maurice and Georgios Kyriazis. Cartels: Proof and Procedural Issues. *Fordham International Law J.* 16:266.

Handler, Milton. The Shift from Substantive to Procedural Innovations in Antitrust Suits. *Columbia Law Review* 1 (1971):71.

Hay, George A. and Daniel Kelley. An Empirical Survey of Price Fixing Conspiracies. *Journal of Law and Economics* 17 (1974): 13-38.

Hay, George A. The Meaning of "Agreement" under the Sherman Act: Thoughts from the "Facilitating Practices" Experience. *Review of Industrial Organization* 16 (2000): 113-129.

Hayes, Peter. *Industry and Ideology*. New York: Cambridge University Press (1987).

Henahan. John F. Depression and Revival. *Chemical Week* (February 18, 1976): 48.

Herling, John. *The Great Price Conspiracy: The Story of the Antitrust Violations in the Electrical Supply Industry*. Washington, DC: Robert B. Luce, Inc. (1962).

Higby, Gregory J. and John Scarborough. In the Literature. *Pharmacy in History* 23 (1990): 138-139.

Hirth, Hans. Cartel Stability and Product Differentiation. *Jahrbucher für Nationalökonomie und Statistik* 218(3-4):325-45 (March 1999).

Hollis, Nicholas E. Archer Daniels Midland: A Case Study of Corruption in the Ag/Food Sector, speech at the Economic Crime Summit, St. Louis, MO, April 28, 1998.

Hovenkamp, H. *Federal Antitrust Policy: The Law of Competition and its Practice*. St. Paul, MN: West Publishing (1994).

HRA. *The North American Corn Wet Milling Industry*. Prairie Village, KS: HRA, Inc. (July 1992).

Hui, Y.H. (editor). *Encyclopedia of Food Science and Technology*. New York: John Wiley & Sons (1992).

Hviid, Morten. Endogenous Cartel Formation with Private Information. *Canadian Journal of Economics* 25(4):927-82 (November 1992).

ICPAC. *Final Report of the International competition Policy Advisory Committee to the Attorney General*. Washington, D.C.: U.S. Department of Justice (2000).

IDCH. *International Directory of Company Histories*. Detroit: St. James Press (published annually since 1988).

Iyori, H. and A. Uesugi. *The Antimonopoly Laws and Policies of Japan*. Federal Legal Publications, New York (1994).

Jacquemin, A., T. Nambu, and I. Dewez. A Dynamic Analysis of Export Cartels: The Japanese Case. *Economic Journal* 91 (1981): 685-696.

Jacquemin, Alexis and Margaret E. Slade. Cartels, Collusion, and Horizontal Merger, in *Handbook of Industrial Oranigzation: Vol. 1*, edited by Richard Schmalensee and Robert D. Willig. Amsterdam: North-Holland (1989).

Jonas, Daniel S. Some Thoughts on the New Federal Sentencing Guidelines for Organizations. *The Legal Intelligencer* (January 29, 1992):6.

Kahn, E.J. *Supermarketer to The World: The Story of Dwayne Andreas, CEO of Archer Daniels Midland*. New York: Warner Books (1991).

Kanne, Michael S., Ilana Diamond Rovner, and Terence T. Evans. *Opinion, U.S. Court of Appeals for the Seventh Circuit in U.S. v. Michael D. Andreas and Terrance S. Wilson* (2000 U.S. App. LEXIS 14572). Chicago, Illinois (June 26, 2000).

Kelley, Michael S. and Bilal Sayyed. Treble for You, for Me Rethinking the Clayton Act's Damage Provisions. *New Jersey Law Journal* 159 (January 17, 2000): 33.

Kiple, Kenneth F. and Kriemhild Coneè Ornelas (editors). *The Cambridge World History of Food*. Cambridge: Cambridge University Press (2000).

Klawiter, Donald C. Criminal Antitrust Comes to the Global Market. *St. John's Journal of Legal Commentary* 13 (1998): 201-222.

Klein, Joel I. Testimony of Joel I. Klein, Assistant Attorney General, Antitrust Division before the Senate Committee on the Judiciary Subcommittee on Antitrust. Washington, DC, February 26, 1998.

Klein, Joel I. Luncheon Address, International Anti-Cartel Enforcement Conference. Washington, D.C. (September 30, 1999).

Knetter, Michael M. International Comparisons of Pricing-to-Market Behavior. *American Economic Review* 83 (June 1993): 473-486.

Knetter, Michael M. Price Discrimination by U.S. and German Exporters. *American Economic Review* 79 (1989): 198-210.

Korah, V. *An Introductory Guide to EC Competition Law and Practice*. Oxford: Hart Publishing (1997).

Korah, Valentine. Lesson from America. *Financial Times* (London) September 9, 1997: 30.

Krepps, Matthew B. Another Look at the Impact of the National Industrial Recovery Act on Cartel Formation and Maintenance Costs. *Review of Economics and Statistics* 79(1):151-54 (February 1997).

Krugman, Paul R. Pricing to Market When the Exchange Rate Changes, in *Real-Financial Linkages Among Open Economies*, S.W. Arndt and J.D. Richardson (editors). Cambridge: MIT Press (1987).

Krugman, Paul R. How Copper Came a Cropper. *Slate* (www.slate.com).

Kudō, Akira and Terushi Hara (editors). *International Cartels in Business History*. Tokyo: University of Tokyo Press (1991).

Kwoka, John and Lawrence J. White. *The Antitrust Paradox.* New York: Prentice-Hall (1989).

Lambertini, Luca. Cartel Stability and the Curvature of Market Demand. *Bulletin of Economic Research* 48(4):329-34 (October 1996).

Lande, Robert H. Are Antitrust 'Treble" Damages Really Single Damages? *Ohio State Law Journal.* 115(1993):54.

Lanzilotti, Robert. The Great School Milk Conspiracies of the 1980s. *Review of Industrial Organization* 11 (1996): 413-458.

Lassar, Scott R. and James M. Griffin. *Government's Proffer of Co-Conspirator Statements* in *United States of America versus Michael D. Andreas, et al.* Chicago, Illinois: Office of the U.S. Attorney and U.S. Department of Justice (May 6, 1998), 54 pages.

Lassar, Scott R., Joel I. Klein, *et al. Brief for Appellee and Cross-Appellant United States of America* in *U.S. v. Michael D. Andreas*, U.S. Court of Appeals, Seventh Circuit (October 19, 1999).

Lean, David F., Jonathan D. Ogur, and Robert P. Rogers. Does Collusion Pay . . . Does Antitrust Work? *Southern Economic Journal* 51 (1985): 828-841.

Levenstein, Margaret. *Vertical Restraints in the Bromine Cartel: The Role of Distributors in Facilitating Collusion*, National Bureau of Economic Research, Working Paper Series on Historical Factors in Long Run Growth 49 (July 1993).

Lieber, James B. *Rats in the Grain: The Dirty Tricks of "Supermarket to the World."* New York: Four Walls Eight Windows (2000).

Lieber, James B. and April L. Boyer. *Attacking International Price Fixing Conspiracies: ADM Executives on Trial*, paper presented at the Allied Social Sciences Association annual meeting, New York City, January 5, 1999.

Lundqvist, Torbjorn. The Making of a National Cartel in the Swedish Brewing Industry, 1885-1908. *Scandinavian Economic History Review* 46 (1998): 42-63.

Madison, James A. *Eli Lilly: A Life*. Indianapolis: Indiana Historical Society (19989).

Manning, Blanche. Various Rulings in *U.S. v. Michael Andreas et al.* Chicago: U.S. District Court (1998-1999).

Markham, Jesse W. *Competition in the Rayon Industry*. Cambridge: Harvard University Press (1952).

Marquez, J. *Life Expectancy of International Cartels: An Empirical Analysis*, Discussion Paper No. 439. Washington, DC: Board of Governors, Federal Reserve System (1992).

März, U. *The Global Market for Vitamins in Food, Feed, Pharma, and Cosmetics* (GA-096). Norwalk, Connecticut: Business Communications Company, Inc. (November 1996).

McChesney, F.S. and W.F. Shughart (editors). *The Causes and Consequences of Antitrust.* Chicago: University of Chicago Press (1995).

McCuskey, Michael P. *ADM v. Mark Whitacre*: *Opinions*. Urbana, Illinois: U.S. District Court for the Central District of Illinois, Danville/Urbana Division (1998-1999).

McCutcheon, B. Do Meetings in Smoke-Filled Rooms Facilitate Collusion? *Journal of Political Economy.* 105 (1997): 330-350.

Mendel, Scott and Erik Dyhrkopp. DOJ Goal: Assistance Abroad. *The National Law Journal*, (November 9, 1998): B5.

Mihm, Michael M. *In re High Fructose Corn Syrup Antitrust*: *Opinions*. Peoria, Illinois: U.S. District Court for the Central District of Illinois, Peoria Division (1996-1999).

Morse, B. Adair and Jeffrey Hyde. *Estimation of Cartel Overcharges: The Case of Archer Daniels Midland and the Market for Lysine*. Staff Paper 00-8. W. Lafayette, IN, Department of Agricultural Economics, Purdue University (October 2000).

Morton-Scott, Fiona M. *Entry and Predation: British Shipping Cartels 1879-1929.* Stanford Graduate School of Business Research Paper 1396 (June 1996).

Mueller, Willard F., Bruce Marion, and Maqbool H. Sial. Price Leadership on the National Cheese Exchange. *Review of Industrial Organization* 12(1997): 145-170.

Muller, Willard F. and Bruce Marion. Market Power in the Cheese Industry: Further Evidence. *Review of Industrial Organization* 17 (2000): 177-191.

Mullenix, Linda. The Art of Intervening. *The National Law Journal* (January 18, 1999):B17.

Nicol, John and Jock Ferguson. The Price Fixers. *Maclean's* (February 22, 1999):48-52.

Nocke, Volke. Cartel Stability under Capacity Constraints: The Traditional View Restored. Unpublished manuscript (2000).

Norr, Knut Wolfgang. Law and Market Organization: The Historical Experience in Germany from 1900 to the Law Against Restraints of Competition. *Journal of Institutional and Theoretical Economics*, 151(1)5-20 (March 1995.

Nussbaum, Helga. International Cartels and Multinational Enterprises, in Alice Teichova, *et al.* (editors) *Multinational Enterprises in Historical Perspective*. Cambridge: Cambridge University Press (1986).

Ostertag, Carlos F. World Production and Marketing of Starch, Chapter 13 of *Cassava Flour and Starch: Progress in Research and Development*, D. Defour, G.M. O'Brien, and R. Best (editors). Cali, Columbia: CIAT (1996).

Page, William H. (editor). *Proving Antitrust Damages: Legal and Economic Issues*. Chicago, Ill.: Section of Antitrust Law, American Bar Association (1996).

Park, Timothy A. and Daniel H. Pick. The Competitive Structure of U.S. Agricultural Exports. *American Journal of Agricultural Economics* 73 (1991): 134-141.

Patterson, Paul M., Alejandro Reca, and Phillip C. Abbott. Price Discrimination by U.S. High-Valued Food Product Exporters, in *Industrial Organization & Trade in the Food Industries*, Ian M. Sheldon and Phillip C. Abbott (editors). Boulder: Westview Press (1996).

Pearce, David. Repeated Games: Cooperation and Rationality, in Jean-Jacques Lafont (editor) *Advances in Economic theory: Sixth World Congress*, Vol. I, pp. 132-74 (1992).

Peters, Lon L. Managing Competition in German Coal, 1893-1913. *Journal of Economic History* 49 (1989): 419-433.

Peterson, Everett B. and John M. Connor. Consumer Welfare Loss Estimates in Differentiated Food Product Markets. *Review of Agricultural Economics* 18 (1996): 233-246.

Phillips, Almarin. An Econometric Study of Price-Fixing, market Structure, and Performance in British Industry in the Early 1950s, in Keith Cowling (editor), *Market Structure and Corporate Behavior*. London: Gray-Mills (1972), pp. 177-192.

Phlips, Louis. *Competition Policy: A Game-Theoretic Perspective*, Cambridge University Press, Cambridge, MA (1995).

Podolny, Joel M. and Fiona M. Scott Morton. Social Status, Entry and Predation: The Case of Shipping Cartels 1879-1929. *Journal of Industrial Economics* 47(1):41-67 (March 1999).

Porter, Robert H. On the Incidence and Duration of Price Wars. *Journal of Industrial Economics* 33 (June 1985): 415-426.

Porter, Robert H. A Study of Cartel Stability: The Joint Executive committee, 1880-1886. *Bell Journal of Economics* 14(2):301-14 (Autumn 1983).

Posner, Richard A. Oligopoly and the Antitrust Laws: A Suggested Approach. *Stanford Law Review* 21 (1969): 1562-1606.

Posner, Richard A. *Antitrust Law: An Economic Perspective*. Chicago: University of Chicago Press (1976).

Posner, Richard A. Optimal Sentences for White-Collar Crime. *American Criminal Law Review* 17 (1980): 409-418.

Posner, Richard A. The Social Costs of Monopoly and Regulation. *Journal of Political Economy* 83 (1975): 807-827.

Preston, Warren P. and John M. Connor. An Economic Evaluation of Federal Antitrust Activity in the Manufacturing Industries, 1980-1985. *Antitrust Bulletin* 34 (Winter 1992): 696-996.

Rahl, James. International Cartels and their Regulation, in Oscar Schachter and Robert Hellawell (editors), *Competition in International Business*. New York: Columbia Univ. Press (1981).

Rakoff, Jed S. The Corporation as Policemen: At What Price? *New York Law Journal* (January 9, 1992): 3.

Robinson, Sue L. *Decision in Ajinomoto Co. Inc. v. Archer-Daniels-Midland Co.*, Civil Action 95-666-SLR, U.S. District Court for the District of Delaware (March 13, 1998).

Rodger, Barry J. and Angus MacCulloch. Community Competition Law Enforcement Deregulation and Reregulation. *Columbia Journal of European Law* 4 (Summer 1998): 579-612.

de Roos, Nicolas. Examining Models of Collusion: The market for Lysine, unpublished paper (October 2000). (www.econ.yale.edu/~njd7/papers.html).

de Roos, Nicholas. A Model of Collusion Timing, unpublished paper (October 1999). (www.econ.yale.edu/~njd7/papers.html).

de Roos, Nicolas. *Examining Models of Collusion: The Market for Lysine*, Ph.D. dissertation. New Haven: Yale University (2001 forthcoming).

Rosenbaum, David I. and Azzedine A. Azzam. Collusion over the Business Cycle: An Empirical Test. Unpublished manuscript (March 2000).

Rotemberg, Julio J. and Garth Saloner. A Supergame Theoretic Model of Price Wars During Booms, *American Economic Review* 76(3):390-407 (June 1986).

Rotemberg, Julio J. and Garth Saloner. The Relative Rigidity of Monopoly Pricing, *American Economic Review* 77(5): 917-26 (December 1987).

Rotemberg, Julio J. and Garth Saloner. The Cyclical Behavior of Strategic Inventories. *Quarterly Journal of Economics* 104(1) (February 1989):73-97.

Rotemberg, Julio J. and Garth Saloner. Collusive Price Leadership. *Journal of Industrial Economics* 39(1):93-111 (September 1990).

Rotemberg, Julio and Garth Saloner. *Leadership Style and Incentives*. Stanford Graduate School of Business Research Paper No. 1153 (August 1991).

Rothschild, R. Cartel Stability When Costs Are Heterogeneous. *International Journal of Industrial Organization* 17(5):717-34 (July 1999).

Round, David K. and John J. Siegfried. Horizontal Price Agreements in Australian Antitrust: Combating Anti-competitive Corporate Conspiracies of Complicity and Connivance. *Review of Industrial Organization* 9(5):569-606 (October 1994).

Sansavini, S. and D. Verzoni. *The Functional Properties of Starches as a Means to Expanding Their Market,* Working Document 3. Bologna: Department of Horticulture - FAO (forthcoming June 1998).

Scherer, F.M. and David Ross. *Industrial Market Structure and Economic Performance* (Third Edition). Boston: Houghton Mifflin (1990).

Schmitt, Nicolas and Rolf Weder. Sunk Costs and Cartel Formation: Theory and Application to the Dyestuff Industry, *Journal of Economic Behavior and Organization* 36(2):197-220 (August 1998).

Schwartzman, David. *The Japanese Television Cartel: A Study Based on Matsushita v. Zenith.* Ann Arbor: The University of Michigan Press (1993).

Selten, R. A Simple Model of Imperfect Competition, Where 4 Are Few and 6 Are Many. *International Journal of Game Theory* 2 (1973): 141-201.

Shapiro, Carl. Theories of Oligopoly Behavior, in *Handbook of Industrial Organization* I, edited by Richard Schmalensee and Robert Willig. Amsterdam: North-Holland (1989).

Shepherd, William G. General Editor's Introduction: The Role of Economists at the Antitrust Division since 1974. *Review of Industrial Organization* 16 (2000): 107-111.

Shepherd, William G. *Public Policy Toward Business, 7th Edition.* Homewood, IL: Irvin (1985).

Sjostrom, William. Competition Law in the European Union and the United States. *New Palgrave Dictionary of Economics and the Law.* Peter Newman (ed.). London: MacMillan (1998).

Slottje, Daniel J. (editor). *The Role of the Academic Economist in Litigation Support: Contributions to Economic Analysis 240.* Amsterdam: Elsevier (1999).

Smith, Fern M. *Decision, In re Citric Acid Antitrust Litigation*, MDL 1092. San Francisco: U.S. District Court (January 23, 1998).

Smith, R.A. The Incredible Electrical Conspiracy. *Fortune* (April-May 1961): 172.

Smith, W. James, Michael B. Vaughan and John P. Formby. The Role of Fines in Deterring Violations at the Margin. *Southern Economic Journal* 53(4):985-96 (April 1987).

Spratling, Gary R. Remarks before the National Institute on White Collar Crime, San Francisco, (March 6, 1998). (http://www.usdoj.gov/atr/speeches/grs97221.htm).

Spratling, Gary R. International Cartels, speech before the American Conference Institute's 7th National Conference on Foreign Corrupt Practices Act. Washington, D.C. (December 9, 1999).

Spratling, Gary R. The Race for Amnesty in International Antitrust. *International Enforcement Law Reporter* 16 (April 2000).

Sproul, M.F. Antitrust and Prices. *Journal of Political Economy.* 101 (1993): 741-754.

Staiger, Robert W. and Frank A. Wolak. Vancouver's Gasoline-Price Wars: An Empirical Exercise in Uncovering Supergame Strategies. *Review of Economic Studies* 59(2):257-76 (April 1992).

Stat-USA. On line service for U.S. international trade statistics maintained by the U.S. Census Bureau.

Stigler, George J. A Theory of Oligopoly. *Journal of Political Economy 72 (1964): 44-61.*

Stocking, George W. and Myron R. Watkins. *Cartels in Action: Case Studies in International Business Diplomacy.* New York: The Twentieth Century Fund (1947).

Stocking, George W. and Myron R. Watkins. *Cartels or Competition?* New York: The Twentieth Century Fund (1948).

Sullivan, Lawrence A. and Wolfgang Fikentscher. On the Growth of the Antitrust Idea. *Berkley Journal of International Law* 16 (1988): 197-223.

Sultan, Ralph G. M. *Pricing in the Electrical Oligopoly.* Boston: Harvard Business School Division of Research (1974).

Sutton, John. *Sunk Costs and Market Structure.* Cambridge: MIT Press (1991).

Swann, John P. In Search of the Historical Record. *Pharmacy in History* 41 (1999): 131-136.

Tannahill, Reay. *Food in History.* New York: Three Rivers Press (1988).

Tr. Transcript of *U.S. v. Michael D. Andreas, et al.* U.S. District Court, Northern District of Illinois, Eastern Division, No. 96 CR 762 (July to September 1998).

Trager, James. *The Food Chronology*. New York: Henry Holt (1995).

Ulton, Michael. Fifty Years of UK Competition Policy. *Review of Industrial Organization* 16 (2000): 267-285.

United States Sentencing Commission. *Guidelines Manual*. Washington, D.C.: U.S. Sentencing Commission (November 1997).

USITC. *Synthetic Organic Chemicals: United States Production and Sales, 1994*. Washington, D.C.: U.S. International Trade Commission (1996).

Varian, Hal. Price Discrimination, Chapter 10 in *Handbook of Industrial Organization*, Richard Schmalensee and Robert D. Willig (editors). Amsterdam: North-Holland (1989).

Venit, James S. EU Competition Law B Enforcement and Compliance: An Overview: *Antitrust Law Journal* 65 (Fall 1996): 81.

Victor, A. Paul. Jurisdiction and Enforcement: the Growth of International Criminal Antitrust Enforcement. *George Mason University Law Review* 6:493-503.

Voight, Fritz. German Experience with Cartels and Their Control During Pre-War and Post-War Periods, in J.P. Miller (editor), *Competition, Cartels, and Their Regulation*. Amsterdam: North-Holland (1962): 169-208.

Wallance, Gregory J. Antitrust Penalties Are Stiffer Than Other Corporate Sanctions. *National Law Journal* (October 28, 1999): 17.

Walton, Clarence C. and Frederick W. Cleveland, Jr. *Corporations on Trial: The Electric Cases*. Belmont, California: Wadsworth (1964).

Warin, F. Joseph and Jerry S. Fowler. New Risks in Nolo Pleas for Antitrust Defendants. *Legal Times* (January 27, 1997): 28.

Warren-Boulton, Fredrick R. An Evaluation of "The Cost to U.S. Animal Feeds Manufacturers of an Alleged Price-Fixing Conspiracy by Lysine Manufacturers, 1992-1995," In Re Amino Acid Lysine Antitrust Litigation, Master File 95-C-7679, U.S. 7th District Court, Eastern Division (1995).

Webb, Steven B. *Cartels and Business Cycles in Germany, 1880 to 1914*. Cheltenham, UK: Elgar (1997).

Wengenroth, Ulrich. *Enterprise and Technology: The German and British Steel Industries, 1865-1895*, Cambridge University Press, Cambridge, MA (1994).

Werden, Gregory I. And Marylin J. Simon. Why Price Fixers Should Go to Jail. *Antitrust Bulletin* 32 (1987): 917-937.

Whish, R. and B. Sufrin. *Competition Law*. London: Butterworths (1993).

Whitacre, Mark. My Life as a Corporate Mole for the FBI. *Fortune* (September 4, 1995): 52-68.

White, Lawrence J. *International Trade in Ocean Shipping Services*. Cambridge: Ballinger (1988).

White, Lawrence J. (ed.). *Private Antitrust Litigation: New Evidence, New Learning*. Cambridge:MIT Press (1988).

White, Lawrence J. Declaration of Lawrence J. White, In Re Amino Acid Lysine Antitrust Litigation, Master File 95-C-7679, U.S. 7th District Court, Eastern Division (1995).

White, Lawrence J. Economic Analysis in Antitrust Litigation Support, Chapter 2 in Slottje (1999).

Wiley, John Shepard, Jr. Economic Crime: Antitrust Offenses, in *Encyclopedia of Crime and Justice: Second Edition*, Joshua Dressler (editor). New York: Macmillan (2001).

Wilke, John R. U.S. Court Rules Antitrust Laws Apply to Foreigners. *Wall Street Journal* (March 19, 1997): B5.

WSJ. (Scores of articles by Scott Kilman, Thomas Burton, Viveca Novak, Edward Felsenthal, Joan Lublin, and Laurie Cohen). *Wall Street Journal* (June 1995-1998).

INDEX

FSC
www.fsc.org
MIX
Papier | Fördert
gute Waldnutzung
FSC® C083411

Kolibri 360 GmbH
Ferdinand-Jühlke-Straße 7
99095 Erfurt, Deutschland
produktsicherheit@kolibri360.de